Lecture Notes in Computer Science 11702

More information about this series at http://www.springer.com/series/7409

Maribel Acosta · Philippe Cudré-Mauroux ·
Maria Maleshkova · Tassilo Pellegrini ·
Harald Sack · York Sure-Vetter (Eds.)

Semantic Systems

The Power of AI and Knowledge Graphs

15th International Conference, SEMANTiCS 2019
Karlsruhe, Germany, September 9–12, 2019
Proceedings

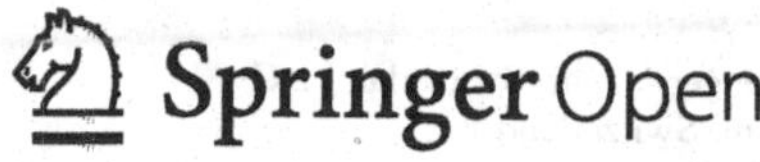

Editors
Maribel Acosta
Karlsruhe Institute of Technology
Karlsruhe, Germany

Maria Maleshkova
University of Bonn
Bonn, Germany

Harald Sack
FIZ Karlsruhe – Leibniz Institute
for Information Infrastructure
Eggenstein-Leopoldshafen, Germany

Philippe Cudré-Mauroux
University of Fribourg
Fribourg, Switzerland

Tassilo Pellegrini
St. Pölten University
of Applied Science
St. Pölten, Austria

York Sure-Vetter
Karlsruhe Institute of Technology
Karlsruhe, Germany

ISSN 0302-9743 ISSN 1611-3349 (electronic)
Lecture Notes in Computer Science
ISBN 978-3-030-33219-8 ISBN 978-3-030-33220-4 (eBook)
https://doi.org/10.1007/978-3-030-33220-4

LNCS Sublibrary: SL3 – Information Systems and Applications, incl. Internet/Web, and HCI

This Springer imprint is published by the registered company Springer Nature Switzerland AG
The registered company address is: Gewerbestrasse 11, 6330 Cham, Switzerland

Preface

SEMANTiCS 2019 took place during September 9–12, 2019, in Karlsruhe, Germany. SEMANTiCS offers a forum for the exchange of latest scientific results in semantic systems and complements these topics with new research challenges in areas like data science, machine learning, logic programming, content engineering, social computing, Semantic Web, and many more. This year was the 15th edition of the SEMANTiCS conference series, which has developed into an internationally visible and professional academic event.

Participants learn from top researchers and industry experts about emerging trends and topics in the wide area of semantic computing. The SEMANTiCS community is highly diverse; attendees have responsibilities in interlinking areas such as artificial intelligence, knowledge discovery and management, big data analytics, e commerce, enterprise search, technical documentation, document management, business intelligence, and enterprise vocabulary management.

This year the SEMANTiCS conference's subtitle was "The Power of AI and Knowledge Graphs," and especially welcomed submissions to the following hot topics:

- Web Semantics and Linked (Open) Data
- Enterprise Knowledge Graphs, Graph Data Management, and Deep Semantics
- Machine Learning and Deep Learning Techniques
- Semantic Information Management and Knowledge Integration
- Terminology, Thesaurus, and Ontology Management
- Data Mining and Knowledge Discovery
- Reasoning, Rules, and Policies
- Natural Language Processing
- Data Quality Management and Assurance
- Explainable Artificial Intelligence
- Semantics in Data Science
- Semantics in Blockchain and Distributed Ledger Technologies
- Trust, Data Privacy, and Security with Semantic Technologies
- Economics of Data, Data Services, and Data Ecosystems

We additionally issued calls for two special tracks:

- Digital Humanities and Cultural Heritage
- LegalTech

Following the great success of SEMANTiCS 2018 in Vienna, we received 88 submissions. In order to properly provide high-quality reviews to these submissions, we set up a Program Committee (PC) comprising of 111 members to help us select the papers with the highest impact and scientific merit. For each submission, at least three reviews were written independently from the assigned reviewers in a single-blind review process (author names are visible to reviewers, but reviewers stay anonymous).

After all reviews were submitted, the PC chairs compared the reviews and discussed discrepancies and different opinions with the reviewers to facilitate a meta-review and suggest a recommendation to accept or reject the paper. Overall, we accepted 20 full papers and 8 short papers from the 88 submissions which resulted in a full paper acceptance rate of 23%.

The program of SEMANTiCS 2019 was structured as follows. In the main conference, the contributors of full papers including posters and industry talks gave their presentations in thematically grouped sessions. These presentations covered a broad palette on current trends and developments in semantic technologies. To support the knowledge transfer between the academic and industrial communities, scientific papers and industry papers were grouped according to the following thematic sessions:

- Semantic Information Management
- Knowledge Discovery and Semantic Search
- Knowledge Graphs
- Knowledge Extraction
- Natural Language Processing
- Thesaurus and Ontology Management
- Linked Data and Data Integration
- Distributed Ledger Technologies
- Smart Connectivity and Interlinking
- Special Track: LegalTech
- Special Track: Digital Humanities and Cultural Heritage
- Special Track: Knowledge Organization and Application for Complex Industry Settings

The Posters and Demos Track provided an opportunity to present late-breaking research results, smaller contributions, and innovative work in progress. 29 original submissions and 2 re-submissions from the research track were accepted to this track, selected with a peer-reviewing process from a total of 47 poster and demo submissions. The reviewing committee, which included 88 members, provided at least three reviews per submission. The accepted works have been published within the CEUR Workshop Proceedings series.

Besides the scientific track of the conference, a call for industry presentations was launched, which resulted in 47 submissions of which 37 were accepted for presentation in the industry track. Additionally, an exhibition took place where organizations presented their semantics-based products and services.

Deliberate long breaks, in a well-suited venue, took place throughout the conference and social events provided excellent opportunities for networking with people interested in semantics-related topics from different disciplines and parts of the world.

We are grateful to our keynote and invited speakers for sharing their ideas about the future development of knowledge management, new media, and semantic technologies with our attendees:

Keynote Speakers:

- Michael J. Sullivan (Oracle): “Hybrid Knowledge Management Architectures”
- Michel Dumontier (Maastricht University): “Accelerating Biomedical Discovery with an Internet of FAIR Data and Services”
- Andy Boyd and Brendan Nielsen (Shell): “High-grading Business Decisions through Semantic Technology”
- Valentina Presutti (Consiglio Nazionale delle Ricerche): “Looking for Common Sense in the Semantic Web”
- Katja Hose (Aalborg University): “Querying the Web of Data”

Invited Speakers:

- Andreas Harth (Fraunhofer Institute): “From Representing Knowledge to Representing Behaviour”
- Christian Dirschl (Wolters Kluwer): “LegalTech – To whom it may concern”

Many thanks also go to all authors who submitted papers and of course to the PC who provided careful reviews in a quick turnaround time.

Special thanks go to Christian Dirschl (Wolters Kluwer Germany) and Andreas Blumauer (Semantic Web Company) who organized all industry related activities. We also would like to thank Thomas Thurner and Martin Kaltenböck from the Semantic Web Company for providing the organizational infrastructure and taking care of all the operational tasks. Additionally, we would also like to thank our local organization team Stefan Summesberger, Viviene Vetter, and Julia Holze, as well as all those helpful hands that are too many to name for supporting this year’s conference and turning it into a success.

We would also like to thank our sponsors (i.a.o.):

- Premium Sponsors: eccenca, PoolParty, FIZ Karlsruhe, and CAS
- Gold Sponsors: Semiodesk, metaphacts, and i-views
- Silver Sponsors: Siemens, Ontotext, Franz Inc., Allegrograph, Enterprise Knowledge, Deloitte, and HP Motion Content
- Bronze and Research: CID, Fraunhofer IAIS, Bosch, inovex, Oracle, Prêt-à-LLOD, STI Innsbruck, GNOSS, Klarso, Ontopic, and SICK

Special thanks also go to the partners of the conference who are:

University of Basel, BID - Bibliothek & Information International, Cefriel, Connected Data London, Consiglo Nazionale delle Ricerche, Cyberforum, DBpedia, eccenca, FIZ Karlsruhe, GFWM, IBM, KIT - Karlsruhe Institute of Technology, TIB, University of Paderborn, University of Fribourg, Springer LNCS, Wolters Kluwer, and WU Vienna.

We hope that SEMANTiCS 2019 will provide you with new inspirations for your research and with opportunities for partnerships with other research groups, academic, and industrial participants.

September 2019

Maribel Acosta
Philippe Cudré-Mauroux
Maria Maleshkova
Tassilo Pellegrini
Harald Sack
York Sure-Vetter

Organization Chairs

Conference Chairs

Harald Sack	FIZ Karlsruhe – Leibniz Institute for Information Infrastructure, Germany
York Sure Vetter	Karlsruhe Institute of Technology, Germany
Tassilo Pellegrini	St. Pölten University of Applied Sciences, Austria

Research and Innovation Chairs

Maribel Acosta	Karlsruhe Institute of Technology, Germany
Philippe Cudré-Mauroux	Université de Fribourg, Switzerland

Special Track Chairs

Sabrina Kirrane	Institute for Information Business of WU Wien, Austria
Victor de Boer	Vrije Universiteit Amsterdam, The Netherlands

Industry and Use Case Chairs

Christian Dirschl	Wolters Kluwer Germany, Germany
Andreas Blumauer	Semantic Web Company, Austria

Poster and Demo Track Chairs

Mehwish Alam	FIZ Karlsruhe – Leibniz Institute for Information Infrastructure, Germany
Ricardo Usbeck	Paderborn University, Germany

Workshop and Satellite Events Chairs

Anna Lisa Gentile	IBM Almaden Research Center, USA
Irene Celino	Cerfriel, Politecnico di Milano, Italy

Proceedings Chairs

Maria Maleshkova	University of Bonn, Germany
Tassilo Pellegrini	St. Pölten University of Applied Sciences, Austria

Promotion Chairs

Thomas Thurner	Semantic Web Company, Austria
Julia Holze	AKSW, InfAI, Leipzig University, Germany
Stefan Summesberger	plantsome communication, Austria

Local Chairs

Thomas Thurner	Semantic Web Company, Austria
Vivien Vetter	FIZ Karlsruhe – Leibniz Institute for Information Infrastructure, Germany

Sponsoring Chair

Stefan Summesberger	plantsome communication, Austria

Permanent Advisory Board

Sören Auer	Fraunhofer Institute for Intelligent Analysis and Information Systems, Germany
Andreas Blumauer	Semantic Web Company, Austria
Tobias Bürger	BMW Group, Germany
Christian Dirschl	Wolters Kluwer Germany, Germany
Victor de Boer	Vrije Universiteit Amsterdam, The Netherlands
Anna Fensel	Semantic Technology Institute (STI) Innsbruck, Austria
Dieter Fensel	Semantic Technology Institute (STI) Innsbruck, Austria
Mike Heininger	GfWM Austria, Austria
Sebastian Hellmann	Institute of Applied Informatics e.V. at the University of Leipzig, Germany
Ute John	GfWM Germany, WissensWertSchöpfung, Germany
Martin Kaltenböck	Semantic Web Company, Austria
Elmar Kiesling	TU Wien, Austria
Tassilo Pellegrini	St. Pölten University of Applied Sciences, Austria
Axel Polleres	Institute for Information Business of WU Wien, Austria
Felix Sasaki	DFKI, W3C Fellow, Germany
Harald Sack	FIZ Karlsruhe – Leibniz Institute for Information Infrastructure and Karlsruhe Institute of Technology (KIT), Germany

Program Committee - Research and Innovation Track and Special Tracks

Harith Alani	The Open University
Vito Walter	Anelli Politecnico di Bari
Luigi Asprino	University of Bologna, STLab (ISTC-CNR)
Sören Auer	TIB, University of Hannover

Nathalie Aussenac-Gilles	IRIT, CNRS
Sebastian Bader	Fraunhofer-Institut für Intelligente Analyse- und Informationssysteme IAIS
Stefan Bischof	Siemens AG Österreich
Carlos Bobed	everis, NTT Data
Loris Bozzato	Fondazione Bruno Kessler
Carlos Buil-Aranda	Universidad Técnica Federico Santa María
Paul Buitelaar	Insight Centre for Data Analytics, National University of Ireland Galway
Irene Celino	Ceriel
Davide Ceolin	Vrije Universiteit Amsterdam
Pierre-Antoine Champin	Liris, Université Claude Bernard Lyon1
Vinay Chaudhri	SRI International, USA
Ioannis Chrysakis	FORTH-ICS, Greece
Ioana-Georgiana Ciuciu	Babes-Bolyai University
Oscar Corcho	Universidad Politécnica de Madrid
Gianluca Correndo	University of Southampton
Enrico Daga	The Open University
Ben De Meester	Ghent University
Elena Demidova	L3S Research Center
Sylvie Despres	Laboratoire d'Informatique Médicale et de BIOinformatique (LIM&BIO)
Chiara Di Francescomarino	Fondazione Bruno Kessler-Irst
Stefan Dietze	GESIS - Leibniz Institute for the Social Sciences
Anastasia Dimou	Ghent University
Jens Dörpinghaus	Fraunhofer
Mauro Dragoni	Fondazione Bruno Kessler-Irst
Anca Dumitrache	Vrije Universiteit Amsterdam
Jérôme Euzenat	Inria, University of Grenoble Alpes
Victoria Eyharabide	STIH Laboratory, Sorbonne University
Michael Färber	University of Freiburg
Catherine Faron Zucker	Université Nice Sophia Antipolis
Said Fathalla	University of Bonn
Ingo Feinerer	University of Applied Sciences Wiener Neustadt
Javier D. Fernández	Vienna University of Economics and Business
Agata Filipowska	Poznan University of Economics
Nuno Freire	INESC-ID
Roberto Garcia	Universitat de Lleida
Raúl García-Castro	Universidad Politécnica de Madrid
Daniel Garijo	Information Sciences Institute
Annalisa Gentile	IBM
Jose Manuel Gomez-Perez	ExpertSystem
Michael Granitzer	University of Passau
Alasdair Gray	Heriot-Watt University
Paul Groth	University of Amsterdam
Peter Haase	metaphacts

Benjamin Heitmann	RWTH Aachen University
Lars Heling	Karlsruhe Institute of Technology
Eelco Herder	Radboud University
Pieter Heyvaert	IDLab Ghent University – imec, Belgium
Rinke Hoekstra	University of Amsterdam
Geert-Jan Houben	Delft University of Technology
Zhisheng Huang	Vrije Universiteit Amsterdam
Shimaa Ibrahim	Bonn University
Marc Jacobs	Fraunhofer
Tobias Käfer	Karlsruhe Institute of Technology
Lucie-Aimée Kaffee	University of Southampton
Elias Kärle	STI-Innsbruck
Tomi Kauppinen	Aalto University School of Science
Dimitris Kontokostas	University of Leipzig
Efstratios Kontopoulos	Information Technologies Institute, Centre for Research & Technology – Hellas, Greece
Tobias Kuhn	Vrije Universiteit Amsterdam
Christoph Lange	Fraunhofer FIT, Germany
Maxime Lefrançois	MINES Saint-Etienne
Isaac Lera	UIB
Steffen Lohmann	Fraunhofer
Vanessa Lopez	IBM
Vincent Lully	Sorbonne Université, France
Nicole Merkle	FZI Forschungszentrum Informatik am KIT
Lyndon Nixon	MODUL Technology GmbH
Leo Obrst	MITRE
Jan Oevermann	University of Bremen, German Research Center for Artificial Intelligence (DFKI)
Harshvardhan Jitendra Pandit	ADAPT, Trinity College Dublin
Heiko Paulheim	University of Mannheim
Catia Pesquita	LaSIGE, Universidade de Lisboa
Jasmin Pielorz	Austrian Institute of Technology
Jędrzej Potoniec	Poznan University of Technology
Cédric Pruski	Luxembourg Institute of Science and Technology
Filip Radulovic	Sépage in Paris, France
Alessandro Raganato	University of Helsinki
Artem Revenko	Semantic Web Company GmbH
Giuseppe Rizzo	LINKS Foundation
Oscar Rodríguez Rocha	Inria
Anisa Rula	University of Milano-Bicocca
Marta Sabou	Vienna University of Technology
Vadim Savenkov	Vienna University of Economics and Business (WU)
Stefan Schlobach	Vrije Universiteit Amsterdam
Pavel Shvaiko	Informatica Trentina
Ruben Taelman	Ghent University – imec

Sanju Tiwari	Ontology Engineering Group
Konstantin Todorov	LIRMM, University of Montpellier
Riccardo Tommasini	Politecnico di Milano
Jürgen Umbrich	Vienna University of Economy and Business (WU)
Victoria Uren	Aston University
Mathias Uslar	OFFIS
Herbert Van De Sompel	Data Archiving Networked Services
Frank Van Harmelen	Vrije Universiteit Amsterdam
Maria Esther Vidal	Universidad Simon Bolivar
Joerg Waitelonis	yovisto GmbH
Shenghui Wang	OCLC Research
Ziqi Zhang	Sheffield University

Additional Reviewers

Wazed Ali	TIB
Imran Asif	Heriot Watt University
Javad Chamanara	L3S
Andrea Cimmino Arriaga	Universidad de Sevilla
Diego Collarana	IAIS Fraunhofer
Mirette Elias	University of Bonn
Simon Gottschalk	L3S
Prashant Khare	The Open University
Allard Oelen	TIB
Nicolas Tempelmeier	L3S

Contents

Web Semantics and Linked (Open) Data

Machine Learning and Deep Learning Techniques

Semantic Information Management and Knowledge Integration

Terminology, Thesaurus and Ontology Management

Data Mining and Knowledge Discovery

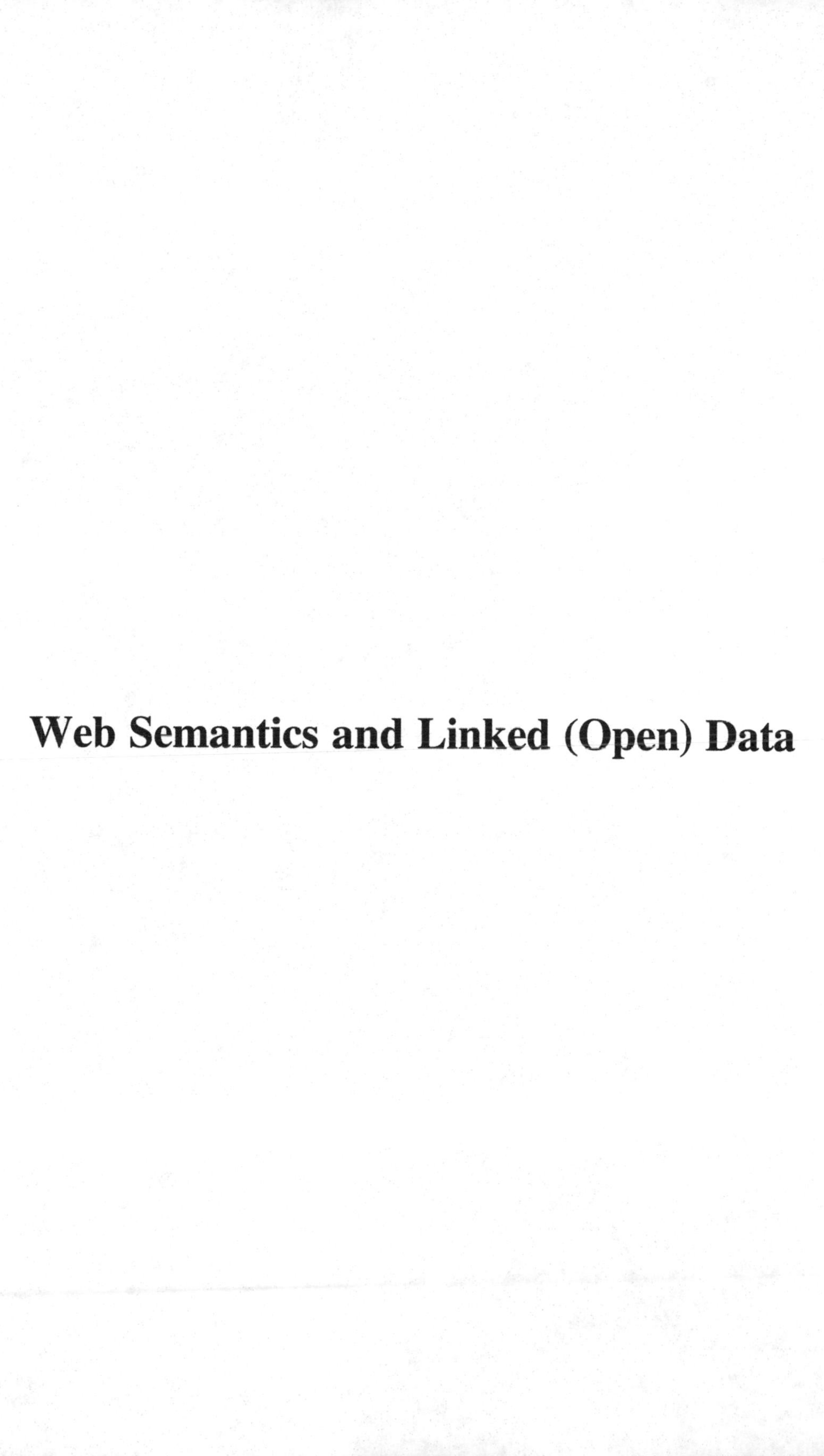

Web Semantics and Linked (Open) Data

Usage of Semantic Web in Austrian Regional Tourism Organizations

Christina Lohvynenko and Dietmar Nedbal(✉)

University of Applied Sciences Upper Austria,
Wehrgrabengasse 1-3, 4400 Steyr, Austria
christina-lohvynenko@gmx.at,
dietmar.nedbal@fh-steyr.at

Abstract. Tourism is one of the most important economic sectors in Austria. Given the high internationality degree of Austrian visitors, the websites of regional tourism organizations (RTOs) are an essential source of information. A state-of-the-art tourism website should include semantic markup for touristic topics so that search engines and other intelligent software applications can access and understand the presented data. This paper empirically studies the usage of Semantic Web formats, ontologies and topics relevant for tourism on the websites of all 137 Austrian RTOs. Results show that 59% of the RTOs use semantic markup. Most regions adhere to the recommendations of leading search engines utilizing ontologies such as Schema.org and the formats Microdata and JSON-LD. While most semantic markup incorporates basic information (e.g. navigation, addresses, corporate data), only few Austrian RTOs annotate touristic relevant topics that would contribute to unlock the full potential of the Semantic Web such as regional events, accommodations, blog posts, images or social media.

Keywords: Semantic Web · Regional tourism organizations · Survey · Austria

1 Introduction

With nearly 45 million resident and non-resident guests in 2018, tourism is one of the most important Austrian economic sectors [1]. In the last years, the tourism and leisure industry contributed around 16% to the Austrian gross domestic product through direct and indirect effects [2]. Even in international comparison, the country occupies an important place among the top 20 tourism destinations [3]. The tourism regions, which are in the midst of the hierarchical organization of this industry in Austria, contribute significantly to the promotion of certain tourism destinations and to addressing a broad target group [4]. These regional tourism organizations (RTO) are also given an important role in the possible weakening of dependence on international online travel agencies (OTA), which dominate the tourism market. Given the growth of the Internet usage and due to the high internationality degree of Austrian visitors, the websites of tourism providers are becoming increasingly important. A state-of-the-art website that implements innovative web technologies is therefore essential [5, 6].

M. Acosta et al. (Eds.): SEMANTiCS 2019, LNCS 11702, pp. 3–18, 2019.
https://doi.org/10.1007/978-3-030-33220-4_1

The use of Semantic Web and Linked Data has long been a standard in website optimization and intends to make important content-bearing elements of web pages machine-readable by means of semantic markup so that access to data for search engines and other intelligent software applications is facilitated. The semantic annotation of structured data to a website is one of the most common search engine optimization practices, which is also recommended by leading search engines. Thus, it can increase the online visibility of the web page and the sales figures on the Internet [7–9]. However, the empirical analysis of the use of Semantic Web by the hotel websites in Austria has shown that the use of direct providers in contrast to OTAs is very moderate and often flawed [6, 10]. Such a weak use of structured data in the hotel industry suggests that the Semantic Web has not yet become a standard in Austria's tourism industry.

With the RTOs playing an important role in the Austrian tourism, the current paper aims to elucidate the usage status of the Semantic Web among these websites. It first discusses the background and related work on the use of structured data in tourism in Sect. 2. Further, the results on an empirical investigation are reported. For this purpose, the selection of the examination objects and preparation of the data for analysis are described in Sect. 3. The results of the evaluation are presented in Sect. 4, followed by a discussion (Sect. 5). Finally, Sect. 6 provides concluding remarks.

2 Background and Related Work

One of the most important communication channels of a tourism organization is the website, which should adhere the current state-of-the-art. In this context it has been recognized that innovative software providing interoperability through ontologies is critical for further innovation in the tourism industry [11]. Although there has been progress in the last ten years, a recent study highlights the still current and growing importance of semantics and ontologies in tourism. The authors further state that academic research in these disciplines is still in its infancy [12].

Website owners and content managers of tourism regions face several challenges when attempting to semantically enrich data on their website. First of all the selection of the appropriate vocabulary, format and content is not a trivial task. In addition to common vocabularies independent of the domain, several domain-specific ontologies for tourism have also been developed which makes it difficult to select the most suitable and, at the same time, a future-proof vocabulary. The Linked Open Vocabularies project, for example, provides a central information point about well-documented vocabularies [13]. The constantly growing website lists 660 high quality vocabularies as of Feb. 2019. Measured by the number of vocabularies that reuse the vocabulary, the most popular ontologies are Dublin Core Metadata Terms (dcterms), Dublin Core Metadata Element Set (dce), Friend of a Friend vocabulary (foaf), A vocabulary for annotating vocabulary descriptions (vann), Simple Knowledge Organization System (skos), Creative Commons Rights Expression Language (cc), SemWeb Vocab Status ontology (vs) and Schema.org vocabulary (schema) [14]. The problem of common vocabularies often lies in the level of precision over domain-specific ontologies. For example, until version 3.0, Schema.org lacked the ability to describe the number of beds in a room, or whether pets are allowed or not [15]. One of the main goals of tourism-specific vocabularies is to achieve a better interoperability and integration of travel information systems [16]. Several researches have focused on the design of semantic vocabularies for the tourism and travel industry [17] (e.g. Harmonise [18], QALL-ME [19], cDott [20], Accommodation Ontology [21], Tourpedia [22]).

Given the amount and diversity of available ontologies, an industry wide adoption is crucial for a future-proof vocabulary. The Web Data Commons project features the largest publicly available collection of structured data from a non-profit organization [23], allowing researchers to analyze the adoption of structured data across the Web. An analysis for the period 2010 to 2013 showed that the use of the Semantic Web, its formats and data classes has been steadily increasing. The comparison of the 2012 and 2013 datasets revealed that the number of websites using Microdata has even grown by more than factor four in just one year. The topics that received the most attention through semantic markup were people and organizations, blog articles, navigation information, product and event data [23]. In another study focusing only on the adoption of Schema.org, it was shown that about half of the elements of this vocabulary have not been used in any of the websites from the Web Data Commons dataset [24].

Since a website is one of the most important means of communication for tourism organizations, several studies have addressed the quality of touristic websites. International online travel agencies have heavily dominated the tourism sector in recent years. Tourism organizations in Austria are also suffering from this online competition and are trying to counteract this competition by means of innovative technologies and intelligent advertising of products and services on several channels. When comparing the quality of content and services offered on official websites of tourism organizations with online travel agencies' websites, OTA websites have often received better results. Tourism websites often do not follow state-of-the-art online developments, therefore OTAs have the lead in terms of technology usage, according to the studies [6, 10, 25]. As far as Austria is concerned, studies in recent years have distinguished a good performance and numerous innovative integrated services on the websites of official Austrian tourism organizations in international comparison [26, 27].

The use of well-documented structured markup should enable error-free annotation and improve the quality of the website. Unfortunately, a large variety of erroneous and restricted usage in the semantic markup are made in practice when using vocabularies like Schema.org, which hinders real-life applications to use the data [10, 28]. To counteract this problem, Şimşek et al. described an approach that validates Schema.org markup in terms of completeness of the annotations for a specified domain and semantic consistency [29] that was implemented in an online-tool semantify.it [30].

Benefits when using Semantic Web technology include better visibility in the search results of leading search engines [7], as well as better online visibility of the promotions being advertised [5]. This further helps reducing reliance on OTAs, enables the use of structured data by emerging intelligent applications (e.g. chatbots and voice search) and improves interoperability among market participants [31–33].

The literature review has shown that the topic of using the Semantic Web has a long history and great potential for the industry. Studies indicate that the tourism sector often lacks expertise and knowledge of the correct use of Semantic Web technology. Furthermore, research on the use of semantic technologies in Austrian tourism organizations focuses mostly on either the hotel sector or individual tourism organizations. A recent study of the usage of Semantic Web comprising all Austrian regional tourism organizations could not be identified during the literature search.

3 Methodology

The methodology for the empirical investigation started with a definition and selection of the examination objects. This is followed by a description of the data extraction process and the preparation of semantic markup for the actual analysis. It is also detailed, how incomplete and erroneous annotations were identified and how they were assigned to groups that emerged during this analysis.

3.1 Selection of the Examination Objects

Austrian regional tourism organizations are well suited as examination objects for this analysis, as they usually have an established website with comparable contents of the region. However, the number of these organizations is not constant in Austria, which makes objective analysis more difficult.

The organization of Austrian tourism has a hierarchical structure. The basis of the tourism market is provided by the 65,000 tourism businesses, most of which operate in municipalities that are classified as tourism-intensive municipality with at least 1,000 overnight stays per year. Of the 1,568 Austrian tourism-intensive municipalities, 151 were categorized as tourism regions in 2008 [34]. At the state level, tourism in Austria is divided into the respective offices of the nine state governments with one national tourism organization ("Austrian National Tourist Office") on the top, working closely together with the tourism regions. Therefore, in this work, the tourism regions together with the nine state tourism organizations and the national tourism organization are referenced to as regional tourism organizations (RTO) in the following.

As mentioned, the number of RTOs varies over time. For example, in Upper Austria, a new tourism law came into force, according to which the number of tourism associations (and thus also the RTOs) must be reduced from 100 to 20 by the year 2020. There are tourism associations that have already merged, but still have separate websites (e.g. "Wels" and "Sattledt") and others that have no joint website (e.g. "Oberes Mühlviertel") as of June 15, 2018. For this research, the list of RTOs to be examined has been determined in a top-down approach. Starting from the actual references on the nine state tourism organizations websites, an initial list of 117 regional websites was gathered (3 organizations in Burgenland, 6 in Lower Austria, 26 in Upper Austria, 14 in Carinthia, 17 in Salzburg, 9 in Styria, 35 in Tyrol, 6 in Vorarlberg). After examining the individual websites of these 117 organizations, the following changes were made: Two Upper Austrian RTOs without own website ("Nationalpark Region Ennstal" and "Steyrtal") were removed and RTOs with separate individual websites were added in Carinthia (1 RTO split into 3 websites), Styria (1 RTO split into 2 websites), and Tyrol (2 RTOs split into 7 websites). In total, 133 websites (one national, nine state and 123 regional tourist organization websites) were included, all of which are subsequently referred to as RTO.

3.2 Data Extraction Process

For this research we used data from Web Data Commons [23], making raw web page data, extracted metadata, and snippets of individual web pages available to the public. The data collection entitled "WDC RDFa, Microdata, Embedded JSON-LD, and Microformats Data Sets (November 2017)" was used as basis for data extraction. The original record contains 8,433 files, each around 100 MB in size. The data in the collection is represented in the form of RDF quads with subject, predicate, and object as well as the URL of the web page from which the data was extracted as fourth element.

With the help of a shell script, the downloaded files were unpacked and examined for the presence of semantic annotations of one of the 133 defined RTOs. The script generates plain text files and can be downloaded from the URL https://t1p.de/shellscript . The duration of the script was approximately 48 h, with ten tasks run simultaneously on several machines.

3.3 Preparation of Semantic Markup

The preparation of the data for the actual evaluation was done using Microsoft Excel 2016. The first step was to create 133 Excel spreadsheets, one for each tourism region from the text files generated by the shell script using an Excel macro. With the help of conditional formatting, regular expressions, and filtering rules in Excel, duplicated annotations and mentions were removed (repeated use of the same annotation on the same web page) and the markup of all subdomains of the respective RTO were checked and adjusted if necessary. Thus, only those data remained, where the fourth part of the RDF quad contained the domain of one of the 133 RTOs defined.

After all tables were cleaned up with irrelevant data, all individual tables containing structured data were combined in two files (one own Excel file containing "wien.info" markup and one for the remaining 77 websites). This subdivision was necessary due to the limited number of rows in this version of Excel.

In order to be able to identify different types of structured data in websites of Austrian tourism regions, the table has been extended with additional information. The final analysis table can be downloaded from the URL http://t1p.de/analysistable as Microsoft Excel file. It contains the following columns:

- The first column contains the relevant RDF quads (430,894 in Vienna and 769,824 in the file for all remaining regions).
- The second column ("Region") contains the domain of the respective tourism region, gathered from the URL.
- The third column ("Federal State") allows the assignment to one of the nine federal states and to the national tourism organization of Austria (austriatourism.com).
- The fourth column "Format" contains the format used for a specific semantic markup. This information was taken from the Web Data Commons file name from which the respective RDF quad was extracted (e.g. file "dpef.html-embedded-jsonld.nq" contains the semantic annotations carried out by JSON-LD).

- The “Namespace & data type” column represents the predicate of the respective triples and contains, in addition to the namespace of the ontology, the names of the data classes and data properties used. The namespaces were determined by means of the Excel filter function from the first column containing the RDF quads.
- The “Ontology” column captures the name of the ontology, which was determined by the namespace in the “Namespace & data type” column.
- The “Class” column contains the data classes used and the “Property” column lists the data properties used by the RDF quad. The data on classes and properties was determined using the Excel filter function from the RDF quads themselves or from the “Namespace & data type” column.
- The “Topics” column contains aggregated information of the data classes from various ontologies used into subject areas, containing similar or related objects (cf. Sect. 4.4).
- The last column “Remark” was used to take notes about found errors or incomplete semantic annotations, most of which were previously described in the study of Meusel and Paulheim [28]. Mistakes found include missing slash, incorrect upper or lower case, missing or incorrect use of a data types, incorrect use of namespace, property mapped to an incorrect class or data type, incorrect use of property values, and incomplete/wrong specification of namespace.

4 Analysis Results

This section contains the main findings of the survey on the use of Semantic Web technology by Austrian RTOs. First, an overview of the top 20 RTOs using semantic markup is given. This is followed by a brief analysis of the formats and ontologies used. Finally, insight into the topics that were annotated by the RTOs is provided.

4.1 Amount of RTOs Using Semantic Annotations

A total of 78 Austrian RTOs (59%) use Semantic Web annotations in their websites, while the remaining 55 RTO websites did not show any semantic markup in the course of this analysis.

Figure 1 shows the top 20 RTOs, measured by the absolute number of RDF quads identified. The leading RTO is Vienna (domain: wien.info), which has 430,894 RDF quads integrated into its website. Second place in this ranking is occupied by zillertalarena.com with 129,320 RDF quads. The other 18 RTOs shown in the figure each use more than 10,000 RDF quads. The structured data from wien.info alone make up 36% of the entire data set; zillertalarena.com added another 11% and the remaining 18 RTOs from the top 20 list sum up to 42% of all annotations. The top 20 regions thus make 89% of the total amount of semantic markup.

4.2 Formats

The use of the Semantic Web formats shows a clear preference of the Microdata format (93,9%) by the number of absolute uses in the RDF quads. JSON-LD was used in 3% and microformats in 2.8% of the RDF quads. The use of RDFa is only at 0.3% and includes almost only the Open Graph protocol (OGP).

53.8% of the 78 RTOs with structured data use Microdata as the only format for semantic annotation of website content. The use of multiple formats by RTO is heterogeneous: 10.3% use Microdata and Microformats at the same time, another 9% Microdata and JSON-LD. The three formats Microdata, Microformats and JSON-LD are simultaneously used by 7.7% of the RTOs. RDFa alone is used by four RTOs (5.1%). All four formats are used by three RTOs (3.8%). The remaining 10.3% of the RTOs use a combination of five different formats.

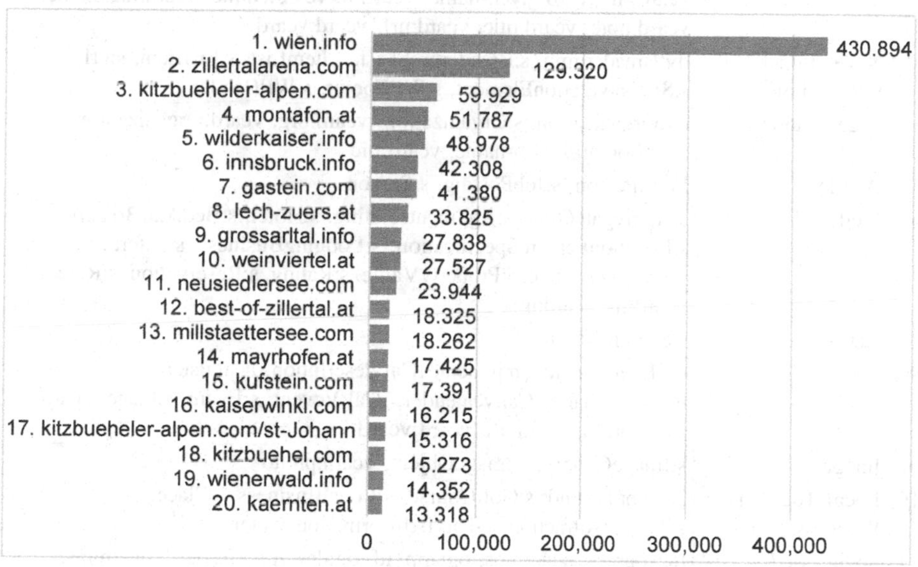

Fig. 1. Top 20 Austrian RTOs by absolute number of RDF quads.

4.3 Structured Data Markup: Ontologies

The examined websites use a total of eight different ontologies. The most used ontology is Schema.org with 63.7% by the number of absolute uses in the RDF quads. In second place (18.2% of the RDF quads) is Data Vocabulary. Dublin Core terms are used by a large number of RTOs (61 websites) but account to only 3.3% of the overall RDF quads. The remaining four ontologies (hCard, OGP, iCal Schema, XFN, FOAF) are all referenced by less than 3% semantic markup. Interestingly, none of the vocabularies developed specifically for tourism were found in the examined objects.

4.4 Topics

Since same or similar content can be annotated using various ontologies and data classes, an overview of the topics that have been covered by the RTOs needs additional consolidation. For this reason, the thematically related objects of a tourism site website were subsequently grouped into similar topics, representing subject areas or categories.

Table 1. Topics and their associated ontologies and data classes.

#	Topic	Ontologies and data classes
1	Addresses	s:GeoCoordinates, s:PostalAddress, vcard:Address, vcard:adr, vcard: addressType, vcard:country-name, vcard:email, vcard:locality, vcard: postal-code, vcard:region, vcard:street-address, vcard:tel
2	Blogs	s:Article, s:Blog, s:CreativeWork, s:BlogPosting, vcard:family-name, vcard:fn, vcard:given-name, vcard:n, vcard:Name, vcard:nickname, vcard:note, vcard:title, vcard:url, vcard:vcard
3	Navigational Information	dv:Breadcrumb, s:BreadcrumbList, s:ItemList, s:ListItem, s:url, s:SiteNavigationElement, s:WPFooter, s:WPHeader
4	Organization	dv:Organization, s:Organization, vcard:org, vcard:Organization, vcard:organization-name, vcard:uid
5	People	Foaf:Person, s:JobPosting, s:Person
6	Product Data	s:AggregateOffer, s:AggregateRating, s:Hotel, s:BedAndBreakfast, s:LocationFeatureSpecification, s:LodgingBusiness, s:Offer, s:Product, s:Date, s:PropertyValue, s:Rating, s:Reservation, s:Review, vcard:fn, vcard:n
7	Action	s:SearchAction
8	Event	dv:Event, iCal:component, iCal:description, iCal:dstart, iCal:summary, iCal:vcalender, iCal:Vevent, s:Event, s:Place, vcard: fn, vcard:n, vcard:url, vcard:vcard
9	Images	s:ImageGallery, s:ImageObject, vcard:photo
10	Local Tourism Business	s:Campground, s:GolfCourse, s:LocalBusiness, s:Place, s:TouristAttraction, s:TouristInformationCenter
11	Social Media	dc:source, og:admins, og:app_id, og:description, og:fbmladmins, og:image, og:site_name, og:title, og:type, og:url, s:sameAs, xfn:mePage, xfn:me-hyperlink
12	Website Information	dc:title, s:Language, s:WebPage, s:WebSite

Table 1 presents the twelve topics identified during the analysis, including the list of data classes that make up each group. The first six topics were taken from the study of Meusel et al. [23]. The remaining groups were defined on the basis of the examined data of the RTOs. The ontologies are abbreviated as follows: "s:" stands for Schema. org, "dv:" for Data Vocabulary, "dc:" for Dublin Core, and "og:" for OGP followed by the respective data class.

The subdivision into these twelve topics unfortunately does not guarantee that there is no overlapping in the content. For example, many blog articles contained information on tourist attractions (topic "Local Tourism Business"), pictures in the category "Images" were occasionally identical to the image properties of individual topics such as "Organization", "Event", "Local Tourism Business", or "Blogs" and several classes are also described by properties that contain address information. The Schema.org class "s:Place" has been divided manually into two topics: on the one hand in "Event", if the information was about an event location, and on the other hand in "Local Tourism Business". The analysis of the use of topics is presented in Table 2; details on the topics are presented in the following.

Table 2. Use of topics by the 78 RTOs using semantic annotations.

Topic	RDF quads	RTOs
Navigational Information	398,947 (33.2%)	41 (52.6%)
Addresses	176,755 (14.7%)	35 (44.9%)
Local Tourism Business	134,577 (11.2%)	20 (25.6%)
Event	94,827 (7.9%)	20 (25.6%)
Product Data	63,670 (5.3%)	24 (30.8%)
Website Information	63,130 (5.3%)	68 (87.2%)
Blogs	52,307 (4.4%)	29 (37.2%)
Organization	24,182 (2.0%)	29 (37.2%)
Images	22,301 (1.9%)	13 (16.7%)
Social Media	21,799 (1.8%)	20 (25.6%)
Action	4,837 (0.4%)	15 (19.2%)
People	1,446 (0.1%)	10 (12.8%)

Navigational Information. Every third semantic markup is made for the purpose of presenting the breadcrumb and list items that help navigate the website. Nearly 56% of this topic is annotated using Schema.org and 44% using Data Vocabulary. Only about 0.1% of the markup is made using JSON-LD and Microdata. A total of eight RTOs account for 81% of the data in the category, of which RTO "zillertalarena.com" alone uses 40% of the annotations. Most commonly used are the classes "dv:Breadcrumb" and "s:SiteNavigationElement".

Addresses. Almost 15% of the markup contains various address details. The annotations use Schema.org and Microdata in 96% of the cases, the remainder is annotated using the Microformat hCard. 41% of the RTOs annotate address data of the region where the company or local providers are located; the exact address (either street and house number or latitude and longitude) is awarded by 45% of the RTOs. 15% of the RTOs use this topic for specific contact information such as telephone, fax, e-mail or URL.

Local Tourism Business. 11.2% of the RDF quads represent information on this topic. Four RTOs (wien.info, weinviertel.at, innsbruck.info, gastein.com) contribute 84.1% of the data in this topic. The only ontologies used here are Schema.org and Microdata.

Events. Almost 8% of the data represent events in the region. Annotations are made at 98% by means of Schema.org and Microdata, the remainder by the Microformats hCalender and hCard. The most used property is the start date of an event, followed by the name, image, location, URL, description, address and the special offers. Overall, only two RTOs (wien.info and lech-zuers.at) have made 87.3% of all annotations in this topic.

Product Data. This topic describes both the "Product" and "Offer" data classes as well as various types of accommodation that can be considered as the product of an RTO. 5.3% of all RDF quads found are subsumed under this topic. RTOs adopted Schema. org and Microdata ontologies. Most used annotations (over 1,000 each) include the LodgingBusiness, AggregateRating, LocationFeatureSpecification, Offer, Hotel, Product, and Review classes. Three RTOs (wien.info, montafon.at, kitzbuehel.com) made a total of 91% of all semantic markup of this topic.

Website Information. This topic describes various elements such as the title, alternative names, languages used and individual elements of a website. 62% of the RDF quads were annotated using Dublin Core, the rest by means of Schema.org. The use of Microdata dominated the format use (93%), with JSON-LD making up the remaining 7%. Although 68 RTOs are using this topic, more than half of the RDF quads in this category were annotated by wien.info.

Blogs. In this section, blog, press and web pages published on the website, including author data, titles, descriptions and evaluations, are subsumed. Four regions (best-of-zillertal.at, wien.info, mayrhofen.at and grossarltal.info) out of 29 make 81% of all RDF quads of this topic. Almost half of all annotations are made using Schema.org and Microdata, the rest using hCard. Typical semantic information include headline, description, author name and URL.

Organization. This topic is used to present information about the website operator such as name, logo and VAT number. 96% of the annotations are done using Schema. org, the rest using Data Vocabulary and Microformats. Microdata is used in 69% of annotations, followed by JSON (28%) and the Microformat hCard (4%). The use of this topic is dominated by four RTOs (nationalpark.at, oetztal.com, stantonamarlberg.com and neusiedlersee.com).

Images. This topic contains various pictures and collections of pictures. 99% of the annotations use Schema.org (mainly Microdata), the rest the Microformat hCard. Four RTOs (kaernten.at, kitzbuehel.com, montafon.at and tennengau.com) account to 85% of all annotated images.

Social Media. Social media annotations are made using four different ontologies (primarily OGP and Schema.org, but also Dublin Core and XFN) in all four formats. The most common purpose is to link to the social media presence: 10 RTOs link to their page on Facebook, five on Instagram, four on YouTube, three on Google+, two on Twitter, and one each on Pinterest and Flickr. Almost 70% of all annotations were made by the RTO neusiedlersee.com.

Action. This topic is used to mark the entries in the search fields or forms that are used by the search engines primarily to provide users with an opportunity to search the content of a website directly on the search results page in their own search window. Four RTOs (grossarltal.info, austriatourism.com, reutte.com and bregenzerwald.at) out of 15 account for 91.5% of the markup in this topic, which are made exclusively using JSON-LD and Schema.org.

People. This topic subsumes individuals (article authors, team members, etc.) and company job offers. Most annotations are based on Schema.org and Microdata. Three out of ten RTOs (lech-zuers.at, hoch-koenig.at and mayrhofen.at) make up 94% of all RDF quads in this topic.

5 Discussion

The analysis revealed that the use of Semantic Web in Austrian RTOs complies with the recommendations of leading search engines such as Google, Yahoo, Bing and Yandex. The majority of semantic annotations by tourism regions are made using Microdata and JSON-LD. In addition, considering a total of eight ontologies that are used, the recommended Schema.org is preferred, along with its predecessor, Data Vocabulary, in over 80% of all annotations.

The grouping of semantic markup in twelve thematically related topics allowed an overview of all structured data specifically for Austrian tourism regions - regardless of the formats and ontologies used. The analysis showed that, with the exception of the three general topics ("Navigational Information", "Addresses", and "Website Information"), the annotation of RTO's specific tourism information is strongly influenced by only a few RTOs. While general information is important to search engines as well as various software agents, specific tourism content should also be semantically annotated to exploit the full potential of the Semantic Web.

For tourism, relevant Schema.org classes and properties are distributed in different parts of this ontology [16]. However, Austrian RTOs use only a few data types and properties of Schema.org intended for the tourism industry. For example, no annotations for food establishments ("FoodEstablishments" class with possible types "Bakery", "BarOrPub", "Brewery", "CafeOrCoffeeShop", "FastFoodRestaurant", "IceCreamShop", "Restaurant", "Winery", etc.) or ski resorts ("SportsActivityLocation", "SkiResort" classes) were found, although such content is available on the websites.

The analysis of the topic "Product Data" revealed that the possibility of specifying specific types of accommodation are hardly used by the RTOs. The Schema.org type "LodgingBusiness" can be used, for example or the more specific subtypes "Hostel", "Hotel", "Motel", "Resort", "Campground", or "BedAndBreakfast". The three types "Hotel", "Campground" and "BedAndBreakfast" together with the type "LocationFeatureSpecification" are only used by one RTO (montafon.at). Furthermore, none of the RTOs annotate specific events such as “MusicEvent”, “SocialEvent”, “SportsEvent”, etc. Nevertheless, a precise classification is particularly important for tourism organizations for all available content and such generic classes should be avoided [32].

Detailed information on accommodations that are relevant for a user’s booking decision and also contribute to specific search results (e.g. Schema.org properties like “amenityFeature”, “availability”, “price”, “offer”, “paymentAccepted”, “petsAllowed”, “priceCurrency”, “priceRange”, “availability”) were used by 13 RTOs. Taking a closer look, 92% of RDF quads with such detailed information came from only one region (montafon.at). The remaining twelve RTOs used the properties mentioned only sporadically. As a result, applications need additional data extraction and fusion techniques to understand the content of these sites (e.g. to find out which RTO offers a specific type of accommodation with specific equipment). Thus, the integration of multiple data items representing the same real-world object into a single, consistent, and precise representation remains challenging [9].

6 Conclusion

The present work empirically studies the use of structured data on the websites of Austrian tourism regions. According to the results of this analysis, 59% of the tourism organizations surveyed use the Semantic Web, which is a high ratio in international and industry comparison. However, the use is designed according to the Pareto principle: 20% of the tourism regions account for 82% of all semantic markup. Most tourism regions adhere to the recommendations of the search engines and use the ontology Schema.org and the formats Microdata and JSON-LD. While semantic markup of basic information such as addresses, corporate and website data is necessary, many areas that would contribute to unlock the full potential of the Semantic Web are neglected by Austrian RTOs. The use of touristic relevant topics, such as regional events, accommodations, blog posts, images or social media is dominated by a few RTOs. None of the special tourism ontologies were applied and also only a few classes and properties that are typical for this type of industry are used by a large number of tourism regions. Many tourism-relevant data, such as points of interest, ski resorts, user reviews, restaurants, job descriptions, accommodation equipment including dynamic content such as prices or availability is available on websites, but are only used sporadically by RTOs. Despite the comparable contents on the websites of RTO and a common objective to achieve the highest possible online visibility and better presentation in the search results and thus a higher booking and attendance rate, the usage scenarios of Semantic Web differ in Austrian tourism regions.

The findings of this study are based on a secondary source. This implies that the number of items of investigation was limited from the start. It has not been investigated whether the sites selected for this analysis were included in the original 3.2 billion site list. In addition, only the websites with a maximum of four website navigation levels were included in the original data set. The original record may also exclude websites that prohibit the browsing of their contents by the unknown web crawlers, which was also not checked during this analysis. Furthermore, the structured data was extracted from the dataset for November 2017 at a single point in time, making it impossible, for example, to check some records in real time. An interesting research approach for the future would be to repeat the same study at a periodic interval to see if the use of Semantic Web technology has changed over time.

Another limitation of this study is the fact that several errors in the semantic annotations on the websites were found when preparing the source data for analysis. Such mistakes not only complicate data analysis but also may fail the very purpose of structured data. Since systematically error detection was not subject of this work, these may bias the analysis results through wrong classification or incorrect detection of semantic markup. Future research should focus more on error analysis in semantic annotations and how these errors could be avoided (e.g. through semantic annotation tools).

The analysis results may have further been influenced by the non-differentiation of language variants of a website. Thus, tourist regions with a large number of indexed pages on search engines, representing many touristic objects in multiple languages show better results in this analysis. In addition, the proportion of structured data that was used only on the subdomains of the websites of RTO has not been determined. It is thus possible that a whole tourist region shows better results, even though semantic annotations were only made on a few subdomains. Thus, an international comparison that copes with different languages and/or subdomains would be of interest. This would allow identifying best practices and recommended actions specifically for the tourism organizations in a certain country.

Even though tourism-specific semantic markup is not widely used in Austrian RTO websites, it can be expected that with the increasing spread of intelligent web applications and services, more and more content owners will deal with this subject. A better visibility of the services and offers of the touristic region through semantic annotations helps in the dissolution of dependence on international online intermediaries and should therefore be more widespread in the websites of Austrian tourism organizations.

References

1. Statistics Austria: Arrivals, Overnight Stays. http://www.statistik.at/web_en/statistics/Economy/tourism/accommodation/arrivals_overnight_stays/index.html. Accessed 05 Feb 2019
2. Statistics Austria: A tourism satellite account for Austria. http://www.statistik.at/web_en/statistics/Economy/tourism/tourism_satellite_accounts/value_added/index.html. Accessed 05 Feb 2019
3. UNWTO: World Tourism Barometer **16**(1), 1–26 (2018)
4. Franch, M., Martini, U., Inverardi, P.L.N., Buffa, F.: The role of the regional tourist boards in the destination marketing policies. The case of the dolomites. Int. Rev. Public Nonprofit Mark. **1**, 113–124 (2004)

5. Fensel, A., Kärle, E., Toma, I.: TourPack: packaging and disseminating touristic services with linked data and semantics. In: Hölldobler, S., Liang, Y. (eds.) Proceedings of the 1st International Workshop on Semantic Technologies (IWOST), pp. 43–54. CEUR-WS.org (2015)
6. Stavrakantonakis, I., Toma, I., Fensel, A., Fensel, D.: Hotel websites, Web 2.0, Web 3.0 and online direct marketing: the case of Austria. In: Xiang, Z., Tussyadiah, I. (eds.) Information and Communication Technologies in Tourism 2014, pp. 665–677. Springer, Cham (2013). https://doi.org/10.1007/978-3-319-03973-2_48
7. Toma, I., Stanciu, C., Fensel, A., Stavrakantonakis, I., Fensel, D.: Improving the online visibility of touristic service providers by using semantic annotations. In: Presutti, V., Blomqvist, E., Troncy, R., Sack, H., Papadakis, I., Tordai, A. (eds.) ESWC 2014. LNCS, vol. 8798, pp. 259–262. Springer, Cham (2014). https://doi.org/10.1007/978-3-319-11955-7_31
8. Kärle, E., Fensel, D.: Annotation based automatic action processing. In: Nikitina, N., Song, D., Fokoue, A., Haase, P. (eds.) Proceedings of the ISWC 2017 Posters & Demonstrations and Industry Tracks (2017)
9. Bizer, C., Heath, T., Berners-Lee, T.: Linked data - the story so far. Int. J. Semant. Web Inf. Syst. **5**, 1–22 (2009)
10. Kärle, E., Fensel, A., Toma, I., Fensel, D.: Why are there more hotels in Tyrol than in Austria? Analyzing Schema.org usage in the hotel domain. In: Inversini, A., Schegg, R. (eds.) Information and Communication Technologies in Tourism 2016, pp. 99–112. Springer, Cham (2016). https://doi.org/10.1007/978-3-319-28231-2_8
11. Buhalis, D., Law, R.: Progress in information technology and tourism management: 20 years on and 10 years after the Internet—The state of eTourism research. Tour. Manag. **29**, 609–623 (2008)
12. Navío-Marco, J., Ruiz-Gómez, L.M., Sevilla-Sevilla, C.: Progress in information technology and tourism management: 30 years on and 20 years after the internet - Revisiting Buhalis & Law's landmark study about eTourism. Tour. Manag. **69**, 460–470 (2018)
13. Vandenbussche, P.-Y., Atemezing, G.A., Poveda, M., Vatant, B.: Linked Open Vocabularies (LOV): a gateway to reusable semantic vocabularies on the Web. Semantic Web **8**, 437–452 (2017)
14. Linked Open Vocabularies (LOV). https://lov.linkeddata.es/dataset/lov. Accessed 18 Feb 2019
15. Kärle, E., Simsek, U., Akbar, Z., Hepp, M., Fensel, D.: Extending the Schema.org vocabulary for more expressive accommodation annotations. In: Schegg, R., Stangl, B. (eds.) Information and Communication Technologies in Tourism 2017, pp. 31–41. Springer, Cham (2017). https://doi.org/10.1007/978-3-319-51168-9_3
16. Soualah-Alila, F., Faucher, C., Bertrand, F., Coustaty, M., Doucet, A.: Applying semantic web technologies for improving the visibility of tourism data. In: Balog, K., Dalton, J., Doucet, A., Ibrahim, Y. (eds.) Proceedings of the Eighth Workshop on Exploiting Semantic Annotations in Information Retrieval - ESAIR 2015, pp. 5–10. ACM Press, New York (2015)
17. Jakkilinki, R., Sharda, N.: A framework for ontology-based tourism application generator. In: Pease, W., Rowe, M., Cooper, M. (eds.) Information and Communication Technologies in Support of the Tourism Industry, pp. 26–49. Idea Group Pub, Hershey (2007)

18. Fodor, O., Werthner, H.: Harmonise: a step toward an interoperable e-tourism marketplace. Int. J. Electron. Commer. **9**, 11–39 (2005)
19. Ou, S., Pekar, V., Orasan, C., Spurk, C., Negri, M.: Development and alignment of a domain-specific ontology for question answering. In: Proceedings of the 6th Edition of the Language Resources and Evaluation Conference, LREC 2008 (2008)
20. Barta, R., Feilmayr, C., Pröll, B., Grün, C., Werthner, H.: Covering the semantic space of tourism. In: Gómez-Pérez, J.M. (ed.) Proceedings of the 1st Workshop on Context, Information and Ontologies, CIAO 2009, Heraklion, Greece, 1 June 2009, pp. 1–8. ACM Press, New York (2009)
21. Hepp, M.: Accommodation Ontology Language Reference. http://purl.org/acco/ns. Accessed 18 Feb 2019
22. Gazzè, D., Lo Duca, A., Marchetti, A., Tesconi, M.: An overview of the tourpedia linked dataset with a focus on relations discovery among places. In: Hellmann, S., Parreira, J.X., Polleres, A. (eds.) SEMANTiCS Vienna 2015. Proceedings of the 11th International Conference on Semantic Systems: 16th–17th of September 2015, Vienna, Austria, pp. 157–160. The Association for Computing Machinery, New York (2015)
23. Meusel, R., Petrovski, P., Bizer, C.: The WebDataCommons microdata, RDFa and microformat dataset series. In: Mika, P., et al. (eds.) ISWC 2014. LNCS, vol. 8796, pp. 277–292. Springer, Cham (2014). https://doi.org/10.1007/978-3-319-11964-9_18
24. Meusel, R., Bizer, C., Paulheim, H.: A web-scale study of the adoption and evolution of the schema.org vocabulary over time. In: Akerkar, R., Dikaiakos, M., Achilleos, A., Omitola, T. (eds.) Proceedings of the 5th International Conference on Web Intelligence, Mining and Semantics, WIMS 2015. ACM Press, New York (2015)
25. Cao, K., Yang, Z.: A study of e-commerce adoption by tourism websites in China. J. Destin. Mark. Manag. **5**, 283–289 (2016)
26. del Carmen Calatrava Moreno, M., Hörhager, G., Schuster, R., Werthner, H.: Strategic E-Tourism alternatives for destinations. In: Tussyadiah, I., Inversini, A. (eds.) Information and Communication Technologies in Tourism 2015, pp. 405–417. Springer, Cham (2015). https://doi.org/10.1007/978-3-319-14343-9_30
27. Luna-Nevarez, C., Hyman, M.R.: Common practices in destination website design. J. Destin. Mark. Manag. **1**, 94–106 (2012)
28. Meusel, R., Paulheim, H.: Heuristics for fixing common errors in deployed *schema.org* microdata. In: Gandon, F., Sabou, M., Sack, H., d'Amato, C., Cudré-Mauroux, P., Zimmermann, A. (eds.) ESWC 2015. LNCS, vol. 9088, pp. 152–168. Springer, Cham (2015). https://doi.org/10.1007/978-3-319-18818-8_10
29. Şimşek, U., Kärle, E., Holzknecht, O., Fensel, D.: Domain specific semantic validation of schema.org annotations. In: Petrenko, Alexander K., Voronkov, A. (eds.) PSI 2017. LNCS, vol. 10742, pp. 417–429. Springer, Cham (2018). https://doi.org/10.1007/978-3-319-74313-4_31
30. Kärle, E., Şimşek, U., Fensel, D.: semantify.it, a platform for creation, publication and distribution of semantic annotations. In: Homenda, W., Roman, D. (eds.) The 11th International Conference on Advances in Semantic Processing (SEMAPRO), pp. 22–30 (2017)
31. Hepp, M., Siorpaes, K., Bachlechner, D.: Towards the semantic web in e-tourism: can annotation do the trick? In: ECIS 2006 Proceedings (2006)

32. Akbar, Z., Kärle, E., Panasiuk, O., Şimşek, U., Toma, I., Fensel, D.: Complete Semantics to empower Touristic Service Providers. In: Panetto, H., et al. (eds.) OTM 2017, vol. 10574, pp. 353–370. Springer, Cham (2017). https://doi.org/10.1007/978-3-319-69459-7_24
33. Zanker, M., Fuchs, M., Seebacher, A., Jessenitschnig, M., Stromberger, M.: An automated approach for deriving semantic annotations of tourism products based on geospatial information. In: Höpken, W., Gretzel, U., Law, R. (eds.) Information and Communication Technologies in Tourism, pp. 211–221. Springer, Vienna (2009). https://doi.org/10.1007/978-3-211-93971-0_18
34. Krajasits, C., Andel, A., Wach, I.: Stellenwert der Gemeinden für den österreichischen Tourismus. https://www.oir.at/files/download/projekte/Raumplanung/Tourismusgemeinden_EB_Sep08.pdf. Accessed 07 Feb 2019

Test-Driven Approach Towards GDPR Compliance

Harshvardhan J. Pandit[✉], Declan O'Sullivan, and Dave Lewis

ADAPT Centre, Trinity College Dublin, Dublin, Ireland
{pandith,declan.osullivan,dave.lewis}@tcd.ie

Abstract. An organisation using personal data should document its data governance processes to maintain and demonstrate compliance with the General Data Protection Regulation (GDPR). As processes evolve, their documentation should reflect these changes with an assessment showing ongoing compliance. Through this paper, we show how semantic representations of processes are useful towards maintaining ongoing GDPR compliance by using a test-driven approach that generates and checks constraints for adherence to GDPR requirements. We first check whether all required information has been documented, and then whether it is compliant. We prototype our testing approach using a real-world website's consent mechanism for GDPR compliance, and persist results towards generating documentation. We use previously-published ontologies to represent processes (GDPRov), consent (GConsent), and GDPR (GDPRtEXT), with SHACL used to test requirement constraints.

Paper and Resources: https://w3id.org/GDPRep/semantic-tests.

Keywords: GDPR · GDPR compliance · Consent · SHACL

1 Introduction

Demonstrating compliance towards the General Data Protection Regulation (GDPR) [17] requires documenting information regarding how its various obligations and requirements were met. GDPR explicitly requires documentation of information for records of processing activities (R82, A30), consent (R42, A7-1), and impact assessment (DPIA (A35)). It also requires controllers to implement and periodically review appropriate measures regarding processing (A5-1, A24). Therefore the process of assessing, maintaining, and demonstrating compliance with the GDPR is tightly coupled with operational workflows involving personal data.

Processes change and evolve over time - such as the purpose may change, or the same process is used for other additional purposes, or the assigned processor changes. For GDPR compliance, each such change needs to be documented as a temporally versioned record of processing to demonstrate compliance regarding processing activities at that period in time. It would be considered prudence or good practice to show that the specific change was assessed and verified to be

M. Acosta et al. (Eds.): SEMANTiCS 2019, LNCS 11702, pp. 19–33, 2019.
https://doi.org/10.1007/978-3-030-33220-4_2

compliant before proceeding with it. This is mandatory under GDPR for certain situations requiring a DPIA (A35).

Semantics, and by extension the semantic-web, has been demonstrated to be of assistance in the management of GDPR compliance. Existing work addresses modelling machine-readable metadata for compliance [8,11,13,14], querying for compliance-related information [16], and maintaining compliant processing logs [8]. Interoperable semantics are beneficial when information is shared between stakeholders such as - controllers and processors, or controllers and certification bodies or supervisory authorities. The interoperability is also helpful towards transparency regarding processing activities to address the discrepancy between requirements of an organisation and compliance [18]. A discussion of four areas where automation can be applied [7], one of which is compliance using checklists, shows possible avenues for further incorporating semantics into the compliance process.

In this paper, we show how semantic representation of processes are useful in a test-driven approach for documenting ongoing compliance with the GDPR. We describe our approach towards generating and testing constraints based on requirements gathered from GDPR and the use of semantics to generate documentation linked with the GDPR. The paper also presents an application of this approach by testing a website's consent mechanism for GDPR compliance and generating compliance documentation. For this, we build on our previous work including ontologies to represent processes (GDPRov [14]), consent (GConsent [12]), and GDPR (GDPRtEXT [13]), and an approach to turn compliance questions into semantic queries [16]. An overview of this was presented in a prior publication [15].

2 Approach

2.1 Generating Constraints from Requirements

The first step towards compliance is selecting applicable clauses from the GDPR and converting them into tangible requirements. Resources useful for this include information and guidance provided by Data Protection Authorities and professional institutes. Information pertaining to the fulfilment of these requirements is required for compliance documentation.

The next step is to identify information required to assess whether requirements have been met, and then generate constraints that check (a) presence of that information, and (b) verify its correctness. For the purposes of this paper, we focus on the legal basis of given consent, with a subset of the requirements and constraints presented in Table 1. Checking for presence of information before verification of correctness follows a closed-world assumption where absence of information indicates non-compliance.

Constraints that verify correctness, or rather conformance, to requirements are required to be implemented based on underlying information representations (e.g. ontology). Some constraint assessments can be automated whereas others require human intervention, particularly where qualitative requirements

Table 1. Subset of Constraints and Assumptions regarding Given Consent

GDPR	Constraint
A4-11	Consent must be associated with only one Data Subject
R32,A4-11	Consent must have one or more categories or types of personal data associated with it
R32,R42	Consent must have one or more purposes associated with it
R32,A4-11	Consent must have one or more processing associated with it
A7-3	Consent must have one and only one state/status
A7-2	Consent is given by exactly one Person
	Given consent must have information on how it was obtained
	Consent must have artefacts associated with how it was obtained
	Consent must have information on what choices provided
	Consent must have statement or affirmative action
	Consent must have information about right to withdraw
R32,A7-2	Consent must not have more than one medium it was provided
	Consent must have a timestamp indicating when it was given
	Purpose or processing associated with Third Party must specify role played by the Third Party
	If data is being stored, it must have information on how long it will be stored for
	Storage of data must have information on its storage location
R71,A9-2c,A22-2	Automated processing of personal data must be clearly indicated
R111,A49-1a	Data transfer to third country or international organisation must specify identity of recipient
R51,A8-2a	Personal data belonging to a special category must be clearly indicated

are involved. For example, informed consent requires the request to be clear and unambiguous - which needs to be evaluated manually[1].

A test for compliance contains verification of (one or more) constraints where results indicate compliance with identified requirements. By linking the constraint with relevant points or concepts within GDPR, it is possible to generate and document 'coverage' of compliance. For example, for constraints generated from identified requirements, by having their results linked to the GDPR, the number of tests passed indicates compliance with set of linked GDPR points or articles.

Constraints can be linked to each other to formulate dependency relationships. This can make testing for compliance more efficient by identifying common dependencies. It also allows creating logical groupings of related constraints. Such groupings can be based on functionality or relation to GDPR such as association

[1] While it may be possible to use NLP-based approaches to evaluate the complexity of language to determine whether it is clear and unambiguous, such approaches cannot be assumed to be universally applicable, and therefore require a manual assessment.

with one concept or one specific article. For example, requirements for validity of consent are grouped from individual constraints for each requirement (e.g. clear, unambiguous), with requirements for explicit consent containing only additional constraints along with the group for valid consent.

2.2 Model of Processes

Representing a model or template of processes as machine-readable metadata has advantages in terms of ex-ante verification of compliance. This allows creating constraints that specifically check whether the model of processes follows the requirements gathered from GDPR. This is distinct from verification of compliance using records or logs of processing which constitute as ex-post compliance. For example, verifying whether the consent collection mechanism follows requirements for valid consent is done by representing the mechanism as a model and checking constraints associated with validity of given consent.

The model also allows testing for existence of internal processes regarding handling of data subject rights and data breaches. The metadata representation of model enables creating a persistent snapshot of processes for planning, conducting an impact assessment (DPIA), and inspecting past compliance. Additionally, creating and testing a model allows abstraction of information common to instances such as notice or dialogue for consent - which is common to all or a significant number of data subjects. By abstracting such common information into the model of the process, actual instances of given consent need to be linked only with the relevant attributes and can refer to the model for more information regarding compliance.

Using models also makes the testing process more efficient in terms of reducing the number of tests to be conducted. If a model is verified to be compliant using prior testing, then its instances can be verified to be compliant using only the constraints specific to the instance. For example, when verifying compliance for processing using given consent as a legal basis, the validity of given consent also needs to be evaluated. By abstracting the model of collecting consent and verifying it to be compliant, the given consent used in processing is assumed to be valid. The only constraint that needs to be tested is therefore whether the processing is permitted based on the interpretation of given consent.

2.3 Testing and Documentation

The requirements and constraints by themselves are universal in that they can be expressed without dependence on any technology or information representation. Adapting constraints into an testing framework requires basing it on the underlying models and information representations. For example, where information is defined using RDF+OWL, the testing framework is created using relevant technologies that can query and validate RDF+OWL - such as using SPARQL [19] and SHACL [9] respectively. In this case, the information format (RDF) itself enables the use of semantics which assists in linking the information, constraints, and results with points of relevance within the GDPR. Where the underlying information format does not inherently supporting semantics, these can be added as metadata to the test results to link them with GDPR.

Having the information or metadata format be machine-readable and interoperable allows taking advantage of querying and validation. The testing framework needs to be aware of the vocabularies and technologies used to represent the information and should persist results using machine-readable metadata. Tests should be defined at a granular level to enable actionable constraints such as "personal data (category) should have a source". These are then combined to create larger and more complex tests, which is similar to the creation of 'unit' tests and combining them into modules to test complex functionality. For example, testing whether personal data collected from users and shared with a third party with legal basis of consent adheres to given consent requires verification using constraints that test - (a) source of personal data (user) (b) third party identity (c) legal basis, and (d) matching processing with given consent.

The results of tests are associated with articles or concepts within GDPR based on the requirements used to generate constraints. Depending on the extent of machine-readable information used, it is possible to also include information such as (a) representation of processes (b) testing constraints (c) results of internal evaluations (d) text of GDPR. The end result of the testing process is a report that lists compliance with GDPR in the form of requirements (un-)fulfilled.

3 Demonstration Using Use-Case

3.1 Creating the Data Graph

For the use-case, we chose the consent mechanism on quantcast.com website, depicted in Fig. 1, and modelled the data graph based on information presented in the consent dialogue and the website. The choice of website was made based on Quantcast being a provider of GDPR consent collection mechanism using the IAB consent framework[2]. The website was also one of the few (to the authors' knowledge) that allows changing/withdrawing consent using the same dialogue. We chose to include information from the website about analytics services provided by Quantcast as it uses personal data. More information on the creation of data graph is available online[3].

We used GDPRov[4] (which extends PROV-O [10] and P-Plan [3]) to model personal data and consent workflows, and GConsent[5] to model consent attributes and given consent. GDPRov allowed representing processes and personal data mentioned in the consent dialogue as models. GConsent allowed expressing consent using attributes such as medium and status. Where there was an overlap, such as for personal data and purpose, we used both to define the instance.

[2] IAB Transparency and Consent Framework https://advertisingconsent.eu/.
[3] Paper and Resources https://w3id.org/GDPRep/semantic-tests.
[4] GDPRov Ontology https://w3id.org/GDPRov.
[5] GConsent Ontology https://w3id.org/GConsent.

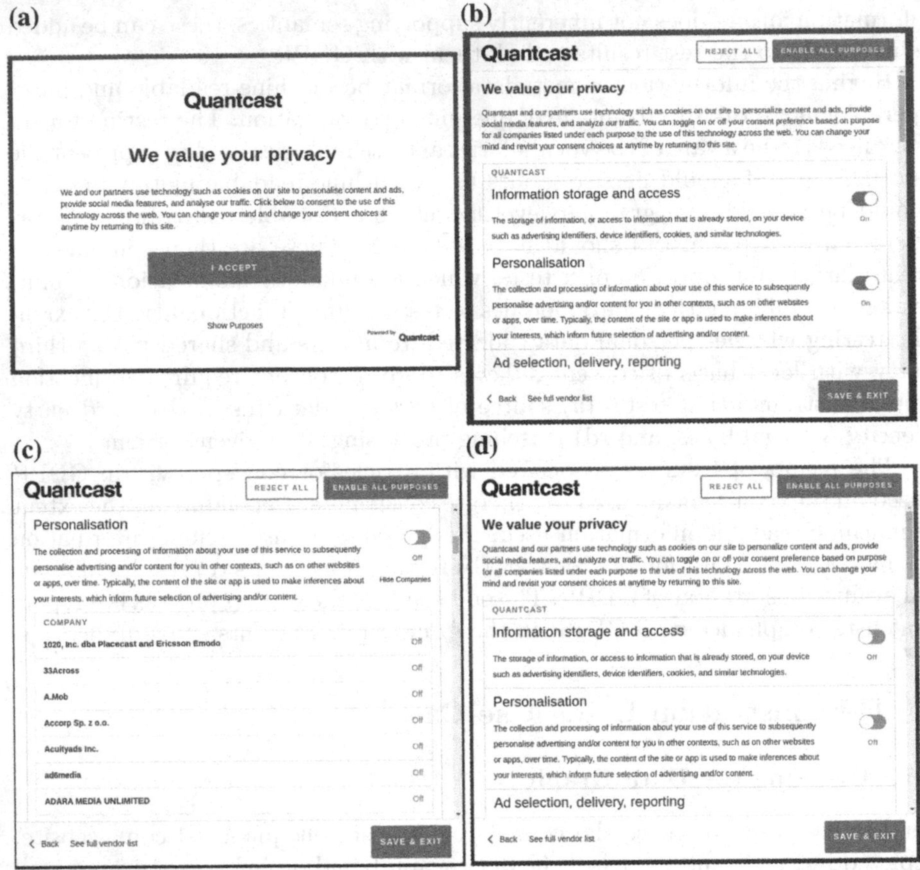

Fig. 1. Consent dialogues on quantcast.com (clockwise from top-left) (a) first screen (b) default options on selecting "I Accept" (c) default options on selecting "Show Purposes" (c) Third parties listed for purpose "Personalisation"

We collected personal data categories from the descriptions in the consent dialogue as well as other pages on the website describing various products and services offered by Quantcast. We defined the source of personal data as 'user' where data collection was mentioned in the consent dialogue, and 'third party' where explicitly defined. We defined processes for addressing the rights provided by GDPR using descriptions provided in the privacy policy. Where a URL or email address was provided regarding rights, we defined it as the IRI of the process for handling that right. We defined the IRI for DPO using the contact point provided in the policy.

We represented the consent collection mechanism on the website as an instance of *gdprov:ConsentAcquisitionStep*. This was defined as a step in the process *QChoice* representing the product Quantcast Choice. Similar processes were defined for Marketing, Advertisement, and Measurement identified from the information on the website. Each top-level description in the consent dialogue, e.g. Personalisation, was modeled as *gdprov:Purpose* and *gc:Purpose* with processing and personal data modeled from its description. The legal basis was defined using GDPRtEXT[6] and was associated at the process (purpose) or step (processing) level. We used given consent as the legal basis for purposes mentioned in the consent dialogue and legitimate interest otherwise.

In the consent dialogue, the use of independent radio buttons was interpreted as allowing the user to consent and withdraw for each individual purpose, which was represented by creating separate instances of consent for each choice. We modelled the dialogue as an instance of *gdprov:ConsentAgreementTemplateBundle* consisting of several *gdprov:ConsentAgreementTemplate* instances to represent multiple individual consent entities. We had difficulty in interpreting the language used for third parties as it suggests the user is giving consent directly to third parties rather than to Quantcast. Pending clarification from legal experts, we chose to represent these as data recipients rather than as Controllers or Joint-Controllers for ease of testing. This allowed us to represent the data sharing processes in a concise manner with each purpose being associated with the hundreds of third parties listed in the consent dialogue rather than defining a separate consent representation for every third party. For testing, we defined an instance of given consent (see Fig. 2.) which was then later withdrawn. All resources associated with the data, constraints, and queries are available online(see footnote 3).

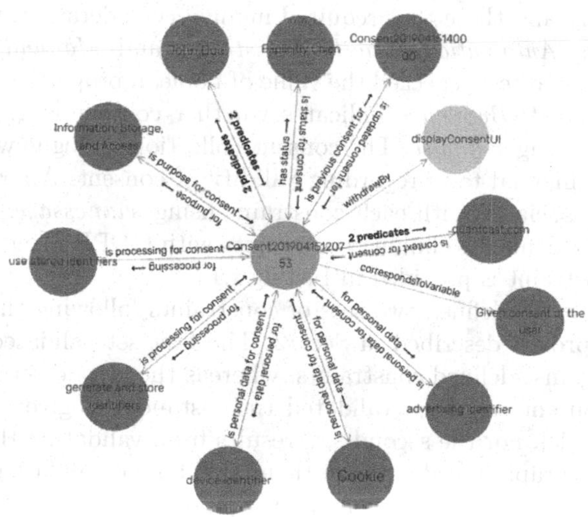

Fig. 2. Visualisation of Given Consent in the data graph (using GraphDB)

[6] GDPRtEXT Ontology and Resource https://w3id.org/GDPRtEXT.

```
:WithdrawConsentConstraints a sh:NodeShape ;
    sh:targetClass m:ManualTest ;
    sh:property :WithdrawConsentEase ;
    sh:property :WithdrawConsentInformation ;
    rdfs:label "Withdraw Consent Constraints" .
:WithdrawConsentEase a sh:PropertyShape , :ManuallyCheckedConstraint ;
    :linkToGDPR gdpr:article7-3 ;
    sh:name "Ease of Withdraw Consent" ;
    sh:path m:withdrawingConsentIsAsEasyAsGivingConsent ;
    sh:hasValue true ;
    sh:message "(M) Consent should be as easy to withdraw as it is to give" .
:WithdrawConsentInformation
    a sh:PropertyShape , :ManuallyCheckedConstraint ;
    :linkToGDPR gdpr:article7-3 ;
    sh:name "Withdraw Consent Information" ;
    sh:path m:withdrawingConsentInformationBeforeGivingConsent ;
    sh:hasValue true ;
    sh:message "(M) Information about withdrawal should be provided before giving
        consent" .
```

Listing 1.1. SHACL constraints for manual tests regarding consent withdrawal

3.2 Testing Data Graph for Compliance

We defined constraints over the data graph using SHACL and its extension SHACL-SPARQL [9]. For testing, we used the SHACL validator binary provided by TopBraid[7]. To distinguish between constraints that could be verified automatically and those that required manual consideration, we subclassed *sh:NodeShape* as *AutomaticallyCheckedConstraint* and *ManuallyCheckedConstraint* where manual tests checked the value of boolean properties. For example, the value of *consentIsBySilence* indicates whether consent is given by silence with valid value being *xsd:false*. The consent collection dialogue was considered as the input for manual tests regarding validity of consent. Appropriate result messages were associated with each constraint using *sh:message*. The property *linkToGDPR* was defined to linking constraints with GDPR using GDPRtEXT. An example constraint is provided in Listing 1.1.

For evaluation, we defined two sets of constraints following the outline provided in the approach described in Sect. 2. The first set validated instances of given consent against defined constraints, whereas the second set first validated the model of consent and then validated the instances of given consent using the validated model. For the second set, results from validating the model were persisted in data graph in order to use them as input to validate given consent. A simple bash script was used to construct a pipeline that executed constraints and stored results as a *rdf/turtle* file.

For ease of evaluation, we generated a combined data graph consisting of data from Quantcast and ontologies used (GDPRov, GConsent, GDPRtEXT). We added this data graph along with results of SHACL validation to a triple-store (GraphDB Free Edition[8]) under separate graphs. We then executed SPARQL queries to query the data graph and generate reports.

[7] TopBraid SHACL https://github.com/TopQuadrant/shacl/.
[8] GraphDB Triple-Store http://graphdb.ontotext.com/.

We used three separate queries to facilitate different actions associated with compliance. The first query listed the distinct messages from failing tests as actionable items. The second query listed the compliance of applicable GDPR articles using links from constraints and their verification. The third query, shown in Listing 1.2, generated a test report, depicted in Table 2, containing the constraint description, type - automatic (A) or manual (M), link to GDPR, result - pass (P) or fail (F), node (instance in data graph), and failure message (not shown in table). The results from these queries were then used to generate a compliance report to document the state of maintaining compliance and actions required. The report contains results of queries related to compliance [16]. The documentation regarding creating the data graph, constraints, and testing, along with the SPARQL queries and generated report is available online (see footnote 3) Fig. 3.

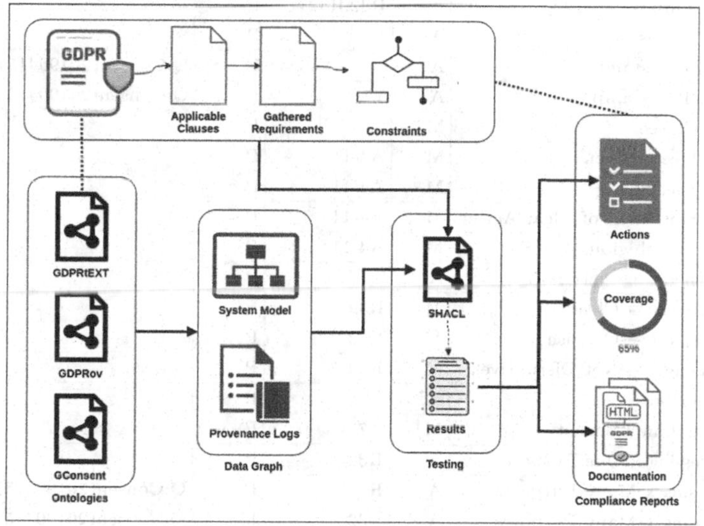

Fig. 3. Overview of testing process

4 Related Work

The approach presented in this paper acts on machine-readable metadata representation of processes and workflows associated with personal data and consent. An alternative to this is an approach that uses ODRL policies [5] for assessment of compliance using questions constructed from GDPR [1]. The ODRL policy consists of constraints classified as *Feature*, *Discretional*, and *Dispensation* with *Rule* used to specify them as *Permission*, *Prohibition*, or *Duty*. The policies are linked to the relevant text in GDPR using RDF properties similar to the use of GDPRtEXT in this paper. The questions are used in a tool that incorporates

Table 2. Report showing constraints, validation results, and link to GDPR

Name	Type	GDPR	Result	Node
Consent ≠ Inactivity	M	R32	P	
Consent ≠ Pre-ticked Boxes	M	R32	P	
Consent ≠ Silence	M	R32	P	
Consent → Data Subject	A	A4-11	P	
Consent → Given To	A		P	
Consent → Location	A		P	
Consent → Medium	A	A7-2	P	
Consent → Personal Data	A	A4-11,R32	P	
Consent → Processing	A	A4-11,R32	P	
Consent → Provided By	A	A7-2	P	
Consent → Purpose	A	R32,R42	P	
Consent → Status	A		P	
Consent → Timestamp	A		F	Q:Consent20190415120753
Consent → Timestamp	A		F	Q:Consent20190415140000
Consent ≡ Choice	M		P	
Consent ≡ Freely Given	M	A4-11	P	
Consent ≡ Specific	M	A4-11	P	
Consent ≡ Statement of Clear Action	M	A4-11	P	
Consent ≡ Unambigious	M	A4-11	P	
Consent Generating Activity	A		P	
Consent Request ≡ Clear	M	R32	P	
Consent Request ≡ Concise	M	R32	P	
Consent Request ≡ Not Disruptive	M	R32	P	
Consent Template	A		P	
Ease of Withdraw Consent	M	A7-3	P	
Many Processing x One Purpose	A	R32	P	
One Processing x Many Purposes	A	R32	F	Q:Consent20190415120753
One Processing x Many Purposes	A	R32	F	Q:Consent20190415140000
Personal Data → Storage Period	A	A13-2-a	F	Q:CATQInfoStorageAccess
Personal Data → Storage Period	A	A13-2-a	F	Q:CATTPInfoStorageAccess
Personal Data → Storage Period	A	A13-2-a,R39	F	Q:Consent20190415120753
Personal Data → Storage Period	A	A13-2-a,R39	F	Q:Consent20190415140000
Right to Withdraw	A	A7-3	P	
Separation of Processing	M	R43	P	
Third Party Categories	A	A44	P	
Third Party Identities	A	A13-1-e	P	
Third Party Identities	A	A30-1-d	P	
Third Party Identities	A	A44	P	
Third Party Safeguards	A		P	
Withdraw Consent Information	M	A7-3	P	

```
PREFIX c: <http://example.com/Quantcast/shapes#>
PREFIX sh: <http://www.w3.org/ns/shacl#>
SELECT DISTINCT ?name ?test ?gdpr ?result ?node ?msg
WHERE {
    ?x a c:Constraint .
    ?x sh:name ?name .
    BIND(
        IF(EXISTS{?x a c:AutomaticallyCheckedConstraint},
            "Automatic"^^xsd:string, "Manual"^^xsd:string)
        as ?test)
    OPTIONAL { ?x c:linkToGDPR ?gdpr }
    BIND(
        IF(EXISTS{?y sh:sourceConstraint ?x},
            "FAIL"^^xsd:string, "PASS"^^xsd:string)
        as ?result)
    OPTIONAL {
        FILTER EXISTS { ?y sh:sourceConstraint ?x } .
        ?y sh:focusNode ?node .
        ?y sh:resultMessage ?msg . }
} ORDER BY ?name
```

Listing 1.2. SPARQL query for report listing validation results linked with GDPR

human feedback and generates an assessment report. This is useful to incorporate the manual testing requirements from our approach, as well as to present the results from validation as a feedback process.

The Scalable Policy-aware Linked Data Architecture For Privacy, Transparency and Compliance (SPECIAL) is an European H2020 project that provides a semantic-web framework for the generation of logs that enable ex-post GDPR compliance verification [8]. Their compliance engine can also be used to perform ex-ante compliance checks [2] using a model-based approach similar to the one advocated by GDPRov. The compliance assessment in SPECIAL focuses on determining whether the specified use of purposes, processes, and personal data is allowed by the specified legal basis such as consent. This can be incorporated in our approach to determine the validity of constraints related to use of given consent for data processing operations.

Other related work includes PrOnto [11] - a legal ontology of concepts related to privacy agents, personal data types, processing operations, rights and obligations. Based on the examples shown in its associated publications, PrOnto can be used to define the underlying data graph and the constraints for compliance validation. The W3C Community Group for Data Protection Vocabularies and Controls[9] (DPVCG) is currently working on taxonomies for purposes, data processing, consent, personal data, technical and organisational measures, and legal basis which will provide a vocabulary for the representation and documentation of such processes. Layered Privacy Language (LPL) [4] can be used to model privacy properties such as personal privacy, user consent, data provenance, and retention management for the GDPR, and can be used to define the constraints using its authorisation-based modeling.

[9] DPVCG https://www.w3.org/community/dpvcg/.

5 Discussion

In this section, we provide a broad discussion of how our test-driven approach can be used as a practical tool by stakeholders and the challenges in its adoption for real-world cases. Considering that processes and activities in an organisations are traditionally documented without semantics, it could be tedious and cumbersome to adopt the semantic-web based framework described in this paper. However, as mentioned earlier, the test-based approach can also be used with existing representations by adding semantics to the test results and reports to link them with relevant information such as the articles in GDPR. This is also applicable towards persisting outputs of reports generated from tools [1] and conformity assessments (CAP) [6].

The advantages of representing processes with semantics goes beyond testing for compliance as representation of processes are also useful for planning of operations and internal documentation. Semantic representations of processes can assist in automating the generation of documentation such as privacy policies where processes are listed along with their purpose, legal basis, and use of personal data. Privacy policy generators that generate boilerplate policies exist online, but do not incorporate semantics. The use of semantics allows queryable machine-readable metadata that can be used in tools towards understanding and evaluating complex policies for users and authorities.

The modeling of third parties as data recipients in Sect. 3.1 shows the challenges in representing complexities when it comes to GDPR compliance. A report of cases regarding data protection [20] further shows instances where individual use-cases differ significantly, which could indicate that an universal ontology to represent such processes may not be feasible. A more practical approach could be to create taxonomies and use them in ontology design patterns for compliance. The DPVCG taxonomies could be used alongside existing ontologies to create compliance design patterns to address GDPR requirements. This follows open technological solutions such as the SPECIAL project that drive adoption of semantics in the regulatory compliance space.

6 Conclusion

This paper demonstrates the benefits of using a test-driven approach towards maintaining ongoing GDPR compliance by using semantic representations of processes. The approach generates and checks constraints for adherence to GDPR requirements and persists the results towards compliance documentation. The prototype demonstration provides an example of testing using a real-world website's consent mechanism using previously-published ontologies to represent processes (GDPRov), consent (GConsent), and GDPR (GDPRtEXT), with SHACL used to test requirement constraints.

In conclusion, the generation of compliance reports by incorporating semantics into the testing process is useful to maintain and document the state of compliance at a given time as well as to demonstrate the ongoing compliance for changes to the data processes within an organisation. While the demonstration in this paper only covers a small set of requirements for GDPR, namely those associated with given consent, it is sufficient to demonstrate the value of the approach and the use of semantics for compliance.

Acknowledgements. This work is supported by the ADAPT Centre for Digital Content Technology which is funded under the SFI Research Centres Programme (Grant 13/RC/2106) and is co-funded under the European Regional Development Fund.

References

1. Agarwal, S., Steyskal, S., Antunovic, F., Kirrane, S.: Legislative compliance assessment: framework, model and GDPR instantiation. In: Medina, M., Mitrakas, A., Rannenberg, K., Schweighofer, E., Tsouroulas, N. (eds.) APF 2018. LNCS, vol. 11079, pp. 131–149. Springer, Cham (2018). https://doi.org/10.1007/978-3-030-02547-2_8
2. Fernández, J.D., Ekaputra, F.J., Ruswono, P., Kiesling, E., Azzam, A.: Privacy-aware linked widgets. In: 1st Workshop on Fairness, Accountability, Transparency, Ethics, and Society on the Web. In Conjunction with The Web Conference 2019, p. 8 (2019)
3. Garijo, D., Gil, Y.: The P-Plan Ontology, March 2014. http://vocab.linkeddata.es/p-plan/
4. Gerl, A., Bennani, N., Kosch, H., Brunie, L.: LPL, towards a GDPR-compliant privacy language: formal definition and usage. In: Hameurlain, A., Wagner, R. (eds.) Transactions on Large-Scale Data- and Knowledge-Centered Systems XXXVII. LNCS, vol. 10940, pp. 41–80. Springer, Heidelberg (2018). https://doi.org/10.1007/978-3-662-57932-9_2
5. Iannella, R., Villata, S.: ODRL Information Model 2.2, February 2018. https://www.w3.org/TR/odrl-model/
6. Kamara, I., Leenes, R., Lachaud, E., Stuurman, K., van Lieshout, M., Bodea, G.: Data protection certification mechanisms - study on articles 42 and 43 of the Regulation (EU) 2016/679. Technical report, Directorate -General for Justice and Consumers, Unit C.3 Data Protection and Unit C.4 International Data Flows and Protection, February 2019
7. Kingston, J.: Using artificial intelligence to support compliance with the general data protection regulation. Artif. Intell. Law **25**(4), 429–443 (2017). https://doi.10/gfxvtc, https://doi.org/10.1007/s10506-017-9206-9
8. Kirrane, S., et al.: A scalable consent, transparency and compliance architecture. In: Gangemi, A., et al. (eds.) ESWC 2018. LNCS, vol. 11155, pp. 131–136. Springer, Cham (2018). https://doi.org/10.1007/978-3-319-98192-5_25
9. Knublauch, H., Kontokostas, D.: Shapes Constraint Language (SHACL). https://www.w3.org/TR/shacl/
10. Lebo, T., et al.: PROV-O: The PROV Ontology (2013)
11. Palmirani, M., Martoni, M., Rossi, A., Bartolini, C., Robaldo, L.: PrOnto: privacy ontology for legal reasoning. In: Kő, A., Francesconi, E. (eds.) EGOVIS 2018. LNCS, vol. 11032, pp. 139–152. Springer, Cham (2018). https://doi.org/10.1007/978-3-319-98349-3_11

12. Pandit, H.J., Debruyne, C., O'Sullivan, D., Lewis, D.: GConsent - a consent ontology based on the GDPR. In: Hitzler, P., et al. (eds.) ESWC 2019. LNCS, vol. 11503, pp. 270–282. Springer, Cham (2019). https://doi.org/10.1007/978-3-030-21348-0_18
13. Pandit, H.J., Fatema, K., O'Sullivan, D., Lewis, D.: GDPRtEXT - GDPR as a linked data resource. In: Gangemi, A., et al. (eds.) ESWC 2018. LNCS, vol. 10843, pp. 481–495. Springer, Cham (2018). https://doi.org/10.1007/978-3-319-93417-4_31
14. Pandit, H.J., Lewis, D.: Modelling provenance for GDPR compliance using linked open data vocabularies. In: Proceedings of the 5th Workshop on Society, Privacy and the Semantic Web - Policy and Technology (PrivOn2017) (PrivOn) (2017). http://ceur-ws.org/Vol-1951/PrivOn2017_paper_6.pdf
15. Pandit, H.J., O'Sullivan, D., Lewis, D.: Exploring GDPR compliance over provenance graphs using SHACL. In: Proceedings of the Posters and Demos Track of the 14th International Conference on Semantic Systems co-located with the 14th International Conference on Semantic Systems (SEMANTiCS 2018), Vienna, Austria (2018). http://ceur-ws.org/Vol-2198/paper_120.pdf
16. Pandit, H.J., O'Sullivan, D., Lewis, D.: Queryable provenance metadata For GDPR compliance. In: Procedia Computer Science. Proceedings of the 14th International Conference on Semantic Systems 10th - 13th of September 2018 Vienna, Austria, vol. 137, pp. 262–268, January 2018. http://doi.org/10/gfdc6r, http://www.sciencedirect.com/science/article/pii/S1877050918316314
17. Regulation (EU) 2016/679 of the European Parliament and of the Council of 27 April 2016 on the protection of natural persons with regard to the processing of personal data and on the free movement of such data, and repealing Directive 95/46/EC (General Data Protection Regulation). Off. J. Eur. Union **L119**, 1–88, May 2016. http://eur-lex.europa.eu/legal-content/EN/TXT/?uri=OJ:L:2016:119:TOC
18. Schiffner, S., et al.: Towards a roadmap for privacy technologies and the general data protection regulation: a transatlantic initiative. In: Medina, M., Mitrakas, A., Rannenberg, K., Schweighofer, E., Tsouroulas, N. (eds.) APF 2018. LNCS, vol. 11079, pp. 24–42. Springer, Cham (2018). https://doi.org/10.1007/978-3-030-02547-2_2
19. SPARQL 1.1 Query Language. https://www.w3.org/TR/sparql11-query/
20. Zanfir-Fortuna, G.: Processing personal data on the basis of legitimate interests under the GDPR: Practical Cases. Technical report, Nymity (2018)

Linked Data Supported Content Analysis for Sociology

Tabea Tietz[1,2(✉)] and Harald Sack[1,2(✉)]

[1] FIZ Karlsruhe – Leibniz Institute for Information Infrastructure, Karlsruhe, Germany
{tabea.tietz,harald.sack}@fiz-karlsruhe.de
[2] Karlsruhe Institute for Technology, Institute AIFB, Karlsruhe, Germany

Abstract. Philology and hermeneutics as the analysis and interpretation of natural language text in written historical sources are the predecessors of modern content analysis and date back already to antiquity. In empirical social sciences, especially in sociology, content analysis provides valuable insights to social structures and cultural norms of the present and past. With the ever growing amount of text on the web to analyze, also numerous computer-assisted text analysis techniques and tools were developed in sociological research. However, existing methods often go without sufficient standardization. As a consequence, sociological text analysis is lacking transparency, reproducibility and data re-usability.

The goal of this paper is to show, how Linked Data principles and Entity Linking techniques can be used to structure, publish and analyze natural language text for sociological research to tackle these shortcomings. This is achieved on the use case of constitutional text documents of the Netherlands from 1884 to 2016 which represent an important contribution to the European cultural heritage. Finally, the generated data is made available and re-usable as Linked Data not only for sociologists, but also for all other researchers in the digital humanities domain interested in the development of constitutions in the Netherlands.

Keywords: Cultural heritage · Sociology · NLP · Linked Data · DBpedia

1 Introduction

Since the earliest existence of writing, text served as a means of human to human communication and is firmly established in human cultures [39]. The development of the Web and (for instance) the establishment of optical character recognition (OCR) and automated speech recognition (ASR) technologies increased the amount and diversity of natural language text available to humans and machines. Cultural heritage often is manifested in text and by now, numerous means to explore cultural heritage exist to make the data accessible and explorable to a broad audience, including interactive visualizations and recommendation systems. However, in order to understand cultural heritage scientifically, fields like digital humanities and social science exist. For sociologists,

M. Acosta et al. (Eds.): SEMANTiCS 2019, LNCS 11702, pp. 34–49, 2019.
https://doi.org/10.1007/978-3-030-33220-4_3

this unthinkable expanse of information captured in the form of text provides an important entry to social realty [27]. Sociological content analysis therefore also represents a necessary gateway to understanding cultural heritage and the social reality cultural heritage data captures. The mentioned cultural heritage exploration tools created for a broad audience however, are often not sufficient for sociologists to perform a scientific content analysis with. Instead, tools are needed to process, store, model, annotate (*code*) and analyze the data in order to develop new theories or test existing theories. With the increasing amount of text to be analyzed, also more technologies have been created to fulfill these tasks. In sociology, computer-assisted content analysis started out with (from today's perspective) simple frequency and valence analyses during the 1950s [35] and grew to more sophisticated statistical Natural Language Processing (NLP) approaches which became increasingly accurate and efficient in a way that they supported to uncover linguistic structures as well as semantic associations [11]. By now, a broad range of interesting and promising methods of computer assisted data acquisition and analysis have established. However, [29] criticizes that especially in social scientific research, no standardized and systematic means of the analysis of complex text material has emerged. [27] emphasizes the necessity to establish universal standards for a sustainable computer assisted text mining in sociology. Another problem in sociology regards data sharing, which is to this day widely not standardized and often not practiced at all [17,44]. According to [4], this lack of transparency lowers the integrity and interpretability of the performed research and its results. Another widely discussed issue in sociology is the re-use of research data, especially qualitative data [30]. A study by [6] suggests that sociologists generally welcome re-using research data in sociology, but certain aspects which includes the difficulty of finding and accessing these data often prevents them to do so.

The Semantic Web provides "a common framework for the liberation of data" [1] by giving data an independent existence [13]. As the Linked Open Data Cloud[1] visualizes, numerous domains have already not only firmly established methods to utilize the possibilities provided by Linked Data, they have also found ways to take part in the development, providing new applications based on the general idea. However in the field of sociological content analysis, Linked Data has so far not played an important role despite the promising standards and principles it entails.

The goal of this paper is to leverage Linked Data and its principles for computer-assisted sociological content analysis. Furthermore, it is demonstrated how this field of research can benefit from the mentioned data liberation process. Thereby, open research problems in both, the Linked Data and social science communities are discussed which (if solved) may improve the process of content analysis in the future. A lesson learned here is that in order to better understand cultural heritage data and its meaning for the society it originated in, the Linked Data research community is challenged to support sociologists in improving their research process to be more transparent, reproducible and re-usable.

[1] https://lod-cloud.net/, last accessed: May 12, 2019.

This paper demonstrates and discusses intersection points between Linked Data and content analysis in sociology on the foundation of the use case of constitutional text documents of the Netherlands from 1884 to 2016. The use case is generalizable and integrates Linked Data in sociological text analysis on a real world research example and thereby utilizes and discusses knowledge engineering, Named Entity Linking (NEL), and querying. Building on the previous work achieved in [41], the presented paper takes the Linked Data perspective instead of the sole sociological view.

This paper is structured as follows. In the following Sect. 2, relevant previous works on the intersection between social science and Linked Data are presented. Section 3 presents the use case of constitutional text documents and on this foundation, sociological content analysis techniques in combination with Linked Data technologies are discussed in Sect. 4.3. Section 5 closes this paper.

2 Related Work

To the best of our knowledge, no previous work exists which discusses the intersection between content analysis in sociology and Linked Data in the hereby presented depth. [13] motivated this work mostly, because the author pointed out the possibilities and necessity of Semantic Web technologies in this sociological analysis process. [2] defines annotation requirements to be implemented in cultural heritage annotation projects. The results are based on case studies at the National Library of Latvia. While the results are insightful, they do not completely apply to the process of content analysis in sociology. [11] emphasizes the foundations and applications of text mining in sociology, however, without discussing Linked Data applications. The use case to reveal intersection points between sociologists and the Linked Data community involves Dutch constitution documents. These documents were converted from their original XML format into RDF. The constitute project[2] as presented by [10] aimed at creating a platform for professionals drafting constitutions, and thus requiring to read and compare constitutions of various countries with each other. The main differences to the work presented here are (1) that the data is modeled not for constitution drafting but for a scientific content analysis and (2) the documents by [10] represent the latest version of a constitution and not all historical editions as it is the case in this presented paper.

3 Use Case

To asses the feasibility and benefits of modeling, storing, annotating and querying documents for sociological content analysis based on Linked Data, a generalizable research example of constitutional documents was chosen. The original document corpus was created by [23]. It consists of 20 XML documents with each one version of the Dutch constitution from 1884 to 2016 in German language.

[2] https://www.constituteproject.org/ontology/, last visited: May 12, 2019.

The previous work achieved by the authors is as important as it was cumbersome, since no machine-readable and chronological dataset of European constitutions is publicly available on the Web. Even though an HTML representation of these constitutions in German language exists on the Web[3], the information which changes appeared in which constitution edition is presented in an unstructured way. In sociological research, constitution texts enable to learn about state identities, definitions of affiliations (e.g. citizens, foreigners, heads of state) and their change over time [3,12,28]. Constitutions can be viewed as a mirror of society and as a self-description of the state in the context of global societies [14] and therefore represent an important contribution to cultural heritage. Sociological research questions involving constitution texts include the modeling of the relationship between the state and the citizen [23], the modeling of gender in a state [16,20] and religious freedom [26,40]. Constitutions follow a strict structure and hierarchy. Each document is divided into several main chapters which are furthermore divided into paragraphs, articles and sections. As often required in sociological content analysis, studying constitutional documents requires to research their structure, their content as well as their changes over time. Even though this use case covers only one domain of research for sociologists, it poses versatile research problems and is generalizable to a broad range of cultural heritage texts used for content analysis in sociology.

4 Linked Data Enabled Content Analysis for Sociology

In sociological research, data sharing and publishing is neither standardized nor is it widely practiced. Studies by [44] and [17] show that social science journals have just been starting to slowly adapt data sharing policies and most journals which enforce data publishing policies do so mostly in an incomplete and varied way. The problem gets more clear when having a look at the research process itself. In sociology, content analysis is generally performed in a process in which data is pre-processed (this can involve digitizing content as well as transforming the data into the needed format for analysis), followed by a coding process (i.e. categorizing the data in varying depth) and an analysis of the produced data to establish first hypotheses or test theories. However, as mentioned in Sect. 1, this process lacks standardized methods and reproducibility which jeopardizes the integrity of research results. This section addresses all three steps in this research process and shows how Linked Data can help to improve its reproducibility and transparency based on the use case scenario described in Sect. 3. Moreover, a number of insufficiencies are discussed which pose interesting long-term research questions for interdisciplinary research.

4.1 Modeling and Publishing Documents

The corpus introduced in Sect. 3 was originally created and made available as XML by [23]. While XML provides a number of benefits regarding the way data

[3] http://www.verfassungen.eu/, last accessed: May 12, 2019.

can be encoded syntactically, the format also has many disadvantages in contrast to RDF, especially in terms of re-usability, data extension and linking to external resources [8]. [10] specifically point out the benefits of publishing constitutional documents as RDF rather than XML. The data from the presented use case were converted to Linked Data according to the best practices specified by the W3C [19]. The Constitute Project already developed an ontology for this domain of constitution documents, which was reused and adapted. The ontology treats all parts of a constitution in the same way, regardless of its structural element (e.g article, section, paragraph). However, the information whether a piece of text belongs to a specific paragraph or a chapter is needed for querying in the context of a sociological analysis, therefore the ontology was adapted accordingly. Furthermore, the ontology by [10] models the year the respective constitution was created in, but often several constitution versions are created in the same year. The ontology was adapted accordingly for the presented use case. [23] created the constitutional XML documents which were utilized in the presented work. As a contribution for this paper, the data were modeled and published as Linked Open Data. As a result, anyone is now able to re-use the data, query the data using the standardized SPARQL query language as opposed to proprietary XML parsers, and to reference each single semantic unit of a document separately. An example snippet of the generated RDF data is depicted in Fig. 1. All generated RDF data are made available on Github[4]. For sociologists to model and publish their data as Linked Data for content analysis to become better reproducible and re-usable, this process seems straight forward. In order to find existing vocabularies for re-use, several tools exist, including Linked Open Vocabularies[5] or Prefix.cc[6]. Furthermore, there are a number of tools and guides to support researchers in the development and reuse of ontologies, e.g. [18,32,37].

4.2 Semantic Annotation

As mentioned above, a major part of the analysis of textual content in sociology is referred to as *coding*. This process means to categorize texts for analysis in order to develop new theories or test existing ones. One issue in this process is that often closed source tools are used which store the resulting data in proprietary formats (e.g. MAXQDA[7] or ATLAS.ti[8]). If neither the textual mentions the code is referring to nor the terms or categories used for coding (and their relationships) are made available immediately together with the concluding text drawn from the analysis, the research is not reproducible. One solution is to implement semantic annotation which makes use of ontologies, which explicitly structure knowledge and define relationships between concepts and individuals. On the example of the described use case, this section demonstrates and discusses semantic annotation for the content analysis process in sociology.

[4] https://github.com/tabeatietz/semsoc, last accessed: May 12, 2019.
[5] https://lov.linkeddata.es/dataset/lov/, last visited: May 12, 2019.
[6] http://prefix.cc/, last visited: May 12, 2019.
[7] https://www.maxqda.com/, last accessed: May 12, 2019.
[8] https://atlasti.com/, last accessed: May 12, 2019.

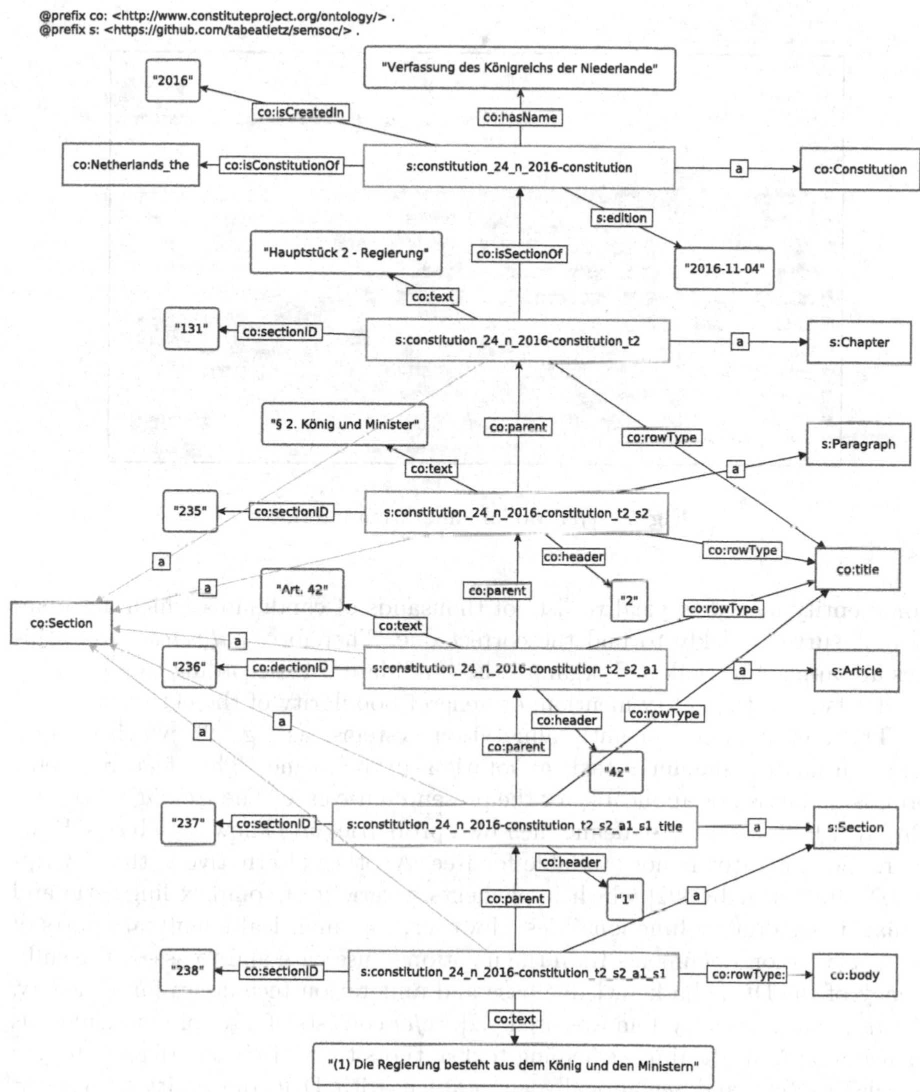

Fig. 1. Visualization of a subset of the generated RDF graph

Annotation System. Manual or semi-automatic annotation of text with entities from a large knowledge base like DBpedia requires an efficient user interface. The task of the user interface is to suggest possible entity candidates to the annotating user based on an input text. One of the major challenges is to present the entities in a way that users unfamiliar with Linked Data (lay-users) are able to make use of the interfaces. Lay-users typically have no further insight about what the content of a knowledge base is or how it is structured, which has to be considered when suggesting the entities the user should choose from [38].

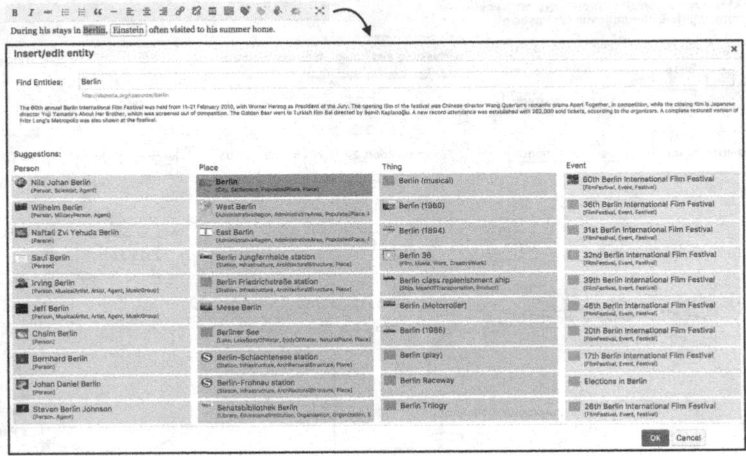

Fig. 2. *refer* Modal annotation interface

Some entity mentions yield to lists of thousands of candidates which a human cannot survey quickly to find the correct one. Therefore, *autosuggestion* utilities are applied to rank and organize the candidate lists according to e. g. string similarity with the entity mention, or general popularity of the entity [34].

There exist many semantic annotation systems, as e.g. [9], which enables semi-automated semantic text annotation in real-time. This feature seems promising but is not applicable for the presented use case. The *Pundit Annotator Pro* by [31] allows users to define their own properties and knowledge bases. However, the annotator is not available for free. Another alternative is the INCEpTION annotator by [22] which implements a variety of complex linguistic and semantic annotation functionalities. However, to semantically annotate parts of the constitution documents from the mentioned use case and to assess the sufficiency of the DBpedia knowledge base and annotation techniques for sociology, the *refer* annotation system was used [42]. *refer* consists of a set of powerful tools focusing on NEL. It aims at helping text authors to semi-automatically analyze textual content and semantically annotate it with DBpedia entities. In *refer*, automated NEL is complemented by manual semantic annotation supported by sophisticated autosuggestion of candidate entities. *refer* is chosen for this task, because it fulfills all annotation criteria mentioned by [21], is publicly available[9], and configurable. Furthermore, a user study focusing on lay-users has shown that the *refer* annotation interface is easy to use and enables a sophisticated annotation process for lay users [42]. The user can choose between a manual and automated annotation process. For automated annotation, *refer* deploys KEA-NEL [43]. For manual (or semi-automated) annotations, the *refer* annotator includes two configurable interfaces for creating or correcting annotations: the Modal annotator, shown in Fig. 2 and an the Inline annotator. The interface

[9] https://www.refer.cx/, last accessed: May 12, 2019.

leaves sufficient space for displaying relevant entities and additional information. Also, it provides a useful parallel view of all available categories. While this manual method seems (and is) cumbersome, it enables to evaluate the feasibility of DBpedia for constitution documents in depth.

Annotation Criteria. For the presented annotation task, several annotation criteria were defined, crucial for reproducibility. For sociological text analysis, it is generally assumed that rigid as well as non-rigid designators are important [25]. The rationale here is to generate as much knowledge as possible from the text to be able to analyze the data from multiple perspectives. Further entity annotation criteria regard entity specificity and completeness. It was defined to annotate textual mentions with semantic entities as specific and as complete as possible. A'Not In List' (NIL) entity was created and included in the configurable annotation interface. Whenever the annotating user encountered an entity not available in the knowledge base, the NIL entity was used to assess the level of completeness of the annotations and the sufficiency of the knowledge base. When annotating historical text documents for scientific analysis, it is especially important to acknowledge the entities' temporal role. That means, if a text in a Dutch constitution document edition from the year 2016 mentions a term like'*der König*' (the King), the term was annotated with the DBpedia resource dbr:Willem-Alexander_of_the_Netherlands. This task of temporal role detection is part of current research in NLP. Advances in this field have been accomplished by [24], the topic is also tackled in a current research project led by the University of Zurich[10]. Even though the NLP and NEL technologies are constantly improving, this rather difficult task of disambiguation has not yet been solved in a way that it can be easily implemented in any domain. This aspect also affirmed the decision to proceed with a manual annotation process in this use case.

Result. Parts of three constitutional documents were semantically annotated with DBpedia entities according to the criteria and method discussed above. The RDFa output created with *refer* was converted into NIF2 to ensure interoperability between language resources and annotations [15]. Overall, 1.175 annotations were created in three constitution documents using 218 distinct DBpedia entities. This means that on average, each DBpedia entity was used around five times. Over all documents, 242 NIL annotations were used, which means that around 20% of all named entities in the documents were not in the knowledge base (or could not be found). All annotations and a list of NIL annotation surface forms is presented on Github[11].

[10] http://www.cl.uzh.ch/en/research/completed-research/hist-temporal-entities.html, last accessed: May 12, 2019.

[11] https://github.com/tabeatietz/semsoc, last accessed: May 12, 2019.

Lessons Learned. Overall, it can be concluded that semantic annotations significantly improve the reproducibility of the research process, especially using ontologies like NIF2 or Open Annotation [36], because each conclusion drawn from the annotation (or coding) process can be proven directly in the annotation document up to character level. Data re-use is also ensured, especially if the annotation criteria are listed in the research process. The created annotations may be re-used in form of RDFa, useful for HTML pages, or NIF2 useful for querying and further adaptation. In general if the annotations are created thoroughly, they can furthermore function as a gold standard for computer scientists to improve and test NEL systems, especially with regard to the annotation criteria mentioned above. However, the process also revealed insufficiencies in terms of the underlying knowledge base, language problems and process automation. In the following, these shortcomings are listed and discussed with the goal to stress on their importance in future research work.

1. **Knowledge Graph:** Choosing DBpedia to annotate constitution documents seems reasonable, because the text corpus deals with constitutions, i.e. country specific information and facts about state leaders. These topics are generally well represented in Wikipedia. However, for 20% of all annotations NIL-entities were used. Therefore it can be concluded that solely using DBpedia is not enough for a profound annotation of these documents. One reason for this may be the systemic bias in Wikipedia [33]. It is easy to imagine that this problem does not only exist for constitution related documents but for a broad range of topics and domains. In general, solving this problem in the long term is crucial to enable sociologists to reliably use the knowledge base for their research process. In future work, also Wikidata should be tested as a knowledge base sufficient for the analysis, but to the best of our knowledge we could not find a user interface for annotating text with Wikidata items similar to *refer*. However, sociologists also need to partake in the process of creating knowledge graphs which fulfill their annotation needs. This way, the entire Linked Data community can benefit from this interdisciplinary approach as well.
2. **Language Issues:** Most NEL systems are created for English language text. This is a major problem when large non-English text corpora have to by analyzed. If non-English cultural heritage content is supposed to be analyzed and understood by sociologists and in any other domain, this is an important research task for the future. One prominent automated NEL system for German language text is DBpedia Spotlight [7]. However, initial experiments with the system revealed that the annotations did not meet the criteria mentioned above. Therefore it was eliminated from the research process.
3. **Historical Text:** The fact that the corpus in the use case includes documents dating back to 1884 further complicates the annotation process. For instance, it was important to map entities according to their temporal role. So far, there is no NEL system available which allows to annotate these temporal roles in German language with a decent quality. Apart from the temporal role disambiguation in this work, one challenge this corpus also provides is the changing style of language in the documents over time.

Even though these insufficiencies evolved during the annotation of constitutional texts, the problems are generalizable to a broad range of cultural heritage data. If these open research problems are resolved, social scientists seeking to understand large text corpora are able to use semantic annotation systems for their analysis process in a more automated manner.

4.3 Querying

When analyzing historical content in sociology, its changes over time as well as their causes and effects with regard to the society in which they appeared are crucial information to be studied. These changes may appear in the structure of a document as well as in the content itself. In this section it will be discussed on the example of the use case, how the previous data modelling and semantic annotation supports the analysis process. For this purpose all previously generated data was imported into the Blazegraph triple store[12] to be queried using SPARQL.

Time Based Analysis. Figure 3 visualizes an example of the analysis process which is enabled by previously modeling the data as Linked Data and querying. The different constitution editions are placed on a timeline along with information on structural changes and DBpedia context information. Constitutional documents follow a strict formal hierarchy. Each document is organized into several units, being the chapters, paragraphs, articles, and sections. A constitution's

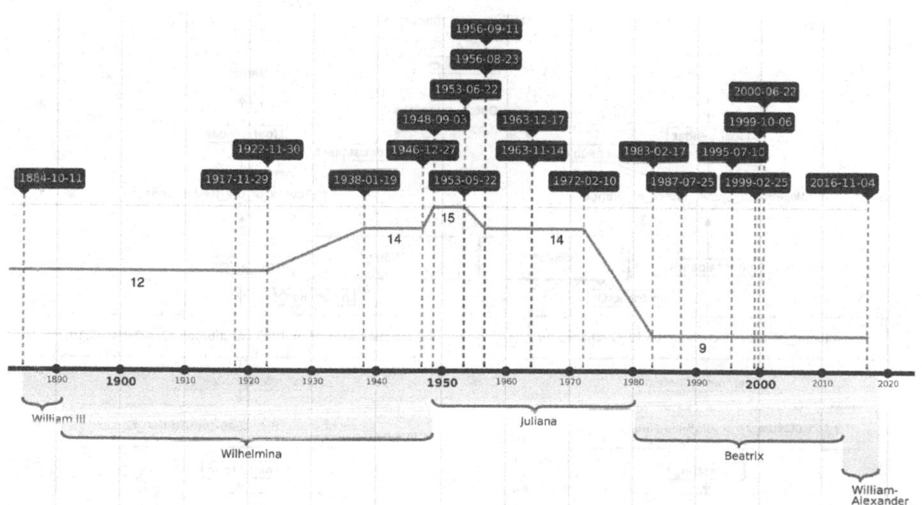

Fig. 3. Timeline of constitution editions, chapter numbers and context information (Color figure online)

[12] https://www.blazegraph.com/, last accessed: May 13, 2019.

chapter as the top level structural unit sets the entire framework of the constitution. Therefore querying and visualizing the changes of chapter numbers in constitutions (cf. red line) already reveal significant changes made in each document and allow the sociologist to focus on specific editions in the further analysis. Via federated querying, context information can be integrated into the process. In this case, information on the respective Dutch monarch was integrated via DBpedia, which may provide hints on the causes or effects on constitutional changes for further investigation.

Knowledge Graph Structure. Linked Data enabled sociological content analysis is especially useful when DBpedia entities are not only included into the analysis to widen the context, but also the underlying graph structure is utilized, as visualized in Fig. 4. In constitution texts, the monarch is named "King" at all times. Even if the monarch was a women (Queen). In sociology, the information of the monarch's gender is vital [5]. With the temporal role annotations as described in Sect. 4.2, the respective constitution editions can be aggregated in

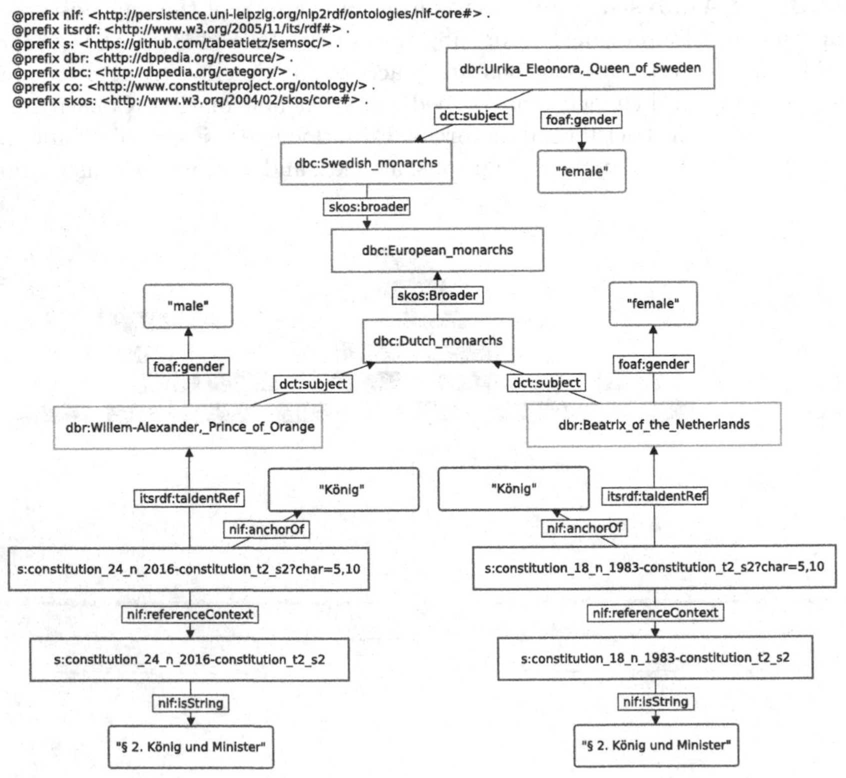

Fig. 4. In two separate constitution versions, "König" (King) was annotated with their respective DBpedia entity (Beatrix and Willem) which allowes to exploit the graph structure of DBpedia.

a more meaningful manner. When only taking into account the Dutch constitution, this possibility seems rather unspectacular, but being able to aggregate all European constitutions according to the gender of the head of state emphasizes how useful Linked Data can be in this analysis process.

Visual Aids. The RDFa enrichment created with *refer* enables to visualize additional information about annotated entities directly within the context of the document which has proven to be useful for the research process. When the annotated text is published within Wordpress (as it is the case with *refer*), the annotations are immediately presented in the document's HTML code. On mouseover, a so-called *infobox* as shown in Fig. 5 is displayed below the annotated text fragment. It contains basic information about the entity derived from DBpedia, e.g. a thumbnail and additional data from the entity RDF graph put in a table layout. When exploring an annotated document corpus of interest, sociologists can make use of these infobox visualizations to learn more about the data in front of them without having to leave the original context of the text. This can support a better understanding of the text, for instance if a certain term is unknown to them or, as shown in Fig. 5, they want to learn about the temporal roles of entities.

Fig. 5. Infobox visualization of former Prime Minister Ruud Lubbers

Discussion. Querying the documents for sociological content analysis with SPARQL revealed that the created data model and semantic annotations are immensely useful and allow to not only the aggregation of the data in the corpus on its own but also through the exploitation of DBpedia's graph structure. Using SPARQL on a RDF dataset which is shared with the research community also enables to share each query which led to the respective results. To make these benefits available to a large number of sociologists, a task for interdisciplinary future work is to create effective interactive visualizations for content analysis. These visualizations can be timelines which also incorporate context information from an external knowledge graph as well as relationship visualizations.

This section demonstrated the benefits of applying Linked Data standards to the different tasks of content analysis in sociology. This involves data modeling and publishing, annotation and querying. Major open research problems include the extension and improvement of existing knowledge graphs, the improvement of NEL systems for non-English texts and the possibility to annotate entities with respect to their temporal roles. Furthermore, meaningful visualizations may be developed to enable a better scientific exploration for non-technical users.

5 Conclusion

Content analysis in sociology is a gateway to understanding cultural heritage data. While a number of methods evolved to contribute to this process of modeling, annotating and analyzing textual content, most methods lack sufficient standardization which results in a research process where the results are often not reproducible and the data cannot be reused. Linked Data may be one way to counter these problems. The goal of this paper was therefore to present and discuss intersection points between Linked Data and content analysis in sociology. On the use case of historical Dutch constitutional documents, it was shown how Linked Data can enhance the entire research process by modeling and distributing research data in RDF, by semantically annotating texts e.g. with DBpedia entities and by querying the documents using SPARQL. One contribution of this paper is to provide lessons learned from the process, which revealed important and interesting open problems to be solved in interdisciplinary research between Linked Data experts and sociologists. Finally, it became apparent that in order to better understand cultural heritage data and its meaning for society, the Linked Data research community is challenged to support sociologists in improving their research to be more transparent, reproducible and re-usable.

References

1. Berners-Lee, T., Hall, W., Hendler, J.A., O'Hara, K., Shadbolt, N., Weitzner, D.J., et al.: A framework for web science. Found. Trends Web Sci. **1**(1), 1–130 (2006)
2. Bojārs, U., Rašmane, A., Žogla, A.: The requirements for semantic annotation of cultural heritage content. In: Proceedings of the 2nd Workshop on Humanities in the Semantic Web (WHiSe 2017). CEUR WS Proceedings. vol. 2014, pp. 69–79 (2017)
3. Boli-Bennett, J.: The ideology of expanding state authority in national constitutions, 1870–1970. National Development and the World System, pp. 212–237 (1979)
4. Büthe, T., Jacobs, A.M., Bleich, E., Pekkanen, R.J., Trachtenberg, M.: Qualitative & Multi-method Research (2008)
5. Crawford, K.: Perilous Performances: Gender and Regency in Early Modern France, vol. 145. Harvard University Press, Cambridge (2009)
6. Curty, R.G.: Factors influencing research data reuse in the social sciences: an exploratory study. IJDC **11**(1), 96–117 (2016)

7. Daiber, J., Jakob, M., Hokamp, C., Mendes, P.N.: Improving efficiency and accuracy in multilingual entity extraction. In: Proceedings of the 9th International Conference on Semantic Systems (I-Semantics), pp. 121–124 (2013)
8. Decker, S., Melnik, S., Van Harmelen, F., Fensel, D., Klein, M., Broekstra, J., Erdmann, M., Horrocks, I.: The semantic web: the roles of xml and rdf. IEEE Internet Comput. **4**(5), 63–73 (2000)
9. Eldesouky, B., Bakry, M., Maus, H., Dengel, A.: Seed, an end-user text composition tool for the semantic web. In: Groth, P., et al. (eds.) ISWC 2016. LNCS, vol. 9981, pp. 218–233. Springer, Cham (2016). https://doi.org/10.1007/978-3-319-46523-4_14
10. Elkins, Z., Ginsburg, T., Melton, J., Shaffer, R., Sequeda, J.F., Miranker, D.P.: Constitute: the world's constitutions to read, search, and compare. Web Semant.: Sci. Serv. Agents World Wide Web **27**, 10–18 (2014)
11. Evans, J.A., Aceves, P.: Machine translation: mining text for social theory. Annu. Rev. Sociol. **42**, 21–50 (2016)
12. Go, J.: A globalizing constitutionalism?: views from the postcolony, 1945–2000. Int. Sociol. **18**(1), 71–95 (2003)
13. Halford, S., Pope, C., Weal, M.: Digital futures? sociological challenges and opportunities in the emergent semantic web. Sociology **47**(1), 173–189 (2013)
14. Heintz, B., Schnabel, A.: Verfassungen als spiegel globaler normen? 58, 685–716 (2006)
15. Hellmann, S., Lehmann, J., Auer, S., Brümmer, M.: Integrating NLP using linked data. In: Alani, H., et al. (eds.) ISWC 2013. LNCS, vol. 8219, pp. 98–113. Springer, Heidelberg (2013). https://doi.org/10.1007/978-3-642-41338-4_7
16. Hergenhan, J.: Geschlechterdemokratie i. d. postrevolutionären Verfassung Tunesiens. Femina Politica-Zeitschrift f feministische Politikwiss **24**(1), 65–72 (2015)
17. Herndon, J., O'Reilly, R.: Data sharing policies in social sciences academic journals: evolving expectations of data sharing as a form of scholarly communication. The Academic Data Librarian in Theory and Practice, Databrarianship (2016)
18. Horridge, M., Knublauch, H., Rector, A., Stevens, R., Wroe, C.: A practical guide to building owl ontologies using the protégé-owl plugin and co-ode tools edition 1.0. University of Manchester (2004)
19. Hyland, B., Atemezing, G., Villazón-Terrazas, B.: Best Practices for Publishing Linked Data. W3C Recommendation, W3C (2014)
20. Kameri-Mbote, P.: Constitutions as pathways to gender equality in plural legal contexts. Oslo Law Rev. **5**(01), 21–41 (2018)
21. Khalili, A., Auer, S.: User interfaces for semantic authoring of textual content: a systematic literature review. Web Semant.: Sci. Serv. Agents World Wide Web **22**, 1–18 (2013)
22. Klie, J.C., Bugert, M., Boullosa, B., de Castilho, R.E., Gurevych, I.: The inception platform: machine-assisted and knowledge-oriented interactive annotation. In: Proceedings of the 27th International Conference on Computational Linguistics: System Demonstrations. pp. 5–9. Association for Computational Linguistics (2018)
23. Knoth, A., Stede, M., Hägert, E.: Dokumentenarbeit mit hierarchisch strukturierten texten: eine historisch vergleichende analyse von verfassungen. In: Vogeler, G. (ed.) Kritik der digitalen Vernunft. Abstract zur Jahrestagung des Verbandes Digital Humanities im deutschsprachigen Raum, pp. 196–203. University Köln (2018)

24. Koutraki, M., Bakhshandegan-Moghaddam, F., Sack, H.: Temporal role annotation for named entities. In: Proceedings of the 14th International Conference on Semantic Systems. (to be published) (2018)
25. Kripke, S.A.: Naming and necessity. Semantics of Natural Language, vol. 40, pp. 253–355. Springer, Dordrecht (1972). https://doi.org/10.1007/978-94-010-2557-7_9
26. Lagler, W.: Gott im grundgesetz? zur bedeutung des gottesbezugs in unserer verfassung und zum christlichen hintergrund der grund-und menschenrechte (2000)
27. Lemke, M., Wiedemann, G.: Einleitung text mining in den sozialwissenschaften. Text Mining in den Sozialwissenschaften, pp. 1–13. Springer, Wiesbaden (2016). https://doi.org/10.1007/978-3-658-07224-7_1
28. Lorenz, A.: How to measure constitutional rigidity: four concepts and two alternatives. J. Theor. Politics **17**(3), 339–361 (2005)
29. Mayring, P.: Qualitative Inhaltsanalyse, 12th edn. Beltz, Weinheim (2015)
30. Moore, N.: (re)using qualitative data? Sociol. Res. Online **12**(3), 1–13 (2007)
31. Morbidoni, C., Piccioli, A.: Curating a document collection via crowdsourcing with pundit 2.0. In: Gandon, F., Guéret, C., Villata, S., Breslin, J., Faron-Zucker, C., Zimmermann, A. (eds.) ESWC 2015. LNCS, vol. 9341, pp. 102–106. Springer, Cham (2015). https://doi.org/10.1007/978-3-319-25639-9_20
32. Musen, M.A.: The protégé project: a look back and a look forward. AI Matters **1**(4), 4–12 (2015)
33. Oeberst, A., Cress, U., Back, M., Nestler, S.: Individual versus collaborative information processing: the case of biases in Wikipedia. In: Cress, U., Moskaliuk, J., Jeong, H. (eds.) Mass Collaboration and Education. CCLS, vol. 16, pp. 165–185. Springer, Cham (2016). https://doi.org/10.1007/978-3-319-13536-6_9
34. Osterhoff, J., Waitelonis, J., Sack, H.: Widen the peepholes! entity-based auto-suggestion as a rich and yet immediate starting point for exploratory search. In: Proceedings of 2nd Workshop Interaction and Visualization in the Web of Data (IVDW). Gesellschaft für Informatik (2012)
35. Popping, R.: Computer-Assisted Text Analysis. Sage, Newcastle Upon Tyne (2000)
36. Sanderson, R., Ciccarese, P., Young, B.: Web Annotation Ontology (2016). https://www.w3.org/ns/oa#. Last accessed 19 July 2018
37. Schandl, T., Blumauer, A.: PoolParty: SKOS thesaurus management utilizing linked data. In: Aroyo, L., et al. (eds.) ESWC 2010. LNCS, vol. 6089, pp. 421–425. Springer, Heidelberg (2010). https://doi.org/10.1007/978-3-642-13489-0_36
38. Shneiderman, B., Plaisant, C., Cohen, M.S., Jacobs, S., Elmqvist, N., Diakopoulos, N.: Designing the User Interface: Strategies for Effective Human-Computer Interaction. Prentice Hall, Pearson (2016)
39. Silberman, N.A.: The Oxford Companion to Archaeology. 1. Ache-Hoho, vol. 1. Oxford University Press, Oxford (2012)
40. Starck, C.: Staat und religion. Juristenzeitung pp. 1–9 (2000)
41. Tietz, T.: The Application of Semantic Web Technologies to Content Analysis in Sociology. Master's thesis (2018)
42. Tietz, T., Jäger, J., Waitelonis, J., Sack, H.: Semantic annotation and information visualization for blogposts with refer. In: Workshop on Visualization and Interaction for Ontologies and Linked Data, co-located with ISWC, pp. 28–40 (2016)

43. Waitelonis, J., Sack, H.: Named entity linking in #tweets with kea. In: Proceedings of 6th Workshop on 'Making Sense of Microposts', Named Entity Recognition and Linking (NEEL) Challenge in conjunction with 25th International WWW Conference CEUR-WS (2016)
44. Zenk-Möltgen, W., Lepthien, G.: Data sharing in sociology journals. Online Inf. Rev. **38**(6), 709–722 (2014)

LinkedSaeima: A Linked Open Dataset of Latvia's Parliamentary Debates

Uldis Bojārs[1,2(✉)], Roberts Darģis[2], Uldis Lavrinovičs[3], and Pēteris Paikens[2]

[1] Faculty of Computing, University of Latvia, Raina bulvaris 19, Riga 1459, Latvia
uldis.bojars@lu.lv

[2] Institute of Mathematics and Computer Science, University of Latvia, Raina bulvaris 29, Riga 1459, Latvia
{roberts.dargis,peteris.paikens}@lumii.lv

[3] SIA LETA Innovation Labs, Marijas iela 2, Riga 1050, Latvia
uldis.lavrinovics@leta.lv

Abstract. This paper describes the LinkedSaeima dataset that contains structured data about Latvia's parliamentary debates from 1993 until 2017. This information is published at http://dati.saeima.korpuss.lv as Linked Open Data. It is a part of the Corpus of Saeima (the Parliament of Latvia) released as open data for multidisciplinary research. The data model of LinkedSaeima follows the data structure of the LinkedEP dataset with a few modifications. The dataset is augmented with links to the Wikidata knowledge base that provide additional information about the speakers and named entities mentioned in the corpus.

Keywords: Linked Open Data · Parliament debate corpus · Named entity linking · Open government data · RDF

1 Introduction

To ensure transparency of political and legislative processes, parliament proceedings and debate transcripts are usually made public. Saeima – the Parliament of the Republic of Latvia – publishes plenary transcripts on its website as unstructured text[1]. In 2016 we published this as a text corpus with speaker annotations and other metadata [1].

With the increasing availability of corpora in different languages we realized that unannotated corpora are not enough to address various researchers' needs such as comparative research across multiple languages. The 2018 release of the Corpus of Saeima attempted to address this concern by adding multiple additional annotation layers including named entity mentions, automated English translation and morphosyntactic information for linguistic analysis [2]. This release is available in multiple

[1] http://www.saeima.lv/lv/transcripts/category/21.

M. Acosta et al. (Eds.): SEMANTiCS 2019, LNCS 11702, pp. 50–56, 2019.
https://doi.org/10.1007/978-3-030-33220-4_4

commonly used formats: as a text corpus in NoSketch query software[2], as syntactically parsed data and as Linked Open Data [3].

This paper describes LinkedSaeima[3] – a Linked Data representation of the Corpus of Saeima containing structured information about Saeima proceedings and the entities mentioned in the proceedings, represented using Wikidata identifiers [4]. Linked Data allows us to represent structured information about parliamentary debates by describing the properties of the objects from the domain of parliamentary meetings and relations between these objects.

2 Parliamentary Speech Corpus

The source of data for this corpus is the Saeima website that contains transcripts of all parliament sessions in text format. These transcripts are processed using a semi-automatic pipeline to identify the boundaries of speeches and the speakers.

The Corpus of Saeima contains information about debates from seven parliamentary terms (5th–12th Saeima) covering years 1993–2017. The transcriptions of this corpus contain 38 million tokens and 497 thousand utterances. The available metadata for each utterance includes the date and type of the parliamentary session and speakers' names and affiliations. A subset of speeches, starting from 2015, were translated from Latvian to English using a neural machine translation system [5]. The unreviewed machine-generated translation is included in the corpus for quantitative analysis purposes and to aid searchability and understanding for international researchers. However, the text quality of automated translation is not sufficient for qualitative analysis of the Saeima corpus.

The named entities mentioned in this corpus were automatically linked to Wikidata as the entity knowledge base [4]. The named entity recognition system is based on a full text search of Wikidata entity names, extending these aliases by generating a heuristic list of alternative variants for organization and people names, and inflecting them through a custom Latvian phrase inflection system built upon the Latvian morphosyntactic tagger [6]. As the goal of named entity recognition was primarily to provide a mapping to Wikidata, no technical means were applied to recognize entities without relevant Wikidata entries, however, in order to improve the coverage of entity linking, Wikidata entries for historical members of parliament and other officials were created (if not already existant) and populated with data based on open access sources available from Saeima. For the purposes of disambiguation of entities with overlapping names, the most likely entity was chosen based on a cosine similarity metric with respect to structured Wikidata information extracts, adapting a system developed earlier for news corpora analysis [7].

2 NoSketch interface for this corpus: http://dati.saeima.korpuss.lv/nosketch/.

3 http://dati.saeima.korpuss.lv/.

3 LinkedSaeima Dataset

This paper focuses on LinkedSaeima – the Linked Data representation of the Saeima speech corpus. The current version of the dataset, published in May 2019, consists of approx. 4.9 million RDF triples[4]. Since the original January 2018 release we have fixed the identified issues with its RDF representation and improved the usability of the human-readable view of the dataset.

The dataset contains 497221 speeches (utterances) from 1293 parliament meetings. These speeches were given by 690 speakers with 162 speaker roles and contain 392530 mentions of 2998 unique Wikidata entities. It includes information about the following classes of objects:

- Meeting (*lpv_eu:SessionDay*) – a top-level concept representing one parliament plenary meeting usually consisting of multiple Speeches;
- Speech (*lpv_eu:Speech*) – an individual speech (utterance) given at a Meeting by a single Speaker in a particular Role;
- Speaker (*lpv:Speaker*) – a person giving a speech;
- Role (*lpv:PoliticalFunction*) – a role which the person represented when giving a Speech (e.g. the Prime Minister). A person may appear in multiple roles.

http://dati.saeima.korpuss.lv/entity/speech/2015_02_05_284-seq43

AN ENTITY OF TYPE: **Speech**

lpv:**number**	43	xsd:integer
dc:**date**	2015-02-05	xsd:date
lpv:**spokenText**	Mans mērķis, kad es ierosināju atteikties no dalības projektā, bija nedot iespēju izšķērdēt valsts līdzekļus. Un apstāties pie tā, kas jau šobrīd ir izdarīts [...] @lv	
dc:**language**	lv	xsd:language
lpv:**translatedText**	My goal, when I proposed to opt out of the draft membership, had withheld the possibility of wasting public resources and Un stop at what is already done [...] @en	
rdf:**type**	lpv_eu:Speech	
dcterms:**isPartOf**	<http://dati.saeima.korpuss.lv/entity/meeting/2015_02_05_284>	
lpv:**spokenAs**	<http://dati.saeima.korpuss.lv/entity/role/103> ↳ Government of Latvia | Minister of Economy	
lpv:**speaker**	<http://dati.saeima.korpuss.lv/entity/speaker/Dana_Reizniece-Ozola-1981> ↳ Dana Reizniece-Ozola	

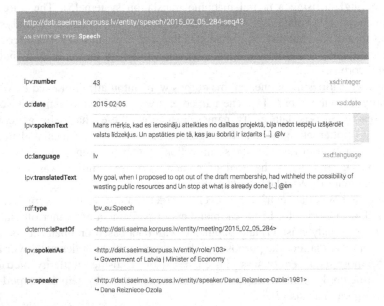

Fig. 1. LinkedSaeima information about a speech (in LodView browser). (http://dati.saeima.korpuss.lv/entity/speech/2015_02_05_284-seq43)

[4] LinkedSaeima RDF dump is available at http://saeima.korpuss.lv/datasets/rdf/.

Figure 1 shows an example of a Speech. Its properties include date (*dc:date*), sequence number (*lpv:number*), spoken (*lpv:spokenText*) and translated (*lpv:translatedText*) text, and it is related to the SessionDay it is a part of (*dct:isPartOf*), to the Speaker (*lpv:speaker*), its Role (*lpv:spokenAs*) and to the named entities recognized in the text.

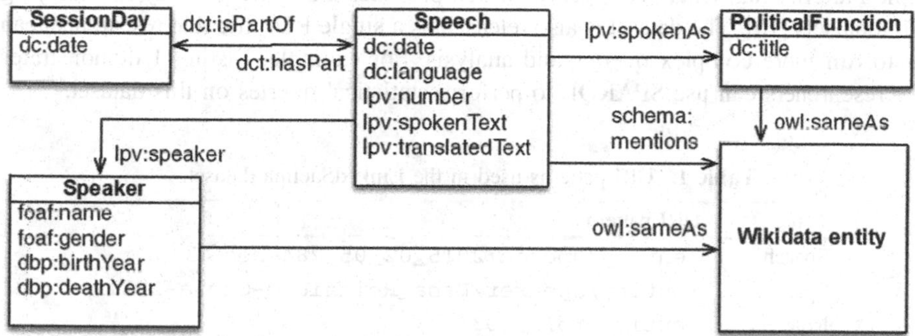

Fig. 2. The data model of the LinkedSaeima dataset.

The data model of the LinkedSaeima dataset, shown in Fig. 2, follows the model of the LinkedEP project and the Linkedpolitics vocabulary used in it, referenced in this paper using vocabulary prefixes *lpv* and *lpv_eu* [8]. The main innovation of this dataset, compared to LinkedEP, is the addition of named entity information, represented using the *schema:mentions* property pointing to entity Wikidata indentifiers. Another difference is that we "materialize" speaker Roles extracted from the corpus by giving them URI identifiers that can be used for querying the dataset (e.g. for speeches by Ministers of Foreign Affairs) and linking them to other datasets. Speaker roles (*lpv:PoliticalFunction*) may also contain links to matching entities in Wikidata.

There is ongoing work for standardization of corpora of parliamentary proceedings based on TEI [9]. Our approach could be applied to other parliamentary speech corpora by implementing a transformation from the TEI standard once it is finalized in order to make these resources available as Linked Data.

4 Data Access and Implementation

The LinkedSaeima dataset can be accessed:

- as Linked Data (published using LodView);
- using a Triple Pattern Fragments server and user interface[5];
- as a single RDF file[6].

[5] http://dati.saeima.korpuss.lv/ldf/saeima.

[6] http://saeima.korpuss.lv/datasets/rdf/.

The dataset is published as Linked Data, all its objects have HTTP URIs and information about them can be retrieved by looking up their URIs. The Linked Data interface is implemented using the LodView linked data browser[7] that can serve data in RDF, HTML and multiple other formats. The URI patterns used in the dataset, illustrated by examples, are listed in Table 1.

In order to provide a lightweight query interface, the dataset is published using the Triple Pattern Fragments (TPF) server which provides a lightweight way for querying RDF datasets [10]. The dataset is also released as a single RDF file that researchers can use to run more complex queries and analysis. For example, Listing 1 demonstrates how researchers can use SPARQL to perform statistical queries on this dataset.

Table 1. URI patterns used in the LinkedSaeima dataset.

Type	URI pattern
Speech	/entity/speech/2015_02_05_284-seq 43
Speaker	/entity/speaker/Dana_Reizniece-Ozola-1981
Role	/entity/role/103
SessionDay	/entity/meeting/2015_02_05_284

Listing 1. A query for the yearly statistics of speeches by the Minister of Foreign Affairs

```
PREFIX lpv: <http://purl.org/linkedpolitics/vocabulary/>
PREFIX lpv_eu: <http://purl.org/linkedpolitics/vocabulary/eu/plenary/>
PREFIX saeima_role: <http://dati.saeima.korpuss.lv/entity/role/>
PREFIX dc: <http://purl.org/dc/elements/1.1/>

SELECT ?year (COUNT(?speech) AS ?count)
WHERE {
  ?speech a lpv_eu:Speech .
  ?speech lpv:spokenAs saeima_role:23 .
  ?speech dc:date ?date .
  BIND (year(?date) as ?year) .
}
GROUP BY ?year
ORDER BY ?year
```

[7] LodLive linked data browser: https://github.com/dvcama/LodLive/.

5 Conclusions

In this paper we described LinkedSaeima – a Linked Data representation of the dataset of Latvia's parliamentary debates extended with NLP annotation layers. We hope that its Linked Data representation and the new annotation levels (entity references and translation) will allow researchers from other countries to use this resource in their studies, comparing Latvia's parliamentary data with data from other national parliaments and to provide users with new ways of exploring this information.

Expected future work includes extending the LinkedSaeima dataset with additional types of structured information, for example, voting data, and adding automated translations for the whole historical dataset. Improvements to entity recognition and morphosyntatic tagging are being carried out as part of related research projects.

By publishing this parliamentary corpus as Linked Open Data and by including links to Wikidata entities we hope to facilitate the development of a global network of linked political and legal information, and to provide an example to other implementers.

Acknowledgments. This research has been partially supported by the University of Latvia project AAP2016/B032 "Innovative information technologies", the European Regional Development Fund under the grant agreement No. 1.1.1.1/16/A/219 and the research project "Competence Centre of Information and Communication Technologies" of EU Structural funds, IT Competence Centre contract No. 1.2.1.1/18/A/003 research project No. 2.4 "Platform for the semantically structured information extraction from the massive Latvian news archive".

References

1. Dargis, R., Rābante-Buša, G., Auziņa, I., Kruks, S.: ParliSearch - A system for large text corpus discourse analysis. Frontiers in Artificial Intelligence and Applications, vol. 289, pp. 115–121 (2016)
2. Dargis, R., Auziņa, I., Bojārs, U., Paikens, P., Znotiņš, A.: Annotation of the corpus of the Saeima with multilingual standards. In: Proceedings of the Eleventh International Conference on Language Resources and Evaluation (LREC 2018) (2018)
3. Heath, T., Bizer, C.: Linked Data: Evolving the Web into a Global Data Space. Synthesis Lectures on the Semantic Web, 1st edn., vol. 1, no. 1, pp. 1–136. Morgan & Claypool (2011)
4. Ismayilov, A., Kontokostas, D., Auer, S., Lehmann, J., Hellmann, S.: Wikidata through the Eyes of DBpedia. Semant. Web **9**(4), 493–503 (2018)
5. Barone, A.V.M., Helcl, J., Sennrich, R., Haddow, B., Birch, A.: Deep architectures for neural machine translation. In: Proceedings of the Second Conference on Machine Translation, Vol. 1: Research Papers, pp. 99–107. Association for Computational Linguistics (2017)
6. Paikens, P.: Deep neural learning approaches for Latvian morphological tagging. In: Proceedings of Human Language Technologies - The Baltic Perspective, pp. 119–125 (2016)
7. Paikens, P.: Latvian newswire information extraction system and entity knowledge base. In: Proceedings of Human Language Technologies - The Baltic Perspective, pp. 119–125 (2014)

8. van Aggelen, A., Hollink, L., Kemman, M., Kleppe, M., Beunders, H.: The debates of the European parliament as linked open data. Semant. Web **8**(2), 271–281 (2017)
9. Erjavec, T., Pančur, A.: Parla-CLARIN: a TEI schema for corpora of parliamentary proceedings (2019). https://clarin-eric.github.io/parla-clarin/
10. Verborgh, R., et al.: Triple pattern fragments: a low-cost knowledge graph interface for the web. J. Web Semant. **37**, 184–206 (2016)

MusicKG: Representations of Sound and Music in the Middle Ages as Linked Open Data

Victoria Eyharabide[1(✉)], Vincent Lully[1], and Florentin Morel[2]

[1] STIH Laboratory, Sorbonne University, Paris, France
{maria-victoria.eyharabide, vincent.lully}@sorbonne-universite.fr
[2] IRcMus Laboratory, Sorbonne University, Paris, France
florentin.morel@etu.sorbonne-universite.fr

Abstract. The World Wide Web is one of the main ways of accessing knowledge in cultural heritage. Recently, several projects in digital humanities have emerged; however only a few are specialized in musicology. In this paper, we present MusicKG, a multilingual knowledge graph about medieval musicology and musical iconography. A specific ontology has been designed to integrate data from several iconographic and musicology databases. In addition, MusicKG is connected to the Linked Open Data cloud with a significant part of its classes, properties and instances being linked to Wikidata, Getty Vocabularies, MIMO, Iconclass and GeoNames. MusicKG is accessible and reusable by three means: a downloadable RDF dump, a Virtuoso faceted browser and a public SPARQL endpoint. Some representative SPARQL query examples are given to illustrate the scope of MusicKG and to show the potential impact on the research work in medieval musicology.

Keywords: Knowledge graph · Linked Open Data · Ontology · Musicology · Cultural heritage · Musical iconography

1 Introduction

The conservation of cultural heritage is very important for humankind. Today, many cultural organizations and actors store and maintain cultural data in digital forms. Applications like virtual visit of museums and culture search portal have been developed to provide digital experiences and interactions with cultural data.

Semantic Web technologies have been used in the cultural heritage field since more than a decade. An important amount of semantic data models, vocabularies and knowledge graphs (KG) have flourished. On the data model and vocabularies side, we can mention CIDOC Conceptual Reference Model [3], Cultural-ON [8], Sampo [6] and the Getty vocabularies[1]. With its own data model [7], Europeana tries to facilitate the

[1] http://www.getty.edu/research/tools/vocabularies/lod/.

M. Acosta et al. (Eds.): SEMANTiCS 2019, LNCS 11702, pp. 57–63, 2019.
https://doi.org/10.1007/978-3-030-33220-4_5

discoverability of cultural resources by collecting the resources'metadata and by centralizing them [5].

On the knowledge graph side, the Amsterdam Museum's Linked Open Data comprises the entire collection of the Amsterdam Museum consisting of more than 70,000 object descriptions [2]. ArCo[2] is a knowledge graph containing around 800.000 catalogue records of Italian cultural heritage entities (ex. archeological objects, numismatic objects). In the music domain which concerns more directly our work, we can mention the LinkedBrainz[3] project that helps MusicBrainz (an open music encyclopedia that collects music metadata) publish its database as Linked Data. Last, the DOREMUS knowledge graph [1] describes classical music works and their associated events (e.g. performances in concerts). The data come from three major French cultural institutions: the French National Library, Radio France and the Philharmonie de Paris.

In this paper, we introduce MusicKG, a unique cultural heritage knowledge graph containing representations of sound and music in the Middle Ages. In Sect. 2, we describe the source data of MusicKG. In Sect. 3, we detail the ontology underlying MusicKG. In Sect. 4, we show how MusicKG is connected to the Linked Open Data cloud. In Sect. 5, we illustrate the data scope of MusicKG with several SPARQL query examples. Section 6 discusses the potential impact of MusicKG on the research in medieval musicology and concludes the paper.

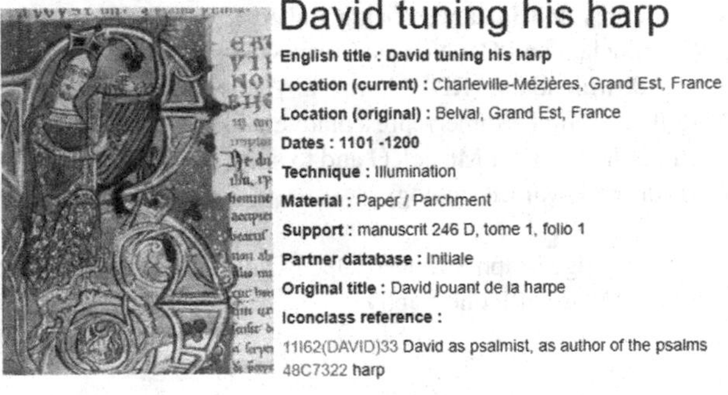

Fig. 1. King David tuning his harp - http://musiconis.huma-num.fr/en/fiche/39/x.html

[2] http://wit.istc.cnr.it/arco/.

[3] http://linkedbrainz.org/.

2 Source Data

The data in MusicKG comes from Musiconis, a database of musical iconographies created from several partner databases[4]: Musicastallis, Vitrail, Metropolitan Museum (NY), Mandragore, Initiale, Sculpture, Gothic Ivories, Et Stalla, and Romane. Each of the partner databases has its own specificity, generally related to the material support of its representations. For example, the Musicastallis database catalogs musical iconographic representations presented on the carved choir stalls of religious buildings. Currently, the Musiconis database contains 2154 iconographic representations whose scenes not only contain musical but also vocal, acrobatic or choreographic performances. These scenes are deeply analyzed and each instrument is described with organological details. Figure 1 depicts a Musiconis illumination representing King David tuning his harp. In this illumination of the character "B", it is possible to observe many details: the number of strings, the tuning key, the characteristics and the detailed form of the instrument.

3 MusicKG Data Model

We follow the W3C recommendation about "Data on the web best practices" [4]. We reuse vocabularies and resources as much as possible, including Wikidata from which the P… and Q… items listed below are taken from. In this section, we present the MusicKG data model which depicts representations of sound and music in the Middle Ages. The main class of our model is **Visual artwork** (Q4502142) (herein "artwork")

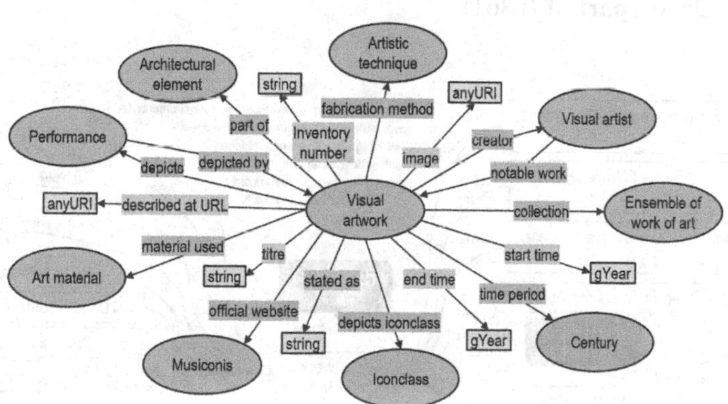

Fig. 2. The Visual artwork entity with its corresponding relations in our KG

[4] http://www.plm.paris-sorbonne.fr/musicastallis/, http://e-chastel.huma-num.fr/xmlui/handle/123456789/3, https://www.metmuseum.org, http://mandragore.bnf.fr/html/accueil.html, http://initiale.irht.cnrs.fr, http://www.gothicivories.courtauld.ac.uk, https://www.ru.nl/ckd/databases/stalla/introductie/.

which represents a visual artistic work or creation (see Fig. 2). Each **Visual artwork** instance (see example in Fig. 3) is connected to the original sources through several predicates: **official website** (P856), **collection** (P195), **inventory number** (P217) and **described at URL** (P973). Also, each artwork instance has a title from the Musiconis database and a title from its original database described by **title** (P1476) and **stated as** (P1932) respectively.

Images are essential for iconographic data. Generally, several **images** (P18) are associated with an artwork to capture all the details from different angles and with different resolutions. Regarding dates, each artwork has three different properties: **start time** (P580); **end time** (P582) and **time period** (P2348) that indicate the century, the date on which the artist began and finished creating the artwork respectively.

The class **Visual artist** (Q3391743) refers to the artist who made the artwork. An artwork is associated to its creator with the relation **creator** (P170). Each artist entity is portrayed with the properties **birth name** (P1477) and **notable work** (P800). In addition, we added two relations to each artwork instance: **material used** (P186) and **fabrication method** (P2079). In one hand, the relation **material used** describes the material an artwork is made of. This relation associates instances of artwork with **Art materials** (Q15303351) such as **Wood** (Q287) or **Ivory** (Q82001) for sculptures; **Textile** (Q28823) for embroideries and tapestry weavings; or **Glass** (Q11469) for stained glasses. On the other hand, the relation fabrication method relates an artwork with its **Artistic technique** (Q11177771), such as **Sculpture technique** (Q21711025) or **Painting technique** (Q1231896). In many cases, we have the information about the **manuscript** (Q87167) or the **Architectural element** (Q391414) to which a certain artwork belongs to. Examples of architectural elements are **archivolts** (Q636008), **misericords** (Q1938805), among many others. In those cases, we relate both entities through the relation **part of** (P361).

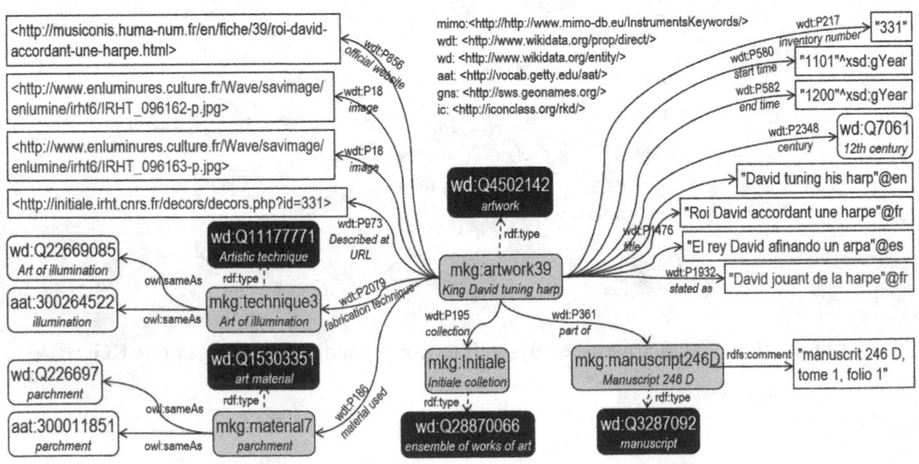

Fig. 3. Representation of the artwork instance describing the example of Fig. 1.

4 Linking MusicKG to the Linked Open Data Cloud

The singularity of MusicKG is its analysis of performances and the relationships between performances. This is one of the main contributions of our Knowledge Graph since, as far as we know, there are no other works that describe to this level of detail the relationships between entities within iconographic representations. Moreover, our model has been enriched with additional information coming from other popular Knowledge Graphs: Wikidata, Getty Vocabularies, Iconclass, MIMO and Geonames. Figure 4 shows an example of the interconnections between MusicKG and the aforementioned Knowledge Graphs.

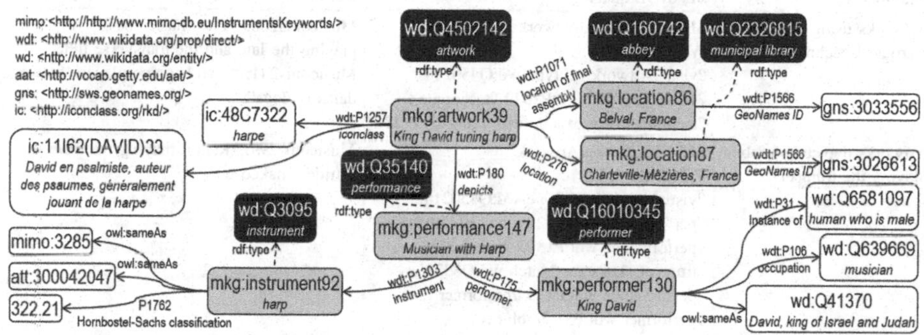

Fig. 4. Example of links between MusicKG and external KGs on the LOD cloud

We used the Wikidata entity Q35140 to represent **performances**. All performances are related to one or several **performers** (Q16010345) through the relation **performer** (P175) and **practiced by** (P3095) respectively. In our KG there are instrumental, vocal, choreographic and acrobatic performances. In the case of instrumental performances, the relation **instrument** (P1303) is used to associate a performance with the **instrument** (Q3095) played.

The property **occupation** (P106) establishes a relationship between a **performer** and a **profession** (Q35140) that represents their occupation or the activity they perform in the artwork. Some of the sixteenth century professions represented in our Knowledge Graph are: acrobat, singer, dancer, animal trainer, conjurer, juggler, pedagogue or partition holder. In addition, a performer may be an **instance of** (P31) an **animal** (Q729), **adult** (QQ9584157) or **mythical entity** (Q24334685); or have a **sex or gender** (P21) such as **male** (Q6581097) or **female** (Q6581072).

5 SPARQL Query Examples

MusicKG can be accessed by three means: a downloadable data dump, a Virtuoso faceted browser and a public SPARQL endpoint. All the information and links are available online[5]. MusicKG is oriented towards visual artworks, performances, performers and instruments. Users can specify techniques, materials, historical periods, etc. To illustrate the data we may retrieve from MusicKG, in Table 1, we provide two representative examples with their associated SPARQL query and result.

Table 1. Representative competency questions, SPARQL queries and results

Example	SPARQL query	Result
Artworks using the marquetry technique	SELECT ?visualArtwork WHERE { ?visualArtwork rdf:type wd:Q4502142 . ?visualArtwork wdt:P2079 ?technique . ?technique skos:exactMatch wd:Q1049923 .}	Musiconis100: "Two musicians playing the lute and the transverse flute" Musiconis241: "Two bagpipe players & two dancing dogs"
Artworks depicting a rabbit playing the trumpet	SELECT ?visualArtwork WHERE { ?visualArtwork rdf:type wd:Q4502142 . ?performance wdt:P1299 ?visualArtwork . ?performance wdt:P1303 ?trumpet . ?trumpet skos:exactMatch wd:Q8338 . ?performance wdt:P175 ?performer . ?performer wdt:P31 ?rabbit . ?rabbit skos:exactMatch wd:Q9394 .}	Musiconis299: "Rabbit playing the trumpet astride a naked man"

6 Conclusion and Future Work

In this paper, we presented MusicKG, a multilingual cultural heritage knowledge graph containing representations of sound and music in the Middle Ages. We presented respectively the source data, the ontology data model, how it is connected to external sources in the Linked Open Data Cloud and representative SPARQL queries. MusicKG may have a great impact on the research in medieval musicology, and more particularly, in musical iconography. The SPARQL endpoint allows to make more precise queries and to retrieve more accurate results. Furthermore, the connection with the LOD cloud may bring several benefits that we envisage exploiting. Wikidata items have known multilingual labels and aliases. We plan to retrieve these data more exhaustively to enable the multilingual display of the knowledge graph. We consider making the MusicKG searchable in multiple languages so that more people can access easily this unique cultural heritage database. As Wikidata is becoming the central hub for cultural heritage datasets with lots of institutions publishing their catalogue data, we will study the ingestion of MusicKG into Wikidata.

[5] https://github.com/victoriaeyharabide/MusicKG.

References

1. Achichi, M., Lisena, P., Todorov, K., Troncy, R., Delahousse, J.: DOREMUS: a graph of linked musical works. In: Vrandečić, D., et al. (eds.) ISWC 2018. LNCS, vol. 11137, pp. 3–19. Springer, Cham (2018). https://doi.org/10.1007/978-3-030-00668-6_1
2. de Boer, V., et al.: Amsterdam museum linked open data. Semant. Web **4**(3), 237–243 (2013)
3. Doerr, M.: The CIDOC conceptual reference module: an ontological approach to semantic interoperability of metadata. AI Mag. **24**(3), 75 (2003)
4. Farias Lóscio, B., Burle, C., Calegari, N. (eds.): Data on the Web Best Practices. W3C Recommendation, 31 January 2017. https://www.w3.org/TR/dwbp/
5. Freire, N., Meijers, E., Voorburg, R., Isaac, A.: Aggregation of cultural heritage datasets through the Web of Data. Procedia Comput. Sci. **137**, 120–126 (2018)
6. Hyvönen, E.: Cultural heritage linked data on the semantic web: three case studies using the sampo model. Artium, Vitoria-Gasteiz, Spain, 19–20 October 2016 (2016)
7. Isaac, A., Haslhofer, B.: Europeana linked open data–data.europeana.eu. Semant. Web **4**(3), 291–297 (2013)
8. Lodi, G., et al.: Semantic web for cultural heritage valorisation. In: Vrandečić, D., et al. (eds.) Data Analytics in Digital Humanities, pp. 3–37. Springer, Cham (2018). https://doi.org/10.1007/978-3-319-54499-1_1

Machine Learning and Deep Learning Techniques

Improving NLU Training over Linked Data with Placeholder Concepts

Tobias Schmitt[1], Cedric Kulbach[2], and York Sure-Vetter[1,2(✉)]

[1] Karlsruhe Institute of Technology (KIT), Karlsruhe, Germany
tobias.s.schmitt@web.de, york.sure-vetter@kit.edu

[2] FZI Research Center for Information Technology, Karlsruhe, Germany
kulbach@fzi.de

Abstract. Conversational systems, also known as dialogue systems, have become increasingly popular. They can perform a variety of tasks e.g. in B2C areas such as sales and customer services. A significant amount of research has already been conducted on improving the underlying algorithms of the natural language understanding (NLU) component of dialogue systems. This paper presents an approach to generate training datasets for the NLU component from Linked Data resources. We analyze how differently designed training datasets can impact the performance of the NLU component. Whereby, the training datasets differ mainly by varying values for the injection into fixed sentence patterns. As a core contribution, we introduce and evaluate the performance of different placeholder concepts. Our results show that a trained model with placeholder concepts is capable of handling dynamic Linked Data without retraining the NLU component. Thus, our approach also contributes to the robustness of the NLU component.

Keywords: Natural Language Understanding · Named Entity Recognition · Chatbots · Linked Data

1 Introduction

Modern conversational systems, also called dialogue systems (DS), are gaining access into peoples day-to-day lives and are offering an increasing number of services, especially known to the public audience in the form of chatbots. The standard DS consists of three components: the Natural Language Understanding (NLU) component, which identifies the meaning behind the incoming message and extracts relevant parts called entities, the Dialogue Manager (DM), which determines the corresponding action based on the output from the NLU, and the Natural Language Generator (NLG), which generates the response that is transmitted to the user [11].

In DS the NLU component mostly uses standard concepts from *Natural Language Processing (NLP)* tasks. It mainly consists of an *intent classifier* and a *named entity recognition (NER)* component. Both components make use of

M. Acosta et al. (Eds.): SEMANTiCS 2019, LNCS 11702, pp. 67–82, 2019.
https://doi.org/10.1007/978-3-030-33220-4_6

machine learning technologies, which mostly need to be trained supervised (s. Sect. 1.1). More and more data is published as Linked Data, which forms a suitable knowledge base for NLP tasks. In the context of chatbots a key challenge is developing intuitive ways to access this data to train an NLU pipeline and to generate answers for NLG purposes. Using the same knowledge base for NLU and NLG provides a self-sufficient system. An NLU component identifies the intents and entities which the NLG component requires for generating the response. However, the challenge becomes apparent when the knowledge base changes and the already trained NLU model deteriorates in the detection of intents and entities. Training on more general training data could avoid computational expensive retraining and make the NLU component more robust against changes in the knowledge base and unclear requests. In this context, we define the robustness of an NLU through the metrics of the NLU on not yet seen entity values. As a more general approach to create appropriate training data for the NLU we propose the placeholder concept where placeholder values are used as entity values instead of real ones taken from a related knowledge base. These values are then filled into predefined sentence patterns to generate the final dataset for training the NLU components. As a key result, we show which type of entity values (placeholder or database values) work best for training a NER algorithm or an intent classifier.

In a first step, we present the typical process that can be used when designing an NLU in the chatbot context. After a motivating example in Sect. 1.2 the procedure for the construction of training data for an NLU pipeline (Sect. 2) is shown. To compare the performance of the two conceptual approaches to create the NLU training dataset, we created a set of experiments that are described in Sect. 3. After evaluating the performance results of the conducted experiments in Sect. 4, we bring the paper into the context of related work (Sect. 5). An outlook is given in Sect. 6.

1.1 NLU in Chatbot Context

In current DS architectures the NLU component is the most critical component to the success of chatbots or question answering (Q&A) [6]. It aims to identify the meaning behind the user's input and extracts all the custom entity values in the incoming utterance [23]. Identifying the intent of the interlocutor is a classification problem that can be solved using supervised machine learning techniques. Available classifiers include Support Vector Machines (SVM) [3,13], deep neural networks [18,19] and embedding models [24]. The classifier is trained to predict to which of the learned intent classes the incoming utterance belongs to and to assign this label to the utterance so that it can be used by the next component [20]. All the intents that the system shall be able to match to user inputs have to be included in the training dataset. If the user input does not correspond to any of the learned intent labels, the model will still match it to one of them [16]. In closed domain DS this behavior leads to a chatbot that will answer every question, which must be taken into account during the creation process of the training dataset.

The second task of the NLU is to extract custom entities using sequence-labeling techniques. Conditional Random Fields (CRF) and Recurrent Neural Network (RNN) are most commonly used to label each unit in an utterance to determine the words that correspond to each of the learned entity types [10]. This is achieved by extracting features from the surrounding words (context) so that the system can predict not only the entity values present in the training data but also new values that users might use in their messages. Both components form an NLU. Examples of available NLUs include Microsoft's LUIS,[1] IBM's Watson[2] and RASA's NLU[3] [4].

```
"text"      :  "Where is the lecture Web Science taking place?",
"intent"    :  " location_of_lecture ",
" entities" :  [
{
"start"  :  21,
"end"    :  32,
"value"  :  "Web Science",
"entity":   "lecture"
}]
```

Listing 1.1. Example of a labelled utterance used to train the intent classifier and entity extractor of the NLU.

Example of a data point that can be either used for training or testing the NLU is presented in Listing 1.1 (s. Sect. 2). To generate the training data like the one shown, we create a set of utterances related to each intent and integrate the entity values from either a knowledge base or placeholder values at the designated places. This approach not only provides a semi-automated way for generating training datasets, such as the one depicted in Listing 1.1, it further provides the first step towards an integration of Semantic Question Answering (SQA) [21] tasks into chatbots. By generating training data as described in this work, the aim is to analyze how well a system can be trained if little or no information is available about the entity values that users might use in their utterances. In summary, we provide contributions to the following questions:

RQ 1 Which type of entity values work best for training the entity recognition algorithm?

RQ 2 Which type of entity values work best for training different intent classifiers?

RQ 3 How can linked data improve NLU performances?

1.2 Motivating Example

We describe an example that motivates our approach and experiments. The handbook for the study program *Industrial Engineering and Management* at

[1] https://www.luis.ai/home, accessed on 11.12.2018.

[2] https://console.bluemix.net/developer/Watson/documentation, accessed on 11.12.2018.

[3] https://rasa.com, accessed on 11.12.2018.

KIT is publicly available as a *.pdf* version. In order to make this information accessible by a computer program, such as a dialogue system, the relevant data were extracted and transformed to RDF. The domain of a DS trained with the RDF triplestore is defined by *lectures*, *lecturers*, *location* and *semesters*, where each *person*(lecturer) can lecture a *lecture* from a specific *module* in a given *room/building* (*location_of_lecture*) at a given *date/semester*. To answer a question like *'Where is the lecture Web Science taking place'* (*Q1*) the NLU needs to detect the intent *location_of_lecture* and the entity *lecture* with the value *'Web Science'*. Remarking that the question for a *location* is related to the entities found in the question (in *Q1 lecture*). This problem is addressed by *relation linking* (RL) [7]. Before the RL problem can be resolved, however, it must first be ensured that the correct intents and entities are found. To train the NLU a set of utterances for each intent is defined (s. Listing 1.1). In a closed domain DS the entries from the knowledge base can be used to generate utterances by replacing the entities (e.g. *"Web Science"* in Listing 1.1) from the utterances with the entries from the knowledge base. For example, with the help of the sentence pattern *'Where is the lecture lecture taking place?'* and the knowledge base, data points can be generated automatically from the *lectures* property. Whereby, *lecture* is a placeholder for the *lectures* entries from the triple store or other values. We call this concept the domain or placeholder concept (s. Sect. 2.1). The results are multiple data points with the same structure, but different entities. Taking into account that the entity values (i.e. for the entity *lecture*) can change over time, the NLU has the task of identifying intents and entities that did not exist before. We address this problem by providing a robust NLU (definition in Sect. 1) from the beginning.

2 Construction of Training Data

In the first part the general design approach is described before presenting a holistic approach that can be used to systematically create a DS and its matching training dataset.

2.1 Training Data Design Approaches

In this work, we aim to optimize the performance of the two tasks of the NLU (Intent classification and entity recognition) by optimizing the dataset that is used to train the system. Therefore we created two different design approaches that can be applied to create the training dataset for a domain-specific NLU. In this work, we focus on how the performance of the trained NLU is impacted if different types of entity values are used to create the training dataset.

Before going into the specifics of the approaches it has to be noticed that the utterance patterns have to be created. This is necessary so that the entity values can later be filled in automatically. For each of the defined intents, a set of utterances have to be created, where each one contains one or more entity values that the system shall learn to detect. Because we want to be able to insert different types of values automatically, an empty slot of matching type is inserted at the position where an entity value shall be inserted during the creation of the training data. Looking at utterance from the motivating example, we replaced the value of type lecture (*Web Science*) by an empty slot of type lecture (*'Where is the lecture {lecture} taking place'*). Now we are able to insert different types of entity values into the utterances without having to change the utterances manually. Both approaches use the same utterances for each intent but are filled with different kinds of entity values.

The two approaches described in the following are called the **Domain Concept** and **Placeholder Concept**. As the names suggest, we used entity values from a related knowledge base to create the training dataset within the database concept and placeholder values in the placeholder concept to create the dataset for training the NLU.

Looking at the domain concept, it can be seen that the related knowledge database is queried for each of the defined entity types with the goal to extract all available values and store them into a list. These values are then used to fill the empty slots in the utterances, with respect to the entity type restriction. Table 1 shows how both concepts work and further depicts an example for each of them. The example shows how one of the entity values of type *lecture* is used to fill the empty slot of matching type in the example utterance. This utterance together with the appropriate labels can then be used to train the component of the NLU.

Table 1. Conceptual approaches used to create the dataset for training and testing the NLU of the task-oriented component-based dialogue system.

Concept	**Domain Concept (DM Concept)**	**Placeholder Value Concepts**	
		Identical Pl. Values (PH Type 1)	Different Pl. Value (PH Type 2)
Entity value generation	Domain Entity Values	One random character sequence for all entity types	Random character sequence for each entity type
List of entity values	**Entity Type** / **Entity Values** Type1 / [List of values] Type2 / [List of values] ... / ...	**Entity Type** / **Entity Values** Type1 / Type2 / Random Value ...	**Entity Type** / **Entity Values** Type1 / Random Value 1 Type2 / Random Value 2 ... / ...
Utterance	<beginning of utterance> <entity type x> <...> <entity type y> <end of utterance>		
Example	Entity Type: lecture Entity Values: [**Web Science**, ...]	Entity Type: lecture Entity Value: x	Entity Type: lecture, ... Entity Value: v
	Where is the lecture <**lecture**> taking place?		

The second approach is called **Placeholder Concept** and refers to the fact that instead of real values, taken from some knowledge database, placeholder values are inserted into the utterances to create the dataset for training the NLU. In general, the placeholder values are values which consist of one or multiple random words of varying length. The random words used in this work have e.g. been created by randomly selecting one or multiple letters from the English alphabet. Within this concept, we followed two different ways of creating the dataset. The first one called **Identical Placeholder Values Concept (PH Type 1)**. As the name suggests in this approach only one random value is created and used to fill all the empty slots in the utterances regardless of the entity type. In the example shown in Table 1 the letter x was selected to fill all of the empty slots. The second approach is called **Different Placeholder Value Concept (PH Type 2)**. In this approach different random values are used to fill the different types of empty slots. For each of the defined entity types, one unique random value is created and used to fill the corresponding empty slots.

With the experiments described in Sect. 3 we aim to determine which design concept is best for training a domain-specific NLU. Based on the design specification of the concepts it can be assumed that if a dataset is created that contains all available entity values the results are likely to be highest.

In the next part of the section, we introduce a holistic approach that can be used to create the dataset matching the requirements of a domain-specific NLU of a task-oriented DS.

2.2 Training Data Creation Process

In this subsection, we describe an approach that can be used to design the NLU of a task-oriented DS and to create a dataset matching the requirements. The complete approach is depicted in Fig. 1 and is based on the procedure described by Grötz [8].

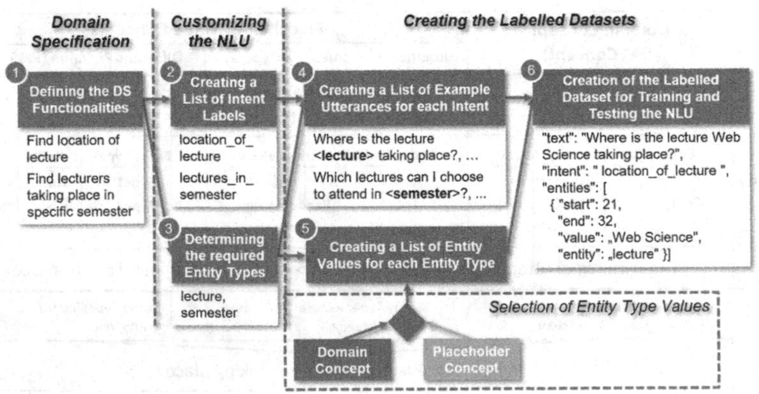

Fig. 1. Process for designing a customized NLU and creating the corresponding labeled dataset to train and test the system

The process consists of six processing steps which can be categorized into three areas. The first area focuses on defining the functions/tasks of the DS. The processes in the second area are to derive a set of intent and entity type labels that the NLU needs to be able to assign to an incoming utterance. In the processes of the last area, the previously defined intents and entity types are used to create a matching dataset for training (and testing) the NLU.

The first area is called **Domain Specification** and consists of one process during which a set of functions/tasks are defined that the dialogue system shall be able to handle. According to Grötz [8], it is recommended to start with a small set of functions and to use the collected experience over time to improve them and to successively add new ones. In this work, we created the NLU of a DS which aims to support students at the KIT in acquiring information related to their study program (s. Sect. 1.2). Two of the defined functions, depicted in Fig. 1, aim to find the location where a certain lecture takes place and to identify lectures that take place in a specific semester. In our approach, the information required to answer the students' questions are stored within an RDF knowledge base. SPARQL queries are used to extract the demanded information from the incoming question.

The second area is called **Customizing the NLU** during which a list of intent labels and entity type labels has to be defined that the NLU shall be able to assign to the incoming utterances. Within the second process step called *Creating a List of Intent Labels*, one intent label is created for each of the previously defined functions. Following the example depicted in Fig. 1, one intent label is created for each of the two functions. The intent label related to the first function is called *location_of_lecture* and the one related to the second function is called *lectures_in_semester*. In the third step, the types of entity values are determined which the NLU needs to be able to extract from the incoming utterances. These values are required to perform the functions defined in the first process step. The types of entity values that the NLU has to be able to extract can e.g. be derived from the underlying SPARQL queries. This is essential since the entity values are required to perform the query in order to retrieve the demanded information from the knowledge base. In the presented example, entity values of type *lecture* or of type *semester* are required to execute the underlying query.

After having defined the required parameters, the process steps within the third area focus on creating an optimal dataset for training the NLU. Within the fourth step, a list of utterances is created for each of the defined intents following the procedure described in the previous section. At the positions in the utterances where an entity value of a certain type shall be inserted, an empty slot of matching type is placed. Furthermore, the utterances have to match the language usage of the target users (e.g. formal or informal) [8]. In Fig. 1 one utterance for each of the two intents is depicted where each includes one of the two defined entity types. In the sixth step, a list of entity values for each type is created that is then used to fill the empty slots in the utterances in order to create the final dataset. As explained in the previous section there are two approaches that can be applied for replacing the empty slots in the utterances. The first one is depicted in step 5.1 where a list of 'real' entity values is extracted from a related knowledge base. As described in Sect. 1.2 we created a RDF knowledge graph that contains all information related to the industrial engineering and management study program at the KIT. The second option is to use placeholder values instead of real values. One value is assigned to each of the entity types, which can be either identical or different as shown in Table 1.

In the last process step the empty slots in the utterances from step 4 are replaced using one of the lists created in step 5. At last information about the two sets of labels are added to each utterance. This includes the intent label, the entity type, the entity value and the position at which the entity values can be found in the utterance. This information is stored in one of the formats such as JSON.

3 Experiments

Based on the previously introduced approach we created a task-oriented NLU to determine which of the approaches from Subsect. 2.1 is best for training such a system. In the first part, we describe the development of the training datasets which were used to train the NLU, which we then evaluated to compare the performance that can be achieved by following the different design approaches. The applied pipeline of the NLU is described as part of the state of the art within the context of related work (s. Sect. 5).

3.1 Creation of Domain Specific Dataset

In order to evaluate the different approaches previously described, we created several datasets to train the NLU of the DS introduced in Sect. 1.2. Following the process from Sect. 2.2 we first defined the functionality of our DS and used these to derive a set of intents and entity types for creating the NLU. Next, we created a set of utterances with empty slots for each intent and created three entity type lists with different values to fill the empty slots. In the last part of the section we describe the experimental datasets used to evaluate the design approaches from Sect. 2.1

System Specification and Creation of Utterances. Following the process described in Fig. 1 we defined 16 functions that our DS shall be able to perform. For the configuration of the NLU, we created one intent label per function, which the intent classifier shall be able to assign to incoming utterances after training. In addition, we derived the types of entity values that are required to perform the succeeding processing step, such as making a database inquiry (not realized in this work). In total, the NER component of the NLU needs to be able to recognize and extract six different types of entity values. An extract of the complete list of the intents and the corresponding entity values can be seen in Table 2. The first column shows the name of the intent and the last column the entity value type that is required for further processing.

Furthermore, the table shows how many utterances have been manually created for each intent. As described in Subsect. 2.1 we inserted empty slots at the position in the utterance where one of the entity values shall be included in the final step. In total 299 utterances were created, which were split into a train (80%) and a test (20%) set. These utterances are used by both design approaches to create the final datasets for training and testing the NLU.

Table 2. Number of training utterances created for each intent and their corresponding entity types.

Intent	Utterance			Entity type
	Train (80%)	Test (20%)	Combined	
lecturer_of_lecture	18	5	23	lecture
lectures_in_the_current_semester	8	3	11	semester, subject
semester_of_lecture	8	2	10	lecture, semester
subject_of_lecture	8	2	10	lecture, subject
modules_within_subject	16	4	20	subject
subject_affiliation_of_module	16	5	21	module
location_of_room	19	5	24	building
office_of_lecturer	16	4	20	person
...	...	...	...	...
Total	**234**	**65**	**299**	

Entity Values. As explained in Sect. 2.1 there are two options to replace the empty slots with a corresponding entity value. Following the domain concept, we extracted all values related to each of the six entity types from a related RDF file as explained in the motivating example. The values were retrieved by using one SPARQL query for each type, which was then stored into a list. One list was created for each entity type where all matching values were stored. As with the utterance, each entity list was split into a training and testing set. The combined set included all values found. Table 3 depicts the number of values found in the RDF file which relates to one of the six entity types. The second column in the table indicates how many empty slots in the utterances exist, which need to be filled in order to create the final dataset. Having extracted all possible values that the system needs to be able to recognize, the empty slots were replaced by looping through the created entity list and filling in a value of the matching type into the existing utterances. If there were more empty slots than unique entity values, some values were used more then once which were selected randomly. If there were more unique entity values than empty slots, some utterances were used more than once. In that case, we randomly selected a matching number of utterances from the list of utterances that only have an empty slot of that specific type. Those were then used to fill in the remaining utterances to finish the replacement process.

To create the utterances following the placeholder concept we created two sets of placeholder values. The type 1 consists of one value which is used to replace all empty slots in the utterances independent of the type. The type 2 list contains one unique value for each entity type, which is then used to replace the empty slots of matching type. The values we used to create our datasets are depicted in the last two columns of Table 3. In the last step, the previously created lists with entity value(s) can now be used to create the datasets for training and testing the different NLUs.

Table 3. Placeholder values and unique domain values used to replace the empty slots.

Entity type	Empty slots	Domain values			Placeholder values	
		Train (80%)	Test (20%)	Combined	Type 1	Type 2
lecture	137	69	18	87	x	v
person	46	36	10	46	x	p
semester	21	11	3	14	x	s
subject	41	4	1	5	x	f
module	61	44	11	55	x	m
building	24	19	5	24	x	g
Total	**330**	**183**	**48**	**231**	**1**	**6**

Experimental Datasets. In order to answer the research questions introduced in Sect. 1.1 we conducted a total of five experiments. Thereby we want to determine which type of entity values are best suited to create the training data and how the trained NLU performs of different test datasets.

The datasets for training the NLU have been created by filling the designated training utterances with some related entity values, as described in Subsect. 2.2. Table 4 contains an overview of the experiments and the datasets used to evaluate the performance of the NLU. The first two experiments are related to the domain concept. In the first experiment (EX 1) the training dataset contains a subset of the entity values that have been extracted from the available knowledge base. Thereby we want to analyze how well the NLU can perform the two tasks if the test set contains unknown utterances and unknown values taken from the knowledge base. In addition, we want to determine how well the NLU performs if the utterances are filled with entity values taken from another domain, in this case, the DBpedia knowledge graph. To determine how well the NLU performs if all domain related entity values are used for training, we conducted the second experiment (EX 2).

The third and fourth experiments (EX 3 and 4) have been created to evaluate how the performance of the NLU changes if placeholder values are used to train the system. In EX 3 the train utterances have been filled with the PH Type 1 values and in EX 4 they have been filled with PH Type 2 values.

In the last experiment, we filled the train utterances with the values extracted from the DBpedia and merged this one with the EX 1 dataset. Thereby we aim to determine if the performance can be approved when the dataset is enriched with values taken from another domain. Because we were not able to extract entity values form all of the six types, we only used the utterances that contain an entity type of at least one of the following types: lecture, building or person.

The datasets used to test the performance has been created by using either the test set of the domain values or the test set of the DBpedia values to fill the test utterances. Because the DBpedia set does not contain values of type semester, subject and module the domain values of those types have been used to create the *Test DBpedia* dataset. For determining and evaluating the performance of the different conceptual approaches we calculated the precision, recall and F1-score of the trained NLUs. No cross-validation has been applied to evaluate the performance.

Table 4. Utterances and entity values used to create the experimental datasets.

Training datasets	
EX 1	Train Utterances + Test Domain Entity Values
EX 2	Train Utterances + All Domain Entity Values
EX 3	Train Utterances + PH Type 1 Entity Values
EX 4	Train Utterances + PH Type 2 Entity Values
EX 5	EX1 extended by
	Train Utterances + Train DBpedia Entity Values
Testing datasets	
Domain test	Test Utterances + Test Domain Entity Values
DBpedia test	Test Utterances + Test DBpedia Entity Values

4 Evaluation Results

In this chapter, the results of the different experiments are evaluated. Table 5 provides an overview of the performance values that have been used to measure the performance of the NER and the intent classifier of the NLU. In the first part of the section, we analyze the results of the NER and intent classifier before giving a recommendation about which approach to use for training the two components of the NLU.

4.1 Performance NER

The first part of Table 5 shows the results when using the Domain Test dataset for evaluating the performance of the differently trained NLUs and the second part shows the results when using the DBpedia test dataset for testing. The first part of the table clearly shows that the datasets related to EX 1, 2 and 5 lead to the best NER performances. From those, it can be derived that using more unique entity values lead to better results. If all potential entity values that an NLU shall be able to extract are known in advance it is best to use them all for training. Enlarging the training dataset with utterances that are filled with values from another domain does not lead to better results. When using the DBpedia test dataset for evaluating the results clearly show that the F1-score of EX 5 is highest and therefore most suited for training. The results related to EX 1 and 2 are in this case far lower. In this case, the discrepancy between EX 1 and 2 and EX 5 is between 11.7 and 15.6% points. In the previous test, the results were much closer with a discrepancy between 3.2 and 6.1% points. In both cases training the NER with placeholder values lead to the lowest results. Although using PH type 1 values lead so slightly higher results the performance is still much lower than that of the other approaches. Due to the low results which are more than 50% lower, compared to the other approaches, they are not suited for training the NER component of the NLU.

Based on these results we recommend to use the approach related to EX 1 or 2 for training the NER component if the NLU shall be optimized for a certain domain. If instead, the NLU shall perform well on several domains we recommend to merge the datasets following the approach described in EX 5 to maximize the NER's performance.

Table 5. Performance results of the conducted experiments.

	NER			Embedding classifier		
	Precision	Recall	F1-Score	Precision	Recall	F1-Score
	Domain test					
EX 1	0.995	0.895	0.940	0.8626	0.8458	0.8452
EX 2	1.000	0.967	0.979	0.8497	0.8151	0.8101
EX 3	0.893	0.286	0.428	0.8663	0.8308	0.8288
EX 4	0.928	0.220	0.351	0.8311	0.8151	0.8029
EX 5	0.991	0.856	0.918	0.8657	0.8308	0.8269
	DBpedia test					
EX 1	0.878	0.770	0.812	0.8448	0.8151	0.8103
EX 2	1.000	0.806	0.851	0.8522	0.8151	0.8170
EX 3	0.835	0.312	0.451	0.8907	0.8769	0.8722
EX 4	0.848	0.220	0.351	0.8317	0.8151	0.8024
EX 5	0.992	0.950	0.968	0.8479	0.8308	0.8185

4.2 Performance Intent Classifier

The performance results of the different experiments when using the domain test for the evaluation show, that overall all different approaches perform well with F1-scores greater than 80%. By comparing EX 1 and 2 it can be noticed that when more unique entity values are used for training the performance of the classifier decreases. We assume this to be the case because several entity values are used multiple times within different utterances that belong to different intents. Because the classifier learns which words relate to which intent, we assume that this approach causes a distortion of the vector space which results in lower performance results. Therefore EX 1 performs better than EX 2 and is overall the best approach for training a domain-specific intent classifier. It has to be noticed that when using the other dataset for testing, the results of EX 2 are slightly higher than that of EX 1, which could indicate that there are other factors that have a significant impact of the performance.

Looking at the performance of the experiments that applied the placeholder concept, the results show that this approach is highly applicable for training a high-performance intent classifier. Especially when using PH type 1 values the discrepancy between EX 1 and EX 3 is only 1.64% points. Furthermore, it is possible to train a much more robust classifier using PH type 1 values. As can be seen from the results where the DBpedia test dataset has been used for testing the trained classifiers, the one which has been trained using PH type 1 values performs better than all the other trained classifiers. Therefore it can be said that this approach is better suited when we want to train a classifier that can perform well in several domains. This approach increases the robustness of the NLU which performs best when entity values form the DBpedia domain are used in the test utterances.

Based on the results at hand, we recommend applying the domain approach following the EX 1 construction when training an intent classifier that shall only perform well in a certain domain. When aiming towards training a more robust and open domain intent classifier we recommend to used PH type 1 values to construct the training dataset. Although the performance in some domains might be lower, compared to using domain-specific values for training, the performance overall domains will be higher.

In order to optimize the performance of the placeholder concept, differently designed placeholder values can be tested. We created values of different word length and also created values which consisted of two or more random words. Although we were not able to increase the performance, it might be possible to find values that can be used to increase the performance.

5 Related Work

Our contribution in training an NLU targets the research field of chatbots, as well as SQA. While most chatbot frameworks (IBM Watson, Microsoft Bot Service) are based on deep learning technologies for Intent and Entity Recognition as one NLU component, most SQA systems use static n-gram strategy [22] or Entity Linking Tools [5]. The *DBpedia Bot* [1] is one example for a rule-based, static SQA realization. This static approach of Q&A over knowledge graphs (KGs) has the disadvantage of only being able to react conditionally to sentence conversions. The idea of the *Frankenstein* Framework [22] is to link these static approaches by generalizing SQA into 3 steps (Named Entity Recognition and Disambiguation, Relation Linking and Query Building). Considering the SQA task our work addresses the NER and NED component, whereby an intent classification task is also taken into account and could improve the query building component. In general, it is possible to train multiple closed domain systems, which would make the NLU applicable in multiple domains [17]. For the present study, the closed domain knowledge is stored in a database and used to create the training data for the NLU. The database contains all entity values that users might use in their utterances.

Bapat et al. [2] already presented an end-to-end pipeline for simplifying the NLU training process, where the first sentences are defined and extended for the following training. While the extension of the training dataset is skipped and only classified into 5 categories of possible extension methods, our approach mainly targets the class of generating big pools of parameter values. The following NLU training was conducted by using the state-of-the-art and open-source software of the Berlin-based company Rasa [16]. The extraction of entities and the classification of intents can be regarded as two separate tasks that can be achieved by two different pipelines that are merged into one coherent NLU pipeline. The intent classification pipeline uses the tokenized utterances created by the spaCy model [9]. During training, each token and intent label is represented as a feature vector, except for digits, all of which are assigned to the same feature vector. The embeddings model is based on the StarSpace model developed by Facebook [24]. During training, the embeddings classifier learns its own embeddings for each of the words in the training dataset, thereby taking into account domain-specific uses of words [15]. The created feature vectors are enriched by an additional three dimensions using the *intent_featurizer_ngrams*. Again, the three most common n-grams in the training data are determined and the three added dimensions are used to indicate whether a given token includes one of these n-grams. The NER pipeline tokenizes the incoming utterance into its elements by also using the spaCy model and automatically assigns POS tags to each word in the utterance. Since only CRF [12] is supported as a NER algorithm in Rasa, it was applied for the experiments. Placeholder concepts could be considered as a way to increase the number of training examples and thus improve the NLU performance.

6 Conclusion and Outlook

Three different design approaches for creating labeled training datasets were developed and integrated into a holistic development process to design the NLU of a task-oriented DS and to create a corresponding dataset for training the component. While the experiments for RQ 1 clearly show that using more unique Entities improves the performance of the NER component, a placeholder concept only affects the intent classifier (RQ 2) slightly. In terms of robustness, the evaluation of EX 5 on different test datasets shows, that the performance of the NER component can be increased by including train datasets from different domains. With placeholder values from different domains, we show how Linked Data can help to increase (RQ 3) not only NLU robustness but also overall performance in open domains.

A challenge that appears with RQ 1–2 is the generalizability of the proposed concepts. We mainly address small, domain-specific databases, whereby an evaluation on larger datasets with multiples domains could lead to synergy effects within the creation of the NLU training dataset. For further research, the NLU component could be integrated into the Frankenstein framework and evaluated on the SQA challenge dataset [14].

References

1. Athreya, R.G., Ngomo, A.N., Usbeck, R.: Enhancing community interactions with data-driven chatbots-the DBpedia chatbot (2018). https://doi.org/10.1145/3184558.3186964

2. Bapat, R., Kucherbaev, P., Bozzon, A.: Effective crowdsourced generation of training data for chatbots natural language understanding (2018). https://doi.org/10.1007/978-3-319-91662-0_8
3. Bocklisch, T., Faulkner, J., Pawlowski, N., Nichol, A.: Rasa: open source language understanding and dialogue management. CoRR abs/1712.05181 (2017)
4. Braun, D., Hernandez-Mendez, A., Matthes, F., Langen, M.: Evaluating natural language understanding services for conversational question answering systems (2017)
5. Buscaldi, D., Rosso, P., Soriano, J.M.G., Sanchis, E.: Answering questions with an n-gram based passage retrieval engine. J. Intell. Inf. Syst. **34**(2), 113–134 (2010). https://doi.org/10.1007/s10844-009-0082-y
6. Diefenbach, D., Lopez, V., Singh, K., Maret, P.: Core techniques of question answering systems over knowledge bases: a survey. Knowl. Inf. Syst. **55**, 529–569 (2018)
7. Dubey, M., Banerjee, D., Chaudhuri, D., Lehmann, J.: EARL: joint entity and relation linking for question answering over knowledge graphs. CoRR abs/1801.03825 (2018)
8. Grötz, R.: Sprich mit mir! iX - Magazin für Professionelle Informationstechnik **6**, 50 (2018). https://www.heise.de/-4054854
9. Honnibal, M., Montani, I.: spaCy 2: natural language understanding with bloom embeddings, convolutional neural networks and incremental parsing (2017)
10. Huang, Z., Xu, W., Yu, K.: Bidirectional LSTM-CRF models for sequence tagging. CoRR abs/1508.01991 (2015)
11. Jurafsky, D., Martin, J.H.: Speech and Language Processing: An Introduction to Natural Language Processing, Computational Linguistics, and Speech Recognition. Prentice Hall Series in Artificial Intelligence, 2nd edn. Prentice Hall Pearson Education International, Upper Saddle River (2009)
12. Lafferty, J., McCallum, A., Pereira, F.C.N.: Conditional Random Fields: Probabilistic Models for Segmenting and Labeling Sequence Data, p. 10 (2001)
13. de Mori, R., Bechet, F., Hakkani-Tur, D., McTear, M., Riccardi, G., Tur, G.: Spoken language understanding. IEEE Signal Process. Mag. **25**(3), 50–58 (2008). https://doi.org/10.1109/MSP.2008.918413
14. Napolitano, G., Usbeck, R., Ngomo, A.N.: The scalable question answering over linked data (SQA) challenge 2018 (2018). https://doi.org/10.1007/978-3-030-00072-1_6
15. Nichol, A.: Supervised word vectors from scratch in Rasa NLU
16. Petraityte, J.: Deprecating the state machine: building conversational AI with Rasa stack (PyData 2018)
17. Ramesh, K., Ravishankaran, S., Joshi, A., Chandrasekaran, K.: A survey of design techniques for conversational agents. In: Kaushik, S., Gupta, D., Kharb, L., Chahal, D. (eds.) ICICCT 2017. CCIS, vol. 750, pp. 336–350. Springer, Singapore (2017). https://doi.org/10.1007/978-981-10-6544-6_31
18. Ruder, S.: An overview of multi-task learning in deep neural networks. CoRR abs/1706.05098 (2017)
19. Sarikaya, R., Hinton, G.E., Deoras, A.: Application of deep belief networks for natural language understanding (2014). https://doi.org/10.1109/TASLP.2014.2303296
20. Serban, I.V., Lowe, R., Henderson, P., Charlin, L., Pineau, J.: A survey of available corpora for building data-driven dialogue systems (2018)
21. Shen, D., Lapata, M.: Using semantic roles to improve question answering (2007)
22. Singh, K., et al.: Why Reinvent the Wheel: Let's Build Question Answering Systems Together, Lyon, France (2018). https://doi.org/10.1145/3178876.3186023

23. Wang, X., Yuan, C.: Recent advances on human-computer dialogue. CAAI Trans. Intell. Technol. **1**(4), 303–312 (2016). https://doi.org/10.1016/j.trit.2016.12.004
24. Wu, L., Fisch, A., Chopra, S., Adams, K., Bordes, A., Weston, J.: StarSpace: Embed all the things! CoRR abs/1709.03856 (2017)

Using Weak Supervision to Identify Long-Tail Entities for Knowledge Base Completion

Yaser Oulabi(✉) and Christian Bizer

Data and Web Science Group, University of Mannheim,
B6 26, 68159 Mannheim, Germany
{yaser,chris}@informatik.uni-mannheim.de

Abstract. Data from relational web tables can be used to augment cross-domain knowledge bases like DBpedia, Wikidata, or the Google Knowledge Graph with descriptions of entities that are not yet part of the knowledge base. Such long-tail entities can include for instance small villages, niche songs, or athletes that play in lower-level leagues. In previous work, we have presented an approach to successfully assemble descriptions of long-tail entities from relational HTML tables using supervised matching methods and manually labeled training data in the form of positive and negative entity matches. Manually labeling training data is a laborious task given knowledge bases covering many different classes. In this work, we investigate reducing the labeling effort for the task of long-tail entity extraction by using weak supervision. We present a bootstrapping approach that requires domain experts to provide a small set of simple, class-specific matching rules, instead of requiring them to label a large set of entity matches, thereby reducing the human supervision effort considerably. We evaluate this weak supervision approach and find that it performs only slightly worse compared to methods that rely on large sets of manually labeled entity matches.

1 Introduction

Cross-domain knowledge bases like YAGO [8], DBpedia [9], Wikidata [20], or the Google Knowledge Graph are being employed for an increasing range of applications, including natural language processing, web search, and question answering. The entity coverage of knowledge bases is far from complete [4,16]. YAGO and DBpedia e.g. rely on data extracted from Wikipedia and as a result cover mostly head instances that fulfill the Wikipedia notability criteria [12]. As the utility of a knowledge base increases for many tasks with its completeness, adding long-tail entities to a knowledge base is an important task.

Web tables [3], which are relational HTML tables extracted from the Web, contain large amounts of structured information, covering a wide range of topics. In previous work [12], we proposed a method for extracting long-tail entities and showed that web tables are a promising source for augmenting knowledge bases

M. Acosta et al. (Eds.): SEMANTiCS 2019, LNCS 11702, pp. 83–98, 2019.
https://doi.org/10.1007/978-3-030-33220-4_7

with new and formerly unknown entities. For this, we trained models using large sets of manually labeled class-specific entity matches. Given that knowledge bases can have many classes, manual labeling limits the usefulness of automatic knowledge base augmentation from web tables.

Weak supervision approaches aim at reducing labeling effort by using supervision that is more abstract or noisier compared to traditional manually labeled high-quality training examples (strong supervision) [14]. Data programming [15] is a paradigm, where experts are tasked with codifying any form of weak supervision into labeling functions. These functions are then employed within a broader system to generate training data by assigning labels and confidence scores to unlabeled data. Recently, various different systems based on the data programming paradigm have been suggested [1,14,19].

For many types of entities, humans generally possess knowledge about when entities definitely match, and what are strong signals that entities do not match. Writing down this general knowledge in the form of simple bold matching rules requires far less effort than labeling many individual positive and negative entity matches. Building on this observation and the data programming paradigm, this paper investigates for the task of long-tail entity extraction whether strong supervision in the form of positive and negative entity matches can be replaced by a set of simple bold matching rules. In order to make it easy to write down such rules, we restrict the rule format to conjuncts of equality tests. These tests are expressed using the schema of the knowledge base without requiring experts to assign weights or specify similarity metrics. Additionally, we introduce a bootstrapping method that exploits the matching rule sets to generate training data and train a supervised machine learning algorithm. Using these approaches, we are able to significantly reduce supervision effort compared to manually labeling positive and negative entity matches, while achieving a comparable performance.

Our contributions are (1) a weak supervision approach that substitutes manually labeled training pairs by a set of bold matching rules, (2) a bootstrapping approach which uses weak supervision to generate training data for a supervised matching method, and (3) an evaluation that compares strong and weak supervision for the task of long-tail entity extraction.

The remainder of this paper is structured as follows. First, we describe our long-tail entity extraction method, including the experimental setup and a summary of results when using strong supervision. Section 3 describes our weak supervision methodology, while Sects. 4 and 5 present and discuss our experiments. Section 6 compares our approach to the related work. The results presented in this paper are fully reproducible, as we publicly provide all code and datasets.[1]

2 Long-Tail Entity Extraction

In previous work, we proposed and evaluated a method for long-tail entity extraction from web tables [12]. This section summarizes the proposed approach, describes our experimental setup, and presents results achieved using manually labeled training data.

[1] http://data.dws.informatik.uni-mannheim.de/expansion/LTEE/.

2.1 Methodology

Extracting long-tail entities from web tables for knowledge base augmentation is a non-trivial task. It consists of two subtasks: (1) identifying entities that are not yet part of the knowledge base and (2) compiling descriptions for those new entities from web table data according to the schema of the knowledge base.

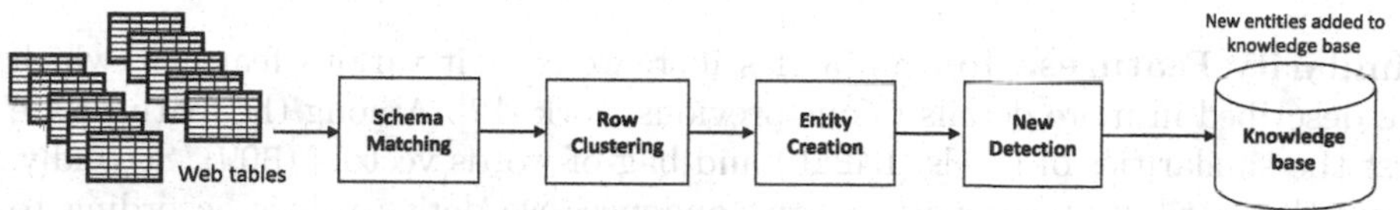

Fig. 1. Pipeline for extending a knowledge base with long-tail entities from web tables.

Long-Tail Entity Extraction Pipeline. Figure 1 gives an overview of our suggested approach. It is a pipeline that starts with web tables and ends by adding new entities to a cross-domain knowledge base. We first cluster all rows that describe the same real-world instance together. From these clusters we then create entities by compiling descriptions from web table data. Finally, the new detection component determines which entities are new, given a specific target knowledge base. As a result, we are able to perform the two subtasks of identifying new entities and compiling their descriptions.

Schema Matching. The first component of the pipeline is schema matching. It creates a mapping between web tables and the knowledge base schema. This includes matching web tables to classes and web table columns to properties. The latter, termed attribute-to-property correspondences [17], allow us to semantically understand cell values. They are exploited by the entity creation component to compile description according to the schema of the knowledge base and by both, the row clustering and new detection components, as similarity features.

Performing Row Clustering and New Detection. For both, row clustering and new detection, we train random forest classifiers that perform entity matching. For row clustering, the classifier compares a row pair to determine if the two rows describe the same entity, while for new detection this is done for a pair of a created entity and a candidate instance from the knowledge base.

Comparing all possible row pairs or entity-instance-pairs would not scale. We therefore utilize a label-based blocking approach using a Lucene index to find candidates to be compared.

Each matching decision is also given a confidence score. For row clustering, we use the confidence scores to perform correlation clustering and generate the row clusters. For new detection, we return an entity as new, only if all candidate instances from the knowledge base were classified as clear non-matches.

Table 1. Overview of the number of labels in the T4LTE gold standard.

Label type	GF-Player	Song	Settlement	Sum
Row pair	1,298	231	2,768	**4,297**
Entity-instance-pair	80	34	51	**165**
New entity classification	17	63	23	**103**
Sum	**1,395**	**328**	**2,842**	**4,565**

Similarity Features. To train a classifier, we exploit various features, which are described in more details in our previous work [12]. Among the features are first the similarities of labels (LABEL) and bag-of-words vectors (BOW). Secondly, using the attribute-to-property correspondences we derive values according to the knowledge base schema, which we compare using data-type-specific similarity functions (ATTRIBUTE). Using the knowledge base we also derive for each table implicit attributes about the entities described in the table, giving us another set of values by knowledge base property that we compare using data-type-specific similarity functions (IMPLICIT_ATT). For row clustering, we additionally exploit the PHI correlation of row labels (PHI) and penalize rows which occur in the same table (SAME_TABLE). For new detection, we additionally exploit type overlap between a created entity and a candidate knowledge base instance (TYPE), and the popularity of a candidate knowledge base instance (POPULARITY).

For each row pair or entity-instance-pair most features return a single normalized similarity score. For ATTRIBUTE and IMPLICIT_ATT, we return for a pair two scores for each property from the knowledge base schema. One score measures the confidence of the pair having equal values given that property, the other of the pair having unequal values.

2.2 Experimental Setup and Results

We employ the 2014 release of DBpedia [9] as the target knowledge base and evaluate our methods on the task of extending the DBpedia classes GridironFootballPlayer (GF-Player), Song[2], and Settlement with additional entities. To ensure diversity among the classes, we selected each from a different first-level class, i.e. Agent, Work, and Place.

We utilize the English-language relational tables set of the Web Data Commons 2012 Web Table Corpus.[3] The set consists of 91.8 million tables. For every table we assume that there is one column that contains the labels of the instances described by the rows. The remaining columns contain values, which potentially can be matched to properties in the knowledge base schema.

For training and evaluation we built the *Web Tables for Long-Tail Entity Extraction*[4] (T4LTE) gold standard. Table 1 provides an overview of the number of labels in T4LTE. Creating this dataset was rather laborious, as we

[2] The class Song also includes all instances of the class Single.

[3] http://webdatacommons.org/webtables/#toc3.

[4] http://webdatacommons.org/T4LTE/.

labeled 4,297 matching row pairs, 165 entity-instance-pairs and 103 new entity classifications.

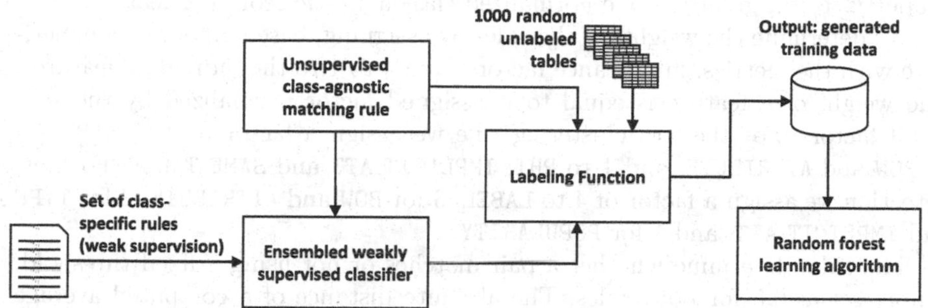

Fig. 2. Our overall methodology of introducing weak supervision using class-specific rule sets and bootstrapping a supervised learning algorithm using a labeling function.

When evaluating the pipeline using the T4LTE gold standard using cross-validation, we were able to achieve an F1 score in the task of finding new entities of 0.80. When running the pipeline on the whole web table corpus, we were able to add 14 thousand new gridiron football players and 187 thousand new songs to DBpedia, an increase of 67% and 356% respectively [12].

3 Methodology

This section describes our approaches for the task of reducing labeling effort using weak supervision. The overall methodology is illustrated in Fig. 2.

We first introduce as a baseline two unsupervised class-agnostic matching rules for row clustering and new detection. These rules exploit the similarity features described above and aggregate them using a weighted average.

We then introduce an approach that exploits user-provided class-specific rule sets as weak supervision. These rules have a high accuracy, but low coverage, which is why we ensemble them with the unsupervised matching rule to derive weakly supervised classifiers for both row clustering and new detection.

Both, the unsupervised matching rules and the weakly supervised classifiers can be used in our pipeline directly. We additionally introduce an approach that exploits these methods as labeling functions to bootstrap a supervised learning algorithm. This is done by using a set of unlabeled web tables to label training pairs for both row clustering and new detection. The labeled data is then used to train random forest classifiers to be used in our pipeline.

3.1 Unsupervised Class-Agnostic Matching Rule

We suggest two unsupervised matching rules that aggregate using a weighted average the individual scores generated by the features described in Sect. 2.1.

To be used in a rule, all features must produce scores that are normalized and class-agnostic. This already applies to all features except `ATTRIBUTE` and `IMPLICIT_ATT`, where, given a pair, we normalize by averaging the individual property scores, giving us one normalized class-agnostic score per feature.

We determine the weights of the rules by assigning, based on our own experience with the metrics, importance factors from 4 to 1 to the individual features. The weight of a feature is equal to it assigned factor normalized by the sum of all factors. For the row clustering rule we assign a factor of 4 to `LABEL`, 2 to `BOW` and `ATTRIBUTE`, and 1 to `PHI`, `IMPLICIT_ATT` and `SAME_TABLE`. For new detection we assign a factor of 4 to `LABEL`, 3 for `BOW` and `ATTRIBUTE`, 2 for `TYPE` and `IMPLICIT_ATT`, and 1 for `POPULARITY`.

The rules determine whether a pair matches or not using a fixed threshold, simply set at 0.5 for both rules. The absolute distance of a computed average from the threshold determines the confidence of a matching decision.

3.2 Class-Specific User-Provided Matching Rules

Humans often possess general knowledge about which conditions need to be fulfilled for entities of a certain domain to clearly match or clearly not match. Based on this observation, we suggest as weak supervision a set of user-provided bold class-specific rules that classify a given candidate pair as a match or non-match. They can codify obvious knowledge, e.g. that a settlement can not be in two different countries, or non-obvious knowledge, e.g. that only one unique football athlete can be drafted in the same year with the same pick number.

The rules consists of conjunctions of attribute tests, expressed using the schema of the knowledge base. It is only required that the provided rules be accurate, regardless of their coverage. This makes it a simple task to identify suitable rules and is the reason why we term these rules as bold. For our experiments, we created per class four rules. For **GF-Player** we came up with two matching and two non-matching rules:

$$(\text{draftYear} = \text{Equal}) \wedge (\text{draftPick} = \text{Equal}) \rightarrow \text{Match} \tag{1}$$

$$(\text{LABEL} = \text{Equal}) \wedge (\text{birthDate} = \text{Equal}) \rightarrow \text{Match} \tag{2}$$

$$(\text{draftYear} = \text{Unequal}) \rightarrow \text{Non-Match} \tag{3}$$

$$(\text{draftPick} = \text{Unequal}) \rightarrow \text{Non-Match} \tag{4}$$

For **Song** we also came up with two matching and two non-matching rules:

$$(\text{LABEL} = \text{Equal}) \wedge (\text{artist} = \text{Equal}) \wedge (\text{releaseDate} = \text{Equal}) \rightarrow \text{Match} \tag{5}$$

$$(\text{LABEL} = \text{Equal}) \wedge (\text{artist} = \text{Equal}) \wedge (\text{album} = \text{Equal}) \rightarrow \text{Match} \tag{6}$$

$$(\text{artist} = \text{Unequal}) \rightarrow \text{Non-Match} \tag{7}$$

$$(\text{releaseYear} = \text{Unequal}) \rightarrow \text{Non-Match} \tag{8}$$

Finally, for **Settlement** we have three matching and one non-matching rule:

$$(\text{country} = \text{Equal}) \wedge (\text{postalCode} = \text{Equal}) \rightarrow \text{Match} \tag{9}$$

$$(\text{LABEL} = \text{Equal}) \wedge (\text{isPartOf} = \text{Equal}) \rightarrow \text{Match} \tag{10}$$

$$(\text{LABEL} = \text{Equal}) \wedge (\text{postalCode} = \text{Equal}) \rightarrow \text{Match} \tag{11}$$

$$(\text{country} = \text{Unequal}) \rightarrow \text{Non-Match} \tag{12}$$

The effort spent creating these rules is minuscule compared to manually labeling the correspondences in the gold standard. While for each class we created only 4 rules, they are tested to substitute 1,395, 328, and 2,842 labels for the classes GF-Player, Song, and Settlement respectively.

To apply a rule we exploit the equal and unequal scores generated by the `ATTRIBUTE` and `IMPLICIT_ATT` features, as described in Sect. 2.1, and the `LABEL` feature using a data-type specific equivalence threshold [12]. A rule fires, when all tests within the rule have scores higher than zero. From these scores we also derive for each rule firing a confidence score, which equals the product of all scores used within the rule.

As the rules fire only when certain conditions are met, the set of rules is not exhaustive and only covers a subset of compared pairs. We therefore ensemble the rules with the unsupervised matching rule through averaging. Given a compared pair, we first check how many rules fire. If no rule fires, we simply return the output of the unsupervised matching rule. If multiple rules fire, which is possible as the rules are not mutually exclusive, we consider only the rule with the highest confidence, preferring negative rules in case of a tie. If the confidence of this rule is higher than the confidence of the output of the unsupervised matching rule, the outputs of both are averaged and returned. Otherwise, we simply return the output of the unsupervised matching rule.

3.3 Bootstrapping Approach

In our experiments, we, on the one hand, directly apply the unsupervised rule and the weakly supervised ensembled classifier to our test data. On the other hand, following the data-programming paradigm, we employ both methods as labeling functions to label row pairs and entity-instance-pairs derived from 1000 randomly selected web tables as matches or non-matches. Additionally, the labeling functions assign weights to the training examples using the confidence scores returned by the underlying method. Using these labels we train a random forest classifier, which is then applied to our test data.

To derive pairs to be labeled, we employ label-based blocking using Lucene for both row clustering and new detection. We additionally include random pairs to be labeled, for row clustering as many as there are positive pairs, and for new detection 8 random instances selected from the knowledge base from within the same class of an entity or its parent classes. Overall, this leads to 2.8 m row pairs and 1.27 m entity-instance-pairs selected to be labeled.

For row clustering, we use the confidence scores to additionally perform correlation clustering. A row pair labeled as a match but not part of the same cluster, is not included as a positive training example. Similarly, a row pair labeled as a non-match, but placed in the same cluster, is not considered as a negative training example.

For new detection, when multiple entity-instance-pairs of the same entity are labeled as matching, which can not be correct, we only include the entity-instance-pair with the highest score as a positive training example.

Table 2. Row clustering performance for runs with various types of supervision.

Method	Average			GF-Player	Song	Settlement
	PCP	AR	F1	F1	F1	F1
Unsupervised	0.76	0.86	0.80	0.90	0.65	0.86
+ Bootstrapping	0.78	0.88	0.83	0.89	0.73	0.86
Weak supervision	0.83	0.89	0.86	0.93	0.81	0.84
+ Bootstrapping	0.83	0.90	0.86	0.89	0.83	0.86
Strong supervision	0.86	0.90	0.88	0.91	0.84	0.90
+ Bootstrapping	0.85	0.90	0.87	0.92	0.79	0.91

When bootstrapping for new detection, we also need a set of row clusters from which we create entities. Using these entities we can then generate training examples using entity-instance-pairs and our labeling function. To create these clusters, we use the supervised model trained by bootstrapping from a labeling function of equal supervision, i.e. when we are bootstrapping a supervised learning algorithm for new detection using the unsupervised rule, we use the clustering method also trained using bootstrapping and the unsupervised rule.

Given the labeled pairs, we train a random forest classifier. Per forest, we train 2000 trees. To reduce correlation between trees, we set the features available at each split to 2, and reduce the sample size used to train each tree to 66% of the total number of pairs. We sample with replacement and using weights, so that higher weighted examples are considered more often during training.

4 Evaluation and Results

In this section, we evaluate, using the T4LTE gold standard, the approaches described above and compare them to a model trained with manually labeled data. As for the latter, the gold standard is also used for training, we apply three-fold cross-validation throughout all experiments. Additionally, we will evaluate the effectiveness of the user-provided rule sets and our bootstrapping approach.

4.1 Row Clustering Evaluation

To evaluate row clustering, we employ the evaluation metric proposed by Hassanzadeh et al. [7,12]. It emphasizes replicating the exact number of clusters in the evaluation set by first computing a one-to-one mapping between returned clusters and clusters in the evaluation set. Only rows of clusters with a mapping contribute towards recall, while the pairwise clustering precision is penalized by the difference between the number of clusters in the evaluation set and the number of returned clusters, or the clusters with a mapping, whichever is higher.

Table 2 shows row clustering performance for different types of supervision. The first two rows show performances when using the unsupervised matching rule alone, while the following two rows show the performances when using the weakly supervised ensembled classifier. The final two rows show the performances when using strong supervision. For each supervision type we apply and evaluate the underlying method directly on the test set, and then use it as a labeling function to bootstrap a random forest, which we then also apply and evaluate on the test set. For strong supervision, the bootstrapped method resembles a semi-supervised learning approach.

From the table, we can see that the difference in average F1 between a model trained using strong supervision, which has an F1 of 0.88, and the unsupervised rule without bootstrapping is 8 pp. We find that using bootstrapping with the unsupervised matching rule allows us to increase F1 by 3 pp on average, with an increase of 8 pp for the class Song. Using user-provided class-specific rule sets, we achieve an average F1 score of 0.86, which is a large increase of overall 6 pp from the unsupervised rule and very close to the performance when using strong supervision. Applying bootstrapping on the weakly supervised method does not increase average F1 further, mainly because we lose performance for the class GF-Player, while gaining performance in the other two classes. This is similarly the case when bootstrapping from a model trained using strong supervision, except we also lose one percentage point in average F1.

When bootstrapping, the labeling functions were given overall 2.8 m row pairs to label, which were selected either by the label-based blocker or chosen randomly. Given as labeling function the weakly supervised ensembled classifier, 275 thousand pairs were labeled as matches, while 2.54 m pairs were labeled as non-matches. For this output, the user-provided matching rules fire in total 37 thousand times, whereas the non-matching rules fire 500 thousand times.

4.2 New Detection Evaluation

We evaluate a new detection method using both, the existing and the new entities labeled in the gold standard. Precision equals the proportion of entities returned as new by the method, that are actually new, while recall equals the proportion of new entities in the testing set, that were returned as new by the method.

Table 3 shows new detection performance for runs with various types of supervision, similar to Table 2. We first find that a model trained using the provided strong supervision outperforms the unsupervised matching rule in F1 by 7 pp on

Table 3. New detection performance for runs with various types of supervision.

Method	Average			GF-Player	Song	Settlement
	P	R	F1	F1	F1	F1
Unsupervised	0.87	0.76	0.80	0.82	0.68	0.89
+ Bootstrapping	0.86	0.86	0.85	0.86	0.78	0.90
Weak supervision	0.87	0.81	0.83	0.82	0.78	0.89
+ Bootstrapping	0.87	0.90	0.87	0.87	0.85	0.90
Strong supervision	0.82	0.94	0.87	0.88	0.92	0.81
+ Bootstrapping	0.81	0.97	0.88	0.88	0.92	0.83

average, and by 24 points for the class Song. On the other hand, the unsupervised matching rule outperforms the model trained using strong supervision by 8 pp for the class Settlement, indicating that the trained model highly overfits. By employing the user-provided rule sets as weak supervision, we are able to increase average F1 by 3 pp.

Unlike for row clustering, bootstrapping is consistently effective for new detection. It increases average F1 in the unsupervised case by 5, and in the weakly supervised case by 3 pp. The latter allows us to achieve an equal average F1 to that of strong supervision, albeit a large part is due to the Settlement class, while for Song we are still lacking 7 points in F1. Bootstrapping is also effective when used with a model trained using strong supervision.

When bootstrapping, a sum of 1.27 m entity-instance-pairs are given to the labeling functions to be labeled. When using the ensembled classifier, we find that 26 thousand pairs were labeled as matches, and the remainder as non-matches. Within the ensembled classifier, the user-provided matching rules fire 13 thousand times, whereas the non-matching rules fire 150 thousand times.

4.3 End-To-End Evaluation

We will now evaluate a full run of the pipeline using weak supervision. As this runs row clustering and new detection sequentially, the errors of the methods tend to accumulate and reduce overall end-to-end performance [12].

To evaluate how well new entities were found, we utilize precision and recall. To compute precision, we determine the proportion of entities returned as new that are correct. An entity is only correctly new, if its cluster includes the majority of the rows of a new cluster in the gold standard, and these rows at the same time form the majority within the entity's cluster. Recall is the fraction of new entities in the gold standard for which a correct new entity was returned.

Table 4 shows end-to-end performance for different types of supervision similar to Table 2. From the table we can see that the highest performance is achieved by the model trained using strong supervision. It achieves an average F1 of 0.81. The highest performance achieved by the methods without strong supervision

Table 4. End-to-end evaluation for various types of supervision.

Method	Average			GF-Player	Song	Settlement
	P	R	F1	F1	F1	F1
Unsupervised	0.71	0.71	0.69	0.76	0.50	0.82
+ Bootstrapping	0.71	0.81	0.74	0.79	0.60	0.82
Weak supervision	0.72	0.77	0.74	0.76	0.63	0.82
+ Bootstrapping	0.72	0.86	0.78	0.81	0.72	0.80
Strong supervision	0.73	0.93	0.81	0.84	0.78	0.81
+ Bootstrapping	0.68	0.93	0.78	0.84	0.69	0.80

is 0.78 for the weak supervision method with bootstrapping. The lowest performance of 0.69 is achieved by the unsupervised method without bootstrapping. Overall, we find that we are able to achieve a performance quite close to that when using strong supervision, and much better than a simple unsupervised matching rule. As a result, we can successfully perform long-tail entity extraction with significantly reduced labeling effort. While on average, we lose recall with almost no loss in precision, the actual effect differs per individual class.

The user-provided rule sets have a strong positive impact on performance, increasing F1 by 5 pp. Bootstrapping also increases average F1 by 5 and 4 pp for the unsupervised and weakly supervised runs respectively. Overall, we achieve an increase of 9 points when comparing a weakly supervised bootstrapped method with an unsupervised non-bootstrapped method. The effect is especially large for Song, where we gain 22 pp in F1.

Bootstrapping from a strongly supervised method is not effective and reduces overall performance. This is because, bootstrapping had mixed results when it comes to row clustering for both, weak and strong supervision. This is especially the case for the class Song, where a method bootstrapped from strong supervision produces 29 bad clusters, leading to a significant drop in end-to-end performance.

Finally, we notice that precision is continuously lower than recall. For GF-Player and Settlement we have e.g. precisions of 0.68 and 0.70, with recalls of 1.00 and 0.92 respectively. This problem is caused by bad clustering, primarily for existing entities, which are then classified as new by the new detection component, thereby reducing precision, without affecting recall. When summing numbers for all testing folds, we are missing for football players 8 existing clusters, meaning the rows were incorrectly included in other existing clusters, causing them to be impure. In the case of settlements we have overall generated 16 extra existing clusters. This leads for GF-Player and Settlements to 8 and 9 clusters respectively, being incorrectly determined to be new. This shows, that errors in the pipeline accumulate and that there is a need for an additional component in the pipeline that detects and filters out bad clusters. While this pattern does not exist for class Song, it is because it suffers from bad clustering for new and existing clusters, leading to lower recall and precision. As a result, even the class Song would benefit from a bad cluster filtering component.

5 Discussion

Ensembling the user-provided rule sets with an unsupervised matching rule, yields a quite effective method that requires minimal supervision. The unsupervised rule, while class-agnostic and simple, still provides an acceptable baseline performance, and more importantly, full coverage to our method. This allows us to require that the rules only be accurate, but not exhaustive, even when the number of provided rules is small. Additionally, these rules are not only easily created by an expert, but could also be mined from or tested on the knowledge base, further reducing supervision effort. A big limitation of our approach is that the rule sets require web tables to describe entities using useful knowledge base properties. This is not the case for settlements, where we find that the number and density of attributes in the web tables are limited [12].

While bootstrapping produces mixed results for row clustering, its impact on new detection and end-to-end performance is positive. There are several factors that possibly contribute to this positive effect. First, a random forest is more expressive than either, the unsupervised matching rule or the user-provided rule sets. It also exploits a larger feature set than both, especially making use of the class-specific scores returned by the `ATTRIBUTE` and `IMPLICIT_ATT` features. By weighting training pairs, we ensure that pairs with a higher confidence are given a higher importance, while less certain pairs are still considered. As bootstrapping works within the context of a component, i.e. row clustering or new detection, it can make use of component-specific characteristics. For example, given one created entity, only one knowledge base instance can possibly be a correct match. This allows us to eliminate likely incorrect training examples during bootstrapping for new detection by keeping for one entity only the matching entity-instance-pair with the highest confidence.

6 Related Work

Various methods exist to reduce effort spent on manual labeling. Semi-supervised methods use a small set of labeled and a larger set of unlabeled examples to train a model. This includes for example co-training and self-training, which train models on data that they labeled themselves, using initially a small number of seed examples. Another approach to reducing labeling effort is active learning, where a user is queried to label examples that are chosen to provide the most information when labeled [6].

Weak supervision approaches exploit supervision at a higher abstraction or that is noisier in nature to efficiently generate a large number of training examples, even if those are of a lower quality [14,15]. This includes letting non-experts generate labels through crowdsourcing or employing rules and heuristics for labeling data. Multiple weak supervision approaches can be combined to overcome the possibly lower accuracy and coverage of weak supervision [14].

One method of weak supervision is distant supervision [11], where a knowledge base or any other external resource is used to train a supervised algorithm.

While originally applied in the context of relation extraction from text, it has been used for the task of augmenting a knowledge base from semi-structured web data, including web tables [4,10]. Bizer et al. [2] make use of schema.org annotations extracted from 43 thousand e-shops to distantly supervise a deep neural network for product matching. To generate training pairs, they make use of generic product identifies that are often provided along the annotations.

Ratner et al. [15] introduce the data programming paradigm, where any weak supervision strategy, including domain heuristics and distant supervision, can be codified into individual low-coverage labeling functions. The authors focus on denoising noisy and conflicting labels, by assigning accuracies to labeling functions using a generative algorithm. In contrast, we do not label using the individual rules, but first ensemble a set of rules and an unsupervised weighted average rule to create one labeling function per class. While we attempt to overcome the low coverage of our rules using ensembling, the authors do not suggest an approach to overcome the possible low coverage of their labeling functions. Snorkel is a system that enables the use of weak supervision based on the data programming paradigm [14]. Snorkel Drybell adapts Snorkel to exploits diverse organizational knowledge resources. Its effectiveness is evaluated in a large-scale case-study at Google [1].

Snuba [19] is a weak supervision system that uses a small set of labeled data to derive heuristics to generate training data and train a machine learning model. The heuristics are similar in purpose to our rule sets, and the authors also limit themselves to what they term *primitive features*, which in their case are bag-of-words representation for text or bounding box attributes for images. In our case, we limit our self to attribute tests using the schema of a knowledge base. As in our case, training a machine learning model yield an increase in performance, which the authors similarly contribute to the fact that learned models are more expressive and can exploit more features. Snuba still requires hundreds of manually labeled training examples to derive heuristics, whereas in our case experts only need to provide a small number of bold matching rules.

Shen et al. [18] introduce constraint-based entity matching, where they suggest a probabilistic framework within which domain-specific constraints can be exploited to perform entity matching without the need for manual labeling. The introduced constraint are of a broad-variety, and not limited to a specific format. Their work differs from ours, as, first of all, their constraints are generally more complex and not based on simple attribute tests using a predefined schema. This makes providing supervision less straight-forward and possibly more laborious for experts. Additionally, they only provide a matching method that uses the constraints directly, and do not consider using them to bootstrap a supervised machine learning algorithm.

To bootstrap supervised learning, a small number of labeled seed examples are often used [11,13], but there have also been approaches that use alternatives to seeds, e.g. domain-independent patterns [5]. We bootstrap by using a classifier that ensembles a heuristic domain-agnostic matching rule and a limited set of user-provided class-specific matching rule sets.

7 Conclusion

This work investigates the possibility of reducing the effort spent on manually labeling training data for the task of augmenting knowledge bases with long-tail entities from web tables. For this, we introduce and evaluate a weak supervision approach that exploits more efficient supervision at a higher level of abstraction.

Specifically, we suggest, as an alternative to manually labeling thousands of entity matching pairs, the use of a small set of bold user-provided class-specific matching rules. These rules are built upon properties from the schema of a knowledge base class, making them universal and semantically easy to understand. More importantly, these rules require considerably less effort to create. To overcome the possibly limited coverage of these rules, we suggest a method to ensemble these class-specific matching rules with a class-agnostic unsupervised matching model. This yields an effective weakly supervised method for long-tail entity extraction.

We then introduce an approach to bootstrap a supervised learning algorithm by using the weakly supervised method as a labeling function and a set of unlabeled web tables. We find that with bootstrapping, we are able to achieve a performance close to that of supervision with manually labeled data. As a result, we are able to perform long-tail entity extraction with considerably reduced effort spent on supervision.

Our weak supervision approach can be highly useful for a variety of tasks. In case where recall is a secondary objective, our approach can be tuned towards precision and used to add highly accurate, albeit fewer, long-tail entities to a knowledge base. The approach can also be used to facilitate generating training data for manual labeling, where experts must only correct generated labels instead of creating them. This would considerably reduce the effort required for manually labeling training data.

We believe that an interesting direction for future work would be combining weakly supervised labeling functions and active learning. The labeling functions could be used to reduce the effort spent of learning initial models. These models can afterwards be refined by labeling individual examples chosen by the active learning method.

References

1. Bach, S.H., et al.: Snorkel drybell: a case study in deploying weak supervision at industrial scale. In: 2019 International Conference on Management of Data, SIGMOD 2019, pp. 362–375. ACM (2019)
2. Bizer, C., Primpeli, A., Peeters, R.: Using the semantic web as a source of training data. Datenbank-Spektrum **19**(2), 127–135 (2019)
3. Cafarella, M.J., Halevy, A.Y., Zhang, Y., Wang, D.Z., Wu, E.: Uncovering the relational web. In: 11th International Workshop on the Web and Databases, WebDB 2008 (2008)
4. Dong, X., et al.: Knowledge vault: a web-scale approach to probabilistic knowledge fusion. In: 20th ACM SIGKDD International Conference on Knowledge Discovery and Data Mining, KDD 2014, pp. 601–610. ACM (2014)

5. Etzioni, O., et al.: Methods for domain-independent information extraction from the web: an experimental comparison. In: Nineteenth National Conference on Artificial Intelligence, AAAI 2004, pp. 391–398 (2004)
6. Han, J., Kamber, M., Pei, J.: Data Mining: Concepts and Techniques, 3rd edn. Morgan Kaufmann, Boston (2012)
7. Hassanzadeh, O., Chiang, F., Lee, H.C., Miller, R.J.: Framework for evaluating clustering algorithms in duplicate detection. Proc. VLDB Endow. **2**(1), 1282–1293 (2009)
8. Hoffart, J., Suchanek, F.M., Berberich, K., Weikum, G.: Yago2: a spatially and temporally enhanced knowledge base from wikipedia. Artif. Intell. **194**, 28–61 (2013)
9. Lehmann, J., et al.: Dbpedia - a large-scale, multilingual knowledge base extracted from wikipedia. Semant. Web **6**(2), 167–195 (2015)
10. Lockard, C., Dong, X.L., Einolghozati, A., Shiralkar, P.: Ceres: distantly supervised relation extraction from the semi-structured web. Proc. VLDB Endow. 11(10) (2018)
11. Mintz, M., Bills, S., Snow, R., Jurafsky, D.: Distant supervision for relation extraction without labeled data. In: Joint Conference of the 47th Annual Meeting of the ACL and the 4th International Joint Conference on Natural Language Processing of the AFNLP. vol. 2, pp. 1003–1011 (2009)
12. Oulabi, Y., Bizer, C.: Extending cross-domain knowledge bases with long tail entities using web table data. In: 22nd International Conference on Extending Database Technology, EDBT 2019, pp. 385–396 (2019)
13. Pennacchiotti, M., Pantel, P.: A bootstrapping algorithm for automatically harvesting semantic relations. In: Fifth International Workshop on Inference in Computational Semantics, ICoS 2006 (2006)
14. Ratner, A., Bach, S.H., Ehrenberg, H., Fries, J., Wu, S., Ré, C.: Snorkel: rapid training data creation with weak supervision. Proc. VLDB Endow. **11**(3), 269–282 (2017)
15. Ratner, A.J., De Sa, C.M., Wu, S., Selsam, D., Ré, C.: Data programming: creating large training sets, quickly. In: Advances in Neural Information Processing Systems, NIPS 2016, vol. 29, pp. 3567–3575 (2016)
16. Ringler, D., Paulheim, H.: One knowledge graph to rule them all? analyzing the differences between dbpedia, yago, wikidata & co. In: KI 2017: Advances in Artificial Intelligence - 40th Annual German Conference on AI, pp. 366–372 (2017)
17. Ritze, D., Bizer, C.: Matching web tables to dbpedia - a feature utility study. In: 20th International Conference on Extending Database Technology, EDBT 2017, pp. 210–221 (2017)
18. Shen, W., Li, X., Doan, A.: Constraint-based entity matching. In: 20th National Conference on Artificial Intelligence, AAAI 2005, vol. 2, pp. 862–867 (2005)
19. Varma, P., Ré, C.: Snuba: automating weak supervision to label training data. Proc. VLDB Endow. **12**(3), 223–236 (2018)
20. Vrandečić, D., Krötzsch, M.: Wikidata: a free collaborative knowledgebase. Commun. ACM **57**(10), 78–85 (2014)

Semantic Information Management and Knowledge Integration

Evaluating Generalized Path Queries by Integrating Algebraic Path Problem Solving with Graph Pattern Matching

Abhisha Bhattacharyya[1(✉)], Ilya Baldin[2], Yufeng Xin[2], and Kemafor Anyanwu[1]

[1] North Carolina State University, Raleigh, NC 27695, USA
{abhatt22,kogan}@ncsu.edu
[2] RENCI/UNC-Chapel Hill, Chapel Hill, NC 27517, USA
{ibaldin,yxin}@renci.org

Abstract. Path querying on Semantic Networks is gaining increased focus because of its broad applicability. Some graph databases offer support for variants of path queries e.g. shortest path. However, many applications have the need for the set version of various path problem i.e. finding paths between multiple source and multiple destination nodes (subject to different kinds of constraints). Further, the sets of source and destination nodes may be described declaratively as patterns, rather than given explicitly. Such queries lead to the requirement of integrating graph pattern matching with path problem solving. There are currently existing limitations in support of such queries (either inability to express some classes, incomplete results, inability to complete query evaluation unless graph patterns are extremely selective, etc).

In this paper, we propose a framework for evaluating *generalized path queries - gpqs* that integrate an algebraic technique for solving path problems with SPARQL graph pattern matching. The integrated algebraic querying technique enables more scalable and efficient processing of gpqs, including the possibility of support for a broader range of path constraints. We present the approach and implementation strategy and compare performance and query expressiveness with a popular graph engine.

Keywords: Algebraic interpretation · Path query · Graph pattern matching

1 Introduction

Many applications have to find connections between entities in datasets. In graph theoretic terms, this amounts to querying for paths in graphs, between multiple sources and destinations. Often the sets of sources and destinations cannot be easily given explicitly but rather in terms of patterns to be matched in graphs. For example, to assess security risks for flights, security officials may want to

M. Acosta et al. (Eds.): SEMANTiCS 2019, LNCS 11702, pp. 101–116, 2019.
https://doi.org/10.1007/978-3-030-33220-4_8

know about relationships between $p1$ = *passengers on any flights to a particular destination within a particular time window who purchased one-way tickets by cash*, and $p2$ = *countries on the CIA watchlist.* Here $p1$ and $p2$ are patterns describing the set of sources and destinations of interest. Such inquiries also commonly occur when dealing with biological networks as well as in several non-traditional emerging applications e.g. networking. For the latter example, suppose there is a network composed of SDN ASs (Autonomous Systems), where an AS controller may want to *compute a domain-level path from one node to another* for an application where the query includes constraints related to *business relationships with potential transit domains.* Another feature of path queries as demonstrated by the networking example is that, there can be constraints on paths e.g. *avoid domains of type T* or *constraints on path disjointedness (link- or node-disjoint for specific resilience level)* or other *structural constraints.* Such constraints are more expressive than the property path queries which require a regular expression of the properties in path being searched for. In a sense, these queries are traditional path queries generalized to include graph patterns and path constraints. We refer to such queries as *Generalized Path Queries - gpqs.*

Property path expressions in SPARQL are also motivated by the need for graph traversal queries. However, they are fundamentally different from path queries in that the result of a property path expression is not paths but rather sets of endpoint nodes connected by paths that match the property path pattern. G-Core [15] presents a good discussion of different classes of graph queries. Existing graph-based query engines such as Neo4j [9], StarDog [13], Allegrogaph [14], AnzoGraph [6], Virtuoso [18] provide varying degrees of support for path querying. Some other platforms such as [19,21–24,30] have focused exclusively on the path querying.

A common thread across existing path querying evaluation strategies is that they are built on traditional graph algorithms. The challenge with graph theoretic interpretations of such queries is that the different constraints in gpqs may translate to different classes of graph problems, requiring different algorithms. For example, shortest path algorithms vs. subgraph isomorphism algorithms vs. subgraph homeomorphism, etc. From the point of view of query processing, this is a limited approach because of the limited opportunity for decomposition and reusability. On the other hand, adopting an algebraic perspective allows problems to be interpreted in a more generalized form. This also allows for more natural integration with algebraic graph pattern query engines. Considering such a strategy makes sense once one observes that gpqs are essentially comprised of four elements: graph pattern matching, joining/filtering of graph patterns, path computation, path filtering. Some existing platforms like [13] do partially interpret gpq-like queries algebraically. However, the absence of a complete algebraic query interpretation framework results on falling back on traditional graph algorithms in many situations.

In this paper, we propose an algebraic query evaluation technique for gpqs that delineates the four gpqs subquery elements and their mapping to algebraic query operations so that gpqs query planning translates to composition and ordering of query operations. More specifically, the paper presents.

- a conceptual query evaluation model that integrates algebraic graph pattern matching with algebraic path problem solving.
- an implementation model that perturbs the plan for graph pattern matching query generated by a SPARQL query compiler by splicing in algebraic path querying operators to produce a gpqs query plan. Another advantage of this strategy is that current SPARQL parsers and existing graph pattern matching compiler can be adopted without modification. An example implementation strategy using Apache Jena's query compiler and Apache Tez' DAG for physical execution is presented.
- comparison of the performance and expressiveness of the integrated platform with a popular engine.

Section 2 presents the background on algebraic path problem solving and graph pattern matching. The relevant work, existing graph querying engines and their limitations are provided in Sect. 3. Section 4 discusses our approach both conceptually as well as the implementation model with evaluation presented in Sect. 5. Conclusion is in Sect. 6.

2 Background

2.1 Algebraic Path Problem Solving in Directed Graphs

We begin with a brief review of an efficient algebraic path problem solving approach due to [34]. An edge e in a directed labeled graph $G = (V, E)$ is denoted as $e = (v_1, v_2)$ with label $\lambda(e) = l_e$, where $v_1, v_2 \in V$ and $e \in E$. A path p, in this graph $G = (V, E)$, is defined as an alternating sequence of nodes and edge labels terminating in a node $p = \{v_1, l_{e_1}, v_2, l_{e_2}, ..., v_n, l_{e_n}, v_{n+1}\}$, where $v_1, v_2, ..., v_n, v_{n+1} \in V$ and $e_1, e_2, ..., e_n \in E$. A path expression of type (s, d), PE(s, d) [34] is a 3-tuple ⟨s, d, R⟩, where R is a regular expression over the set of edges defined using the standard operators union($\cup$), concatenation($\bullet$) and closure($*$) such that the language L(R) of R represents paths from s to d, where $s, d \in V$. For example in Fig. 1(a) borrowed from [21], PE(2, 7) = $\langle 2, 7, ((b \bullet c \bullet f) \cup (i \bullet f))\rangle$ is path expression of type (2,7) (for brevity, only edges are captured in the regular expression, no nodes). Path expressions may or may not be complete in terms of the subset of paths represented. For example, PE(2, 7) only represents two of the several paths between 2 and 7.

If a graph is ordered using any numbering scheme, path information can be represented using a particular ordering of path expressions called a *Path-Sequence (PS)* [21,34]. Figure 1(b) shows the path-sequence that represents the example graph in Fig. 1(a). It can be observed that some path expressions are simple, e.g. representing only a single edge, while others are more complex. The formalization of a path sequence [34] defines what path expressions are in a path sequence. A particularly appealing property of a path-sequence is that many path problems can be solved using a simple propagation *SOLVE algorithm* [21,34], that assembles path information as it scans the path-sequence from left

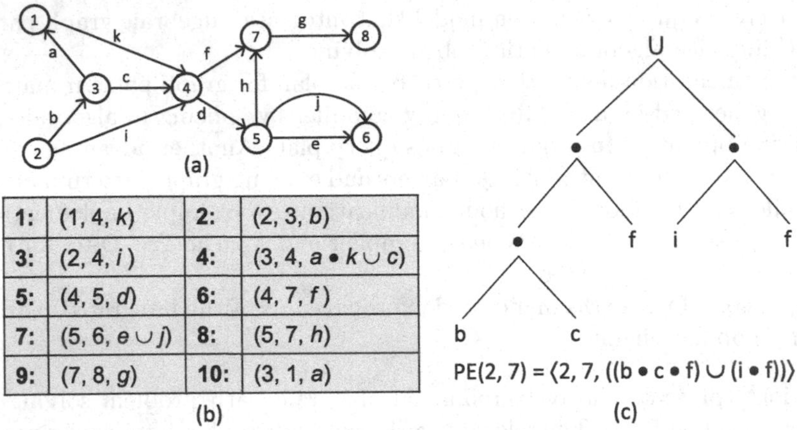

(a)

1:	(1, 4, *k*)	2:	(2, 3, *b*)
3:	(2, 4, *i*)	4:	(3, 4, *a* • *k* ∪ *c*)
5:	(4, 5, *d*)	6:	(4, 7, *f*)
7:	(5, 6, *e* ∪ *j*)	8:	(5, 7, *h*)
9:	(7, 8, *g*)	10:	(3, 1, *a*)

(b)

PE(2, 7) = ⟨2, 7, ((b • c • f) ∪ (i • f))⟩

(c)

Fig. 1. Example explaining path-sequence and expression (a) Example graph (b) Path-sequence for the graph (c) Partial path expression for paths between nodes 2 to 7

to right. At every iteration of the *SOLVE algorithm* the following step is performed $PE(s, w_i) \cup (PE(s, v_i) \bullet PE(v_i, w_i)) -> SA[w_i]$, where an existing path expression for (s, w_i) is extended using concatenation of two subpath expressions and/or union of new path expression capturing additional paths for (s, w_i). At the end of the scan and propagation phase, we are guaranteed completeness of the source node used to drive the propagation phase. The original single source *SOLVE* algorithm was generalized in [21] to multiple sources, with a particular emphasis on sharing computation across sources where subexpressions were common.

One of the main issues with graph computation is that every problem requires a different algorithm. A nice property of this algebraic framework as shown by [34] is that multiple path problems can be solved using the same algorithm by interpreting Union(∪) and concatenation(•) operators appropriately. For example, the shortest path problem has a very straightforward interpretation in terms of the Union(∪) operator, where rather than union multiple path expressions you ignore all but that with the least cost. Some problems can also be interpreted in terms of manipulation of the path expression produced by the unconstrained path problem. [17,21,23] all describe some examples. For problems in this category, a critical issue is that computationally efficient representations of path expressions are used rather than mere string representations. For example, there is a natural mapping from regular expressions to abstract syntax trees (AST) where the operators like union(∪) and concatenation(•) form the internal nodes while the edges form the leaves of the tree. Figure 1(c) shows the AST for the PE shown earlier. In this context, path filter operators can then be defined in terms of manipulation of path expression representations.

2.2 Algebraic Query Evaluation of Graph Pattern Matching

It is well known that RDF admits a directed graph model. SPARQL [29] is the standard RDF query language with its main query primitive being a *graph pattern*. Evaluation of graph pattern matching query is usually performed using operators with an algebraic query plan where we typically use relational-like query operators. The graph patterns are compiled into an algebraic logical plan representation, which is generally a sequence of query operators with an implied execution ordering. For example, Jena ARQ [4,28] is a popular query engine that supports SPARQL queries and it creates a SPARQL Syntax-Expression(SSE) as an algebraic logical query plan. The last step in query evaluation is transforming the logical plan to a physical plan which depends on the physical execution environment.

3 Related Work

[16,35] provides a good survey of graph query languages. For running queries that have both graph pattern matching and path computation components, in most cases, users have to use two different platforms. Those platforms that do allow both components mostly focus on finding shortest paths and not necessarily all paths. Platforms like Virtuoso [18], RDFPath [30], Blazegraph [5] use property paths [12] supported by SPARQL 1.1 [25]. However, using property paths, it is only possible to know the specific sources and destination, but not the exact paths. Also, the users would need to write a regular expression of the properties in the paths they are looking for, requiring the user to know the exact properties in the path as well as have some idea of the sequence of these properties. Gremlin [32], the query language for JanusGraph [8] and Neptune [2] also requires the predicates of the path to be specified in the query. Oracle's PGQL [10,11,31,33] finds paths using general expressions over vertices and edges of the graph. The user needs to have knowledge of the sequence of edges in the paths being searched for in this case as well.

Neo4j [9], AgensGraph [1] use Cypher [7,20] as their query language. Cypher uses a fast bidirectional breadth-first search algorithm for optimizing path queries. However, this fast algorithm is used only in certain scenarios like finding shortest path. When finding all paths, Cypher uses a much slower exhaustive depth-first search algorithm. Even for shortest path queries, the fast algorithm is used only if the predicates in the path query can be evaluated on the fly. For path queries, with predicates for which they need to examine the whole path before making a decision on filtering, Cypher's query evaluation falls back to exhaustive search. Cypher has another drawback, where its shortest path algorithm produces incomplete results when the start and end nodes are the same. Such a scenario might occur when performing a shortestPath search where the sources and destinations are overlapping sets of nodes.

Stardog [13] uses more traditional SPARQL operators for query evaluation. For any path query with start and end variable patterns Stardog first finds all possible paths that match *PQ* which is a regular expression similar to that used

Original query

```
PREFIX akt:<http://www.aktors.org/ontology/
portal#>
PREFIX rdf:<http://www.w3.org/1999/02/22-rdf-
syntax-ns#>

SELECT * WHERE {
   ?s1 rdf:type akt:Affiliated-Person .
   ?s1 akt:full-name "Wendy E. Mackay" .
   ?s akt:has-author ?s1 .
   ?s2 akt:full-name "Irene Greif" .
   ?s2 akt:has-affiliation ?d .

   ?s ?pathVar ?d .
}
```

(a)

SSE produced by Jena after parsing and compiling

```
(prefix ((akt:http://www.aktors.org/ontology/portal#)
         (rdf:http://www.w3.org/1999/02/22-rdf-syntax-ns#))
  (project (?s1 ?s)
    (product
      (join
        (BGP
          [triple ?s1 rdf:type akt:Affiliated-Person]
          [triple ?s1 akt:full-name "Wendy E. Mackay"])
        (BGP
          [triple ?s akt:has-author ?s1]
        ))
      (BGP
        [triple ?s2 akt:full-name "Irene Greif"]
        [triple ?s2 akt:has-affiliation ?d]))
```

(b)

Fig. 2. (a) An example path query in our implementation of the integrated platform. (b) The SSE produced by Jena's parser and compiler

by property paths. The resulting set of paths is then joined with the end graph pattern, followed by the start graph pattern. This approach of applying filter first and then joining with source and destination patterns might be useful when the filter is highly restrictive. However, if the path query filter is not restrictive it will produce a large resultset resulting in poor performance when joining with the start and end patterns.

4 Approach

Introducing a new query class would typically require the extension of query language and processing framework. However, we adopted an approach of introducing a syntactic sugar that avoided the need for changing SPARQL's query syntax. A second simplifying but reasonable strategy is the use of a fixed order between the graph pattern matching phase and the path computation phase. The rationale here is that in gpqs, pattern matching serves to compute the set of sources, destinations and/or intermediate nodes in constraints. In other words, the output of graph pattern matching can be seen as input to the path problem phase. Interpreting this in terms of query plans implies that the path computation and path filter operators will always be at the root of the tree for any gpqs query plans. In the sequel, we elaborate our realization of the above implied strategy.

4.1 Identifying GPQ Sub-Query Components in SPARQL* Queries

Our syntactic sugar is based on adopting a pre-defined variable name **?pathVar** as the path operator. We acknowledge the risk of other users using this variable in their queries, but assume this risk to be small. Since this a legal variable that is recognized by the graph pattern matching platform's parser, the unaltered parser can parse and compile path queries without failing due to syntax issues. Here, we refer to SPARQL with our pre-defined variable **?pathVar** as SPARQL*.

Implementation Strategy: In this section, we describe the approach followed to identify the source and destination variables using the pre-defined path variable **?pathVar** and then project them out from the graph patterns. The last triple pattern in example query in Fig. 2(a), ⟨**?s ?pathVar ?d**⟩ denotes the path computation between all bindings to the variable **?s** and the variable **?d**. Presence of the **?pathVar** variable in the predicate position implies that it is a path query. Now, we must keep track of the position of the source and destination variables in the graph patterns and finally, after all the joins have taken place we must project out only the bindings of the source and destination variables. These bindings would then go into the path operator. To do this, we create the required datastructures to hold the position information of the source and destination variables in the query. This information will be later required when we create the final physical plan of the query.

For our proof-of-concept prototype, we implemented by integrating **Semstorm** [27] as the graph pattern matching platform and **Serpent** [21,23] as the path query computation platform. Semstorm uses the below two main datastructures as query plan representation to hold the position information of the different triple patterns in the submitted query.

- **subjObjListMap** holds the mapping between the subjects and the corresponding objects in the query. The subjObjListMap for the query in Fig. 2(a) would be

  ```
  subjObjListMap: {?s=[[?s1]], ?s1=[["Wendy E. Mackay"]],
                   ?s2=[["Irene Greif"], [?d]]}
  ```

- **subjPropListMap** holds the mapping between the subjects and the properties or predicates in the triple patterns in the query. The subjPropListMap of the query in Fig. 2(a) would be

  ```
  subjPropListMap: {?s=[has-author], ?s1=[full-name],
                    ?s2=[full-name, has-affiliation]}
  ```

In addition to these, the following datastructures have been added to facilitate path computation and provide required location information to the path operator.

- **pathSrcDst** is a map that shows the mapping between the source variable and its corresponding destination variable. For the query in Fig. 2(a), the pathSrcDst would be

  ```
  pathSrcDst: {?s=[?d]}
  ```

- **srcMap** contains the source variable in the key position and a list of integers in the value position. The list of integers denote the exact position of the source variable in the subjObjListMap datastructure. The srcMap of the query in Fig. 2(a) would be

  ```
  srcMap: {?s=[[0, -1]]}
  ```

- **dstMap** is similar to the srcMap, except that its key contains the destination variable and the list of integers in its value position denote the position of the destination variable. The dstMap of the query in Fig. 2(a) would be

```
dstMap: {?d=[[2, 1]]}
```

- **cndMap** is also same as the srcMap and dstMap except that it hold the constraints information. For example, some query might want to restrict paths to the ones which contain at least one **akt:has-affiliation** property or predicate. Then, this triple will be a part of the constraints and the position of this triple would be captured in the cndMap. The query in Fig. 2(a) is not a constrained query and hence, its cndMap would be empty.

The list of integers in the value position of the **srcMap, dstMap** and **cndMap** all denote the position of the respective variables in subjObjListMap. For example, {?s = [[0, − 1]]} means the variable **?s** is in the first BGP of subjObjListMap (indexing starts at 0) and −1 denotes that it is the subject of the BGP. {?d = [[2, 1]]} means that the variable **?d** is in the third BGP and it is the second object of that BGP. Sometimes these variables might also be the join variable between two graph patterns and so, they can exist in multiple BGPs and the value of the respective maps will have a list of integer pairs, identifying the position of the variable in subjObjListMap.

4.2 Logical Query Plan Transformation

Our query planning approach is based on transforming the query plan produced by graph pattern matching engine. The intuition is that the subqueries which are the graph patterns defining the sets of sources, destinations, etc for path computation can be translated to query plans in the usual manner. However, the semantics of such queries will usually imply a cross-product of intermediate results (since the subgraph patterns will be disconnected). We illustrate this idea with the example query in Fig. 2(a) (but ignoring the last triple pattern ⟨`?s ?pathVar ?d`⟩ which is our syntactic sugar for the path variable triple pattern). Figure 2(b) shows the SSE created by Jena's parser and compiler and

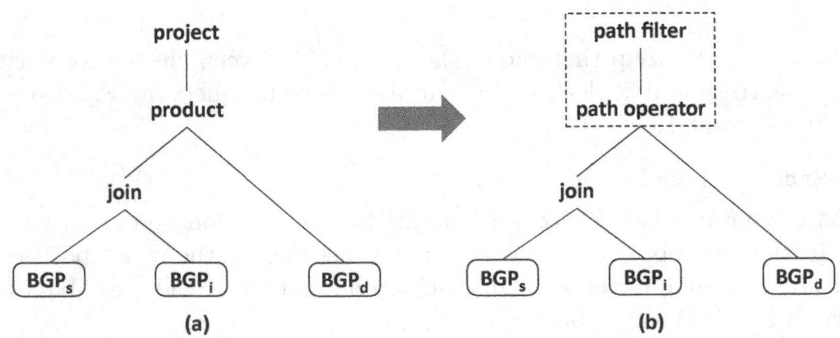

Fig. 3. Query plan transformation from graph pattern matching query to ggpq

Fig. 3(a) shows the SSE as a tree. To achieve the correct query semantics, the cross-product and projection operators have to be removed and query operators associated with path computation introduced. The final operator in the plan is a path filter operator (if path filtering constraints are specified - absent in example). The newly introduced components of the query plan are enclosed in a dotted box in Fig. 3(b).

Implementation Strategy: Our graph pattern matching platform, Semstorm [27] is an RDF processing platform that is targeted for Cloud-processing and uses Apache Hadoop/Tez execution environment. Semstorm's compiler builds on Jena's parser, using Jena's SSE to create a Tez [3] DAG as the physical query plan based on Semstorm's query algebra. To achieve an equivalent physical query plan transformation, similar to the logical plan transformation in Fig. 3, new physical query operators have to be introduced. Since our physical execution environment is Tez, the new physical operators are nothing but new Tez Vertices. The following new Tez vertex types were added that act as the physical query operators.

- **Annotator Vertex for Source, Destination and Constraint Variables.** Semstorm is meant to run *SELECT * WHERE* queries and so, it propagates the data for all of the variables in the query. However, the path computation platform Serpent expects three lists of nodes that denote sources, destinations and constraints respectively. Hence, annotators were required to identify the source, destination or constraint variables and then, allow only the bindings

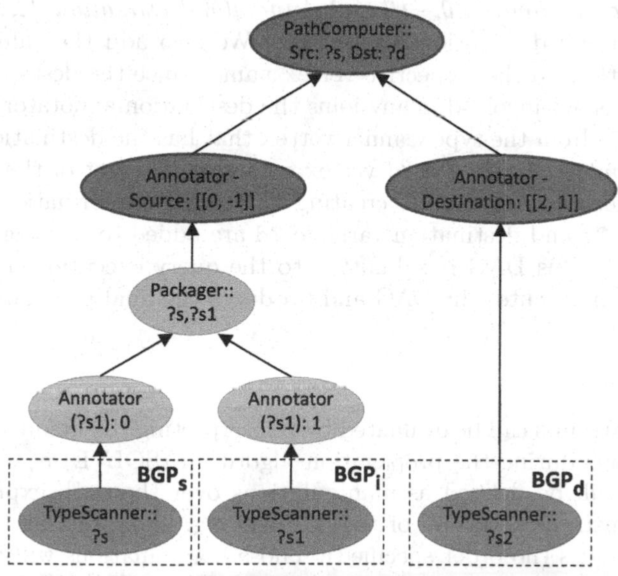

Fig. 4. The Tez DAG representating the physical plan for the query shown in Fig. 2

for that variable to pass through, discarding the rest of the bindings. While this might seem to be a less optimized method, it must be noted that bindings to other variables cannot be discarded before all joins have completed since the source, destination or constraint variable may not always be the join variable.

- **PathComputer Vertex.** This is the path operator which performs the path computation. It takes the sources, destinations and constraints as input, converts these into three String arrays as is required by Serpent and then calls the appropriate method in the Serpent platform. For every path query DAG this vertex will always be at the root.

Figure 4 shows the final Tez DAG that needs to be generated for the example query in Fig. 2(a). The *TypeScanner::?s* vertex in the DAG identifies and reads all triples that match the pattern {`?s akt:has-author ?s1`} from the data file. Similarly, the other TypeScanner vertices read the respective matching triples. The output of the *TypeScanner::?s* and *TypeScanner::?s1* vertices go to *Annotator(?s1):0* and *Annotator(?s1):1* vertices respectively. These annotator vertices identify the join variable and its position in the graph pattern. The *Packager::?s,?s1* vertex performs the actual join operation between the two graph patterns and provides the joined output of the two input graph patterns.

If a simple pattern matching query is submitted to Semstorm, it would add a *Producter* vertex that would take inputs from the *Packager::?s,?s1* and *TypeScanner::?s2* vertices and the output of the *Producter* vertex would go into a *Flattener* vertex which would write out the final query output to an output file on disk. In our integrated version, we created a fork at this point, where for a path query, we do not add the *Producter* and *Flattener* vertices. After joins, we add the *Annotator- Source:[[0,−1]]* and *Annotator-Destination:[[2,1]]* to annotate the source and destination respectively. We also add the value from the `srcMap` and `dstMap` to the respective vertex name. Since the destination vertex in our example is not involved in any joins the destination annotator vertex gets its input directly from the typeScanner vertex that has the destination variable. The *PathComputer::Src:?s, Dst:?d* vertex comes at the root of the DAG since this will be executed last. While creating this vertex, information about the source variable `?s` and destination variable `?d` are added to it using the configuration payload. This DAG is submitted to the query execution framework of Semstorm, which executes the DAG and produces the final path output.

4.3 Path Constraints

Some path constraints can be evaluated by reinterpreting the union and concatenation operations during the propagation algorithm (SOLVE) e.g. for shortest paths. Others will be defined as manipulations over the path expression produced by unconstrained version of the problem e.g. finding paths that contain a given set of nodes (no order specified). Those manipulations will be encapsulated in operators that are parent nodes of the pathComputer node in operator plan tree. The efficiency of the such operations will depend on the nature of

Number of sources and Destinations					
Queries	Sources	Destinations	Queries	Sources	Destinations
SmallQuery_1	25	2	LargeQuery_1	13641	907
SmallQuery_2	4	6	LargeQuery_2	29974	32583
SmallQuery_3	4	3	LargeQuery_3	11793	6
SmallQuery_4	29	7	LargeQuery_4	29974	2290
SmallQuery_5	26	31	LargeQuery_5	2290	32582

Fig. 5. Size of source and destination sets for each query

path expression representation e.g. a binary encoded representation. However, a detailed discussion path constraints is outside scope of this paper.

5 Evaluation

5.1 Test Setup

The primary goal of our evaluation was to compare our integrated system with an existing platform on the following parameters.

1. Query compilation time comparison for our platform with and without path operator.
2. Performance, i.e., time taken to run the same queries.
3. Completeness of results, i.e., whether the platform returns all paths expected.
4. Expressiveness, i.e., what level of queries can be expressed in each platform.

Dataset and Queries: Our queries were ran on the BTC500M dataset [26] (size 0.5 GB, 2.5 million triples). While formulating queries, we focused on finding paths that are at least three hops long. The queries we ran varies from small set of sources and destinations to very large set of sources and destinations. We ran five small queries and five large queries where small and large indicate the size of the set of sources and destinations shown in Fig. 5. In the charts Small Queries and Large Queries have been abbreviated to SQ and LQ respectively. The same queries were modified to add constraints to run constrained query experiments.

All the comparisons have been done with Stardog. We also considered Neo4j, but while trying to run queries using Cypher we found that all-paths queries on this dataset were running indefinitely and causing the Neo4j server to crash. We were able to run shortest path queries on Neo4j but that result is not included in this paper as finding shortest path was not an evaluation goal for this paper.

Hardware Configuration: Evaluation was conducted on single node server running HDFS in a privately owned RedHat Enterprise Server server, housed in the University's server lab. The server is equipped with Xeon octa core x86_64 CPU (2.33 GHz), 40 GB RAM, and two HDDs (3.6 TB and 445 GB). All results have been averaged over five trials. In all the charts our platform has been labelled as "Sem-Ser".

5.2 Evaluation Results

Query Compilation Time Comparison: Figure 6 shows the time taken for query compilation on our platform for queries which have the path operator compared with the same queries without the path operator. The path operator does not have much effect on the query compilation time and in most cases the compilation time increased by less than one second.

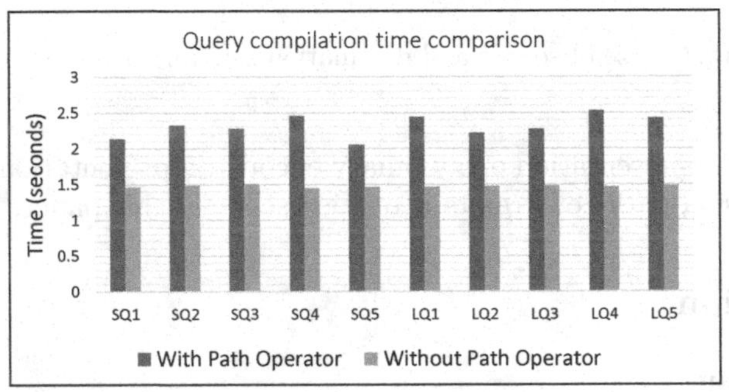

Fig. 6. Chart showing compilation time comparison

Performance Evaluation: When comparing absolute time taken by our platform with that of Stardog, we found that Stardog performed better in all queries except for SQ_1, LQ_1 and LQ_2. LQ_2 timed out and produced only partial results on Stardog and took the longest time (5.5 min) and produced the largest number of paths (0.8 million paths) on our platform. This is mainly because the graph patterns provided for the source and destination nodes was quite general, thus, leading to large number of matching sources and destinations. Consequently, there were a large number of paths connecting these nodes.

Completeness of Results: Figure 7(a) and (b) show the number of paths identified by small and large queries respectively. LQ_2 has been marked with an asterix since it did not finish in Stardog and hence, all the charts have only one value for this query. For all the queries, Stardog produced incomplete results and also duplicate paths. This dataset has a lot of triples such as ⟨`acm:58567 akt:has-publication-reference acm:58567`⟩. In this triple the subject and the object is the same uri `acm:58567` and hence, this is called a *loop* or *self-loop*. The BTC dataset has a lot of such triples and Stardog does not consider the self loops in the paths it identifies. For example, suppose we have an RDF graph consisting of the triples ⟨`A p1 A`⟩ ⟨`A p2 B`⟩ ⟨`B p3 B`⟩ and a path query with `A` as source node and `B` as destination node. On execution of the path query Stardog will ignore the self-loops ⟨`A p1 A`⟩ and ⟨`B p3 B`⟩ and will output only one path (`A p2 B`). However, our platform will find four paths (`A p2 B`), (`A p1 A p2 B`), (`A p2 B p3 B`) and (`A p1 A p2 B p3 B`). This is the reason behind Stardog mostly finding less paths as compared to our platform.

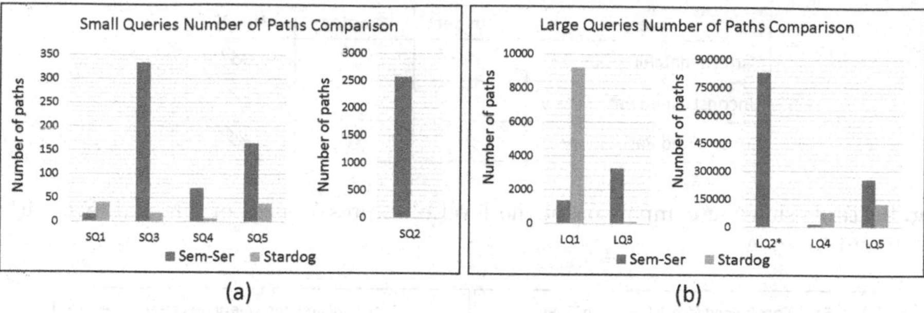

Fig. 7. Chart showing comparison of number of paths identified

In some queries (SQ_1, LQ_1), Stardog does find more number of paths. However, these results contain duplicate paths. For example, although Stardog produces 40 paths for SQ_1 the number of unique paths is 6. Since there was a huge mismatch between the number of paths found by our platform and Stardog we compared the time taken per path identified rather than the absolute time taken for executing each query. Figure 8(a) and (b) shows the time per path comparison for the small and large queries respectively.

Expressiveness: All types of graph patterns can be expressed in Neo4j, Stardog as well as our platform. However, Stardog does not support constraints such as *ALL, ANY, NONE.* Figure 9 shows the comparison of the expressiveness of our platform with that of Stardog and Neo4j. Neo4j has predicate functions (all, any, exists, none, single) which can be used for the same purpose of filtering. However, since we were not able to run all paths queries on Neo4j it was not possible to compare constrained queries on our platform with that on Neo4j.

Figure 10 shows the time taken for constrained queries as compared to unconstrained queries on our platform. All of the constrained queries understandably taken longer time to complete query execution, since these queries include an

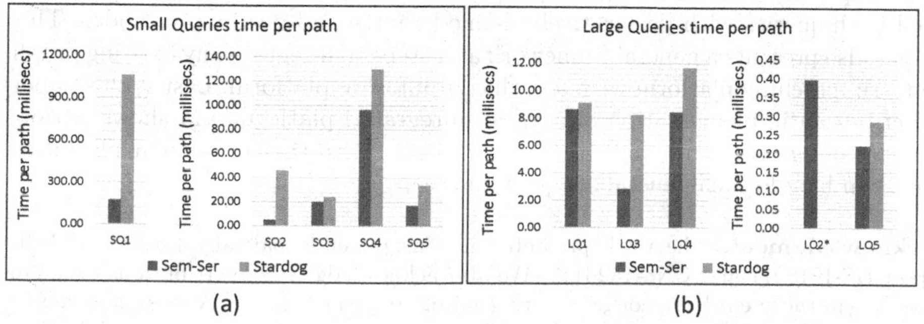

Fig. 8. Chart showing the comparison of time taken per path identified

Query	Sem-Ser	Stardog	Neo4j
Pattern matching Query	✓	✓	✓
Unconstrained Path Query	✓	✓	✓
Constrained Path Query	✓	✗	✓

Fig. 9. Table showing comparison of the level of expressiveness of our platform with Neo4j and Stardog

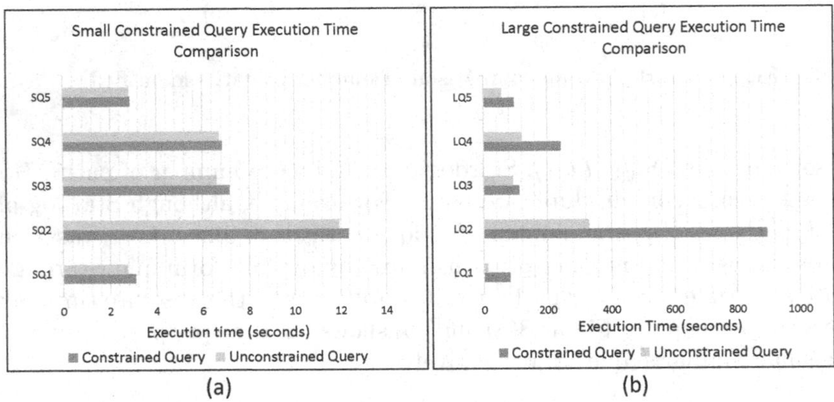

Fig. 10. Execution Time of constrained queries vs unconstrained queries

extra filtering step. For all of the small queries, the increase in execution time is minimal mainly because the size of the resulting set of paths before filtering is also small. For the large queries, the increase in execution time is more noticeable due to the larger size of the resultset prior to filtering.

6 Conclusion

This paper presents an algebraic query evaluation strategy to evaluate generalized path queries with declaratively defined source and destination nodes. This paper also presents a general framework and steps to integrate any existing graph pattern matching platform with a path computation platform. Lastly, this paper describes an implementation of such an integrated platform and shows performance comparison with this integrated platform with that of popular platforms that can handle such generalized path queries.

Acknowledgment. The work presented in this paper is partially funded by NSF grant IIS-1218277 and CNS-1526113. We also acknowledge the contributions of Sidan Gao {sgao@ncsu.edu}, HyeongSik Kim {hkim22@ncsu.edu} and Arunkumar Krishnamoorthy {akrish12@ncsu.edu} who did part of the work for this paper while they were students at North Carolina State University.

References

1. AgensGraph Enterprise Edition. https://bitnine.net/
2. Amazon Neptune. https://aws.amazon.com/neptune/
3. Apache Tez. https://tez.apache.org/
4. ARQ - A SPARQL Processor for Jena. https://jena.apache.org/
5. Blazegraph. https://www.blazegraph.com/
6. Cambridge Semantics: AnzoGraph. https://www.cambridgesemantics.com/product/anzograph/
7. Cypher for Apache Spark (2017). https://github.com/opencypher/cypher-for-apache-spark
8. JanusGraph. https://janusgraph.org/
9. Neo4j Graph Platform. https://neo4j.com/
10. Oracle: Oracle Big Data Spatial and Graph (2017). https://oracle.com/technetwork/database/database-technologies/bigdata-spatialandgraph/
11. Oracle 2017: PGQL 1.1 Specication (2017). https://pgql-lang.org/spec/1.1/
12. SPARQL 1.1 Property Paths. https://www.w3.org/TR/sparql11-property-paths/
13. Stardog: The Enterprise Knowledge Graph Platform. https://www.stardog.com/
14. Aasman, J.: Allegro Graph: RDF Triple Database. Oakland Franz Incorporated, Cidade (2006)
15. Angles, R., et al.: G-core: a core for future graph query languages. In: Proceedings of the 2018 International Conference on Management of Data, pp. 1421–1432. ACM (2018)
16. Angles, R., Gutierrez, C.: Survey of graph database models. ACM Comput. Surv. (CSUR) **40**(1), 1 (2008)
17. Anyanwu, K., Maduko, A., Sheth, A.: Sparq2l: towards support for subgraph extraction queries in RDF databases. In: Proceedings of the 16th International Conference on World Wide Web, pp. 797–806. ACM (2007)
18. Erling, O., Mikhailov, I.: RDF support in the virtuoso DBMS. In: Networked Knowledge - Networked Media, Studies in Computational Intelligence, vol. 221 (2009)
19. Fionda, V., Gutierrez, C., Pirró, G.: Extracting relevant subgraphs from graph navigation. In: Proceedings of the 2012th International Conference on Posters & Demonstrations Track, vol. 914, pp. 81–84. Citeseer (2012)
20. Francis, N., et al.: Cypher: an evolving query language for property graphs. In: Proceedings of the 2018 International Conference on Management of Data, pp. 1433–1445. ACM (2018)
21. Gao, S., Anyanwu, K.: Prefixsolve: efficiently solving multi-source multi-destination path queries on RDF graphs by sharing suffix computations. In: Proceedings of the 22nd International Conference on World Wide Web, pp. 423–434. ACM (2013)
22. Gao, S., Fu, H., Anyanwu, K.: An agglomerative query model for discovery in linked data: semantics and approach. In: Proceedings of the 13th International Workshop on the Web and Databases, p. 2. ACM (2010)
23. Gao, S., Shrivastava, S., Ogan, K., Xin, Y., Baldin, I.: Evaluating path query mechanisms as a foundation for SDN network control. In: 4th IEEE Conference on Network Softwarization and Workshops, NetSoft 2018, Montreal, QC, Canada, June 25–29, 2018. pp. 28–36 (2018). https://doi.org/10.1109/NETSOFT.2018.8460116
24. Gubichev, A., Neumann, T.: Path Query Processing on Very Large RDF Graphs. Citeseer, Princeton (2011)

25. Harris, S., Seaborne, A.: SPARQL 1.1 Query Language - W3C Recommendation (2013). https://www.w3.org/TR/sparql11-query/
26. Harth, A.: Billion triples challenge data set (2011)
27. Kim, H., Ravindra, P., Anyanwu, K.: Type-based semantic optimization for scalable RDF graph pattern matching. In: Proceedings of the 26th International Conference on World Wide Web, WWW 2017, Perth, Australia, April 3–7, 2017. pp. 785–793 (2017). https://doi.org/10.1145/3038912.3052655
28. McBride, B.: Jena: A Semantic Web Toolkit. Internet Computing, IEEE 6 (2002)
29. Prud'Hommeaux, E., Seaborne, A., et al.: Sparql query language for RDF. W3C recommendation 15 (2008)
30. Przyjaciel-Zablocki, M., Schätzle, A., Hornung, T., Lausen, G.: RDFPath: path query processing on large RDF graphs with MapReduce. In: García-Castro, R., Fensel, D., Antoniou, G. (eds.) ESWC 2011. LNCS, vol. 7117, pp. 50–64. Springer, Heidelberg (2012). https://doi.org/10.1007/978-3-642-25953-1_5
31. van Rest, O., Hong, S., Kim, J., Meng, X., Chafi, H.: PGQL: a property graph query language. In: Proceedings of the Fourth International Workshop on Graph Data Management Experiences and Systems, p. 7. ACM (2016)
32. Rodriguez, M.A.: The gremlin graph traversal machine and language (invited talk). In: Proceedings of the 15th Symposium on Database Programming Languages, pp. 1–10. ACM (2015)
33. Sevenich, M., Hong, S., van Rest, O., Wu, Z., Banerjee, J., Chafi, H.: Using domain-specific languages for analytic graph databases. Proc. VLDB Endowment **9**(13), 1257–1268 (2016)
34. Tarjan, R.E.: Fast algorithms for solving path problems. Stanford University California Department of Computer Science, Technical report (1979)
35. Wood, P.T.: Query languages for graph databases. ACM SIGMOD Record **41**(1), 50–60 (2012)

Building a Conference Recommender System Based on SciGraph and WikiCFP

Andreea Iana[1(✉)], Steffen Jung[1], Philipp Naeser[1], Aliaksandr Birukou[2,3], Sven Hertling[1], and Heiko Paulheim[1]

[1] Data and Web Science Group, University of Mannheim, Mannheim, Germany
andreeaiana@gmail.com, mail@jung.vision, pnaeser@mail.uni-mannheim.de, {sven,heiko}@informatik.uni-mannheim.de

[2] Springer Nature, Heidelberg, Germany
Aliaksandr.Birukou@springer.com

[3] Peoples' Friendship University of Russia (RUDN University), Moscow, Russia

Abstract. SciGraph is a Linked Open Data graph published by Springer Nature which contains information about conferences and conference publications. In this paper, we discuss how this dataset can be utilized to build a conference recommendation system, yielding a recall@10 of up to 0.665, and a MAP of up to 0.540, generating recommendations based on authors, abstracts, and keywords. Furthermore, we show how the dataset can be linked to WikiCFP to recommend upcoming conferences.

Keywords: Recommender system · SciGraph · Scientific publications

1 Introduction

Bibliographic datasets form a major topic in the Linked Open Data Cloud[1], accounting for a total of 12–13% of all datasets [15]. One of those datasets is SciGraph[2], which is published by Springer Nature and is the successor of Springer's Linked Open Data Conference Portal [3], comprising 7.2M articles and 240k books published by Springer Nature, and totaling to 1B triples.

In this paper, we aim at exploiting SciGraph to provide users with recommendations of conferences to submit their publications to, utilizing SciGraph for information on past conferences and publications, and WikiCfP for information on upcoming conferences.

[1] https://lod-cloud.net/.
[2] https://www.springernature.com/de/researchers/scigraph.

The publication has been prepared with the support of the "RUDN University Program 5-100".

M. Acosta et al. (Eds.): SEMANTiCS 2019, LNCS 11702, pp. 117–123, 2019.
https://doi.org/10.1007/978-3-030-33220-4_9

2 Related Work

The idea of building recommender systems for scholarly content goes back almost 20 years [2,7]. More recently, Linked Open Data has been recognized as a valuable source for building recommender systems. In particular, content-based recommender systems, which focus on the items to be recommended and their interrelations, can benefit strongly from detailed descriptions of those items in open datasets [4,5].

Similar to the task in this paper, several approaches have been proposed for the recommendation of *research papers* (see [1] for a comprehensive survey). Although sharing the same domain, the setup is slightly different here – in our scenario, both the input data (i.e., authors, a textual abstract, keywords), and the prediction target (conferences instead of individual papers) are different.

3 Approach

3.1 Datasets

The main dataset used to train the recommender system is SciGraph. For training, we use publications from the years 2013–2015, whereas for evaluation, publications from the year 2016 are used. In total, SciGraph contains 240,396 books, however, only a fraction out of those correspond to the proceedings of a single conference. Moreover, it contains 3,987,480 individual book chapters, again, a fraction of which correspond to papers published at conferences. Additionally, SciGraph provides a taxonomy of research topics, called *Product Market Codes* (PMCs). In total, 1,465 of those PMCs are included in the hierarchy and assigned to books. Only 89 of those PMCs are related to computer science.

The second dataset we use is WikiCfP[3], a website which publishes calls for papers. Since there is no downloadable version of the data (although the CC-BY-SA license allows for reusing the dataset), we built a crawler to create a dataset of CfPs, containing names, acronyms, dates, locations, and submission deadlines (which we consider mandatory attributes), as well as links to the conference page, the conference series, categorization in WikiCfP, and textual description (which we consider optional attributes). Overall, we crawled data for 65,714 CfPs in July 2018. The crawled data was linked to SciGraph using string similarity between the conference names. This leads to 53.1% of the CfPs linked to SciGraph.

3.2 Recommendation Techniques

We use three main families of recommendation techniques, i.e., recommendations based on authors, abstracts, and keywords. Furthermore, we also use an ensemble strategy. Generally, the recommendation strategies either exploit some notion of similarity (e.g., recommending conferences which contain publications with similar abstracts), or model the problem as a machine learning problem (i.e., since we have 742 conference series in our training set, we train a multi-label classifier for 742 classes).

[3] http://www.wikicfp.com.

Author-based recommendations are computed based on the authors of an application. Essentially, we count the number of papers per conference series which share at least one author with the authors given in the abstract, and use that count as a score.[4]

Abstract-based recommendations compare the abstracts of publications in SciGraph with the abstract given by the user. Overall, we use two different approaches: the *max* strategy finds single publications with the highest abstract similarity and proposes the corresponding conference, while the *concat* strategy concatenates all abstracts related to a conference to a virtual document, and compares the given abstract to those virtual documents.

Different variants for generating recommendations are used. We utilize standard TF-IDF, as well as TF-IDF based on word n-grams, LSA and LSA based on word n-grams [10], and pLSA [6]. Furthermore, we utilize similarity based on word embeddings, based on word2vec [11], GloVe [13], and FastText [8], using both pre-trained embeddings, as well as embeddings trained on the SciGraph collection of abstracts. While all those approaches are based on similarities, we also tried directly predicting the conferences using a convolutional neural network (CNN) approach, which takes the self-trained word2vec embeddings as representations for words, as discussed in [9].

Keyword-based recommendations are based on *Product Market Codes* in SciGraph. Such product market codes are defined by Springer Nature and resemble other categorization systems in computer science, such as the ACM computing classification system. A second keyword-based model uses a script to identify Computer Science Ontology (CSO) [14] terms in the abstract entered by the user.

4 Evaluation

As sketched above, publication data from 2013–2015 were used as training data for the recommender system, whereas publications from 2016 were used for testing. For each publication in the test set, we try to predict the conference at which it has been published, and compare the results to the gold standard (i.e., the conference in which it has actually been published). We create 10 recommendations with each technique[5], and report recall@10 and mean average precision (MAP).

Table 1 shows some basic statistics of the training and test set. In total, the recommender system is trained on 742 conference series and 555,798 papers written by 110,831 authors. As far as the abstracts are concerned, only little

[4] We do not disambiguate authors here, since no further clues for disambiguation, such as organizations, or unique IDs, such as ORCID, are present in SciGraph.

[5] The only exception are recommendations based on authors, which may create shorter lists in cases where all authors altogether have published at less than 10 conferences contained in SciGraph.

Table 1. Characteristics of the training and test set

	Training (2013–2015)	Test (2016)	Overlap
Distinct conference series ID	742	526	405
Distinct author names	110,831	53,862	20,529
Product market codes	155	150	115
Papers	555,798	200,502	–
English abstracts	57,797	21,323	–

Table 2. Results of the best performing individual recommendation techniques. For each individual technique, we only report the results of the best performing strategy (max or concat).

Method	Recall@10	MAP
Author-based	0.372	0.284
Abstract-based TF-IDF (concat)	0.461	0.237
Abstract-based n-gram TF-IDF (concat) w/ cosine similarity	0.490	0.270
Abstract-based n-gram TF-IDF (concat) w/ Multinomial Naive Bayes	0.494	0.273
Abstract-based LSA (concat)	0.461	0.237
Abstract-based n-gram LSA (concat)	0.490	0.270
Abstract-based pLSA (concat)	0.369	0.172
Abstract-based Glove pre-trained (max)	0.229	0.097
Abstract-based word2vec self-trained (max)	0.346	0.154
Abstract-based word2vec plus CNN (concat)	0.405	0.201
Abstract-based doc2vec (concat)	0.352	0.164
Keyword-based SciGraph market codes (max)	**0.665**	**0.522**
Keyword-based CSO (max)	0.201	0.081
Ensemble TF-IDF & word2vec plus CNN (10)	0.498	0.250
Ensemble TF-IDF & word2vec plus CNN & SciGraph market codes (10)	0.648	0.509
Ensemble TF-IDF & word2vec plus CNN & SciGraph market codes (100)	0.662	0.539
Ensemble TF-IDF & word2vec plus CNN & SciGraph market codes (1,000)	0.661	0.540

more than 10% of all the papers have an English language abstract.[6] The average length of an abstract is 136 words.

Table 2 summarizes the results of the best performing models for recommendations based on authors, abstracts, and keywords. Generally, abstracts work better than authors, and keywords work better than abstracts. For abstracts, TF-IDF using single tokens yields a recall@10 of 0.461 and a MAP of 0.237. For using TF-IDF with n-grams, we explored different variants: we varied the upper limit for n between 2 and 5, and evaluated the approach with the 500k and 1M most frequent n-grams, as well as with all n-grams. The best results were obtained when using the 1M most frequent n-grams of size 1 to 4, outperforming the standard TF-IDF approach.

[6] For a larger fraction of papers in SciGraph, no abstract is contained in the dataset.

In addition, we also evaluated a few ensemble setups. These were built by combining recommendation lists of length 10, 100, and 1,000, given by different base recommenders, and using a logistic regression as a meta learner [16] to generate a recommendation list of length 10 as in the setups above. We can observe that combining two abstract-based techniques (TF-IDF and word2vec plus CNN, which were very diverse in their predictions), outperforms the two individual techniques in both recall@10 and MAP.

Building ensembles incorporating SciGraph market codes yields no significantly better results than using keywords alone, demonstrating that those keywords are in fact the most suitable indicator for recommending conferences. Generally, extending the base recommendation lists beyond 100 elements does not change the results much, because conferences predicted on a position higher than 100 are unlikely to be considered in the final result list of size 10.

The recall figures reported in Table 2 do not exceed 0.665, but this result should be considered in a broader context. In total, only 77% of all conferences in the test set are also contained in the training set, i.e., we do not have any training signals for the remaining conferences. Since we can only use previous publications of proceedings for generating training features, the approaches discussed in this paper can only recommend conferences known from the training set, i.e., the maximum recall we could reach with these methods would be 0.815.

In general, we can see that keyword-based models are the best performing ones. However, they are also the least user-friendly ones, since product market codes are assigned by editors at Springer Nature (more recently, using automated tools [12]). While end users might be able to assign them at a decent quality, the actual recommendation quality with user-assigned keywords might actually be lower than the one based on editor-assigned product market codes. Another possible issue is that by selecting up to seven keywords out of 1,465, one could easily create pseudo-keys for conferences (i.e., each conference can be uniquely identified by its keywords), so overfitting might also be an issue for those models.

Another observation we have made in our experiments is that there is a strong bias towards machine learning and neural networks related conferences. As the corpus is focused on computer science conferences, and the training dataset is from the past few years (an informal inspection of the data in SciGraph yielded that roughly half of the papers in the graph are related to artificial intelligence), this topic is over-represented in our training dataset. Hence, the system is likely to create more recommendations for such conferences.

5 Conclusion

In this paper, we have introduced a recommendation system for conferences, based on abstracts, authors, and keywords.[7] The system can be used by authors searching for upcoming conferences to publish at. The recommendations are computed based on SciGraph, with submission deadlines added from WikiCfP.

[7] A prototype is available at http://confrec.dws.uni-mannheim.de/.

We have observed that the best signal for creating recommendations are keywords, in particular market codes in SciGraph, which, however, are not often easy to select for laymen users. With those keywords, a recall@10 of up to 0.665 and a MAP of up to 0.522 can be reached. Recommendations based on authors (recall@10 of 0.372 and MAP of 0.284) and abstracts (recall@10 up to 0.494, MAP up to 0.273) are clearly inferior, where the best results for the latter are obtained with TF-IDF based on word n-grams. Moreover, the good results obtained with vector space embeddings pre-trained on other text categories (e.g., news articles or Wikipedia texts) could not be reproduced on a target corpus of abstracts of scientific texts from various research fields.

References

1. Beel, J., Langer, S., Genzmehr, M., Gipp, B., Breitinger, C., Nürnberger, A.: Research paper recommender system evaluation: a quantitative literature survey. In: International Workshop on Reproducibility and Replication in Recommender Systems Evaluation, pp. 15–22. ACM (2013)
2. Birukou, A., Blanzieri, E., Giorgini, P.: A multi-agent system that facilitates scientific publications search. In: Fifth International Joint Conference on Autonomous Agents and Multiagent Systems, pp. 265–272. ACM Press (2006)
3. Birukou, A., Bryl, V., Eckert, K., Gromyko, A., Kaindl, M.: Springer LOD conference portal. In: International Semantic Web Conference, Posters and Demos (2017)
4. Di Noia, T., Mirizzi, R., Ostuni, V.C., Romito, D., Zanker, M.: Linked open data to support content-based recommender systems. In: Proceedings of the 8th International Conference on Semantic Systems, pp. 1–8. ACM (2012)
5. Heitmann, B., Hayes, C.: Using linked data to build open, collaborative recommender systems. In: AAAI Spring Symposium (2010)
6. Hofmann, T.: Probabilistic latent semantic analysis. In: 15th Conference on Uncertainty in Artificial Intelligence, pp. 289–296. Morgan Kaufmann (1999)
7. Janssen, W.C., Popat, K.: UpLib: a universal personal digital library system. In: ACM Symposium on Document Engineering, pp. 234–242. ACM (2003)
8. Joulin, A., Grave, E., Bojanowski, P., Mikolov, T.: Bag of tricks for efficient text classification. arXiv preprint arXiv:1607.01759 (2016)
9. Kim, Y.: Convolutional neural networks for sentence classification. In: Proceedings of the 2014 Conference on Empirical Methods in Natural Language Processing (EMNLP), pp. 1746–1751 (2014)
10. Landauer, T.K., Foltz, P.W., Laham, D.: An introduction to latent semantic analysis. Discourse Process. **25**(2–3), 259–284 (1998)
11. Mikolov, T., Sutskever, I., Chen, K., Corrado, G.S., Dean, J.: Distributed representations of words and phrases and their compositionality. In: Advances in Neural Information Processing Systems, pp. 3111–3119 (2013)
12. Osborne, F., Salatino, A., Birukou, A., Motta, E.: Automatic Classification of Springer Nature Proceedings with Smart Topic Miner. In: Groth, P., et al. (eds.) ISWC 2016. LNCS, vol. 9982, pp. 383–399. Springer, Cham (2016). https://doi.org/10.1007/978-3-319-46547-0_33
13. Pennington, J., Socher, R., Manning, C.: GloVe: global vectors for word representation. In: Proceedings of the 2014 Conference on Empirical Methods in Natural Language Processing (EMNLP), pp. 1532–1543 (2014)

14. Salatino, A.A., Thanapalasingam, T., Mannocci, A., Osborne, F., Motta, E.: The computer science ontology: a large-scale taxonomy of research areas. In: Vrandečić, D., et al. (eds.) ISWC 2018. LNCS, vol. 11137, pp. 187–205. Springer, Cham (2018). https://doi.org/10.1007/978-3-030-00668-6_12
15. Schmachtenberg, M., Bizer, C., Paulheim, H.: Adoption of the linked data best practices in different topical domains. In: Mika, P., et al. (eds.) ISWC 2014. LNCS, vol. 8796, pp. 245–260. Springer, Cham (2014). https://doi.org/10.1007/978-3-319-11964-9_16
16. Wolpert, D.H.: Stacked generalization. Neural Netw. **5**(2), 241–259 (1992)

V4Ann: Representation and Interlinking of Atom-Based Annotations of Digital Content

Georgios Meditskos(✉), Stefanos Vrochidis, and Ioannis Kompatsiaris

Information Technologies Insititute, Centre for Research and Technology Hellas, Thessaloniki, Greece
{gmeditsk,stefanos,ikom}@iti.gr

Abstract. There is a great potential in creative industries, such as architecture and video game design, for re-using and re-purposing of digital content. Paintings, archival footage, documentaries, movies, reviews or catalogues, and various other forms of artwork can serve as sources of inspiration and design direction towards innovative designs and new concepts. In this paper, we present V4Ann, an ontology-based framework for semantically representing, aggregating and combining annotations (atoms) coming from visual and textual analysis of digital content. The aim is to structure and link data in such a way so as to facilitate the systematic process, integration and organisation of information and establish innovative value chains and end-user applications. The framework is part of the V4Design platform that aims to re-use and re-purpose existing heterogeneous multimedia content by semantically enriching and transforming assets into a 3D representation, so as to inspire and support the design, architecture, as well as 3D and VR game industries.

Keywords: Annotations · Ontologies · Reasoning · Semantic enrichment · Multimodal data

1 Introduction

Vast amounts of multimedia content is being produced, archived and digitised, resulting in great troves of data of interest. Examples include user-generated content, such as images, videos, text and audio posted by users on social media and wikis, or content provided through official publishers and distributors, such as digital libraries, organisations and online museums. This digital content can serve as a valuable source of inspiration to the cultural and creative industries to produce new assets or to enhance and (re-)use the already existing ones.

However, the re-use and re-purposing of digital content is mainly realised based on individual designers skills and a variety of non-interlinked heterogeneous tools. To this end, the content remains largely under-exploited, despite its great potential for re-use and re-purpose, due to the lack of appropriate solutions for its retrieval and integration into the design process. For example, existing

M. Acosta et al. (Eds.): SEMANTiCS 2019, LNCS 11702, pp. 124–139, 2019.
https://doi.org/10.1007/978-3-030-33220-4_10

heterogeneous multimedia content, such as video and images of buildings and objects, can be collected and transformed (e.g. into 3D models[1]), so as to inspire and support the creation of new content in creative industries. One of the main challenges in this area is to maximise the potential for re-purposing of digital content through the development of innovative technologies to systematically analyse, combine, link and foster searchability and reusability of heterogeneous multimedia content in different contexts.

In this paper we describe V4Ann, an ontology-based framework for capturing and interlinking digital assets and duly annotations at two levels: (a) *content analysis level*, during which visual and textual content is analysed to extract labels, called *atoms*; and (b) *retrieval and repurposing level*, where the assets (e.g. 3D models and images) are interlinked and contextually enriched to facilitate their discovery. At the content analysis level, V4Ann provides the conceptual structures to capture and interlink multimedia analysis results on digital content, such as video, image and text. During retrieval and repurpose, V4Ann provides practical retrieval capabilities, allowing users, e.g. game designers, to search for assets relevant to their needs. V4Ann is part of the V4Design platform[2], enriching multimedia processing with a semantic annotation layer.

The contribution of our research can be summarised in the following:

- We describe a resource annotation model that implements the W3C standard for defining annotations (Web Annotation Data Model [17]).
- We define a core set of rules that perform valid inferences for annotation propagation and interlinking, as well as for validity checking.
- We propose an atom similarity metric along with a searching algorithm for keyword-based digital asset retrieval.

The rest of the paper is structured as follows: Sect. 2 presents related work. Section 3 gives an overview of the framework and presents our motivation. In Sect. 4 we describe the basic concepts of the V4Ann annotation model, while in Sect. 5 we elaborate on the inference and validation capabilities. Section 6 describes the atom similarity metric and the searching functionality. In Sect. 7 we present evaluation results and, finally, in Sect. 8 we conclude our work.

2 Related Work

Annotations are typically used to convey information about a resource or associations between resources. Simple examples include a comment or tag on a single web page or image, video or a blog post about a news article. In 2017, the Web Annotation Data Model (WADM) [17] became the W3C recommendation for defining annotations. It provides an extensible, interoperable framework for expressing annotations, such that they can easily be shared between platforms[3].

---

[1] https://pro.europeana.eu/project/3d-content-in-europeana.

[2] https://v4design.eu/.

[3] https://www.w3.org/TR/annotation-vocab/.

In the domain of digital libraries, the Europeana Data Model (EDM) [4] adopts an open and scalable approach that can accommodate the range and level of details of particular standards, such as LIDO for museums, EAD for archives or METS for digital libraries. EDM is not built on any particular standard, however it is conceptually in line with WADM and the ORE[4] initiative.

The Open Provenance Model (OPM) [11] enables to specify what caused "things" to be, i.e., how "things" depended on others and resulted in specific states. In essence, it allows provenance information to be exchanged between systems, by means of a compatibility layer based on a shared provenance model. OPM predates PROV-O [9], and has a very similar approach to modelling provenance by relating agents, artifacts and processes and the concepts of OPM are covered by equivalent PROV-O concepts. PAV [3] extends PROV-O and specifies Provenance, Authoring and Versioning information.

The Dublin Core metadata (DCMI) standard[5] is a simple yet effective general-purpose set of 15 elements for describing a wide range of networked resources. Although DCMI favors document-like objects, it can be applied to other resources as well. The SKOS Core Vocabulary [10] is a model for expressing the basic structure and content of concept schemes. Specifically for multimedia, the Ontology for Media Resources[6] was developed by the W3C Media Annotations Working Group to identify a minimum set of core properties to describe and retrieve information about media resources. VidOnt [18] provides a formally grounded core reference ontology for video representation. Several attempts have been made to map the XML Schema of MPEG-7 to RDFS and OWL [19] and X3D to OWL (OntologyX3D [6]) and the 3D Modeling Ontology (3DMO[7]).

V4DAnn aims to serve as the semantic annotation layer of multimedia processing results for fostering data exchange among analysis services and for human consumption. In order to promote interoperability and extensibility, it implements the WADM pattern, introducing the concept of atoms and providing several annotation entities and properties. In contrast to existing models that mostly focus on metadata defined by data providers and curators, V4Ann aims to capture content analysis results (e.g. visual and textual analysis), serving as a semantic middleware for metadata exchange. For example, EDM views refer to digital representations, whereas in V4Ann a view represents an atom-based interpretation of a content analysis procedure, e.g. aesthetics extraction. However, V4Ann provides alignments to conceptual structures of existing models, such as the EDM, ORE and SKOS (see Sect. 4 for more details).

As far as semantic enrichment and retrieval are concerned, recent advances in machine learning and especially deep learning have provided us with tools like word representations (e.g. word2vec [20] and Glove [14]), which led to the development of more recent and powerful analysis models [15]. In addition, several approaches have been proposed for question answering over Semantic

[4] http://www.openarchives.org/ore/1.0/vocabulary.
[5] http://dublincore.org/documents/dces/.
[6] http://www.w3.org/TR/mediaont-10.
[7] http://3dontology.org.

Web knowledge bases and Linked Data. Most of them generate one or more queries, while others opt for graph-based approaches to mitigate the rigidness often entailed in formulating appropriate SPARQL queries. Examples include EARL [5] and VoxEL [16]. V4Ann aims to provide a practical context enrichment framework to facilitate basic asset discovery, rather than proposing a fully fledged question answering framework. To this end, it introduces the notions of atom similarity and local contexts.

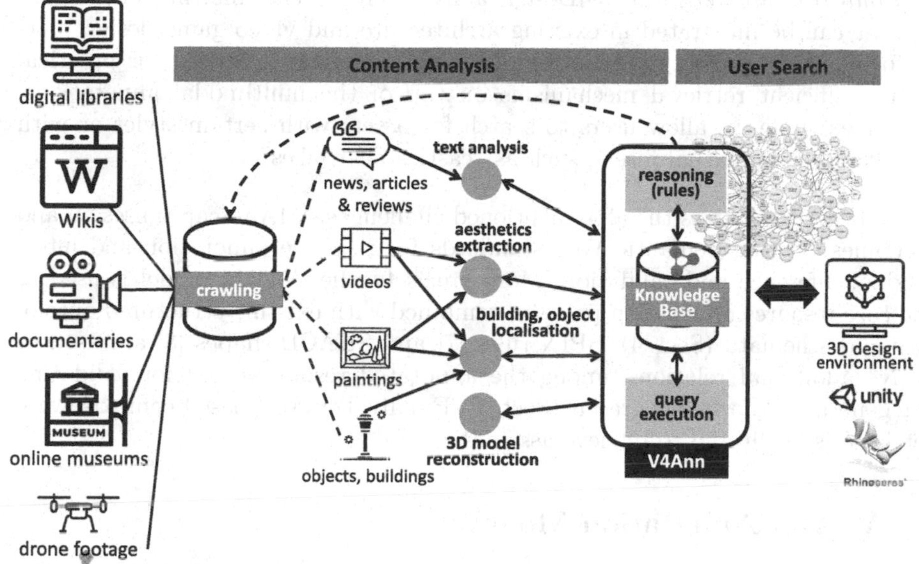

Fig. 1. The position of V4Ann in the integrated V4Design platform.

3 Key Concepts and Motivation

In a world where visual and textual data are in abundance, creative industries need to re-use and re-purpose them so as to remain competitive to other industries and provide to society and creativity a novel financial prism. V4Design is an H2020 project that aims at exploiting state-of-the-art digital content analysis techniques to generate 3D models, extract aesthetic and stylistic information from paintings and videos, localise buildings and objects of interest within visual content, and integrate it with textual information so as to inspire and support the design, architecture, as well as 3D and VR game industries.

V4Ann aims to enrich V4Design with a semantic annotation layer. From one hand, V4Ann acts as the semantic middleware, capturing, interlinking and serving analysis results to multimedia analysis services. On the other hand, it provides the semantic atom-based query infrastructure to retrieve generated assets. The conceptual architecture of V4Design, along with the position of V4Ann, is depicted in Fig. 1. All in all, V4Ann aims to address the following challenges:

- *Annotation propagation and linking:* In a multimodal content analysis setting, like in V4Design, a single media type can be analysed by multiple technologies. For example, an image can be used for extracting building masks, as well as for aesthetics (style) extraction. Also, in many cases, there are interdependencies among the components, e.g. 3D model reconstruction needs as input video frame masks extracted by building localisation. It is important to have an efficient and interoperable way to represent, exchange and further link metadata, both structurally and semantically.
- *Context-aware retrieval:* V4Design aims to create new multimedia content that can be integrated in existing architecture and video game design platforms, such as Unity[8] and Rhino[9]. Therefore, there is a need for practical and efficient retrieval mechanisms on top of the multimodal annotations. For example, to allow users to search for assets with certain styles or with advanced contextual filters, such as "castles near lakes".

In order to address the aforementioned challenges, V4Ann capitalises on and combines existing Semantic Web standards for resource annotation and interlinking, inference and validation. More precisely, the WADM model is used as the core resource annotation pattern, combined with existing structured ontologies and schemata (Sect. 4). SPIN rules [7] and SHACL shapes [8] are used to derive additional relations among the annotated resources and for validating the generated knowledge graphs (Sect. 5). Finally, keyword-based context-aware retrieval is facilitated to retrieve assets (Sect. 6).

4 V4Ann Annotation Model

Figure 2 illustrates the upper-level concepts of the V4Ann annotation model. The conceptual model revolves around the notions of *annotations*, *media types*, *views* and *atoms*. Annotations serve as resource containers, implementing the annotation pattern of WADM. Each annotation associates a media type (image, video, text, 3D model) with a view, which encapsulates a set of atoms. Each view defines one or more atoms, e.g. entities, tags, styles, etc. that are derived from multimedia content analysis. These atoms describe: (a) Aesthetics, i.e. architectural styles and creators that are extracted from images and videos; (b) Object and building types that are recognised in images and videos; (c) Named entities and concepts that are extracted from textual descriptions, e.g. image captions; (d) images and video frames used to reconstruct a 3D model. All atoms derived by aesthetics, localisation and text analysis are disambiguated, i.e. they are already mapped to WordNet, BabelNet or DBpedia resources by the content analysis services. Figure 2 also presents SKOS mappings to the ORE specification, as well as subclass and subproperty relations to WADM and EDM. In the following we describe in details each key concept.

[8] https://unity3d.com/.
[9] https://www.rhino3d.com/.

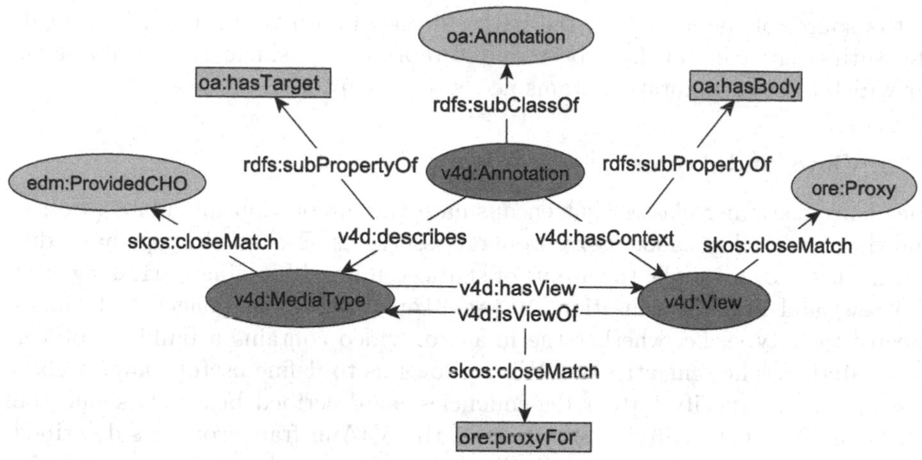

Fig. 2. The core concepts of the V4Ann annotation model defined as specialisation of WADM (`oa` namespace). Mappings to other models are also depicted, such as to Europeana Data Model (EDM) and Object Reuse and Exchange (ORE) initiative.

4.1 Annotation Resources

Four domain-specific annotation classes are defined for attaching atom views to media types[10]: `LocalisationAnnotation`, `TextualAnnotation`, `Aesthetics-Annotation` and `3DModelAnnotation`. According to the WADM specification, an annotation has 0 or more *bodies* (`oa:hasBody`), which encapsulate descriptive information, and a 1 or more *targets* (`oa:hasTarget`) that the bodies describe. V4Ann defines two subproperties to restrict the values of these properties, associating the targets (i.e. the media types) with view atoms. Intuitively, a V4Ann annotation has a *context* that *describes* a *media type* using *views*. In terms of OWL 2 semantics, the `hasContext` ($\sqsubseteq$ `oa:hasBody`) property takes as values only instances of the `View` class and the `describes` ($\sqsubseteq$ `oa:hasTarget`) property at least one `MediaType` value. The `Annotation` class is defined as:[11]

$$\begin{aligned}\texttt{Annotation} \sqsubseteq\ & \texttt{oa:Annotation} \sqcap \\ & \exists \texttt{describes.MediaType} \sqcap \forall \texttt{hasContext.View}\end{aligned} \tag{1}$$

4.2 Media Types

In order to define the targets of annotations (`describes` property assertions), V4Ann provides the `MediaType` upper-level class. There are four media types for annotations: `Video`, `Text`, `Image`, `Mask` $\sqsubseteq$ `Image`, `Texture` $\sqsubseteq$ `Image` and `3DModel`. Each media type can be associated with additional descriptive information, such

[10] In the rest of the paper, we omit the `v4d` namespace.
[11] We use Description Logics [2] to represent the semantics.

as the source of the asset (e.g. the URL), license information, date of retrieval, etc. Intuitively, each media type resource represents a single multimedia asset for which a set of annotation atoms needs to be captured.

4.3 Views and Atoms

Views are container classes that encapsulate the annotation metadata (atoms) and they are used in `hasContext` property assertions. Each media type has a different view. For example, the atoms of spatio-temporal building (`BuildingView` $\sqsubseteq$ `View`) and object localisation (`ObjectView` $\sqsubseteq$ `View`) in images and videos specify their type, i.e. whether the image or video contains a building, object or a painting. The semantics of OWL 2 allows us to define useful complex class descriptions to specify further dependencies, as described below. It should be noted that content analysis is not part of the V4Ann framework. As described in Sect. 3, V4Ann aims to semantically capture the results of content analysis, which is part of the overall V4Design platform [1].

Aesthetics. Aesthetics extraction refers to the categorisation of the aesthetics of paintings and images that contain architecture objects and buildings based on their style (e.g. impressionism, cubism and expressionism), the creator (mainly for paintings) and emotion that they evoke to the viewer. Two properties are defined for creators (`v4d:creator` $\equiv$ `schema:creator`) and styles (`v4d:style`), whose domain is the `v4d:AestheticsView` class.

$$\begin{aligned}&\texttt{AestheticsAnnotation} \sqsubseteq \texttt{oa:Annotation} \sqcap \\ &\quad \exists \texttt{describes}.\{\texttt{Image} \sqcup \texttt{Video}\} \sqcap \forall \texttt{hasContext}.\texttt{AestheticsView}\end{aligned} \tag{2}$$

$$\texttt{AestheticsView} \sqsubseteq \forall \texttt{creator}.\texttt{Creator} \sqcap \forall \texttt{style}.\texttt{Style} \tag{3}$$

The `Creator` and `Style` classes serve as container classes, allowing the capturing of data-specific properties, such as the classification confidence, as well as contain links to DBpedia and BabelNet. Figure 3 presents an aesthetics annotation example (left part). The image depicts the Tholos of Delphi that has been given the atom (style) "Greek Architecture".

Object and Building Localisation. Building and interior objects localisation on art and architecture-related movies, documentaries and multiple art-images, aims to extract content that can be re-purposed and re-used in a meaningful and innovative way. Examples include buses, trains, as well as statues, buildings, etc.

The extracted atoms (labels) are mapped to the V4Ann annotation model in terms of generated *masks* and *tags*. In videos, the results are also associated with frame(s) to capture the temporal aspects of localisation.

$$\begin{aligned}&\texttt{LocalisationAnnotation} \sqsubseteq \texttt{oa:Annotation} \sqcap \\ &\quad \exists \texttt{describes}.\{\texttt{Image} \sqcup \texttt{Video}\} \sqcap \forall \texttt{hasContext}.\texttt{LocalisationView}\end{aligned} \tag{4}$$

$$\texttt{LocalisationView} \sqsubseteq \exists \texttt{hasTag}.\texttt{Tag} \sqcap \forall \texttt{hasFrame}.\texttt{integer} \tag{5}$$

Text Analysis. Text analysis provides the atoms that are derived from textual content. For example, in addition to annotating images with building and objects, the assets are further enriched with named entities and concepts extracted from captions, titles and descriptions. V4Ann captures these atoms and associate them with the media type (video or image) that the textual content is relevant to through instantiations of the `TextAnalysisView` class. Example atoms include `name`, `title`, `date`, `creator`, `designer`, `artist`, `location`, etc., defined as subproperties of `Tag`.

$$\begin{aligned}\texttt{TextAnnotation} \sqsubseteq\ & \texttt{oa:Annotation} \sqcap \\ & \exists \texttt{describes}.\{\texttt{Image} \sqcup \texttt{Video}\} \sqcap \forall \texttt{hasContext}.\texttt{TextView}\end{aligned} \tag{6}$$

$$\texttt{TextView} \sqsubseteq \exists \texttt{hasTag}.\texttt{Tag} \tag{7}$$

3D Reconstruction. 3D reconstruction converts input video and images into 3D point clouds and meshes. Apart from the actual 3D object, this process generates a variety of metadata, such as the number of point clouds, number of faces, textures, etc. The most important atom is the source of reconstruction, i.e. the video or the images the 3D model has been extracted from.

$$\begin{aligned}\texttt{3DModelAnnotation} \sqsubseteq\ & \texttt{oa:Annotation} \sqcap \\ & \exists \texttt{describes}.\texttt{3DModel} \sqcap \forall \texttt{hasContext}.\texttt{3DModelView}\end{aligned} \tag{8}$$

$$\texttt{3DModelView} \sqsubseteq \exists \texttt{hasSource}.\{\texttt{Images} \sqcup \texttt{Video}\} \tag{9}$$

A 3D annotation example is depicted in Fig. 3 (right part). The annotation of the 3D model of Tholos is associated ($\texttt{image} \sqsubseteq \texttt{hasSource}$) with the images that have been used for the reconstruction. It is assumed that the example image for aesthetics extraction is part of the set, demonstrating the way multimodal analysis results are interlinked. As we describe in the next section, these links are used to materialise additional relationships in the form of inference rules.

5 Inference and Validation

5.1 Implicit Relationships

Additional inferences are derived by combining native OWL 2 RL reasoning and custom rules. The former is based on the OWL 2 RL profile semantics (OWL 2 RL/RDF rules [12]), which is implemented by state-of-the-art triple stores, such as GraphDB. However, the semantics OWL 2 is limited. For example, only instances connected in a tree-like manner can be modelled [13]. V4Ann implements domain rules on top of the graphs to express richer relations. SPARQL-based `CONSTRUCT` graph patterns are used that identify the valid inferences that can be made on the annotation graphs. It is beyond the scope of the paper to include an extensive coverage of relevant reasoning capabilities. In the following we present the concept of *atom propagation* that illustrates the principle idea.

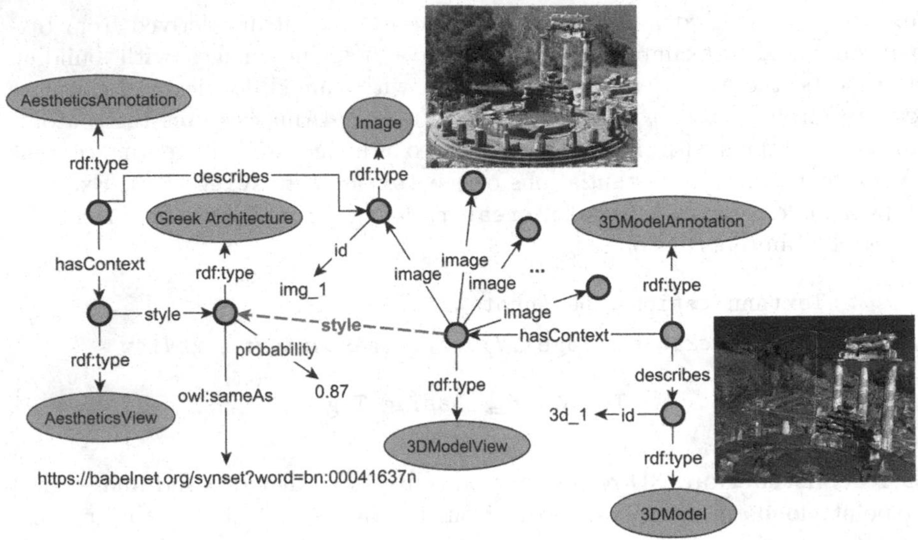

Fig. 3. Example of atom propagation. The dashed arrow illustrates the enrichment of the 3D annotation resource with the aesthetics `style` derived from visual analysis.

Since V4Ann follows a standard-based annotation pattern, additional relations can be further derived. For example, the aesthetics atoms extracted from video frames can be used to annotate the 3D models that have been reconstructed using those frames. The principle idea is that atoms can be *propagated* among one or more views, provided that their annotations are associated.

Figure 3 illustrates atom propagation between an aesthetics and 3D model annotations. The two annotations are connected at the view level, since the aesthetics annotation describes an image (`img_1`) that has been used to generate the 3D model of Tholos (id `3d_1`). In this case, the view that describes the 3D model inherits the atom (style) of the image (`Greek Architecture`). The corresponding SPARQL graph pattern is given bellow.

```
CONSTRUCT {
   ?view :style ?atom .
} WHERE {
   ?a1 a :AestheticsAnnotation;
      :describes ?img; :hasContext [:style ?atom] .
   ?a2 a :3DModelAnnotation; :hasContext ?view .
   ?view :image ?img .
}
```

5.2 Validation and Consistency Checking

The validation process checks the consistency, structural and syntactic quality of the metadata. We use both native ontology consistency checking (e.g. OWL

2 DL reasoning) and custom SHACL validation rules, following the closed-world paradigm. The former handles validation taking into account the semantics at the terminological level (TBox), e.g. checking class disjointness. The latter detects constraint violations, e.g. missing values and cardinality violations. An example SHACL shape is given below that represents a constraint that all 3D model views should include references to the atoms (images) used to the 3D reconstruction.

```
v4d:3DModelView
   rdf:type sh:NodeShape ;
   sh:property [
      rdf:type sh:PropertyShape ; sh:path v4d:image ;
      sh:class v4d:MediaType ; sh:minCount 1 ;
      sh:name "one or more images" ; sh:nodeKind sh:IRI ;
   ] .
```

6 Context-Based Asset Retrieval

In Sect. 4 we described the process of creating the V4Ann annotation graphs, which involves the representation and further interlinking (e.g. through annotation propagation) of media type atoms. In this section we describe the approach of V4Ann towards enabling keyword-based context-aware retrieval of assets, capitalising on the concept of *local context.*

Definition 1. *The local content l_t of an atom t is defined as the tuple $\langle t, r_t, he_t, ho_t\rangle$, where r_t is the set of conceptually relevant terms, he_t is the set of hypernyms and ho_t is the set of hyponyms of t.*

Intuitively, a local context of an atom constitutes an enriched, pre-constructed semantic signature of this atom, taking into account conceptual and lexical relations from existing semantic networks and datasets, such as WordNet, BabelNet and ConceptNet (Fig. 4). In the case of hypernyms and hyponyms, we use the threshold h to specify the maximum level of relevant atoms. All in all, the retrieval mechanism of V4Ann aims to match incoming local contexts of query atoms (keywords) against local contexts of annotation atoms.

6.1 The $\mathcal{AH}$ Metric

The $\mathcal{AH}$ metric represents the similarity of two atoms taking into account their local context. It depends on a term similarity function S, and on a set F of local context filters. In the following, we assume that $S(A, B)$ denotes the similarity of two atoms A and B, with respect to the function S, and that $S(A, B) \in [0..1]$, with 1 denoting absolute match. We use the notation $A \overset{f}{\sim} B$ to denote that A matches to B, with respect to one of the following filters f:

1. *exact (e).* The two atoms should have either the same URI, or they should be equivalent concepts, that is, $A \overset{e}{\sim} B \Leftrightarrow A = B \vee A \equiv B$.

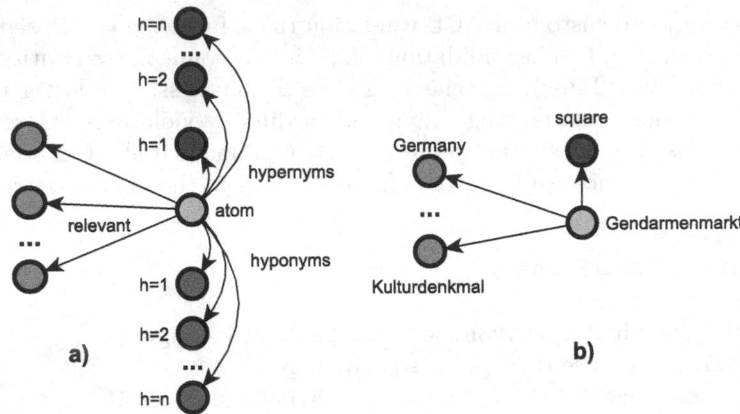

Fig. 4. (a) Generic local context of atom: relevant atoms are extracted from ConceptNet and BabelNet properties, hypernyms stem from WordNet and IS-A BebelNet relationships, hyponyms stem from WordNet; (b) example local context for "Gendarmenmarkt".

2. *plugin (p)*. The atom B should belong to the set of hypernyms of A (he_A) or to the set of relevant concepts of A (r_A), that is, $A \overset{p}{\sim} B \Leftrightarrow B \in he_A \vee B \in r_A$.
3. *subsume (su)*. The atom B should belong to the set of the hyponyms of A, that is, $A \overset{su}{\sim} B \Leftrightarrow B \in ho_A$.

We generalize the $A \overset{f}{\sim} B$ relation to a set of filters F and we define that the atom A matches the atom B, with respect to a filter set F, if and only if there is at least one filter f in F, such that $A \overset{f}{\sim} B$, that is:

$$A \overset{F}{\sim} B \Leftrightarrow \exists f \in F : A \overset{f}{\sim} B.$$

Definition 2. *The $\mathcal{AH}$ similarity of two atoms X and Y is the normalized value to* [0..1] *that is defined, with respect to a function S and a filter set F, as*

$$\mathcal{AH}(X,Y,F) = \begin{cases} S(X,Y) & \textit{if}\, X \overset{F}{\sim} Y \\ 0 & \textit{otherwise}. \end{cases} \tag{10}$$

We generalize (10) on two sets S_A, S_B of atoms as

$$\mathcal{AH}_{set}(S_A, S_B, F) = \frac{\sum\limits_{\forall B \in S_B} \max\limits_{\forall A \in S_A} [\mathcal{AH}(B, A, F)]}{|S_B|} \tag{11}$$

Intuitively, for each atom $B \in S_B$ there should be at least one atom $A \in S_A$ relevant to B, with respect to the filter set F. Otherwise, $\mathcal{AH}_{set}$ returns 0 (absolute mismatch). The overall $\mathcal{AH}_{set}$ similarity is computed as the mean value of the sum of the maximum $\mathcal{AH}$s for each atom B, since each B may have more than one relevant atoms in S_A. In V4Ann, S_A represents the atoms that are associated with an asset, while S_B is the set of keywords.

6.2 Atom Similarity S

As a similarity function $S(A, B)$, V4Ann uses a heuristic function that takes into account the information captured in local contexts of A and B, i.e. in the sets r, he and ho (see Definition 1). The implementation of S is summarised in the following priority rules r_i, where $r_1 > r_2 > r_3 > r_4$.

r_1: if $A = B \vee A \equiv B$, then $S(A, B) = 1$.
r_2: if $B \in hy_A \vee B \in r_A$, then $S(A, B) = a$.
r_3: if $B \in ho_A$, then $S(A, B) = b$.
r_4: $S(A, B) = 0$.

Currently, a and b ($a > b$) are defined manually based on domain knowledge regarding the quality of multimedia analysis that produces the atoms (e.g. aesthetics extraction). The empirical definition of these values (currently $a = 0.7$ and $b = 0.3$) aims to promote plugin matches (r_2) over subsumed (r_3).

7 Evaluation and Discussion

7.1 Digital Content

Deutsche Welle (DW) and Europeana are two key content providers in V4Design. DW provides selected parts of their documentary and movie archives so as to localise building structures and objects. Europeana provides their large archive of paintings, pictures of contemporary artwork and related critics, for stylistic and aesthetics extraction and textual analysis. The generated V4Ann annotation graphs contain the atoms that have been extracted from the analysis components, along with interconnections among the annotation resources. Table 1 provides some statistics for the annotation graphs.

7.2 Evaluation

User-Centred. A user-centred evaluation has been performed with a twofold purpose. First, to collect qualitative feedback on the results, as well as on non-functional aspects, such as query response time. Second, and most important, to generate an annotation dataset and assess the performance of V4Ann.

Participants were invited to evaluate the current implementation by performing keyword-based queries. A list of relevant resources has been provided, such as square names, monuments, building types, etc., in order to help them conduct relevant queries. Users filled in a five-point scale questionnaire (1-completely agree, 5-completely disagree). Sample questions are depicted in Table 2. The feedback can be summarised as it follows:

Table 1. The number of annotations and atoms in the V4Ann annotation graphs, along with the average size of local context for each atom ($r + hy + ho$).

#annotations	#atoms	Avg. local context size
17245	154610	17 per atom

Table 2. Example questions answered by users.

#	Question	Mean (SD)
Q1	Atoms that are derived from visual analysis are most of the time correct	1.7 ± 0.83
Q2	Atoms that are derived from text analysis are most of the time correct	2.34 ± 0.79
Q3	Many times irrelevant results are top-ranked	3.97 ± 1.29
Q4	There are many irrelevant results	2.43 ± 1.41
Q5	It takes too long for the system to provide a response	4.04 ± 0.99
Q6	There are too many "No results" responses	4.08 ± 0.45

- **Quality of atoms:** The quality and relevance of local contexts depends on the performance of content analysis, e.g. visual and textual analysis. Table 2 shows that visual analysis provides, in principle, better results than text analysis (Q1, Q2).
- **Retrieval results:** According to Q3, the system achieves good top-ranked accuracy, however the complete set of the results contain quite a lot irrelevant entries (Q4). As we explain in the next section, this is mainly relevant to the context provided in the query (i.e. number of keywords). Due to the local context, the system was able to provide a response in most cases (Q6), even partially correct (Q4).
- **Response time:** The response time of the system was positively assessed (Q5). The average response time was 4.1 seconds, which includes query analysis, building of local context and searching algorithm execution.

System Evaluation. We manually annotated the relevance sets of the performed queries, so as to quantitatively assess performance. Table 3 depicts the average precision and recall achieved for $h = 1$ and $h = 3$ and using different searching filters (Sect. 6.1). As expected, the stricter the filter is, the more accurate results we obtain (high precision) with low, however, recall. On the other hand, the more relax is the filter, the higher recall is achieved with a negative impact on the precision. This is due to the fact that with a strict filter (i.e. exact), the probability of finding the correct annotation is higher compared to a relaxed filter (i.e. subsume), since in the second case, impartial matches are also allowed.

It should be noted that the overall performance of V4Ann strongly depends on the quality of the atoms, which in turn depends on the quality of the results provided to V4Ann. For example, if the wrong style for a painting is provided by aesthetics, this will affect precision, since V4Ann does not aim at improving the classification of incoming atoms. However, we plan to integrate multimodal data aggregation and fusion techniques to derive the most plausible classification of atoms and help improve the contextual information captured in local contexts.

Another interesting finding involves the threshold h. We observed that for $h = 1$ the framework provides better results than using $h = 3$, i.e. by enriching the local context with additional atoms, up to the third level. Intuitively, h allows to control the amount of contextual information taken into account during the definition of local contexts. A higher h value leads to more generic local contexts that affect precision. For example, the third-level WordNet hypernym of "tower" is "unit", which is too generic, obfuscating the semantics of the atom. The optimal value of h depends on the concreteness of the atoms extracted from content analysis: the more specific is the label/atom, the more room for additional context exists. In our experiments, the labels we get tend to be generic, therefore the best performance is achieved with $h = 1$.

Table 3. Average precision and recall (top-20 results).

	$h = 1$		$h = 3$	
	Recall	Precision	Recall	Precision
exact	0.59	**0.77**	0.44	0.51
plugin	0.67	0.69	0.52	0.48
subsume	**0.73**	0.61	0.59	0.42

8 Conclusion

In this paper we presented V4Ann, an ontology-based framework for representing, linking and enriching results of multimedia analysis on digital content. V4Ann generates annotation graphs of image, video, textual analysis and 3D model reconstruction, so as to facilitate the systematic process, integration and organisation of information and establish practical repurposing mechanisms.

The annotation model of V4Ann reuses existing standards and schemata, building the atom-based annotations graphs on top of standard ontologies, controlled vocabularies and patterns. The vocabularies are defined in OWL 2 and atoms are associated with assets using the WADM pattern. As such, it promotes interoperability, as well as fosters the use of declarative languages to identify further inferences and ensure the semantic consistency of the knowledge graphs. We also elaborated on the concept of local contexts, as well as on the $\mathcal{AH}$ metric for asset retrieval. We evaluated the framework using actual multimedia content and atoms provided by the V4Design modules and discussed the findings.

V4Ann is accessible through Rhinoceros 3D (Rhino)[12] and Unity plugins developed in the V4Design project through which users (architects and video games designers) can search for assets and import them in the scene. For future work we plan to implement context-aware algorithms to improve the classification accuracy of incoming atoms, as well as to extend the context-aware retrieval algorithm with more sophisticated similarity metrics and functions.

[12] https://gitlab.com/v4designEU/v4d4rhino.

Acknowledgments. This work was supported by the EC funded projects V4Design (H2020-779962) and MindSpaces (H2020-825079).

References

1. Avgerinakis, K., Meditskos, G., Derdaele, J., Mille, S., et al.: V4design for enhancing architecture and video game creation. In: IEEE International Symposium on Mixed and Augmented Reality, pp. 305–309 (2018)
2. Baader, F., Calvanese, D., McGuinness, D.L., et al.: The Description Logic Handbook: Theory, Implementation and Applications. Cambridge University Press, Cambridge (2003)
3. Ciccarese, P., Soiland-Reyes, S., Belhajjame, K., Gray, A.J., Goble, C., Clark, T.: PAV ontology: provenance, authoring and versioning. J. Biomed. Semant. **4**(1), 37 (2013)
4. Doerr, M., Gradmann, S., Hennicke, S., Isaac, A., Meghini, C., Van de Sompel, H.: The Europeana data model (EDM). In: World Library and Information Congress: 76th IFLA General Conference and Assembly, pp. 10–15 (2010)
5. Dubey, M., Banerjee, D., Chaudhuri, D., Lehmann, J.: EARL: joint entity and relation linking for question answering over knowledge graphs. In: Vrandečić, D., et al. (eds.) ISWC 2018. LNCS, vol. 11136, pp. 108–126. Springer, Cham (2018). https://doi.org/10.1007/978-3-030-00671-6_7
6. Kalogerakis, E., Christodoulakis, S., Moumoutzis, N.: Coupling ontologies with graphics content for knowledge driven visualization. In: IEEE Virtual Reality, vol. 2006, p. 6 (2006)
7. Knublauch, H., Hendler, J., Idehen, K.: SPIN - Overview and Motivation (2011). https://www.w3.org/Submission/spin-overview/
8. Knublauch, H., Ryman, A.: Shapes Constraint Language (SHACL) (2015). https://www.w3.org/TR/shacl/
9. Lebo, T., Sahoo, S., McGuinness, D.: PROV-O: The PROV Ontology. W3C Recommendation (2013). https://www.w3.org/TR/prov-o/
10. Miles, A.: SKOS Core Vocabulary Specification. English, pp. 1–28, November 2005. https://www.w3.org/TR/swbp-skos-core-spec/
11. Moreau, L., Clifford, B., Freire, J., Futrelle, J., et al.: The Open provenance model core specification (v1.1). In: Future Generation Computer Systems (2011)
12. Motik, B., Grau, B.C., Horrocks, I., Wu, Z., Fokoue, A., Lutz, C.: OWL 2 WebOntology Language Profiles (2012). https://www.w3.org/TR/owl2-profiles/
13. Motik, B., Grau, B.C., Sattler, U.: Structured objects in OWL: representation and reasoning. 17th International World Wide Web Conference, pp. 555–564 (2008)
14. Pennington, J., Socher, R., Manning, C.: Glove: global vectors for word representation. In: Empirical Methods in Natural Language Processing (2014)
15. Peters, M., et al.: Deep contextualized word representations. In: Computational Linguistics: Human Language Technologies, pp. 2227–2237, June 2018
16. Rosales-Méndez, H., Hogan, A., Poblete, B.: VoxEL: a benchmark dataset for multilingual entity linking. In: Vrandečić, D., et al. (eds.) ISWC 2018. LNCS, vol. 11137, pp. 170–186. Springer, Cham (2018). https://doi.org/10.1007/978-3-030-00668-6_11
17. Sanderson, R., Ciccarese, P., Young, B.: Web Annotation Data Model. W3C, pp. 1–56 (2016). https://www.w3.org/TR/annotation-model/
18. Sikos, L.F.: VidOnt: a core reference ontology for reasoning over video scenes. J. Inf. Telecommun. **2**, 192–204 (2018)

19. Sikos, L.F., Powers, D.M.: Knowledge-driven video information retrieval with LOD. In: Exploiting Semantic Annotations in Information Retrieval, pp. 35–37 (2015)
20. Zhao, H., Lu, Z., Poupart, P.: Efficient estimation of word representations in vector space. In: IJCAI International Joint Conference on Artificial Intelligence (2015)

RSP-QL*: Enabling Statement-Level Annotations in RDF Streams

Robin Keskisärkkä[1(✉)], Eva Blomqvist[1,2], Leili Lind[1,2], and Olaf Hartig[1]

[1] Linköping University, Linköping, Sweden
{robin.keskisarkka,eva.blomqvist,leili.lind,olaf.hartig}@liu.se
[2] RISE Research Institutes of Sweden AB/Division ICT SICS East, Linköping, Sweden
{eva.blomqvist,leili.lind}@ri.se

Abstract. RSP-QL was developed by the W3C RDF Stream Processing (RSP) community group as a common way to express and query RDF streams. However, RSP-QL does not provide any way of annotating data on the statement level, for example, to express the uncertainty that is often associated with streaming information. Instead, the only way to provide such information has been to use RDF reification, which adds additional complexity to query processing, and is syntactically verbose. In this paper, we define an extension of RSP-QL, called RSP-QL*, that provides an intuitive way for supporting statement-level annotations in RSP. The approach leverages the concepts previously described for RDF* and SPARQL*. We illustrate the proposed approach based on a scenario from a research project in e-health. An open-source implementation of the proposal is provided and compared to the baseline approach of using RDF reification. The results show that this way of dealing with statement-level annotations offers advantages with respect to both data transfer bandwidth and query execution performance.

Keywords: RSP-QL* · RDF* · RDF Stream Processing · e-health

1 Introduction

Recent years have seen an increasing interest in processing and analyzing streaming information as it is generated by applications, services, sensors, and smart devices. RDF Stream Processing (RSP) leverages the principles of Linked Data and the Semantic Web to cope with heterogeneity in data, but employs strategies inspired from stream processing to cope with high velocity data streams. During the last decade, several RSP systems and models have been proposed, which have all provided their own syntax, semantics, and underlying assumptions about the nature of RDF streams [6,7]. The RSP community group[1] was formed to define a common model for producing, transmitting and continuously querying RDF streams. The first version of this common query model (RSP-QL)

[1] https://www.w3.org/community/rsp/.

M. Acosta et al. (Eds.): SEMANTiCS 2019, LNCS 11702, pp. 140–155, 2019.
https://doi.org/10.1007/978-3-030-33220-4_11

was proposed by Dell'Aglio et al. in 2014 [7], and the draft of the abstract syntax and semantics was published by the RSP community group in 2016 [2].

Data generated by sensors is almost always coupled with provenance information, or a level of uncertainty representing, for instance, lack of precision or a knowledge gap. For example, all values reported by a temperature sensor may be associated with some error describing a probability distribution. The RDF specification provides a vocabulary that allows metadata to be represented about RDF triples using *RDF reification* [11]. In practice, however, this is not widely adopted as a standard for representing and managing such metadata on the Semantic Web [8]. RDF* was recently proposed as a way to support a concise representation of statement-level metadata, while remaining backwards compatible with standard RDF [9,10]. By enclosing a triple using the strings '<<' and '>>', the extension allows it to be used in the subject or object position of other triples. This allows statement-level metadata to be provided directly. For example, the triple *:bob :knows :alice* could be annotated with the source *wikipedia* as follows: *<<:bob :knows :alice>> :source :wikipedia*. Similarly, the authors' propose SPARQL* as an extension of SPARQL for querying RDF* data, where SPARQL* supports similar nesting of triple patterns.

We propose an extension to RSP-QL that leverages RDF*/SPARQL* for annotating and querying streaming data. We show that the proposed approach has several benefits over RDF reification when it comes to statement-level annotations. The approach is motivated based on a use case from a current research project, where we attempt to detect abnormal situations in an e-health scenario.

The rest of the paper is organized as follows. Section 2 briefly discusses the relevant related work, while Sect. 3 describes a use-case scenario that both motivates the proposed approach and exemplifies the requirements addressed by the proposal. Section 4 describes the proposed approach informally, and Sects. 5 and 6 provide the necessary formal definitions, where Sect. 5 defines the data model and Sect. 6 defines the syntax and semantics of the proposed RSP-QL extension. Section 7 provides an application-based evaluation of the approach. Section 8 describes a prototype implementation and a performance evaluation of the implemented system. Section 9 discusses the impact of the presented work and Sect. 10 summarizes the main conclusions of the paper.

2 Related Work

Over the past decade, there has been a growing interest in providing models and languages for combining the principles of the Semantic Web with streaming information. RDF Stream Processing (RSP) systems aim to provide extensions to RDF and SPARQL for representing and querying streaming data. However, though several RSP systems have emerged that provide extensions and operators for this purpose [1,3,4,13,18], they typically provide different languages, constructs, operators, and evaluation semantics [7]. The W3C RSP community group was formed to define a common model for representing and querying streaming RDF data. The proposed model and language, RSP-QL [7], can be used to model the behavior of most of the current RSP systems, and provides well-defined semantics for explaining query execution. However, none of the existing RSP approaches have given much attention to aspects related to representing metadata in streams, such as uncertainty or provenance. The RSP-QL stream model allows such annotations to be provided on the graph level, but annotations on the triple level are not supported.

The term *statement-level metadata* refers to data that captures information about a single statement or fact. The RDF specification includes the notion of *RDF reification* that lets a set of RDF triples describe some other RDF triple [11]. The approach requires the inclusion of four additional RDF triples for every statement where metadata is to be provided. Another approach is to leverage *named graphs*, where the identifier of the graphs can be used to attach metadata to statements [12]. However, this approach has the disadvantage of inhibiting the application of named graphs for other uses. Finally, *singleton properties* have been proposed as an alternative approach, where a distinct property is provided for each triple to be annotated [15]. The singleton properties proposal introduces a large number of unique predicates, which is atypical for RDF data, and disadvantageous for common SPARQL optimization techniques [19]. Additionally, these approaches result in verbose queries [9]. For standard RDF, there therefore exists no convenient way of annotating data with metadata on the statement level [10]. The RDF*/SPARQL* approach was proposed as a way of supporting a more intuitive representation, by allowing triples in the subject and object positions of RDF statements [9,10]. In this paper, we propose to extend RSP-QL based on this approach.

3 Use-Case Scenario

In this section, we describe a use-case scenario to exemplify the kinds of requirements that may be addressed by combining RSP-QL with RDF*/SPARQL*. The scenario originates from an ongoing research project, E-care@home[2], in which the aim is to develop privacy-preserving AI-solutions for home care of elderly patients. In addition to developing technical solutions, the project has put great emphasis on studying the requirements of stakeholders. These requirements have been documented in a project deliverable [14]. As part of this deliverable, a number of personas and use-case scenarios were also developed, including the following description of a scenario involving the patient Rut who has advanced chronic obstructive pulmonary disease (COPD) and is multimorbid.

"The system can automatically sense abnormal situations, e.g. when certain health parameters deviate from the normal values, or when the overall situation as assessed by a multitude of sensors appears abnormal. When the system detects such situations, it sends out an alarm to a suitable recipient based on the severity of the deviation (e.g., emergency dispatch for a life-threatening deviation, the patient's physician if no immediate action is required, or next-of-kin if suitable). [...] Today the system has detected an abnormal state. Rut appears to have been

[2] http://ecareathome.se/.

sitting in the same position in a chair in the living room for an unusually long time given that there are no entertainment devices turned on at the moment. Her heart rate is above normal, but her breathing is slower than normal. Small motions indicate that she is not asleep, yet she is not moving much. Her oxygen levels are about normal. The system decides to classify this as a low-emergency abnormal state. The system also knows that Rut's partner has left the house a few hours ago. It therefore sends an alert to him [...] the alert reaches Rut's partner as he is already on his way home. He hurries home and opens the door only to find out that Rut is in good health and has been enjoying a paperback copy of the latest crime novel by a famous Swedish author for the past few hours" [14].

Like any health-care system, the one envisioned by E-care@home sets high requirements in terms of patient safety, system reliability, and transparency. To this end, all the data that the system uses to draw conclusions and to generate suggestions, or even to take action, must be accompanied by some assessed confidence. For instance, in the scenario above, to put patient safety first the system cannot afford to miss an abnormal and highly dangerous situation, but on the other hand it needs to be able to disregard observations that are not reliable. As an example, whenever a pulse oxymeter reports the oxygen saturation of a patient, the system also needs to know the confidence that the system can put in this value. The sensor may have a fixed confidence value, but the system may also derive an adjusted value that takes into account contextual factors of the measurement, such as the position of the sensor and the activity of the patient at measurement time. Regardless of how the confidence value is derived, it needs to be reported as part of the reported observation.

4 Overview of RSP-QL*

The main difference between RSP and traditional RDF/SPARQL processing is that the former introduces a time dimension to processing [6]. The time dimension in RSP-QL is managed by allowing *windows* to define discrete subsets over *RDF streams*, and at any point in time, a window can be queried as a regular RDF dataset. The approach proposed in this paper extends RSP-QL in two fundamental ways: RDF streams are extended to support RDF*, and the supported graph patterns in RSP-QL are extended to support those in SPARQL*. The example in Listing 1.1 shows an RSP-QL* query that illustrates the main features and language constructs.

The registered query is evaluated every 10 seconds. It defines a time-based window with a width of 1 min that slides every 10 s over the heart-rate stream. The query then matches the heart-rate value and confidence of each observation in the window using an RDF* pattern [9]. This is the only difference between RSP-QL and RSP-QL* in this query. The results are then filtered based on a threshold, and the heart-rate value and timestamp of the matched observations are reported. There are conceptually no limitations on the complexity of the provided annotations, and they can, e.g., instead be represented as confidence intervals or distributions rather than single values.

```
PREFIX ex: <http://www.example.org/ontology#>
PREFIX sosa: <http://www.w3.org/ns/sosa/>
REGISTER STREAM <heart-rate/alert> COMPUTED EVERY PT10S AS
SELECT ?hr ?time
FROM NAMED WINDOW <window/1> ON <http://stream/heart-rate> [RANGE PT1M STEP PT10S]
WHERE {
    WINDOW <window/1> {
        GRAPH ?g {
            <<?obs sosa:hasSimpleResult ?hr>> ex:Confidence ?confidence .
            FILTER(?confidence > 0.9 && ?hr > 120)
        }
        ?g <generatedAt> ?time .
    }
}
```

Listing 1.1. Example of an RSP-QL* query.

5 Data Model

This section defines the concepts that capture the notion of streams considered by our approach. We begin with the basic notions of RDF and RDF*.

As usual [5,16], we assume three pairwise disjoint, countably infinite sets $\mathcal{I}$ (IRIs), $\mathcal{B}$ (blank nodes), and $\mathcal{L}$ (literals). Then, an *RDF triple* is a tuple $(s,p,o) \in (\mathcal{I} \cup \mathcal{B}) \times \mathcal{I} \times (\mathcal{I} \cup \mathcal{B} \cup \mathcal{L})$, and an *RDF graph* is a set of RDF triples. For such a triple (s,p,o), s is called the *subject*, p the *predicate*, and o the *object*.

RDF* extends this notion of triples by allowing the subject or the object to be another triple [9]. This form of nesting of triples, which may be arbitrarily deep, allows for statements to capture metadata about other statements. Formally, an *RDF* triple* is defined recursively as follows [9]: (i) any RDF triple is an RDF* triple, and (ii) given two RDF* triples t and t', and the RDF terms $s \in (\mathcal{I} \cup \mathcal{B})$, $p \in \mathcal{I}$, and $o \in (\mathcal{I} \cup \mathcal{B} \cup \mathcal{L})$, the tuples (t,p,o), (s,p,t), and (t,p,t') are RDF* triples. Furthermore, a set of RDF* triples is called an *RDF* graph*.

The concept of an *RDF dataset* has been introduced to represent collections of RDF graphs [5]. We extend this concept to cover RDF* graphs.

Definition 1. *A* ***named RDF* graph*** *is a pair* $(n, G^\star)$ *where* $n \in (\mathcal{I} \cup \mathcal{B})$, *which is called the* graph name, *and* $G^\star$ *is an RDF* graph. An* ***RDF* dataset*** *is a set* $D = \{G^\star_0, (n_1, G^\star_1), (n_2, G^\star_2), ..., (n_i, G^\star_i)\}$, *where* $G^\star_0$ *is an RDF* graph, called the* default graph *of* D, *and* $(n_k, G^\star_k)$ *is a named RDF* graph for all* $k \in \{1, 2, ..., i\}$.

While the RDF model is atemporal, the notion of an RDF stream has been introduced to capture the dynamic nature of streaming RDF data [7]. Along the same lines, we define an *RDF* stream* as a time-ordered sequence of elements that are captured by a specific form of RDF* datasets.

Definition 2. *Let* p *be an IRI that denotes a predicate to capture timestamps for named RDF* graphs. Then, an* ***RDF* stream element*** E *is an RDF* dataset that consists of a default graph* $G^\star_o$ *and exactly one named RDF* graph* $(n, G^\star)$ *such that the default graph* $G^\star_o$ *contains one RDF triple of the form* (n, p, τ), *where* τ *is a timestamp. To denote this timestamp* τ *in* E *we write* $\tau(E)$.

Definition 3. *An **RDF* stream** S is a potentially unbounded sequence of RDF* stream elements such that for every pair of such elements E_i and E_j, where E_i comes before E_j (i.e., $S = (..., E_i, ..., E_j, ...)$), the following properties hold:*

1. $\tau(E_i) \leq \tau(E_j)$, *and*
2. *the names of the single named RDF* graph $(n_i, G_i^\star)$ in E_i and of the single named RDF* graph $(n_j, G_j^\star)$ in E_j are different (i.e., $n_i \neq n_j$).*

*A **named RDF* stream** is a pair (n, S) where $n \in \mathcal{I}$ and S is an RDF* stream.*

We also need to define a notion of windows over such streams as a way of referencing discrete portions of potentially infinite data streams [7].

Definition 4. *A **window** W over an RDF* stream S is a finite set of RDF* stream elements from S.*

In this paper, we focus explicitly on temporal window operators (other window operators, such as count-based windows, can be defined in a similar manner). To this end, we define a *time-based window* of an RDF* stream as a contiguous set of elements from the stream whose timestamp is in a given interval.

Definition 5. *Given a time interval $[l, u)$, the **time-based window** over an RDF* stream S for $[l, u)$, denoted by $\mathcal{W}(S, l, u)$, is a window over S that is defined as follows: $\mathcal{W}(S, l, u) = \{E \mid E \text{ is in } S \text{ and } l \leq \tau(E) < u\}$.*

Finally, we shall need a function that represents any window as an RDF* dataset. Informally, this dataset consists of all the named RDF* graphs of all RDF* stream elements within the window, and the default graph of this dataset is constructed from the default graphs in all these RDF* stream elements.

Definition 6. *Let $\mathcal{W} = \{E_1, E_2, ..., E_n\}$ be a window over some RDF* stream. The **dataset representation** of $\mathcal{W}$, denoted by $DS(\mathcal{W})$, is the RDF* dataset that is constructed as follows:*

- *the default graph of $DS(\mathcal{W})$ is $G_0^\star = \bigcup_{\{G_{dflt}^\star, (n, G^\star)\} \in \mathcal{W}} G_{dflt}^\star$, and*
- *the set of named RDF* graphs in $DS(\mathcal{W})$ is $\{(n, G^\star) \mid \{G_{dflt}^\star, (n, G^\star)\} \in \mathcal{W}\}$.*

6 Syntax and Semantics of RSP-QL*

This section defines RSP-QL*, which is an RDF*-aware extension of RSP-QL. RSP-QL, in turn, is an extension of SPARQL. Hence, our definitions in this section extend RSP-QL [7] along the lines of how SPARQL* extends SPARQL [9, 10], and by also taking into account the abstract syntax and semantics draft of the W3C RSP community group [2]. For the SPARQL-specific constructs we adopt the algebraic SPARQL syntax introduced by Pérez et al. [16]. Due to space constraints, we limit ourselves to presenting only the core concepts of the language.

6.1 Syntax of RSP-QL⋆ Queries

RSP-QL is an extension of SPARQL [17], and the basic building block is a *basic graph pattern* (BGP), that is, a finite set of *triple patterns*. A triple pattern is a tuple $(s, p, o) \in (\mathcal{V} \cup \mathcal{B} \cup \mathcal{I}) \times (\mathcal{V} \cup \mathcal{I}) \times (\mathcal{V} \cup \mathcal{B} \cup \mathcal{I} \cup \mathcal{L})$, where $\mathcal{V}$ is a countably infinite set of query variables that is disjoint from $\mathcal{B}$, $\mathcal{I}$, and $\mathcal{L}$, respectively.

Like SPARQL⋆ [9,10], RSP-QL⋆ extends these notions further by supporting the concept of *triple⋆ patterns*, which add the possibility to nest triple patterns (arbitrarily deep), and which are defined recursively as follows [9,10]:

- any triple pattern is a triple⋆ pattern, and
- given two triple⋆ patterns tp and tp', and $s \in (\mathcal{I} \cup \mathcal{B} \cup \mathcal{V})$, $p \in (\mathcal{I} \cup \mathcal{V})$, and $o \in (\mathcal{I} \cup \mathcal{B} \cup \mathcal{L} \cup \mathcal{V})$, then (tp, p, o), (s, p, tp), and (tp, p, tp') are triple⋆ patterns.

A finite set of triple⋆ patterns is referred to as a *BGP⋆*.

On top of BGPs, RSP-QL supports all the other forms of graph patterns that have been introduced for SPARQL, and RSP-QL adds a new form to match data within windows of streaming data. We define a corresponding notion of patterns for RSP-QL⋆, but for brevity we here focus only on the core constructs.

Definition 7. *An* ***RSP-QL⋆ pattern*** *is defined recursively as follows:*

1. *Any BGP⋆ is an RSP-QL⋆ pattern.*
2. *If $n \in (\mathcal{V} \cup \mathcal{I})$ and P is a RSP-QL⋆ pattern, then (WINDOW n P) and (GRAPH n P) are RSP-QL⋆ patterns.*
3. *If P_1 and P_2 are RSP-QL⋆ patterns, then (P_1 AND P_2), (P_1 OPT P_2), and (P_1 UNION P_2) are RSP-QL⋆ patterns.*

In addition to such patterns, every RSP-QL⋆ query may declare windows over named RDF⋆ streams, which we capture by the concept of window declarations.

Definition 8. *A* ***window declaration*** *is a tuple $(u_S, \alpha, \beta, \tau_0)$ where $u_S \in \mathcal{I}$ is an IRI (representing the name of a named RDF⋆ stream), α is a time duration (representing a window width), β is a time duration (representing a slide parameter), and τ_0 is a timestamp (representing a start time).*

We now have everything required to define RSP-QL⋆ queries, which consist of an RSP-QL⋆ pattern and window declarations that are associated with IRIs to serve as names for the corresponding windows in the query.

Definition 9. *An* ***RSP-QL⋆ query*** *is a pair (ω, P) where ω is a partial function that maps some IRIs in $\mathcal{I}$ to a window declaration, respectively, and P is an RSP-QL⋆ pattern such that for every sub-pattern (WINDOW n P') in P it holds that if $n \in \mathcal{I}$, then ω is defined for n, i.e., $n \in \mathrm{dom}(\omega)$.*

6.2 Semantics of RSP-QL* Queries

We now define the semantics of RSP-QL* queries, for which we have to introduce some concepts used to define the query semantics of SPARQL and of SPARQL*.

The query semantics of SPARQL is based on the notion of *solution mappings* [16] that map query variables to blank nodes, IRIs, or literals. For SPARQL*, this notion has been extended to also be able to map to RDF* triples. That is, a *RSP-QL** is a partial function $\eta : \mathcal{V} \rightarrow (\mathcal{T} \cup \mathcal{I} \cup \mathcal{B} \cup \mathcal{L})$ where $\mathcal{T}$ denotes the set of all RDF* triples [9,10]. The standard notions of *compatibility*, *merging* and *application* of solution mappings can then be adapted as follows.

Definition 10. *Two solution* mappings* η, η' *are* ***compatible*** *if* $\eta(v) = \eta'(v)$ *for every variable* $v \in dom(\eta) \cap dom(\eta')$.

Definition 11. *The* ***merge*** *of two compatible solution* mappings* η *and* η', *denoted by* $\eta \cup \eta'$, *is a solution* mapping* η'' *with the following three properties:*

- $dom(\eta'') = dom(\eta) \cup dom(\eta')$,
- $\eta''(v) = \eta(v)$ *for all* $v \in dom(\eta)$, *and*
- $\eta''(v) = \eta'(v)$ *for all* $v \in dom(\eta)' \setminus dom(\eta)$.

Definition 12. *The* ***application*** *of a solution* mapping* η *to an RSP-QL* pattern* P, *denoted by* $\eta[P]$, *is the RSP-QL* pattern obtained by replacing all variables in* P *according to* η.

We now define the corresponding algebra operators *join*, *union*, and *left join*.

Definition 13. *Let* Ω_1 *and* Ω_2 *be sets of solution* mappings.*

$\Omega_1 \bowtie \Omega_2 = \{\eta_1 \cup \eta_2 \mid \eta_1 \in \Omega_1, \eta_2 \in \Omega_2,\ \eta \text{ and } \eta' \text{ are compatible}\}$
$\Omega_1 \cup \Omega_2 = \{\eta \mid \eta \in \Omega_1 \text{ or } \eta \in \Omega_2\}$
$\Omega_1 ⟕ \Omega_2 = (\Omega_1 \bowtie \Omega_2) \cup \{\eta \in \Omega_1 \mid \forall \eta' \in \Omega_2 : \eta \text{ and } \eta' \text{ are not compatible}\}$

Based on these algebra operators, RSP-QL* patterns are evaluated over a background dataset and a set of named windows at a given timestamp.

Definition 14. *Let* W *be a partial function that maps some IRIs in* $\mathcal{I}$ *to a window over some RDF* stream, respectively, and* P *be an RSP-QL* pattern such that for every sub-pattern* (*WINDOW* n P') *in* P *with* $n \in \mathcal{I}$, *it holds that* W *is defined for* n, *i.e.,* $n \in \mathrm{dom}(W)$. *Furthermore, let* D *be an RDF* dataset,* G *be an RDF* graph, and* τ *be a timestamp. Then, the* ***evaluation of P*** *over* D *and* W *at* τ *with* G, *denoted by* $[\![P]\!]_G^{D,W,\tau}$, *is defined recursively as follows:*

1. *If* P *is a triple* pattern* tp, *then* $[\![P]\!]_G^{D,W,\tau} = \{\eta \mid dom(\eta) = var(tp) \text{ and } \eta(tp) \in G\}$ *where* $var(tp)$ *denotes the set of variables occurring in* tp.
2. *If* P *is* (*GRAPH* u P'), *then* $[\![P]\!]_G^{D,W,\tau} = [\![P']\!]_{G'}^{D,W,\tau}$ *where* $(u, G') \in D$
3. *If* P *is* (*GRAPH* $?x$ P'), *then* $[\![P]\!]_G^{D,W,\tau} = \bigcup_{(u,G') \in D} [\![GRAPH\ u\ P']\!]_{G'}^{D,W,\tau}$
4. *If* P *is* (*WINDOW* u P'), *then* $[\![P]\!]_G^{D,W,\tau} = [\![P']\!]_{G'}^{DS(\mathcal{W}),\emptyset,\tau}$ *where* $\mathcal{W} = W(u)$ *and* G' *is the default graph of the RDF* dataset* $DS(\mathcal{W})$

5. *If P is (WINDOW ?x P′), then* $[\![P]\!]_G^{D,W,\tau} = \bigcup_{u \in \mathrm{dom}(W)} [\![\mathit{WINDOW}\ u\ P']\!]_G^{D,W,\tau}$
6. *If P is (P1 AND P2), then* $[\![P]\!]_G^{D,W,\tau} = [\![P1]\!]_G^{D,W,\tau} \bowtie [\![P2]\!]_G^{D,W,\tau}$
7. *If P is (P1 UNION P2), then* $[\![P]\!]_G^{D,W,\tau} = [\![P1]\!]_G^{D,W,\tau} \cup [\![P2]\!]_G^{D,W,\tau}$
8. *If P is (P1 OPT P2), then* $[\![P]\!]_G^{D,W,\tau} = [\![P1]\!]_G^{D,W,\tau} ⟕ [\![P2]\!]_G^{D,W,\tau}$

It remains to define the semantics of RSP-QL* queries, which contain window declarations in addition to an RSP-QL* pattern (cf. Definition 9).

Definition 15. *Let $\mathcal{S}$ be a finite set of named RDF* streams and $q = (\omega, P)$ be an RSP-QL* query such that for every IRI $u_S \in \mathrm{dom}(\omega)$ there exists a named RDF* stream $(u_S, S) \in \mathcal{S}$. Furthermore, let D be an RDF* dataset and τ be a timestamp. The* ***evaluation of q*** *over D and $\mathcal{S}$ at τ, denoted by $[\![q]\!]^{D,\mathcal{S},\tau}$, is defined as $[\![q]\!]^{D,\mathcal{S},\tau} = [\![P]\!]_G^{D,W,\tau}$ where G is the default graph of D and W is a partial function such that $\mathrm{dom}(W) = \mathrm{dom}(\omega)$ and for every IRI $u \in \mathrm{dom}(W)$, it holds that $W(u)$ is the time-based window $\mathcal{W}(S, x - \alpha, x)$ with $(u_S, S) \in \mathcal{S}$, $(u_S, \alpha, \beta, \tau_0) = \omega(u)$ and $x = \tau_0 + \alpha + \beta \times i$ for the greatest possible $i \in \mathbb{N}$ for which $x < \tau$.*

7 Application-Based Evaluation

In this section, we evaluate RSP-QL* based on the application use-case scenario introduced in Sect. 3. To this end, we make three assumptions: First, we assume that all parameters about the patient are provided in separate streams.

Second, the thresholds for the physiological parameters are context dependent, and we assume that the background data contains information about Rut's expected values with respect to some activity. Third, we assume that all physiological parameters are reported with a confidence value representing some inherent uncertainty of the sample.

Listing 1.2 illustrates a typical query for the application scenario. For the sake of readability, we have simplified the query slightly compared to the actual project application. Additional optimization strategies would also be employed in practice to provide improved scalability.

The inputs to the query are 5 different streams that report data about the patient's current heart rate, breathing rate, oxygen saturation, location (of both Rut and Rut's partner), and current activity, respectively. The activity stream might have been created by another reasoning mechanism in the system, which infers activities of daily life based on sensor inputs and the context. For each window, the values are filtered for specific values or a confidence threshold, and then the aggregated data is checked against the threshold values specific to the current context of the patient (e.g., including the type of activity). If these conditions are met, we consider it a low-emergency situation, as described in the scenario outlined in Sect. 3. The resulting event is pushed to another stream upon which the system can act appropriately. In our use-case scenario, the system would first contact Rut's partner. Similar queries could be set up to deal with other situations that the system should be able to detect.

```
BASE <http://base/>
PREFIX ex: <http://www.example.org/ontology#>
PREFIX foaf: <http://xmlns.com/foaf/0.1/>
PREFIX sosa: <http://www.w3.org/ns/sosa/>

REGISTER STREAM <alert/lowEmergencyAbnormalState> COMPUTED EVERY PT10S AS

SELECT ?activity (AVG(?hr) AS ?avgHr) (AVG(?br) AS ?avgBr) (AVG(?ox) AS ?avgOx)
FROM NAMED WINDOW <w/1> ON <s/activity>  [RANGE PT10M STEP PT10S]
FROM NAMED WINDOW <w/2> ON <s/location>  [RANGE PT10M STEP PT10S]
FROM NAMED WINDOW <w/3> ON <s/heart>     [RANGE PT1M STEP PT10S]
FROM NAMED WINDOW <w/4> ON <s/breathing> [RANGE PT1M STEP PT10S]
FROM NAMED WINDOW <w/5> ON <s/oxygen>    [RANGE PT1M STEP PT10S]
WHERE {
    ?person a foaf:Person ;
       foaf:name "Rut" ;
       ex:home ?home ;
       ex:partner ?partner .

    [] a ex:NormalSituation ;
       ex:forPerson ?person ;
       ex:forActivity ?activity ;
       ex:expectedHeartRate [ ex:upperBound ?hrMax ] ;
       ex:expectedBreathingRate [ ex:lowerBound ?brMin ] ;
       ex:expectedOxygenSaturation [ ex:lowerBound ?oxMin ; ex:upperBound ?oxMax ] .

    WINDOW <w/1> { # Current activity, reported by the system
        GRAPH ?g1 {
            [ a sosa:Observation ;
              sosa:featureOfInterest ?person ;
              sosa:hasSimpleResult ?activity ] .
        }
    }
    WINDOW <w/2> { # Location of Rut's partner
        GRAPH ?g2 {
            [ a sosa:Observation ;
              sosa:featureOfInterest ?partner ;
              sosa:hasSimpleResult ?loc ] .
            FILTER(?loc != ?home)
        }
    }
    WINDOW <w/3> { # Heart rate
        GRAPH ?g3 {
            ?o3 a sosa:Observation ;
                sosa:featureOfInterest ?person .
            <<?o3 sosa:hasSimpleResult ?hr>> ex:confidence ?c3 .
            FILTER(?c3 > 0.95)
        }
    }
    WINDOW <w/4> { # Breathing rate
        GRAPH ?g4 {
            ?o4 a sosa:Observation ;
                sosa:featureOfInterest ?person .
            <<?o4 sosa:hasSimpleResult ?br>> ex:confidence ?c4 .
            FILTER(?c4 > 0.95)
        }
    }
    WINDOW <w/5> { # Oxygen saturation
        GRAPH ?g5 {
            ?o5 a sosa:Observation ;
                sosa:featureOfInterest ?person .
            <<?o5 sosa:hasSimpleResult ?ox>> ex:confidence ?c5 .
            FILTER(?c5 > 0.95)
        }
    }
}
GROUP BY ?activity ?hrMax ?brMin ?oxMin ?oxMax
HAVING(?avgHr > ?hrMax && ?avgBr < ?brMin && ?oxMin <= ?avgOx && ?avgOx <= ?oxMax)
```

Listing 1.2. The RSP-QL* query used in the use-case evaluation.

The application of RSP-QL* to this project use case shows that it is possible to express the queries needed, and that the proposed language thereby fulfills our use-case based requirements. In particular, it is worth noting the compactness and relative readability of the query in Listing 1.2, as compared to the corresponding RDF reification query[3] (excluded to space constraints).

8 Performance Evaluation

In this section, we begin by briefly describing a prototype implementation of the proposed approach. We then report on the effects of the proposed RDF stream model with respect to data bandwidth, and compare it with a baseline approach of using RDF reification. Finally, we compare the query execution performance of the prototype when using RDF* as opposed to RDF reification, while varying the number of annotated triples per streamed element.

All experiments were run on a MacBook Pro with 16 GB 1600 MHz DDR3 memory, and a 2.8 GHz Intel Core i7. The experiments were run using Java 1.8.0 with 2048 MB allocated for the JVM. All experiments were preceded by warm-up runs and averages for execution times were collected only after memory usage had stabilized.

8.1 Prototype Implementation

We implemented the prototype using Apache Jena[4] and RDFstarTools[5], where the latter provides a collection of Java libraries for processing RDF* data and SPARQL* queries. Additionally, we implemented a separate RSP-QL* query parser and integrated it with the standard Jena architecture, along with an extension of Jena's query class to support the additional syntax elements defined in RSP-QL*.

For the query execution, the implementation provides an extension of Jena's query engine and query execution, supporting the new query operators. During query execution, all windows over streams are materialized as individual RDF* datasets. The execution's active dataset then changes as needed when a window operation is evaluated. To improve evaluation efficiency, all parsed nodes are encoded as integers in one of two dictionaries: the *node dictionary* or the *reference dictionary*. Regular RDF nodes are added to the node dictionary, while triple nodes are added to the reference dictionary, which (recursively) encodes each separate node of the triple. All nodes, regardless of type, are internally represented as an integer, where the most significant bit signals whether the ID represents a regular node or a reference triple. This allows the system to quickly check how a node should be decoded. Encoding and decoding iterators

[3] https://github.com/keski/RSPQLStarEngine/tree/master/publications/semantics2019.

[4] https://jena.apache.org/ (version 3.8.0).

[5] https://github.com/RDFstar/RDFstarTools (version from 2019-02-28).

are provided to support moving between ID-based iterators, and Jena's standard iterator implementations.

The prototype is provided as open-source[6] under the MIT License. The underlying data structures can easily be changed by providing alternative implementations for the corresponding interfaces.

8.2 Serialization Overhead

One of the side-effects of using RDF reification to annotate triples is that it increases the size of the dataset, since for each reification triple four additional triples have to be added. Thus, one of the benefits of the proposed extension is the reduced overhead involved in transferring statement-level annotations in data streams. To compare the impact on bandwidth requirements, we compared the overhead in terms of bytes for each of the two approaches. The data was serialized using TriG*, which is an extension of Turtle* [9] for supporting named graphs, and compressed[7].

The amount of metadata per annotated triple impacts the relative overhead of the two approaches. For this evaluation, the TriG* serialization of each RDF* stream element contains declarations of one prefix, a base IRI, and a single metadata statement per annotated triple. Figure 1 shows the bandwidth required by the approaches as a function of the number of annotated triples per streamed element. The results show that the amount of bytes required when using RDF* is around half of what is required when using RDF reification.

8.3 Query Execution Performance

The performance of the approach was evaluated on the prototype implementation. The streamed elements contained a single confidence annotated triple, where the number of additional triples annotated with some other metadata predicate varied between experiments runs. A single evaluation query was used to match and filter all triples annotated with the confidence value. We compared query execution times when representing the metadata using RDF* and querying it using RSP-QL* versus representing the metadata using RDF reification and querying it using pure reification-based RSP-QL queries. The prototype applies no specific optimization techniques for the queries; thus, the two approaches differ only with respect to how statement-level metadata is represented internally. The RDF reification approach simply uses regular triple-pattern matching, whereas the RDF* approach represents the annotated triples as resources on the physical level. For the RDF reification query, we provided an additional version of the query optimized based on the heuristics described by Tsialiamanis et al. [19], where the order of the matched triple patterns was determined based on selectivity. Figure 2 presents the average query execution times. The results

---

6 https://github.com/keski/RSPQLStarEngine.

7 Compression here included the removal of excessive whitespace characters, the use of prefixes, and the use of predicate lists where appropriate.

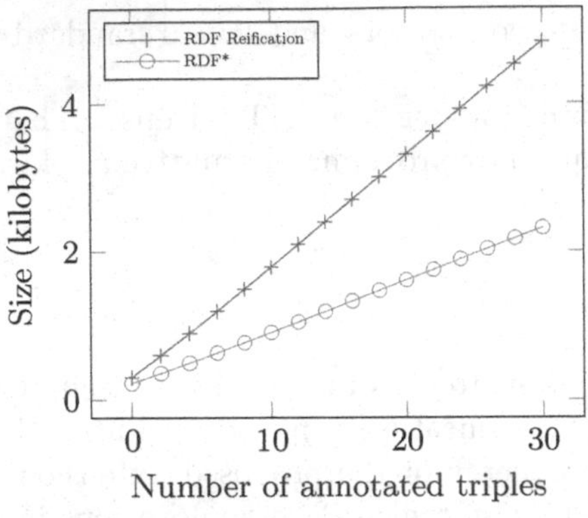

Fig. 1. Byte size of a serialized RDF* stream element as a function of the number of triples in it, where each triple is annotated with exactly one metadata triple.

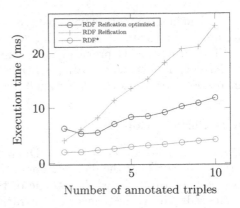

Fig. 2. Average query execution times of the prototype implementation when using either RDF*, reification, or reification with query optimization based on selectivity.

show that the advantage of the proposed approach grows with the number of distinct triples annotated in each streamed element, but that this difference can potentially be reduced by applying established optimization heuristics.

9 Discussion

The proposed approach provides a compact and intuitive way for both representing and querying annotated triples. Other approaches that could be considered for this purpose include single-triple named graphs [12], singleton properties [15], and RDF reification [11], but these approaches come with various drawbacks.

The application of named graphs inhibits the use of the graph name for other purposes, which means it is not compatible with the structure of RDF stream elements. Singleton properties introduce large numbers of unique predicates, which can adversely affect query execution performance. RDF reification, on the other hand, is both part of the RDF standard and can be supported in RSP-QL. However, RDF reification is verbose, both with respect to representing and querying data.

We note that RDF* and SPARQL* may be understood simply as syntactic sugar on top of RDF and SPARQL [9], and by extension this applies to the approach presented in this paper. However, the evaluation of the prototype implementation illustrates that representing annotated triples as resources on the physical level can have positive effects on the query execution level. When matching a single RDF reification triple, a total of four additional triple patterns have to be evaluated. In fact, due to this inefficiency, many RDF stores implement specific strategies for representing annotated triples [8]. For example,

Virtuoso[8] encodes RDF reification statements as quads, Apache Jena[9] provides an implementation of a node type with direct access to the statement it reifies, and Blazegraph[10] uses an approach similar to the one implemented in our prototype.

RDF* and SPARQL*, and thus RSP-QL*, simplifies the representation of complex scenarios, both from the perspective of modeling and of querying annotated metadata. For example, we may want to treat an RDF statement differently depending on whether the uncertainty associated with it has been automatically generated by a sensor, or if it originates from a physician. Querying this using RSP-QL* simply involves having a triple* pattern with two layers of nesting.

As part of future work, we plan on relaxing some of the assumptions made in the semantics, and add support for additional features defined in RSP-QL, such as count-based window operators and output stream operators.

10 Conclusion

In this paper, we have presented a novel way of annotating and querying statement-level metadata in RDF Stream Processing (RSP), and formally defined the new continuous query language RSP-QL*. The approach extends RDF streams to allow triples to directly use other triples in the subject and object positions, and similarly extends the current version of RSP-QL to query these, by leveraging and building on the concepts previously proposed for RDF* and SPARQL* [9,10].

The proposed approach was applied in a use case from an e-health research project, where multiple data streams have to be queried in parallel, and over extended periods of time, to detect possibly abnormal situations. The results show that RSP-QL* meets all our use-case requirements, and provides a compact and intuitive way of expressing and querying statement-level metadata, compared with the baseline approach of using RDF reification. Furthermore, the prototype implementation presented in the paper, which is provided as open-source, demonstrates benefits over the baseline approach, both with respect to the bandwidth required for data transfer and with respect to query execution performance over statement-level annotations. RDF* is a syntactically more compact way to express metadata annotations, and our experiments show that this difference is large enough to have an impact in deployed real-world systems and applications, where bandwidth may be limited. Although our prototype implementation is not optimized for query performance, we were able to demonstrate that the approach was faster with respect to query execution performance, when compared to using standard RDF reification.

This is the first work on RSP that has focused on supporting annotations on the statement level. We believe that the proposed approach provides an

[8] https://virtuoso.openlinksw.com/.

[9] https://jena.apache.org/.

[10] https://wiki.blazegraph.com/.

intuitive and compact way for representing and querying statement-level metadata, and that this work provides a good foundation for future research on efficient management of, e.g., uncertainty and provenance, in RDF data streams.

Acknowledgements. This research was supported by E-care@home, a "SIDUS – Strong Distributed Research Environment" project, funded by the Swedish Knowledge Foundation (KK-stiftelsen, Dnr: 20140217). Project website: http://ecareathome.se/. Olaf Hartig's work on this paper has been funded by the CENIIT program at Linköping University (project no. 17.05).

References

1. Anicic, D., Fodor, P., Rudolph, S., Stojanovic, N.: EP-SPARQL: a unified language for event processing and stream reasoning. In: Proceedings of the 20th International Conference on World Wide Web (2011)
2. Athan, T., Anderson, J., Ortner, P.W.B.: RDF Stream Abstract Syntax and Semantics: Draft Community Group Report 22 August 2016 (2016)
3. Barbieri, D.F., Braga, D., Ceri, S., Valle, E.D., Grossniklaus, M.: Querying RDF streams with C-SPARQL. ACM SIGMOD Rec. **39**(1), 20–26 (2010)
4. Calbimonte, J.-P., Corcho, O., Gray, A.J.G.: Enabling ontology-based access to streaming data sources. In: Patel-Schneider, P.F., et al. (eds.) ISWC 2010. LNCS, vol. 6496, pp. 96–111. Springer, Heidelberg (2010). https://doi.org/10.1007/978-3-642-17746-0_7
5. Cyganiak, R., Wood, D., Lanthaler, M.: RDF 1.1 Concepts and Abstract Syntax. Technical report W3C (2014). http://www.w3.org/TR/rdf11-concepts/
6. Dell'Aglio, D., Calbimonte, J.-P., Della Valle, E., Corcho, O.: Towards a unified language for RDF stream query processing. In: Gandon, F., Guéret, C., Villata, S., Breslin, J., Faron-Zucker, C., Zimmermann, A. (eds.) ESWC 2015. LNCS, vol. 9341, pp. 353–363. Springer, Cham (2015). https://doi.org/10.1007/978-3-319-25639-9_48
7. Dell'Aglio, D., Della Valle, E., Calbimonte, J.P., Corcho, O.: RSP-QL semantics: a unifying query model to explain heterogeneity of RDF stream processing systems. Int. J. Semant. Web Inf. Syst. **10**(4), 17–44 (2014)
8. Frey, J., Müller, K., Hellmann, S., Rahm, E., Vidal, M.E.: Evaluation of metadata representations in RDF stores. Semant. Web J. **10**, 205–229 (2017)
9. Hartig, O.: Foundations of RDF* and SPARQL* - an alternative approach to statement-level metadata in RDF. In: Proceedings of the 11th Alberto Mendelzon International Workshop on Foundations of Data Management and the Web (2017)
10. Hartig, O., Thompson, B.: Foundations of an Alternative Approach to Reification in RDF. CoRR abs/1406.3399 (2014)
11. Hayes, P.J., Patel-Schneider, P.F.: RDF 1.1 Semantics. Technical report, W3C (2014). https://www.w3.org/TR/rdf11-mt/
12. Hernández, D., Hogan, A., Krötzsch, M.: Reifying RDF: what works well with Wikidata? In: Proceedings of the 11th International Workshop on Scalable Semantic Web Knowledge Base Systems (SSWS) (2015)
13. Le-Phuoc, D., Dao-Tran, M., Xavier Parreira, J., Hauswirth, M.: A native and adaptive approach for unified processing of linked streams and linked data. In: Aroyo, L., et al. (eds.) ISWC 2011. LNCS, vol. 7031, pp. 370–388. Springer, Heidelberg (2011). https://doi.org/10.1007/978-3-642-25073-6_24

14. Lind, L., Prytz, E., Lindén, M., Kristoffersson, A.: Use cases unified description. E-care@home project Milestone Report MSR5.1b (Project Internal) (2017)
15. Nguyen, V., Bodenreider, O., Sheth, A.: Don't like RDF reification?: making statements about statements using singleton property. In: Proceedings of the 23rd International Conference on World Wide Web (2014)
16. Pérez, J., Arenas, M., Gutierrez, C.: Semantics and Complexity of SPARQL. ACM Trans. Database Syst. **34**(3) (2009)
17. Prud'hommeaux, E., Harris, S., Seaborne, A.: SPARQL 1.1 Query Language. Technical report, W3C (2013). http://www.w3.org/TR/sparql11-query
18. Rinne, M., Nuutila, E., Törmä, S.: INSTANS: high-performance event processing with standard RDF and SPARQL. In: ISWC 2012 Posters & Demos Track (2012)
19. Tsialiamanis, P., Sidirourgos, L., Fundulaki, I., Christophides, V., Boncz, P.: Heuristics-based query optimisation for SPARQL. In: Proceedings of the 15th International Conference on Extending Database Technology (2012)

Terminology, Thesaurus and Ontology Management

The Semantic Asset Administration Shell

Sebastian R. Bader[1(✉)] and Maria Maleshkova[2]

[1] Fraunhofer Institute for Intelligent Analysis and Information Systems IAIS, Schloss Birlinghoven, 53757 Sankt Augustin, Germany
sebastian.bader@iais.fraunhofer.de

[2] University of Bonn, Endenicher Allee 19a, 53115 Bonn, Germany
maleshkova@cs.uni-bonn.de

Abstract. The disruptive potential of the upcoming digital transformations for the industrial manufacturing domain have led to several reference frameworks and numerous standardization approaches. On the other hand, the Semantic Web community has made significant contributions in the field, for instance on data and service description, integration of heterogeneous sources and devices, and AI techniques in distributed systems. These two streams of work are, however, mostly unrelated and only briefly regard the each others requirements, practices and terminology. We contribute to this gap by providing the Semantic Asset Administration Shell, an RDF-based representation of the Industrie 4.0 Component. We provide an ontology for the latest data model specification, created a RML mapping, supply resources to validate the RDF entities and introduce basic reasoning on the Asset Administration Shell data model. Furthermore, we discuss the different assumptions and presentation patterns, and analyze the implications of a semantic representation on the original data. We evaluate the thereby created overheads, and conclude that the semantic lifting is manageable, also for restricted or embedded devices, and therefore meets the conditions of Industrie 4.0 scenarios.

Keywords: Industrie 4.0 · Data lifting · Asset Administration Shell

1 Introduction

Even though the various digital developments and internet-based technologies have attracted great attention in the manufacturing industry, a common understanding of the resulting requirements and implications has not been reached. The number of different terms, which are being used in this context, reflects this challenge – Internet of Things (IoT), Industrial Internet, Cyber-physical Systems, Digital Twins and many more have slightly overlapping scopes but still depict different applications and features. Still, the primary target is always the effective integration and interoperability of industrial devices, services and data sources. Therefore, the actual implementations require clear specifications of the used data formats, interfaces, and semantic meaning of the referenced objects and attributes.

M. Acosta et al. (Eds.): SEMANTiCS 2019, LNCS 11702, pp. 159–174, 2019.
https://doi.org/10.1007/978-3-030-33220-4_12

IoT data is currently mainly exchanged in either JSON or XML. These commonly used data formats ease the serialization and parsing by providing specifications for the syntactic structure of the data objects. Additional information on the meaning of keys/values is usually specified in customized data models and schemata. The latest specification of the Plattform Industrie 4.0 Asset Administration Shell (AAS) also follows this convention [1]. The AAS is promoted as the digital twin for the German Plattform Industrie 4.0 and encompasses the interpretation of the digital representation of any production-related asset. As such, materials and products, devices and machines but also software and digital services have a respective digital version.

While the predefined structure and the usage of specific keys reduce the heterogeneity inherent in the data exchange processes of current industrial scenarios, all real-world scenarios still require a thorough understanding of the specific terms and values. Therefore they are dependent on extensive manual work and understanding of the extended AAS model, followed by a time consuming data mapping. A semantic formalization of entities and data objects has several advantages in this context. The mature Semantic Web technology stack around RDF enables clear references to classes, properties and instances in the form of URIs, beyond the scope of single AAS objects but also across applications, domains, and organizations. The defined meaning of the used entities further allows its combination with predefined logical axioms, which allow the automatic derivation of new knowledge.

We contribute to the state of the art by presenting a mapping from the latest AAS data model to RDF. Thus we provide a data model as an openly accessible ontology and create SHACL shapes for all classes to enable schema validation. We outline the various pitfalls, especially the different patterns to identify, and refer to encoded entities and to links to remote resources. Based on the inherent Web nature of RDF, we show how the transformation to the semantic data model decreases the amount of required storage space. Furthermore, we present patterns to directly insert the RDF translation into the original XML and JSON files and discuss their implications. Relying on the RDF/XML and JSON-LD serializations, we are able to merge the predefined data structure with the semantically defined data. We show that the provided extension points in the form of submodel elements are suitable for this task and that the output AAS files are still processable by existing software, therefore the risk of compatibility issues is manageable.

The applicability of the presented approach is evaluated by determining the necessary overhead in terms of both storage and computation effort, and by a detailed discussion of the restrictions of the RDF version. We show that some semantic constructs are more efficient than the originally specified ones, whereas others are not directly compatible with the data structure of RDF and some are even not expressible at all.

In this context the paper makes the following contributions: (1) an RDF data model of the Semantic Asset Administration Shell *SAAS*, (2) a mapping from XML Asset Administration Shell representations to *SAAS*, (3) a set of preliminary reasoning axioms in order to explicitly derive implicitly encoded information from the data model, and (4) a validation model for this data model, encoded through SHACL shapes.

The remainder of this paper is organized as follows. Section 2 contains an overview on similar efforts in the field. Section 3 introduces a formalization of the regarded domain followed by the presentation of the RAMI ontology and an RML mapping in Sect. 5. Section 6 briefly examines several axioms for automated reasoning on top of the SAAS, while Sect. 7 illustrates the provided SHACL Shapes for schema validation. We use several use cases (Sect. 8) to evaluate our approach (Sect. 9). Finally, we conclude with a discussion on the potential of the SAAS and outline further research gaps.

2 Related Work

In this section, we discuss three areas of related work – the data model of the Asset Administration Shell, the existing mappings towards a semantic representation and related mappings of Industrie 4.0 data models to RDF.

Barnstedt et al. define the data model of the Asset Administration Shell [1], the form of identifiers, access rights and roles, as well as XML and JSON serializations and their transport. The textual documentation of the model is enhanced with XML and JSON schemata. The model defines a basic set of keys and properties, and outlines defined points for custom vocabularies and terminologies. Part 2 of specification will further determine the APIs and interaction functions of the Asset Administration Shell, and how operations can be provided and described for the Industrie 4.0 (Fig. 1).

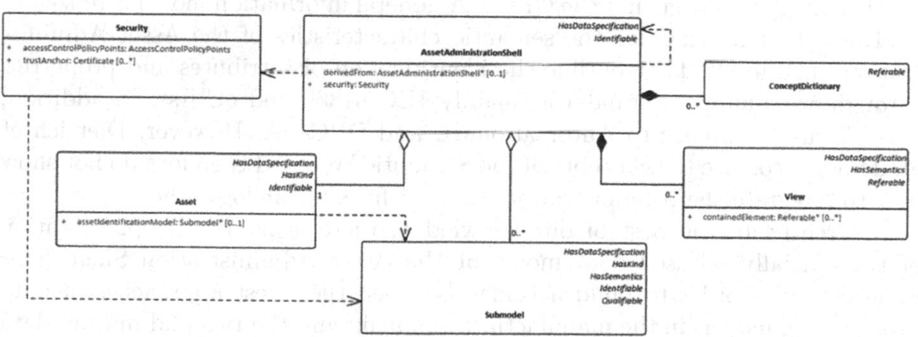

Fig. 1. Sections of the Asset Administration Shell Data Model according to [1] (page 44).

Grangel-González provide a first RDF data model for the Administration Asset Shell and the respective technical standards as published by ISO, IECC, and DIN [6]. They further extended the work in [5] with a formalized model of the Reference Architecture for Industrie 4.0 (RAMI4.0) and entities for units of measurements and provenance, and show a prototypical mapping using R2RML. However, the mapping itself was not generally applicable to other Asset Shells as a common data model was not specified at this time.

Tantik and Anderl [11] present an analysis how recommendations of the World Wide Web Consortium (W3C) fit to the guidelines of the Plattform Industrie 4.0. They outline various suggestions how standardized Web technologies can be integrated into Asset Shells. The authors present best practices and integration methods through a sample implementation scenario but do not discuss the implications on the data model itself.

Mappings of relational or otherwise formatted data to RDF are possible with the RDB to RDF Mapping Language R2RML [2] or the broader applicable RDF Mapping Language RML [4], which also enables mappings from JSON, XML or CSV to RDF. The desired transformations are also formulated in RDF by defining the output graph structure by so-called Maps and URI templates. While R2RML strictly relies on tables, and uses column names as resource and attribute identifiers of row-based data objects, RML also transforms JSON and XML data by identifying objects according to their keys. Even though some tools have been introduced in order to support the creation of mappings for both approaches, the possibility to collaboratively work on mappings was not part of the design requirements and is still missing.

Katie et al. [8] show by integrating the machine-to-machine communication protocol OPC-UA for servers and clients how semantic descriptions, in particular SAWSDL annotations, bridge the gap between the heterogeneous devices of the shop floor. The use of uniquely identified semantic descriptions supports the automatic orchestration of decoupled Cyber-physical Systems. However, only the specific input and output requirements of the OPC-UA methods are described. Neither the data objects nor the OPC-UA general information model is reflected.

Dietrich et al. examine the semantic characteristics of the Asset Administration Shell in [3]. They outline the identification of attributes and properties through cross-industry standards, mainly IEC 61360 and eCl@ss. In addition, they discuss mappings to AutomationML and OPC-UA. However, Dietrich et al. do not recognize the concepts of the Semantic Web and therefore do not show how to integrate the Administration Shell with its technology stack.

Currently, to the best of our knowledge, there is no RDF representation of the officially released data model of the Asset Administration Shell. This is necessary in order to build a bridge between the latest approaches of data provisioning models in the manufacturing domain and the rich and mature data integration and formalization capabilities of the Semantic Web. As such, an RDF data model has the potential to ease the information exchange but also provides the capabilities to introduce logical reasoning to the Asset Administration Shell.

3 Methodology

The data model for the Industrie 4.0 component aims to provide high coverage of the different modeling variants. RDF on the other hand has specific conditions how data is presented (triple-based structure, URI as identifier). In order to structure the contribution of this paper, the parts of the respective data models are defined as follows:

AAS captures the information about the Administration Asset Shell itself. In this regard, *AAS* is the digital representation or Digital Twin of the Asset. Information from *AAS*, therefore, refers to the information object or document and only indirectly to the original asset. Examples are the creation date of the digital representation, manuals, or how the AAS was generated or modified. It is important to note that the same reference is used to denote both the Administration Asset Shell itself and the set of information contained by it.

A captures the information about the actual asset. The asset can be anything of interest in the context of a digital production setting. Even though assets are usually embedded devices or internet-capable components, any physical object, such as materials, production goods or machines, can be seen as an asset too. In addition, assets also include software components and any digital service or intangible thing, which is necessary to model a manufacturing use case.

S denotes the submodel of the asset shell. Submodels partition the provided information and categorize facts according to their usage, for instance as part of a documentation submodel or a submodel for quality testing. Submodels are further separated into SubmodelElements, which are either themselves collections of SubmodelElements or the final bearer of key-value-encoded facts. As any combination of different submodels can be included in the Asset Administration Shell, the set S^k represents the superset, including all possible submodels.

I is the set of identifiers for data objects. Specifically $I = I_{glob} \cup I_{loc}$ where I_{glob} contains all globally valid identifiers, while the elements of I_{loc} are only valid in their context, in particular inside the AAS, which uses them.

The concept descriptions denoted with ***CD*** may provide further definitions about the used concepts, mainly attributes and data types. While concept descriptions are optional components of an AAS, they give the ability to place necessary explanations especially for entities with local identifiers close to the data. Similarly to submodels, concept descriptions are not limited in their appearance, therefore the superset CD^l is used.

An instance *aas* of an AAS is, therefore, defined by the union of the mentioned sets:

$$aas \in AAS \cup A \cup S^k \cup CD^l \quad (1)$$

The identifiers appear in all sets and are therefore not mentioned separately. They connect the objects of the different sets with each other. However, the nature of identifiers in the AAS data model is mostly the one of foreign keys, which do not link directly to the intended object. We define two types of functions on the administration shell. First, a serialization *ser* transforms each administration shell to a representation in a data format, in particular JSON and XML: $ser : AAS \rightarrow D = \{XML, JSON, ...\}$

Second, a mapping is a transformation m from the data model AAS to the Semantic Asset Administration Shell $SAAS$. $SAAS$ is defined as

$$SAAS = AAS_{RDF} \cup A_{RDF} \cup S^k_{RDF} \cup CD^l_{RDF} \quad (2)$$

Using these definitions, an AAS in XML undergoes several steps (see Fig. 2). A created SAAS object using the provided mapping (Sect. 5) can be sent to a reasoning engine (Sect. 6) to enrich it with additional facts. Both the native $SAAS_{RDF}$ and the enriched $SAAS^{+}_{RDF}$ can be forwarded to a validation module (Sect. 7). The validation module creates a validation report, containing the errors and inconsistencies against the SAAS schema. Of course, also otherwise created SAAS objects can be sent to the reasoning or validation modules (bottom lane).

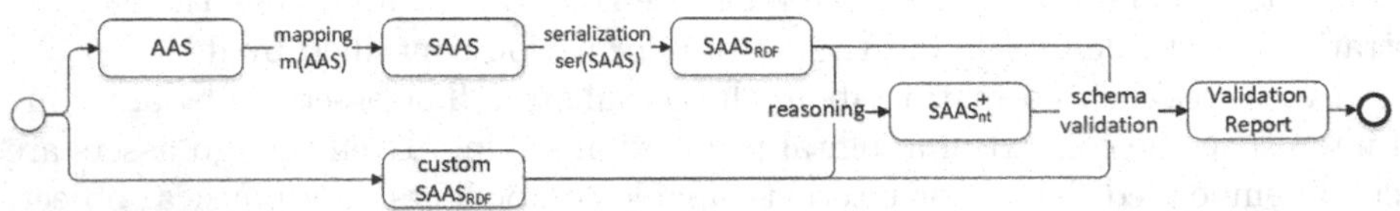

Fig. 2. Process steps through the provided modules.

4 The SAAS Data Model

In the following we present the *SAAS* data model as an RDF ontology[1]. As mentioned, the ontology is an advanced version of the RAMI ontology [6] and, therefore, the namespace *rami* is used. For each class from [1] a corresponding OWL Class has been created and every attribute has been mirrored with either an ObjectProperty or a DataProperty, except for the 'semanticId'. The reason for the later is that 'semanticId' links to the unique identifier for the entity. In RDF, this is the entity URI itself and therefore does not need to be repeated (Fig. 3).

All RDF entities are supplied with (sub)class assertions, labels and comments. The SAAS classes reflect the original ones in most cases and form a subclass hierarchy based on the inheritance specification of the AAS data model. However, neither RDF nor OWL know abstract classes. AAS uses abstract class constructs to partition certain attribute requirements and characteristics. For instance, the 'Has Kind' class covers all realizations, which contain a 'kind' attribute. This attribute encodes whether a certain entity is either referring to a concrete instance (the explicit machine installed in a shop floor) or is related to a whole type (machine type A can be installed in a certain setting). The data model reflects the abstract nature through *:class skos:note "abstract"* statements.

While the existing schemes for XML and JSON are based on a tree-structure, the RDF data model supports a more generic graph structure. While this might lead to the conclusion that for every model from AAS_{xml} or AAS_{json} a corresponding RDF serialization must be possible, therefore $AAS \subseteq SAAS$, we will show that some limitations exist and actually $AAS \supset SAAS$ is the case.

[1] https://github.com/i40-Tools/RAMIOntology.

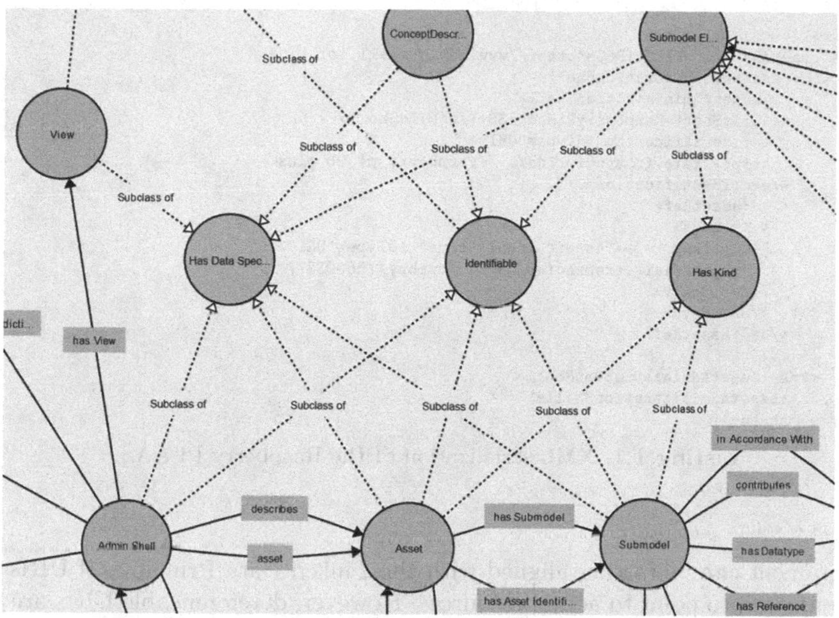

Fig. 3. Overview on the most important classes and properties of the SAAS (For full visualization see http://www.visualdataweb.de/webvowl/#iri=https://raw.githubusercontent.com/i40-Tools/RAMIOntology/master/rami.ttl).

5 Mapping to RDF

The Administration Shell object (*AAS*) is the root of every Asset Administration Shell. Listing 1.1 shows an example XML snippet. As the root entity, it is also the entrypoint for traversing the SAAS graph. A native mapping is always possible if the identifier is already applied in the form of an URI. However, also International Registration Data Identifiers (IRDI) and any other custom format is allowed. While IRDIs in case of the wide-spread eCl@ss system can – with significant additional efforts – being mapped to URIs, this is in general a very hard and error-prone challenge[2]. This becomes even harder when regarding proprietary or custom identifiers. In addition, custom identifiers may contain special characters as spaces or several hash signs. These characters are percent encoded (*# → %23*, changing the appearance of identifiers. As a result, only native URI identifiers can be mapped without risk, not only for AAS identifiers but also for the other sets in the following.

A consequence of this decision is also that the 'Has Semantics' class and the 'semanticId' property of the AAS data model becomes native to all objects. Moreover, it implies that all URIs are not only uniquely identifying its data object but also supply the semantic definition of their meaning. This rather strict

[2] For instance, templates for eCl@ss IDs, e.g. 26-04-07-02 (High-voltage current), may map to https://www.eclasscontent.com/index.php?id=26040702.

```xml
<?xml version="1.0"?>
<aas:aasenv xmlns:IEC61360="http://www.admin-shell.io/...">
  <aas:assetAdministrationShells>
    <aas:assetAdministrationShell>
      <aas:idShort>RaspberryPiModel3B+</aas:idShort>
      <aas:identification idType="URI">
        http://iais.fraunhofer.de/.../raspberry_pi_3b_plus
      </aas:identification>
      <aas:assetRef>
        <aas:keys>
          <aas:key type="Asset" local="true" idType="URI">
          https://iais.fraunhofer.de/.../rspbry/755003377
          </aas:key>
        </aas:keys>
      </aas:assetRef>
      ...
    </aas:assetAdministrationShell>
  </aas:assetAdministrationShells>
</aas:aasenv>
```

Listing 1.1. XML serialization of the Raspberry Pi AAS.

requirement can be further aligned with the Linked Data Principles if URIs are also enforced to point to actual resources. However, dereferencable URIs are not a requirement for now but should be seen as a preferable best practice.

The asset objects (A) constitute the link from the AAS to the real-world thing. As assets themselves only contain a very brief description, only the class assertions (rdf:type), the name (rdfs:label), descriptions (rdfs:comment) and the kind attribute are translated to A_{RDF}.

Submodels (S) and SubmodelElements are the core information carrier of the Asset Administration Shell. The basic structure of the submodel serves as a bracket for several SubmodelElements. Abstract SubmodelElements can be realized by Operations, ReferenceElements, Files, binary objects (Blob) and Properties. Properties have further attributes such as a key, value, value type and several others. In order to align the Property class with the graph model of RDF, each instance is transformed to a respective rdf:Property. Therefore, a distinct class 'Property' does not exist in SAAS. The alternative usage of n-ary relations, which would further allow the linking of more attributes to the relation, was discarded in order to sustain cleaner graphs. Consequently, not all Property objects can be translated to the SAAS model.[3]

Mainly, attributes and properties are converted to triples and identifiers are restricted to URIs. Therefore, all identifiers of attributes become globally valid, as URIs are globally valid. It has been deliberately decided against n-ary constructs with blank nodes and an explicit property class, which would have been closer to the XML and JSON influenced data model. The reason is that an

[3] Examples can be found at https://github.com/i40-Tools/RAMIOntology/tree/master/AssetAdministrationShell_examples.

```
_:AssetShellMap a rr:TriplesMap ;
  ...
    rr:subjectMap   [
        rml:reference "identification" ;
        rr:class rami:AdminShell ] ;
    rr:predicateObjectMap    [
        rr:predicateMap [ rr:constant rdfs:label ] ;
        rr:objectMap    [
            rml:reference "idShort" ;
            rr:termType rr:Literal ;
            rr:datatype xsd:string ]
    ] ; ...
```

Listing 1.2. Example RML TriplesMap excerpt.

```
<http://iais.fraunhofer.de/en/aas/examples/raspberry_pi_3b_plus> a rami:AssetShell;
  rdfs:label "RaspberryPiModel3B+";
  rami:hasAsset "http://iais.fraunhofer.de/en/aas/devices/rspbry/755003377"; ...
```

Listing 1.3. Equivalent representation to Listing 1.1 as RDF/Turtle.

thereby created graph increases in complexity while its comprehensibility significantly decreases and the information content stays the same.[4]

Concept description objects (CD) serve as local dictionaries for used entities. As the proliferation of definitions and metadata directly with the productive data eases its interpretation, Concept Descriptions increase the degree of interoperability between AAS providing and consuming components. RDF and Linked Data however propagate the usage of dereferencing URIs in order to retrieve metadata. In that sense, Linked Data conventions can reduce the amount of transmitted data. On the other hand, not all relevant Industrie 4.0 components are able to actively request such metadata. The possibility to independently open outgoing interactions beyond the restricted shop floor network is usually also a security risk and is not a good practice. Therefore, Concept Descriptions are a valuable feature to ship metadata and to ensure a common understanding on the shipped AAS. The mapping itself is provided as RML TripleMaps (see Listing 1.2) and can be executed with the open-source tool RMLMapper[5].

6 Reasoning

RDF and RDFS already contain trivial entailment rule sets[6]. As RDF and RDFS are very general vocabularies, the allowed reasoning focuses on the syntactic position (subject, predicate, object) of entities in RDF graphs. For instance, the information that p is an instance of the class Property can be inferred from the fact that a triple with p at the predicate position exists. Although rule

[4] Full example: https://github.com/i40-Tools/RAMIOntology/tree/master/rml_mapping/mapping_examples.

[5] Accessible at https://github.com/RMLio/rmlmapper-java.

[6] https://www.w3.org/TR/rdf11-mt/.

entailments of this kind are certainly correct, the created amount of explicit data increases significantly while the information content stays nearly the same.

In order to illustrate the power of reasoning based on the SAAS, selected rule sets using owl:sameAs and rdfs:subClassOf properties have been prepared. The rules are encoded in N3 according to Stadtmüller et al. in order to use their Linked Data Integration and Reasoning Engine [10]. In addition to the two entailment regimes, both consisting of several single rules[7], the SAAS ontology with its inherent axioms is integrated on the fly. Section 9.3 presents the results.

7 Schema Validation

The AAS presents a closed-world model. As such, the definitions of classes and properties must be regarded as restrictions and simply reusing properties, which were introduced for class A, for class B usually causes a violation of the model. RDF on the other hand does by default allow all not excluded patterns. Nevertheless, industrial use cases require verifiable statements on the data content but also its structure.

The Shapes Constraint Language (SHACL) [9] introduces a W3C recommendation for validation mechanisms on RDF graphs. The definition of required attributes, cardinality of relations or datatype restrictions in the form of shapes is an important aspect to enable data quality assurance in any productive system. Some tools are already created to assist the creation of SHACL shapes, e.g. a Protégé plugin and as a part of TopBraid Composer. As SHACL shapes are also defined in RDF, they share the same format as the validated data in contrast to e.g. plain SPARQL Rules. This eases the required technology stack and reduces the amount of used libraries.

The SAAS supplies respective shapes for all its classes[8]. These shapes mainly check for mandatory properties but also check the existence of label and comment annotations. In addition, the shapes are essential in order to check the incoming data during the exchange of Asset Administration Shells. Furthermore, the shapes can also be used to describe input and output specifications. For instance, an Industrie 4.0 component can postulate that its API requires data objects conforming to the Asset Shape and will output Submodel objects as defined by the Submodel Shape.

8 Use Cases

We use three different Asset Administration Shells in order to evaluate our approach. All of them are reflecting the specifications from [1] and are in the AASX file format. The corresponding descriptions are included in XML files contained in the AASX files.

[7] rdfs9 and rdfs11 from [7], transitivity, symmetry and replaceability characteristic for owl:sameAs.

[8] https://github.com/i40-Tools/RAMIOntology/tree/master/schema.

Raspberry Pi. The first Asset Administration Shell represents a Raspberry Pi 3B+ (see Listing 1.1). Three Submodels are included, namely one for the technical characteristics, one containing documentation material as the product sheet and a usage manual, as well as one submodel explaining the asset itself. Here, the asset is one specific Raspberry Pi (kind=instance) and not referring to the type of product of all Raspberry Pis, which have been produced or will ever be produced (kind=type). Therefore, the description is only valid for one and only one Raspberry Pi. The AAS delivers 52 SubmodelElements.

Automation Controller. AAS2 describes an electronic controller for automation facilities. As it is not approved as an official artifact, the providing company as well as its details can unfortunately not be published. AAS2 contains one asset, three submodels and more than 100 SubmodelElements.

Multi-protocol Controller. The third use case (AAS3) represents an internet-capable controller unit with multiple protocol support. Like AAS2, this Asset Administration Shell is not officially published yet. However, none of the authors of this paper was involved in the creation of either AAS2 or AAS3. The third use case includes one Asset with eight Submodels and more than 150 SubmodelElements.

9 Experimental Evaluation

We evaluate the AAS to SAAS mapping by examining the results and the performance of the three use cases (see Table 1). As a reference to estimate the information coverage, the number of XML nodes of the AAS serializations are provided. In addition, the amount of unique leaves of the three XML trees are noted, as these numbers better reflect the single information content of the AAS. Table 1 also presents the numbers of generated triples by the RMLMapper. The comparison indicates, as already mentioned, that not the whole expressiveness of AAS can be transported to the SAAS version. This is due to the fact that some constructs can not being represented sufficiently in RDF (for instance the Property class) but also many original entities contain redundant information. Especially the ConceptDescriptions repeat many attributes, which are collapsed by the mapping process and only added once.

Table 1. Results of the SAAS mapping and RDF serialization.

	#XML Leaves / #XML Nodes	AAS (XML)	#Triples	SAAS (XML)	SAAS (nquad)	SAAS (turtle)	SAAS (JSON-LD)
RaspberryPi	1161/2864	148 KB	510	40 KB	86 KB	32 KB	51 KB
AAS2	925/2604	91 KB	459	17 KB	58 KB	12 KB	20 KB
AAS3	2651/6743	313 KB	1154	43 KB	156 KB	31 KB	52 KB

9.1 Mapping Time

The necessary overhead in terms of computation time measured in milliseconds is presented in Fig. 4, in addition to the average mapping times outlined in the last column of Table 1. The time was measured on a regular laptop (Win10, 16 GB, Intel i5-7300 2,60 GHz) using a bash emulation. The different RDF serializations do influence the execution time, indicating that the writing is not the bottleneck. While the average mapping time of the Raspberry Pi AAS (2,7 s) and AAS2 (3,1 s) are rather close, the duration for AAS3 (5,7 s) is significantly higher. The variation between the selected use cases reflects the differences in their XML file size. This could indicate that the overall behavior is nearly linear. However, each of the 19 TripleMaps leads to a reloading and reiteration of the whole XML file. Overcoming this expensive process would speed up the process significantly but is out of the scope for this paper.

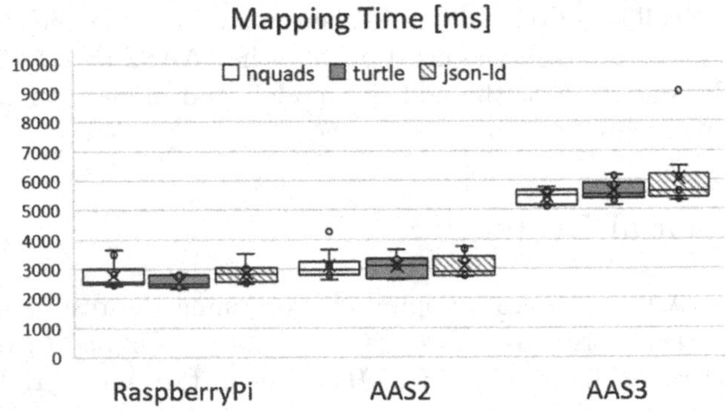

Fig. 4. Mapping times for the three Asset Administration Shells.

9.2 Data Overhead

RDF is in general not an effective data format in terms of storage efficiency. Nevertheless, the syntax requirements of the AAS and especially its XML schema create already significant overhead for the original AAS model. As depicted in Table 1, all RDF serializations reduce the necessary storage size. Especially noteworthy is the difference between the original XML file size and the RDF/XML serialization. This is mostly due to the usage of namespaces in the RDF/XML version, which reduces the noted URIs. It should be mentioned that for all serializations the mapping step (m) and the serialization (ser) were executed directly by the mapping engine.

Nevertheless, the resulting costs in terms of storage requirements and communication bandwidth do not exceed the ones created by the original Asset Administration Shells. Consequently, all devices and scenarios capable of handling AAS are also sufficient for the operation of SAAS. Furthermore, the possible serialization of SAAS as both XML and JSON should enable AAS implementations to quickly adapt to SAAS objects in their original file format.

Table 2. Added triples by the different rule sets.

	Triples (original)	sameAs (triples)	sameAs (time)	subClassOf (triples)	subClassOf (time)	both (triples)	both (time)
RaspberryPi	510	959	2,760 ms	771	2,719 ms	1,217	2,808 ms
AAS2	459	452	3,057 ms	367	2,368 ms	570	2,313 ms
AAS3	1154	1,115	2,776 ms	818	2,677 ms	1,343	2,668 ms

9.3 Reasoning

Three different rule sets have been applied to all use cases. All rule sets contain a web request to the ontology source file in order to load the class hierarchy and any other relevant axioms of the data model itself. The first one also adds several rules reflecting the symmetry and transitivity of owl:sameAs as well as the fact that same instances share all properties and annotations of each other. The second rule set contains subclass statements as encoded by the rules rdfs9 and rdfs11 [7]. The third set combines both to the most expressive reasoning set. Table 2 gives an overview of the amount of created triples. *rdfs:subClassOf*, *owl:sameAs* and the combination of both entailments are shown with the amount of uniquely added triples and the average reasoning time.

We use the Linked Data-Fu engine [10]. The preparation of the reasoning engine, involving the parsing of the rule files, takes around 1 s. The following web request, the download of the ontology, the evaluation of the rules and the serialization to a n-triple file is then executed. The duration distribution of ten repetitions is shown in Fig. 5. One can see that the whole process takes between 2,3 and 3,3 s, nearly independently of the amount of inputs (AAS3 is significantly larger than the graph for the Raspberry Pi) and the expressiveness of the rule sets (the second set is leading to way less results than the others).

As the rule sets are only regarding the structure of the ontology, the inferencing of context-dependent knowledge is not yet possible. In order to reach productively usable information, domain-specific axioms tailored to the actually contained or expected data is necessary. However, we can show that the reasoning process with complex rules is applicable in an acceptable amount of time.

9.4 Schema Validation

The evaluation times of the SHACL shapes are shown in Fig. 6. On average, the execution of all shapes takes 46,2 s and the execution of one single shape 1,8 s. All shapes have been executed a total of ten times.

About 2 s are required for setting up the validation tool and parsing the data shape (the Asset Administration Shell) and the single class shape. The size of the Asset Administration Shell has no significant impact on the achieved results. Regarding these conditions, we claim that the necessary effort is acceptable for a typical Industrie 4.0 scenario as the validation itself is not necessary for every restricted devices. This is due to the fact that the validation of data takes either

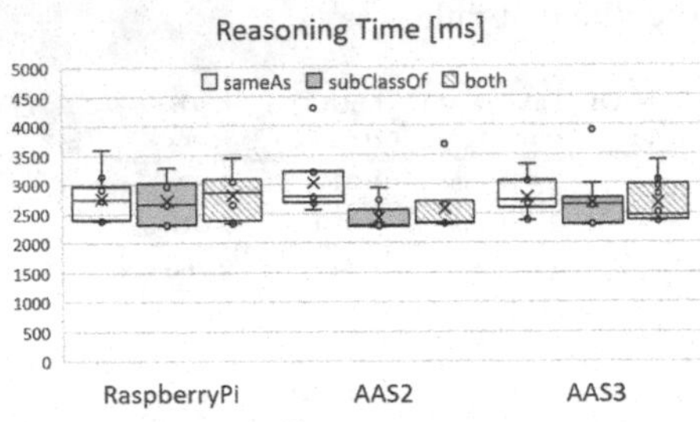

Fig. 5. SAAS Reasoning duration.

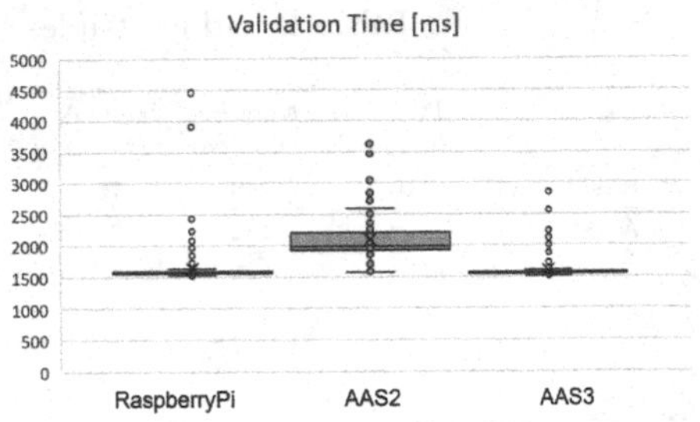

Fig. 6. Schema validation performance.

place at development or deployment time where time is not critical. In addition, the validation is important for the higher-level data analytical services which usually run on more powerful machines or are even hosted in the cloud.

10 Conclusion and Outlook

We presented a semantic version of the Administration Admin Shell, a mapping from its XML serialization to any RDF serialization, schema validation shapes and a brief set of reasoning rules. In that sense, we showed the lifting process of the AAS data to a semantic integration layer.

This is one step to an automated integration of Industrie 4.0 components. We showed how existing, non-customized tools can work with the RDF model of the AAS and execute their task without prior configuration. This enables the implementation of real interoperable pipelines and data-driven workflows, not only on the data format and syntax level but also regarding the meaning of the data. Furthermore, the examined overhead of the SAAS model and showed that the requirements do not exceed the requirements set by the original AAS model.

The mapping provided in this paper outlines the data lifting to the SAAS RDF model. The lowering of RDF to the original AAS data model has not yet been achieved. Furthermore, the main benefit of the semantic model is, besides its formalized meaning, the interlinking with other definitions and the integration of additional sources.

For now, only the data provisioning capabilities of the AAS are defined. In the next step, the provisioning and invocation of operations through Asset Administration Shells will be specified. Using semantically defined descriptions of the respective interfaces, their input and output parameters and the provided services will allow the Industrie 4.0 community to rely on the huge amount of expertise and experience with Web Services and Semantic Web Services in particular. This way, the goal of truly interoperable and flexible manufacturing workflows, where software and hardware, materials and products, costumers and suppliers form on demand information chains, benefits from the huge amount of existing research in the area.

We will further extend our work in order to keep the semantic models aligned with the progress of the Asset Shell specification. Furthermore, we provide feedback and outline established best practices to the manufacturing community. Furthermore, we see two main challenges which must be tackled by the semantic community. First, the core potential of the semantic web – the seamless integration of heterogeneous devices, services and data sources – still lacks sufficient numbers of implemented use cases and deployed scenarios in practice. Second, the reoccurring discussion on identifiers in distributed settings is a huge chance for the established practices of the Semantic Web and Linked Data in particular. However, the benefits of (dereferencable) URIs are still underestimated in the manufacturing community, mostly because of missing experiences.

References

1. Barnstedt, E., et al.: Details of the Asset Administration Shell. Technical Report Part 1, Plattform Industrie 4.0 (2018). https://www.plattform-i40.de/PI40/Redaktion/DE/Downloads/Publikation/2018-verwaltungsschale-im-detail.html
2. Das, S., Sundara, S., Cyganiak, R.: R2RML: RDB to RDF Mapping Language, W3C Recommendation. World Wide Web Consortium (W3C), Cambridge, MA (2012). www.w3.org/TR/r2rml
3. Diedrich, C., et al.: Semantic interoperability for asset communication within smart factories. In: 22nd International Conference on Emerging Technologies and Factory Automation (ETFA), pp. 1–8. IEEE (2017)
4. Dimou, A., Vander Sande, M., Colpaert, P., Verborgh, R., Mannens, E., Van de Walle, R.: RML: a generic language for integrated RDF mappings of heterogeneous data. In: LDOW (2014)
5. Grangel-González, I., Halilaj, L., Auer, S., Lohmann, S., Lange, C., Collarana, D.: An RDF-based approach for implementing Industry 4.0 Components with Administration Shells. In: 21st International Conference on Emerging Technologies and Factory Automation (ETFA), pp. 1–8. IEEE (2016)
6. Grangel-González, I., Halilaj, L., Coskun, G., Auer, S., Collarana, D., Hoffmeister, M.: Towards a semantic administrative shell for industry 4.0 components. In: International Conference on Semantic Computing (ICSC), pp. 230–237 (2016)
7. Hayes, P.J., Patel-Schneider, P.F.: Rdf 1.1 Semantics. W3C Recommendation (2014). https://www.w3.org/TR/rdf11-mt/
8. Katti, B., Plociennik, C., Ruskowski, M., Schweitzer, M.: SA-OPC-UA: introducing semantics to OPC-UA application methods. In: 14th International Conference on Automation Science and Engineering (CASE), pp. 1189–1196. IEEE (2018)
9. Knublauch, H., Kontokostas, D.: Shapes Constraint Language (SHACL). W3C Candidate Recommendation **11**(8) (2017)
10. Stadtmüller, S., Speiser, S., Harth, A., Studer, R.: Data-fu: a language and an interpreter for interaction with read/write linked data. In: Proceedings of the 22nd International Conference on World Wide Web. ACM (2013)
11. Tantik, E., Anderl, R.: Integrated data model and structure for the asset administration shell in industrie 4.0. Procedia CIRP **60**, 86–91 (2017)

BY

Taxonomy Extraction for Customer Service Knowledge Base Construction

Bianca Pereira[1(✉)], Cecile Robin[1], Tobias Daudert[1], John P. McCrae[1], Pranab Mohanty[2], and Paul Buitelaar[1]

[1] Insight Centre for Data Analytics, Data Science Institute, National University of Ireland Galway, Galway, Ireland
{bianca.pereira,cecile.robin,tobias.daudert,john.mccrae, paul.buitelaar}@insight-centre.org

[2] Fidelity Investments, Boston, USA
pranab.mohanty@fmr.com

Abstract. Customer service agents play an important role in bridging the gap between customers' vocabulary and business terms. In a scenario where organisations are moving into semi-automatic customer service, semantic technologies with capacity to bridge this gap become a necessity. In this paper we explore the use of automatic taxonomy extraction from text as a means to reconstruct a customer-agent taxonomic vocabulary. We evaluate our proposed solution in an industry use case scenario in the financial domain and show that our approaches for automated term extraction and using in-domain training for taxonomy construction can improve the quality of automatically constructed taxonomic knowledge bases.

Keywords: Taxonomy extraction · Knowledge base construction · Conversational agents

1 Introduction

Customer service agents are charged with the role of identifying the intention behind customer questions, retrieving the relevant business information that address those queries, and expressing it in a form that the customer is able to understand. However, the increasing demand for customer services and the necessity to scale up a human workforce are an ongoing challenge for businesses. To address that, organisations are turning to semi-automatic customer service through the use of digital conversational agents (DCAs, also referred to as chatbots) for primary contact with customers, leaving human agents to deal mostly with unusual or more complex customer queries.

Some of the challenges faced by DCAs are: the acquisition of domain knowledge, and knowledge representation that can be audited by the business. Whereas human agents may pass through training programmes to understand the business they are working with, DCAs not only need to acquire knowledge about the

M. Acosta et al. (Eds.): SEMANTiCS 2019, LNCS 11702, pp. 175–190, 2019.
https://doi.org/10.1007/978-3-030-33220-4_13

business but also about the way customers express their informational needs. Further, while it is expected that human agents would be responsible for the provision of the correct information needed by the customer, DCAs cannot be held legally responsible. Instead, businesses need to have means to audit the knowledge used by these DCAs in order to minimise the error in the retrieval of information. Therefore, DCAs need to make use of knowledge representation mechanisms that are applicable to their tasks but also interpretable by humans.

In this paper we propose a solution for the automatic generation of taxonomies from customer service dialogue data. Such solution contributes to the conversational agent use case by taking advantage of existing dialogues between customers and agents as learning data about the domain, and by automatically generating taxonomies as semantic structures for auditing the knowledge used by the conversational agent. The main contributions of this paper are: the comparison of state-of-the-art Term Extraction features, the proposal of Taxonomy Likelihood Scores to measure how likely a tree represents an actual taxonomy, and the applicability of our solution to an anonymised financial customer service use case provided by Fidelity Investments.

2 Related Work

DCAs need to have domain-specific knowledge in order to be effective interfaces for human-computer interaction. Most attempts to represent such knowledge have been based on extracting information directly from textual sources, such as online discussion forums [19]. However, it has been identified that a structured form of knowledge can provide a useful intermediate step. Sánchez-Díaz et al. [26] used a logical representation to apply chatbots as intelligent tutors, whereas Semantic Web representations have been used in OntBot [3], through manually designed ontologies, and DBpedia bot [7], by using an open domain knowledge graph. However, none of these solutions is based on automatically generated domain-specific taxonomies. (See Abdul-Kader et al. [1] for a survey.)

The approach we have defined in this paper consists of two steps. First we extract the terms that are most relevant to the domain, a task referred to as automatic term recognition (ATR). Current approaches to this task have employed a varied suite of methods for extracting terms from text based on parts of speech and metrics for assessing 'termhood' [15,29], domain modelling [11], and the composition of multiple metrics in an unsupervised manner [5]. More recently, these methods have been combined into off-the-shelf tools such as ATR4S [7] and JATE [31], and our system is a similar implementation to ATR4S.

The second step organizes these terms into a taxonomy. Although similar to hypernym learning [28], the challenges it proposes are quite different (see [10]). Multiple string and grammar-based methods have been proposed, where baseline systems have used string-based metrics with Hearst-like patterns learned from text [23], while more advanced ones have been based on the concept of *endocentricity* of terms to indicate a hypernym-like relationship [30]. Other methods not based on grammar such as genetic algorithms [14] or word embeddings [17,27] have also been explored. We include these approaches in our system thus providing an integrated solution to both term and taxonomy extraction.

3 Task Definition

Taxonomy extraction consists of extracting a set of terms from a corpus and organising them into a taxonomic structure [10], i.e. a hierarchical tree structure where terms closer to the root of the tree are considered broader[1] than terms farther to the root.

Our framework for taxonomy extraction from text is divided into two steps: automatic term recognition and taxonomy construction. The term recognition step aims at detecting the most relevant terms (also referred to as keyphrases) for a domain represented by a corpus. Based on this list of terms, the taxonomy construction step aims at finding a suitable taxonomy that maintains the correct broad/narrow relationship between terms.

Definition 1. *Given a set of terms T in which each $t \subset T$ is represented by a label t_l. A* ***taxonomy****, $\mathcal{T} = (T, \sqsubseteq)$, is then defined as a partial ordering of a set of terms, T, satisfying the following constraints:*

- *(Reflexivity)* $t \sqsubseteq t \; \forall t \in T$
- *(Antisymmetry)* $t_1 \sqsubseteq t_2$ *and* $t_2 \sqsubseteq t_1$ *if and only if* $t_1 = t_2 \; \forall t_1, t_2 \in T$
- *(Transitivity)* $t_1 \sqsubseteq t_2$ *and* $t_2 \sqsubseteq t_3$ *implies* $t_1 \sqsubseteq t_3 \; \forall t_1, t_2, t_3 \in T$
- *(Unique parent) if* $t_1 \sqsubseteq t_2$ *and* $t_1 \sqsubseteq t_3$ *then* $t_2 \sqsubseteq t_3$ *or* $t_3 \sqsubseteq t_2 \; \forall t_1, t_2, t_3 \in T$
- *(Single root) There is some element* $r \in T$ *such that* $t \sqsubseteq r \; \forall t \in T$

4 Automatic Term Recognition

Our proposed solution for term recognition uses a corpus-based approach based on a pipeline of four consecutive steps (Fig. 1): (i) identification of candidate terms, (ii) scoring, (iii) ranking, and (iv) filtering.

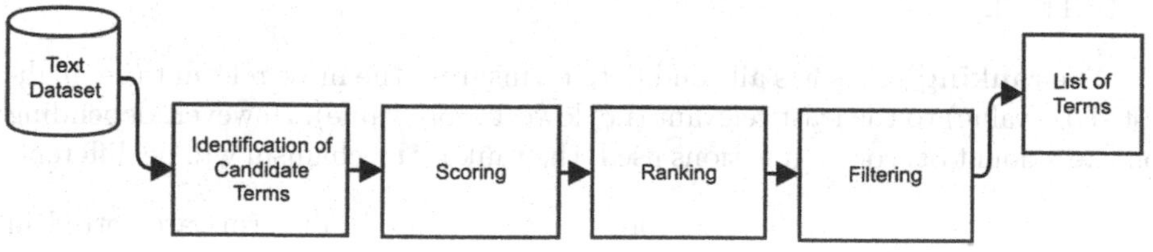

Fig. 1. Automatic term recognition pipeline.

The **identification of candidate terms** consists of identifying the key terms appearing within each document. This is accomplished by detecting all noun phrases appearing in the corpus that:

[1] By 'broader' we do not mean hypernymy, but that the topic has a wider scope.

- Contain a minimum and a maximum number of n-grams.
- Do not either start or end with a stopword [20].
- Follows a set of part-of-speech patterns empirically found to be associated with terms [9,20].
- Occurs within the corpus at least a given number of times.

The **scoring** step provides a quantitative measurement for the relevance of each candidate term to the domain in the corpus. As the notion of relevance changes from one application area to another, the scoring step can make use of one or multiple scoring functions more suitable for the underlying domain and task. In this work we will explore the use of multiple combinations of scoring functions for the choice of terms in the financial customer service domain.

Formally, consider C a corpus and $t \in C$ a candidate term extracted in the step for identification of candidate terms. The score for a given term t is a n-tuple $score(t) = (f_1(t), f_2(t), ..., f_n(t))$ given by a set of functions that indicate the relevance of t in C for a task T.

In this work we evaluate scoring functions within four categories:

- *Frequency of occurrences*: scoring functions that consider only frequencies of candidate terms within the corpus and/or frequency of words occurring within candidate terms (TF-IDF, Residual IDF [13], C Value [4], ComboBasic [6]).
- *Context of occurrences*: scoring functions that follow the distributional hypothesis [18] to distinguish terms from non-terms by considering the distribution of words in their contexts (PostRankDC [11]).
- *Reference corpora*: scoring functions based on the assumption that terms can be distinguished from other words and collocations by comparing occurrence statistics in the dataset against statistics from a reference corpus - usually of general language/non specific domain (Weirdness [2], Relevance [24]).
- *Topic modelling*: scoring functions based on the idea that topic modelling uncovers semantic information useful for term recognition, in particular that the distribution of words over the topics found by the topic modelling is a less noisy signal than the simple frequency of occurrences (Novel Topic Model (NTM) [21]).

The **ranking** step sorts all candidate terms from the most relevant (i.e. highest score value) to the least relevant (i.e. lowest score value). However, depending on the amount of scoring functions used, the ranking mechanism will be different:

- *Single score*: where only one score function is used, all terms are sorted in ascending order of their associated score value.
- *Voting*: when more than one scoring function is used, the ranking is based on the voting mechanism from [32] and happens in two steps. In the first step, the single score procedure is applied to each scoring function used, resulting in a set of ranked lists R – one list per scoring function. Next, the final ranking position for a candidate term t is given by Eq. 1 where n is the number of scoring functions used and $R_i(t)$ is the rank position of t as provided by the scoring function i.

$$rank(t) = \sum_{i}^{n} \frac{1}{R_i(t)} \tag{1}$$

Last, the **filtering** step keeps only the top n terms after the ranking step (where n is a parameter provided to the algorithm).

5 Taxonomy Construction

Taxonomy construction aims to build a taxonomy based on the terms extracted by the automatic term recognition algorithm. The proposed pipeline consists of two consecutive steps (Fig. 2): (i) pairwise scoring, and (ii) search. In the first step, each pair of terms extracted $\{\forall(c,d) \in T | c \neq d\}$ will receive a score referring to the estimated probability $p(c \sqsubseteq d)$ that c is a narrower term than d. This score will be based on the terms themselves and on their corpus frequency. Based on this set of scores, the second step will search for a tree structure that maximises the likelihood of it being a taxonomy, according to a pre-defined taxonomy likelihood score. The result of this process is a taxonomy $\mathcal{T}$ containing all the terms provided as input.

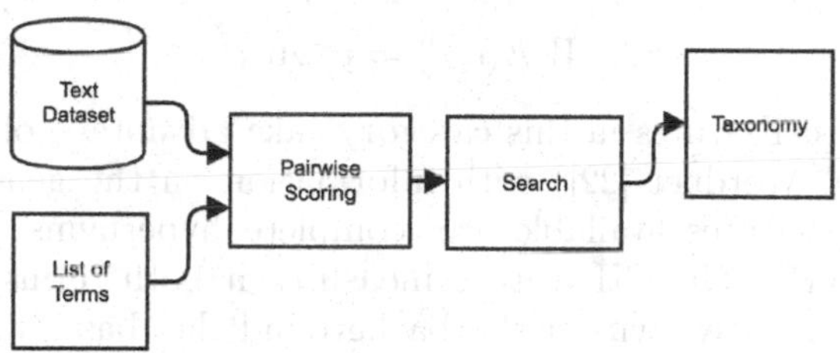

Fig. 2. Taxonomy construction pipeline.

5.1 Pairwise Scoring

Pairwise scoring aims at identifying, for a pair of terms (c,d) where $c \neq d$, if c is a narrower concept than d ($c \sqsubseteq d$). In this work we accomplished this by using a supervised learning setting.

For each pair of terms (c,d) a feature vector is created with features from the following four categories:

- *String-based features:* Features in this category presume that shorter terms embedded within longer ones are more general. For instance, ‘funds’ is more general than ‘mutual funds’. Features in this category are: Inclusion, overlap, and longest common substring (LCS). Inclusion is +1 if c is totally contained within d, −1 if d is totally contained within c, or 0 otherwise. Overlap represents how many words are shared between two terms. Last, LCS measures the longest string of characters shared by two terms.

- *Frequency-based features:* This category assumes that the generality or specificity of a term influences its frequency in the domain corpus. Features in this category are: relative frequency and term difference. Relative frequency measures the difference between the frequency of two terms (Eq. 2 where $f(x)$ denotes the frequency of term x). Term difference measures the difference in the distribution of two terms (Eq. 3 where $D(x)$ denotes the number of documents in which the term x appears).

$$relativeFrequency(c, d) = log(\frac{f(d)}{f(c)}) \tag{2}$$

$$termDifference = \frac{|D(c) \cap D(d)|}{|D(d)|} \tag{3}$$

- *Word embedding features:* Features in this category intend to capture the generality of a term by the relation it has with other terms in a shared latent semantic space. For that, GloVe [25] vectors are gathered for each word within a term c in order to generate a vector v_c for the whole term using Single Value Decomposition (SVD) [27]. Two approaches are used, each one leading to a different word embedding feature: SVD average and SVD minmax. The word embedding (WE) features used for pairwise scoring between a pair (c, d) will be calculated according to Eq. 4.

$$WE(c, d) = v_c^T A v_d \tag{4}$$

- *Lexical features:* Features in this category take advantage of existing lexical databases (e.g. Wordnet [22]) with information on the generality of terms (i.e. $c \sqsubseteq d$). Features available are: complete hypernyms (CH) and word hypernyms (WH). The CH feature measures if both terms appear related (directly or indirectly) within the background database, whereas the WH feature measures the presence of relations between any two pairs of words in terms c and d according to Eq. 5.

$$WH(c, d) = \frac{\#words(t_c) + \#words(t_d)}{2} \sum CH(w_c, w_d) \tag{5}$$

A SVM (Support Vector Machine) classifier[2] is then trained using a manually created taxonomy with an associated corpus in the same domain. Each pair of terms (c, d) where $c \neq d$ and c is a child of d in the training taxonomy is labelled with $+1$, otherwise the pair is labelled as -1. The result of the classification is the probability estimation for the class $+1$ which is then given as the estimate for $p(c \sqsubseteq d)$.

5.2 Search

Based on the pairwise score between any two terms provided as input to the taxonomy construction, the search step aims at identifying a tree structure that

[2] Earlier versions of the system experimented with other classifiers, however we have found that SVMs provide higher quality and robust performance.

represents a taxonomy of these terms. In order to identify how close a tree structure is to a valid taxonomy, a taxonomy likelihood score was designed. In this work we design and evaluate three score functions: transitive, non-transitive, and Bhattacharyya-Poisson. The goal for the search is to find a tree-structure that maximises the taxonomy likelihood score. Here we also experimented with two types of search methods: greedy and beam.

Taxonomy Likelihood Score

Transitive. The transitive score (Eq. 6) just follows the basic assumption that the best taxonomy is the one that maximises the product of all $p(c \sqsubseteq d)$ for all (c, d) pairs of terms. In practice, we take logs of the probabilities and maximise the resulting sum (Eq. 7).

$$S(T) = \prod_{c \sqsubseteq d} p(c \sqsubseteq d) \tag{6}$$

$$\max_T S(T) = \max_T \sum_{c \sqsubseteq d} \log p(c \sqsubseteq d) \tag{7}$$

Non-transitive. In practice, the transitive score is not expected to work well since it is maximised by taxonomies for which there are as few as possible pair of terms (c, d) such that $c \sqsubseteq d$. The most trivial case is when a taxonomy is composed only by a single root term and all other terms are a direct child of it. As such, taxonomies that are constructed from maximising the transitive score tend to have a very large number of average children. In order to avoid that, the non-transitive score (Eq. 8) considers only the set of direct children, which are denoted by $c \leq d$ and should satisfy the following constraints:

- $c \leq d$ implies $c \sqsubseteq d$.
- $c \sqsubseteq d$ implies there exists c such that $c \leq e$ and $e \sqsubseteq d$.
- For all, $c \leq d$ there does not exist e, $e \neq d$, $e \neq c$, such that $c \leq e$ and $e \leq d$.

$$S_{nonTransitive}(T) = \prod_{c \leq d} p(c \sqsubseteq d) \tag{8}$$

Bhattacharyya-Poisson. Despite the possible improvement given by the non-transitive likelihood function, it may still lead to a single path (i.e. a tree with just one branch), what differs from usual expectations for taxonomies as more balanced trees (i.e. tree structures with multiple branches). In order to address this, the Bhattacharyya-Poisson likelihood score takes into account the number of children of each node in the tree.

Formally, let n_c denote the number of terms in a taxonomy that have exactly c children. If the tree was to be constructed in a truly random fashion we would expect n_c to be distributed according to a binomial distribution (Eq. 9). However, in a completely balanced tree of N terms there are $N - 1$ direct children so that the number of children in each branch is $p = \frac{(N-1)}{b}$, where b is the number of branches. In order to allow us to vary the average number of children in each branch (λ), since taxonomies do not need to be completely balanced, we use the Poisson distribution as an approximation for the binomial distribution (Eq. 10). However, the constraints on what constitutes a taxonomy fix this value to very near 1 and we wish to vary this in order to control the taxonomy structure. We thus ignore the leaf nodes in the taxonomy (i.e., we ignore n_0).

$$p(n_c = m) = choose(N, m)p^m(1-p)^{N-m} \tag{9}$$

$$p(n_c = m) \simeq \frac{\lambda^m e^{-\lambda}}{m!} \tag{10}$$

In order to measure the similarity of the candidate taxonomy with this theoretical probability value we use the Bhattacharyya distance [8] that measures the similarity of two (discrete) probability distributions p and q as provided in Eq. 11. If we compare this to the actual children count in a taxonomy, we can score a taxonomy as provided in Eq. 12. Finally, this is interpolated with the previous metric to score a taxonomy as provided in Eq. 13.

$$B(p, q) = \sum_i \sqrt{p_i qi} \tag{11}$$

$$BP(T) = \sum_{i=1}^{N} \frac{n_i \lambda^{n_i} e^{-\lambda}}{(N - n_0)n_i!} \tag{12}$$

$$S_{BP}(T) = \prod_{c \leq d} p(c \sqsubseteq d) + \alpha N \times BP(T) \tag{13}$$

Search Method. Having chosen the likelihood score, the next step is to use a search strategy that optimises this likelihood score. We used two search strategies: (i) greedy, and (ii) beam.

Greedy. In this method, provided the pairwise scores for all pairs of terms, the pair that has the maximal score for $p(c \sqsubseteq d)$ is added as $c \leq d$. This process is repeated until a full taxonomy is constructed, that is we take pairs $c \leq d$ that satisfy the first four axioms of the taxonomy, from the first (reflexivity - unique parent) until the final axiom is satisfied (single root), which means the taxonomy is complete.

Beam. In contrast to the greedy method, where only a single partially constructed taxonomy is maintained, this method keeps a list of the top scoring possible solutions. This list (also called beam) is of a fixed size, thus the addition of a new partial solution may cause the least scoring partial solution to be dropped. Complete solutions are stored in a separate beam and the algorithm proceeds until it has considered all possible pairs of concepts and returns the highest scoring complete solution found.

6 Experiments

6.1 Automatic Term Recognition

Our experiments were performed on an anonymised customer service chat-log dataset containing 300,000 conversations provided by Fidelity Investments, where any personal information was removed prior to using the data for this project. In order to use such dataset, first we need to decide what is the unit of analysis or, in other words, what would be considered a document in the corpus. There are two obvious options: each interaction made by a customer or an agent, or the whole customer-agent conversation. In our experiments we decided to use the whole conversation as unit of analysis for two reasons: (i) to give priority to terms frequent in conversations rather than those cited multiple times only in a single conversation; and (ii) because different elements in a conversation could provide contextual information for the terms extracted.

Also, in order to protect customers' identities and personal data, the corpus provided is full of anonymisation tokens, i.e. tokens that were put in place of what would be sensitive information (e.g. name, email address, etc.). Before conducting any experiment, a list of stopword terms was compiled containing all anonymisation tokens appearing in the corpus so that these would not be captured as terms due to their potential high frequency in the corpus.

After preprocessing the corpus, several experiments were conducted in order to identify the most suitable configuration for automatic term recognition in the customer-agent interaction scenario. First, we adjusted the hyper-parameters for identification of candidate terms: the part-of-speech patterns used are given by the literature [9,20], the list of stopwords includes common English stopwords and the anonymisation tokes extracted, a relevant term should have frequency higher than 2, and it should not have an unlimited size so we choose a maximum of 4-grams and we varied the minimum n-gram between 1 and 2. Table 1 summarises the configuration of each experiment.

For scoring functions we choose TF-IDF as a baseline due to its common use in measuring relevant terms in a corpus. We also opted to have settings with one function from each category to measure how they behave independently, except the reference corpora category since using Wikipedia as background corpus could give a high number of false positive terms if used alone. Also, we included a configuration (TE_1 and TE_2) that has demonstrated positive results in previous experiments. And last, due to the positive results of the use of ComboBasic (TE_2 long) we experimented combining it with a reference corpora scoring function.

Table 1. Configuration of each automatic term recognition experiment

Experiment	n-gram		Scoring function				Ranking
	Min	Max	Frequency	Context	Reference corpora	Topic modelling	
TE baseline	1	4	tf-idf	-	-	-	Single
TE baseline long	2	4	tf-idf	-	-	-	Single
TE_1	1	4	tf-idf Residual Idf C Value ComboBasic	-	Weirdness	-	Voting
TE_1 long	2	4	tf-idf Residual Idf C Value ComboBasic	-	Weirdness	-	Voting
TE_2	1	4	ComboBasic	-	-	-	Single
TE_2 long	2	4	ComboBasic	-	-	-	Single
TE_3 long	2	4	ComboBasic	-	Relevance	-	Voting
TE_4	1	4	-	PostRankDC	-	-	Single
TE_4 long	2	4	-	PostRankDC	-	-	Single
TE_5	1	4	-	-	-	NTM	Single
TE_5 long	2	4	-	-	-	NTM	Single

Results and Discussion. The evaluation of the automatic term recognition experiments was based on the manual evaluation of a list of terms. A group of domain experts from Fidelity Investments who are familiar with financial industry taxonomies were asked to evaluate the relevance of each term to the financial domain according to a 5-point Likert-type scale (from irrelevant to very relevant). Any term rated as either 4 or 5 by a majority of annotators (i.e. at least four annotators) was considered a relevant term in the financial domain.

The list of terms for evaluation was generated by merging the top 100 terms extracted by each experiment, removing duplicates and ranking them using the Mean Reciprocal Rank [16]. The final list was then limited to a manageable number of terms (200 terms) sent for manual validation by a team of experts in the financial customer service domain. Since each term may appear in more than one experiment, Table 1 reports how much of the evaluation list is covered by each experiment. The result of each experiment is then evaluated using precision, i.e. the proportion of correct terms among those appearing in the evaluation set. Based on this evaluation, the experiments TE_2 log and TE_3 were the ones to provide the best results in our experiments (Table 2).

The positive results using the ComboBasic feature are mostly due to its ability to remove conversational words (such as "good morning", "thanks"). Because greetings do not appear in the corpus either as part of longer combination of words (e.g. "good morning" will not typically be a substring of any longer noun phrase), or as an aggregation of smaller and frequent terms (e.g. "morning" is not a frequent term in the corpus and "good" is not even considered a term for

Table 2. Evaluation of automatic term recognition experiments

Experiment	Coverage (%)	Precision (%)
TE baseline	36	48.6
TE baseline long	38.5	59.7
TE_1	47	50.0
TE_1 long	41.5	59.0
TE_2	30.5	54.1
TE_2 long	37.5	**65.3**
TE_3 long	37.5	**65.3**
TE_4	45	56.7
TE_4 long	30.5	62.3
TE_5	21.5	30.2
TE_5 long	21.5	30.2

being an adjective), then the requirements for frequency and term embeddedness expected by ComboBasic will be less likely to consider greetings as terms.

The drawback of using ComboBasic, on the other hand, is that it fails to retrieve terms of different lengths. In fact, only the experiment TE_5 retrieved a mix of single and multi-word terms. Also, other irrelevant terms that could have been removed by filtering out common out-of-domain terms using the weirdness feature (TE_3 long) did not have the expected result. The interpretation we give is that Wikipedia is not the most suitable corpus for this use case. Instead, in future work, we would like to experiment with customer service data in other domains so that we could remove terms that are common to customer service domain in general while keeping those that are specific to customer service in the financial domain. The difficulty lies in the availability of such datasets.

6.2 Taxonomy Construction

The objective of our taxonomy construction experiments are twofold: (i) to evaluate the combination of likelihood score and search methods that generate the best taxonomy structure; and (ii) to verify the impact of using an in-domain taxonomy as training data for the pairwise scoring function.

In order to separate the error generated by the automatic term recognition from the results of the taxonomy construction, we did not use the terms extracted previously. Instead, three manually constructed financial taxonomies provided by Fidelity Investments (financial products, financial sectors, and financial topics) were used to inform the terms to be used in each experiment. The products taxonomy was used to train the in-domain model for pairwise scoring while the remaining taxonomies were used as gold standard for evaluation.

First, two pairwise scoring models were trained using LibSVM [12], a library for support vector classification. The first model is trained on an out-of-domain taxonomy (food domain) and background corpus provided by the TexEval challenge [10]. The second model is trained using the products taxonomy and the pages in the Fidelity.com website as a corpus for extraction of features required by the Pairwise Scoring algorithm. All relationships between terms (c, d) appearing in the training taxonomy are given as positive examples (+1) and any other combination of terms is a negative example (−1). As the negative class sample is very large we perform negative sampling, with a fixed ratio of 5 negative examples to each positive one. The pairwise scoring uses the probability estimation in LibSVM by returning the probability that the class is +1 as $p(c \sqsubseteq d)$.

The workflow for comparison of taxonomy construction configurations using the different models is the following:

- *Step1.* The term extraction algorithm was used to extract from the chatlog dataset the frequency of each term in the gold standard T_{GOLD} taxonomy.
- *Step2.* The taxonomy construction algorithm was applied using the term frequencies from step 1, varying the configuration (Table 3) and model to be evaluated.

Table 3. Configuration of each taxonomy construction experiment

	Likelihood score		
Search	Transitive	Non-transitive	Bhattacharyya-Poisson
Greedy	TA_1	TA_2	TA_3
Beam	TA_4	TA_5	TA_6

The unit of analysis for our evaluation is each pair of concepts x and y where there is a relation $x \sqsubseteq y$. Note that transitivity was not taken into consideration, therefore only direct connection between terms was considered. The results of each run were evaluated using link precision as described in Eq. 14, where T is the resulting taxonomy provided by the taxonomy construction algorithm, and T_{GOLD} is the taxonomy provided as the expected result.

$$precision(T, T_{GOLD}) = \frac{|\{(x \sqsubseteq y) \in T \wedge (x \sqsubseteq y) \in T_{GOLD}\}|}{|\{(x \sqsubseteq y) \in T\}|} \quad (14)$$

Results and Discussion. The problem of taxonomy construction is very challenging, and previous evaluations such as TexEval [10] have only reported precision as high as 30%. One challenge is that the structure of multiple taxonomies in the same domain may vary considerably, therefore it is difficult to take advantage of the overall structure of one taxonomy when the best structure in another occasion may be completely different. Therefore, due to the multiple challenges in the automatic generation of a taxonomy structure (see [10]), a precision measure of 20% can already be considered as a strong result.

From the perspective of the logical connection between terms in the taxonomy, the best performing setting (Table 4) was the one using the Bhattacharyya-Poisson likelihood score function, greedy search strategy, and the in-domain model (using the products taxonomy as background knowledge). This setting consistently gave better results than all the others on the three taxonomies available. It is important to note, however, that only the sectors and topics taxonomies were used as gold standard since the products taxonomy was the one used as training data. The results using the products taxonomy are displayed only to contrast the impact of using an in-domain taxonomy versus using an out-of-domain one to train the pairwise scoring model. In fact, the results suggest that the choice of likelihood score and search method have a higher contribution to the quality of the final taxonomy than the domain of the taxonomy used to train the pairwise scoring algorithm. Therefore, we infer that the taxonomy construction framework can be successfully applied to other customer service domains where there is no background taxonomy to train the pairwise scoring model.

Table 4. Precision (%) of taxonomy construction algorithm

Search method	Likelihood score function	Out-of-Domain model			In-Domain model		
		Products	Sectors	Topics	Products	Sectors	Topics
Greedy	Transitive	16.86	11.25	11.41	7.28	8.75	7.38
	Non-Transitive	17.62	12.50	11.41	21.84	15.00	13.42
	BP	17.62	12.50	12.08	22.22	16.25	13.42
Beam	Transitive	4.21	1.25	1.34	3.83	1.25	0.67
	Non-Transitive	16.86	11.25	10.74	16.48	8.75	8.72
	BP	18.01	12.50	10.74	15.33	8.75	9.40

In general, the pairwise scoring model is just one element that impacts on the final taxonomy built from text. In some cases its use provided better results and in some cases not. Overall, the choices of likelihood score function and search strategy had a higher impact on the quality of the final taxonomy than the taxonomy provided for pairwise scoring training. Nonetheless, the use of a domain taxonomy as background knowledge showed between 10% and 25% improvement in the precision when using the non-transitive score or BP functions with the greedy search.

7 Conclusion and Future Work

In this paper, we presented a solution for the automatic extraction of taxonomies, motivated by its use by conversational agents, and applied this solution to an anonymised customer service dialogue data provided by Fidelity Investments.

We evaluated multiple methods for automatic term recognition, where ComboBasic was the most suitable term scoring function for the dataset used.

Also, we introduced multiple functions to evaluate the likelihood that a tree structure is a taxonomy and evaluated their efficacy in taxonomy extraction. Furthermore, our results suggest that despite our approach benefiting from in-domain data, it does not require the taxonomy used for training to be in the same domain of the business, which makes our solution applicable to customer service domains where a manually created taxonomy is not available.

In future work, we plan to explore: the use of customer service text datasets in other domains as background knowledge to remove greetings and other out-of-domain terms, the design of likelihood scores that take into consideration the desired graph structure of the taxonomy, and the application of the extracted taxonomy in a conversational agent.

References

1. Abdul-Kader, S.A., Woods, J.: Survey on chatbot design techniques in speech conversation systems. Int. J. Adv. Comput. Sci. Appl. **6**(7) (2015)
2. Ahmad, K., Gillam, L., Tostevin, L., et al.: University of surrey participation in TREC8: weirdness indexing for logical document extrapolation and retrieval (wilder). In: TREC, pp. 1–8 (1999)
3. Al-Zubaide, H., Issa, A.A.: Ontbot: ontology based chatbot. In: International Symposium on Innovations in Information and Communications Technology, pp. 7–12. IEEE (2011)
4. Ananiadou, S.: A methodology for automatic term recognition. In: COLING 1994, vol. 2: The 15th International Conference on Computational Linguistics. vol. 2 (1994)
5. Astrakhantsev, N.: Automatic term acquisition from domain-specific text collection by using wikipedia. Proc. Inst. Syst. Program. **26**(4), 7–20 (2014)
6. Astrakhantsev, N.: Methods and software for terminology extraction from domain-specific text collection. Ph.D. thesis, Ph. D. thesis, Institute for System Programming of Russian Academy of Sciences (2015)
7. Athreya, R.G., Ngonga Ngomo, A.C., Usbeck, R.: Enhancing community interactions with data-driven chatbots-the DBpedia chatbot. In: Companion of the The Web Conference 2018 on The Web Conference 2018, pp. 143–146. International World Wide Web Conferences Steering Committee (2018)
8. Bhattacharyya, A.: On a measure of divergence between two statistical populations defined by their probability distributions. Bull. Calcutta Math. Soc. **35**, 99–109 (1943)
9. Bordea, G.: Domain adaptive extraction of topical hierarchies for expertise mining. Ph.D. thesis (2013)
10. Bordea, G., Lefever, E., Buitelaar, P.: SemEval-2016 task 13: taxonomy extraction evaluation (TexEval-2). In: Proceedings of the 10th International Workshop on Semantic Evaluation (SemEval-2016), pp. 1081–1091 (2016)
11. Buitelaar, P., Bordea, G., Polajnar, T.: Domain-independent term extraction through domain modelling. In: The 10th International Conference on Terminology and Artificial Intelligence (TIA 2013), Paris, France. 10th International Conference on Terminology and Artificial Intelligence (2013)
12. Chang, C.C., Lin, C.J.: LIBSVM: a library for support vector machines. ACM Trans. intell. Syst. Technol. (TIST) **2**(3), 27 (2011)

13. Church, K.W., Gale, W.A.: Poisson mixtures. Nat. Lang. Eng. **1**(2), 163–190 (1995)
14. Cleuziou, G., Moreno, J.G.: QASSIT at SemEval-2016 Task 13: on the integration of semantic vectors in pretopological spaces for lexical taxonomy acquisition. In: 10th International Workshop on Semantic Evaluation (SemEval-2016), pp. 1315–1319 (2016)
15. Cram, D., Daille, B.: Terminology extraction with term variant detection. In: Proceedings of ACL-2016 System Demonstrations, pp. 13–18 (2016)
16. Craswell, N.: Mean reciprocal rank. In: Encyclopedia of Database Systems, pp. 1703–1703 (2009)
17. Fu, R., Guo, J., Qin, B., Che, W., Wang, H., Liu, T.: Learning semantic hierarchics via word embeddings. In: Proceedings of the 2014 Conference of the Association for Computational Linguistics, pp. 1199–1209 (2014)
18. Harris, Z.S.: Distributional structure. Word **10**(2–3), 146–162 (1954)
19. Huang, J., Zhou, M., Yang, D.: Extracting chatbot knowledge from online discussion forums. IJCAI **7**, 423–428 (2007)
20. Hulth, A.: Enhancing linguistically oriented automatic keyword extraction. In: Proceedings of HLT-NAACL 2004: Short Papers (2004)
21. Li, S., Li, J., Song, T., Li, W., Chang, B.: A novel topic model for automatic term extraction. In: Proceedings of the 36th International ACM SIGIR Conference on Research and Development in Information Retrieval, pp. 885–888. ACM (2013)
22. Miller, G.: WordNet: An Electronic Lexical Database. MIT Press, Cambridge (1998)
23. Panchenko, A., et al.: TAXI at SemEval-2016 Task 13: a taxonomy induction method based on lexico-syntactic patterns, substrings and focused crawling. In: 10th International Workshop on Semantic Evaluation (SemEval-2016) (2016)
24. Peñas, A., Verdejo, F., Gonzalo, J.: Corpus-based terminology extraction applied to information access. In: Proceedings of Corpus Linguistics. vol. 2001, p. 458. Citeseer, Priceton (2001)
25. Pennington, J., Socher, R., Manning, C.: GloVe: global vectors for word representation. In: Proceedings of the 2014 Conference on Empirical Methods in Natural Language Processing (EMNLP), pp. 1532–1543 (2014)
26. Sánchez-Díaz, X., Ayala-Bastidas, G., Fonseca-Ortiz, P., Garrido, L.: A knowledge-based methodology for building a conversational chatbot as an intelligent tutor. In: Batyrshin, I., Martínez-Villaseñor, M.L., Ponce Espinosa, H.E. (eds.) MICAI 2018. LNCS (LNAI), vol. 11289, pp. 165–175. Springer, Cham (2018). https://doi.org/10.1007/978-3-030-04497-8_14
27. Sarkar, R., McCrae, J.P., Buitelaar, P.: A supervised approach to taxonomy extraction using word embeddings. In: Proceedings of the Eleventh International Conference on Language Resources and Evaluation (LREC-2018) (2018)
28. Snow, R., Jurafsky, D., Ng, A.Y.: Learning syntactic patterns for automatic hypernym discovery. In: Advances in Neural Information Processing Systems, pp. 1297–1304 (2005)
29. Spasić, I., Greenwood, M., Preece, A., Francis, N., Elwyn, G.: Flexiterm: a flexible term recognition method. J. Biomed. Semant. **4**(1), 27 (2013)
30. Tan, L., Bond, F., van Genabith, J.: USAAR at SemEval-2016 Task 13: Hyponym endocentricity. In: 10th International Workshop on Semantic Evaluation (SemEval-2016) (2016)

31. Zhang, Z., Gao, J., Ciravegna, F.: Jate 2.0: Java automatic term extraction with apache SOLR. In: Proceedings of the Tenth International Conference on Language Resources and Evaluation (LREC-2016) (2016)
32. Zhang, Z., Iria, J., Brewster, C., Ciravegna, F.: A comparative evaluation of term recognition algorithms. In: Proceedings of the Sixth International Conference on Language Resources and Evaluation (LREC-2008), vol. 5 (2008)

An Ontology Alignment Approach Combining Word Embedding and the Radius Measure

Molka Tounsi Dhouib[1,2(✉)], Catherine Faron Zucker[1(✉)], and Andrea G. B. Tettamanzi[1(✉)]

[1] University Cote d'Azur, Inria, CNRS, I3S, Sophia Antipolis, France
{dhouib,faron,tettamanzi}@i3s.unice.fr
[2] Silex France, Gentilly, France

Abstract. Ontology alignment plays a key role in achieving interoperability on the semantic Web. Inspired by the success of word embedding techniques in several NLP tasks, we propose a new ontology alignment approach based on the combination of word embedding and the radius measure. We tested our system on the OAEI (http://oaei.ontologymatching.org/) conference track and then applied it to aligning ontologies in a real-world case study. The experimental results show that using word embedding and the radius measure make it possible to determine, with good accuracy, not only equivalence relations, but also hierarchical relations between concepts.

Keywords: Ontology alignment · Word embedding

1 Introduction

The Silex[1] company develops a SaaS sourcing tool for the identification of the service providers that are best suited to meet some service requests. The Silex platform allows companies to provide a textual description of their professional activities, their offers and the services they are looking for. The work presented in this paper has been carried out in the context of a collaboration between Silex and the I3S research laboratory, to add a semantic layer to the Silex B2B platform, in order to be able to automatically process the descriptions of service requests and improve the recommendation of relevant providers. An ontology engineering work has been conducted to semantically annotate the text descriptions of companies, offers, and service requests, with three kinds of knowledge: skills, occupations, and business sectors. We developed the Silex ontology by combining several meta-data repositories: ESCO,[2] ROME,[3] Cigref,[4]

[1] https://www.Silex-france.com/Silex/.
[2] https://ec.europa.eu/esco/portal/home.
[3] http://www.pole-emploi.org/accueil/mot-cle.html?tagId=94b2eaf6-d7bd-4244-bddc-01415605563b.
[4] http://cigref.hr-ingenium.com/accueil.aspx.

M. Acosta et al. (Eds.): SEMANTiCS 2019, LNCS 11702, pp. 191–197, 2019.
https://doi.org/10.1007/978-3-030-33220-4_14

NAF,[5] UNSPSC[6], Kompass[7] and an internal `Silex` business sectors repository. Currently, the `Silex` ontology covers only the Computer Science (CS) field [1]. Our aim now is to automatically align the entire vocabularies to extend the Silex ontology to all business sectors.

In this paper, we present a new approach to ontology alignment based on word embedding and inspired by an existing proposals [6]. We consider word embedding to represent concepts and we use it to compute not only equivalence relations between concepts but also hierarchical relations. We report our experiments on several open datasets from the Ontology Alignment Evaluation Initiative (OAEI) benchmark and the `Silex` use case.

This paper is organized as follows: related work is discussed in Sect. 2. Section 3 describes our algorithm for ontology alignment. Section 4 reports and discusses the results of our experiments on the Silex use case. Section 5 draws some conclusions and discusses our perspectives as future work.

2 Related Work

The main issue when using several ontologies is to deal with their semantic heterogeneity when combining them: each ontology has its own designer, its own knowledge area and its own level of details. Ontology alignment is thus a crucial yet difficult task to achieve interoperability on the semantic Web. It aims to discover the correspondences between the entities of different ontologies, and express them as equivalence or hierarchical relations.

There are two main ontology alignment techniques [2]: (i) Element-level techniques are meant to discover correspondences by calculating the surface similarity between lexical information of entities (usually labels), (ii) Structure-level techniques rely on the analysis of the neighbourhood of two entities in order to determine their similarity. Both techniques suffer from their weakness in capturing the semantics of lexical information of entities, and have been extended by exploiting external information sources, such as WordNet or Wikipedia. However, these auxiliary resources still suffer from the incompleteness and non exhaustiveness of their entries. To overcome this problem, the approach presented in [6] uses word embedding to preserve the semantic and syntactic similarities between words. This work mainly extract the lexical information (names, labels and comments of an entity) and search equivalence relations between this informations based on word embeddings similarity. In our work, we have been inspired by [6] to calculate the similarites between entities based only on their labels. We extended this approach by using cluster's radius to find equivalence and hierarchical relations between concepts.

[5] https://www.insee.fr/fr/information/2406147.
[6] https://www.unspsc.org/.
[7] http://www.kompass-international.com/Corporate/home.html.

3 Overview of Our Approach to Ontology Alignment

Our alignment process is based on a set of rules exploiting the word embedding similarity to discover the alignment. Our process is divided into four successive steps described in the following subsections. Our system supports two types of input (OWL ontologies and SKOS vocabulary), and two languages (French and English). But we can't work with both languages at the same time as we have a different word embedding model per language.

3.1 Extracting Lexical and Structural Information from Ontologies

We started by extracting two types of information from inputs: (i) lexical information (e.g., labels of concepts) and (ii) structural information (e.g., to associate the labels of all child entities to their parent entities). To achieve this, the two inputs (OWL or SKOS) are parsed with rdflib and queried with a SPARQL query. The Listing 1.1 shows an example of queries that handle with SKOS input and french language. The same query is used for owl ontologies by replacing *rdfs:label* instead of *skos:prefLabel* to extract the label of the class or the properties, and *rdfs:subClass* or *rfs:subproperties* instead of *skos:broader* to get the hierarchical relation between classes or properties.

Listing 1.1. SPARQL query to extract lexical and structural information from skos vocabulary

```
SELECT ?uri ?label
       (group_concat(DISTINCT ?mid_label; separator=":")
       AS ?lineage)
WHERE {
   ?uri skos:prefLabel ?label FILTER (lang(?label)='fr')
   ?uri ^skos:broader* ?mid. ?mid skos:prefLabel ?mid_label.
   FILTER (lang(?mid_label)='fr')
} GROUP BY ?mid ORDER BY count(?label)
```

3.2 Computing Word Embedding Representations of Concepts

The second step of our approach is to compute the vector representations of concepts. We used a pre-trained word vectors for French and English, learned using fastText.[8] The French model contains 1,152,449 tokens, and the English model contains one million tokens. Both of them are mapped to 300-dimensional vectors [3].

The vector representation of a concept is constructed by averaging the word embedding vectors along each dimension of all the terms contained in its label and occurring in the dictionary $conceptWordEmbedding(c) = \frac{1}{n}\sum_{i=1}^{n} w_i$, where n is the number of words in the dictionary occurring in the label of a concept c and $w_i \in \mathbb{R}^{300}$ denotes the word embedding vector of the ith word. If a term does not appear in the dictionary, it is just ignored.

[8] https://fasttext.cc/docs/en/pretrained-vectors.html.

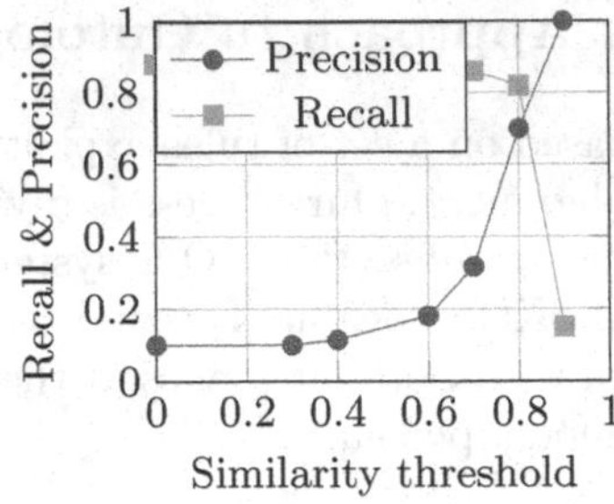

Fig. 1. Precision and recall as a function of the similarity threshold.

In the case of structural information, the vector representation of a cluster is given by averaging the word embedding vector representation of the label of the root concept (which is itself an average) with the vector representations of its child concepts $clusterWordEmbedding(cl) = \frac{1}{k}\sum_{i=1}^{k} conceptWordEmbedding(c_i)$, where k is the number of concepts in cluster cl.

3.3 Searching for Matching Concepts

We match every concept in the source ontology O_1 with the similar concept in the target ontology O_2 using the cosine similarity between vector representations of concept and cluster. The correspondence is then added to the alignment list based on the similarity threshold. Our algorithm aims at collecting all the possible correspondences between concepts. We empirically chose the threshold, by varying its value and calculating for each one the recall and precision measures. Figure 1 shows that an optimal trade-off of performance is achieved by setting the similarity threshold equal to 0.8.

3.4 Refining the Nature of the Relationship Between Two Matching Concepts

The result of the previous step is a list of matching concepts whose relationship must be made more precise. To link two concepts that are sufficiently similar, we used *skos:closeMatch* for SKOS and *owl:sameAs* for OWL. To define a hierarchical mapping link between two concepts, we used *skos:broader* or *skos:narrower* for SKOS and *rdfs:subClassOf* or *rdfs:subPropertiesOf* for OWL.

This relationship between two matching concepts is refined by comparing the radii of their respective embedding vector clusters formed mainly using structural information. The radius of a cluster is the maximum distance between all the vector representing the terms and the centroid. We define the radius of a cluster of concepts as the standard deviation of their cosine dissimilarity with respect to the centroid: $radius = \sqrt{\frac{1}{N}\sum_{i=1}^{N}\left(1 - \frac{w_i \cdot \overline{w}}{|w_i| \cdot |\overline{w}|}\right)^2}$, where $w_i \in \mathbb{R}^{300}$ is the vector representation of the $i$the concept in the cluster, N is the size of the cluster, and $\overline{w} \in \mathbb{R}^{300}$ is the centroid of the cluster, defined as $\overline{w} = \frac{1}{N}\sum_{i=1}^{N} w_i$. We suppose that the cluster whose result has the lowest average distance between a point and the centroid is in broader relation with the cluster which have the biggest radius. We decide of the relationship holding between two similar concepts by comparing their radii based on the following rules:

$$|radius(C1) - radius(C2)| < 0.1 \Rightarrow C1\ closeMatch\ C2 \quad (1)$$

$$|radius(C1) - radius(C2)| > 0.1 \Rightarrow C1\ narrowMatch\ C2 \wedge C2\ broadMatch\ C1 \quad (2)$$

4 Experiments

To evaluate the effectiveness of our approach, we performed experiments on two alignment datasets: (i) Task-oriented complex alignment on conference organisation and (ii) the Silex use case. The performances of our approach are measured by calculating precision, recall and F-measure [4].

4.1 Experiments on Task-Oriented Complex Alignment on Conference Organisation

To validate the proposed approach, we experimented it on a conference complex alignment benchmark[9], [10] for ontology merging, which has been constructed within the framework of the OAEI. This data set contains 57 correspondences made on five owl ontologies. Following the evaluation process presented in [5], we have taken into account only the alignments that exist in the complex data set and we ignored the alignment of simple data set. We assume that if our system is able to find the correct match between a proposed list, we consider that the entire proposed list is correct. This decision is justified by the fact that our system was designed to support end-users by presenting a list of possible matches. We compared our matching results with the results of three state-of-the-art systems that were mentioned in [5]: Our system clearly outperforms the others on this benchmark, with a precision value equals to O.89 and recall value equals to 0.69 compared to 0.83, and 0.13 for the best state-of-the-art system. Many reasons can explain our result: (i) the cosine similarity between classes is much smaller, as a consequence this match gets discarded than the threshold (cosine similarity ('chair main', 'demo chair' = 0)). (ii) Our system is not designed to test hierarchical relations between two leaf nodes. This type of relationship must pass through the structural information to calculate the radius and, thus, infer the relationship. (iii) Based on Eq. 1, our system can assign equivalence relation instead of hierarchical relation because the threshold of the difference of radius between two classes is smaller than 0.1.

[9] Thieblin, Elodie (2019): Task-oriented complex alignments on conference organisation. figshare. Dataset.

[10] https://doi.org/10.6084/m9.figshare.4986368.v8.

4.2 Experiments on the Silex Use Case

The second data set used in this evaluation is the vocabularies gathered for the Silex use case in the CS field: we tried to match (i) ESCO (160 concepts to represent occupations) to Cigref (42 concepts), (ii) ESCO to ROME (117 concepts), (iii) NAF to kompass (574 concepts) and (iv) NAF to Silex activity domains (14 concepts). A gold standard of each matching case was provided by an expert in the Silex company. Depending on the vocabularies to be aligned, the precision value ranges between (i) 0.71 and 0.8 for the closeMatch relation, (ii) 0.7 and 0.83 for the narrowMatch relation and (iii) 0.73 and 1 for the broadMatch relation. On the other hand, the recall value ranges between (i) 0.6 and 0.95 for the closeMatch relation, (ii) 0.69 and 1 for the narrowMatch relation and (iii) 0.68 and 1 for the broadMatch relation. For example, the ROME concept "computer developer" is stated to be broader than the ESCO concept of "Applications programmers" which is in broad relation with the ESCO concept of "Usability designer", "System programmer", "System developer".

5 Conclusion

In this paper, we reported the results of a novel ontology alignment method, capable of distinguishing between equivalence and hierarchical relationships. Our first challenge was to answer on the real-world use case encountered by the Silex company. These results show that the proposed approach to ontology alignment based on a vector representation of the concepts to be matched is promising. As future work, we aim at defining a specific set of pre-trained word vectors that best covers the Silex B2B use case. We also aim at performing an empirical study to define the optimal threshold for radius difference.

References

1. Dhouib, M., Zucker, C.F., Tettamanzi, A.: Construction d'ontologie pour le domaine du sourcing. In: 29es Journées Francophones d'Ingénierie des Connaissances, IC 2018, pp. 137–144 (2018)
2. Euzenat, J., Shvaiko, P., et al.: Ontology Matching, vol. 18. Springer, Heidelberg (2007). https://doi.org/10.1007/978-3-540-49612-0
3. Mikolov, T., Sutskever, I., Chen, K., Corrado, G.S., Dean, J.: Distributed representations of words and phrases and their compositionality. In: Advances in Neural Information Processing Systems, pp. 3111–3119 (2013)
4. Ochieng, P., Kyanda, S.: Large-scale ontology matching: state-of-the-art analysis. ACM Comput. Surv. (CSUR) **51**(4), 75 (2018)
5. Thiéblin, É., Haemmerlé, O., Hernandez, N., Trojahn, C.: Task-oriented complex ontology alignment: two alignment evaluation sets. In: Gangemi, A., et al. (eds.) ESWC 2018. LNCS, vol. 10843, pp. 655–670. Springer, Cham (2018). https://doi.org/10.1007/978-3-319-93417-4_42
6. Zhang, Y., et al.: Ontology matching with word embeddings. In: Sun, M., Liu, Y., Zhao, J. (eds.) CCL/NLP-NABD -2014. LNCS (LNAI), vol. 8801, pp. 34–45. Springer, Cham (2014). https://doi.org/10.1007/978-3-319-12277-9_4

Ontology Design Rules Based on Comparability via Particular Relations

Philippe A. Martin[1,2(✉)], Olivier Corby[3], and Catherine Faron Zucker[3]

[1] EA2525 LIM, ESIROI I.T., University of La Réunion, 97490 Sainte Clotilde, France
Philippe.Martin@univ-reunion.fr
[2] School of I.C.T., Griffith University, Gold Coast, Australia
[3] Wimmics Team, INRIA/Université CoTe d'Azur, CNRS, I3S, Sophia Antipolis, France
olivier.corby@inria.fr, faron@i3s.unice.fr

Abstract. The difficulty of representing and organizing knowledge in reasonably complete ways raises at least two research questions: "how to check that particular relations are systematically used not just whenever possible but whenever relevant for knowledge providers?" and "how to extend best practices, ontology patterns or methodologies advocating the systematic use of particular relations and, at the same time, automatize the checking of compliance with these methods?". As an answer, this article proposes a generic "ontology design rule" (ODR). A general formulation of this generic ODR is: in a given KB, for each pair of knowledge base objects (types or individuals) of a given set chosen by the user of this ODR, there should be *either* statements connecting these objects by relations of particular given types *or* statements negating such relations. This article further specifies this ODR and shows its interests for subtype relations and other transitive relations, e.g. part relations and specialization relations with genus & differentia. This article shows how this ODR can be implemented via OWL and SPARQL, at least for common simple cases (and, generically, via an higher-order logic based language).

Keywords: Ontology design patterns · Ontology completeness · OWL · SPARQL

1 Introduction

Representing and organizing knowledge within or across knowledge bases (KBs) is a fundamental and difficult task for knowledge sharing and inferencing, and thereby for knowledge retrieval and exploitation. At least three kinds of research avenues (relevant to refer to in this article) guide this task. The first are ontologies made for reuse purposes (with methodologies implicitly or explicitly based on these ontologies, e.g. the Ontoclean methodology): foundational ontologies such as DOLCE and BFO; task-oriented ones such as OWL-S; general ones such as DBpedia and Schema.org; domain-oriented ones such as those from BioPortal. The second are catalogs of best practices

M. Acosta et al. (Eds.): SEMANTiCS 2019, LNCS 11702, pp. 198–214, 2019.
https://doi.org/10.1007/978-3-030-33220-4_15

[1, 2] and ontology patterns [3, 4] or anti-patterns [5, 6]. The third are ontology/KB evaluation criteria and measures [7], e.g. for knowledge connectedness, precision, consistency, conciseness and completeness. The results of these three kinds of research avenues are especially helpful for building reusable ontologies.

These three kinds of research avenues advocate the use of relations of particular types between *objects* of particular types. In the RDF terminology, one would say that these three kinds of research avenues advocate the use of properties to connect *resources* of particular classes – e.g. the use of subClassOf or equivalentClass relations between classes or other objects, whenever this is relevant. *However*, often, only a knowledge provider knows when it is relevant to use a particular property. This limits the possibilities of checking or guiding the use of the advocated properties. *Furthermore*, it may also be useful that the knowledge provider represents when the advocated properties do not or cannot occur. E.g., representing disjointWith or complementOf relations between classes to express that subClassOf or equivalentClass relations cannot occur between these classes has many advantages that Sect. 2 illustrates. Using all these relations is especially useful between top-level classes since many inference engines can exploit the combination of these relations, e.g. via inheritance mechanisms. *Finally*, checking that particular relations are represented as either existing or forbidden can be done automatically. *Thus*, as an answer to the research questions "how to check that particular relations are systematically used not simply whenever this is possible but whenever this is relevant for the knowledge providers?" and "how to extend best practices, ontology patterns or methodologies that advocate the systematic use of particular relations, and make the compliance with these methods easier to check?", this article proposes the following *generic "ontology design rule" (ODR)*. A first general formulation of this generic ODR is: *in a given KB, for each pair of objects of a given set chosen by the user of this ODR, there should be either statements connecting these objects by relations of particular given types or statements negating such relations, i.e. expressing that these relations do not or cannot occur in the given KB.* A negated relation can be expressed directly via a negated statement or indirectly, e.g. via a disjointWith relation that forbids the existence of such a relation.

In its more precise version given in the next page, we call this ODR the "comparability via particular relation types" ODR, or simply the "comparability ODR". We call it an ODR, not a pattern nor a KB evaluation criteria/measure because this is something in between. As above explained, it is always automatically checkable. It is also reusable for evaluating a KB for example by applying it to all its objects and dividing the number of successful cases by the number of objects. An example of KB evaluation criteria that can be generalized by a reuse of this ODR is the "schema-based coverage" criteria of [1] which measures the percentage of objects using the relations that they should or could use according to schemas or relation signatures. Examples of methodologies, best practices or ontology patterns that can be generalized via the use of this ODR are those advocating the use of tree structures or of genus & differentia when organizing or defining types. (Sections 2.3 and 3.3 detail this last point.)

Before formulating this ODR more precisely, it seems interesting to further detail its application to the OWL properties subClassOf or equivalentClass – along with those that negate or exclude them, e.g. disjointWith and complementOf. Using all these properties whenever relevant, as this applied ODR encourages, will for example lead the authors of a KB to organize the direct subtypes of each class – or at least each top-level class – into "complete sets of exclusive subtypes" (each of such sets being a subclass partition, or in other words, a disjoint union of subtypes equivalent to the subtyped class), and/or "incomplete sets of exclusive subtypes", and/or "(in-)complete sets of subtypes that are not exclusive but still different and not relatable by subClassOf relations", etc. The more systematic the organization, the more a test of whether a class is *subClassOf_or_equivalent* (i.e. is subClassOf, equivalentClass or sameAs) another class will lead to a *true/false result, not an "unknown" result*. In other words, the more such a test will lead to a true/false result without the use of "negation as failure" (e.g. via the "closed-world assumption": any statement not represented in the KB is considered to be false) or the use of the "unique name assumption" (with which different identifiers are supposed to refer to different things). Since most inferences are based on such subClassOf_or_equivalent tests, the more systematic the organization, the more inferences will be possible without having to use negation as failure. This is interesting since using negation as failure implies making an assumption about the content of a KB whereas adding subClassOf or disjointWith relations means adding information to a KB.

The next two sections illustrate some of the many advantages of the more systematic organization resulting from the application of this ODR: for inferencing or querying, for avoiding what could have otherwise been implicit redundancies or inconsistencies and, more generally, for improving the completeness, consistency and precision of a KB. These advantages are not restricted to subClassOf_or_equivalent relations. They apply to all *specializationOf_or_equivalent* relations, i.e. specializationOf relations (they generalize subClassOf relations), equivalence relations or sameAs relations. As we shall see, most of these advantages also apply to other transitive relations such as *partOf_or_equivalent* (i.e. isSubPartOf, equivalentClass or sameAs). We call "speciali-zation of an object" any other object that represents or refers to more information on the same referred object. This covers all subtype relations but also specialization relations between individuals, e.g. between the statements "some cars are red" and "John's car is dark red". We call "statement" a relation or a set of connected relations.

We adopt the following "comparability" related definitions. Two objects are "*comparable via a relation of a particular type*" (or, more concisely, "comparable via a particular relation type") if they are *either identical (sameAs), equivalent (by intension, not extension) or connected by a relation of this type*. Two objects are "uncomparable via a relation of a particular relation type" (or, more concisely, "uncomparable via a particular property") if they are different and if some statement in the KB forbids a relation of this type between these two objects. Given these definitions, the comparability ODR can be defined as testing whether "*each object (in the KB or a part of the KB selected by the user of this ODR) is defined as either comparable or uncomparable to each other object* (or *at least some object*, if the user prefers) *via each of the tested relation types*". In a nutshell, the comparability ODR checks that between particular selected objects there is "either a comparability or an uncomparability via particular relations". This ODR does not rely on particular kinds of KBs or inference engines but powerful engines may be relevant for checks if they infer more relations.

Stronger versions of this ODR can be used. E.g., for a more organized KB, some users may wish to have "either comparability or *strong* uncomparability" via relations of particular types between any two objects. Two objects are "strongly uncomparable via a relation of a particular type" if they are different and if some statement in the KB forbids the existence of a relation of this type between the two objects *as well as* between their specializations. E.g., disjoint classes are strongly uncomparable since they cannot have shared instances or shared subclasses (except for `owl:Nothing`).

A more general version of this ODR could also be defined by using "equivalence by intension or extension" instead of simply "equivalence by intension". In this article, "equivalence" means "equivalence by intension" and "specialization" is also "specialization by intension". This article also assumes that the equivalence or specialization relations (or their negations) which are automatically detectable by the used inference engine are made explicit by KB authors and thus can be exploited via SPARQL queries. In a description logics based KB, this can be achieved by performing type classification and individual categorization before checking the ODR.

Figure 1 shows a simple graphic user interface for selecting various *options or variants* for this ODR. With the shown selected items (cf. the blue items in Fig. 1 and the words in italics in the rest of this sentence), this interface generates a function call or query to check that each object (in the *default KB*) which is instance of *owl:Thing* is either *comparable or uncomparable* via *specialization* relations and *part* relations to *each* other object in the *default KB*. Figure 1 shows a function call. After the conversion of its last three parameters into more formal types, a similar call can be made to a generic function. [8] is an extended version and on-line companion article for this one. In its appendix, [8] defines this generic function and the types it exploits. To achieve this, these definitions are written in a higher-order logic based language.

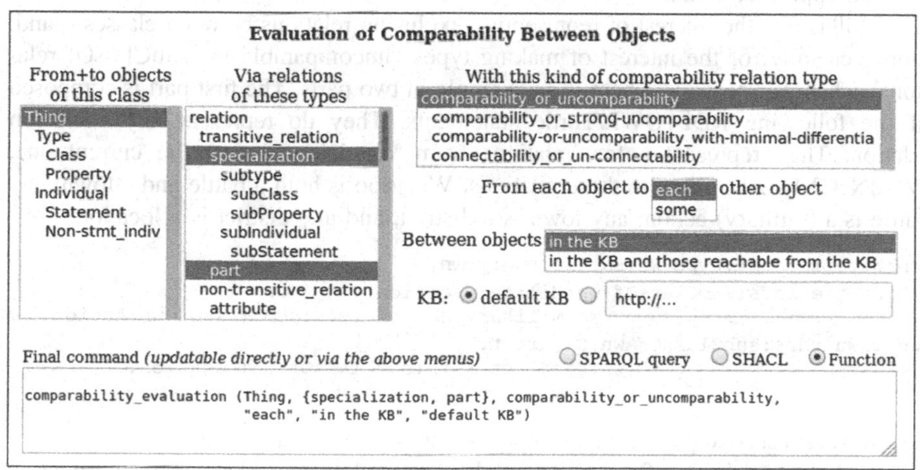

Fig. 1. A simple interface for object comparability/connectability evaluation (Color figure online)

With the *comparability_or_uncomparability* option (hence with the *comparability* ODR), equivalence or sameAs relations are always exploited in addition to the specified relations. When it is not relevant to also exploit equivalence or sameAs relations, the *connectability_or_un-connectability* option shown in Fig. 1 should be selected.

The next two sections show the interests of this ODR for, respectively, (i) subtype relations, and (ii) other relations, e.g. part relations and specialization relations with genus & differentia. When relevant, these sections present type definitions in OWL, as well as SPARQL queries or update operations, to illustrate how this ODR can be implemented. Figure 1 shows that SHACL (a constraint language proposed by the W3C) may also be exploited when its expressiveness is sufficient to express the constraint that needs to be represented. However, this exploitation is not described in this article. Section 4 provides more comparisons with other works and concludes.

2 Comparability of Types via Subtype Relations

2.1 Representation via OWL

In this document, OWL refers to OWL-2 (OWL-2 DL or OWL-2 Full) [9] and OWL entities are prefixed by "`owl:`". All the types that we propose in this article are in http://www.webkb.org/kb/it/o_knowledge/d_odr_content/sub/ and the "`sub`" namespace is here used to abbreviate this URL. Unless otherwise specified, the syntax used for defining these types is Turtle, and the syntax used for defining queries or update operations is SPARQL. SPARQL uses Turtle for representing relations. For clarity purposes, identifiers for relation types have a lowercase initial while other identifiers have an uppercase initial.

To illustrate the interest of representing exclusion relations between classes – and, more generally, of the interest of making types "uncomparable via subClassOf relations" whenever possible – here is an example in two parts. The first part is composed of the following RDF+OWL/Turtle statements. They do represent any exclusion relation. They represent a few relations from WordNet 1.3 (not the current one, WordNet 3.1). According to these relations, Waterloo is both a battle and a town, any battle is a (military) action, any town is a district, and any district is a location.

```
wn:Waterloo rdf:type wn:Battle, wn:Town.
wn:Battle rdfs:subClassOf wn:Military_action.
                          wn:Military_action rdfs:subClassOf wn:Action.
wn:Town rdfs:subClassOf wn:District.
                        wn:District rdfs:subClassOf wn:Location.
```

Now, as a second part of the example, a disjointWith relation is added between two top-level classes: the one for actions and the one for locations. This exclusion relation between actions and locations has not been made explicit in WordNet but is at least compatible with the informal definitions associated to categories in WordNet. *Given all these relations*, an OWL inference engine (that handles disjointWith relations) *detects* that the categorization of Waterloo as both a battle and a town is *inconsistent*. As illustrated in Sect. 2.3, many other possible problems in WordNet 1.3 were similarly detected. Most of them do not exist anymore in the current WordNet.

```
wn:Action owl:disjointWith wn:Location.
```

OWL DL is sufficient for representing statements implying that particular *classes* are "comparable via subClassOf (relations)" or "strongly uncomparable via subClassOf". For this second case, which amounts to state that two classes are disjoint, the properties `owl:AllDisjointClasses`, `owl:complementOf`, `owl:disjointWith` and `owl:disjointUnionOf` can be used. OWL Full [9] is necessary for setting `owl:differentFrom` relations between *classes*, and hence, as shown in the next page, for defining the property `sub:different_and_not_subClassOf` as a sub-property of `owl:differentFrom`. In turn, this property is necessary for representing statements implying that particular classes are *weakly uncomparable*, i.e. uncomparable but not strongly uncomparable (hence not disjointWith nor complementOf). OWL Full is also necessary for defining the properties `sub:different_and_not_equivalentClass` and `sub:proper-subClassOf` (alias, `sub:subClassOf_and_not-equivalentClass`). With all the above cited types, it is possible for KB authors to express any relationship of "comparability or uncomparability via subClassOf".

OWL inference engines generally cannot exploit OWL Full and hence do not enforce nor exploit the semantics of definitions requiring OWL Full. When inference engines do not accept OWL Full definitions, the above cited "sub:" properties have to be solely *declared* (as being properties) instead of being *defined* via relations (hence by a logic formula). However, when inference engines do not accept or do not exploit OWL Full definitions, the loss of inferencing possibilities due to the non-exploitation of the above cited "sub:" properties is often small. When the goal is simply to detect whether the comparability ODR is followed, if the SPARQL query proposed in the next subsection is used to achieve that goal, it does not matter whether the above cited "sub:" properties are declared or defined.

Making *every* pair of classes in a KB comparable or uncomparable via subClassOf is cumbersome without the use of properties that create (in-)complete sets of (exclusive) subclasses. We propose such properties, e.g. `sub:complete_set_of_uncomparable-subClasses`, `sub:incomplete_set_of_uncomparable-subClasses` and `sub:proper-superClassOf_uncomparable_with_its_siblings`. Such complex properties cannot be defined in OWL. However, as illustrated below, SPARQL update operations can be written to replace the use of these complex properties by the use of simpler properties that OWL inference engines can exploit

```
sub:proper-subClassOf  rdfs:subPropertyOf  rdfs:subClassOf;
  owl:propertyDisjointWith owl:equivalentClass .
#a "proper subClass" is a "strict subClass" (a direct or indirect one)

sub:proper-subPropertyOf  rdfs:subPropertyOf  rdfs:subPropertyOf;
  owl:propertyDisjointWith owl:equivalentProperty .

sub:different_and_not_subClassOf  rdfs:subPropertyOf  owl:differentFrom;
  owl:propertyDisjointWith  rdfs:subClassOf .

sub:different_and_not_equivalentClass rdfs:subPropertyOf owl:differentFrom;
  owl:propertyDisjointWith  owl:equivalentClass .

sub:proper-superClassOf  owl:inverseOf  sub:proper-subClassOf .
sub:proper-superClassOf_uncomparable_with_its_siblings
  rdfs:subPropertyOf  sub:proper-superClassOf .  #partial definition only

#Example of a SPARQL update operation to replace the use of
# sub:proper-superClassOf_uncomparable_with_its_siblings relations
# by simpler relations:
DELETE
{ ?c sub:proper-superClassOf_uncomparable_with_its_siblings ?sc1, ?sc2 }
INSERT { ?c sub:proper-superClassOf ?sc1, ?sc2 .
         ?sc1 sub:different_and_not_subClassOf ?sc2 .
         ?sc2 sub:different_and_not_subClassOf ?sc1 }
WHERE{?c sub:proper-superClassOf_uncomparable_with_its_siblings ?sc1, ?sc2
      FILTER (?sc1 != ?sc2) }
```

Similarly, to state that particular properties are (strongly or at least weakly) "uncomparable via `rdfs:subPropertyOf` relations", OWL DL is sufficient. For strong uncomparability, `owl:propertyDisjointWith` relations can be used. Defining that particular properties are only *weakly uncomparable*, i.e. uncomparable but not strongly uncomparable, is possible in OWL Full, exactly as for subClassOf relations: to define these properties, it is sufficient to replace every occurence of "class" by "property" in the above code. As for classes too, if these "sub:" properties are only declared instead of being defined, the loss of inferencing possibilities is small.

2.2 Checking via SPARQL

Using SPARQL (1.1) [10] to check the "comparability of classes via subClassOf relations" means finding each class that does not follow this ODR, i.e. that each class that is *neither* comparable *nor* uncomparable via subClassOf relations to *each/some other* class in selected KBs ("each/some" depending on what the user wishes to test).

The next page shows a SPARQL query for the "*each* other class" choice, followed by a SPARQL query for the "*some* other class" choice. In any case, if instead of the "comparability_or_uncomparability" option (the default option selected in Fig. 1), the user prefers the "comparability_or_strong-uncomparability" option, the two lines about `sub:different_and_not_subClassOf` relations should be removed. For the "connectability_or_un-connectability" option, the line about `owl:equivalentClass` and `owl:sameAs` relations should instead be removed.

```
SELECT distinct ?c1 ?c2 WHERE   #query for the "each other class" choice
{ ?c1 a owl:Class.  ?c2 a owl:Class. FILTER(?c1 != ?c2)

  #skip comparable objects (here, classes comparable to ?c1):
  FILTER NOT EXISTS{ ?c1 rdfs:subClassOf|^rdfs:subClassOf ?c2 }
  FILTER NOT EXISTS{ ?c1 owl:equivalentClass|owl:sameAs ?c2 }

  #skip strongly uncomparable objects:
  FILTER NOT EXISTS{ ?c1 owl:complementOf|owl:disjointWith ?c2 }
  FILTER NOT EXISTS{ [] rdf:type owl:AllDisjointClasses;
                        owl:members/rdf:rest*/rdf:first ?c1,?c2 }
  FILTER NOT EXISTS{ [] owl:disjointUnionOf/rdf:rest*/rdf:first ?c1,?c2 }

  #skip remaining uncomparable objects that are only weakly uncomparable:
  FILTER NOT EXISTS { ?c1 owl:differentFrom ?c2 }
} #no need to use sub:different_and_not_subClassOf here since, at this
  #  point, subClassOf relations have already been filtered out


SELECT distinct ?c1 WHERE    #query for the "some other class" choice
{ ?c1 a owl:Class.   #for each class ?c1

  #skip comparable objects (here, classes comparable to ?c1):
  FILTER NOT EXISTS{?c1 rdfs:subClassOf|owl:equivalentClass|owl:sameAs ?c2
                    FILTER ((?c1!=?c2) && (?c2!=owl:Nothing)) }

  #skip strongly uncomparable objects:
  FILTER NOT EXISTS{ ?c1 owl:complementOf|owl:disjointWith ?c2
                        FILTER ((?c1!=?c2) && (?c2!=owl:Nothing)) }
  FILTER NOT EXISTS{ [] rdf:type owl:AllDisjointClasses;
                        owl:members/rdf:rest*/rdf:first ?c1,?c2 }
  FILTER NOT EXISTS{ [] owl:disjointUnionOf/rdf:rest*/rdf:first ?c1,?c2 }

  #skip remaining uncomparable objects that are only weakly uncomparable:
  FILTER NOT EXISTS { ?c1 owl:differentFrom ?c2 }
}
```

Checking the "comparability of properties via subPropertyOf relations" is similar to checking the "comparability of classes via subClassOf relations". The above SPARQL query can easily be adapted. The first adaptation to make is to replace every occurence of "class" by "property", to replace "disjointWith" by "propertyDisjointWith" and to replace "complementOf" by "inverseOf". The second adaptation to make is to remove the lines about "AllDisjointClasses" and "disjointUnionOf" since in OWL these types do not apply to properties and have no counterpart for properties.

Dealing with Several Datasets. A KB may reuse objects defined in other KBs; object identifiers *may* be URIs which refer to KBs where more definitions on these objects can be found. We abbreviate this by saying that these other KBs or definitions are reachable from the original KB. Similarly, from this other KB, yet other KBs can be reached. One feature proposed in Fig. 1 is to check all objects "in the KB and those *reachable* from the KB". Since comparability checking supports the detection of particular inconsistencies and redundancies (cf. next subsection and next section), the above cited feature leads to the checking that a KB does not have particular inconsistencies or redundancies with the KBs reachable from it. This feature does not imply *fully* checking these other KBs. The above presented SPARQL query does not support this feature since it checks classes in the dataset of a *single* SPARQL endpoint. Implementing this feature via SPARQL while still benefiting from OWL inferences unfortunately requires the SPARQL engine and the exploited OWL inference engine to work on a merge of all datasets reachable from the originally queried dataset. For small datasets, one way to achieve this could be to perform such a merge beforehand via SPARQL insert operations. However, when it is not problematic to give up OWL inferences based on knowledge from other datasets, an alternative is to use a SPARQL query where (i) "SPARQL services" are used for accessing objects in other datasets, and (ii) transitive properties such as rdfs:subClassOf are replaced by property path expressions such as "`rdfs:subClassOf+`".

2.3 Advantages for Reducing Implicit Redundancies, Detecting Inconsistencies and Increasing Knowledge Querying Possibilities

Within or across KBs, hierarchies of types (classes or properties) may be *at least partially redundant*, i.e. they could be at least partially derived from one another if particular type definitions or transformation rules were given. Implicitly redundant type hierarchies, i.e. non-automatically detectable redundancies between type hierarchies, are reduced and easier to merge (manually or automatically) when types are related by *subtypeOf_or_equivalent* relations, e.g. subClassOf, subPropertyOf, equivalentClass or equivalentProperty relations. Using such relations is also a cheap and efficient way of specifying the semantics of types.

Relating types by *not_subtypeOf-or-equivalent* relations – e.g. disjointWith or complementOf relations – permits the detection or prevention of incorrect uses of such relations and of instanceOf relations. These incorrect uses are generally due to someone not knowing some particular semantics of a type, because this someone forgot this semantics or because this semantics was never made explicit. The two-point list below gives some examples extracted from [11]. In this article, the author – who is also the first author of the present article – reports on the way he converted the noun related part of WordNet 1.3 into an ontology. Unlike for other such conversions, the goal was to avoid modifying the meanings the conceptual categories of WordNet as specified by their associated informal definitions and informal terms. The author reports that, after adding disjointWith relations between top-level *conceptual categories* which according to their informal definitions seemed exclusive, his tool automatically detected 230 violations of these exclusions by lower-level categories. In the case of WordNet, what these violations mean is debatable since it is not an ontology. However, like all such violations, they can at least be seen as heuristics for bringing more precision and structure when building a KB. The authors of WordNet 1.3 were sent the list of the 230 detected possible problems. Most of these possible problems do not occur anymore in the current WordNet (3.1).

- Many of the 230 possible problems were detected via the added exclusion relations between *the top-level category for actions* and other top-level categories which seemed exclusive with it, based on their names, their informal definitions and those of their specializations. Via the expression "informal definition" we refer to the description in natural language that each WordNet category has. Via the expression

"categorized as" we refer to the generalization relations that an object has in WordNet. The above mentioned added exclusion relations led to the discovery of categories – e.g. those for some of the meanings of the words "epilogue" and "interpretation" – which were (i) categorized and informally defined as action results/attributes/descriptions, (ii) seemingly exclusive with actions (given how they were informally defined and given they were not also informally defined as actions), and (iii) (rather surprisingly) *also* categorized as actions. Given these last three points, [11] removed the "categorization as action" of these action result/attribute/description categories. Based on the content of WordNet 3.1, it appears that the authors of WordNet then also made this removal.
- Other causes for the 230 violations detected via the added exclusion relations between top-level categories came from the fact that WordNet uses *generalization relations* between categories instead of other relations. E.g., instead of location/place relations: in WordNet 1.3, many categories informally defined as battles were classified as both battles and cities/regions (this is no more the case in WordNet 3.1). E.g., instead of member relations: in WordNet, the classification of species is often intertwined with the classification of genus of species.

Several research works in knowledge acquisition, model-driven engineering or ontology engineering, e.g. [12–15], have advocated the use of *tree* structures when designing a subtype hierarchy, hence the use of (i) single inheritance only, and (ii) multiple tree structures, e.g. one per *view* or *viewpoint*. They argue that each object of the KB has a *unique place* in such trees and thus that such trees can be used as decision trees or ways to avoid redundancies, normalize KBs and ease KB searching/handling. This is true but the same advantages can be obtained by creating subtypes *solely via sets of disjoint (direct) subtypes*. Indeed, to keep these advantages, it is sufficient (and necessary) that *whenever* two types are disjoint, this disjointness is specified. With tree structures, there are no explicit disjointWith relations but the disjointness is still (implicitly) specified. Compared to the use of multiple tree structures, the use of disjoint subtypes and multiple inheritance has the advantages of (i) not requiring a special inference engine to handle "tree structures with bridges between them" (e.g. those of [12, 16]) instead of a classic ontology, and (ii) generally requiring less work for knowledge providers than creating and managing many tree structures with bridges between them. Furthermore, when subtype partitions can be used, the completeness of these sets supports additional inferences for checking or reasoning purposes. The above rationale do not imply that views or tree structures are not interesting, they only imply that sets of disjoint subtypes are good alternatives when they can be used instead.

Methods or patterns to fix (particular kinds of) detected conflicts are not within the scope of this article. Such methods are for example studied in the belief set/base revision/contraction as well as in KB debugging. [17] proposes an adaptation of base revision/debugging for OWL-like KBs. The authors of [18] have created ontology design patterns that propose systematic ways to resolve some particular kinds of inconsistencies, especially the violation of exclusion relations.

As illustrated in Sect. 2.1, the OWL properties usable to express that some types are "comparable or uncomparable via subtypeOf" – e.g. subClassOf, subPropertyOf, equivalentClass, equivalentProperty, disjointWith and complementOf relations – can be combined to define or declare properties for creating (un-)complete sets of (non-) disjoint subtypes or, more generally, for creating more precise relations which better support the detection of inconsistencies or redundancies. E.g., `sub:proper-subClassOf` can be defined and used to prevent unintended subClassOf cycles.

Advantages for Knowledge Querying. Alone, subtypeOf_or_equivalent relations only support the search for specializations (or generalizations) of a query statement, i.e. the search for objects comparable (via subtype relations) to the query parameter. The search for objects "not uncomparable via specialization" to the query parameter – i.e. objects that are or could be specializations or generalizations of this parameter – is more general and sometimes useful.

- Assume that a KB user is searching for lodging descriptions in a KB where sports halls are not categorized as lodgings but are not exclusive with them either, based on the fact that they are not regular lodgings but that they can be used as such when natural disasters occurs. Also assume that the user intuitively shares such views on lodgings and sports halls. Then, querying the KB for (specializations of) "lodgings" will not retrieve sports halls. On the other hand, querying for objects not uncomparable to "lodgings" will return sports halls; furthermore, if lodgings have been defined as covered areas, such a query will not return uncovered areas such as open stadiums. Thus, assuming that the term "lodging" in this previous querying has been used because the author of the query was looking for covered areas only, this person will only get potentially relevant results.
- More generally, when a person does not know which exact type to use in a query or does not know what kind of query to use – e.g. a query for the specializations or the generalizations of the query parameter – a query for objects "not uncomparable" to the query parameter may well collect all and only the objects the person is interested in, if in the KB all or most types are either comparable or uncomparable via subtype relations.

The more systematically the types of a KB are comparable via subtype relations, the more the statements of the KB – as well as other if they have a definition – will be retrievable via comparability or uncomparability based queries.

3 Other Interesting Cases of Comparability

The previous section was about the comparability of types via subtype relations. This subsection generalizes the approach to other types of relations.

3.1 Comparability via "Definition Element" Relations

In this article, an object definition is a logic formula that all specializations of the object must satisfy. A full definition specifies necessary and sufficient conditions that the specializations must satisfy. In OWL, a full definition of a class is made by relating this class to a class expression via an `owl:equivalentClass` relation. Specifying only necessary conditions – e.g. using `rdfs:subClassOf` instead of `owl:equivalentClass` – means making only a partial definition. An "element of a definition" is any target domain object which is member of that definition, except for objects of the used language (e.g. quantifiers and logical operators). A "definition element" relation is one that connects the defined object to an element of the definition. E.g., if a *Triangle* is defined as a "Polygon that has as part 3 Edges and 3 Vertices", *Triangle* has as *definition elements* the types *Polygon*, *Edge*, *Vertex* and *part* as well as the value *3*. The property `sub:definition_element` – one of the types that we propose – is the type of all "definition element" relations that can occur with OWL-based definitions. We have fully defined sub:definition_element in [8] based on the various ways definitions can be made in OWL; one of its subtypes is `rdfs:subClassOf`. This subsection generalizes Sect. 2 since a definition may specify other relations than subClassOf relations, as illustrated by the above definition of Triangle. A "definition-element exclusion" relation is one that connects an object O to another one that could not be used for defining O. This property can be defined based on the "definition element" relation type. E.g.:

```
sub:definition-element_exclusion   #reminder: "has_" is implicit
  rdfs:subPropertyOf  owl:differentFrom ;
  owl:propertyDisjointWith  sub:definition_element ;
  owl:propertyDisjointWith [owl:inverseOf sub:definition_element].
```

As explained in Sect. 2.3, checking that types in a KB are either comparable or uncomparable via subtype relations *reduce* implicit redundancies between type hierarchies. As illustrated by the later paragraph titled "Example of implicit potential redundancies", this checking is not sufficient for finding *every* implicit potential redundancy resulting from a lack of definition, hence for finding every specialization hierarchy that could be derived from another one in the KB if particular definitions were given. However, this new goal can be achieved by generalizing the previous approach since this goal implies that for every pair of objects (in the KB or a selected KB subset), *either* one of these objects is defined using the other *or* none can be defined using the other. In other words, this goal means checking that for every pair of objects in the selected set, these two objects are either comparable or uncomparable via "definition element" relations. To express that objects are strongly uncomparable in this way – and hence *not* potentially redundant – "definition-element exclusion" relations can be used.

The above cited new goal implies that, from every object, *every other object* in the KB is made comparable or uncomparable via "definition element" relations. This is an enormous job for a KB author and very few current KBs would satisfy this ODR. However, given particular reasons and techniques described in [8], a KB contributor/evaluator *may* choose to assume that for avoiding *a good enough amount of* implicit potential redundancies between type hierarchies, it is sufficient to check that from every object, *at least one other object* in the KB is made comparable or uncomparable via "definition element" relations (thus, using the "some other object" option given in Fig. 1, instead of the "every other object" option). As explained in [8], this saves a lot of work to the KB contributors and may avoid generating a large number of "definition-element exclusion" relations.

Example of Implicit Potential Redundancies. It is often tempting to specialize particular types of processes or types of physical entities according to particular types of attributes, without explicitly declaring these types of attributes and organizing them by specialization relations. E.g., at first thought, it may sound reasonable to declare a process type Fair_process without relating it to an attribute type Fairness (or Fair) via a definition such as "any Fair_process has as attribute a Fairness". However, Fair_process may then be specialized by types such as Fair_process_for_utilitarianism, Fair_process_wrt_Pareto-efficiency, Fair_bargaining, Fair_distribution, Fair_distribution_wrt_utilitarianism, Fair_distribution_for_prioritarianism, Fair_distribution_wrt_Pareto-efficiency, etc. It soon becomes apparent that this approach is not relevant since (i) every process type can be specialized wrt. a particular attribute type or any combination of particular attribute types, and (ii) similar specializations can *also* be made for function types (e.g. starting from Fair_function) and attribute types (starting from Fairness). Even if the KB is not a large KB shared by many persons, many beginnings of such parallel categorizations may happen, without them being related via definitions. Indeed, the above example with process types and attribute relations to attributes types can be replicated with any type and any relation type, e.g. with process types and agent/object/instrument/time relation types or with physical entity types and mass/color/age/place relation types.

Ensuring that objects are either comparable or uncomparable via "definition element" relations is a way to prevent such (beginnings of) implicitly potentially redundant type hierarchies: all/most/many of them depending on the chosen option and assumption. As with disjointWith relations, the most useful "definition-element exclusion" relations are those between some top-level types. To normalize definitions in the KB, e.g. to ease logical inferencing, a KB owner may also use "definition-element exclusion" relations to forbid particular kinds of definitions, e.g. forbid processes to be defined wrt. attributes or physical entities. Each definition for a type T sets "definition element" relations to *other types*, and these relations also apply to the subtypes of T. A special "definition element" relation type may also be used to reach not just the above cited *other types* but their subtypes too. Otherwise, most types would need to be defined if few "definition-element exclusion" relations are set between top-level types.

3.2 Comparability via Other Transitive Relations, Especially Part Relations

Ensuring that objects are either comparable or uncomparable via specialization relations via specialization relations has many advantages which were illustrated in Sects. 2.3 and 3.1. Similar advantages exist with all transitive relations, not just specialization relations, although to a lesser extent since less inferences – and hence less error detection – can be made with other transitive relations.

Part properties – e.g. for spatial parts, temporal parts or sub-processes – are *partial-order* properties that are often exploited. Unlike subtype relations, they connect individuals. Nevertheless, for checking the "comparability of individuals via part relations (let us assume sub:part relations)", the SPARQL query given in Sect. 2.2 can be adapted. Below is this adapted query for the "*each* other object" choice. The adaptation to make for the "*some* other object" choice is similar to the one in Sect. 2.2. Two objects that are "comparable via part relations" if one is fully part of the other (or if they are identical). They are "strongly uncomparable via part relations" if they do not share any part (and hence the respective parts of these two objects do not have shared parts either). Two objects that are "weakly uncomparable via part relations" share some parts but none is fully part of the other.

```
SELECT distinct ?i1 ?i2 WHERE #individuals (as checked by the next 2 lines)
{ ?i1 rdf:type ?c1.   FILTER NOT EXISTS { ?i1 rdf:type owl:Class }
  ?i2 rdf:type ?c2.   FILTER NOT EXISTS { ?i2 rdf:type owl:Class }

  #skip comparable objects:
  FILTER NOT EXISTS { ?i1 owl:sameAs|sub:part+|(^sub:part)+ ?i2 }

  #skip strongly uncomparable objects:
  FILTER NOT EXISTS { ?i1 sub:part_exclusion ?i2 }

  #skip remaining uncomparable objects that are only weakly uncomparable:
  FILTER NOT EXISTS { ?i1 owl:differentFrom ?i2 } #as in Section 2.2
} #with:     sub:part rdfs:subPropertyOf owl:differentFrom ;
  #                   rdf:type owl:TransitiveProperty .
  #          sub:part_exclusion  rdfs:subPropertyOf  owl:differentFrom ;
  #                              owl:propertyDisjointWith  sub:part .
```

3.3 Comparability via Transitive Relations Plus Minimal Differentia

When defining a type, a good practice is to specify (i) its similarities and differences with each of its direct supertypes (e.g., as in the genus & differentia design pattern), and (ii) its similarities and differences with each of its siblings for these supertypes. This is an often advocated best practice to improve the understandability of a type, as well as enabling more inferences. E.g., this is the "Differential Semantics" methodology of [13]. Several ODRs can be derived from this best practice, depending on how "difference" is defined. In this article, the term "minimal-differentia" refers to a difference of at least one (inferred or not) relation in the compared type definitions: one more relation, one less or one with a type or destination that is different (semantically, not just syntactically). Furthermore, to check that a class is different from each of its superclasses (i.e. to extend the genus & differentia method), an rdfs:subClassOf relation between the two classes does not count as "differing relation". When relevant, this ODR can be generalized to use other transitive relations between objects, e.g. partOf relations.

For the "comparability relation type", Fig. 1 proposes the option "comparability-or-uncomparability_with-minimal-differentia". For supporting this option when checking "comparability via subClassOf relations" between any pair of classes in a KB, the code of the SPARQL query of Sect. 2.2 can be adapted by adding some lines before the filters testing whether the classes are comparable or uncomparable: below, see the FILTER block from the 3rd line to the "...". This block checks that there is a "minimal-differentia" between the tested classes. The retrieval of automatically inferred relations relies on the use of a relevant entailment regime.

```
SELECT distinct ?c1 ?c2 WHERE
{ ?c1 rdf:type owl:Class.   ?c2 rdf:type owl:Class.  FILTER (?c1 != ?c2)
  FILTER (!            #skip classes satisfying the following conditions:
   ( (EXISTS
       { ?c1 ?p1 ?v1 .                  #?c1 has at least one property
         FILTER(?p1!=rdfs:subClassOf) #         that is not rdfs:subClassOf
         FILTER                         #and
         ( NOT EXISTS { ?c2 ?p1 ?v2 } #   ?p1 is not in ?c2
           ||  EXISTS { ?c2 ?p1 ?v2    #or ?p1 ?v1 is not in ?c2
                        FILTER (?v1 != ?v2) }
           ||  EXISTS { ?c2 ?p2 ?v2    #or ?p2 ?v2 is not in ?c1
                        FILTER NOT EXISTS { ?c1 ?p2 ?v2 }  } )
      })
     || ((NOT EXISTS                    #or
           { ?c1 ?p1 ?v1                #  ?c1 has no property, except may be
             FILTER((?p1!=rdfs:subClassOf) #  an rdfs:subClassOf property
                    && (?v1 != ?c2))}      #  to ?c2
        ) && EXISTS{?c2 ?p2 ?v2})     #  and ?c2 has (other) properties
   ))
  ... #same filtering for (un-)comparable objects as in Section 2.2
}
```

4 Other Comparisons with Other Works and Conclusion

As previously illustrated, the "comparability ODR" generalizes – or permits one to generalize – some best practices, ontology patterns or methodologies that advocate the use of particular relations between particular objects, and supports an automated checking of the compliance with these practices, patterns or methodologies. This leads to the representation of knowledge that is more connected and precise, or with less redundancies. Since the comparability ODR can be used for evaluating a KB – e.g. by applying it to all its objects and dividing the number of successful cases by the number of objects – it can also be used to create KB evaluation criteria/measures, typically for measuring the *(degree of) completeness of a KB, with respect to some criteria*.

As noted in [7], a *survey* on quality assessment for Linked Data, *completeness* commonly refers to a *degree* to which the "information *required* to satisfy some given criteria or a given query" are present in the considered dataset. To complement this very general definition, we distinguish two kinds of completeness.

- *Constraint-based completeness* measures the percentage of elements in a dataset that satisfy *explicit* representations of what – or how – information *must* be represented in the dataset. These representations are constraints such as integrity constraints or, more generally, constraints expressed by database schemas, structured document schemas, or schemas enforcing ontology design patterns. E.g., in a particular dataset, the constraint that at least one movie must be associated to each movie actor, or the constraint that all relations must be binary.

- *Real-world-based completeness* measures the degree to which particular kinds of real-world information are represented in the dataset. E.g., regarding movies associated to an actor, calculating this completeness may consist in dividing "the number of movies associated to this actor in the dataset" by "the number of movies he *actually* played in, *i.e. in the real world*". Either the missing information are found in a *gold standard dataset* or the degree is estimated via *completeness oracles* [19], i.e. rules or queries estimating what is missing in the dataset to answer a given query correctly. Tools such as SWIQA and Sieve help perform measures for this kind of completeness.

All the completeness criteria/measures collected by [7] – *schema/property/population/interlinking* completeness – "assume that a gold standard dataset is available". Hence, they are all subkinds of *real-world based completeness*. However, constraint-based completeness is equally interesting and, for its subkinds, categories named *schema/property/population/interlinking completeness* could also be used or have been used [1, 4]. What the comparability ODR can be reused for to ease the measure of completeness is about *constraint-based completeness*. As illustrated in this article, checking such a completeness may lead the KB authors to represent information that increase the KB precision and then enable the finding of yet-undetected problems. Increasing such a completeness does not mean increasing inferencing speed.

This article showed how SPARQL queries could be used for implementing comparability ODRs. More generally, most *transformation languages or systems* that exploit KRs could be similarly reused. [20] and [21] present such systems. The proposed SPARQL queries have been validated experimentally (using Corese [21], a tool which includes an OWL-2 inference engine and a SPARQL engine). Unsurprisingly, in the tested existing ontologies, many objects were not compliant with the ODRs.

References

1. Mendes, P.N., Bizer, C., Miklos, Z., Calbimonte, J.P., Moraru, A., Flouri G.: D2.1 Conceptual model and best practices for high-quality metadata publishing. Delivery 2.1 of PlanetData, FP7 project 257641 (2012)
2. Farias Lóscio, B., Burle, C., Calegari, N.: Data on the Web Best Practices. W3C Recommendation, 31 January 2017 (2017). https://www.w3.org/TR/dwbp/
3. Presutti, V., Gangemi, A.: Content ontology design patterns as practical building blocks for web ontologies. In: Li, Q., Spaccapietra, S., Yu, E., Olivé, A. (eds.) ER 2008. LNCS, vol. 5231, pp. 128–141. Springer, Heidelberg (2008). https://doi.org/10.1007/978-3-540-87877-3_11
4. Dodds, L., Davis, I.: Linked Data Patterns – a pattern catalogue for modelling, publishing, and consuming Linked Data, 56 pages (2012). http://patterns.dataincubator.org/book/
5. Ruy, F.B., Guizzardi, G., Falbo, R.A., Reginato, C.C., Santos, V.A.: From reference ontologies to ontology patterns and back. Data Knowl. Eng. **109**(C), 41–69 (2017)
6. Roussey C., Corcho Ó, Vilches Blázquez L.M.: A catalogue of OWL ontology antipatterns. In: K-CAP 2009, Redondo Beach, CA, USA, pp. 205–206 (2009)
7. Zaveri, A., Rula, A., Maurino, A., Pietrobon, R., Lehmann, J., Auer, S.: Quality assessment for linked data: a survey. Semant. Web **7**(1), 63–93 (2016)

8. Martin, Ph., Corby, O.: Ontology Design Rules Based On Comparability Via Particular Relations. Extended version and on-line companion article for this present article (2019). http://www.webkb.org/kb/it/o_knowledge/d_odr_content_article.html
9. Hitzler, P., Krötzsch, M., Parsia, B., Patel-Schneider, P.F., Rudolph, S.: OWL 2 Web Ontology Language Primer (Second Edition). W3C Recommendation, 11 December 2012 (2012).. https://www.w3.org/TR/owl2-primer/
10. Harris, S., Seaborne, A.: SPARQL 1.1 Overview. W3C Recommendation, 21 March 2013 (2013). https://www.w3.org/TR/2013/REC-sparql11-overview-20130321/
11. Martin, Ph.: Correction and extension of WordNet 1.7. In: Ganter, B., de Moor, A., Lex, W. (eds.) ICCS 2003. LNCS (LNAI), vol. 2746, pp. 160–173. Springer, Heidelberg (2003). https://doi.org/10.1007/978-3-540-45091-7_11
12. Marino, O., Rechenmann, F., Uvietta, P.: Multiple perspectives and classification mechanism in object-oriented representation. In: ECAI 1990, 425–430. Pitman Publishing London, Stockholm (1990)
13. Bachimont, B., Isaac, A., Troncy, R.: Semantic commitment for designing ontologies: a proposal. In: Gómez-Pérez, A., Benjamins, V.R. (eds.) EKAW 2002. LNCS (LNAI), vol. 2473, pp. 114–121. Springer, Heidelberg (2002). https://doi.org/10.1007/3-540-45810-7_14
14. Dromey, R.G.: Scaleable formalization of imperfect knowledge. In: AWCVS 2006, 1st Asian Working Conference on Verified Software, Macao SAR, China, pp. 29–31 (2006)
15. Rector, A., Brandt, S., Drummond, N., Horridge, M., Pulestin, C., Stevens, R.: Engineering use cases for modular development of ontologies in OWL. Appl. Ontol. **7**(2), 113–132 (2012)
16. Djakhdjakha, L., Mounir, H., Boufaïda, Z.: Towards a representation for multi-viewpoints ontology alignments. IJMSO Int. J. Metadata Semant. Ontol. **9**(2), 91–102 (2014)
17. Corman, J., Aussenac-Gilles, N., Vieu, L.: Prioritized base debugging in description logics. In: JOWO@IJCAI (2015)
18. Djedidi, R., Aufaure, M.: Ontology change management. In: I-SEMANTICS 2009, 611–621 (2009)
19. Galárraga, L., Hose, K., Razniewski, S.: Enabling completeness-aware querying in SPARQL. In: WebDB 2017, Chicago, IL, USA, 19–22 (2017)
20. Zamazal, O., Svátek, V.: PatOMat – versatile framework for pattern-based ontology transformation. Comput. Inform. **34**(2), 305–336 (2015)
21. Corby, O., Faron-Zucker, C.: STTL: a SPARQL-based transformation language for RDF. In: WEBIST 2015, 11th International Conference on Web Information Systems and Technologies, Lisbon, Portugal (2015)

From Monolingual to Multilingual Ontologies: The Role of Cross-Lingual Ontology Enrichment

Shimaa Ibrahim[1,2](✉), Said Fathalla[1,3], Hamed Shariat Yazdi[1], Jens Lehmann[1,4], and Hajira Jabeen[1]

[1] Smart Data Analytics (SDA), University of Bonn, Bonn, Germany
{ibrahim,fathalla,shariat,jens.lehmann,jabeen}@cs.uni-bonn.de
[2] Institute of Graduate Studies and Research, University of Alexandria, Alexandria, Egypt
[3] Faculty of Science, University of Alexandria, Alexandria, Egypt
[4] Enterprise Information Systems Department, Fraunhofer IAIS, Sankt Augustin, Germany

Abstract. While the multilingual data on the Semantic Web grows rapidly, the building of multilingual ontologies from monolingual ones is still cumbersome and hampered due to the lack of techniques for cross-lingual ontology enrichment. Cross-lingual ontology enrichment greatly facilitates the semantic interoperability between different ontologies in different natural languages. Achieving such enrichment by human labor is a time-consuming and error-prone task. Thus, in this paper, we propose a fully automated ontology enrichment approach using cross-lingual matching (OECM) approach, which builds a multilingual ontology by enriching a monolingual ontology from another one in a different natural language using a cross-lingual matching. OECM selects the best translation among all available translations of ontology concepts based on their semantic similarity with the target ontology concepts. We present a use case of our approach for enriching English Scholarly Communication Ontologies using German and Arabic ontologies from the MultiFarm benchmark. We have compared our results with the results from the Ontology Alignment Evaluation Initiative (OAEI 2018). Our approach has higher precision and recall in comparison to five state-of-the-art approaches. Additionally, we recommend some linguistic corrections in the Arabic ontologies in Multifarm which have enhanced our cross-lingual matching results.

Keywords: Cross-lingual ontology enrichment · Cross-lingual matching · Multilingual ontology · Ontology engineering · Knowledge management

1 Introduction

The wide proliferation of multilingual data on the Semantic Web results in many ontologies scattered across the web in various natural languages. According to

M. Acosta et al. (Eds.): SEMANTiCS 2019, LNCS 11702, pp. 215–230, 2019.
https://doi.org/10.1007/978-3-030-33220-4_16

the Linked Open Vocabularies (LOV)[1], the majority of the ontologies in the Semantic Web are in English, however, ontologies in other Indo-European languages also exist. For instance, out of a total 681 vocabularies found in LOV, 500 are in English, 54 in French, 39 in Spanish, and 33 in German. Few ontologies exist in non-Indo-European languages, such as 13 in Japanese and seven in Arabic. Monolingual ontologies with labels or local names presented in a certain language are not easily understandable to speakers of other languages. Therefore, in order to enhance semantic interoperability between monolingual ontologies, approaches for building multilingual ontologies from the existing monolingual ones should be developed [26]. Multilingual ontologies can be built by applying *cross-lingual ontology enrichment* techniques, which expand the target ontology with additional concepts and semantic relations extracted from external resources in other natural languages [23]. For example, suppose we have two ontologies; Scientific Events Ontology in English (SEO_{en}) and Conference in German ($Conference_{de}$). Both SEO_{en} and $Conference_{de}$ have complementary information, i.e. SEO_{en} has some information which does not exist in $Conference_{de}$ and vice versa. Let us consider a scenario where a user wants to get information from both SEO_{en} and $Conference_{de}$ to be used in an ontology-based application. This may not be possible without a cross-lingual ontology enrichment solution, which enrich the former by the complementary information in the latter. Manual ontology enrichment is a resource demanding and time-consuming task. Therefore, fully automated *cross-lingual* ontology enrichment approaches are highly desired [23]. Most of the existing work in ontology enrichment focus on enriching English ontologies from English sources only (monolingual enrichment) [23]. To the best of our knowledge, only our previous work [1,14] has addressed the cross-lingual ontology enrichment problem by proposing a semi-automated approach to enrich ontologies from multilingual text or from other ontologies in different natural languages.

In this paper we address the following research question; *how can we automatically build multilingual ontologies from monolingual ones?* We propose a fully automated ontology enrichment approach in order to create multilingual ontologies from monolingual ones using cross-lingual matching. We extend our previous work [14] by: (1) using the semantic similarity to select the best translation of class labels, (2) enriching the target ontology by adding new classes in addition to all their related subclasses in the hierarchy, (3) using ontologies in non-Indo-European languages (e.g., Arabic), as the source of information, (4) building multilingual ontologies, and (5) developing a fully automated approach. OECM comprises six phases: (1) *translation*: translate class labels of the source ontology, (2) *pre-processing*: process class labels of the target and the translated source ontologies, (3) *terminological matching*: identify potential matches between class labels of the source and the target ontologies, (4) *triple retrieval*: retrieve the new information to be added to the target ontology, (5) *enrichment*: enrich the target ontology with new information extracted from the source ontology, and (6) *validation*: validate the enriched ontology. A noticeable feature of

[1] https://lov.linkeddata.es/dataset/lov/vocabs.

OECM is that we consider multiple translations for a class label. In addition, the use of semantic similarity has significantly improved the quality of the matching process. We present a use case for enriching the Scientific Events Ontology (SEO) [9], a scholarly communication ontology for describing scientific events, from German and Arabic ontologies. We compare OECM to five state-of-the-art approaches for cross-lingual ontology matching task. OECM outperformed these approaches in terms of precision, recall, and F-measure. Furthermore, we evaluate the enriched ontology by comparing it against a Gold standard created by ontology experts. The implementation of OECM and the datasets used in the use case are publicly available[2].

The remainder of this paper is structured as follows: we present an overview of related work in Sect. 2. Overview of the proposed approach is described in Sect. 3. In order to illustrate possible applications of OECM, a use case is presented in Sect. 4. Experiments and evaluation results are presented in Sect. 5. Finally, we conclude with an outline of the future work in Sect. 6.

2 Related Work

A recent review of the literature on multilingual Web of Data found that the potential of the Semantic Web for being multilingual can be accomplished by techniques to build multilingual ontologies from monolingual ones [12]. Multilingual enrichment approaches are used to build multilingual ontologies from different resources in different natural languages [5,6,24]. Espinoza et al. [6] has proposed an approach to generate multilingual ontologies by enriching the existing monolingual ontologies with multilingual information in order to translate these ontologies to a particular language and culture (ontology localization). In fact, ontology enrichment depends on matching the target ontology with external resources, in order to provide the target ontology with additional information extracted from the external resources.

All the literature have focused on the cross-lingual ontology matching techniques which are used for matching different natural languages of linguistic information in ontologies [12,26]. Meilicke et al. [20] created a benchmark dataset (MultiFarm) that results from the manual translations of a set of ontologies from the conference domain into eight natural languages. This dataset is widely used to evaluate the cross-lingual matching approaches [7,15,16,28]. Manual translation of ontologies can be infeasible when dealing with large and complex ontologies. Trojahn et al. [27] proposed a generic approach which relies on translating concepts of source ontologies using machine translation techniques into the language of the target ontology. In the translation step, they depend on getting one translation for each concept (one-to-one translation), then they apply monolingual matching approaches to match concepts between the source ontologies and the translated ones. Fu et al. [10,11] proposed an approach to match English and Chinese ontologies by considering the semantics of the target ontology, the mapping intent, the operating domain, the time and resource

[2] https://github.com/shmkhaled/OECM.

constraints and user feedback. Hertling and Paulheim [13] proposed an approach which utilizes Wikipedia's inter-language links for finding corresponding ontology elements. Lin and Krizhanovsky [18] proposed an approach which use Wiktionary[3] as a source of background knowledge to match English and French ontologies. Tigrine et al. [25] presented an approach, which relies on the multilingual semantic network BabelNet[4] as a source of background knowledge, to match several ontologies in different natural languages. In the context of OAEI 2018 campaign[5] for evaluating ontology matching technologies, AML [7], KEPLER [16], LogMap [15] and XMap [28] provide high-quality alignments. These systems use terminological and structural alignments in addition to using external lexicon, such as WordNet[6] and UMLS-lexicon[7] in order to get the set of synonyms for the ontology elements. In order to deal with multilingualism, AML and KEPLER rely on getting (one-to-one translation) using machine translation technologies, such as Microsoft translator, before starting the matching process. LogMap and XMap do not provide any information about the utilized translation methodology. Moreover, LogMap is an iterative process, that starts from initial mappings ('almost exact' lexical correspondences) to discover new mappings. It is mentioned in [15] that the main weakness of LogMap is that it can not find matching between ontologies which do not provide enough lexical information as it depends mainly on the initial mappings. A good literature of the state-of-the-art approaches in cross-lingual ontology matching is provided in [26].

Most of the literature have focused on enriching monolingual ontologies with multilingual information in order to translate or localize these ontologies. In addition, in the cross-lingual ontology matching task, there is a lack of exact one-to-one translation between terms across different natural languages which negatively affects the matching results. We address this limitations in our proposed approach by building multilingual ontologies, where a class label is presented by several natural languages, from monolingual ones. Such approach support the ontology matching process with multiple translations for a class label in order to enhance the matching results.

3 The Proposed Approach

Goal: Given two ontologies S and T, in two different natural languages L_s and L_t respectively, as RDF triples $\langle s, p, o \rangle \in \mathcal{C} \times \mathcal{R} \times (\mathcal{C} \cup \mathcal{L})$ where $\mathcal{C}$ is the set of ontology domain entities (i.e. classes), $\mathcal{R}$ is the set of relations, and $\mathcal{L}$ is the set of literals. We aim at finding the complementary information $\mathcal{T}_e = S - (S \cap T)$ from S in order to enrich T.

The proposed approach comprises six phases (Fig. 1): translation, preprocessing, terminological matching, triple retrieval, enrichment, and validation.

[3] https://www.wiktionary.org/.
[4] https://babelnet.org/.
[5] http://oaei.ontologymatching.org/2018/results/multifarm/index.html.
[6] https://wordnet.princeton.edu/.
[7] https://www.nlm.nih.gov/research/umls/.

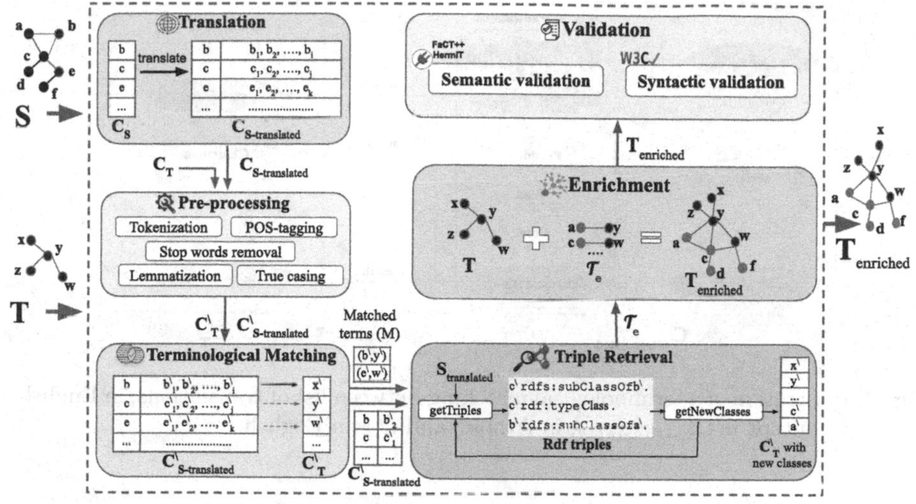

Fig. 1. The workflow of OECM.

The input is the two ontologies in two different natural languages, i.e. the target ontology T and the source ontology S. The output is the multilingual enriched ontology $T_{enriched}$ in two different natural languages L_1 and L_2. In the following subsections, we describe each of these phases in details.

3.1 Translation

Let $\mathcal{C}_S$ and $\mathcal{C}_T$ be the set of classes in S and T respectively. Each class is represented by a label or a local name. The aim of this phase is to translate each class in $\mathcal{C}_S$ to the language of T (i.e. L_t). Google Translator[8] is used to translate classes of source ontologies. All available translations are considered for each class. Therefore, the output of the translation is $\mathcal{C}_{S-translated}$ which has each class, in S, associated with a list of all available translations. For example, the class `Thema` in German has a list of English translations (Subject and Topic), and the class label "مراجعة" in Arabic has a list of English translations such as "Review, Revision, Check". The best translation will be selected in the terminological matching phase (Subsect. 3.3).

3.2 Pre-processing

The aim of this phase is to process classes of $\mathcal{C}_T$ and lists of translations in $\mathcal{C}_{S-translated}$ by employing a variety of natural language processing (NLP) techniques, such as tokenization, POS-tagging (part-of-speech tagging), and lemmatization, to make it ready for the next phases. In order to enhance the similarity

[8] https://translate.google.com/.

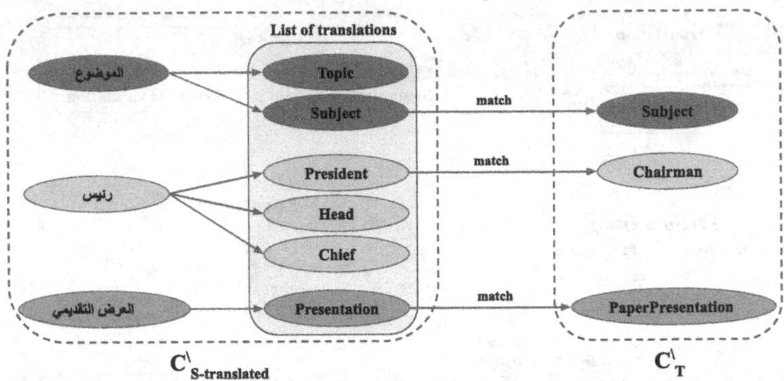

Fig. 2. Illustration of a terminological matching between list of translations, in English, for every concept in $\mathcal{C}'_{S-translated}$, in Arabic, and $\mathcal{C}'_T$ in English

results between $\mathcal{C}_T$ and $\mathcal{C}_{S-translated}$, stop words are removed and normalization methods and regular expressions are used to remove punctuation, symbols, additional white spaces, and to normalize the structure of strings. Furthermore, our pre-processing is capable of recognizing classes such as camel cases "ReviewArticle" and adds a space between lower-case and upper-case letters "Review Article" (i.e. true casing technique). The output of this phase is $\mathcal{C}'_T$, which has pre-processed translations of classes in T, and $\mathcal{C}'_{S-translated}$, which has pre-processed translations for each class in S.

3.3 Terminological Matching

The aim of this phase is to identify potential matches between class labels of S and T. We perform a pairwise lexical and/or semantic similarity between the list of translations of each class in $\mathcal{C}'_{S-translated}$ and $\mathcal{C}'_T$ to select the best translation for each class in S that matches the corresponding class in T (see Algorithm 1). Jaccard similarity [22] is used to filter the identical concepts instead of using semantic similarity from the beginning because there is no need for extra computations to compute semantic similarity between two identical classes. The reason behind choosing the Jaccard similarity is that according to the experiments conducted for the ontology alignment task for the MultiFarm benchmark in [2], Jaccard similarity has achieved the best score in terms of precision. For non-identical concepts, we compute the semantic similarity using the path length measure, based on WordNet, which returns the shortest path between two words in WordNet hierarchy [3]. If two words are semantically equivalent, i.e., belonging to the same WordNet synset, the path distance is 1.00. We use a specific threshold θ in order to get the set of matched terms (matched classes) M. We obtained the best value of $\theta = 0.9$ which has the best matching results after running the experiments for ten times. If no match is found, we consider this class as a new class that can be added to T and we consider its list of translations as synonyms for that class. Generally, class labels have more than one

Algorithm 1. Terminological Matching

Data: $\mathcal{C}'_{S-translated}$, $\mathcal{C}'_{T}$, θ similarity threshold
Result: M matched terms, $\mathcal{C}'_{S-translated}$

1 **foreach** $c_s \in \mathcal{C}'_{S-translated}$, $t \in listOfTranslations$, $c_t \in \mathcal{C}'_T$ **do**
2 $\quad$ $similarityScore \leftarrow$ getSimilarity(t,c_t)
3 $\quad$ **if** $similarityScore \geq \theta$ **then**
4 $\quad\quad$ $M ::= (t, c_t)$
5 $\quad\quad$ $\mathcal{C}'_{S-translated}$ = update($\mathcal{C}'_{S-translated}$,$M$)
6 **Function** **getSimilarity**(*sentence*1, *sentence*2)**:double**
7 $\quad$ $similarity \leftarrow$ getJaccardSimilarity(*sentence*1, *sentence*2)
8 $\quad$ **if** $similarity \neq 1$ **then**
9 $\quad\quad$ $similarity \leftarrow$ (sentenceSimilarity(*sentence*1,*sentence*2)
10 $\quad\quad$ + sentenceSimilarity(*sentence*2,*sentence*1))/2
11 $\quad$ **return** *similarity*
12 **Function** **sentenceSimilarity**(*sentence*1, *sentence*2)**:double**
13 $\quad$ $simScore \leftarrow 0.0$
14 $\quad$ $count \leftarrow 0.0$
15 $\quad$ **foreach** $w_i \in$ *sentence*1*.split(" ")* **do**
16 $\quad\quad$ **foreach** $w_j \in$ *sentence*2*.split(" ")* **do**
17 $\quad\quad\quad$ $pathSim ::=$ getPathSimilarity(w_i,w_j)
18 $\quad\quad$ $simScore+ = pathSim.max$
19 $\quad\quad$ $count+ = 1$
20 $\quad$ $simScore \leftarrow simScore/count$
21 $\quad$ **return** *simScoure*

word, for example "InvitedSpeaker", therefore, the semantic similarity between sentences presented in [21] is adapted as described in Algorithm 1 - line 9. Given two sentences *sentence*1 and *sentence*2, the semantic similarity of each sentence with respect to the other is defined by: for each word $w_i \in sentence1$, the word w_j in *sentence*2 that has the highest path similarity with w_i is determined. The word similarities are then summed up and normalized with the number of similar words between the two sentences. Next, the same procedure is applied to start with words in *sentence*2 to identify the semantic similarity of *sentence*2 with respect to *sentence*1. Finally, the resulting similarity scores are combined using a simple average. Based on the similarity results, the best translation is selected and $\mathcal{C}'_{S-translated}$ is updated. For example, in Fig. 2, the class "رئيس" in Arabic, has a list of English translations such as "President, Head, Chief". After computing the similarity between $\mathcal{C}'_{S-translated}$ and $\mathcal{C}'_T$, "President" has the highest similarityScore of 1.00 with the class "Chairman", in $\mathcal{C}'_T$, because they are semantically equivalent. Therefore, "President" is selected to be the best translation for "رئيس". The output of this phase is the list of matched terms M between $\mathcal{C}'_T$ and the updated $\mathcal{C}'_{S-translated}$.

Algorithm 2. Triple Retrieval

Data: S, $\mathcal{C}'_{S-translated}$, $\mathcal{C}'_T$, M
Result: $\mathcal{T}_e$ triples to be enriched

$S_{translated} \leftarrow$ translateOntologyClasses(S, $\mathcal{C}'_{S-translated}$)
$newClasses \leftarrow M$
while *!newClasses.isEmpty()* **do**
  $tempTriples \leftarrow$ getTriplesForNewClasses($S_{translated}$, $newClasses$)
  $newClasses \leftarrow$ getClasses($tempTriples$).subtract($newClasses$)
  $newTriples \leftarrow newTriples$.union($tempTriples$)
$otherLangTriples \leftarrow$ getOtherLangTriples($newTriples$, $\mathcal{C}'_{S-translated}$)
$\mathcal{T}_e \leftarrow newTriples$.union($foreignLanguageTriples$)

3.4 Triple Retrieval

The aim of this phase is to identify which and where the new information can be added to T. Each class in S is replaced by its best translation found in $\mathcal{C}'_{S-translated}$ from the previous phase in order to get a translated ontology $S_{translated}$ (see Algorithm 2). We design an iterative process in order to obtain $\mathcal{T}_e$, which is represented by $\langle s, p, o \rangle$, that has all possible multilingual information from S to be added to T. We initiate the iterative process with all matched terms ($newClasses = M$) in order to get all related classes, if exist. The iterative process has three steps: (1) for each class $c \in newClasses$, all triples $tempTriples$ are retrieved from $S_{translated}$ where c is a subject or an object, (2) a new list of new classes is obtained from $tempTriples$, (3) $tempTriples$ is added to $newTriples$ which will be added to T. These three steps are repeated until no new classes can be found ($newClasses$.isEmpty() $= true$). Next, we retrieve all available information from the other language for each class in $newTriples$ such as ⟨president, `rdfs:label`, "رئيس"@ar⟩. The output of this phase is $\mathcal{T}_e$ which contains all multilingual triples (i.e., in L_s and L_t languages) to be added to T.

3.5 Enrichment

The aim of this phase is to enrich T using triples in $\mathcal{T}_e$. By using OECM, the target ontology can be enriched from several ontologies in different natural languages sequentially, i.e. one-to-many enrichment. In this case, $T_{enriched}$ can have more than two natural languages. For instance, English T can be enriched from a German ontology, then the enriched ontology can be enriched again form a different Arabic ontology, i.e. the final result for $T_{enriched}$ is presented in English, German, and Arabic. With the completion of this phase, we have successfully enriched T and create a multilingual ontology from monolingual ones.

3.6 Validation

The aim of this phase is to validate the enriched ontology, which is a crucial step to detect inconsistencies and syntax errors, which might be produced during

```
### https://w3id.org/seo#Publisher
seo:Publisher rdf:type owl:Class ;
        rdfs:subClassOf <http://xmlns.com/foaf/0.1/Organization> ;
        rdfs:comment "The publisher of the event proceedings."@en ;
        rdfs:label "Publisher"@en .
                   "Herausgeber"@de .

### http://conference_de#CommitteeMember
conference_de:CommitteeMember rdf:type owl:Class ;
        rdfs:subClassOf <http://xmlns.com/foaf/0.1/Person> ;
        rdfs:label "committee member"@en .
                   "Angehörige des Ausschusses"@de .

### https://w3id.org/seo#Chair
seo:Chair rdf:type owl:Class;
        rdfs:subClassOf conference_de:CommitteeMember ;
        rdfs:label "Chair"@en .
                   "Vorsitzender"@de .
```

Fig. 3. Small fragment from SEO_{en-de} ontology after the enrichment. The newly added information is marked in bold.

the enrichment process [8]. There are two types of validations: syntactic and semantic validation. In the syntactic validation, we validate $T_{enriched}$ to conform with the W3C RDF standards using the online RDF validation service[9] which detects syntax errors, such as missing tags. For semantic validation, we use two reasoners, FaCT++ and HermiT, for detecting inconsistencies in $T_{enriched}$ [8].

4 Use Case: Enriching the Scientific Events Ontology

In this use case, we use an example scenario to enrich the SEO_{en}[10] ontology (with 49 classes), in English, using the MultiFarm dataset (see Sect. 5). We use the Conference ontology (60 classes) and the ConfOf ontology (38 classes), in German and Arabic respectively, as source ontologies. This use case aims to show the whole process starting from submitting the source and target ontologies until producing the enriched multilingual ontology. Here, the source ontology is the German ontology Conference_{de} and the target ontology is the English ontology SEO_{en}. The output is the enriched ontology SEO_{en-de}, which becomes a multilingual ontology in English and German. Table 1 demonstrates the enrichment process for SEO_{en} from Conference_{de} and shows the output sample of each phase starting from the translation phase to the produced set of triples which are used to enrich SEO_{en}. In the terminological matching task, the relevant matching results (with similarity scores in bold) are identified with $\theta \geq 0.9$. The iterative process, in the triple retrieval phase, is initiated with the identified matched terms, for example, `person` class. At the first iteration, six triples

[9] https://www.w3.org/RDF/Validator/.
[10] https://w3id.org/seo.

Table 1. Use case: the sample output of each phase, from translation to triple retrieval.

Phase	Output
Translation	(Thema)$_{de}$ → (subject, topic)$_{en}$ (Gutachter)$_{de}$ → (reviewer, expert)$_{en}$ (Herausgeber)$_{de}$ → (publisher, editor)$_{en}$ (Fortschritte der Konferenz)$_{de}$ → (Progress of the conference)$_{en}$
Pre-processing	SizeOrDuration → size duration WorkshopProposals → workshop proposal InvitedSpeaker → invite speaker In-useTrack → use track
Terminological matching score results	(invited speaker, keynote speaker, 0.57) (person, person, **1.00**) (tutorial, tutorial proposals, 0.78) (prize, award, **1.00**) (conference document, license document, 0.61) (publisher, publisher, **1.00**) (conference series, event series, 0.79) (conference series, symposium series, 0.75) (proceedings, proceedings, **1.00**) (poster, posters track, 0.78)
Triple Retrieval (Iterative process)	1st Iteration: ⟨conference contributor, rdfs:subClassOf, person⟩ ⟨committee member, rdfs:subClassOf, person⟩ 2nd Iteration: ⟨committee member, rdf:type, Class⟩ ⟨chairman, rdfs:subClassOf, committee member⟩ ⟨conference contributor, rdf:type, Class⟩ ⟨invited speaker, rdfs:subClassOf, conference contributor⟩ ⟨regular author, rdfs:subClassOf, conference contributor⟩
Triple Retrieval ($\mathcal{T}_e$)	⟨committee member, rdf:type, Class⟩ ⟨committee member, rdfs:label, "committee member"@en⟩ ⟨committee member,rdfs:label,"Angehörige des Ausschusses"@de⟩ ⟨chairman, rdfs:subClassOf, committee member⟩

(not all results are exist in the table because of the limited space) are produced such as ⟨**conference contributor**, rdfs:subClassOf, person⟩, where the matched term person is located at the object position. New classes are determined from the produced triples such as **conference contributor** and **committee member** (in bold). At the second iteration, all triples that have these new classes, as subject or object, are retrieved, for example; for the committee member class, the triples ⟨committee member, rdf:type, Class⟩ and ⟨chairman, rdfs:subClassOf, committee member⟩ are retrieved. This process is repeated again and new classes are identified from the produced triples such as chairman. The iterative process ended at the fifth iteration where three triples are produced without any new classes. The output of this phase is $\mathcal{T}_e$ which has 40 new triples (with 20 new classes and their German labels), to be added to SEO$_{en}$ and produce SEO$_{en-de}$. Figure 3 shows a small fragment of the enriched ontology SEO_{en-de}, in Turtle, after completing the enrichment process. The resulting multilingual ontology contains a newly added class `CommitteeMember` with its English and German labels, a new relation `rdfs:subClassOf` between the two classes `CommitteeMember` and `Chair`, and new German labels such as `Herausgeber` and `Vorsitzender` for classes `Publisher` and `Chair` respectively. Similarly, SEO_{en-de} is enriched from the Arabic ontology ConfOf_{ar}, where all classes with English labels in SEO_{en-de} are matched with class labels in ConfOf_{ar}. The produced $\text{SEO}_{en-de-ar}$ has 113 new triples with 37 new classes with their Arabic labels. Final output results can be found at the OECM GitHub repository.

5 Evaluation

The aim of this evaluation is to measure the quality of the cross-lingual matching process in addition to the enrichment process. We use ontologies in MultiFarm benchmark[11], a benchmark designed for evaluating cross-lingual ontology matching systems. MultiFarm consists of seven ontologies (*Cmt*, *Conference*, *ConfOf*, *Edas*, *Ekaw*, *Iasted*, *Sigkdd*) originally coming from the Conference benchmark of OAEI, their translation into nine languages (Chinese, Czech, Dutch, French, German, Portuguese, Russian, Spanish and Arabic), and the corresponding cross-lingual alignments between them.

Experimental Setup. All phases of OECM have been implemented using Scala and Apache Spark[12]. SANSA-RDF library[13] [17] with Apache Jena framework[14] are used to parse and manipulate the input ontologies (as RDF triples). In order to process the class labels, the Stanford CoreNLP[15] [19] is used. All experiments are carried out on Ubuntu 16.04 LTS operating system with an Intel Corei7-4600U CPU @ 2.10 GHz x 4 CPU and 10 GB of memory. In our experiments, we consider English ontologies as target ontologies to be enriched from German and Arabic ontologies.

Our evaluation has three tasks: (1) evaluating the effectiveness of the cross-lingual matching process in OECM compared to the reference alignment provided in the MultiFarm benchmark, (2) comparing OECM matching results with four state-of-the-art approaches, in addition to our previous work (OECM 1.0) [14], and (3) evaluating the quality of the enrichment process.

Effectiveness of OECM. In this experiment, we use the English version of *Cmt* ontology as the source ontology, and German and Arabic versions of *Conference*, *ConfOf*, and *Sigkdd* ontologies as target ontologies. We match class labels in *Cmt* ontology with class labels of German and Arabic versions of *Conference*, *ConfOf*, and *Sigkdd* ontologies separately. The resulting alignments are compared

[11] https://www.irit.fr/recherches/MELODI/multifarm/.
[12] https://spark.apache.org/.
[13] https://github.com/SANSA-Stack/SANSA-RDF.
[14] https://jena.apache.org/.
[15] https://stanfordnlp.github.io/CoreNLP/.

Table 2. Precision, recall and F-measures for the cross-lingual matching

Ontology pairs	German × English			Arabic × English					
	Precision	Recall	F-measure	Precision		Recall		F-measure	
				Before	After	Before	After	Before	After
Conference × Cmt	1.00	0.38	0.56	1.00	1.00	0.33	0.42	0.50	0.59
ConfOf × Cmt	1.00	0.70	0.82	1.00	1.00	0.30	0.60	0.46	0.75
Sigkdd × Cmt	1.00	0.90	0.95	1.00	1.00	0.40	0.80	0.57	0.89

with the reference alignments, as a gold standard, provided in the benchmark for each pair of ontologies. Table 2 shows the precision, recall and F-measure of the matching process for each pair of ontologies. OECM achieves the highest precision of 1.00 for all pair of ontologies. Meanwhile, OECM achieves the highest recall and F-measure of 0.90 and 0.95 respectively for matching the German *Sigkdd* with the English *Cmt*. As two authors of this work are native speakers of Arabic, we found some linguistic mistakes in the Arabic ontologies which negatively affect the translation and the matching results. Therefore, we correct these mistakes and make it available at the OECM GitHub repository. Matching results *before* and *after* the corrections are presented in the table, where such corrections have greatly improved the matching results in terms of recall and F-measure. For instance, in matching the Arabic *Sigkdd* with the English *Cmt*, recall and F-measure are enhanced by 40% and 32% respectively.

Comparison with the State-of-the-Art. We identified four of the related approaches (AML, KEPLER, LogMap, and XMap) to be included in our evaluation in addition to OECM 1.0. The other related work, neither publish their code, nor their evaluation datasets [10,11,25]. In order to compare our results with the state-of-the-art, we use German (Conference$_{de}$) and Arabic (Conference$_{ar}$) versions of the *Conference* ontology as the source ontologies, and Ekaw$_{en}$ and Edas$_{en}$ ontologies as the target English ontologies. We choose Ekaw$_{en}$ and Edas$_{en}$ ontologies in this evaluation because they are used in the state-of-the-art systems for evaluation, as mentioned in the results of OAEI 2018. We generate the gold standard alignments between each pair of ontologies using the Alignment API 4.9[16], as used by the state-of-the-art systems, in order to compute precision, recall, and F-measures. Table 3 shows the comparison between our results against four state-of-the-art approaches and OECM 1.0 (results for matching English and German ontologies only). In addition, we add the updated Arabic ontology (Conference'$_{ar}$) with our linguistic correction in the matching process in order to show the effectiveness of such corrections. The current version of OECM (OECM 1.1) outperforms all other systems in precision, recall and F-measure. For instance, when matching Conference$_{de}$ × Ekaw$_{en}$, OECM 1.1 outperforms LogMap, the highest precision, recall and F-measure among the others, by 29%, 60% and 58% in terms of precision, recall and F-measure respectively. The use of semantic similarity in OECM 1.1 significantly improves the matching results

[16] http://alignapi.gforge.inria.fr/.

Table 3. State-of-the-art comparison results. Bold entries are the top scores.

Approaches	Conference$_{de}$ × Ekaw$_{en}$			Conference$_{de}$ × Edas$_{en}$		
	Precision	Recall	F-measure	Precision	Recall	F-measure
AML [7]	0.56	0.20	0.29	0.86	0.35	0.50
KEPLER [16]	0.33	0.16	0.22	0.43	0.18	0.25
LogMap [15]	0.71	0.20	0.31	0.71	0.29	0.42
XMap [28]	0.18	0.16	0.17	0.23	0.18	0.20
OECM 1.0 [14]	0.75	0.67	0.71	0.93	0.76	0.84
OECM 1.1	**1.00**	**0.80**	**0.89**	**1.00**	**0.78**	**0.88**
	Conference$_{ar}$ × Ekaw$_{en}$			Conference$_{ar}$ × Edas$_{en}$		
AML [7]	0.64	0.39	0.28	0.71	0.42	0.29
KEPLER [16]	0.40	0.30	0.24	0.40	0.30	0.24
LogMap [15]	0.40	0.13	0.08	0.40	0.18	0.12
XMap [28]	**1.00**	0.0	0.0	**1.00**	0.00	0.00
OECM 1.1	**1.00**	**0.50**	**0.67**	0.86	**0.67**	**0.75**
OECM 1.1	Conference'$_{ar}$ × Ekaw$_{en}$			Conference'$_{ar}$ × Edas$_{en}$		
	0.88	**0.70**	**0.78**	**1.00**	**0.78**	**0.88**

compared to the results of OECM 1.0. For instance, when matching Conference$_{de}$ × Ekaw$_{en}$, matching results in OECM 1.0 have been enhanced by 25%, 13%, and 18% in terms of precision, recall and F-measure respectively. When matching Conference$_{ar}$ × Edas$_{en}$, XMap outperform OECM by 14% in terms of precision, while OECM outperforms it in both recall and f-measure. It is observed that the precision of OECM slightly decreased because of the linguistic mistakes found in Conference$_{ar}$. When considering Conference'$_{ar}$, which has the linguistic correction, as a source ontology in this matching, the matching results are improved.

Evaluating the Enrichment Process. According to [4], the enriched ontology can be evaluated by comparing it against a predefined reference ontology (Gold standard). In this experiment, we evaluate the enriched ontology SEO$_{en-de}$ (cf. Sect. 4). A gold standard ontology has been manually created by ontology experts. By comparing SEO$_{en-de}$ with the gold standard, OECM achieves 1.00, 0.80, and 0.89 in terms of precision, recall, and F-measure respectively. This finding confirms the usefulness of our approach in cross-lingual ontology enrichment.

6 Conclusion

We present a fully automated approach, OECM, for building multilingual ontologies. The strength of our contribution lies on building such ontologies from monolingual ones using cross-lingual matching between ontologies concepts. Indo and non-Indo-European languages resources are used for enrichment in order to illustrate the robustness of our approach. Considering multiple translations of concepts and the use of semantic similarity measures for selecting the best translation have significantly improved the quality of the matching process. Iterative triple retrieval process has been developed to determine which information, from the source ontology, can be added to the target ontology, and where such information should be added. We show the applicability of OECM by presenting a use case for enriching an ontology in the scholarly communication domain. The results of the cross-lingual matching process are found promising compared to five state-of-the-art approaches, involving the previous version of OECM. Furthermore, evaluating the quality of the enrichment process emphasizes the validity of our approach. Finally, we propose some linguistic corrections for the Arabic ontologies in the MultiFarm benchmark that used in our experiment, which considerably enhanced the matching results. In conclusion, our approach provides a springboard for a new way to build multilingual ontologies from monolingual ones. In the future, we intend to further consider properties and individuals in the enrichment process. In addition, we aim to apply optimization methods in order to evaluate the efficiency of OECM when enriching very large ontologies.

Acknowledgments. This work has been supported by the BOOST EU project no. 755175. Shimaa Ibrahim and Said Fathalla would like to acknowledge the Ministry of Higher Education (MoHE) of Egypt for providing scholarships to conduct this study.

References

1. Ali, M., Fathalla, S., Ibrahim, S., Kholief, M., Hassan, Y.F.: CLOE: a cross-lingual ontology enrichment using multi-agent architecture. In: Enterprise Information Systems, pp. 1–21 (2019)
2. Cheatham, M., Hitzler, P.: String similarity metrics for ontology alignment. In: Alani, H., et al. (eds.) ISWC 2013. LNCS, vol. 8219, pp. 294–309. Springer, Heidelberg (2013). https://doi.org/10.1007/978-3-642-41338-4_19
3. Cross, V.: Semantic similarity: a key to ontology alignment. In: Ontology Matching: OM-2018: Proceedings of the ISWC Workshop, p. 61 (2018)
4. Dellschaft, K., Staab, S.: On how to perform a gold standard based evaluation of ontology learning. In: Cruz, I., et al. (eds.) ISWC 2006. LNCS, vol. 4273, pp. 228–241. Springer, Heidelberg (2006). https://doi.org/10.1007/11926078_17
5. Embley, D.W., Liddle, S.W., Lonsdale, D.W., Tijerino, Y.: Multilingual ontologies for cross-language information extraction and semantic search. In: Jeusfeld, M., Delcambre, L., Ling, T.-W. (eds.) ER 2011. LNCS, vol. 6998, pp. 147–160. Springer, Heidelberg (2011). https://doi.org/10.1007/978-3-642-24606-7_12
6. Espinoza, M., Gómez-Pérez, A., Mena, E.: Enriching an ontology with multilingual information. In: Bechhofer, S., Hauswirth, M., Hoffmann, J., Koubarakis, M. (eds.) ESWC 2008. LNCS, vol. 5021, pp. 333–347. Springer, Heidelberg (2008). https://doi.org/10.1007/978-3-540-68234-9_26
7. Faria, D., et al.: Results of AML participation in OAEI 2018. In: Proceedings of the 13th International Workshop on Ontology Matching, pp. 125–131. CEUR-WS (2018)

8. Fathalla, S., Lange, C., Auer, S.: EVENTSKG: a 5-star dataset of top-ranked events in eight computer science communities. In: Hitzler, P., et al. (eds.) ESWC 2019. LNCS, vol. 11503, pp. 427–442. Springer, Cham (2019). https://doi.org/10.1007/978-3-030-21348-0_28
9. Fathalla, S., Vahdati, S., Auer, S., Lange, C.: SEO: a scientific events data model. In: International Semantic Web Conference. Springer (2019, in Press)
10. Fu, B., Brennan, R.: Cross-lingual ontology mapping and its use on the multilingual semantic web. MSW **571**, 13–20 (2010)
11. Fu, B., Brennan, R., O'Sullivan, D.: A configurable translation-based cross-lingual ontology mapping system to adjust mapping outcomes. Web Semant. Sci. Serv. Agents World Wide Web **15**, 15–36 (2012)
12. Gracia, J., Montiel-Ponsoda, E., Cimiano, P., Gómez-Pérez, A., Buitelaar, P., McCrae, J.: Challenges for the multilingual web of data. Web Semant. Sci. Serv. Agents World Wide Web **11**, 63–71 (2012)
13. Hertling, S., Paulheim, H.: Wikimatch: using Wikipedia for ontology matching. In: Ontology Matching, vol. 946 (2012)
14. Ibrahim, S., Fathalla, S., Yazdi, H.S., Lehmann, J., Jabeen, H.: OECM: a cross-lingual approach for ontology enrichment. In: European Semantic Web Conference. Springer (2019, in Press)
15. Jiménez-Ruiz, E., Grau, V.C.: LogMap family participation in the OAEI 2018. In: Proceedings of the 13th International Workshop on Ontology Matching, pp. 187–191. CEUR-WS (2018)
16. Kachroudi, M., Diallo, G., Yahia, S.B.: OAEI 2018 results of KEPLER. In: Proceedings of the 13th International Workshop on Ontology Matching, pp. 173–178. CEUR-WS (2018)
17. Lehmann, J., et al.: Distributed semantic analytics using the SANSA stack. In: d'Amato, C., et al. (eds.) ISWC 2017. LNCS, vol. 10588, pp. 147–155. Springer, Cham (2017). https://doi.org/10.1007/978-3-319-68204-4_15
18. Lin, F., Krizhanovsky, A.: Multilingual ontology matching based on Wiktionary data accessible via SPARQL endpoint. In: RCDL (2011)
19. Manning, C.D., Surdeanu, M., Bauer, J., Finkel, J., Bethard, S.J., McClosky, D.: The Stanford CoreNLP natural language processing toolkit. In: Association for Computational Linguistics (ACL) System Demonstrations, pp. 55–60 (2014). http://www.aclweb.org/anthology/P/P14/P14-5010
20. Meilicke, C., et al.: MultiFarm: a benchmark for multilingual ontology matching. In: Web Semantics: Science, Services and Agents on the World Wide Web, vol. 15, pp. 62–68 (2012)
21. Mihalcea, R., Corley, C., Strapparava, C., et al.: Corpus-based and knowledge-based measures of text semantic similarity. AAAI **6**, 775–780 (2006)
22. Niwattanakul, S., Singthongchai, J., Naenudorn, E., Wanapu, S.: Using of Jaccard coefficient for keywords similarity. In: Proceedings of the International MultiConference of Engineers and Computer Scientists, vol. 1 (2013)
23. Petasis, G., Karkaletsis, V., Paliouras, G., Krithara, A., Zavitsanos, E.: Ontology population and enrichment: state of the art. In: Paliouras, G., Spyropoulos, C.D., Tsatsaronis, G. (eds.) Knowledge-Driven Multimedia Information Extraction and Ontology Evolution. LNCS (LNAI), vol. 6050, pp. 134–166. Springer, Heidelberg (2011). https://doi.org/10.1007/978-3-642-20795-2_6
24. Spohr, D., Hollink, L., Cimiano, P.: A machine learning approach to multilingual and cross-lingual ontology matching. In: Aroyo, L., et al. (eds.) ISWC 2011. LNCS, vol. 7031, pp. 665–680. Springer, Heidelberg (2011). https://doi.org/10.1007/978-3-642-25073-6_42

25. Tigrine, A.N., Bellahsene, Z., Todorov, K.: Light-weight cross-lingual ontology matching with LYAM++. In: Debruyne, C., et al. (eds.) OTM 2015. LNCS, vol. 9415, pp. 527–544. Springer, Cham (2015). https://doi.org/10.1007/978-3-319-26148-5_36
26. Trojahn, C., Fu, B., Zamazal, O., Ritze, D.: State-of-the-art in multilingual and cross-lingual ontology matching. In: Buitelaar, P., Cimiano, P. (eds.) Towards the Multilingual Semantic Web, pp. 119–135. Springer, Heidelberg (2014). https://doi.org/10.1007/978-3-662-43585-4_8
27. Trojahn, C., Quaresma, P., Vieira, R.: A framework for multilingual ontology mapping (2008)
28. Warith Eddine Djeddi, S.B.Y., Khadir, M.T.: XMap results for OAEI 2018. In: Proceedings of the 13th International Workshop on Ontology Matching, pp. 210–215. CEUR-WS (2018)

MELT - Matching EvaLuation Toolkit

Sven Hertling[1(✉)], Jan Portisch[1,2], and Heiko Paulheim[1]

[1] Data and Web Science Group, University of Mannheim, Mannheim, Germany
{sven,jan,heiko}@informatik.uni-mannheim.de

[2] SAP SE Product Engineering Financial Services, Walldorf, Germany
jan.portisch@sap.com

Abstract. In this paper, we present the Ontology Matching EvaLuation Toolkit (MELT), a software toolkit to facilitate ontology matcher development, configuration, evaluation, and packaging. Compared to existing tools in the ontology matching domain, our framework offers detailed evaluation capabilities on the correspondence level of alignments as well as extensive group evaluation possibilities. A particular focus is put on a streamlined development and evaluation process along with ease of use for matcher developers and evaluators. Our contributions are twofold: We present an open source matching toolkit that integrates well into existing platforms, as well as an exemplary analysis of two OAEI 2018 tracks demonstrating advantages and analytical capabilities of MELT.

Keywords: Ontology matching · Evaluation framework · OAEI · SEALS · HOBBIT

1 Introduction

Ontology matching or ontology alignment is the non-trivial task of finding correspondences between entities of a set of given ontologies [10]. The matching can be performed manually or through the use of an automated matching system. For systematically evaluating the quality of such matchers, the Ontology Alignment Evaluation Initiative (OAEI) has been running campaigns [9] every year since 2005. Unlike other evaluation campaigns where researchers submit *data sets* as solutions to report their results (such as Kaggle[1]), the OAEI requires participants to submit a matching *system*, which is then executed on-site. After the evaluation, the results are publicly reported[2]. Therefore, execution and evaluation platforms have been developed and OAEI participants are required to package and submit their matching system for the corresponding platform. Two well-known platforms are used in the ontology matching community: The Semantic Evaluation at Large Scale (SEALS)[3] [12,35] and the more recent Holistic Benchmarking of Big Linked Data (HOBBIT)[4] [24].

[1] https://www.kaggle.com.

[2] http://oaei.ontologymatching.org/2018/results/index.html.

[3] http://www.seals-project.eu.

[4] http://project-hobbit.eu.

M. Acosta et al. (Eds.): SEMANTiCS 2019, LNCS 11702, pp. 231–245, 2019.
https://doi.org/10.1007/978-3-030-33220-4_17

Based on the results of the OAEI 2018 campaign [1], only 4 out of 12 tracks were available in HOBBIT (*LargeBio*, *Link Discovery*, *SPIMBENCH*, *KnowledgeGraph*). Out of 19 matchers that were submitted in the 2018 campaign, only 6 matchers supported both, SEALS and HOBBIT, and 2 supported HOBBIT exclusively. The remaining 11 matchers supported only SEALS. While one reason for the low HOBBIT adoption might be its novelty, it also requires more steps to package a matcher for the HOBBIT platform and knowledge of the Docker[5] virtualization software. In particular for new entrants to the ontology matching community, the existing tooling might appear overwhelmingly complicated. In addition to potential obstacles for matcher development and submission, another observation from the OAEI campaigns is that the evaluation varies greatly among the different tracks that are offered e.g. *Anatomy* results contain *Recall+* as well as alignment coherence whereas the *Conference* track focuses on different reference alignments. Due to limited group evaluation capabilities in existing frameworks, some track organizers even developed their own evaluation systems.

For these reasons we present the *Matching EvaLuation Toolkit* (MELT)[6] – an open source toolkit for ontology matcher development, fine-tuning, submission, and evaluation. The target audience are matching system developers as well as researchers who run evaluations on multiple matching systems such as OAEI track organizers. Likewise, system developers can use this tool to analyze the performance and errors of their systems in order to improve it. Furthermore, they can package and submit the system easily to OAEI campaigns.

The rest of this paper is structured as follows: Sect. 2 describes other work in the field of alignment visualization and evaluation. Section 3 gives an overview of the MELT framework and its possibilities whereas Sect. 4 shows an exemplary analysis of the latest systems submitted to the OAEI. We finish with an outlook on future developments.

2 Related Work

As MELT can be used both for evaluating ontology matching tools, as well as visualizing matching results, we discuss related works in both fields.

2.1 Matching and Alignment Evaluation Platforms

OAEI campaigns consist of multiple problem sets, so called *tracks*. Each track has its organizers who provide the datasets including reference alignments, execute the matching systems, and prepare the results page for the participants and the whole community. The track contains one or more test cases which correspond to a specific matching task consisting of two ontologies and a reference alignment. In 2010, three tracks (*Benchmark*, *Anatomy*, and *Conference*) were adjusted

[5] https://www.docker.com.

[6] https://github.com/dwslab/melt.

to be run with the SEALS platform [8]. One year later, participants of OAEI campaigns had to implement a matching interface and the SEALS client was the main tool used for executing and evaluating matchers. The interface contains a simple method (`align()`) which receives a URL for the source and a URL for the target ontology and has to return a URL which points to a file containing all correspondences in the alignment format[7]. This format is defined and used by the *Alignment API* [5].

Starting from 2017, a second evaluation platform, called *HOBBIT*, was added [18]. One difference compared to SEALS is that the system has to be submitted as a Docker image to a *GitLab* instance[8], and in the corresponding project, a matcher description file has to be created. After submission of the matching system, the whole evaluation runs on servers of the HOBBIT platform. Thus, the source code for evaluating the matchers has to be submitted as a Docker image as well. All Docker containers communicate with each other over a message broker (*RabbitMQ*[9]). Hence, the interface between a system and the evaluation component can be arbitrary. To keep a similar interface to SEALS, the data generation component transfers two ontologies and the system adapter receives the URL to these files. It should return a file similar to the SEALS interface.

Working with alignments in Java code can be achieved with the *Alignment API* [5]. It is the most well-known API for ontology matching and can be used for loading and persisting alignments as well as for evaluating them with a set of possible evaluation strategies. Moreover, it provides some matching systems which are also used in OAEI campaigns as a baseline. Unfortunately, it is not yet enabled to be used with the maven build system[10]. Therefore, instead of using this API, some system developers created their own classes to work with alignments and to store them on disk[11] in order to be compatible with the evaluation interface.

Alignment Visualization. A lot of work has been done in the area of analyzing, editing, and visualizing alignments or ontologies with a graphical user interface. One example is *Alignment Cubes* [15], which allows an interactive visual exploration and evaluation of alignments. An advantage is the fine grained analysis on the level of an individual correspondence. It further allows to visualize the performance history of a matcher, for instance, which correspondences a matcher found in the most recent OAEI campaign but not in the previous one. Another framework for working with alignment files is *VOAR* [28,29]. It is a Web-based system where users can upload ontologies and alignments. *VOAR* then allows the user to render them with multiple visualization types. The upload size of ontologies as well as alignments is restricted so that very large files cannot be uploaded.

[7] http://alignapi.gforge.inria.fr/format.html.
[8] https://master.project-hobbit.eu.
[9] https://www.rabbitmq.com.
[10] https://maven.apache.org/.
[11] https://github.com/ernestojimenezruiz/logmap-matcher/tree/master/src/main/java/uk/ac/ox/krr/logmap_lite/io.

Similar to *VOAR*, the *SILK workbench* [33] is also a Web-based tool with a focus on link/correspondence creation between different data sets in the *Linked Open Data Cloud*[12]. Unlike *VOAR*, it usually runs on the user's computer. Matching operations (such as Levenshtein distance [20]) are visualized as nodes in a computation graph. The found correspondences are displayed and can be modified to further specify which concepts should be matched.

Further visualization approaches were pursued by matching system developers to actually fine-tune their systems. All these visualizations are therefore very specific to a particular matching approach. One such example is *YAM++* [23], which is a matching system based on a machine learning approach. Results are visualized in a split view where the class hierarchy of the two input ontologies is shown on each side lines are drawn between the matched classes. The user can modify the alignment with the help of this GUI. In a similar way, the developers of *COMA++* [2] created a user interface for their results. A visualization of whole ontologies is not implemented by the current tools but can be achieved with the help of *VOWL* [21] or *Web Protégé* [32], for instance.

Our proposed framework MELT allows for detailed and reusable analyses such as the ones presented in this section due to its flexible metrics and evaluators. An overview of the framework is presented in the following section.

3 Matching Evaluation Toolkit

MELT is a software framework implemented in Java which aims to facilitate matcher development, configuration, packaging, and evaluation. In this section, we will first introduce *Yet Another Alignment API*, an API for ontology alignment which is integrated into the framework. Afterwards, the matcher development process in MELT is introduced. Subsections 3.3 and 3.4 cover specific aspects of the framework that have not yet been explicitly addressed in the community: The implementation of matchers outside of the Java programming language Subsect. 3.3 and the chaining matching workflows Subsect. 3.4. After explaining the tuning component of the framework, this section closes with the matcher evaluation process in MELT.

3.1 YAAA: Yet Another Alignment API

To allow for a simple development workflow, MELT contains *Yet Another Alignment API* (YAAA). It is similar to the *Alignment API* presented earlier but contains additional improvements such as maven support and arbitrary indexing possibilities of correspondence elements allowing queries such as "retrieve all correspondences with a specific source". This is very helpful for a fast evaluation of large-scale test cases containing large reference or system alignments. The indexing is done with the *cqengine* library[13]. The API is, in addition, capable

[12] https://lod-cloud.net.
[13] https://github.com/npgall/cqengine/.

of serializing and parsing alignments. It also makes sure that all characters are escaped and that the resulting XML is actually parseable[14]. As explainability is still an open issue in the ontology matching community [7,34], YAAA also allows for extensions to correspondences and alignments. This means that additional information such as debugging information or human-readable explanations can be added. If there is additional information available in the alignment, it will also be printed by the default `CSVEvaluator` which allows for immediate consumption in the analysis and evaluation process and hopefully fosters the usage of additional explanations in the alignment format.

It is important to note that MELT does not require the usage of YAAA for parameter tuning, executing, or packaging a matcher – but also works with other APIs such as the *Alignment API*. This allows to evaluate matchers that were not developed using YAAA (see Sect. 4).

3.2 Matcher Development Workflow

In order to develop a matcher in Java with MELT, the first step is to decide which matching interface to implement. The most general interface is encapsulated in class `MatcherURL` which receives two URLs of the ontologies to be matched together with a URL referencing an input alignment. The return value should be a URL representing a file with correspondences in the alignment format. Since this interface is not very convenient, we also provide more specialized classes. In the `matching-yaaa` package we set the alignment library to YAAA. All matchers implementing interfaces from this package have to use the library and get at the same time an easier to handle interface of correspondences. In further specializations we also set the Semantic Web framework which is used to represent the ontologies. For a better usability, the two most well-known frameworks are integrated into MELT: *Apache Jena*[15] [3] (`MatcherYAAAJena`) and the *OWL API*[16] [14] (`MatcherYAAAOwlApi`). As the latter two classes are organized as separate maven projects, only the libraries which are actually required for the matcher are loaded. In addition, further services were implemented such as an ontology cache which ensures that ontologies are parsed only once. This is helpful, for instance, when the matcher accesses an ontology multiple times, when multiple matchers work together in a pipeline, or when multiple matchers shall be evaluated. We explicitly chose a framework-independent architecture so that developers can use the full functionality of the frameworks they already know rather than having to understand an additional wrapping layer. The different levels at which a matcher can be developed as well as how the classes presented in this section work together, are displayed in Fig. 1.

[14] This is not always the case for other implementations.

[15] https://jena.apache.org.

[16] http://owlcs.github.io/owlapi/.

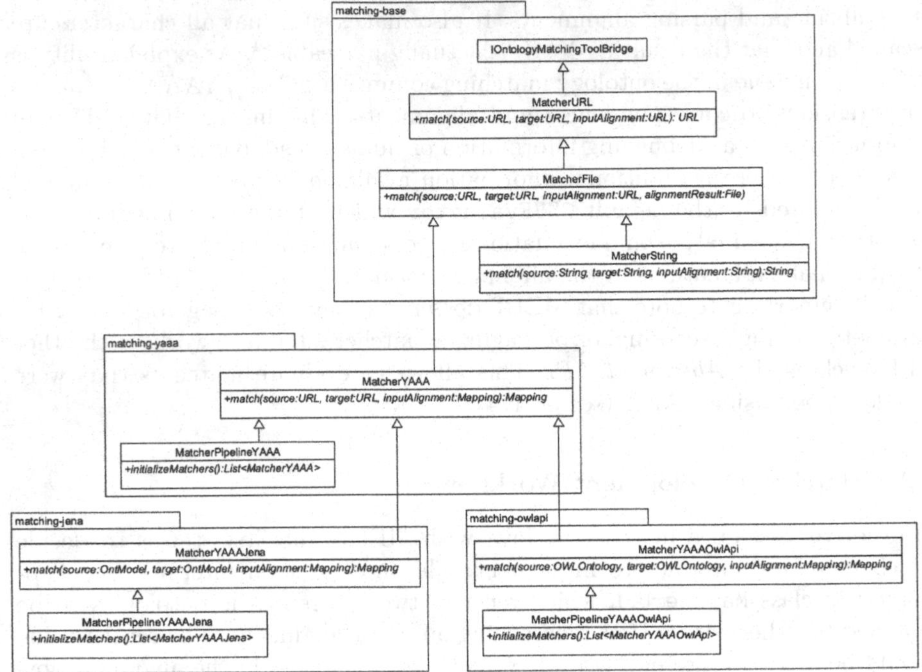

Fig. 1. Different possibilities to implement matchers

3.3 External Matching

The current ontology matching development and evaluation frameworks that are available focus on the Java programming language. As researchers apply advances in machine learning and natural language processing to other domains, they often turn to Python because leading machine learning libraries such as *scikit-learn*[17], *TensorFlow*[18], *PyTorch*[19], *Keras*[20], or *gensim* [26] are not easily available for the Java language. In the 2018 OAEI campaign, the first tools using such frameworks for ontology matching have been submitted [1].

To accommodate for the changes outlined, MELT allows to develop a matcher in any other programming language and wrap it as a SEALS or HOBBIT package. Therefore, class `MatcherExternal` has to be extended. It has to transform the given ontology URIs and input alignments to an executable command line call. The interface for the external process is simple. It receives the input variables via the command line and outputs the results via the standard output of the process – similar to many Unix command line tools. An example for a

[17] https://scikit-learn.org/.
[18] https://www.tensorflow.org/.
[19] https://pytorch.org/.
[20] https://keras.io/.

matcher implemented in Python is available on GitHub[21]. It also contains a simple implementation of the alignment format to allow Python matchers serializing their correspondences.

When executing the matcher with the SEALS client, the matching system is loaded into the Java virtual machine (JVM) of the SEALS client (evaluation code) with a customized class loader. This raises two points: (1) The code under test is executed in the same JVM and can probably access the code for evaluation. (2) The used class loader from the *JCL library*[22] does not implement all methods (specifically `getPackage()` and `getResource()`) of a class loader. However, these methods are used by other Java libraries[23] to load operating system dependent files contained in the jar file. Thus, some libraries do not work when evaluating a matcher with SEALS. Another problem is that all libraries used by the matching system may collide with libraries used by SEALS. This can cause issues with *Jena* and other Semantic Web frameworks because of the same JVM instance. To solve this issue, `MatcherExternal` can not only be used for matchers written in another programming language but also for Java matchers which use dependencies that are incompatible with the SEALS platform.

3.4 Pipelining Matchers

Ontology matchers often combine multiple matching approaches and sometimes consist of the same parts. An example would be a string-based matching of elements, and the application of a stable marriage algorithm or another matching refinement step on the resulting similarity matrix.

Following this observation, MELT allows for the chaining of matchers: The alignment of one matcher is then the input for the next matcher in the pipeline. The ontology caching services of MELT mentioned above prevent performance problems arising from repetitive loading and parsing of ontologies.

In order to execute a matcher pipeline, classes `MatcherPipelineYAAA` (for matchers that use different ontology management frameworks), `MatcherPipelineYAAAJena` (for pure *Jena* pipelines), and `MacherPipelineYAAAOwlApi` (for pure *OWL API* pipelines) can be extended. Here the `initializeMatchers()` method has to be implemented. It returns matcher instances as a `List` in the order in which they shall be executed. These reusable parts of a matcher can easily be uploaded to GitHub to allow other developers to use common functionality[24].

[21] https://github.com/dwslab/melt/tree/master/examples/externalPythonMatcher.

[22] https://github.com/kamranzafar/JCL/blob/master/JCL/src/xeus/jcl/AbstractClassLoader.java.

[23] An example would be class `SQLiteJDBCLoader` in `sqlite-jdbc` which uses these class loader methods.

[24] Other GitHub dependencies can be included by using https://jitpack.io, for instance.

3.5 Tuning Matchers

Many ontology matching systems require parameters to be set at design time. Those can significantly influence the matching system's performance. An example for a parameter would be the threshold parameter of a matcher utilizing a normalized string distance metric. For tuning such a system, MELT offers a `GridSearch` functionality. It requires a matcher and one or more parameters together with their corresponding search spaces, i.e. the values that shall be tested. The Cartesian product of these values is computed and each system configuration (an element of the Cartesian product which is a tuple of values) runs on the specified test case. The result is an `ExecutionResultSet` which can be further processed like any other result of matchers in MELT. To speed up the execution, class `Executor` was extended and can run matchers in parallel. Properties can be specified by a simple string. Therefore, the `JavaBeans` specification[25] is used to access the properties with so called setter-methods. This strategy allows also to change properties of nested classes or any list or map. An example of a matcher tuning can be found in the MELT repository[26].

3.6 Evaluation Workflow

MELT defines a workflow for matcher execution and evaluation. Therefore, it utilizes the vocabulary used by the OAEI: A matcher can be evaluated on a `TestCase`, i.e. a single ontology matching task. One or more test cases are summarized in a `Track`. MELT contains a built-in `TrackRepository` which allows to access all OAEI tracks and test cases at design time without actually downloading them from the OAEI Web page. At runtime `TrackRepository` checks whether the required ontologies and alignments are available in the internal buffer; if data is missing, it is automatically downloading and caching it for the next access. The caching mechanism is an advantage over the SEALS platform which downloads all ontologies again at runtime which slows down the evaluation process if run multiple times in a row.

One or more matchers are given, together with the track or test case on which they shall be run, to an `Executor`. The Executor runs a matcher or a list of matchers on a single test case, a list of test cases, or a track. The `run()` method of the executor returns an `ExecutionResultSet`. The latter is a set of `ExecutionResult` instances which represent individual matching results on a particular test case. Lastly, an `Evaluator` accepts an `ExecutionResultSet` and performs an evaluation. Therefore, it may use one or more `Metric` objects. MELT contains various metrics, such as a `ConfusionMatrixMetric`, and evaluators. Nonetheless, the framework is designed to allow for the further implementation of evaluators and metrics.

---

25 https://www.oracle.com/technetwork/java/javase/documentation/spec-136004.html.

26 https://github.com/dwslab/melt/blob/master/examples/simpleJavaMatcher/src/test/java/de/uni_mannheim/informatik/dws/ontmatching/demomatcher/EvaluateMatcher.java.

After the `Executor` has run, an `ExecutionResult` can be refined by a `Refiner`. A refiner takes an individual `ExecutionResult` and makes it smaller. An example is the `TypeRefiner` which creates additional execution results depending on the type of the alignment (classes, properties, datatype properties, object properties, instances). Another example for an implemented refiner is the `ResidualRefiner` which only keeps non-trivial correspondences and can be used for metrics such as recall+. Refiners can be combined. This means that MELT can calculate very specific evaluation statistics such as the residual precision of datatype property correspondences.

A novelty of this framework is also the granularity at which alignments can be analyzed: The `EvaluatorCSV` writes every correspondence in a CSV format together with further details about the matched resources and the performed refinements. This allows for an in-depth analysis in various spreadsheet applications such as LibreOffice Calc where through the usage of filters analytical queries can be performed such as "false-positive datatype property matches by matcher X on test case Y".

4 Exemplary Analysis of OAEI 2018 Results

In order to demonstrate the capabilities of MELT, a small analysis of the OAEI 2018 results for the *Conference* and *Anatomy* track has been performed and is presented in the following.

The *Conference* track consists of 16 ontologies from the conference domain. We evaluated all matching systems that participated in the 2018 campaign: *ALIN* [30], *ALOD2Vec* [25], *AML* [11], *DOME* [13], *FCAMapX* [4], *Holontology* [27], *KEPLER* [19], *Lily* [31], *LogMap* and *LogMapLt* [17], *SANOM* [22], as well as *XMap* [6].

The *Anatomy* track consists of a mapping between the human anatomy and the anatomy of a mouse. In the 2018 campaign, the same matchers mentioned above participated with the addition of *LogMapBio*, a matcher from the *LogMap* family [17].

First, the resulting alignments for *Anatomy*[27] and *Conference*[28] have been downloaded from the OAEI Web site. As both result sets follow the same structure every year, the MELT functions `Executor.loadFromAnatomyResultsFolder()` and `Executor.loadFromConferenceResultsFolder()` were used to load the results. The resulting `ExecutionResultSet` was then handed over to the `MatcherSimilarityMetric` and rendered using the `MatcherSimilarityLatexHeatMapWriter`. As the *Conference* track consists of multiple test cases, the results have to be averaged. Here, out of the available calculation modes in MELT, micro-average was chosen as this calculation mode is also used on the

[27] http://oaei.ontologymatching.org/2018/results/anatomy/oaei2018-anatomy-alignments.zip.

[28] http://oaei.ontologymatching.org/2018/conference/data/conference2018-results.zip.

official results page[29] to calculate precision and recall scores. Altogether, the analysis was performed with few lines of Java code.[30]

Tables 1 and 2 show the Jaccard overlap [16] of the correspondences rendered as heat map where darker colors indicate a higher similarity. The Jaccard coefficient $J \in [0,1]$ between two alignments a_1 and a_2 with correspondences $corr(a_1)$ and $corr(a_2)$ was obtained as follows:

$$J(a_1, a_2) = \frac{|corr(a_1) \cap corr(a_2)|}{|corr(a_1) \cup corr(a_2)|}$$

In Table 1 it can be seen that – despite the various approaches that are pursued by the matching systems – most of them arrive at very similar alignments. One outlier in this statistic is *Holontology*. This is due to the very low number of correspondences overall found by this matching system (456 as opposed to ALIN, which had the second-smallest alignment with 928 matches).

Similarly, the matching systems of the *Conference* track also show commonalities in their alignments albeit the similarity here is less pronounced compared to the *Anatomy* track: The median similarity (excluding perfect similarities due to self-comparisons) of matching systems for *Anatomy* is $median_{Anatomy} = 0.7223$ whereas the median similarity for *Conference* is $median_{Conference} = 0.5917$. The lower matcher similarity median indicates that *Conference* is a harder matching task because the matching systems have more disagreement about certain correspondences.

In a second step, the same result from the `MatcherSimilarityMetric` has been printed by another writer (`MatcherSimilarityLatexPlotWriter`) which plots the mean absolute deviation (MAD) on the X-axis and the F_1 score on the Y-axis. MAD was obtained for each matcher by applying

$$MAD = \frac{1}{n} \sum_{i=1}^{n} |x_i - mean(X)|$$

where X is the set of Jaccard similarities for a particular matcher. The resulting plots are shown in Figs. 2 and 3. It can be seen that the matchers form different clusters: *Anatomy* matchers with a high F_1 measure have also a high deviation. Consequently, those matchers are likely candidates for a combination to achieve better results. On *Conference*, on the other hand, good combinations cannot be derived because the best matchers measured by their F_1 score tend not to deviate much in their resulting alignments.

In addition to the evaluations performed using the matcher similarity metric, the `EvaluatorCSV` was run using the OAEI 2018 matchers on the *Anatomy* and *Conference* tracks. The resulting CSV file contains one row for each correspondence together with additional information about each resource that is mapped

---

29 http://oaei.ontologymatching.org/2018/results/conference/.

30 The code to run the analysis can be found on GitHub: https://github.com/dwslab/melt/tree/master/examples/analyzingMatcherSimilarity.

Table 1. OAEI anatomy 2018 alignment similarity

	ALIN	ALOD2Vec	AML	DOME	FCAMapX	Holontology	KEPLER	Lily	LogMap	LogMapBio	LogMapLt	POMAP++	SANOM	XMap
ALIN	1	0.93	0.62	0.97	0.72	0.47	0.79	0.63	0.66	0.6	0.81	0.63	0.62	0.65
ALOD2Vec	0.93	1	0.65	0.94	0.77	0.45	0.81	0.67	0.7	0.63	0.84	0.66	0.64	0.68
AML	0.62	0.65	1	0.62	0.76	0.3	0.74	0.72	0.8	0.82	0.72	0.83	0.79	0.83
DOME	0.97	0.94	0.62	1	0.73	0.47	0.79	0.64	0.66	0.6	0.81	0.63	0.62	0.66
FCAMapX	0.72	0.77	0.76	0.73	1	0.35	0.75	0.69	0.82	0.77	0.89	0.77	0.75	0.78
Holontology	0.47	0.45	0.3	0.47	0.35	1	0.38	0.3	0.32	0.29	0.39	0.31	0.3	0.31
KEPLER	0.79	0.81	0.74	0.79	0.75	0.38	1	0.69	0.78	0.72	0.75	0.76	0.71	0.76
Lily	0.63	0.67	0.72	0.64	0.69	0.3	0.69	1	0.7	0.68	0.69	0.72	0.72	0.72
LogMap	0.66	0.7	0.8	0.66	0.82	0.32	0.78	0.7	1	0.9	0.81	0.81	0.8	0.81
LogMapBio	0.6	0.63	0.82	0.6	0.77	0.29	0.72	0.68	0.9	1	0.74	0.8	0.78	0.78
LogMapLt	0.81	0.84	0.72	0.81	0.89	0.39	0.75	0.69	0.81	0.74	1	0.74	0.74	0.75
POMAP++	0.63	0.66	0.83	0.63	0.77	0.31	0.76	0.72	0.81	0.8	0.74	1	0.79	0.83
SANOM	0.62	0.64	0.79	0.62	0.75	0.3	0.71	0.72	0.8	0.78	0.74	0.79	1	0.78
XMap	0.65	0.68	0.83	0.66	0.78	0.31	0.76	0.72	0.81	0.78	0.75	0.83	0.78	1

Table 2. OAEI conference 2018 alignment similarity

	ALIN	ALOD2Vec	AML	DOME	FCAMapX	Holontology	KEPLER	Lily	LogMap	LogMapLt	SANOM	XMap
ALIN	1	0.75	0.65	0.84	0.63	0.77	0.53	0.43	0.72	0.76	0.52	0.6
ALOD2Vec	0.75	1	0.58	0.87	0.67	0.75	0.61	0.37	0.67	0.86	0.5	0.54
AML	0.65	0.58	1	0.61	0.58	0.56	0.53	0.45	0.71	0.59	0.63	0.64
DOME	0.84	0.87	0.61	1	0.67	0.81	0.59	0.39	0.7	0.86	0.52	0.56
FCAMapX	0.63	0.67	0.58	0.67	1	0.6	0.55	0.41	0.62	0.66	0.51	0.53
Holontology	0.77	0.75	0.56	0.81	0.6	1	0.53	0.37	0.64	0.72	0.49	0.52
KEPLER	0.53	0.61	0.53	0.59	0.55	0.53	1	0.41	0.57	0.62	0.5	0.54
Lily	0.43	0.37	0.45	0.39	0.41	0.37	0.41	1	0.46	0.39	0.48	0.51
LogMap	0.72	0.67	0.71	0.7	0.62	0.64	0.57	0.46	1	0.7	0.63	0.66
LogMapLt	0.76	0.86	0.59	0.86	0.66	0.72	0.62	0.39	0.7	1	0.51	0.56
SANOM	0.52	0.5	0.63	0.52	0.51	0.49	0.5	0.48	0.63	0.51	1	0.61
XMap	0.6	0.54	0.64	0.56	0.53	0.52	0.54	0.51	0.66	0.56	0.61	1

(e.g. label, comment, or type) and with additional information about the correspondence itself (e.g. residual match indicator or evaluation result). All files are available online for further analysis on correspondence level.[31]

[31] https://github.com/dwslab/melt/tree/master/examples/analyzingMatcherSimilarity.

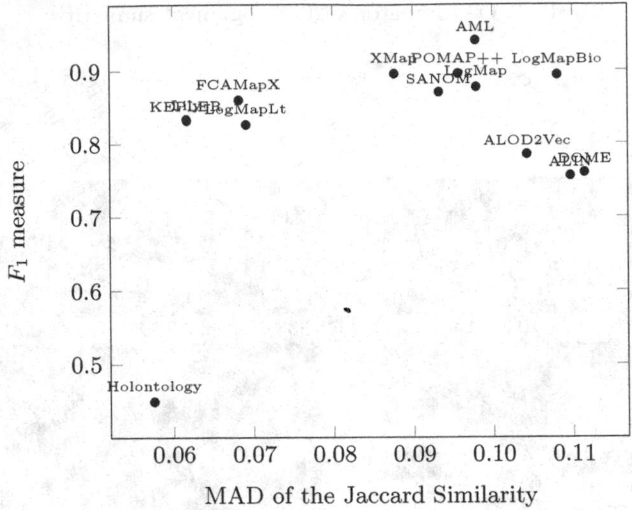

Fig. 2. Matcher comparison using MAD and F_1 on the *Anatomy* data set

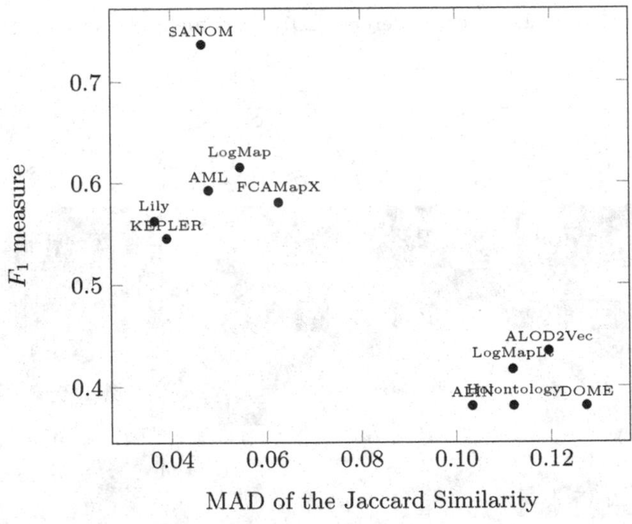

Fig. 3. Matcher comparison using MAD and F_1 on the *Conference* data set

5 Conclusion

With MELT, we have presented a framework for ontology matcher development, configuration, packaging, and evaluation. We hope to lower the entrance barriers into the ontology matching community by offering a streamlined development process. MELT can also simplify the work of researchers who evaluate multiple matchers on multiple data sets such as OAEI track organizers through its rich evaluation capabilities.

The evaluation capabilities were exemplarily demonstrated for two OAEI tracks by providing a novel view on matcher similarity. The MELT framework as well as the code used for the analyses presented in this paper are open-source and freely available.

Future work will focus on adding more evaluation possibilities in the form of further refiners and reasoners, providing more default matching functionalities such as modular matchers that can be used in matching pipelines, and developing visual evaluation support based on the framework to allow for better ontology matcher results comparisons.

References

1. Algergawy, A., et al.: Results of the ontology alignment evaluation initiative 2018. In: OM@ISWC, CEUR Workshop Proceedings, vol. 2288, pp. 76–116 (2018). CEUR-WS.org
2. Aumueller, D., Do, H.H., Massmann, S., Rahm, E.: Schema and ontology matching with COMA++. In: Proceedings of the 2005 ACM SIGMOD International Conference on Management of Data, pp. 906–908. ACM (2005)
3. Carroll, J., Reynolds, D., Dickinson, I., Seaborne, A., Dollin, C., Wilkinson, K.: Jena: implementing the semantic web recommendations. In: Proceedings of the 13th International World Wide Web (WWW) Conference, pp. 74–83. ACM, New York (2004)
4. Chen, G., Zhang, S.: FCAMapX results for OAEI 2018. In: OM@ISWC, CEUR Workshop Proceedings, vol. 2288, pp. 160–166 (2018). CEUR-WS.org
5. David, J., Euzenat, J., Scharffe, F., Trojahn dos Santos, C.: The alignment API 4.0. Semant. Web J. **2**(1), 3–10 (2011)
6. Djeddi, W.E., Yahia, S.B., Khadir, M.T.: XMap: results for OAEI 2018. In: OM@ISWC, CEUR Workshop Proceedings, vol. 2288, pp. 210–215 (2018). CEUR-WS.org
7. Dragisic, Z., Ivanova, V., Lambrix, P., Faria, D., Jiménez-Ruiz, E., Pesquita, C.: User validation in ontology alignment. In: Groth, P., et al. (eds.) ISWC 2016. LNCS, vol. 9981, pp. 200–217. Springer, Cham (2016). https://doi.org/10.1007/978-3-319-46523-4_13
8. Euzenat, J., et al.: Results of the ontology alignment evaluation initiative 2011. In: OM, CEUR Workshop Proceedings, vol. 814 (2011). CEUR-WS.org
9. Euzenat, J., Meilicke, C., Stuckenschmidt, H., Shvaiko, P., Trojahn, C.: Ontology alignment evaluation initiative: six years of experience. In: Spaccapietra, S. (ed.) Journal on Data Semantics XV. LNCS, vol. 6720, pp. 158–192. Springer, Heidelberg (2011). https://doi.org/10.1007/978-3-642-22630-4_6
10. Euzenat, J., Shvaiko, P.: Ontology Matching, 2nd edn. Springer, New York (2013)
11. Faria, D., et al.: Results of AML participation in OAEI 2018. In: OM@ISWC, CEUR Workshop Proceedings, vol. 2288, pp. 125–131 (2018). CEUR-WS.org
12. García-Castro, R., Esteban-Gutiérrez, M., Gómez-Pérez, A.: Towards an infrastructure for the evaluation of semantic technologies. In: eChallenges e-2010 Conference, pp. 1–7. IEEE (2010)
13. Hertling, S., Paulheim, H.: DOME results for OAEI 2018. In: OM@ISWC, CEUR Workshop Proceedings, vol. 2288, pp. 144–151 (2018). CEUR-WS.org

14. Horridge, M., Bechhofer, S., Noppens, O.: Igniting the OWL 1.1 touch paper: the OWL API. In: OWLED 258 (2007)
15. Ivanova, V., Bach, B., Pietriga, E., Lambrix, P.: Alignment cubes: towards interactive visual exploration and evaluation of multiple ontology alignments. In: d'Amato, C., et al. (eds.) ISWC 2017. LNCS, vol. 10587, pp. 400–417. Springer, Cham (2017). https://doi.org/10.1007/978-3-319-68288-4_24
16. Jaccard, P.: Lois de distribution florale dans la zone alpine. Bull. Soc. Vaudoise Sci. Nat. **38**, 69–130 (1902). https://doi.org/10.5169/seals-266762
17. Jiménez-Ruiz, E., Grau, B.C., Cross, V.: Logmap family participation in the OAEI 2018. In: OM@ISWC, CEUR Workshop Proceedings, vol. 2288, pp. 187–191 (2018). CEUR-WS.org
18. Jiménez-Ruiz, E., et al.: Introducing the HOBBIT platform into the ontology alignment evaluation campaign. In: OM@ISWC, CEUR Workshop Proceedings, vol. 2288, pp. 49–60 (2018). CEUR-WS.org
19. Kachroudi, M., Diallo, G., Yahia, S.B.: KEPLER at OAEI 2018. In: OM@ISWC, CEUR Workshop Proceedings, vol. 2288, pp. 173–178 (2018). CEUR-WS.org
20. Levenshtein, V.: Binary codes capable of correcting deletions, insertions, and reversals. Sov. Phys. Dokl. **10**(8), 707–710 (1966)
21. Lohmann, S., Negru, S., Haag, F., Ertl, T.: Visualizing ontologies with VOWL. Semant. Web **7**(4), 399–419 (2016). https://doi.org/10.3233/SW-150200
22. Mohammadi, M., Hofman, W., Tan, Y.: SANOM results for OAEI 2018. In: OM@ISWC, CEUR Workshop Proceedings, vol. 2288, pp. 205–209 (2018). CEUR-WS.org
23. Ngo, D.H., Bellahsene, Z.: YAM++: a multi-strategy based approach for ontology matching task. In: ten Teije, A., et al. (eds.) EKAW 2012. LNCS (LNAI), vol. 7603, pp. 421–425. Springer, Heidelberg (2012). https://doi.org/10.1007/978-3-642-33876-2_38
24. Ngomo, A.C.N., Röder, M.: HOBBIT: holistic benchmarking for big linked data. In: ERCIM News, no. 105 (2016)
25. Portisch, J., Paulheim, H.: ALOD2Vec matcher. In: OM@ISWC, CEUR Workshop Proceedings, vol. 2288, pp. 132–137 (2018). CEUR-WS.org
26. Řehůřek, R., Sojka, P.: Software framework for topic modelling with large corpora. In: Proceedings of the LREC 2010 Workshop on New Challenges for NLP Frameworks, ELRA, Valletta, Malta, pp. 45–50, May 2010. http://is.muni.cz/publication/884893/en
27. Roussille, P., Megdiche, I., Teste, O., Trojahn, C.: Holontology: results of the 2018 OAEI evaluation campaign. In: OM@ISWC, CEUR Workshop Proceedings, vol. 2288, pp. 167–172 (2018). CEUR-WS.org
28. Severo, B., dos Santos, C.T., Vieira, R.: VOAR: a visual and integrated ontology alignment environment. In: Proceedings of the Ninth International Conference on Language Resources and Evaluation, LREC 2014, Reykjavik, Iceland, 26–31 May 2014, pp. 3671–3677 (2014)
29. Severo, B., Trojahn, C., Vieira, R.: VOAR 3.0 : a configurable environment for manipulating multiple ontology alignments. In: International Semantic Web Conference (Posters, Demos & Industry Tracks), CEUR Workshop Proceedings, vol. 1963 (2017)
30. da Silva, J., Revoredo, K., Baião, F.A.: ALIN results for OAEI 2018. In: OM@ISWC, CEUR Workshop Proceedings, vol. 2288, pp. 117–124 (2018). CEUR-WS.org
31. Tang, Y., Wang, P., Pan, Z., Liu, H.: Lily results for OAEI 2018. In: OM@ISWC, CEUR Workshop Proceedings, vol. 2288, pp. 179–186 (2018). CEUR-WS.org

32. Tudorache, T., Vendetti, J., Noy, N.F.: Web-protege: a lightweight OWL ontology editor for the web. In: OWLED, CEUR Workshop Proceedings, vol. 432 (2008). CEUR-WS.org
33. Volz, J., Bizer, C., Gaedke, M., Kobilarov, G.: Silk - a link discovery framework for the web of data. In: LDOW, vol. 538 (2009)
34. Wang, X., Haas, L., Meliou, A.: Explaining data integration. Data Eng. Bull. **41**(2), 47–58 (2018)
35. Wrigley, S.N., García-Castro, R., Nixon, L.: Semantic evaluation at large scale (SEALS). In: Proceedings of the 21st International Conference Companion on World Wide Web - WWW 2012 Companion, pp. 299–302. ACM Press, Lyon (2012)

Data Mining and Knowledge Discovery

Interaction Network Analysis Using Semantic Similarity Based on Translation Embeddings

Awais Manzoor Bajwa[1], Diego Collarana[2](✉), and Maria-Esther Vidal[3,4,5]

[1] University of Bonn, Bonn, Germany
bajwaa@cs.uni-bonn.de

[2] Fraunhofer Institute for Intelligent Analysis and Information Systems, Sankt Augustin, Germany
collaran@cs.uni-bonn.de

[3] TIB Leibniz Information Centre for Science and Technology, Hannover, Germany
maria.vidal@tib.eu

[4] L3S Research Centre, Leibniz University of Hannover, Hannover, Germany

[5] Universidad Simón Bolívar, Caracas, Venezuela

Abstract. Biomedical knowledge graphs such as STITCH, SIDER, and Drugbank provide the basis for the discovery of associations between biomedical entities, e.g., interactions between drugs and targets. Link prediction is a paramount task and represents a building block for supporting knowledge discovery. Although several approaches have been proposed for effectively predicting links, the role of semantics has not been studied in depth. In this work, we tackle the problem of discovering interactions between drugs and targets, and propose SimTransE, a machine learning-based approach that solves this problem effectively. SimTransE relies on translating embeddings to model drug-target interactions and values of similarity across them. Grounded on the vectorial representation of drug-target interactions, SimTransE is able to discover novel drug-target interactions. We empirically study SimTransE using state-of-the-art benchmarks and approaches. Experimental results suggest that SimTransE is competitive with the state of the art, representing, thus, an effective alternative for knowledge discovery in the biomedical domain.

Keywords: Knowledge graphs · Embeddings · Similarity function

1 Introduction

The discovery of interactions among entities is one of the main link prediction tasks over knowledge graphs. Specifically, the problem of drug-target interaction discovery, i.e., proteins that are targets of drugs, is a crucial task, given the fact, that on average, bringing a new drug to the market, costs ≈ $1.8 billion and takes more than 10 years. Several approaches have been defined to tackle the

M. Acosta et al. (Eds.): SEMANTiCS 2019, LNCS 11702, pp. 249–255, 2019.
https://doi.org/10.1007/978-3-030-33220-4_18

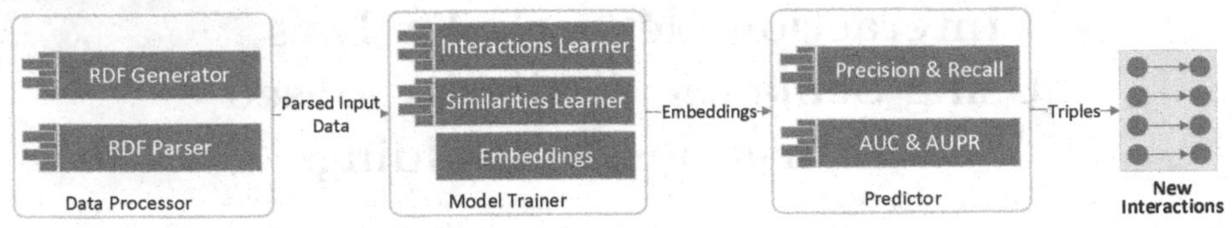

Fig. 1. The Architecture. SimTransE receives an RDF knowledge graph and similarities among its entities. The output is a set of predicted interactions.

problem of drug-target interaction discovery (e.g., [2,4]). Albeit effective, existing approaches are not able to exploit the semantics encoded in the main features of the drugs or targets to enhance prediction. We present SimTransE approach that exploits both similarities between entities, e.g., drugs and target, as well as their connections in a knowledge graph. These features are considered by SimTransE to represent entities into a vector space. SimTransE is based on TransE, which utilizes the gradient descent optimization method to learn the embeddings based on relations stated in a knowledge graphs. Similarly, SimTransE optimizes the distance between embeddings, considering the existing interactions between drugs and targets, but additionally, SimTransE takes into consideration domain similarity values between drugs and between targets. Embeddings generated by SimTransE are utilized to predict new interactions by applying the homophily principle[1]. We conduct an empirical evaluation to assess the quality of SimTransE with respect to TransE and a benchmarks of interactions between drugs and targets. Our observed results suggest that considering similarity empowers SimTransE and allows for the discovery of interactions between drugs and targets that could be identified by baseline version of TransE.

2 The SimTransE Approach

After reviewing different approaches such as [2,4], we realize the benefits that integrating the entity-entity similarity (e.g., target-target, drug-drug, and target-drug) into a learning model can bring. The intuition behind this work is that vector embedding-based approaches effectively combine different dimensions of the input data to learn embeddings. As a result, embeddings merge different dimensions of the data giving a multi-dimensional entity representation. We present SimTransE, an approach that maps each entity into multi-dimensional vector space considering entity-entity similarities to improve the results of the link prediction task. Thus, SimTransE is a vector embedding based machine learning model to learn a bipartite graph interactions and predict unknown interactions.

2.1 Architecture

The SimTransE architecture comprises a pipeline with three main components. Figure 1 shows the interaction between these components and the data flowing

[1] https://en.wikipedia.org/wiki/Homophily.

among them. The *Data Processor* receives an RDF graph and creates dictionaries and matrices understandable by SimTransE. Three sets of *entity dictionaries* are created, i.e., left entities (the subjects), right entities (the objects), and relational entities. These dictionaries are used throughout the pipeline to create vector embeddings. Secondly, two different sets of binary *sparse matrices* are created. One representing the **positive and negative interactions** of entities. Lastly, similarity matrices are built, i.e., given the **m** number of left entities and **n** number of right entities, we prepare two square matrices where the similarity score between entities from **m** to **n** are kept. The *Model Trainer* component receives as input the entity and interaction dictionaries and similarity matrices. The Model Trainer resorts to the **stochastic gradient descent** method to optimize the position and direction of the embeddings in a vector space. The *Model Trainer* uses interactions and similarities between entities to solve the optimization problem, and generates embeddings as output; (Table 1 shows the SimTransE interaction and objective functions). The *Predictor* component takes the generated embedding vectors, interactions, and thresholds. Using the embeddings and thresholds, this component iterates over all the entities and identifies interactions of each entity with every other entity. The *Predictor* component calculates the precision and recall. Additionally, the Area Under Receiver (AUC) and the Area Under the Precision-Recall Curve (AUPRC) are calculated.

2.2 Learning Vector Embeddings

State-of-art approaches use only connectivity patterns between entities to learn the embeddings and perform predictions. Using just interactions among entities is not enough real-world applications where domain-specific knowledge plays a relevant role (e.g., during the prediction of drug-target interactions [8]). There are very few known interactions and the ratio of positive to negative classes is large, impacting, this, in the accuracy of the predictions. To tackle the problem of unbalance ratio of positive to negative classes, SimTransE incorporates not only entities interactions but similarities between entities during the learning process. SimTransE creates duplicate positive classes and adds a set of positive examples, which are generated using the similarity matrices. The similarity score is considered as the weight of example in the learning process.

SimTransE[2] analyses the interactions and similarities between entities to learn the embeddings. SimTransE is based on the work "Translating Embeddings for Modelling Multi-relational Data" (TransE [1]). SimTransE intuition relies on the basic idea of TransE, i.e., if two entities interacts with each other, then the sum of first entity vector and relation vector should be approximately equal to the second vector. If there is no interaction between the two entities, the sum of first entity vector and relation vector will be far from the second entity vector. Using the same principle, SimTransE locates vectors using the similarities as well, and adds a new condition in the learning model that states similar entities

[2] Algorithms are documented in our repository https://github.com/RDF-Molecules/SimTransE.

Table 1. SimTransE interaction and objective function to learn embeddings

Interaction functions	Objective functions
$\begin{cases} h + l \approx t, & \text{if h interacts (l) t} \\ h + l \not\approx t, & \text{otherwise} \end{cases}$	$L_i = \sum_{(h,\ell,t)\in S} \sum_{(h',\ell,t')\in S'_{(h,\ell,t)}} [\gamma + d(h+\ell,t) - d(h'+\ell,t')]_+$
$\begin{cases} h1 + l \approx h2, & \text{if h1 similar h2} \\ h1 + l \not\approx h2, & \text{otherwise} \end{cases}$	$L_s = \sum_{(h,\ell,t)\in S} \sum_{(h',\ell,t')\in SI_{(h,\ell,t)}} [d(h+\ell,t) - d(h'+\ell,t')]_+$

should be closer than the dissimilar ones. Interactions are generated based on the homophily principle that states that similar entities tend to interact with similar entity. Further, we rely on thresholds captured from the meaning of the similarity metrics and to decide when two entities can be considered similar. Then the **stochastic gradient descent** optimization method is performed; a mini-batch of drug-target interactions is generated according to a training set **S** of interactions. The embeddings are updated during the learning process with two objective functions: (1) L_i minimizes the distance whenever this is greater between actual and a corrupted triple with respect to the relation among them; and (2) L_s minimizes the distance according to the similarity between the actual and self-generated similar triples. The learning process stops when reaching the total number of epochs, or depending on a threshold about the distance between the generated embeddings and the training set.

2.3 Predicting Links

The fundamental task of link prediction is to identify a relations between two entities. Yang et al. [9] define the link prediction formally as a task in a network $\mathbf{G} = (\mathbf{V}, \mathbf{E})$ where $\mathbf{V}$ is the set of nodes and $\mathbf{E}$ is the set of edges. The main challenge to be achieved in this task is to predict whether there is or will be a link $e(u, v)$ between a pair of nodes u and v $\in \mathbf{V}$ and $e(u, v) \notin \mathbf{E}$. To perform link prediction, SimTransE uses the trained vector embeddings and calculates the distance of each entity to every other entity with respect to the relation between them. Based on this calculated distance and a given threshold, SimTransE decides if the input entities are or not related. SimTransE ranks each entity on the basis of distance and assigns a probability by comparing it with the distance of other entities. If this probability is greater than the given threshold, then SimTransE considers the link in the output.

To evaluate link prediction we measure: **Precision**, the ratio of correctly predicted interactions to total predictions; **Recall**, the ratio of correctly predicted interactions to expect predictions; **Area under Precision-Recall Curve** , we calculate the area under precision recall curve as the metric to evaluate our model, it does not consider true negatives since neither of both precision and recall consider true negatives; Finally, we measure the **Area under ROC Curve**, to evaluate our method since it works best when the problem of imbalanced classes exist in the dataset [9] (Fig. 2).

3 Empirical Evaluation

We empirically study the effectiveness of SimTransE on the problem of predicting links. We assess the following research questions: **(RQ1)** Is SimTransE able to perform as good as the state-of-the-art similarity measures? **(RQ2)** Does SimTransE perform well on the task of link prediction when applied to data with lots of connections? To answer these questions, we evaluate SimTransE on a state-of-the-art benchmark of drug-target interactions [8]; we report only on the results of interactions between drugs and targets of the type Nuclear Receptor and Ion Channel. TransE [1] is the baseline of the experiment. Additionally, we utilize the link prediction technique, SemEP [4], that extracts interaction from highly connected partitions of a knowledge graph; these interactions are utilized to enhance the set of input interactions. Furthermore, we compute the drug-drug and target-target similarity matrices; drug similarities are computed using SIMCOMP [3] while target similarities are computed using a normalised Smith-Waterman score [5].

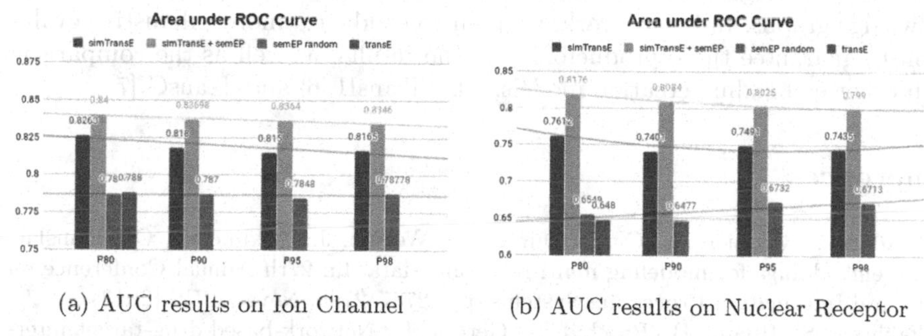

(a) AUC results on Ion Channel

(b) AUC results on Nuclear Receptor

Fig. 2. SimTransE exhibits good performance in both datasets.

Results and Discussion: From the output of SimTransE, we calculated: *true and false positives* and *true and false negatives*. From these values, we derived *Precision*, *Recall*, *AUC*, and *AUPR*[3]. We apply a **blocking** method on the generated similarity-based interactions, through percentiles, i.e., four percentiles are considered: 80, 90, 95, and 100. Link prediction is validated following 10-fold cross-validation, and we report the mean across the results of the ten folds. Based on the observed outcomes, we can positively answer **RQ1**, i.e., SimTransE performs well on all the datasets, and outperforms the baseline method TransE in all cases. These results suggest that similarities between entities, e.g., drugs and targets, have a positive impact on both the learning process and the link prediction tasks. We observe, as well, that by increasing the number of connections between drugs and target (e.g., by using SemEP results) the effectiveness

[3] Source code and formulas to calculate Precision, Recall, AUC, and AUPR are documented in our repository https://github.com/RDF-Molecules/SimTransE.

of the approach improve even further. Few interactions are not predicted properly although they are present in the training set. For most of them, we find that drugs and targets with few numbers of interactions are difficult to train for SimTransE. This situation is improved after using the interactions predicted from SemEP. Therefore, **RQ2** is positively answered too.

4 Conclusions

In this paper, we presented SimTransE, a method to analyze interactions in knowledge graphs to predict links, based on the vectorization of the entities. To learn the embeddings, SimTransE uses not only the interactions among entities but also values of similarity between them. To test the accuracy of SimTransE, we compared its results against TransE, a prediction model for translational embeddings that uses only interactions among entities. SimTransE exhibited high accuracy and competitive result and outperformed TransE, one of the state-of-the-art approaches. The observed results suggest that combining interaction and similarity related semantics in the embeddings empowers the prediction model over knowledge graphs. In future work, we plan to conduct a more exhaustive evaluation to guarantee the reproducibility of the results, as well as the comparison with other embedding creation models, e.g., TransH [6] and TransG [7].

References

1. Bordes, A., Usunier, N., García-Durán, A., Weston, J., Yakhnenko, O.: Translating embeddings for modeling multi-relational data. In: 27th Annual Conference on Neural Information Processing Systems, pp. 2787–2795. Nevada, US (2013)
2. Fakhraei, S., Huang, B., Raschid, L., Getoor, L.: Network-based drug-target interaction prediction with probabilistic soft logic. IEEE/ACM Trans. Comput. Biol. Bioinform. **11**(5), 775–787 (2014)
3. Hattori, M., Okuno, Y., Goto, S., Kanehisa, M.: Development of a chemical structure comparison method for integrated analysis of chemical and genomic information in the metabolic pathways. J. Am. Chem. Soc. **125**(39), 11853–11865 (2003)
4. Palma, G., Vidal, M.-E., Raschid, L.: Drug-target interaction prediction using semantic similarity and edge partitioning. In: Mika, P., et al. (eds.) ISWC 2014. LNCS, vol. 8796, pp. 131–146. Springer, Cham (2014). https://doi.org/10.1007/978-3-319-11964-9_9
5. Smith, T.F., Waterman, M.S.: Identification of common molecular subsequences. J. Mol. Biol. **147**(1), 195–197 (1981)
6. Wang, Z., Zhang, J., Feng, J., Chen, Z.: Knowledge graph embedding by translating on hyperplanes. In: Proceedings of the Twenty-Eighth AAAI Conference on Artificial Intelligence, July 27–31, 2014, pp. 1112–1119. Québec City, Québec, Canada (2014)
7. Xiao, H., Huang, M., Zhu, X.: Transg : a generative model for knowledge graph embedding. In: Proceedings of the 54th Annual Meeting of the Association for Computational Linguistics, ACL 2016, August 7–12, 2016, Berlin, Germany, vol. 1: Long Papers (2016)

8. Yamanishi, Y., Araki, M., Gutteridge, A., Honda, W., Kanehisa, M.: Supplement of paper: prediction of drug-target interaction networks from the integration of chemical and genomic spaces (2018). Last accessed 15 Apr. 2018
9. Yang, Y., Lichtenwalter, R.N., Chawla, N.V.: Evaluating link prediction methods. Knowl. Inf. Syst. **45**(3), 751–782 (2015)

CACAO: Conditional Spread Activation for Keyword Factual Query Interpretation

Edgard Marx[1,2,3](✉), Gustavo Correa Publio[1], and Thomas Riechert[1,2,3]

[1] LiberAI, AKSW, Leipzig University, Leipzig, Germany
{marx,gustavo.publio}@informatik.uni-leipzig.de
[2] HTWK, Leipzig, Germany
{edgard.marx,thomas.riechert}@htwk-leipzig.de
[3] Institute for Digital Technologies, Leipzig, Germany
http://liberai.org, http://ifdt.org/

Abstract. Information retrieval is regarded as pivotal to empower lay users to access the Web of Data. Over the past years, it achieved momentum with a large number of approaches being developed for different scenarios such as entity retrieval, question answering, and entity linking. This work copes with the problem of entity retrieval over RDF knowledge graphs using keyword factual queries. It discloses an approach that incorporates keyword graph structure dependencies through a conditional spread activation. Experimental evaluation on standard benchmarks demonstrates that the proposed method can improve the performance of current state-of-the-art entity retrieval approaches reasonably.

1 Introduction

Over the last years, information aplenty has been published as structured data. The *Resource Description Framework (RDF)*[1] became a standard format for many knowledge graphs (KG) publicly available such as DBpedia [18] and Wikidata [26]. An RDF KG organizes the information in the form of subject-predicate-object statements expressing semantic relations between entities (e.g. persons, organizations, and places) and concepts (e.g. given names, addresses, and locations). Currently, approximately 10.000 RDF KGs are available via public data portals.[2] Together, these graphs compose the so-called Linked Open Data Cloud (LOD).

Ultimately, approaches designed to retrieve or use KG's information has been getting substantial attention. Some of these approaches are Entity Retrieval (ER), Entity Linking (EL), Entity Disambiguation (ED), and Question Answering (QA). ER specifies a category of information retrieval (IR) whereas the result of a natural language search query is an entity or an entity's property rather than a document. ER methods play a fundamental role in IR on KGs. It enables lay

[1] http://www.w3.org/RDF.
[2] http://lodstats.aksw.org/.

M. Acosta et al. (Eds.): SEMANTiCS 2019, LNCS 11702, pp. 256–271, 2019.
https://doi.org/10.1007/978-3-030-33220-4_19

users to access KG's information as well as other approaches on performing EL [7], ED [24,36], and QA [10,33,35] tasks. Improving ER methods can have a substantial impact on the whole IR chain.

ER on RDF KG has peculiar characteristics that make it stand apart from standard document retrieval. The information in KG is structured in entities, attributes, classes, and their relationships. Exploring this structure makes ER a thriving research topic. Early approaches applied bag-of-word document retrieval techniques [4,8,38]. The research has been shifted to explore the KG entities and concepts relations in fields, the field retrieval models [5]. Late studies focus on evaluating the word sequence and property-type influence [2,21,41]. Recently, the use of EL is being considered for ER improvement [14].

This work presents `CACAO`, a novel approach for ER on large[3] and diverse RDF KGs. It relies on a novel spread activation (SA) method to improve information access. SA is a method that iteratively propagates weights in a graph from one node to another [6]. It differs from the previous approaches by evaluating query's intent on entities and concepts rather than fields and avoiding keyword over- and under-relatedness-estimation by accounting only the highly activated ones. The evaluation of the approach in two standard benchmarks shows an f-measure improvement of ≈10%.

The remaining of this work is organized as follows. Section 2 defines RDF KG and states the problem. Section 3 describes the conditional spread activation model entitled `CACAO`. Section 4 presents the evaluation and discusses the results. Section 5 provides a literature overview on related work. Finally, Sect. 6 concludes giving an outlook on approach limitations and potential future work.

2 Preliminaries

An RDF KG can be regarded as a set of triples in the form of $<s,p,o> \in (I \cup B) \times P \times (I \cup L \cup B)$ where: I is the set of all IRIs; B is the set of all blank nodes, $B \cap I = \emptyset$; P is the set of all predicates, $P \subseteq I$; E is the set of all entities, $E = I \cup B \setminus P$; L is the set of all literals, and; R is the set of all resources $R = I \cup B \cup P \cup L$. In this graph, an entity type is specified by the property `rdf:type` while the label, by the property `rdfs:label`. A field of an entity is a predicate object $f = <p,o>$ belonging to an entity triple $<e,p,o>$. The aim of entity retrieval is to recover the `top-K` ranked entities that best address the information need behind a given query as follows.

Definition 1 (Problem Statement). *Formally, a* `top-K` *entity retrieval takes a keyword query* Q*, an integer* $0 < k$*, a set of entities* $E = \{e_1, e_2, ..., e_{|E|}\}$*, and returns the top-k entities based on a scoring function* $S(Q, e)$*.*

3 The Approach

CACAO is an ER approach to facilitate information access using keyword factual queries in RDF knowledge graphs. Factual queries are those whose intent can

[3] We define large KGs as those having over a billion facts.

be formalized by simple Basic Graph Patterns (BGP).[4] Entity retrieval on KGs has been a long-studied research topic for many years. Early approaches rely on bag-of-words models [4,8,38] that suffers from *unrelatedness* [5] and *verbosity* [29]. They were built under the assumption that the distribution of keywords is proportional to its subject relatedness [19]. This idea contradicts with the fact that people can describe things differently. Authors can be more descriptive or verbose than others. Particularly in case of DBpedia, editors' experience or knowledge can unconsciously influence keyword frequency or even graph connectivity. To address the problem of verbosity, researchers proposed to score keywords normalized by the information (entity) length [29]. Other generation of ER approaches focused on the problem of unrelatedness by employing field retrieval models [5]. Late studies focused on evaluating how to weight fields differently so that to improve ER accuracy [2,21,41]. Nevertheless, field retrieval models are unable to relate query keywords with a specific predicate or object because they are treated as one, a bag-of-(field-words). Recent approaches introduced the use of two stage techniques employing ER followed by an Entity Link Retrieval (ELR) [14].

CACAO addresses the ER problem in a different manner. It relies on a SA method that works in threefold. A query triggers an activation function that measures the relatedness of KG resources w.r.t. the query. The resource relatedness values are then spread to their connected entities using a conditionally backward propagation, and, in a latter process, conditionally forward. The individual resource relatedness measurement addresses the problem of finding the query's intent. The conditional propagation avoids the over- and the under-estimation of frequent and rare keywords. The next sections describes how the (1) Activation, (2) Conditional Backward Propagation and (3) Conditional Forward Propagation works.

3.1 Activation

CACAO performs the activation in the resources. It uses the resource label coverage to evaluate its query relatedness. In this judgment, a query containing *birth date* should be more related to the property dbo:birthDate than to the property dbo:deathDate or dbpprop:date, while the query *date* should be more related with the property dbpprop:date than dbo:birthDate. Equation 1 formalizes the evaluation of the query label's coverage. It receives as parameters the query $\overrightarrow{Q}$ and a resource label $\overrightarrow{L}$ represented by bit vectors. In these vectors, keywords are dimensions in which their occurrence are either zero or one.

$$C(\overrightarrow{Q}, \overrightarrow{L}) = \frac{\sum \overrightarrow{Q}_i \overrightarrow{L}_i}{\sum \overrightarrow{L}_i} \qquad (1)$$

Yet, the equation above cannot be used as an activation function, because it measures equally resources with the same query coverage rate. For the sake of

[4] For Basic Graph Pattern definition, visit http://www.w3.org/TR/rdf-sparql-query/#BasicGraphPatterns.

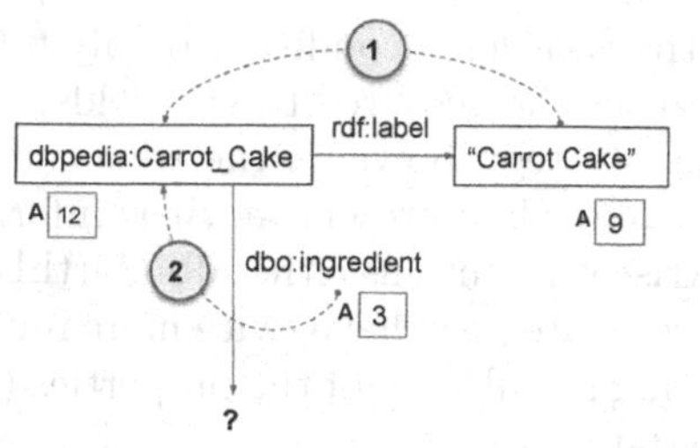

(a) The picture illustrates the conditional backward activation being performed on query "carrot cake ingredients". The activation value of the literal "Carrot Cake" and the property **dbo**:ingredient is being transfered to the entity **dbpedia**:Carrot_Cake ((1)-(2)).

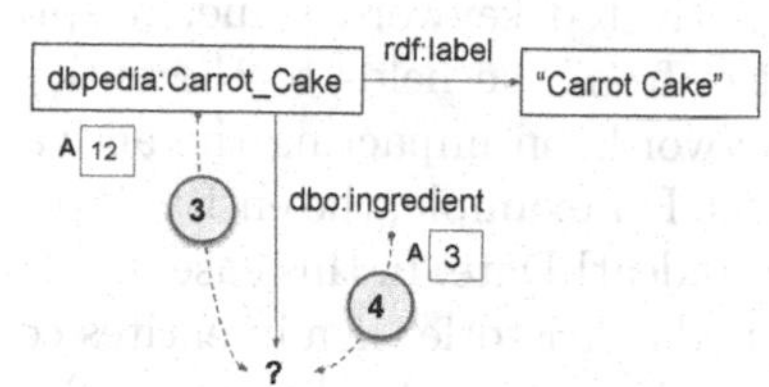

(b) The picture illustrates the conditional forward activation being performed on query "carrot cake ingredients".The activation value of the entity **dbpedia**:Carrot_Cake and the property **dbo**:ingredient is being transfered to the property's entities ((3)-(4)).

Fig. 1. Conditional Spread Activation on query "carrot cake ingredients".

illustration, let us take as an example the query "carrot cake". For this query, either dbr:Carrot, dbr:Cake and dbr:Carrot_Cake are going to have the same coverage value of one, although dbr:Carrot_Cake has two overlapping keywords. Thus, full label-query overlaps are evaluated as the number of query keywords to the power of label keywords, $(\sum \overrightarrow{Q}_i)^{\sum \overrightarrow{L}_i}$. The incomplete overlaps are still considered, but treated with less importance. For those, the query-label intersects over their union suffices (Eq. 2). Equation 3 outlines the activation function. Notice, however, two important properties. First, entities whose resources were activated for mere casualty will always valuate lower than the query length $(\sum \overrightarrow{Q}_i)$. Second, it makes it easier to differentiate among resources with full and partial query coverage.

$$J(\overrightarrow{Q}, \overrightarrow{L}) = \frac{\sum \overrightarrow{Q}_i \overrightarrow{L}_i}{\sum \overrightarrow{L}_i + \sum \overrightarrow{Q}_i - \sum \overrightarrow{L}_i \overrightarrow{Q}_i} \tag{2}$$

$$A(\overrightarrow{Q}, \overrightarrow{L}) = \begin{cases} J(\overrightarrow{Q}, \overrightarrow{L}) & if\ C(\overrightarrow{Q}, \overrightarrow{L}) < 1; \\ (\sum \overrightarrow{Q}_i)^{\sum \overrightarrow{L}_i} & otherwise. \end{cases} \tag{3}$$

3.2 Conditional Backward Propagation

Backward Propagation consists of distributing backward computed values through a network. It is used in neural networks to transfer the errors throughout the network's layers [12]. In CACAO, the backward propagation is used to spread the resource's activation values to their connected entities. By doing so, the approach computes implicitly the relatedness of the entity and its connected resources to the query elements. However, the transfer is conditioned only to the most activated keyword value. It spreads from the resource to the fields, and, likewise, from the fields to the entity. This strategy prevents the frequency of the keywords on impacting the activation value while preserving their informativeness. For example, the entity dbpedia:Aristotle contains either dbo:birthDate and dbo:deathDate. In this case, the keyword "date" will have twice more impact on dbpedia:Aristotle then in entites containing solenly one of the properties (e.g. dbo:birthDate, dbo:deathDate or dbpprop:date).

Previous works demonstrate that scoring fields differently can improve the ER accuracy [2,21,41]. Hence, CACAO employs field weighting as described by Marx et al. [21]. Additionally, a query intent can be one or a set of entities. In the latter case, an important feature is the relevance ranking. As an example, the query "give me all persons" can return more than one million persons if applied to the DBpedia KG. But not all these entities may be relevant to the user. To deal with this problem, each activated entity receives a Page-Rank value normalized lower than a keyword weight. This work uses a modified version of *PageRank* [32] dubbed *DBpedia Page-Rank* which has been shown to produce better estimations [22].

Algorithm 1 describes the computation of the conditional backward propagation formally (Fig. 1a). It starts when function $A^f(\overrightarrow{Q}, f, \overrightarrow{L}^{\ominus})$ receives a bit vector representing the query $\overrightarrow{Q}$, the field, and a set of processed keywords. The activation field value (a_f) is initialized with 0, $R^f_{\blacktriangledown}$ with $\emptyset$, and R^f receives the field's resource list. In sequel, the function iterates over R^f computing the activation value a_f using the vectorized resource label returned by the function $\overrightarrow{V}^L(r)$. In line 19, the function INSERT operates an insertion sort on the list set $R^f_{\blacktriangledown}$. The insertion is performed in the ascending order of the resource's activation value to ensure that only the highly activated keywords have their value transfered to the entity. Subsequently, an iteration operates over the resource sorted list $R^f_{\blacktriangledown}$. The activation a_r is now evaluated over the resource label after removing the keywords that were computed on previous iterations ($\overrightarrow{L}^U_r$). In the last iteration instructions, the resource activation value is transferred to the field a_f (line 25), and the resource keywords are added to the computed keyword list $\overrightarrow{L}^{\ominus}$ (line 26). The function resums adding the field's weight $\phi(f)$ to the final activation value a_f (line 28). Notice that we did not discuss the use of stop words removal or tokenization to describe the algorithm because they are optional and does not influence the overall computation.

The entity activation is computed over the fields' activation as follows. The function $A^r(\overrightarrow{Q}, e)$ receives a vectorized query $\overrightarrow{Q}$ and an entity e. The entity activation value a_e is initialized with 0. The computed keywords $\overrightarrow{L}^{\ominus}$ and the field set $F^e_{\blacktriangledown}$ receives $\emptyset$. The fieldset R^f receives the list of entity fields. Similar to the field activation function $A^f(\overrightarrow{Q}, f, \overrightarrow{L}^{\ominus})$, the entity activation consists in two iterations. The first (line 3) computes the field activation value a_f on every field's keyword, and uses an insertion sort function (line 5) to add them in $F^e_{\blacktriangledown}$ according to their inverse activation value. In this iteration, the computed keywords parameter $\overrightarrow{L}^{\ominus}$ from the field activation function $A^f(\overrightarrow{Q}, f, \overrightarrow{L}^{\ominus})$ receives an empty set (line 5), allowing it to compute the activation on every keyword. It then iterates over the sorted fields $F^e_{\blacktriangledown}$ (line 8) discarding the computed keywords, and transferring the field's activation value to the entity, a_e. The activation value then receives a normalized Page-Rank value returned by the $\psi(e)$ function.

3.3 Conditional Forward Propagation

The forward propagation is only applied when a property contributes to the field's activation. It forwards the entity activation to its activated properties, and from them to their objects. It results in objects having a higher activation value than their associated entity. Let us suppose that an user is looking for "carrot cake ingredients". In case of dbpedia:Carrot_Cake, the label activation will be backward propagated to the entity and then forwarded to the dbo:ingredient fields' object herewith the property activation. Thus, the dbo:ingredients' object on the BGP <dbpedia:Carrot_Cake dbo:ingredient `?object`> is going to have a higher activation value then dbpedia:Carrot_Cake. The Fig. 1b shows the conditional forward propagation for our running example query "carrot cake ingredients".

4 Evaluation

The evaluation was designed to measure the accuracy of `CACAO` compared to other ER, and Entity Linking methods. All output generated by the systems is publicly available at https://github.com/AKSW/irbench. There are several benchmark data sets that could be used on this task, including benchmarks from *Semantic Search* initiatives [13][5] and *QA Over Linked Data (QALD)*.[6] *Semantic Search* is based on user queries extracted from the YAHOO! search log, containing an average distribution of 2.2 words per-query. *QALD* provides both QA and keyword search benchmarks for RDF data. The QALD data sets are the most suitable due to the wide type of queries they contain and also because they make use of *DBpedia*, a very large and diverse KG. In this work, we use the QALD version 2 (QALD-2) data set benchmark from *The Test Collection for Entity Search* (`DBpedia-Entity`) [1], and; QALD version 4 (QALD-4) [34]. Table 1 shows the number of queries evaluated on each of them.

4.1 Experimental Setup

The evaluation contains two setups: The first setup evaluates `CACAO` against state-of-the-art Entity Retrieval (ER) using the QALD-2 from `DBpedia-Entity`. The second setup evaluates `CACAO` using state-of-the-art ER and Entity Linking Retrieval (ELR) for RDF data with the QALD-4. Both setups evaluate the approach with (`CACAO+F`) and without (`CACAO`) forward propagation.

[5] http://km.aifb.kit.edu/ws/semsearch10/.
[6] http://greententacle.techfak.uni-bielefeld.de/~cunger/qald/.

Table 1. Number of queries evaluated on each of the benchmark data sets.

Benchmark	#Queries
QALD-2 (`DBpedia-Entity`)	140
QALD-4	50

Data: $\overrightarrow{Q}$, the query. e, the entity.
Result: The entity final activation value a_e.

Function $A^e(\overrightarrow{Q}, e)$:
    $a_e \leftarrow 0$; $\overrightarrow{L}^{\ominus} \leftarrow \emptyset$; $F^e_{\blacktriangledown} \leftarrow \emptyset$; F^e, the fields in $< e, p, o >$ triples;
    forall $f \in F^e_{\blacktriangledown}$ **do**
        $a_f \leftarrow A^f(\overrightarrow{Q}, f, \overrightarrow{L}^{\ominus})$;
        $\overrightarrow{L}^{\ominus} \leftarrow \emptyset$;
        INSERT$(F^e_{\blacktriangledown}, f, a_f)$;
    end
    forall $f \in F^e_{\blacktriangledown}$ **do**
        $a_e \leftarrow a_e + A^f(\overrightarrow{Q}, f, \overrightarrow{L}^{\ominus})$;
    end
    $a_e \leftarrow a_e + \psi(e)$;
    return a_e;
end

Data: f, the field. $\overrightarrow{Q}$, the query. $\overrightarrow{L}^{\ominus}$, the vector containing the already computed keywords.
Result: The field score a_f.

Function $A^f(\overrightarrow{Q}, f, \overrightarrow{L}^{\ominus})$:
    $a_f \leftarrow 0$; $R^f_{\blacktriangledown} \leftarrow \emptyset$; R^f the list of resources in f;
    forall $r \in R^f$ **do**
        $\overrightarrow{L}_r \leftarrow \overrightarrow{V}^L(r)$;
        $a_r \leftarrow A(\overrightarrow{Q}, \overrightarrow{L}_r)$;
        INSERT$(R^f_{\blacktriangledown}, r, a_r)$;
    end
    forall $r \in R^f_{\blacktriangledown}$ **do**
        $\overrightarrow{L}^r \leftarrow \overrightarrow{V}^L(r)$;
        $\overrightarrow{L}^U_r \leftarrow \overrightarrow{L}_r \wedge \neg \overrightarrow{L}^{\ominus}$;
        $a_r \leftarrow A(\overrightarrow{Q}, \overrightarrow{L}^U_r)$;
        $a_f \leftarrow a_f + a_r$;
        $\overrightarrow{L}^{\ominus} \leftarrow \overrightarrow{L}^{\ominus} \vee \overrightarrow{L}^U_r$;
    end
    $a_f \leftarrow a_f + \phi(f)$;
    return a_f;
end

Algorithm 1. A Conditional Backward Propagation.

First Setup. The first setup evaluates CACAO against thirteen different ER models distributed over three groups (Unstructured, Fielded and Other models) using the QALD-2 DBpedia-Entity data set benchmark. Results are reported using the benchmark standard evaluation metrics: Mean Average Precision (MAP) and Precision at rank 10 (P@10) [20]. The evaluated unstructured retrieval models use flattened entity representation: LM (Language Modeling) [27]; SDM (Sequential Dependence Model) [23], and; BM25 [29]. Five retrieval models employed fielded entity representation: MLM (Mixture of Language Models) [25]; FSDM (Fielded Sequential Dependence Model) [41]; BM25F [5]; MLM-all, with equal field weights, and; PRMS (Probabilistic Model for Semistructured Data) [15]. The LTR (Learning-to-Rank) approach [3] employs 25 features from various retrieval models trained using the RankSVM algorithm. All EL (Entity Link) methods used TAGME [11] for annotating queries with entities, and an URI-only index (with a single catchall field) for computing the EL component. CA suffixes refer to models that are trained using Coordinate Ascent.

Second Setup. The second setup extends the evaluation to QALD-4 benchmark on ER and EL. It measures the performance of eight different Levenshtein, Jaccard, BMF25F and CACAO baseline scoring functions: $Levenshtein_a$ uses the number of matched characters for each matched keyword; $Levenshtein_b$ uses the number of matched characters with the paraphrase disambiguation method proposed by Zhang et al. [40]; $Jaccard_a$ uses the Jaccard distance of matched resources per matched keyword; $Jaccard_b$ uses the disambiguating model implemented by Shekarpour et al. [31]; BMF25F is the ER method proposed by Blanco et al. [2], and; $\texttt{CACAO}_{P65}$ is the CACAO disambiguation model with rule 65 proposed by Shaekapour et al. [31][7]—$J(\overrightarrow{Q}, \overrightarrow{L}) \in [0.65, 1]$—applied only to properties. The idea is that there is a need to address inflections only on properties where verbs occur rather than objects that usually contain proper names. The $Levenshtein_a$ and $Jaccard_a$ methods are used to measure local keyword frequency without global occurrency normalization. CACAO and $\text{Glimmer}_{\text{Y!}}$ [2] performed all queries in OR mode. The performance considers only the *top-K* entries returned by each approach, where k equals to the number of entries in the target test query. The EL evaluation on Table 5 evaluates the mentioned baseline functions as well as the last version of DBpedia Spotlight (version 1.0), AGDISTIS [36] and the state-of-the-art ED MAG [24] in simply BGP queries. This evaluation was designed to measure how accurate CACAO can be when dealing with approaches that use EL on factual keyword queries. We discard queries that can only be answered using classes and properties. We avoid the use of these queries because annotators usually can only handle entities. QALD-4 has ten queries that follow this criteria, Queries 12, 13, 21, 26, 30, 32, 34, 41, 42, and 44. All queries evaluated over DBpedia Spotlight used a refinement operator approach starting from confidence 0.5 in decreasing scale of 0.05 until reaching an annotation—when it was possible—or zero. AGDISTIS [36] and MAG [24] were evaluated over manually marked entity queries.

[7] The optimal value is a range belonging to the interval [0.6, 0.7].

Table 2. Mean Average Precision (**MAP**) achieved by different Entity Retrieval models on QALD-2 *DBpedia-Entity* benchmark data set.

Approach	**MAP**
CACAO	**0.2417**
BM25-CA	0.1939
SDM+EL	0.1887
FSDM+EL	0.1719
BM25F-CA	0.1671
LTR	0.1629
LM+EL	0.1534
SDM	0.1533
LM	0.1424
FSDM	0.1403
MLM-CA	0.1273
PRMS	0.1103
BM25	0.1092
MLM-all	0.1062

Table 3. Precision 10 (**P@10**) achieved by different Entity Retrieval models on QALD-2 *DBpedia-Entity* benchmark data set.

Approach	**P@10**
CACAO	**0.3057**
BM25-CA	0.2527
LM+EL	0.2362
SDM+EL	0.2249
LM	0.2144
FSDM+EL	0.2113
BM25F-CA	0.2053
FSDM	0.2000
SDM	0.1883
PRMS	0.1871
MLM-CA	0.1844
MLM-all	0.1843
LTR	0.1732
BM25	0.0986

Table 4. ***P****recision*, ***R****ecall* and $\boldsymbol{F_1}$*-measure* achieved by different ER approaches on QALD-4 benchmark data set.

Approach	**P**	**R**	$\mathbf{F_1}$
CACAO+F	**0.19**	**0.19**	**0.19**
CACAO	0.11	0.11	0.11
CACAO_{P65}	0.09	0.09	0.09
Levenshtein_b	0.04	0.05	0.04
BM25F [2]	0.03	0.03	0.03
Jaccard_b	0.01	0.04	0.01
Levenshtein_a	0.00	0.00	0.00
Jaccard_a	0.00	0.00	0.00

Table 5. ***P****recision*, ***R****ecall* and $\boldsymbol{F_1}$*-measure* achieved by different EL approaches on QALD 4 benchmark data set.

Approach	**P**	**R**	$\mathbf{F_1}$
CACAO_{P65}	**1**	**1**	**1**
CACAO	0.90	0.90	0.90
MAG [24]	0.80	0.80	0.80
DBpedia Spotlight [7]	0.70	0.70	0.70
Levenshtein_b	0.60	0.60	0.60
Jaccard_b	0.60	0.60	0.60
AGDISTIS [36]	0.30	0.30	0.30
BM25F [2]	0.30	0.30	0.30
Levenshtein_a	0.00	0.00	0.00
Jaccard_a	0.00	0.00	0.00

Query and Resource Parsing. All implemented models (CACAO, CACAO+F, Jaccard and Levenshtein) perform the query and resource parsing extracting individual keywords, removing punctuation and capitalization as well as applying lemmatization.

4.2 Results

The results show that CACAO outperforms the state-of-the-art in both ER and EL tasks with keyword factual queries. It achieved ≈10% more accuracy than ER and EL approaches. Further, as expected, annotators performed better than ER on EL task. Tables 2 and 3 shows resp. the MAP and P@10 performance of CACAO compared to 13 methods. The tables show the score with a precision of four digits. It is possible to notice that MAP@10 scores considerably lower than P@10. That occurs because MAP is calculated on the average entry's precision per question while P is computed only over matching entries. It means that although the entities are retrieved, their query rank can still be improved. Except for CACAO, some methods achieved different position in P@10 and MAP. The outcomes reveal that CACAO could produce more (1) precise and (2) complete results. In general, except SDM, the results confirm previous findings [14] that shows that CA and EL approaches could achieve better performance than their simple version—without—while EL versioned methods performed better than CA ones. CACAO could outperform previous methods because it acts as a resource linking approach. It evaluates resource dependencies rather than bi and trigrams keyword dependencies used in fielded approaches. It also suppresses SDM weakness of sorting entities in relevance order [41] using Page-Rank.

Table 4 shows the Precision, Recall and F-measure achieved by each baseline models on QALD-4. CACAO achieved a better F-measure than $\texttt{CACAO}_{P65}$ mainly because it could overcome the problem of vocabulary mismatch on Query 29 by annotating the keyword "Australian" with dbpedia:Australia, and Query 49, by annotating the keyword "Swedish" with dbpedia:Sweden. As expected, methods empowered by disambiguation ($Levenshtein_a$ and $Jaccard_a$) scores better than bag-of-words ($Levenshtein_b$ and $Jaccard_b$). $Levenshtein_a$ scores better than $Jaccard_a$, confirming previous research conclusion [40]. However, $Jaccard_b$ and $Levenshtein_b$ have their major drawbacks in the path disambiguation level. When retrieval scoring functions consider keywords equally weighted, they cannot disambiguate among resources containing the same keywords. For instance, in case an user query "places", both property dbo:place and the entity-type dbo:Place can be equally weighted, leading those models to retrieve either places as well as the entities connected to the property dbo:place. Not surprisingly, there was an issue related to the local[8] term frequency on BMF25F [2] model. On Query 30, it retrieves the entity dbpedia:Halloween_(Dave_Matthews_Band_song) because the word "halloween" occurs more frequently than in the desired one (dbpedia:Halloween).

[8] Not to confuse with global term frequency.

Table 5 shows the EL evaluation over ten queries. There, $\texttt{CACAO}_{P65}$ achieved the highest F-measure of `1`. `CACAO` achieved an F-measure of `0.90`, obtaining ≈0.10% more accuracy than `MAG`, the third best-performing approach. `CACAO` annotates wrongly Query `21` keyword `bach` by dbpedia:Bachs. $\texttt{CACAO}_{P65}$ applied 65 rule only to the properties, assigning correctly dbpedia:Bach. MAG could not annotate correctly Query `34` and `44`, and; DBpedia Spotlight Queries `12`, `41`, and `42`. The results expose a deficiency of EL systems in dealing with single entity factual queries.

Entity Linking and Disambiguation approaches [7,24] exploit IR for finding the corresponding entity. For these systems, incomplete labels can lead to a non or an inconsistent annotation. For example, in our evaluation DBpedia Spotlight links the keyword "baldwin" in Query `47` with the entity `dbpedia:Baldwin_Locomotive_Works`. Other queries do not generate any annotation. That is the case of Query `36` whereas DBpedia Spotlight does not annotate it using confidence score `0.5`, but annotates it wrongly using confidence `0.45`.[9] The use of the 65 rule, enhanced the results achieved by `CACAO` when applied to subjects, properties, and objects in comparison to when applied to only properties ($\texttt{CACAO}_{P65}$), see Table 4. This happens because it can help to annotate noun resources that are not handled by the lemmatization, i.e., Sweden and Swedish on Query `43`. However, the use of this method decreases the precision of the approach in Entity Linking task (see Table 5) because the 65 rule increases the possible overlaping resources leading to wrong annotations. That's the case of Query `21`.

Complexity Analysis. In general, entity (document) retrieval algorithms can be implemented as an entity- or term-a-time. Entity-a-time retrieval algorithms aggregates scores over entities whereas term-a-time over terms. Term-a-time is the most common retrieval method and relies on posting lists implemented in popular IR frameworks such as Lucene. Intuitively, the complexity of term a time methods are bounded by the size of the posting list matching terms M' and E' matching entities insertions on a tree of size k (top-k) which leads to a complexity of $O(M' + E' \log k)$.[10] Algorithm 1 display a naive implementation of our proposed entity-a-time method. The second `For` instruction (`line 21`) is bounded by the same time complexity of the number of the entity's matched terms, giving an overall collection complexity of $O(M')$. However, when considering the first loop (`line 16`), there is a need for calculating the activation value on every entity's matched term, adding an extra complexity of matched term frequencies Tf'. Thus, the complexity of Algorithm 1 is at least $\Omega(Tf' + M' + E' \log k)$, highlighting a future point of improvement.

5 Related Work

IR. Existing IR approaches commonly aim to retrieve the *top-K* ranked documents for a given NL input query. Term Frequency-Inverse Document Frequency

[9] With confidence 0.45 "pope" is annotated with the entity dbpedia:Pope.

[10] We ignored the existence of fields and resources for simplification.

(TF-IDF) [30] evaluates query keywords based on their local and global frequency. BM25 [28] extends TF-IDF introducing a document length normalization. Field-base extensions from bag-of-words have been proposed for IR on structured data. BM25F [5] is an extension of BM25 to retrieve structured data using different weighted fields. Mixture of Language Models (MLM) [25] extends the Language Model (LM) [27] using a linear combination of query keyword probability in a multi-field language model (MLM). Although individual field weights in BM25F and MLM can be tuned for a particular collection, they are fixed across different query keywords. Probabilistic Retrieval Model for Semistructured Data (PRMS) [16] overcomes this limitation using a probabilistic classification to map query keywords into fields. Other IR approaches extend field retrieval models adding keyword dependencies. The Markov Random Field (MRF) retrieval model [23] proposes three variants of keyword query dependencies: (1) full independence (FIM); (2) sequential dependence (SDM), and; full dependence (FDM). Zhiltsov et al. [41] proposed an fielded ER model based on unigrams and bigrams applied to five different fields (names, categories, similar entity names, related entity names, and other attributes). The model uses different field weights for ordered (e.g., keywords that appear consecutive ly) and unordered bigrams. Koumenides et al. Hasibi et al. [14] shows that entity linking can improve entity retrieval models. Asi et al. [17] gives a comprehensive overview of ER approaches.

Semantic Web. Swoogle [9] introduces a modified version of PageRank that takes into consideration the types of the links between ontologies. Semplore [39], Falcons [4], and Sindice [8] explore traditional document retrieval for querying RDF data. YAHOO! BNC and Umass [13] were respectively the best and second best ER in SemanticSearch'10. YAHOO! BNC uses BM25F aplaying specific boosts on different fields (title, name, dbo:title, others). Blanco et al. [2] uses BM25F boosting important and unimportant fields differently. The proposed adaptation is implemented in the Glimmer$_{Y!}$ engine and is shown to outperform other state-of-the-art methods on the task of ER. Virgilio et al. [37] introduced a distributed technique for ER on RDF data using MapReduce. The retrieval is carried out using only the high ranked (Linear) and all matched fields (Monotonic) strategies. Our work distinguish from the previous by (1) computing the similarity on the individual resources and avoiding the over- and the under-estimation of frequent and rare keywords.

6 Conclusion, Limitations and Future Work.

Whereas recent ER systems gain more precision, retrieving the desired information still imposes a major challenge. This work presented a conditional activation approach for efficient ER over RDF KG using factual query interpretation. The results show a significant improvement of accuracy in comparison to the state-of-the-art ER and EL systems in standard benchmark data sets. In particular, CACAO shows an increase of ≈10% on P@10 and MAP in standard ER benchmark data set. CACAO could outperform other ER and EL methods because it relies on a model that combines two properties: (1) It is a resource-based rather than a fielded retrieval approach, and; (2) It performs a conditional activation that avoids the over- and the under-estimation of frequent and rare keywords.

Nevertheless, there are a few challenges not addressed in the current implementation such as the keyword and character position as well as approach memory and runtime optimizations. Queries such as "peace and war" and "war and peace" can be activated equally. However, one can refer to dbpedia:Peace_and_War whereas the other to dbpedia:War_and_Peace. Recent works [41] have shown promising results in addressing this problem. The evaluation shows that current benchmarks do not address this issue. In future work, we plan to overcome the mentioned challenges. We see this work as the first step of a broader research agenda for designing more accurate ER systems over Linked Data.

Acknowledgments. This work was partly supported by German Research Foundation, project *Professorial Career Patterns of the Early Modern History* grant number 317044652 and CNPq Foundation under (200527/2012-6) and (201808/2015-3).

References

1. Balog, K., Neumayer, R.: A test collection for entity search in DBpedia. In: Proceedings of the 36th International ACM SIGIR Conference on Research and Development in Information Retrieval, SIGIR 2013, pp. 737–740. ACM, New York (2013)
2. Blanco, R., Mika, P., Vigna, S.: Effective and efficient entity search in RDF data. In: Aroyo, L., et al. (eds.) ISWC 2011. LNCS, vol. 7031, pp. 83–97. Springer, Heidelberg (2011). https://doi.org/10.1007/978-3-642-25073-6_6
3. Chen, J., Xiong, C., Callan, J.: An empirical study of learning to rank for entity search. In: Proceedings of the 39th International ACM SIGIR Conference on Research and Development in Information Retrieval, SIGIR 2016, pp. 737–740. ACM, New York (2016)
4. Cheng, G., Qu, Y.: Searching linked objects with falcons: approach, implementation and evaluation. Int. J. Semant. Web Inf. Syst. **5**(3), 49–70 (2009)
5. Craswell, N., Zaragoza, H., Robertson, S.: Microsoft Cambridge at TREC 14: enterprise track. In: Voorhees, E.M., Buckland, L.P. (eds.) TREC, volume Special Publication 500-266. National Institute of Standards and Technology (NIST) (2005)
6. Crestani, F.: Application of spreading activation techniques in information retrieval. Artif. Intell. Rev. **11**(6), 453–482 (1997)
7. Daiber, J., Jakob, M., Hokamp, C., Mendes, P.N.: Improving efficiency and accuracy in multilingual entity extraction. In: Proceedings of the 9th International Conference on Semantic Systems, I-SEMANTICS 2013, pp. 121–124. ACM, New York (2013)
8. Delbru, R., Campinas, S., Tummarello, G.: Searching web data: an entity retrieval and high-performance indexing model. Web Semant. Sci., Serv. Agents World Wide Web **10**, 33–58 (2012)
9. Ding, L., et al.: Swoogle: a search and metadata engine for the semantic web. In: Proceedings of the Thirteenth ACM Conference on Information and Knowledge Management (CIKM), pp. 652–659. ACM (2004)

10. Dubey, M., Dasgupta, S., Sharma, A., Höffner, K., Lehmann, J.: AskNow: a framework for natural language query formalization in SPARQL. In: Sack, H., Blomqvist, E., d'Aquin, M., Ghidini, C., Ponzetto, S.P., Lange, C. (eds.) ESWC 2016. LNCS, vol. 9678, pp. 300–316. Springer, Cham (2016). https://doi.org/10.1007/978-3-319-34129-3_19
11. Ferragina, P., Scaiella, U.: TAGME: on-the-fly annotation of short text fragments (by Wikipedia entities). In: Proceedings of the 19th ACM International Conference on Information and Knowledge Management, CIKM 2010, pp. 1625–1628. ACM, New York (2010)
12. Goodfellow, I., Bengio, Y., Courville, A.: Deep Learning. MIT Press, Cambridge (2016)
13. Halpin, H., et al.: Evaluating ad-hoc object retrieval. In: Proceedings of the International Workshop on Evaluation of Semantic Technologies (IWEST 2010), Shanghai, PR China, 11 2010. 9th International Semantic Web Conference (ISWC2010) (2010)
14. Hasibi, F., Balog, K., Bratsberg, S.E.: Exploiting entity linking in queries for entity retrieval. In: Proceedings of the 2016 ACM International Conference on the Theory of Information Retrieval, pp. 209–218. ACM (2016)
15. Hasibi, F., Balog, K., Bratsberg, S.E.: Entity linking in queries: efficiency vs. effectiveness. In: Jose, J.M., et al. (eds.) ECIR 2017. LNCS, vol. 10193, pp. 40–53. Springer, Cham (2017). https://doi.org/10.1007/978-3-319-56608-5_4
16. Hasibi, F., et al.: DBpedia-entity V2: a test collection for entity search. In: Proceedings of the 40th International ACM SIGIR Conference on Research and Development in Information Retrieval, SIGIR 2017, pp. 1265–1268. ACM, New York (2017)
17. Koumenides, C.L., Shadbolt, N.R.: Ranking methods for entity-oriented semantic web search. J. Assoc. Inf. Sci. Technol. **65**(6), 1091–1106 (2014)
18. Lehmann, J., et al.: DBpedia - a large-scale, multilingual knowledge base extracted from Wikipedia. Semant. Web J. **6**(2), 167–195 (2015)
19. Luhn, H.P.: A statistical approach to mechanized encoding and searching of literary information. IBM J. Res. Dev. **1**(4), 309–317 (1957)
20. Manning, C.D., Raghavan, P., Schütze, H.: Introduction to Information Retrieval. Cambridge University Press, New York (2008)
21. Marx, E., Höffner, K., Shekarpour, S., Ngomo, A.-C.N., Lehmann, J., Auer, S.: Exploring term networks for semantic search over RDF knowledge graphs. In: Garoufallou, E., Subirats Coll, I., Stellato, A., Greenberg, J. (eds.) MTSR 2016. CCIS, vol. 672, pp. 249–261. Springer, Cham (2016). https://doi.org/10.1007/978-3-319-49157-8_22
22. Marx, E., Zaveri, A., Moussallem, D., Rautenberg, S.: DBtrends: exploring query logs for ranking RDF data. In: Proceedings of the 12th International Conference on Semantic Systems, SEMANTiCS 2016, pp. 9–16. ACM, New York (2016)
23. Metzler, D., Croft, W.B.: A Markov random field model for term dependencies. In: Proceedings of the 28th Annual International ACM SIGIR Conference on Research and Development in Information Retrieval, SIGIR 2005, pp. 472–479. ACM, New York (2005)
24. Moussallem, D., Usbeck, R. , Röder, M., Ngonga Ngomo, A.-C.: MAG: a multilingual, knowledge-base agnostic and deterministic entity linking approach. In: K-CAP 2017: Knowledge Capture Conference, p. 8. ACM (2017)

25. Ogilvie, P., Callan, J.: Combining document representations for known-item search. In: Proceedings of the 26th Annual International ACM SIGIR Conference on Research and Development in Informaion Retrieval, SIGIR 2003, pp. 143–150. ACM, New York (2003)
26. Pellissier Tanon, T., Vrandečić, D., Schaffert, S., Steiner, T., Pintscher, L.: From freebase to Wikidata: the great migration. In: Proceedings of the 25th International Conference on World Wide Web, pp. 1419–1428. International World Wide Web Conferences Steering Committee (2016)
27. Ponte, J.M., Croft, W.B.: A language modeling approach to information retrieval. In: Proceedings of the 21st Annual International ACM SIGIR Conference on Research and Development in Information Retrieval, SIGIR 1998, pp. 275–281. ACM, New York (1998)
28. Robertson, S., Zaragoza, H.: The probabilistic relevance framework: Bm25 and beyond. Found. Trends® Inf. Retr. **3**(4), 333–389 (2009)
29. Robertson, S.E., Walker, S., Jones, S., Hancock-Beaulieu, M.M., Gatford, M., et al.: Okapi at trec-3. Nist Spec. Publ. Sp **109**, 109 (1995)
30. Salton, G., Wong, A., Yang, C.S.: A vector space model for automatic indexing. Commun. ACM **18**(11), 613–620 (1975)
31. Shekarpour, S., Marx, E., Ngomo, A.-C.N., Auer, S.: SINA: semantic interpretation of user queries for question answering on interlinked data. J. Web Semant. **30**, 39–51 (2015)
32. Thalhammer, A., Rettinger, A.: Browsing DBpedia entities with summaries. In: Presutti, V., Blomqvist, E., Troncy, R., Sack, H., Papadakis, I., Tordai, A. (eds.) ESWC 2014. LNCS, vol. 8798, pp. 511–515. Springer, Cham (2014). https://doi.org/10.1007/978-3-319-11955-7_76
33. Unger, C., Bühmann, L., Lehmann, J., Ngonga Ngomo, A.-C., Gerber, D., Cimiano, P.: Template-based question answering over RDF data. In: Proceedings of the 21st International Conference on World Wide Web, WWW 2012, pp. 639–648. ACM, New York (2012)
34. Unger, C., et al.: Question answering over linked data (QALD-4). In: Cappellato, L., Ferro, N., Halvey, M., Kraaij, W. (eds.) Working Notes for CLEF 2014 Conference, Sheffield, United Kingdom (2014)
35. Usbeck, R., Ngonga Ngomo, A.-C., Bühmann, L., Unger, C.: HAWK – hybrid question answering using linked data. In: Gandon, F., Sabou, M., Sack, H., d'Amato, C., Cudré-Mauroux, P., Zimmermann, A. (eds.) ESWC 2015. LNCS, vol. 9088, pp. 353–368. Springer, Cham (2015). https://doi.org/10.1007/978-3-319-18818-8_22
36. Usbeck, R., et al.: AGDISTIS - graph-based disambiguation of named entities using linked data. In: Mika, P., et al. (eds.) ISWC 2014. LNCS, vol. 8796, pp. 457–471. Springer, Cham (2014). https://doi.org/10.1007/978-3-319-11964-9_29
37. De Virgilio, R., Maccioni, A.: Distributed keyword search over RDF via MapReduce. In: Presutti, V., d'Amato, C., Gandon, F., d'Aquin, M., Staab, S., Tordai, A. (eds.) ESWC 2014. LNCS, vol. 8465, pp. 208–223. Springer, Cham (2014). https://doi.org/10.1007/978-3-319-07443-6_15
38. Wang, H., et al.: Semplore: a scalable IR approach to search the web of data. J. Web Semant. **7**(3), 177–188 (2009)
39. Zhang, L., Liu, Q.L., Zhang, J., Wang, H.F., Pan, Y., Yu, Y.: Semplore: an IR approach to scalable hybrid query of semantic web data. In: Aberer, K., et al. (eds.) ASWC/ISWC -2007. LNCS, vol. 4825, pp. 652–665. Springer, Heidelberg (2007). https://doi.org/10.1007/978-3-540-76298-0_47

40. Zhang, Y., He, S., Liu, K., Zhao, J.: A joint model for question answering over multiple knowledge bases. In: Proceedings of the Thirtieth AAAI Conference on Artificial Intelligence, AAAI 2016, pp. 3094–3100. AAAI Press (2016)
41. Zhiltsov, N., Kotov, A., Nikolaev, F.: Fielded sequential dependence model for ad-hoc entity retrieval in the web of data. In: Proceedings of the 38th International ACM SIGIR Conference on Research and Development in Information Retrieval, SIGIR 2015, pp. 253–262. ACM, New York (2015)

Fine-Grained Named Entity Recognition in Legal Documents

Elena Leitner, Georg Rehm(✉), and Julian Moreno-Schneider

DFKI GmbH, Alt-Moabit 91c, 10559 Berlin, Germany
{elena.leitner,georg.rehm,julian.moreno_schneider}@dfki.de

Abstract. This paper describes an approach at Named Entity Recognition (NER) in German language documents from the legal domain. For this purpose, a dataset consisting of German court decisions was developed. The source texts were manually annotated with 19 semantic classes: *person*, *judge*, *lawyer*, *country*, *city*, *street*, *landscape*, *organization*, *company*, *institution*, *court*, *brand*, *law*, *ordinance*, *European legal norm*, *regulation*, *contract*, *court decision*, and *legal literature*. The dataset consists of approx. 67,000 sentences and contains 54,000 annotated entities. The 19 fine-grained classes were automatically generalised to seven more coarse-grained classes (*person*, *location*, *organization*, *legal norm*, *case-by-case regulation*, *court decision*, and *legal literature*). Thus, the dataset includes two annotation variants, i.e., coarse- and fine-grained. For the task of NER, Conditional Random Fields (CRFs) and bidirectional Long-Short Term Memory Networks (BiLSTMs) were applied to the dataset as state of the art models. Three different models were developed for each of these two model families and tested with the coarse- and fine-grained annotations. The BiLSTM models achieve the best performance with an 95.46 F_1 score for the fine-grained classes and 95.95 for the coarse-grained ones. The CRF models reach a maximum of 93.23 for the fine-grained classes and 93.22 for the coarse-grained ones. The work presented in this paper was carried out under the umbrella of the European project LYNX that develops a semantic platform that enables the development of various document processing and analysis applications for the legal domain.

Keywords: Language technology · LT · Natural Language Processing · NLP · Named Entity Recognition · NER · Legal processing · Curation technologies · Legal technologies · BiLSTM · CRF

1 Introduction

Named Entity Recognition (NER) is the automatic identification of named entities (NEs) in texts, typically including their assignment to a set of semantic categories [19]. The established classes (for newspaper texts) are *person* `PER`, *location* `LOC`, *organization* `ORG` and *other* `OTH` [3,36,37]. Research on NER has a history

M. Acosta et al. (Eds.): SEMANTiCS 2019, LNCS 11702, pp. 272–287, 2019.
https://doi.org/10.1007/978-3-030-33220-4_20

of more than 20 years and produced approaches based on linear statistical models, e.g., Maximum Entropy Models [1,10], Hidden Markov Models [27], among others. Nowadays, the state of the art results are produced by methods such as CRFs [2,4,16,17] and BiLSTMs [9,20,22,26]. For English news documents, the best models have a performance of approx. 90 F_1 [9,20,22,26,29,38], while the best models for German are not quite as good with approx. 80 F_1 [2,4,16,22]. Based on their very good performance on news documents, we examine the use of CRFs and BiLSTMs in legal documents.

1.1 Application and Project Context

The objective of the project LYNX (Building the Legal Knowledge Graph for Smart Compliance Services in Multilingual Europe), a three year EU project that started in December 2017, is the creation of a legal knowledge graph that contains different types of legal and regulatory data.[1] LYNX aims to help European companies, especially SMEs, that already operate internationally, facing to offer and to promote their products and services in other countries. The project will eventually offer compliance-related services that are currently tested and validated in three use cases. The first pilot is a legal compliance solution, where documents related to data protection are innovatively managed, analysed, and visualised across different jurisdictions. In the second pilot, LYNX supports the understanding of regulatory regimes, including norms and standards, related to energy operations. The third pilot is a compliance solution in the domain of labour law, where legal provisions, case law, administrative resolutions, and expert literature are interlinked, analysed, and compared to define legal strategies for legal practice. The LYNX services are developed for several European languages including English, Spanish and German [32].

Documents in the legal domain contain multiple references to NEs, especially NEs specific to the legal domain, i.e., jurisdictions, legal institutions, etc. Most NER solutions operate in the general or news domain, which makes them not completely suitable for the analysis of legal documents, because they are unable to detect domain-specific entities. The goal is to make knowledge workers, who process and make use of these documents, more efficient and more effective in their day to day work, this also includes the analysis of domain-specific NEs, see [5,31] for related approaches in the area of content curation technologies.

1.2 Research Questions

This article is dedicated to the recognition of NERs and their respective categories in German legal documents. Legal language is unique and differs greatly from newspaper language. This also relates to the use of *person*, *location* and *organization* NEs in legal text, which are relatively rare. It does contain such specific entities as designations of legal norms and references to other legal documents (laws, ordinances, regulations, decisions, etc.) that play an essential role.

[1] http://www.lynx-project.eu.

Despite the development of NER for other languages and domains, the legal domain has not been exhaustively addressed yet. This research also had to face the following two challenges. (1) There is no uniform typology of semantic concepts related to NEs in documents from the legal domain; correspondingly, uniform annotation guidelines for NEs in the legal domain do not exist either. (2) There are no freely available datasets consisting of documents from the legal domain, in which NEs have been annotated.

Thus, the research goal is to examine NER with a specific focus on German legal documents. This includes the elaboration of the corresponding *concepts*, the construction of a *dataset*, developing, evaluating and comparing state of the art *models for NER*. We address the following research questions:

1. Which state of the art approaches are in use for NER? Which approaches have been developed for NER in legal documents? Do these approaches correspond to the state of the art?
2. Which NE categories are typical for legal documents? Which classes are to be identified and classified? Which legal documents can be used for a dataset?
3. What performance do current models have? How are different categories recognized? Which categories are recognized better than others?

2 Related Work

NER in the legal domain, despite its high relevance, is not a well researched area. Existing approaches are inconsistent with regard to the applied methods, techniques, classifications and datasets, which makes it impossible to compare their results adequately. Nevertheless, the developed approaches make an important contribution and form the basis for further research.

The first work in which NER in the legal domain was explicitly defined as a term was described by Dozier et al. [13]. The authors examined NER in US case law, depositions, pleadings and other legal documents, implemented using simple lookups in a list of NEs, contextual rules, and statistical models. Taggers were developed for *jurisdiction*, *court*, *title*, *document type* (e.g., brief, memorandum), and *judge*. The *jurisdiction* tagger performed best with an F_1 of 92. The scores of the other taggers were around 82–85.

Cardellino et al. developed a tool for recognizing, classifying, and linking legal NEs [8]. It uses the YAGO and LKIF ontologies and elaborated four different levels of granularity: NER, NERC, LKIF and YAGO. A Support Vector Machine, Stanford NER [17] and a neural network (NN) were trained and evaluated on Wikipedia and decisions of the European Court of Human Rights. The best result on the Wikipedia dataset was achieved by the NN with F_1 scores for the NERC and YAGO classes of 86 and 69, respectively. For the LKIF classes, Stanford NER was better with F_1 score of 77. The performance was significantly worse on decisions. The F_1 scores varied according to the model and the level of granularity. Stanford NER was able to achieve a maximum F_1 score of 56 with the NERC classes.

Glaser et al. tested three NER systems [18]. The first, GermaNER [4], recognized *person*, *location*, *organization* and *other*. Temporal and numerical expressions were recognized using rule-based approaches, and references using the approach described in Landthaler et al. [23]. The second system was DBpedia Spotlight [11,28], developed for the automatic annotation of DBpedia entities. The third system, Templated, was designed by Glaser et al. [18]. It focused on NER in contracts created using templates. For GermaNER and DBpedia Spotlight a manually annotated corpus was created, which consisted of 500 decisions of the 8th Civil Senate of the German Federal Court of Justice and had reference to tenancy law. GermaNER and DBpedia-Spotlight were evaluated on 20 decisions from the created dataset and Templated was evaluated on five different contracts. GermaNER and DBpedia Spotlight achieved an F_1 of 80 and 87, respectively. The result of Templated NER was 92 F_1.

To adapt categories for the legal domain, the set of NE classes was redefined in the approaches described above. Thus, Dozier et al. [13] focused on legal NEs (e.g., *judge*, *lawyer*, *court*). Cardellino et al. [8] extended NEs on NERC level to *document*, *abstraction*, and *act*. It is unclear what belongs to these classes and how they were separated from each other. Glaser et al. [18] added *reference* [23]. However, this was understood as a reference to legal norms, so that further references (to decisions, regulations, legal literature, etc.) were not covered.

The research of NER in legal documents is also complicated by the fact that there are no freely available datasets, neither for English nor for German. Datasets for newspaper texts, which were developed in CoNNL 2003 or GermEval 2014, again are not suitable in terms of the type of text and the annotated entities. In this context, the need for a manually annotated dataset consisting of legal texts is enormous, requiring the development of a classification of legal categories and uniform annotation guidelines. Such a dataset consisting of documents from the legal domain would make it possible to implement NER with state of the art architectures, i.e., CRF and BiLSTM, and to analyze their performance.

3 A Dataset of Documents from the Legal Domain

3.1 Semantic Categories

Legal documents differ from texts in other domains, and from each other in terms of text-internal, and text-external criteria [7,12,15,21], which has a huge impact on linguistic and thematic design, citation, structure, etc. This also applies to NEs used in legal documents. In law texts and administrative regulations, the occurrence of typical NEs such as *person*, *location* and *organization* is very low. Court decisions, on the other hand, include these NEs, and references to national or supranational laws, other decisions, and regulations. Two requirements for a typology of legal NEs emerge from these peculiarities. First, the categories used must reflect those entities that are typical for decisions. Second, a typology must concern the entities whose differentiation in decisions is highly relevant.

Domain-specific NEs in legal documents can be divided into two basic groups, namely designations and references. For legal norms (i.e., for laws and ordinances) designations are headings for their standard legal texts, which provide information on rank and content [6, Rn. 321 ff.]. Headings are uniform and usually consist of a long title, short title and abbreviation, e.g., the title of the Medicinal Products Act of 12 December 2005 'Gesetz über den Verkehr mit Arzneimitteln (Arzneimittelgesetz – AMG)' (Federal Law Gazette I p. 3394). The short title 'Arzneimittelgesetz' and the abbreviation 'AMG' are in brackets. The citation of the legal norms is also fixed. There are different citation rules for full and short citations [6, Rn. 168 ff.]. The designation and citation of binding individual acts such as regulations or contracts is not uniformly defined.

For our dataset consisting of court decisions, a total of 19 fine-grained classes were developed, which are based on seven coarse-grained classes (see Table 1). As a starting point, the well-researched newspaper domain was used for the elaboration of the typology. The annotation guidelines are based on the ACE guidelines [25] and NoSta-D Named-Entity [3]. The core NEs are typical classes like PER, LOC, and ORG, which are split into fine-grained classes.[2] The coarse- and fine-grained classifications correlate such that, e.g., the coarse-grained class of *person* PER under number 1 in Table 1 contains the fine-grained classes of *judge* RR, *lawyer* AN and other *person* PER (plaintiffs, defendants, witnesses, appraisers, etc.) under numbers 1 to 3. The *location* LOC includes the fine-grained classes of *country* LD (countries, states and city-states), *city* ST (cities, villages and communities), *street* STR (streets, squares, avenues, municipalities and attractions) and *landscape* LDS (continents, mountains, lakes, rivers and other geographical units). The coarse-grained class *organization* ORG is divided into public/social, state and economic institutions. They form the fine-grained classes of *organization* ORG, *institution* INN, and *company* UN. Designations of the federal, supreme, provincial and local courts are summarized in the fine-grained class *court* GRT. Furthermore, *brand*[3] MRK is a separate category.

A fundamental peculiarity of the published decisions is that all personal information is anonymised on account of data privacy reasons. This applies primarily to *person*, *location* and *organization*. NEs are replaced by letters (1) or dots (2).

(1) ... das Land B. **LD** ...

(2) ... unter der Firma C ... AG **UN** ...

In addition to the typical categories, other classes specific to legal documents, i.e., court decisions, are also included in the categories. These are the coarse-grained classes of *legal norm* NRM, *case-by-case regulation* REG, *court decision* RS

[2] The coarse- and fine-grained classes PER and ORG are different despite their identical abbreviations.

[3] From an onomastical point of view, *brand* belongs to object NEs which also contain the coarse-grained class of *organization*. Despite terminological and typological inaccuracy, *brand* was intentionally categorized as a fine-grained class of *organization* and not as independent coarse-grained class (see Table 1).

and *legal literature* `LIT`. The *legal norm* and *case-by-case regulation* include NEs (3) and references (4), but the *court decision* and *legal literature* only references (5). *Legal norm* `NRM` is subdivided according to legal force into the fine-grained classes *law* `GS`, *ordinance* `VO` and *European legal norm* `EUN`. *Case-by-case regulation* `REG`, on the other hand, contains binding individual acts that are below each legal standard. These include the fine-grained classes *regulation* `VS` (administrative regulations, directives, circulars and decrees) and *contract* `VT` (public service contracts, international treaties, collective agreements, etc.). The last two coarse-grained classes, *court decision* `RS` and *legal literature* `LIT`, do not have any fine-grained classes. `RS` reflects references to decisions, and `LIT` summarizes references to legal commentaries, legislative materials, legal textbooks and monographs.

(3) ... ist nach Maßgabe der Gründe mit dem Grundgesetz **GS** vereinbar.

(4) Mit der Neuregelung in § 35 Abs. 6 StVO **VO** ...

(5) ... Klein, in: Maunz/ Schmidt-Bleibtreu/ Klein/ Bethge, BVerfGG, § 19 Rn. 9 **LIT** ...

3.2 Dataset Statistics and Distribution of Semantic Categories

The dataset Legal Entity Recognition (LER) consists of 750 German court decisions published online in the portal 'Rechtsprechung im Internet'.[4] The source texts were extracted from the XML documents and split into sentences and words by SoMaJo [30]. The annotation was performed manually by one Computational Linguistics student using WebAnno [14]. In terms of future work we plan to add annotations from two to three linguists so that we can report inter-annotator agreement. The dataset[5] is freely available for download under the CC-BY 4.0 license[6], in CoNLL-2002 format. Each line consists of two columns separated by a space. The first column contains a token and the second a tag in IOB2 format. The sentence boundary is marked with an empty line.

The dataset consists of 66,723 sentences and 2,157,048 tokens. The percentage of annotations (per-token basis) is approx. 19%. Overall, the dataset includes 53,632 annotated NEs. The dataset has two variants for the classification of legal NEs (Table 1). The *person*, *location* and *organization* make up 25.66% of all annotated instances. 74.34% are specific categories like the *legal norm* `NRM`, *case-by-case regulation* `REG`, *court decision* `RS` and *legal literature* `LIT`. The largest classes are the *law* `GS` (34.53%) and *court decision* `RS` (23.46%). Other entities, i.e., *ordinance*, *European legal norm*, *regulation*, *contract*, and *legal literature*, are less common (between 1 and 6% of all annotations).

[4] http://www.rechtsprechung-im-internet.de.
[5] https://github.com/elenanereiss/Legal-Entity-Recognition.
[6] https://creativecommons.org/licenses/by/4.0/deed.en.

Table 1. Distribution of coarse- and fine-grained classes in the dataset

Coarse-grained classes			#	%	Fine-grained classes			#	%
1	**PER**	Person	3,377	6.30	1	**PER**	Person	1,747	3.26
					2	**RR**	Judge	1,519	2.83
					3	**AN**	Lawyer	111	0.21
2	**LOC**	Location	2,468	4.60	4	**LD**	Country	1,429	2.66
					5	**ST**	City	705	1.31
					6	**STR**	Street	136	0.25
					7	**LDS**	Landscape	198	0.37
3	**ORG**	Organization	7,915	14.76	8	**ORG**	Organization	1,166	2.17
					9	**UN**	Company	1,058	1.97
					10	**INN**	Institution	2,196	4.09
					11	**GRT**	Court	3,212	5.99
					12	**MRK**	Brand	283	0.53
4	**NRM**	Legal norm	20,816	38.81	13	**GS**	Law	18,520	34.53
					14	**VO**	Ordinance	797	1.49
					15	**EUN**	European legal norm	1,499	2.79
5	**REG**	Case-by-case regulation	3,470	6.47	16	**VS**	Regulation	607	1.13
					17	**VT**	Contract	2,863	5.34
6	**RS**	Court decision	12,580	23.46	18	**RS**	Court decision	12,580	23.46
7	**LIT**	Legal literature	3,006	5.60	19	**LIT**	Legal literature	3,006	5.60
		Total	53,632	100			**Total**	53,632	100

4 Evaluation and Results

We used two tools for sequence labeling for our experiments: sklearn-crfsuite[7] and UKPLab-BiLSTM [35]. In total, 12 models were tested, i.e., three CRF and BiLSTM models with coarse- and fine-grained classes. For CRFs, the following groups of features and sources were selected and manually developed:

1. F: features for the current word in a context window between −2 and +2, which are case and shape features, prefixes, and suffixes;
2. G: for the current word, gazetteers of persons from Benikova et al. [4]; gazetteers of countries, cities, streets, landscapes, and companies from GOVDATA[8], the Federal Agency for Cartography and Geodesy[9] and Datendieter.de[10]; gazetteers of laws, ordinances and administrative regulations from the Federal Ministry of Justice and Consumer Protection[11,12]. A detailed description of the gazetteers can be found in the Github project;
3. L: lookup table for the word similarity in a context window between -2 and +2 as in Benikova et al. [4], which contains the four most similar words to the current word.

[7] https://sklearn-crfsuite.readthedocs.io.

[8] https://www.govdata.de/apps/-/details/liste-der-staatennamen.

[9] https://www.bkg.bund.de/DE/Produkte-und-Services/Shop-und-Downloads/Digitale-Geodaten/Geographische-Namen/geographische-namen.html.

[10] https://www.datendieter.de.

[11] https://www.gesetze-im-internet.de.

[12] http://www.verwaltungsvorschriften-im-internet.de.

Three models were designed to chain these groups of features and gazetteers: (1) CRF-F with features; (2) CRF-FG with features and gazetteers; and (3) CRF-FGL with features, gazetteers, and the lookup table; the model names reflect the three groups. As a learning algorithm, the L-BFGS method is used with L1 and L2 regularization parameters, set to the coefficient 0.1. The maximum number of iterations for optimizing the algorithm is set to 100.

For BiLSTM we also use three models: (1) BiLSTM-CRF [20]; (2) BiLSTM-CRF+ with character embeddings from the BiLSTM [22]; (3) BiLSTM-CNN-CRF with character embeddings from CNN [26]. As hyperparameters we used the values that achieved the best NER performance according to Reimers and Gurevych [34]. The BiLSTM models have two BiLSTM layers, each with a size of 100 units and a dropout of 0.25. The maximum number of epochs is 100. At the same time, the tool uses pre-trained word embeddings for German [33].

The results were measured with the micro-precision, -recall and -F_1 measures. In order to reliably estimate their performance, we evaluated the models using stratified 10-fold cross-validation. The dataset is shuffled, sentence-wise, and divided into ten mutually exclusive partial sets of similar size. One iteration uses one set for validation and the rest for training. We iterate ten times, so that each part of the dataset is used nine times for training and once for validation. The distribution of NEs in the training and validation set remain the same over the iterations. The cross-validation prevented overfitting during training and the stratification prevented measurement errors in unbalanced data.

4.1 CRF Models

For the fine-grained classes, CRF-FGL achieved the best performance with an F_1 score of 93.23 (Table 2). The recognition of legal NEs in the different classes had varied levels of success depending on the model. *Lawyer*, *institution*, *court*, *contract* and *court decision* reached the highest F_1 with CRF-F. With the CRF-FG better results could be achieved for *judge*, *city*, *regulation* and *legal literature.* This means that the gazetteers have had a positive impact on the recognition of these NEs. The remaining classes performed better with CRF-FGL. The concatenation of gazetteers and the lookup table for the word similarity has improved the results, but not as much as expected.

For the coarse-grained classes, the CRF-FG and CRF-FGL together achieved the best result with an F_1 value of 93.22 (Table 3). However, *person* was recognized better with CRF-FG and *location* and *organization* better with CRF-FGL. CRF-FG achieved the best result in the *case-by-case regulation* and *court decision*. With CRF-FGL, the values in the *legal norm* and *legal literature* increased. Compared to the fine-grained classes, the better balanced precision and recall were observed and the F_1 increased by max. 0.1 per model.

4.2 BiLSTM Models

For the fine-grained classes, two models with character embeddings have achieved the best result with an F_1 score of 95.46 (Table 4), confirming the positive impact

Table 2. Precision, recall and F_1 values of CRF models for fine-grained classes

Fine-grained classes	CRF-F			CRF-FG			CRF-FGL		
	Prec	Rec	F_1	Prec	Rec	F_1	Prec	Rec	F_1
Person	89.41	83.53	86.32	90.50	83.54	86.83	90.44	84.22	**87.18**
Judge	98.22	97.62	97.92	98.68	97.75	**98.21**	98.55	97.75	98.14
Lawyer	93.14	76.84	**83.73**	89.81	73.51	80.39	92.17	75.04	81.99
Country	96.73	90.42	93.44	97.03	91.98	94.40	96.93	92.62	**94.70**
City	88.99	77.37	82.70	88.27	81.77	**84.77**	88.09	81.82	84.67
Street	88.69	59.58	70.51	87.51	57.95	68.90	90.50	59.85	**71.30**
Landscape	94.34	61.14	73.43	92.63	64.09	75.25	93.33	65.27	**76.08**
Organization	86.82	71.25	78.20	86.71	71.95	78.56	88.84	72.72	**79.89**
Company	92.77	86.04	89.21	93.00	86.18	89.39	93.54	86.85	**90.01**
Institution	92.74	89.49	**91.07**	92.88	89.20	90.98	92.51	89.47	90.96
Court	97.23	96.35	**96.78**	97.03	96.35	96.69	97.19	96.33	96.75
Brand	85.85	56.91	67.85	90.33	56.20	68.82	88.40	58.07	**69.61**
Law	96.86	96.34	96.60	97.00	96.44	96.72	97.02	96.56	**96.79**
Ordinance	91.91	82.23	86.79	91.35	82.85	86.87	91.41	83.49	**87.26**
European legal norm	89.37	86.07	87.67	88.91	85.49	87.14	89.41	86.21	**87.76**
Regulation	83.83	71.38	77.00	84.34	71.03	**77.02**	84.42	70.66	76.85
Contract	90.66	87.72	**89.15**	90.18	87.42	88.76	90.53	87.67	89.06
Court decision	93.35	93.39	**93.37**	93.22	93.34	93.28	93.21	93.29	93.25
Legal literature	92.98	91.28	92.12	92.94	91.42	**92.17**	92.79	91.28	92.02
Total	94.28	91.85	93.05	94.31	91.96	93.12	94.37	92.12	**93.23**

Table 3. Precision, recall and F_1 values of CRF models for coarse-grained classes

Coarse-grained classes	CRF-F			CRF-FG			CRF-FGL		
	Prec	Rec	F_1	Prec	Rec	F_1	Prec	Rec	F_1
Person	94.20	89.43	91.74	94.54	89.99	**92.20**	94.22	90.20	92.16
Location	94.60	84.55	89.26	93.89	85.48	89.45	94.33	86.45	**90.18**
Organization	92.82	89.00	90.87	93.02	89.08	90.99	93.23	89.10	**91.11**
Legal norm	96.19	95.16	95.67	96.29	95.26	95.77	96.28	95.44	**95.86**
Case-by-case regulation	89.29	84.72	86.94	89.28	84.77	**86.96**	88.76	84.15	86.39
Court decision	93.19	93.26	93.23	93.28	93.23	**93.25**	93.08	93.08	93.08
Legal literature	92.72	91.15	91.92	92.99	91.14	92.06	93.11	91.13	**92.11**
Total	94.17	92.07	93.11	94.26	92.20	**93.22**	94.22	92.25	**93.22**

of character level information. A significant improvement with an increase in F_1 by 5–16 (compared to the BiLSTM-CRF without character embeddings) was found in *organization*, *company*, *ordinance*, *regulation* and *contract*. *Judge* and *lawyer* were recognized better by about 1 with the BiLSTM-CRF. *Person*, *country*, *city*, *court*, *brand*, *law*, *ordinance*, *European legal norm*, *regulation* and

Table 4. Precision, recall and F_1 values of BiLSTM models for fine-grained classes

Coarse-grained classes	BiLSTM-CRF			BiLSTM-CRF+			BiLSTM-CNN-CRF		
	Prec	Rec	F_1	Prec	Rec	F_1	Prec	Rec	F_1
Person	89.30	91.08	90.09	90.78	92.24	**91.45**	90.21	92.57	91.35
Judge	98.64	99.48	**99.05**	98.37	99.21	98.78	98.18	99.01	98.59
Lawyer	94.85	84.62	**88.19**	86.18	90.59	87.07	88.02	87.96	87.11
Country	94.66	95.98	95.29	96.52	96.81	**96.66**	95.09	97.20	96.12
City	81.26	86.32	83.48	82.58	89.06	**85.60**	83.21	87.95	85.38
Street	81.70	75.94	78.10	81.82	75.78	77.91	86.24	78.21	**81.49**
Landscape	78.54	79.08	77.57	78.50	80.20	78.25	80.93	81.80	**80.90**
Organization	79.50	74.72	76.89	82.70	80.18	81.28	84.32	81.00	**82.51**
Company	85.81	81.34	83.44	90.05	88.11	89.04	91.72	89.18	**90.39**
Institution	88.88	90.91	89.85	89.99	92.40	91.17	90.24	92.23	**91.20**
Court	97.49	98.33	97.90	97.72	98.24	**97.98**	97.52	98.34	97.92
Brand	78.34	73.11	75.17	83.04	76.25	**79.17**	83.48	73.62	77.79
Law	96.59	97.01	96.80	98.34	98.51	**98.42**	98.44	98.38	98.41
Ordinance	82.63	72.61	77.08	92.29	92.96	**92.58**	91.00	91.09	90.98
European legal norm	90.62	89.79	90.18	92.16	92.63	**92.37**	91.58	92.29	91.92
Regulation	75.58	68.91	71.77	85.14	78.87	**81.63**	79.43	78.30	78.74
Contract	87.12	85.86	86.48	92.00	92.64	**92.31**	90.78	92.06	91.40
Court decision	96.34	96.47	96.41	96.70	96.73	96.71	97.04	97.06	**97.05**
Legal literature	93.87	93.68	93.77	94.34	93.94	94.14	94.25	94.22	**94.23**
Total	93.80	93.70	93.75	95.36	95.57	**95.46**	95.34	95.58	**95.46**

contract were identified better with the BiLSTM-CRF+, and *street*, *landscape*, *organization*, *company*, *institution*, *court decision* and *legal literature* with the BiLSTM-CNN-CRF. Dependencies of the results on character embeddings produced by BiLSTM and CNN were also found. *Brand*, *ordinance* and *regulation* benefited significantly from the use of the BiLSTM. However, recognition of *street* and *landscape* improved with the character embeddings from the CNN.

For the coarse-grained classes, F_1 increased by 0.3–0.9 per model, and precision and recall were also more balanced (Table 5). The best result was produced by the BiLSTM-CRF+ with 95.95. The model had the highest values of more than 90 F_1 in almost all classes. An exception was the BiLSTM-CNN-CRF in *organization*, which increased F_1 by 0.3.

Table 5. Precision, recall and F_1 values of BiLSTM models for coarse-grained classes

Coarse-grained classes	BiLSTM-CRF			BiLSTM-CRF+			BiLSTM-CNN-CRF		
	Prec	Rec	F_1	Prec	Rec	F_1	Prec	Rec	F_1
Person	94.34	95.16	94.74	94.82	96.03	**95.41**	94.09	96.21	95.12
Location	90.85	92.59	91.68	92.60	94.05	**93.31**	91.74	93.45	92.57
Organization	91.82	90.94	91.37	92.87	92.89	92.87	93.80	92.65	**93.21**
Legal norm	97.04	96.50	96.77	97.93	98.04	**97.98**	97.71	97.87	97.79
Case-by-case regulation	86.79	84.15	85.43	90.72	90.53	**90.61**	90.11	90.80	90.43
Court decision	96.54	96.58	96.56	96.93	97.05	**96.99**	96.73	96.83	96.78
Legal literature	93.78	93.91	93.84	94.23	94.62	**94.42**	94.24	93.80	94.02
Total	94.86	94.49	94.68	95.84	96.07	**95.95**	95.71	95.87	95.79

4.3 Discussion

The BiLSTMs achieved superior performance compared to the CRFs. They produced good results even with the fine-grained classes covered poorly in the dataset. The CRF models, on the other hand, delivered values that were about 1–10 lower per class. In addition, some classes are characterized by bigger differences in precision and recall, indicating certain weaknesses of the CRFs. In particular, the recognition of *street* and *brand* with the BiLSTM models improved by values of at least 10. The values for *lawyer*, *landscape* and *ordinance* also increased by a value of 5.

The results also show that the two model families exhibit a similar performance due to the dataset or structure of the data. The models produce their best results with 95 F_1 score in the fine-grained classes *judge*, *court* and *law*. On the one hand, this depends on a smaller number of types compared to tokens in *judge* and *court*. On the other hand, the precise identification of *law* can be explained by its good coverage in the dataset and uniform citation. Incorrect predictions about boundaries are made if references had a different form such as in '§ 7 des Gesetzes (gemeint ist das VersAnstG)' instead of common '§ 7 VersAnstG', 'das zwölfte Kapitel des neunten Sozialgesetzbuches' instead of 'das Kapitel 12 des SGB XII'. There were also incorrect classifications of terms as a NE containing the word 'law', such as 'federal law', 'law of experience', 'criminal law', etc. The recognition of *country*, *institution*, *court decision*, and *legal literature* was also very good with scores higher than 90 F_1. This is also due to a smaller number of types in *country*, *institution* and uniform references of *court decision* and *legal literature*.

However, the recognition of *street*, *landscape*, *organization* and *regulation* is the lowest throughout, amounting to 69–80 with the CRF and 72–83 with the BiLSTM models, caused by inconsistent citation styles. The recognition of *street* and *landscape* is poor because they are covered in the dataset with only about 200 instances, but heterogeneously represented. The worst result, i.e., a maximum F_1 value of 69.61 with the CRFs and of 79.17 with the BiLSTMs, was observed in *brand*. These NEs were also expressed in different contexts, such as the *brand* NE 'Einstein's Garage' and the scientist Albert Einstein. It can be concluded that the differences in the recognition of certain NEs is firstly due to the unbalanced class distribution and secondly to the specifics of the legal documents, in particular because of the coverage in the corpus, the heterogeneity with regard to the form of names or references as well as the context.

Overall, the CRFs and BiLSTMs perform very well, producing state of the art results, which are significantly better than comparable models for newspaper text. This fact can, first, be explained by the size of the dataset which is larger than other NE datasets for German. Second, the form of legal NEs, which also includes references, differs a lot from NEs in newspaper text. The distribution of designations or references in the dataset consisting of documents from the legal domain is greater compared to *person*, *location* or *organization*. Third, the strictly regulated linguistic and thematic design (repeated use of NEs per one decision, repeated use of formulaic, template-like sentences, etc.) and the uniform reference style have had a positive impact on performance. The applied evaluation method made it possible to reliably estimate performance for unbalanced data. Unfortunately, it is not possible to compare our results with other systems for NER in legal documents because they are not freely available.

5 Conclusion

We describe and evaluate a set of approaches for the recognition of semantic concepts in German court decisions. In line with the goals, the characteristic and relevant semantic categories such as *legal norm*, *case-by-case regulation*, *court decision* and *legal literature* were worked out and a dataset of legal documents was built, instances of a total of 19 semantic classes were annotated. For the experiment, CRF and BiLSTM models were selected that correspond to the state of art, and tested with the two sets of classes. The results of both model families demonstrate the superiority of the BiLSTMs models with character embeddings with an F_1 score of 95.46 for the fine-grained classes and 95.95 for the coarse-grained classes. We found that the structure of the data involved in the training process strongly impacts the performance. To improve NER, it is necessary to extend or optimize the unbalanced data. This helps to minimize the specific influencing factors of the legal documents on models. Our results show that there is no universal model that recognizes all classes in the best way. Accordingly, an even better universal system could be built as an ensemble of different models that perform well for particular classes.

Acknowledgments. The project LYNX has received funding from the European Union's Horizon 2020 research and innovation programme under grant agreement no. 780602. More information is available online at http://www.lynx-project.eu. This work was carried out under the umbrella of an internship of the first author at DFKI, which resulted in a Bachelor thesis at the University of Potsdam [24].

References

1. Bender, O., Och, F.J., Ney, H.: Maximum entropy models for named entity recognition. In: Proceedings of the Seventh Conference on Natural Language Learning at HLT-NAACL 2003, vol. 4, pp. 148–151. Association for Computational Linguistics (2003)
2. Benikova, D., Biemann, C., Kisselew, M., Padó, S.: GermEval 2014 named entity recognition shared task: companion paper. In: Proceedings of the KONVENS GermEval Workshop, Hildesheim, Germany, pp. 104–112 (2014)
3. Benikova, D., Biemann, C., Reznicek, M.: NoSta-D named entity annotation for German: guidelines and dataset. In: Calzolari, N., et al. (eds.) Proceedings of the Ninth International Conference on Language Resources and Evaluation, LREC 2014, Reykjavik, Iceland, 26–31 May 2014. pp. 2524–2531. European Language Resources Association (ELRA) (2014)
4. Benikova, D., Yimam, S.M., Santhanam, P., Biemann, C.: GermaNER: free open German named entity recognition tool. In: Proceedings of the International Conference of the German Society for Computational Linguistics and Language Technology, GSCL 2015, University of Duisburg-Essen, Germany, 30 September–2 October 2015, pp. 31–38 (2015)
5. Bourgonje, P., Moreno-Schneider, J., Rehm, G.: Domain-specific entity spotting: curation technologies for digital humanities and text analytics. In: Reiter, N., Kremer, G. (eds.) CUTE Workshop 2017 - CRETA Unshared Task zu Entitätenreferenzen. Workshop bei DHd 2017, Berne, Switzerland, February 2017
6. Bundesministerium der Justiz: Bekanntmachung des Handbuchs der Rechtsförmlichkeit. Bundesanzeiger Jahrgang **60**(160a), 296 (2008)
7. Busse, D.: Textsorten des Bereichs Rechtswesen und Justiz. Text- und Gesprächslinguistik. Ein internationales Handbuch zeitgenössischer Forschung **1**, 658–675 (2000)
8. Cardellino, C., Teruel, M., Alemany, L.A., Villata, S.: A low-cost, high-coverage legal named entity recognizer, classifier and linker. In: Proceedings of the 16th Edition of the International Conference on Artificial Intelligence and Law, ICAIL 2017, pp. 9–18. , ACM, New York (2017)
9. Chiu, J.P.C., Nichols, E.: Named entity recognition with bidirectional LSTM-CNNs. TACL **4**, 357–370 (2016)
10. Clark, A.: Combining distributional and morphological information for part of speech induction. In: Proceedings of the Tenth Conference on European chapter of the Association for Computational Linguistics, vol. 1, pp. 59–66. Association for Computational Linguistics (2003)
11. Daiber, J., Jakob, M., Hokamp, C., Mendes, P.N.: Improving efficiency and accuracy in multilingual entity extraction. In: I-SEMANTICS 2013–9th International Conference on Semantic Systems, ISEM 2013, Graz, Austria, 4–6 September 2013, pp. 121–124 (2013)
12. Deutsch, A.: 5. Schriftlichkeit im Recht: Kommunikationsformen/Textsorten. Handbuch Sprache im Recht **12**, 91–117 (2017)
13. Dozier, C., Kondadadi, R., Light, M., Vachher, A., Veeramachaneni, S., Wudali, R.: Named entity recognition and resolution in legal text. In: Francesconi, E., Montemagni, S., Peters, W., Tiscornia, D. (eds.) Semantic Processing of Legal Texts. LNCS (LNAI), vol. 6036, pp. 27–43. Springer, Heidelberg (2010). https://doi.org/10.1007/978-3-642-12837-0_2

14. Eckart de Castilho, R., et al.: A web-based tool for the integrated annotation of semantic and syntactic structures. In: Hinrichs, E.W., Hinrichs, M., Trippel, T. (eds.) Proceedings of the Workshop on Language Technology Resources and Tools for Digital Humanities, LT4DH@COLING, Osaka, Japan, December 2016, pp. 76–84. The COLING 2016 Organizing Committee (2016)
15. Engberg, J.: Prinzipien einer Typologisierung juristischer Texte. Fachsprache Int. J. Spec. Commun. **15**(1/2), 31–38 (1993)
16. Faruqui, M., Padó, S.: Training and evaluating a german named entity recognizer with semantic generalization. In: Pinkal, M., Rehbein, I., im Walde, S.S., Storrer, A. (eds.) Semantic Approaches in Natural Language Processing: Proceedings of the 10th Conference on Natural Language Processing, KONVENS 2010, Saarland University, Saarbrücken, Germany, 6–8 September 2010, pp. 129–133. universaar, Universitätsverlag des Saarlandes/Saarland University Press/Presses universitaires de la Sarre (2010)
17. Finkel, J.R., Grenager, T., Manning, C.D.: Incorporating non-local information into information extraction systems by Gibbs sampling. In: Knight, K., Ng, H.T., Oflazer, K. (eds.) Proceedings of the Conference on ACL 2005, 43rd Annual Meeting of the Association for Computational Linguistics, 25–30 June 2005, University of Michigan, USA, pp. 363–370. The Association for Computer Linguistics (2005)
18. Glaser, I., Waltl, B., Matthes, F.: Named entity recognition, extraction, and linking in German legal contracts. In: IRIS: Internationales Rechtsinformatik Symposium, pp. 325–334 (2018)
19. Grishman, R., Sundheim, B.: Message understanding conference-6: a brief history. In: Proceedings of the 16th International Conference on Computational Linguistics, COLING 1996, Center for Sprogteknologi, Copenhagen, Denmark, 5–9 August 1996, pp. 466–471 (1996)
20. Huang, Z., Xu, W., Yu, K.: Bidirectional LSTM-CRF models for sequence tagging. CoRR abs/1508.01991 (2015)
21. Kjær, A.: Normbedingte Wortverbindungen in der juristischen Fachsprache (Deutsch als Fremdsprache). Fremdsprachen Lehren und Lernen **21**, 46–64 (1992)
22. Lample, G., Ballesteros, M., Subramanian, S., Kawakami, K., Dyer, C.: Neural architectures for named entity recognition. In: NAACL HLT 2016, The 2016 Conference of the North American Chapter of the Association for Computational Linguistics: Human Language Technologies, San Diego California, USA, 12–17 June 2016, pp. 260–270 (2016)
23. Landthaler, J., Waltl, B., Matthes, F.: Unveiling references in legal texts - implicit versus explicit network structures. In: IRIS: Internationales Rechtsinformatik Symposium, pp. 71–78 (2016)
24. Leitner, E.: Eigennamen- und Zitaterkennung in Rechtstexten. Bachelor's thesis, Universität Potsdam, Potsdam, February 2019
25. Linguistic Data Consortium: ACE (Automatic Content Extraction) English Annotation Guidelines for Entities (2008)
26. Ma, X., Hovy, E.H.: End-to-end sequence labeling via bi-directional lstm-CNNs-CRF. In: Proceedings of the 54th Annual Meeting of the Association for Computational Linguistics, ACL 2016, Volume 1: Long Papers, Berlin, Germany, 7–12 August 2016 (2016)
27. Mayfield, J., McNamee, P., Piatko, C.: Named entity recognition using hundreds of thousands of features. In: Proceedings of the seventh conference on Natural language learning at HLT-NAACL 2003, vol. 4, pp. 184–187. Association for Computational Linguistics (2003)

28. Mendes, P.N., Jakob, M., García-Silva, A., Bizer, C.: DBpedia spotlight: shedding light on the web of documents. In: Ghidini, C., Ngomo, A.N., Lindstaedt, S.N., Pellegrini, T. (eds.) Proceedings the 7th International Conference on Semantic Systems, I-SEMANTICS 2011, Graz, Austria, 7–9 September 2011. . ACM International Conference Proceeding Series, pp. 1–8. ACM (2011)
29. Passos, A., Kumar, V., McCallum, A.: Lexicon infused phrase embeddings for named entity resolution. In: Morante, R., Yih, W. (eds.) Proceedings of the Eighteenth Conference on Computational Natural Language Learning, CoNLL 2014, Baltimore, Maryland, USA, 26–27 June 2014, pp. 78–86. ACL (2014)
30. Proisl, T., Uhrig, P.: SoMaJo: State-of-the-art tokenization for German web and social media texts. In: Cook, P., Evert, S., Schäfer, R., Stemle, E. (eds.) Proceedings of the 10th Web as Corpus Workshop, WAC@ACL 2016, Berlin, 12 August 2016, pp. 57–62. Association for Computational Linguistics (2016)
31. Rehm, G., et al.: Event detection and semantic storytelling: generating a travelogue from a large collection of personal letters. In: Caselli, T., et al. (eds.) Proceedings of the Events and Stories in the News Workshop, co-located with ACL 2017, Vancouver, Canada, August 2017, pp. 42–51. Association for Computational Linguistics (2017)
32. Rehm, G., et al.: Developing and orchestrating a portfolio of natural legal language processing and document curation services. In: Aletras, N., et al. (eds.) Proceedings of Workshop on Natural Legal Language Processing (NLLP 2019), co-located with NAACL 2019, Minneapolis, USA, 7 June 2019, pp. 55–66 (2019)
33. Reimers, N., Eckle-Kohler, J., Schnober, C., Kim, J., Gurevych, I.: GermEval-2014: nested named entity recognition with neural networks. In: Faaß, G., Ruppenhofer, J. (eds.) Workshop Proceedings of the 12th Edition of the KONVENS Conference, Oktober 2014, pp. 117–120. Universitätsverlag Hildesheim (2014)
34. Reimers, N., Gurevych, I.: Optimal hyperparameters for deep LSTM-networks for sequence labeling tasks. CoRR abs/1707.06799 (2017)
35. Reimers, N., Gurevych, I.: Reporting score distributions makes a difference: performance study of LSTM-networks for sequence tagging. In: Proceedings of the 2017 Conference on Empirical Methods in Natural Language Processing, pp. 338–348. Association for Computational Linguistics (2017)
36. Sang, E.F.T.K., Meulder, F.D.: Introduction to the CoNLL-2003 shared task: language-independent named entity recognition. In: Daelemans, W., Osborne, M. (eds.) Proceedings of the Seventh Conference on Natural Language Learning, CoNLL 2003, Held in cooperation with HLT-NAACL 2003, Edmonton, Canada, 31 May–1 June 2003, pp. 142–147. ACL (2003)
37. Tjong Kim Sang, E.F.: Introduction to the CoNLL-2002 shared task: language-independent named entity recognition. In: Proceedings of the 6th Conference on Natural Language Learning, COLING 2002, vol. 20, pp. 1–4. Association for Computational Linguistics, Stroudsburg (2002)
38. Tkachenko, M., Simanovsky, A.: Named entity recognition: exploring features. In: Jancsary, J. (ed.) 11th Conference on Natural Language Processing, KONVENS 2012, Empirical Methods in Natural Language Processing, Vienna, Austria, 19–21 September 2012. Scientific series of the ÖGAI, vol. 5, pp. 118–127. ÖGAI, Wien (2012)

Extracting Literal Assertions for DBpedia from Wikipedia Abstracts

Florian Schrage(✉), Nicolas Heist, and Heiko Paulheim

Data and Web Science Group, University of Mannheim, Mannheim, Germany
florian.schrage@sap.com,{nico,heiko}@informatik.uni-mannheim.de.de

Abstract. Knowledge Graph completion deals with the addition of missing facts to knowledge graphs. While quite a few approaches exist for type and link prediction in knowledge graphs, the addition of literal values (also called instance or entity attributes) is not very well covered in the literature. In this paper, we present an approach for extracting numerical and date literal values from Wikipedia abstracts. We show that our approach can add 643k additional literal values to DBpedia at a precision of about 95%.

Keywords: Knowledge Graph · Completion · Literals · DBpedia

1 Introduction

In the past, adding missing facts to Knowledge Graphs to increase the data quality in knowledge graphs has gained a lot of attention [10]. Most prominently, link prediction using embedding models is a very active field of research [14].

While a lot of research is devoted on missing links, i.e., relations between two entities, the prediction of missing facts involving literals (e.g., numbers or dates), is considerably underrepresented in the current research landscape [10].

In this paper, we aim at closing this gap by identifying and extracting literal values from abstracts in Wikipedia[1]., defining an abstract as the In contrast to standard relation extraction, there are a few additional challenges to face:

- Natural text uses a lot of different number formats (e.g., w.r.t. decimal and thousands separators) [15]. Even within a single Wikipedia article, the number formats may be inconsistent [11].
- Numbers often come with units of measurement, which complicate the extraction, since those units need to be harmonized [13].
- Exact numbers are often rounded in natural text (e.g., *about 3,000* instead of *3,085*, which can make it difficult to assess whether a rounded and an exact number refer to the same or a different fact.

The contribution of this paper is an approach for extracting literal values (numbers and dates) from Wikipedia articles, which can deal with roundings and different units of measurement.

[1] We follow the *long abstract* notion in [9], extracting the "'text before a table of contents"' from a Wikipedia page.

M. Acosta et al. (Eds.): SEMANTiCS 2019, LNCS 11702, pp. 288–294, 2019.
https://doi.org/10.1007/978-3-030-33220-4_21

2 Related Work

There are not many approaches for completing literal values in knowledge graphs. In [12], the use of Web tables as a source for literal values is explored. This setting is different, since the authors work on structured, not unstructured data, so they can use different features.

One of the few closer approaches is presented in [2], where the authors run open relation extraction on Wikipedia text and perform an a posteriori mapping to the DBpedia ontology. Although they do not deal with numbers, their approach can extract date literals and reaches an overall precision of 74.3%[2].

Similarly, the authors of [1] train specific models for DBpedia relations, but only evaluate their approach on two date-valued and one integer-valued relation. They extract 440k date valued literals (birthdate and deathdate) at a precision of 91%, and 237k integer-valued literals (population) at a precision of 70%[3].

In comparison to that state of the art, the approach discussed in this paper yields superior results both in absolute numbers of values extracted, as well as in precision.

For error detection in knowledge graphs, there are approaches based on outlier detection [3], probabilistic data modeling [7] and data fusion [8]. There, it can also be observed that the amount of research directed towards literal values is much underrepresented in comparison to relation assertions between individuals.

3 Approach

Our approach builds on previous works for extracting relation assertions from Wikipedia abstracts [4,5]. That approach exploits *links* in Wikipedia abstracts, learns characteristic patterns for relations (e.g., *The first place linked in the*

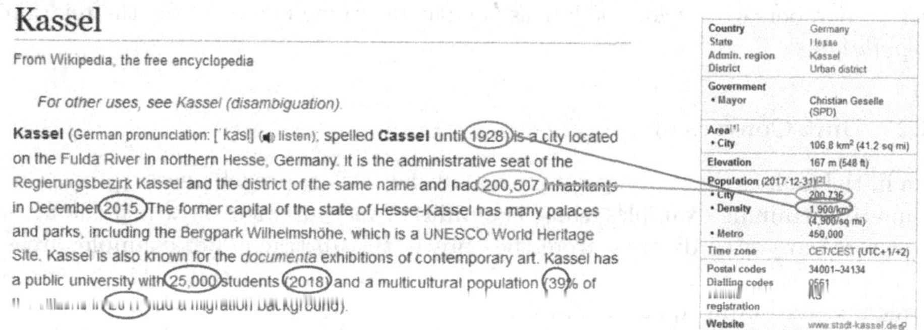

Fig. 1. Example from Wikipedia with a correct and an incorrect example extracted, as well as non-matching literals marked in the abstract.

[2] Their final dataset contains about 5k date literals mapped to properties in the DBpedia ontology.

[3] The totals include both literals contained and not contained in DBpedia.

Wikipedia abstract about a person is that person's birthplace), and then applies the models to extract new statements (e.g., new facts for the relation *birthplace*). For each relation, a separate model is trained and validated on the existing instances, which allows for only applying models that achieve a desired precision.

3.1 Training Data Creation

To create the training data, we use regular expressions to detect and parse numbers in the abstract in various formats (i.e., thousands and decimal separators), and SpaCy[4] and dateparser[5] to detect and parse dates.

With these approaches, we extract the sets of numerical literals N and date literals D from the Wikipedia abstract describing a DBpedia entity e. Since numbers may be rounded, we accept a training example $n \in N$ as positive example for a relation if there is a statement $r(e, v)$ in DBpedia with $n \in [v \cdot (1 - p), v \cdot (1 + p)]$ for a deviation factor of p. We manually examined candidates drawn at deviation factors of 1%, 1.5%, and 2%, and observed that the precision at 1% and 1.5% was 65%, and dropped to 60% when further increasing the deviation factor. Hence, we decided to use a factor of 1.5% in our further experiments.

Figure 1 illustrates this generation of examples. Since DBpedia is constructed from infoboxes in Wikipedia, the values in the infobox on the right hand side correspond to the values in DBpedia. Given the Wikipedia abstract, 200,507 would be extracted as a training example for the relation *population* (correct), while 1928 would be extracted as a training example for the relation *density* (incorrect). The deviation is 0.11% and 1.47%, respectively.

Since dates are not rounded, training data for date valued literals are based on exact matches with DBpedia only[6].

As negative training examples, we use all numbers or dates, respectively, which have been tagged in the abstract which are not identified as positive examples for the relation at hand. In the example depicted in Fig. 1, we would use all numbers except for 200,507 as negative training examples for the relation *population*.

3.2 Unit Conversion

An initial look at the training data revealed that this approach misses quite a few numerical training examples, since the units of measurement in which the facts are stored are often different from the ones in the abstracts. For example, areas (of countries, cities, ...) are stored in DBpedia in square meters, while they are typically written in square kilometers or non-metric units. Therefore, for those relations, the training data sets create are often very small (e.g., for *area*, which is one of the most frequent relations in DBpedia, we initially collected less than 100 training examples).

---

[4] https://spacy.io/.

[5] https://pypi.org/project/dateparser/.

[6] Note that it is not trivial to detect that *1928* in the text is a date, not an integer.

Table 1. Examples for unit conversions learned from the data.

Token	Target unit	Correct factor	Inferred factor	R squared
km^2	m^2	1,000,000	997,097	0.9949
km2	m^2	1,000,000	999,927	0.9999
ha	m^2	10,000	9,467	0.8987
pupils	$	–	13,613	0.9062
kilometers	*m*	1,000	973	0.9347
century	*m*	–	73,453	0.9421

Therefore, we decided to enhance the training example generation with unit conversion. We follow the assumption that (1) units of measurement are typically the token after a number[7], and (2) the function for converting units to their standard unit in DBpedia is usually a simple multiplication by a factor. Thus, we group numeric literals for each relation by the token following the number (e.g., *ha*) and try to learn a regression model for that token. From those regression models, we derive unit conversion rules which are applied to the literals extracted as above before mapping them to relations in DBpedia. Following an initial inspection of the data, we accept unit conversions learned on at least 100 examples and having a coefficient of determination of at least 0.85. Table 1 shows a few example unit conversion factors, including useful rules learned, but also some misleading rules (e.g., converting the "unit" *pupils* to $).

3.3 Feature Extraction

For each positive and negative training example extracted, we create a set of features to feed into a classifier. We use a similar set of features as in [4], e.g., position in the sentence, position of the sentence in the abstract, etc., plus a bag of words representation of the sentence in which the literal is located, and, for numerical literals, the deviation from the mean divided by the standard deviation of all values of the respective relation, in order to discard outliers.

3.4 Model Building

To learn models given the examples and feature vectors, we experimented with different classifiers from the scikit-learn library[8], i.e., SGD, Naive Bayes, SVM, Decision Trees, Random Forest, Extra Trees, Bagging Decision Trees, and XGBoost. Out of those, the latter five delivered the best results in an initial experiment (using split validation on a sample of relations with the most already existing instances), without much variance in quality. Random Forests were chosen because of a good trade-off between runtime and accuracy.

[7] There are rare exceptions, like currencies, which we ignore.

[8] https://scikit-learn.org/.

4 Evaluation

For our evaluation, we used the most recent downloadable version of DBpedia, i.e., DBpedia 2016-10[9] and the abstracts contained therein[10]. We tried to train models for all 405 number and date valued properties in the DBpedia ontology. To learn meaningful models, we discarded all properties that were too small (i.e., less than 100 positive examples), leaving us with 120 properties.

Following the approach in [4], we aimed at achieving a high precision in the extraction in order not to add too much noise to the knowledge graph at hand. Therefore, we validated all models internally using a training (75%) and a test (25%) split, and kept only those models achieving a precision of at least 95%. Out of those 120 properties, we could learn a model at 95% precision in 28 cases.

As shown in Table 2, for those 28 relations, the approach creates almost 9M statements, however, only a smaller fraction (about 7%) is not yet contained in DBpedia. That share of new statements is considerably higher for dates (11%) than for numbers (less than 1%). The majority of the former are birthdates, the majority of the latter are population numbers.

Table 2. Number of statements extracted at 95% precision according to internal validation.

Range	Properties	Statements	New statements
Date	17	5,525,089	621,747
Int	6	224,606	15,326
Float	5	3,185,497	5,955
Total	28	8,955,192	643,030

In order to validate the precision values of the internal validation based on the test set, we randomly sampled 500 of the new statements for manual inspection. This inspection yields a precision of 94.2%, which confirms the estimation based on the internal test set.

In terms of runtime, a complete run on the entire DBpedia and the corresponding Wikipedia abstracts takes about 135 h on a Linux server with 512 GB of RAM. The by far longest time is consumed by the preprocessing of the abstracts, e.g., the date tagging and parsing takes 65 h alone, whereas the model training and statement creation take 1.9 and 3.6 h each.

[9] https://wiki.dbpedia.org/downloads-2016-10.

[10] http://downloads.dbpedia.org/2016-10/core-i18n/en/long_abstracts_en.tql.bz2.

5 Conclusion and Outlook

With this paper, we have aimed at closing a gap in the current research landscape on knowledge graph completion. While research in this field is strongly focused on type and relation prediction, we have shown how numeric and date valued facts can be extracted from Wikipedia abstracts. While there are quite a few challenges, including number and date formats and unit conversions, we have shown that it is possible to achieve an extraction at a precision of about 95%. The code used to create the results reported in this paper is available online[11].

In the future, we plan to apply the approach to other Wiki-based knowledge graphs, such as DBkWik [6].

References

1. Aprosio, A.P., Giuliano, C., Lavelli, A.: Extending the coverage of DBpedia properties using distant supervision over Wikipedia. In: Workshop on NLP & DBPEDIA (2013)
2. Exner, P., Nugues, P.: Entity extraction: from unstructured text to DBpedia RDF triples. In: The Web of Linked Entities Workshop (WoLE 2012), pp. 58–69. CEUR (2012)
3. Fleischhacker, D., Paulheim, H., Bryl, V., Völker, J., Bizer, C.: Detecting errors in numerical linked data using cross-checked outlier detection. In: Mika, P., et al. (eds.) ISWC 2014. LNCS, vol. 8796, pp. 357–372. Springer, Cham (2014). https://doi.org/10.1007/978-3-319-11964-9_23
4. Heist, N., Hertling, S., Paulheim, H.: Language-agnostic relation extraction from abstracts in Wikis. Information **9**(4), 75 (2018)
5. Heist, N., Paulheim, H.: Language-agnostic relation extraction from Wikipedia abstracts. In: d'Amato, C., et al. (eds.) ISWC 2017. LNCS, vol. 10587, pp. 383–399. Springer, Cham (2017). https://doi.org/10.1007/978-3-319-68288-4_23
6. Hertling, S., Paulheim, H.: DBkWik: a consolidated knowledge graph from thousands of Wikis. In: 2018 IEEE International Conference on Big Knowledge (ICBK), pp. 17–24. IEEE (2018)
7. Li, H., Li, Y., Xu, F., Zhong, X.: Probabilistic error detecting in numerical linked data. In: Chen, Q., Hameurlain, A., Toumani, F., Wagner, R., Decker, H. (eds.) DEXA 2015. LNCS, vol. 9261, pp. 61–75. Springer, Cham (2015). https://doi.org/10.1007/978-3-319-22849-5_5
8. Liu, S., d'Aquin, M., Motta, E.: Towards linked data fact validation through measuring consensus. In: Workshop on Linked Data Quality (2015)
9. Morsey, M., Lehmann, J., Auer, S., Stadler, C., Hellmann, S.: DBpedia and the live extraction of structured data from wikipedia. Program **46**(2), 157–181 (2012)
10. Paulheim, H.: Knowledge graph refinement: a survey of approaches and evaluation methods. Semantic Web **8**(3), 489–508 (2017)
11. Paulheim, H.: A robust number parser based on conditional random fields. In: Kern-Isberner, G., Fürnkranz, J., Thimm, M. (eds.) KI 2017. LNCS (LNAI), vol. 10505, pp. 337–343. Springer, Cham (2017). https://doi.org/10.1007/978-3-319-67190-1_29

[11] https://github.com/FlorianSchrage/DBpediaLiteralRelations.

12. Ritze, D., Lehmberg, O., Oulabi, Y., Bizer, C.: Profiling the potential of web tables for augmenting cross-domain knowledge bases. In: Proceedings of the 25th International Conference on World Wide Web, pp. 251–261 (2016)
13. Subercaze, J.: Chaudron: extending DBpedia with measurement. In: Blomqvist, E., Maynard, D., Gangemi, A., Hoekstra, R., Hitzler, P., Hartig, O. (eds.) ESWC 2017. LNCS, vol. 10249, pp. 434–448. Springer, Cham (2017). https://doi.org/10.1007/978-3-319-58068-5_27
14. Wang, Q., Mao, Z., Wang, B., Guo, L.: Knowledge graph embedding: a survey of approaches and applications. IEEE Trans. Knowl. Data Eng. **29**(12), 2724–2743 (2017)
15. Wienand, D., Paulheim, H.: Detecting incorrect numerical data in DBpedia. In: Presutti, V., d'Amato, C., Gandon, F., d'Aquin, M., Staab, S., Tordai, A. (eds.) ESWC 2014. LNCS, vol. 8465, pp. 504–518. Springer, Cham (2014). https://doi.org/10.1007/978-3-319-07443-6_34

Towards a Scalable Semantic-Based Distributed Approach for SPARQL Query Evaluation

Gezim Sejdiu[1(✉)], Damien Graux[2], Imran Khan[1], Ioanna Lytra[1], Hajira Jabeen[1], and Jens Lehmann[1,2]

[1] Smart Data Analytics, University of Bonn, Bonn, Germany
{sejdiu,lytra,jabeen,jens.lehmann}@cs.uni-bonn.de, s6imkhan@uni-bonn.de
[2] Enterprise Information Systems, Fraunhofer IAIS, Sankt Augustin, Germany
{damien.graux,jens.lehmann}@iais.fraunhofer.de

Abstract. Over the last two decades, the amount of data which has been created, published and managed using Semantic Web standards and especially via Resource Description Framework (RDF) has been increasing. As a result, efficient processing of such big RDF datasets has become challenging. Indeed, these processes require, both efficient storage strategies and query-processing engines, to be able to scale in terms of data size. In this study, we propose a scalable approach to evaluate SPARQL queries over distributed RDF datasets using a semantic-based partition and is implemented inside the state-of-the-art RDF processing framework: SANSA. An evaluation of the performance of our approach in processing large-scale RDF datasets is also presented. The preliminary results of the conducted experiments show that our approach can scale horizontally and perform well as compared with the previous Hadoop-based system. It is also comparable with the in-memory SPARQL query evaluators when there is less shuffling involved.

1 Introduction

Recently, significant amounts of data have been created, published and managed using the Semantic Web standards. Currently, the Linked Open Data (LOD) cloud comprises more than 10000 datasets available online[1] using the Semantic Web standards. RDF is a standard that represents data linked as a graph of resources following the idea of the linking structure of the Web and using URIs for representation.

To facilitate better maintenance and faster access to this scale of data, efficient data partitioning is needed. One of such partitioned strategies is semantic-based partitioning. It groups the facts based on the subject and its associated triples. We want to explore and evaluate the effect of semantic-based partitioning on query performance when dealing with such a volume of RDF datasets.

[1] http://lodstats.aksw.org/.

M. Acosta et al. (Eds.): SEMANTiCS 2019, LNCS 11702, pp. 295–309, 2019.
https://doi.org/10.1007/978-3-030-33220-4_22

SPARQL is a W3C standard query language for querying data modeled as RDF. Querying RDF data efficiently becomes challenging when the size of the data increases. This has motivated a considerable amount of work on designing distributed RDF systems able to efficiently evaluate SPARQL queries [6,20,21]. Being able to query a large amount of data in an efficient and faster way is one of the key requirements for every SPARQL engine.

To address these challenges, in this paper, we propose a scalable semantic-based distributed approach[2] for efficient evaluation of SPARQL queries over distributed RDF datasets. The main component of the system is the data partitioning and query evaluation over this data representation.

Our contributions are:

- A scalable approach for semantic-based partitioning using the distributed computing framework, Apache Spark.
- A scalable semantic-based query engine (*SANSA.Semantic*) on top of Apache Spark (under the *Apache Licence 2.0*).
- Comparison with state-of-the-art engines and demonstrate the performance empirically.
- Integration with the SANSA [13][3] framework.

The rest of the paper is structured as follows: Our approach for data modeling, data partitioning, and query translation using a distributed framework are detailed in Sect. 3 and evaluated in Sect. 4. Related work on the SPARQL query engines is discussed in Sect. 5. Finally, we conclude and suggest planned extensions of our approach in Sect. 6.

2 Preliminaries

Here, we first introduce the basic notions used throughout the paper.

Apache Hadoop and MapReduce. Apache Hadoop is a distributed framework that allows for the distributed processing of large data sets across a cluster of computers using the MapReduce paradigm. Beside its computing system, it contains a distributed file system: the Hadoop Distributed File System (HDFS), which is a popular file system capable of handling the distribution of the data across multiple nodes in the cluster.

Apache Spark. Apache Spark is a fast and generic-purpose cluster computing engine which is built over the Hadoop ecosystem. Its core data structure is Resilient Distributed Dataset (RDD) [25] which are a fault-tolerant and immutable collections of records that can be operated in a parallel setting. Apache Spark provides a rich set of APIs for faster, in-memory processing of RDDs.

[2] https://github.com/SANSA-Stack/SANSA-Query/tree/develop/sansa-query-spark/src/main/scala/net/sansa_stack/query/spark/semantic.

[3] http://sansa-stack.net/.

Data Partitioning. Partitioning the RDF data is the process of dividing datasets in a specific logical and/or physical representation in order to ease faster access and better maintenance. Often, this process is performed for improving the system availability, load balancing and query processing time. There are many different data partitioning techniques proposed in the literature. We choose to investigate the so-called *semantic-based partitioning* behaviors when dealing with large-scale RDF datasets. This partitioned technique was proposed in the SHARD [17] system. We have implemented this technique using in-memory processing engine, Apache Spark for better performance. A semantically partitioned fact is a tuple (S, R) containing pieces of information $R \in (P, O)$ about the same S where S is a unique subject on the RDF graph and R represents all its associated facts i.e predicates P and objects O.

3 Approach

In this section, we present the system architecture of our proposed approach, the semantic-based partitioning, and mapping SPARQL to Spark Scala-compliant code.

3.1 System Architecture Overview

The system architecture overview is shown in the Fig. 1.

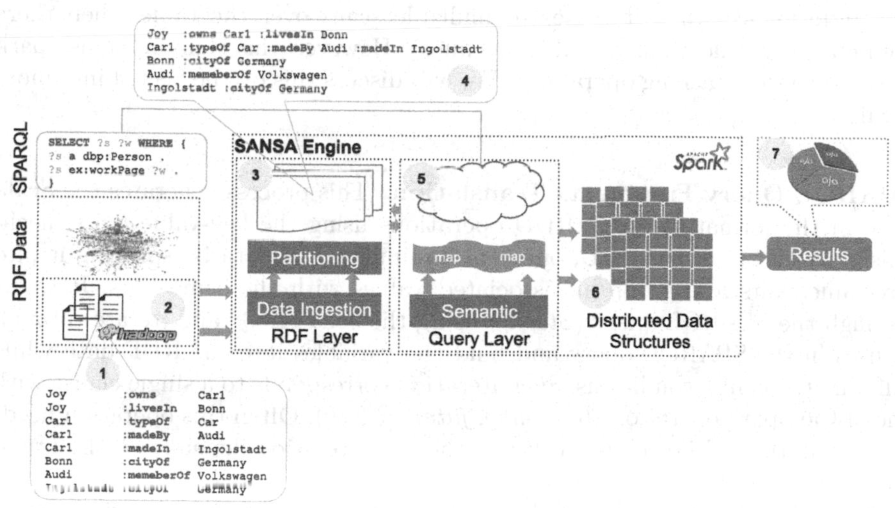

Fig. 1. System architecture overview.

It consists of three main facets: Data Storage Model, SPARQL Query Fragments Translator, and Query Evaluator. Below, each facet is discussed in more details.

Data Storage Model. We model the RDF data following the concept of RDDs. RDDs are immutable collections of records, which represent the basic building blocks of the Spark framework. RDDs can be kept in-memory and are able to operate in parallel throughout the Spark cluster. We make use of SANSA [13]'s data representation and distribution layer for such representation.

First, the RDF data (see *Step 1* as an example) needs to be loaded into a large-scale distributed storage (*Step 2*). We use Hadoop Distributed File-System (HDFS)[4]. We choose HDFS as Spark is capable of performing operations based on data locality in order to choose the nearest data for faster and efficient computation over the cluster. Second, we partition (*Step 3*) the data using semantic-based partitioning (see *Step 4* as an example of such partition). Instead of working with table-wise representation where the triples are kept in the format of $RDD < Triple >$, data is partitioned into subject-based grouping (e.g. all entities which are associated with a unique subject). Consider the example in the Fig. 1 (*Step 2*, first line), which represents two triples associated with the entity `Joy`:

```
Joy :owns Car1 :livesIn Bonn
```

This line represents that the entity `Joy` owns a car entity `Car1`, and that `Joy` lives in `Bonn`.

Often flattening data is considered immature with respect to other data representation, we want to explore and investigate if it improves the performance of the query evaluation. We choose this representation for the reason of easy-storage and reuse while designing a query engine. Although, it slightly degrades the performance when it comes to multiple scans over the table when there are multiple predicates involved in the query. However, this is minimal, as Spark uses in-memory, caching operations. We will discuss this on the Sect. 4 into more detail.

SPARQL Query Fragments Translation. This process generates the Scala code in the format of Spark RDD operations using the key-value pairs mechanism. With Spark pairRDD, one can manipulate the data by splitting it into key-value pairs and group all associated values with the same keys. It walks through the SPARQL query (*Step 4*) using the Jena ARQ[5] and iterate through clauses in the SPARQL query and bind the variables into the RDF data while fulfilling the clause conditions. Such iteration corresponds to a single clause with one of the Spark operations (e.g. *map*, *filter*, *reduce*). Often this operation needs to be materialized i.e the result set of the next iteration depends on the previous clauses and therefore a *join* operation is needed. This is a bottleneck since scanning and shuffling is required. In order to keep these joins as small as possible, we leverage the caching techniques of the Spark framework by keeping the intermediate results in-memory while the next iteration is performed. Finally, the

[4] https://hadoop.apache.org/docs/r1.2.1/hdfs_design.html.

[5] https://jena.apache.org/documentation/query/.

Algorithm 1. Spark parallel semantic-based query engine.

```
  input  : q: a SPARQL query, input: an RDF dataset
  output: result an RDD – list of result set
  /* Loading the graph                                                 */
1 graph = spark.rdf(lang)(input)
  /* Partitioning the graph. See algorithm 2 for more details.         */
2 partitionGraph ← graph.partitonAsSemanticGraph()
  /* Querying the graph. See algorithm 3 for more details.             */
3 result ← partitionGraph.sparql(q)
4 return result
```

Spark-Scala executable code is generated (*Step 5*) using the bindings corresponding the query. Besides simple BGP translation, our system supports **UNION**, **LIMIT** and **FILTER** clauses.

Query Evaluator. The mappings created as shown in the previous section can now be evaluated directly into the Spark RDD executable code. The result set of these operations is distributed data structure of Spark (e.g. RDD) (*Step 6*). The result set can be used for further processing and visualization using the SANSA-Notebooks (*Step 7*) [5].

3.2 Distributed Algorithm Description

We implement our approach using the Apache Spark framework (see Algorithm 1). It constructs the graph (*line 1*) while reading RDF data and converts it into an RDD of triples. Later, it partitions the data (*line 2*, for more details see Algorithm 2) using the semantic-based partitioning strategy. Finally, the query evaluator is constructed (*line 3*) which is detailed in Algorithm 3.

The partition algorithm (see Algorithm 2) transforms the RDF graph into a convenient SP (*line 2*). For each unique triple in the graph in a distributed fashion, it does the following: It gets the values about subjects and objects (*line 3*) and local name of the predicate (*line 4*). It generates the key-value pairs of the subject and its associated triples with predicate and object separated with the space in between (*line 5*). After the mapping is done, the data is grouped by key (in our case *subject*) (*line 6*). Afterward, when this information is collected, the block is partitioned using the *map* transformation function of Spark to refactor the format of the lines based on the above information (*line 7*).

This SPARQL query rewriter includes multiple Spark operations. First, partitioned data is mapped to a list of variable bindings satisfying the first basic graph pattern (BGP) of the query (*line 2*). During this process, the duplicates are removed and the intermediate result is kept in-memory (RDD) with the variable bindings as a key. The consequent step is to iterate through other variables and bind them by processing the upcoming query clauses and/or filtering the

Algorithm 2. partitonAsSemanticGraph: Semantic-based partition algorithm.

```
input  : graph: an RDD of triples
output: partionedData: an RDD of partitions
partitonedData ← ∅
foreach ∀!triple ∈ graph  &&  triple.getSubject ≠ ∅ do
    s ← triple.getSubject;   o ← triple.getObject
    p ← triple.getPredicate.getLocalName
    partitonedData + = (s, p + " " + o + " ")
partitonedData.reduceByKey(_ + _)
               .map(f → (f._1 + " " + f._2))
return partitonedData
```

Algorithm 3. sparql: Semantic-based query algorithm.

```
  input  : partitonedData: an RDD of partitions
  output: result an RDD of result set
1 foreach p ∈ partitionedData do
2     1stVariable ← assignVariablesFor1stClaues()
3     foreach i ∈ getClauses() do
4         iVariable ← assignVariablesForiClaues()
5         mapResult ← mapByKey(getCommonVariables())
6         joinResult ← join(mapResult)
7     joinResult.filter(getSelectVariables())
8     result ← result.join(joinResult)
9 return result
```

other ones unseen on the new clause. These intermediate steps perform Spark operations over both, the partitioned data and the previously bound variables which were kept on Spark RDDs.

The ith step discovers all variables in the partitioned data which satisfy the ith clause appeared and keep this intermediate result in-memory with the key being any variable in the ith step which has been introduced on the previous step. During this iteration, the intermediate results are reconstructed in the way that the variables not seen in this iteration are mapped (*line 5*) with the variables of the previous clause and generate a key-value pair of variable bindings. Afterward, the *join* operation is performed over the intermediate results from the previous clause and the new ones with the same key. This process iterates until all clauses are seen and variables are assigned. Finally, the variable binding (*line 7*) to fulfill the *SELECT* clause of the SPARQL query happens and returns the result (*line 8*) of only those variables which are present in the SELECT clause.

4 Evaluation

In our evaluation, we observe the impact of semantic-based partitioning and analyze the scalability of our approach when the size of the dataset increases.

In the following subsections, we present the benchmarks used along with the server configuration setting, and finally, we discuss our findings.

4.1 Experimental Setup

We make use of two well-known SPARQL benchmarks for our experiments: the *Waterloo SPARQL Diversity Test Suite (WatDiv)* v0.6 [3] and *Lehigh University Benchmark (LUBM)* v3.1 [8]. The dataset characteristics of the considered benchmarks are given in Table 1.

WatDiv comes with a test suite with different query shapes which allows us to compare the performance of our approach and the other approaches. In particular, it comes with a predefined set of 20 query templates which are grouped into four categories, based on the query shape: *star-shaped* queries, *linear-shaped* queries, *snowflake-shaped* queries, and *complex-shaped* queries. We have used *WatDiv* datasets with 10M to 100M triples with scale factors 10 and 100, respectively. In addition, we have generated the SPARQL queries using *WatDiv Query Generator.*

LUBM comes with a *Data Generator (UBA)* which generates synthetic data over the *Univ-Bench* ontology in the unit of a university. *LUBM* provides Test Queries, more specifically 14 test queries. Our *LUBM* datasets consist of 1000, 2000, and 3000 universities. The number of triples varies from 138M for 1000 universities, to 414M triples for 3000 universities.

Table 1. Dataset characteristics (nt format).

	LUBM			Watdiv	
	1K	2K	3K	10M	100M
#nr. of triples	138,280,374	276,349,040	414,493,296	10,916,457	108,997,714
Size (GB)	24	49	70	1.5	15

We implemented our approach using Spark-2.4.0, Scala 2.11.11, Java 8, and all the data were stored on the HDFS cluster using Hadoop 2.8.0. All experiments were carried out on a commodity cluster of 6 nodes (1 master, 5 workers): Intel(R) Xeon(R) CPU E5-2620 v4 @ 2.10 GHz (32 Cores), 128 GB RAM, 12 TB SATA RAID-5. We executed each experiment three times and the average query execution time has been reported.

4.2 Preliminary Results

We run experiments on the same cluster and evaluate our approach using the above benchmarks. In addition, we compare our proposed approach with selected state-of-the-art distributed SPARQL query evaluators. In particular, we compare our approach with SHARD [17] – the original approach implemented on Hadoop MapReduce, *SPARQLGX* [6]'s direct evaluator SDE, and Sparklify [21] and report the query execution time (cf. Table 2). We have selected these approaches as they do not include any pre-processing steps (e.g. statistics) while evaluating the SPARQL query, similar to our approach.

Table 2. Performance analysis on large-scale RDF datasets.

	Queries	Runtime (s) (mean)			
		SHARD	**SPARQLGX-SDE**	**SANSA.Sparklify**	**SANSA.Semantic**
Watdiv-10M	*C*3	n/a	38.79	72.94	90.48
	*F*3	n/a	38.41	74.69	n/a
	*L*3	n/a	21.05	73.16	72.84
	*S*3	n/a	26.27	70.1	79.7
Watdiv-100M	*C*3	n/a	181.51	96.59	300.82
	*F*3	n/a	162.86	91.2	n/a
	*L*3	n/a	84.09	82.17	189.89
	*S*3	n/a	123.6	93.02	176.2
LUBM-1K	*Q*1	774.93	103.74	103.57	226.21
	*Q*2	fail	fail	3348.51	329.69
	*Q*3	772.55	126.31	107.25	235.31
	*Q*4	988.28	182.52	111.89	294.8
	*Q*5	771.69	101.05	100.37	226.21
	*Q*6	fail	73.05	100.72	207.06
	*Q*7	fail	160.94	113.03	277.08
	*Q*8	fail	179.56	114.83	309.39
	*Q*9	fail	204.62	114.25	326.29
	*Q*10	780.05	106.26	110.18	232.72
	*Q*11	783.2	112.23	105.13	231.36
	*Q*12	fail	159.65	105.86	283.53
	*Q*13	778.16	100.06	90.87	220.28
	*Q*14	688.44	74.64	100.58	204.43

Our evaluation results for performance analysis, sizeup analysis, node scalability, and breakdown analysis by SPARQL queries are shown in Table 2, Figs. 2, 3 and 4 respectively. In Table 2 we use "fail" whenever the system fails to complete the task and "n/a" when the task could not be completed due to a parser error (e.g. not able to translate some of the basic patterns to RDDs operations).

In order to evaluate our approach with respect to the *speedup*, we analyze and compare it with other approaches. This set of experiments was run on three datasets, *Watdiv-10M*, *Watdiv-100M* and *LUBM-1K*.

Table 2 presents the performance analysis of the systems on three different datasets. We can see that our approach evaluates most of the queries as opposed to SHARD. SHARD system fails to evaluate most of the *LUBM* queries and its parser does not support *Watdiv* queries. On the other hand, SPARQLGX-SDE performs better than both Sparklify and our approach, when the size of the dataset is considerably small (e.g. less than 25 GB). This behavior is due to the large partitioning overhead for Sparklify and our approach. However, Sparklify performs better compared to SPARQLGX-SDE when the size of the dataset increases (see *Watdiv-100M* results in the Table 2) and the queries involve more joins (see *LUBM-1K* results in the Table 2). This is due to the Spark SQL optimizer and Sparqlify self-joins optimizers. Both SHARD and SPARQLGX-SDE fail to evaluate query *Q2* in the *LUBM-1K* dataset. Sparklify can evaluate the query but takes longer as compared to our approach. This is due to the fact that our approach uses Spark's lazy evaluation and join optimization by keeping the intermediate results in memory.

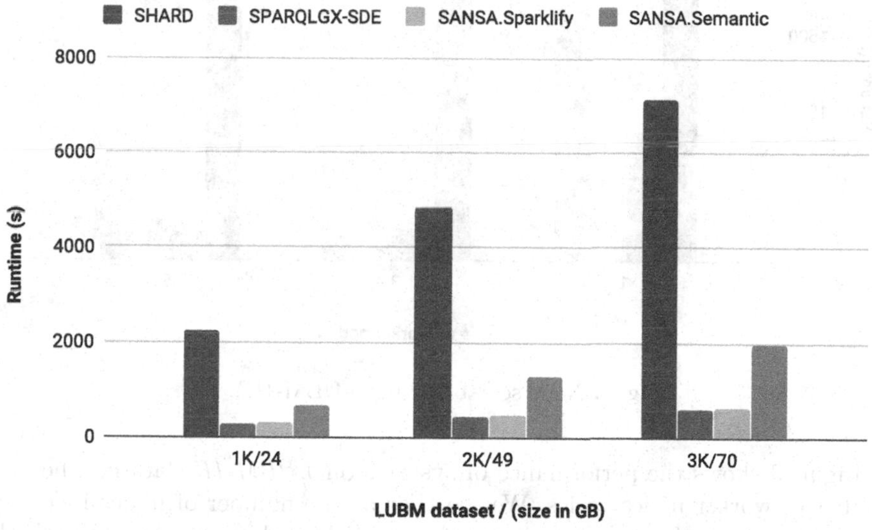

Fig. 2. Sizeup analysis (on LUBM dataset).

Scalability Analysis. In order to evaluate the scalability of our approach, we conducted two sets of experiments. First, we measure the data scalability (e.g. size-up) of our approach and position it with other approaches. As SHARD fails for most of the LUBM queries, we omit other queries on this set of experiments and choose only Q1, Q5, and Q14. Q1 has been chosen due to its complexity while bringing large inputs of the data and high selectivity, Q5 since it has considerably larger intermediate results due to the triangular pattern in the query, and Q14 mainly for its simplicity. We run experiments on three different sizes of *LUBM* (see Fig. 2). We keep the number of nodes constant i.e. 5 worker nodes and increase the size of the datasets to measure whether our approach deals with larger datasets.

We see that the query execution time for our approach grows linearly when the size of the datasets increases. This shows the scalability of our approach as compared to SHARD, in context of the sizeup. SHARD suffers from the expensive overhead of MapReduce joins which impact its performance, as a result, it is significantly worse than other systems.

Second, in order to measure the node scalability of our approach, we increase the number of worker nodes and keep the size of the dataset constant. We vary them from 1, 3 to 5 worker nodes.

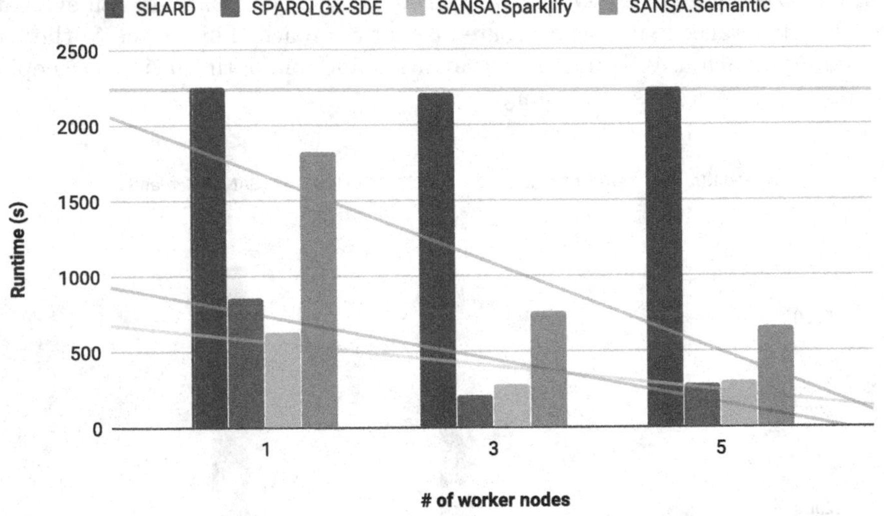

Fig. 3. Node scalability (on LUBM-1K).

Figure 3 shows the performance of systems on *LUBM-1K* dataset when the number of worker nodes varies. We see that as the number of nodes increases, the runtime cost of our query engine decreases linearly as compared with the SHARD, which keeps staying constant. SHARD performance stays constant (high) even when more worker nodes are added. This trend is due to the communication overhead SHARD needs to perform between map and reduce steps. The execution time of our approach decreases about 1.7 times (from 1,821.75 s down to 656.85 s) as the worker nodes increase from one to five nodes. SPARQLGX-SDE and Sparklify perform better when the number of nodes increases compared to our approach and SHARD.

Our main observation here is that our approach can achieve linear scalability in the performance.

Correctness. In order to assess the correctness of the result set, we computed the count of the result set for the given queries and compare it with other approaches. As a result of it, we conclude that all approaches return exactly the same result set. This implies the correctness of the results.

Breakdown by SPARQL Queries. Here we analyze some of the LUBM queries (Q1, Q5, Q14) run on a *LUBM-1K* dataset in a cluster mode on all the systems.

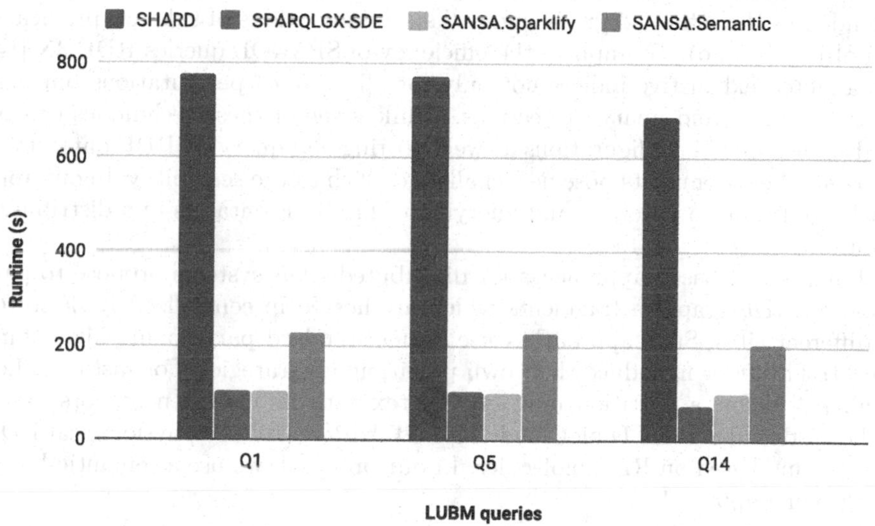

Fig. 4. Overall analysis of queries on LUBM-1K dataset (cluster mode).

We can see from Fig. 4 that our approach performs better compared to Hadoop-based system, SHARD. This is due to the use of the Spark framework which leverages the in-memory computation for faster performance. However, the performance declines as compared to other approaches which use vertical partitioning (e.g., SPARQLGX-SDE on RDD and Sparklify on Spark SQL). This is due to the fact that our approach performs de-duplication of triples that involves shuffling and incurs network overhead. The results show that the performance of SPARQLGX-SDE decreases as the number of triple patterns involved in the query increases (see *Q5*) when compared to Sparklify. However, SPARQLGX-SDE performs better when there are simple queries (see *Q14*). This occurs because SPARQLGX-SDE must read the whole RDF graph each time when there is a triple pattern involved. In contrast to SPARQLGX-SDE, Sparklify performs better when there are more triple patterns involved (see *Q5*) but slightly worse when linear queries (see *Q14*) are evaluated.

Based on our findings and the evaluation study carried out in this paper, we show that our approach can scale up with the increasing size of the dataset.

5 Related Work

Partitioning of RDF Data. Centralized RDF stores use relational (e.g., Sesame [4]), property (e.g., Jena [23]), or binary tables (e.g., SW-Store [1]) for storing RDF triples or maintain the graph structure of the RDF data (e.g., gStore [26]). For dealing with big RDF datasets, vertical partitioning and exhaustive indexing are commonly employed techniques. For instance, Abadi et al. [2] introduce a vertical partitioning approach in which each predicate is mapped to a two-column table containing the subject and object. This approach has been extended in Hexastore [22] to include all six permutations of subject, predicate, and object (s, p, o). To improve the efficiency of SPARQL queries RDF-3X [14] has adopted exhaustive indices not only for all (s, p, o) permutations but also for their binary and unary projections. While some of these techniques can be used in distributed configurations as well, storing and querying RDF datasets in distributed environments pose new challenges such as the scalability. In our approach, we tackle partitioning and querying of big RDF datasets in a distributed manner.

Partitioning-based approaches for distributed RDF systems propose to partition an RDF graph in fragments which are hosted in centralized RDF stores at different sites. Such approaches use either standard partitioning algorithms like METIS [9] or introduce their own partitioning strategies. For instance, Lee et al. [12] define a partition unit as a vertex with its closest neighbors based on heuristic rules while DiploCloud [24] and AdPart [10] use physiological RDF partitioning based on RDF molecules. In our proposal, we use a semantic-based partitioning approach.

Hadoop-Based Systems. Cloud-based approaches for managing large-scale RDF mainly use NoSQL distributed data stores or employ various partitioning approaches on top of Hadoop infrastructure, i.e., the Hadoop Distributed File System (HDFS) and its MapReduce implementation, in order to leverage computational resources of multiple nodes. For instance, Sempala [19] is a Hadoop-based approach which serves as SPARQL-to-SQL approach on top of Hadoop. It uses Impala[6] as a distributed SQL processing engine. Sempala uses unified vertical partitioning based on a single property table to improve the runtime of the star-shaped queries by excluding the joins. The limitation of Sempala is that it was designed only for that particular shape of the queries. PigSPARQL [18] uses Hadoop based implementation of vertical partitioning for data representation. It translates SPARQL queries into Pig[7] LATIN queries and runs them using the Pig engine. A most recent approach based on MapReduce is RYA [16]. It is a Hadoop based scalable RDF store which uses Accumulo[8] as a distributed key-value store for indexing the RDF triples. One of RYA's advantages is the power of performing join reorder. The main drawback of RYA is that it relies on disk-based processing increasing query execution times. Other RDF systems like

[6] https://impala.apache.org/.
[7] https://pig.apache.org/.
[8] http://www.accumulo.apache.org.

JenaHBase [11] and H2RDF+ [15] use the Hadoop database HBase for storing triple and property tables.

SHARD [17] is one approach which groups RDF data into a dedicated partition so-called semantic-based partition. It groups these RDF data by subject and implements a query engine which iterates through each of the clauses used on the query and performs a query processing. A MapReduce job is created while scanning each of the triple patterns and generates a single plan for each of the triple pattern which leads to a larger query plan, therefore, it contains too many Map and Reduces jobs. Our partitioning algorithm is based on SHARD, but instead of creating MapReduce jobs we employ the Spark framework in order to increase scalability.

In-Memory Systems. S2RDF [20] is a distributed query engine which translates SPARQL queries into SQL ones while running them on Spark-SQL. It introduces a data partitioning strategy that extends vertical partitioning with additional statistics, containing pre-computed semi-joins for query optimization. SPARQLGX [6] is similar to S2RDF, but instead of translating SPARQL to SQL, it maps SPARQL into direct Spark RDD operations. It is a scalable query engine which is capable of evaluating efficiently the SPARQL queries over distributed RDF datasets [7]. It uses a simplified VP approach, where each predicate is assigned to a specific parquet file. As an addition, it is able to assign RDF statistics for further query optimization while also providing the possibility of directly query files on the HDFS using SDE. Recently, Sparklify [21] – a scalable software component for efficient evaluation of SPARQL queries over distributed RDF datasets has been proposed. The approach uses Sparqify[9] as a SPARQL to SQL rewriter for translating SPARQL queries into Spark executable code. In our approach, intermediate results are kept in-memory in order to accelerate query execution over big RDF data.

6 Conclusions and Future Work

In this paper, we propose a scalable semantic-based query engine for efficient evaluation of SPARQL queries over distributed RDF datasets. It uses a semantic-based partitioning strategy as the data distribution and converts SPARQL to Spark executable code. By doing so, it leverages the advantages of the Spark framework's rich APIs. We have shown empirically that our approach can scale horizontally and perform well as compared with the previous Hadoop-based system: the SHARD triple store. It is also comparable with other in-memory SPARQL query evaluators when there is less shuffling involved i.e. less duplicate values.

Our next steps include expanding our parser to support more SPARQL fragments and adding statistics to the query engine while evaluating queries. We want to analyze the query performance in the large-scale RDF datasets and explore prospects for the improvement. For example, we intend to investigate the re-ordering of the BGPs and evaluate the effects on query execution time.

[9] https://github.com/SmartDataAnalytics/Sparqlify.

Acknowledgment. This work was partly supported by the EU Horizon2020 projects Boost4.0 (GA no. 780732), BigDataOcean (GA no. 732310), SLIPO (GA no. 731581), and QROWD (GA no. 723088).

References

1. Abadi, D.J., Marcus, A., Madden, S., Hollenbach, K.: SW-Store: a vertically partitioned DBMS for semantic web data management. VLDB J. **18**(2), 385–406 (2009)
2. Abadi, D.J., Marcus, A., Madden, S., Hollenbach, K.J.: Scalable semantic web data management using vertical partitioning. In: Proceedings of the 33rd International Conference on Very Large Data Bases, University of Vienna, Austria, 23–27 September 2007, pp. 411–422 (2007)
3. Aluç, G., Hartig, O., Özsu, M.T., Daudjee, K.: Diversified stress testing of RDF data management systems. In: International Semantic Web Conference (2014)
4. Broekstra, J., Kampman, A., van Harmelen, F.: Sesame: a generic architecture for storing and querying RDF and RDF schema. In: Horrocks, I., Hendler, J. (eds.) ISWC 2002. LNCS, vol. 2342, pp. 54–68. Springer, Heidelberg (2002). https://doi.org/10.1007/3-540-48005-6_7
5. Ermilov, I., et al.: The Tale of Sansa Spark. In: 16th International Semantic Web Conference, Poster & Demos (2017)
6. Graux, D., Jachiet, L., Genevès, P., Layaïda, N.: SPARQLGX: efficient distributed evaluation of SPARQL with Apache Spark. In: Groth, P., et al. (eds.) ISWC 2016. LNCS, vol. 9982, pp. 80–87. Springer, Cham (2016). https://doi.org/10.1007/978-3-319-46547-0_9
7. Graux, D., Jachiet, L., Geneves, P., Layaïda, N.: A multi-criteria experimental ranking of distributed SPARQL evaluators. In: 2018 IEEE International Conference on Big Data (Big Data), pp. 693–702. IEEE (2018)
8. Guo, Y., Pan, Z., Heflin, J.: LUBM: a benchmark for OWL knowledge base systems. J. Web Semant. **3**, 158–182 (2005)
9. Gurajada, S., Seufert, S., Miliaraki, I., Theobald, M.: TriAD: a distributed shared-nothing RDF engine based on asynchronous message passing. In: International Conference on Management of Data, SIGMOD 2014, Snowbird, UT, USA, 22–27 June 2014, pp. 289–300 (2014)
10. Harbi, R., Abdelaziz, I., Kalnis, P., Mamoulis, N., Ebrahim, Y., Sahli, M.: Accelerating SPARQL queries by exploiting hash-based locality and adaptive partitioning. VLDB J. Int. J. Very Large Data Bases **25**(3), 355–380 (2016)
11. Khadilkar, V., Kantarcioglu, M., Thuraisingham, B., Castagna, P.: Jena-HBase: a distributed, scalable and efficient RDF triple store. In: Proceedings of the 2012th International Conference on Posters & Demonstrations Track, ISWC-PD 2012, vol. 914, pp. 85–88 (2012)
12. Lee, K., Liu, L.: Scaling queries over big RDF graphs with semantic hash partitioning. Proc. VLDB Endow. **6**(14), 1894–1905 (2013)
13. Lehmann, J., et al.: Distributed semantic analytics using the SANSA stack. In: Proceedings of 16th International Semantic Web Conference - Resources Track (ISWC 2017) (2017)
14. Neumann, T., Weikum, G.: The RDF-3X engine for scalable management of RDF data. VLDB J. **19**(1), 91–113 (2010)
15. Papailiou, N., Konstantinou, I., Tsoumakos, D., Karras, P., Koziris, N.: H2RDF+: high-performance distributed joins over large-scale RDF graphs. In: Proceedings

of the 2013 IEEE International Conference on Big Data, 6–9 October 2013, Santa Clara, CA, USA, pp. 255–263 (2013)
16. Punnoose, R., Crainiceanu, A., Rapp, D.: Rya: a scalable RDF triple store for the clouds. In: Proceedings of the 1st International Workshop on Cloud Intelligence, Cloud-I 2012, pp. 4:1–4:8. ACM, New York (2012)
17. Rohloff, K., Schantz, R.E.: High-performance, massively scalable distributed systems using the MapReduce software framework: the SHARD triple-store. In: Programming Support Innovations for Emerging Distributed Applications, PSI EtA 2010, pp. 4:1–4:5. ACM, New York (2010)
18. Schätzle, A., Przyjaciel-Zablocki, M., Lausen, G.: PigSPARQL: mapping SPARQL to Pig Latin. In: Proceedings of the International Workshop on Semantic Web Information Management, SWIM 2011, pp. 4:1–4:8. ACM, New York (2011)
19. Schätzle, A., Przyjaciel-Zablocki, M., Neu, A., Lausen, G.: Sempala: interactive SPARQL query processing on Hadoop. In: Mika, P., et al. (eds.) ISWC 2014. LNCS, vol. 8796, pp. 164–179. Springer, Cham (2014). https://doi.org/10.1007/978-3-319-11964-9_11
20. Schätzle, A., Przyjaciel-Zablocki, M., Skilevic, S., Lausen, G.: S2RDF: RDF querying with SPARQL on Spark. Proc. VLDB Endow. **9**(10), 804–815 (2016)
21. Stadler, C., Sejdiu, G., Graux, D., Lehmann, J.: Sparklify: A Scalable Software Component for Efficient evaluation of SPARQL queries over distributed RDF datasets. In: Proceedings of 18th International Semantic Web Conference (2019)
22. Weiss, C., Karras, P., Bernstein, A.: Hexastore: sextuple indexing for semantic web data management. PVLDB **1**(1), 1008–1019 (2008)
23. Wilkinson, K.: Jena property table implementation. In: SSWS, Athens, Georgia, USA, pp. 35–46 (2006)
24. Wylot, M., Cudré-Mauroux, P.: Diplocloud: efficient and scalable management of RDF data in the cloud. IEEE Trans. Knowl. Data Eng. **28**(3), 659–674 (2016)
25. Zaharia, M., et al.: Resilient distributed datasets: a fault-tolerant abstraction for in-memory cluster computing. In: Proceedings of the 9th USENIX Conference on Networked Systems Design and Implementation, USENIX (2012)
26. Zou, L., Mo, J., Chen, L., Özsu, M.T., Zhao, D.: gStore: answering SPARQL queries via subgraph matching. PVLDB **4**(8), 482–493 (2011)

Automatic Facet Generation and Selection over Knowledge Graphs

Leila Feddoul[1,2(✉)], Sirko Schindler[2], and Frank Löffler[1]

[1] Heinz Nixdorf Chair for Distributed Information Systems, Friedrich Schiller University Jena, Jena, Germany
{leila.feddoul,frank.loeffler}@uni-jena.de

[2] Institute of Data Science, German Aerospace Center DLR, Jena, Germany
{leila.feddoul,sirko.schindler}@dlr.de

Abstract. With the continuous growth of the Linked Data Cloud, adequate methods to efficiently explore semantic data are increasingly required. Faceted browsing is an established technique for exploratory search. Users are given an overview of a collection's attributes that can be used to progressively refine their filter criteria and delve into the data.

However, manual facet predefinition is often inappropriate for at least three reasons: Firstly, heterogeneous and large scale knowledge graphs offer a huge number of possible facets. Choosing among them may be virtually impossible without algorithmic support. Secondly, knowledge graphs are often constantly changing, hence, predefinitions need to be redone or adapted. Finally, facets are generally applied to only a subset of resources (e.g., search query results). Thus, they have to match this subset and not the knowledge graph as a whole. Precomputing facets for each possible subset is impractical except for very small graphs.

We present our approach for automatic facet generation and selection over knowledge graphs. We propose methods for (1) candidate facet generation and (2) facet ranking, based on metrics that both judge a facet in isolation as well as in relation to others. We integrate those methods in an overall system workflow that also explores indirect facets, before we present the results of an initial evaluation.

Keywords: Faceted browsing · Facet ranking · Knowledge graph · Exploratory search

1 Introduction

A facet is by definition[1] a particular aspect or feature of something. In the present work, this is applied to a set of resources that could be viewed under different aspects. Each aspect is called a *facet* and consists of several categories, *facet values*, which can be used to filter the initial resource set. The number of resources that are associated with a certain facet value is called *value size*.

[1] Oxford Dictionaries: https://en.oxforddictionaries.com/definition/facet.

M. Acosta et al. (Eds.): SEMANTiCS 2019, LNCS 11702, pp. 310–325, 2019.
https://doi.org/10.1007/978-3-030-33220-4_23

Considering an example, a list of books can be viewed under the aspect of their *genre*. Choosing the facet value *science fiction*, books of this specific *genre* would be selected. The number of selected resources then corresponds to the value size of the facet value *science fiction*. The same list could be viewed under the aspect of their *publication year*, with each sublist containing only books published in one particular year. These two aspects, *genre* and *publication year*, are just two of the many possible facets for books.

To obtain different facets, we assume each resource to have properties assigned, linking them either to other resources (*genre*, with, e.g., a description for itself) or plain literal values (*publication year*). While our method works on any resource set possessing such properties, we use semantic models as rigorous formulation. In particular, we consider knowledge graphs (KGs). They provide significant advantages for the creation of facets: First of all, assuming the resources are drawn from a rich KG, we automatically get a large amount of direct resource information from their properties. The values of those properties may be resources themselves and can be used to generate indirect facets over the initial resource set. For example, an indirect facet for books can be an *author's place of birth*, where *place of birth* is linked to *author*, not to the *book* itself.

However, considering continuously changing and heterogeneous resources, manually predefining facets is often impractical. Using concepts from large KGs, e.g., the Linked Data Cloud, for semantic annotation induces a large number of possible facets. Hence, an automated method has to rank the large number of candidate facets to be able to pick the most suitable ones among them.

Nevertheless, determining the single, best facet is not enough. Users generally expect a list of facets to choose from. Moreover, this list should not be extremely long, and its items should be "useful" both individually and as collection. Were it not for the requirement of usefulness also as collection, simply choosing the top-k highest-ranked facets would be sufficient. However, avoiding facets that are semantically very close to each other is important as well. After their identification, criteria need to be defined to decide which of the candidates to drop to arrive at the final list of facets.

We propose an approach for *dynamic facet generation* and *facet ranking* over KGs. Our ranking is based on intra- and inter-facet metrics to determine the usefulness of a facet, also in the presence of others. A key aspect is exploiting indirect properties to find *better categorizations*. Since inter-facet metrics have not been satisfactorily addressed so far, we present *semantic similarity* as a usefulness criterion.

Based on our previously proposed workflow [1], we integrated all methods into an initial prototypical implementation [2]. While this leverages data from a specific KG, i.e., Wikidata [3], the methods we describe and use are generally applicable without or with only minimal changes to a wide range of KGs. Possible applications include exploratory browsing of a data catalog of semantically annotated datasets, or the reduction of a search result set using facets as filters.

In Sect. 2 we first revisit some of the related works in this direction. We then discuss methods we used for candidate facet generation and ranking in Sect. 3

and propose our workflow in Sect. 4. We present evaluation results in Sect. 5. Finally, we conclude and discuss future work in Sect. 6.

2 Related Work

Faceted browsing over KGs has been the subject of various research efforts, e.g., [4]. Prominent approaches such as *Ontogator* [5] or *mSpace* [6] use *statically predefined* facets for data navigation and do not consider continuously changing data sources. Moreover, their evaluation scenarios suppose data homogeneity and domain-dependent collections like cultural artifacts [5] or classical music [6].

Other projects include *BrowseRDF*, *Parallax*, *gFacet*, *Faceted Wikipedia*, *VisiNav*, *Rhizomer*, *SPARKLIS*, *SemFacet*, *Grafa*, *MediaFaces*, and *Hippalus* ([7–17], resp.). Facets are either *dynamically selected* from a precomputed set of facets or *dynamically generated* on the fly. The latter type of facets relies on building dynamic SPARQL queries and executing them on the respective SPARQL endpoints. *Grafa* [15] proposed a selection strategy to precompute only a subset of possible facets to avoid indexing of all data.

Some of these projects assume a homogeneous data source [7,17], using very specific data sets from the domains of, e.g. species [17], other contributions account for *domain heterogeneity* [8–16] and base their work on large scale KGs such as Wikidata [3], Dbpedia [18], or Freebase [19]. However, in some projects [9,10,12,13], an initial interaction (*resource type specification*) is required, before any facets are generated.

Various aspects of facet generation are discussed. This includes *facet ranking* [7,10–12,15–17], *entity type pivoting*[2] [8,9,11–14], *visualization* [8,9,11–13], *indirect facet generation* [6,7,9,13,14], or *performance issues* [10,13,15].

Facet ranking is of particular importance for dynamic facet generation in order to select from the considerable number of facet candidates. *Frequency-based ranking* was adopted by [10–12,15]. In *Faceted Wikipedia* [10], facet values are ranked based on the value sizes. For facet ranking, the most frequent facets corresponding to the selected type are candidates. They are ranked based on their most frequent facet value. Note that a ranking is applied only in case of resource type selection, otherwise generic facets are displayed. *VisiNav* [11] also adopts a *frequency-based* approach to rank facets and facet values inspired by PageRank [20]. The respective scores are calculated based on the PageRank score of the data sources [21]. *Rhizomer* [12] defines relevant facets based on the properties usage frequency in the resource type instances and the number of different facet values. In *Grafa* [15], facets are ranked according to the number of search result resources that have a value for the specific facet and facet values are ordered by PageRank. *BrowseRDF* [7] proposes three metrics to measure the quality of facets: (1) predicate balance, considering faceted browsing as the operation of traversing a decision tree where the tree should be well balanced (2) object cardinality, the number of facet values as also considered in [12]

[2] Switching the focus type, e.g., from a set of *books* to the set of their *authors*.

(3) predicate frequency similar to [10,12,15]. The metrics are combined to a final score that is used to rank facets. In *MediaFaces* [16], facets are ranked based on the analysis of image search *query logs* and *users tags* of *Flickr*[3] public images. *Hippalus* [17] introduces a different ranking approach involving user interactions where users rank facets and facet values according to their manually defined *preferences*.

We notice that all the previously described efforts concerning facet ranking only involve *intra-facet metrics* that rate facets individually without taking into consideration the significance of facet co-occurrence, or in other words *inter-facet metrics*. To the best of our knowledge, only *Facetedpedia* [22] includes a metric for measuring the collective usefulness of a facets collection. However, it does not take advantage of KGs or semantically annotated collections, but generates facets over Wikipedia[4] pages based on the Wikipedia category system. They consider the *navigational cost*, i.e. the number of edges traversed, as an intra-facet metric that is based on the number of steps required to reach target articles and the number of choices at each step. Furthermore, facets are penalized if they have a low *coverage*, i.e., not all the articles can be reached using the considered facet. Besides the *navigational cost*, the *average pairwise similarity* is proposed as an inter-facet metric. However, the used metric is specifically designed to be applied on the Wikipedia category system and is not generic enough to express *semantic similarity* in the sense of arbitrary KGs.

3 Methods

Before presenting our proposed workflow, this section provides details on the employed methods. This includes initial candidate facet generation, handling of literal facet values, and the metrics used to compare facets. The latter discussion is split into two parts: Intra-facet metrics evaluate a facet in isolation, whereas inter-facet metrics judge facets in relation to others.

3.1 Candidate Facet Generation

We aim to generate facets over a set of resources given by their respective Internationalized Resource Identifiers (IRIs) within the KG. In such a graph we treat the relations of the given resources as their properties and thus any applicable property path is equivalent to a candidate facet. To achieve a better categorization of resources, we consider not only the direct properties (i.e., values that are connected to the resource by a single link), but also indirect properties (i.e., chained links are needed to connect a resource and a value). As an example, consider a set of resources referring to people. A direct property can be derived from a relation *place of birth* pointing to instances of a class *city*. An indirect property could then also exploit an existing link between *city* and *country*[5] to

[3] https://www.flickr.com/.
[4] https://www.wikipedia.org/.
[5] Assuming there is no direct link between persons and their country of birth.

arrange the connected cities into possibly fewer categories[6]. Indirect properties are only possible, if the range of the associated relation is not a literal, as those can not be the subject of further statements in the standard RDF model.

A candidate facet is now given by a property path within the KG. In case of direct properties this path is of length one, whereas for indirect properties any path length greater than one is possible. However, longer paths loosen the connection between resources and facets values. At some point this renders a facet useless for the given task or at least makes it unclear to users how that facet is supposed to support them. Furthermore, longer paths increase the number of candidates and thus require more computations in later phases. For these reasons, we limit the path length for candidates by a threshold τ.

We categorize candidate facets into two types: (1) *Categorical facets* that result from property paths connecting exclusively to other resources and (2) *quantitative facets* whose values are given by literals. While we allow quantitative candidates for numeric or date literals, we exclude string literals. The rationale is that those oftentimes contain labels or descriptions specific to single resources and, hence, are barely shared between different ones. As facets rely on common values to categorize the given input set, these properties will only rarely provide a suitable candidate facet. If a string value is common to multiple resources, there is a high chance, that this should have been modeled as a distinct resource instead of a literal. Of course, resources are often not modeled perfectly. Future work might need to include these to be able to cope with this type of data.

3.2 Clustering of Quantitative Facets

As mentioned before, facets can be created from numeric or date literals. Unlike categorical facets, it is highly unlikely that the number of distinct values is sufficiently small to generate a useful facet. However, these values can be clustered by dividing their continuous range into discrete subranges.

The clustering step is only applied to quantitative facets. It replaces the associated values with value ranges. The number of these clusters is determined by the optimum value cardinality as defined by the respective intra-facet metric (see Subsect. 3.3). The clustering technique itself is a consequence of the rationale behind another intra-facet metric, the value dispersion. It assembles approximately the same number of values in each cluster.

3.3 Intra-Facet Metrics

To select the most useful facets among the candidates, we define metrics to judge their usefulness. The first set of metrics presented here assigns scores to individual candidates independently of each other. Each metric is designed to reflect one intuition of what constitutes a useful facet.

The first requirement concerns the applicability of the facet. For each facet we also include an *unknown* value. This accumulates the resources that do not

[6] Cities belonging to the same country will be grouped into one category.

support the respective property path, i.e., at least one of the corresponding relations is missing for this resource. For heterogeneous resource sets, the *unknown* value size will be non-zero for most facets. However, for a facet to be useful, it should apply to as many resources as possible. So we strive for the value size of *unknown* to be small in comparison with the overall size of the resource set.

These thoughts lead to the definition of *predicate probability* of a facet f, $score_{predicateProb}$, as given in Eq. 1. It calculates, for a randomly chosen resource, the probability to support the property path of a given facet.

$$score_{predicateProb}(f) = \frac{|supporting\ resources|}{|resources|} \tag{1}$$

Our next requirement deals with the number of facet values. We consider a facet with only a single value as not useful, as it can not be used to narrow down the given set of resources. But then again, facets with too many values provide little help as well. Here, users have to scan through a long list of possible options, which may even rival the number of input resources. We believe that there is a number of values that is optimal in the sense that it balances between a concise categorization and a sufficient number of options to choose from.

Following these considerations, we define the *value cardinality*, $score_{valueCard}$, of a facet f with a number of values c_f as given in Eq. 2. The minimum cardinality is denoted by *minCard* and the optimal one by *optCard*. Note that we chose an asymmetric function that favors facets with fewer values rather than more. This follows the intuition that better categorizations tend to have fewer categories. The parameter $\theta \neq 0$ allows to adjust the preference for value sizes between *minCard* and *optCard*.

$$score_{valueCard}(f) = \begin{cases} 0 & \text{if } c_f < minCard \\ e^{\frac{c_f - optCard}{\theta^2}} & \text{if } minCard \leq c_f \leq optCard \\ \frac{1}{1+(c_f - optCard)} & \text{if } c_f > optCard \end{cases} \tag{2}$$

Our final requirement follows the principle of self-balancing search trees: Each decision made while traversing the tree should eliminate roughly the same number of results from consideration. In other words, no leaf node (representing a specific result) is preferred over others in terms of steps needed to reach it from the root node. Similarly, we do not want to favor any specific category.

For a facet, this means that all value sizes within a single facet should be approximately equal[7]. As a measure for the variance in value sizes, we employ the coefficient of variation c_v (see Eq. 3). We chose this coefficient over the plain standard deviation, as it allows to better compare across multiple facets with possibly different value sizes. Using this, we define the *value dispersion*, $score_{dispersion}$,

[7] The subsets induced by the different facet values do not have to be disjoint. A single resource may be linked to several such values. Consider, e.g., the relation *part of* that relates *country* and *continent*. Here, the individual *Russia* is connected to two continents, *Asia* and *Europe*, thus appearing as part of both facet values' results.

as given in Eq. 4. Here, N is the number of facet values, x_i denotes the value size of the ith facet value, and $\overline{x}$ is the average of all value sizes. We exclude the value size of the special facet value *unknown* from this calculation, as this value is already exploited in $score_{predicateProb}$.

$$c_v(f) = \frac{\sqrt{\frac{1}{N} \times \sum_{i=1}^{N}(x_i - \overline{x})^2}}{\overline{x}} \tag{3}$$

$$score_{dispersion}(f) = \frac{1}{1 + c_v(f)} \tag{4}$$

All presented metrics are designed to return only values in the range between zero and one. In order to combine them into a single metric used in the ranking process (see Sect. 4), we can use a weighted average as shown in Eq. 5. With the individual weights summing up to one as well, we assure that the final *score* is also between zero and one.

$$\begin{aligned} score(f) = \; & w_{predicateProb} \times score_{predicateProb} \\ & + w_{dispersion} \times score_{dispersion} \\ & + w_{valueCard} \times score_{valueCard} \\ \text{with} \sum_i w_i = 1 & \end{aligned} \tag{5}$$

3.4 Inter-Facet Metrics

In contrast to their intra-facet counterparts, inter-facet metrics assess the relationship between different candidate facets. We use *semantic similarity* of facets as an inter-facet metric. The motivation is to prevent facets that are too close to one another and thus would provide about the same partitioning of the resource set. Moreover, semantically distant facets increase the chances of meeting users' information need and/or mindset.

Generally, no restrictions are imposed on the *semantic similarity* measure chosen to be included in the current facet generation workflow. However, we base our workflow on a structure-based measure that combines the shortest path length and the depth. In particular, we consider the one proposed by [23] as reference similarity metric between two concepts c_i and c_j, defined as follows:

$$sim(c_i, c_j) = e^{-\alpha \cdot length(c_i, c_j)} \cdot \frac{e^{\beta \cdot depth(c_{lcs})} - e^{-\beta \cdot depth(c_{lcs})}}{e^{\beta \cdot depth(c_{lcs})} + e^{-\beta \cdot depth(c_{lcs})}} \tag{6}$$

where $length(c_i, c_j)$ is the shortest path length between c_i and c_j and $depth(c_{lcs})$ is the shortest path length between the Least Common Subsumer (LCS) of the two concepts, c_{lcs} and the root concept. $\alpha \geq 0$ and $\beta > 0$ are used to adjust the importance assigned to the shortest path length and the depth, respectively. Based on the correlation evaluation conducted by [23], the optimal parameters are $\alpha = 0.2$ and $\beta = 0.6$.

The previously defined *semantic similarity* metric takes a pair of concepts as input. Therefore, a mapping between properties and concepts needs to be available. For this purpose, we exploit a particular characteristic of Wikidata's data model: Properties are annotated with a matching entity. For example, the property *author* (*P50*) is itself linked to the entity *author* (*Q482980*). This allows us to retrieve entities corresponding to the property path of a facet.

When comparing two facets, we first retrieve the respective entities for the first property in their property paths. We then calculate the *semantic similarity* between the entity pair. Two entities are considered similar, if sim is larger than a defined threshold σ. Since we calculate the similarity over Wikidata taxonomy, we only consider links using *subclass of* (*P279*) and *instance of* (*P31*) here.

4 Workflow

We consider the facet generation to be part of larger applications. In particular, we assume that the retrieval of an initial resource set is subject to other independent components. Hence, details of the resource retrieval process are out of scope at this point. For the sake of argument, we base our workflow on the results of a keyword-based full text search over the string properties of entities in the KG. Its result is represented as a set of IRIs, each identifies a single result item or resource and forms the input to our proposed facet generation workflow. We structured the overall process into four phases as shown in Fig. 1.

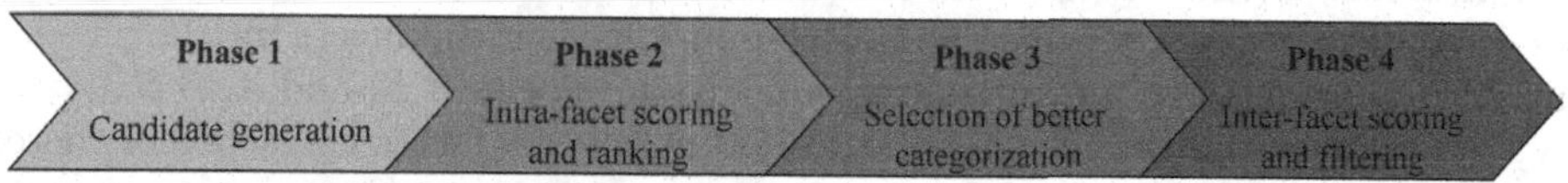

Fig. 1. Phases of the facet generation process.

Phase 1: Candidate Generation
This first phase enumerates possible facets by querying for a list of property-paths associated with the input list of resources. As the predicate probability $score_{predicateProb}$ is a simple metric, we choose to include it as part of the query. Candidates that have a $score_{predicateProb}$ below a predefined threshold, $minPredProb$, are already removed in this phase. This reduces the necessary data transfers and the calculation of computationally expensive metrics. The result is a list of candidates, each comprised of a basic graph pattern (BGP), that describes the facet, and a score to reflect the fraction of resources it applies to.

Phase 2: Intra-Facet Scoring and Ranking
As a prerequisite for the remaining intra-facet metrics, now the facet values along with the respective value size are retrieved from the SPARQL endpoint.

We distinguish between object and data properties[8] at this point. The latter are subjected to the clustering described in Subsect. 3.2 to derive comparable characteristics with regard to intra-facet metrics.

After augmenting the facets with their respective values, the remaining intra-facet metrics, $score_{dispersion}$ and $score_{valueCard}$, are calculated for all candidates. This allows us to compute the final intra-facet score, $score(f)$, and accordingly rank all facets in decreasing order.

Phase 3: Selection of Better Categorization
The number of necessary inter-facet metrics calculations grows quadratically with the remaining number of candidates. To reduce the list of candidates before the next step, we exploit a key characteristic of the semantic similarity metric. The similarity only depends on the first direct property of each facet. Consequently, out of all candidates sharing the direct property, only one will be chosen for the final result, as all others will be too similar to it. Leveraging this observation, we can group the candidates by their direct properties and only choose the best-ranked one within each group.

Phase 4: Inter-Facet Scoring and Filtering
The final result is derived by consecutively applying inter-facet metrics to chosen pairs of candidates. Calculating semantic similarities is rather expensive. To minimize the comparisons required, facets are selected in a greedy fashion.

Let C be the list of candidates in decreasing order w.r.t. the intra-facet metric scoring of Phase 2 and S be the final collection of facets as returned by Phase 4.

(i) Initialize S with the best-ranked facet.
(ii) Take the next facet out of C and compare it with the facets in S.
(iii) If it is not closely semantically similar to any facet in S, add it to S.
(iv) Continue with Step (ii) until the desired number of facets is reached or there are no more candidates left.

Finally, S will contain a subset of facets deemed most suitable for the given input set of resources. The suitability has been determined by employing both the intra- and inter-facet metrics, which can be extended or changed without affecting the corresponding workflow. S can now be presented to users. Note that selecting specific value and subsequently reducing the result set will trigger a new facet generation process, as the basis for our calculations—the input resource set—might have changed substantially.

5 Evaluation

The methods described in Sect. 3 were implemented in a prototype that issues dynamic SPARQL queries to the public SPARQL endpoint of Wikidata (WDQS)[9]. The source code is available online [2], under an MIT license.

---

[8] Data properties using string literals have already been excluded in the candidate generation. That means, only numeric and date literals are considered here.

[9] https://query.wikidata.org/.

Table 1. Number of candidates depending on path length and number of IRIs.

#IRIs	100	1000	2000	3000	4000
$\tau = 1$	37	52	65	66	75
$\tau = 2$	901	1643	2039	2342	2648
$\tau = 3$	16076	31543	39318	44619	50843

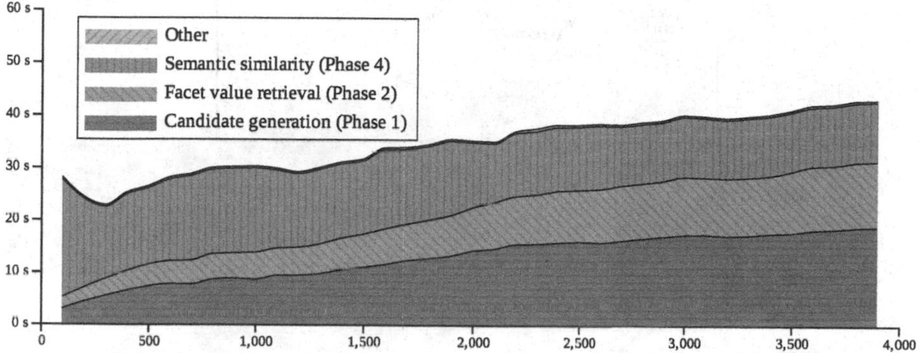

Fig. 2. Benchmark results: average timings depending on the input IRI size.

5.1 Benchmarking

To evaluate the performance of our prototype we used a collection of IRIs extracted from Wikidata (instances of *novel* (Q8261) or its subclasses).

First, we examined the change in the number of candidates depending on the path length τ and number of input IRIs. Results are shown in Table 1. As expected, the number of candidates increases significantly –about 20-fold– for each additional hop in the paths. However, a growth in input IRIs yields only a small effect in comparison. These figures and the considerations of Subsect. 3.1, led to a path length of $\tau = 2$ for the remainder of the evaluation.

Subsequently, we looked at the run-time of our prototype for varying sizes of input IRIs. We fixed the semantic similarity threshold ($\sigma = 0.70$), the parameters for value cardinality scoring ($optCard = 10$, $minCard = 2$, and $\theta = 3$), and the predicate probability threshold ($minPredProb = 0.1$). Figure 2 shows a breakdown of the measured execution times, averaged over about 350 individual measurements over the course of a week. We observe a less than linear growth of run-time depending on the input IRI size. The most expensive operations are (1) *candidate generation*, (2) *facet value retrieval*, and (3) *semantic similarity*. Other operations such as *intra-facet metric* calculation and *selection of better categorization* do not contribute significantly. A detailed analysis revealed that the execution times are largely dominated by querying the SPARQL endpoint.

Overall, we acknowledge that the current performance prohibits any productive use. However, the overwhelming impact of query response times on the

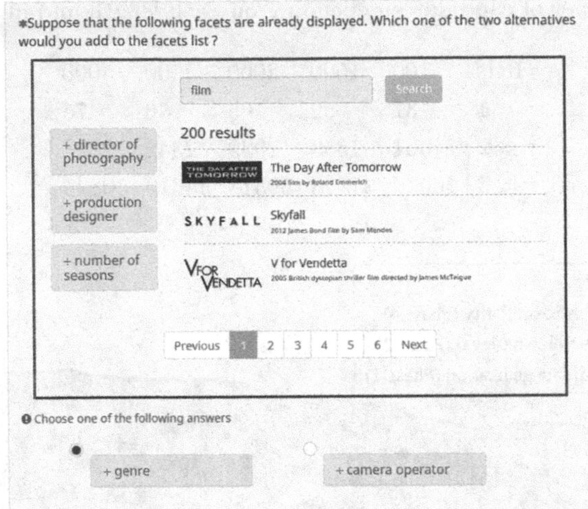

Fig. 3. User evaluation: Fictitious interface for *facet selection* task.

overall execution time indicates potential for improvement. Further parallelization and caching of reoccurring queries might prove fruitful.

5.2 User Evaluation

Setup. In a survey-based user evaluation, we examined whether facets generated by the proposed workflow match user expectations. Based on a fictitious scenario, we assumed an initial search with the keyword "film".

After introducing users to the general concepts of faceted search and the given scenario, we asked for user preferences in a series of questions categorized into two kinds of situations: one for *facet selection* and one for *facet ranking*. In *facet selection* (cf. Fig. 3), users were presented with a static user interface that resembles a common search engine and includes three different facets, e.g., *director of photography*, *production designer*, and *number of seasons*. They were then given two more facets, e.g., *genre* and *camera operator*, and were asked which would be a better addition to the existing three facets. In *facet ranking*, we presented three to four different facets per question and asked users to rate their usefulness in the given scenario using a five point Likert scale [24].

Unlike *facet selection*, where only facet headers are shown, *facet ranking* also includes facet values. Unless noted otherwise, all facets and their values are modeled according to the data present in Wikidata as of February 2019 using a path length of $\tau = 2$. The facets are generated by an initial, prototypical implementation of the workflow, but were manually adapted to reflect the respective evaluation intent to emphasize specific intra-facet scores.

Using these situations, the following order of questions was used in the survey. Overall, we created a pool of 43 questions, out of which a random subset of 15

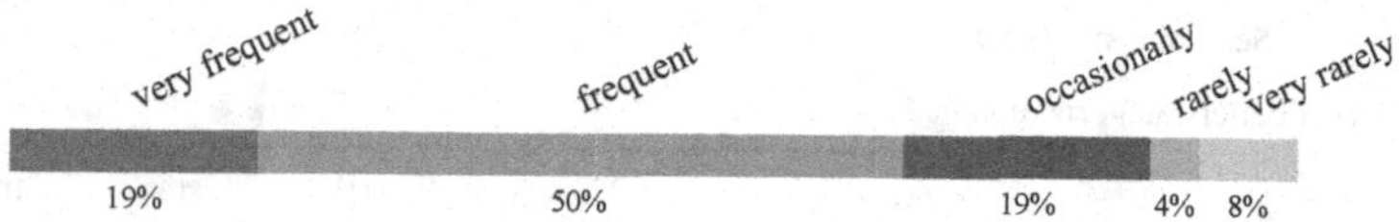

Fig. 4. Usage of facets. An option "never" was provided, but not chosen by any user.

was chosen for each user. This approach is intended to reduce the bias that might arise from certain terms used throughout.

In a first set of questions we focus on inter-facet comparisons using *facet selection*. In particular, this evolves around the *selection of better categorization* (Phase 3 in Sect. 4) and *semantic similarity* (Subsect. 3.4).

A second set of questions uses *facet ranking* with facets modeled after Wikidata. This compares multiple indirect facets with their respective direct counterparts. Here, the indirect facets also vary in their intra-facet scores, allowing us to evaluate our strategy in the *selection of better categorization.*

Finally, we used *facet ranking*, this time with abstract facets, i.e., replacing facet headers with "Facet 1" etc. and values with "Value 1" etc. The reason is again to reduce bias stemming from the actual semantics of the proposed facets. In this last part of the evaluation, we issued questions, where the proposed facets differed only with respect to one intra-facet metric[10]. In a similar fashion, we also examined combinations of two and all three proposed intra-facet metrics.

For the survey, we recruited 26 volunteers differing in age (18–44) and educational background. In total, they performed 130 facet selections and 936 individual facet ratings. Most of the participants stated at least an occasional use of facets, if they are provided (cf. Fig. 4). Consequently, we assume that they are familiar with the general behavior of faceted browsing.

Results. For each question in *facet selection*, we derive the percentage of participant selections that match the system decision. Figure 5 shows the results of the first question set with each dot representing agreement of one particular question[11]. For the *selection of better categorization* we see an overall agreement between the survey users and our system of ~83%.

The average result for *semantic similarity* is mixed (~63%). However, when analyzing the agreement per question, we see a more polarized result. While users most often agree on a specific facet, our system is not always able to concur with this choice. This leads us to believe that the survey responses were driven more by the applicability of the individual facet and not its relation to the already given ones. Yet, this is dependent on the available information and hence, out of control of the proposed workflow.

In *facet ranking*, we are not interested in the specific numerical values each metric provides, but focus on the ranking induced by those metrics. To compare the ranking determined by our system with the ranking induced by the sur-

10 The respective other metrics did not vary within a small error margin.

11 By experiment design, not all questions received the same number of responses.

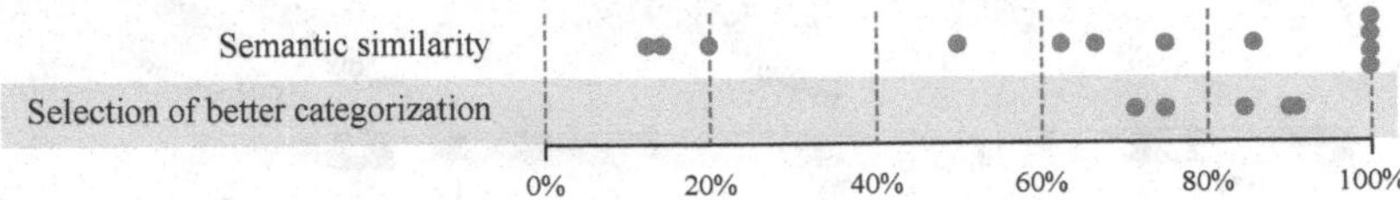

Fig. 5. Agreement of participants and system in *facet selection*. One dot per question.

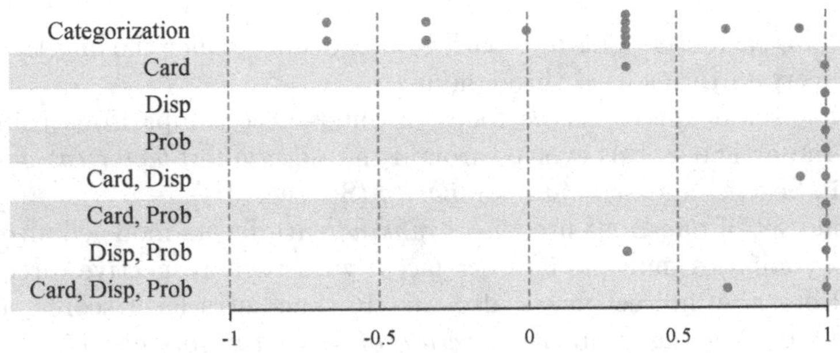

Fig. 6. Rank correlation for *facet ranking* tasks. One dot per survey question. Value Cardinality (*Card*), Value Dispersion (*Disp*), Predicate Probability (*Prop*).

vey responses, we encoded the latter using numerical values and calculated an average rating for each facet. For each question, we ranked the presented facets according to these ratings, which results in a *survey ranking*. We then chose Kendall's Tau-B[12] to compare our *system ranking* with this *survey ranking*.

The survey responses for the second question set, concerned with the selection of better categorization, are shown in the topmost lane of Fig. 6. The overall result shows no clear support for our approach in this step. When there was no (obvious) relation between the indirect property and the initial resource set (e.g., a facet for *country of origin/driving side*), users rated the facet rather low. However, the system sometimes favors these facets, as they oftentimes provide a good categorization with respect to the defined metrics. On other occasions, like the facet *country of origin/continent*, both users and the system agree that this is a helpful facet. This leads us to believe that, although indirect facets are promising, they require additional refinement to ensure their relevancy.

The final question set verified our metrics independent of semantic biases induced by real-world facets. Results are shown in the lower parts of Fig. 6. In general, survey participants agree almost completely with our approach. The only exceptions are due to a tie (*Card, Disp*) or a different opinion about the order of one particular pair of facets (*Disp, Prob* and *Card, Disp, Prob*).

The user evaluation suggests that the technical criteria seem well suited in isolation. However, resulting facets not only have to be evaluated against each

[12] Kendall's Tau-B is a variant of Kendall's Tau that also accounts for possible ties in the ranking. Values range from +1 for identical rankings to −1 for inverse ones. A value of 0 hints towards no correlation between the involved rankings.

other, but also against the semantic context of the input IRIs. While in search tasks user input can be used to assess this intent, it remains open how this can automatically be approximated for arbitrary resource sets.

6 Conclusion

We have proposed methods to enable automatic facet generation and ranking over KGs. In particular, we provided an approach for dynamic candidate facet generation for arbitrary input sets of resources. We defined intra- and inter-facet metrics to rank the candidates and reduce the possible facet space by selecting the most useful ones. We explored indirect properties to find better categorizations and consequently enhance facets' usefulness. We proposed semantic similarity as a criterion to select among multiple candidate facets. Finally, we developed a holistic workflow that integrates all proposed methods.

Initial survey results support the used metrics. While indirect facets show promise as a helpful addition, their relevancy for the initial resource set needs to be ensured. This latter issue is also the main focus of our future efforts: How can we estimate the relatedness to the initial input for indirect facets? Another prime direction is a performance improvement of our initial prototype, to make it applicable for real-world systems (e.g., caching and parallelization of queries).

References

1. Feddoul, L., Schindler, S., Löffler, F.: Semantic relatedness as an inter-facet metric for facet selection over knowledge graphs. In: ESWC 2019 (2019, in press)
2. Schindler, S., Feddoul, L.: Semantic Facets (2019). https://doi.org/10.5281/zenodo.2784142
3. Vrandečić, D., Krötzsch, M.: Wikidata: a free collaborative knowledgebase. Commun. ACM (2014). https://doi.org/10.1145/2629489
4. Tzitzikas, Y., Manolis, N., Papadakos, P.: Faceted exploration of RDF/S Datasets: a survey. J. Intell. Inf. Syst. **48**(2), 329–364 (2016). https://doi.org/10.1007/s10844-016-0413-8
5. Mäkelä, E., Hyvönen, E., Saarela, S.: Ontogator — a semantic view-based search engine service for web applications. In: Cruz, I., et al. (eds.) ISWC 2006. LNCS, vol. 4273, pp. 847–860. Springer, Heidelberg (2006). https://doi.org/10.1007/11926078_61
6. Schraefel, M.C., Smith, D.A., Owens, A., Russell, A., Harris, C., Wilson, M.: The evolving mSpace platform: leveraging the semantic web on the trail of the Memex. In: Proceedings of the Sixteenth ACM Conference on Hypertext and Hypermedia, HYPERTEXT 2005, pp. 174–183. ACM (2005). https://doi.org/10.1145/1083356.1083391
7. Oren, E., Delbru, R., Decker, S.: Extending faceted navigation for RDF data. In: Cruz, I., et al. (eds.) ISWC 2006. LNCS, vol. 4273, pp. 559–572. Springer, Heidelberg (2006). https://doi.org/10.1007/11926078_40
8. Huynh, D., Karger, D.: Parallax and companion: set-based browsing for the data web. Technical report, Metaweb Technologies Inc. (2009)

9. Heim, P., Ziegler, J., Lohmann, S.: gFacet: a browser for the web of data. In: Proceedings of the International Workshop on Interacting with Multimedia Content in the Social Semantic Web (IMC-SSW 2008), Aachen (2008)
10. Hahn, R., et al.: Faceted wikipedia search. In: Abramowicz, W., Tolksdorf, R. (eds.) BIS 2010. LNBIP, vol. 47, pp. 1–11. Springer, Heidelberg (2010). https://doi.org/10.1007/978-3-642-12814-1_1
11. Harth, A.: VisiNav: a system for visual search and navigation on web data. J. Web Semant. **8**(4), 348–354 (2010). https://doi.org/10.1016/j.websem.2010.08.001. Semantic Web Challenge 2009 – User Interaction in Semantic Web research
12. Brunetti, J.M., García, R., Auer, S.: From overview to facets and pivoting for interactive exploration of semantic web data. Int. J. Semant. Web Inf. Syst. **9**(1), 1–20 (2013). https://doi.org/10.4018/jswis.2013010101
13. Ferré, S.: Expressive and scalable query-based faceted search over SPARQL endpoints. In: Mika, P., et al. (eds.) ISWC 2014. LNCS, vol. 8797, pp. 438–453. Springer, Cham (2014). https://doi.org/10.1007/978-3-319-11915-1_28
14. Arenas, M., Grau, B.C., Kharlamov, E., Marciuska, S., Zheleznyakov, D.: Faceted search Over RDF-based knowledge graphs. Web Semant. Sci., Serv. Agents World Wide Web **37**(0) (2016). https://doi.org/10.1016/j.websem.2015.12.002
15. Moreno-Vega, J., Hogan, A.: GraFa: scalable faceted browsing for RDF graphs. In: Vrandečić, D., et al. (eds.) ISWC 2018. LNCS, vol. 11136, pp. 301–317. Springer, Cham (2018). https://doi.org/10.1007/978-3-030-00671-6_18
16. van Zwol, R., et al.: Faceted exploration of image search results. In: Proceedings of the 19th International Conference on World Wide Web, WWW 2010, pp. 961–970. ACM (2010). https://doi.org/10.1145/1772690.1772788
17. Papadakos, P., Tzitzikas, Y.: Hippalus: preference-enriched faceted exploration. In: EDBT/ICDT Workshops. CEUR Workshop Proceedings, vol. 1133, pp. 167–172. CEUR-WS.org (2014)
18. Lehmann, J., et al.: DBpedia - a large-scale, multilingual knowledge base extracted from Wikipedia. Semant. Web J. **6**(2), 167–195 (2015). https://doi.org/10.3233/SW-140134
19. Bollacker, K., Evans, C., Paritosh, P., Sturge, T., Taylor, J.: Freebase: a collaboratively created graph database for structuring human knowledge. In: Proceedings of the 2008 ACM SIGMOD International Conference on Management of Data, SIGMOD 2008, pp. 1247–1250. ACM, New York (2008). https://doi.org/10.1145/1376616.1376746
20. Page, L., Brin, S., Motwani, R., Winograd, T.: The PageRank citation ranking: bringing order to the web. In: Proceedings of the 7th International World Wide Web Conference, Brisbane, Australia, pp. 161–172 (1998)
21. Harth, A., Kinsella, S., Decker, S.: Using naming authority to rank data and ontologies for web search. In: Bernstein, A., et al. (eds.) ISWC 2009. LNCS, vol. 5823, pp. 277–292. Springer, Heidelberg (2009). https://doi.org/10.1007/978-3-642-04930-9_18
22. Li, C., Yan, N., Roy, S.B., Lisham, L., Das, G.: Facetedpedia: dynamic generation of query-dependent faceted interfaces for Wikipedia. In: Proceedings of the 19th International Conference on World Wide Web, WWW 2010, pp. 651–660. ACM, New York (2010). https://doi.org/10.1145/1772690.1772757
23. Li, Y., Bandar, Z.A., Mclean, D.: An approach for measuring semantic similarity between words using multiple information sources. IEEE Trans. Knowl. Data Eng. **15**(4), 871–882 (2003). https://doi.org/10.1109/TKDE.2003.1209005
24. Likert, R.: A technique for the measurement of attitudes. Arch. Psychol. **22**, 5–55 (1932)

Knowledge Graph Exploration: A Usability Evaluation of Query Builders for Laypeople

Emil Kuric[1(✉)], Javier D. Fernández[1,2(✉)], and Olha Drozd[1(✉)]

[1] Vienna University of Economics and Business, Vienna, Austria
emil.kuric@s.wu.ac.at, {jfernand,olha.drozd}@wu.ac.at
[2] Complexity Science Hub Vienna, Vienna, Austria

Abstract. SPARQL enables users to access and browse knowledge graphs in a precise way. However, using SPARQL requires knowledge that many casual users lack. To counter this, specific tools have been created that enable more casual users to browse and query results. This paper evaluates and compares the most prominent techniques, QueryVOWL, SPARKLIS and the Wikidata Query Service (WQS), through a usability evaluation, using a mixed-method evaluation based on usability metrics and heuristics, containing both quantitative and qualitative data. The findings show that while WQS achieved the best results, usability problems were encountered in all tools. Key aspects for usability, extracted from the evaluation, serve as important contributions for future query builders.

Keywords: Knowledge graphs · SPARQL · Query builder · Usability

1 Introduction

Linked Open Data (LOD) describes knowledge graphs (KGs) from open sources, in such a way that data can be interlinked [13]. These KGs are ubiquitous, becoming the de facto standard for heterogeneous data integration [5]. Projects such as DBpedia that converts semi-structured content from Wikipedia [2], or Wikidata that offers an open KG created by volunteers [23], are just two KG examples of many successful stories in the Linked Open Data ecosystem.

Traditionally, SPARQL [12], the W3C recommended structured query language for graphs, enables users to access and browse these KGs in a precise way. However, using SPARQL requires a non-negligible knowledge that many end users do not have [9]. While it is a precise and expressive language, it also needs the user to conform to its complex syntax. In addition, it can be difficult to manipulate the interconnected graphs or to gain satisfying results from queries within them [13]. Therefore, SPARQL is mainly geared towards experienced users (i.e., semantic web practitioners) with prior knowledge or insights regarding the SPARQL query language and the structure of datasets (i.e., the

M. Acosta et al. (Eds.): SEMANTiCS 2019, LNCS 11702, pp. 326–342, 2019.
https://doi.org/10.1007/978-3-030-33220-4_24

underlying data model). To counter this, specific tools have been created that enable more casual users (i.e., laypeople) to browse and query results. These so-called SPARQL query builders enable users to generate queries that provide satisfying results either by suggesting relevant parts of the query or through the use of graphical metaphors [9]. While many of these query builders are available, documentation about the evaluation of their usability is scarce. The evaluation process is often not accurately described and therefore may not lead to meaningful results [9].

This paper aims to fill this gap in the scientific literature by evaluating the usability of the most prominent SPARQL query builders. In particular, we focus on studying the usability of SPARQL query builders with users that are inexperienced and have no prior knowledge of SPARQL. For this purpose, we first analyze existing SPARQL query builders and categorize them based on the querying approach into *form-based*, *graph-based* and *natural language-based* query builders. Then, three query builders, the Wikidata Query Service[1] (WQS), QueryVOWL [11] and SPARKLIS [8] are selected based on factors including their availability, querying approach and expressiveness. We compare them using a mixed-method approach consisting of a combination of quantitative and qualitative methods [10]. We first design three tasks to be performed in each of the three tools, and we then conduct a user study with 15 individuals. Quantitative data, that we gather, include the time per task, completion rate and the amount of hints it took to finish the tasks. Furthermore, we evaluate each tool with a System Usability Scale (SUS) questionnaire [6]. Qualitative data are collected through the use of the think-aloud method [7] and the information is analyzed afterwards by clustering the think-aloud protocols with the usability heuristics [19].

Our results show that the querying approach is not as important for the usability of the tool as it may seem, and user satisfaction and preference were mostly influenced by the interface design and ease of use of the tools. In particular, the form-based WQS approach offered the best usability of the three selected tools, although a majority of participants would prefer traditional keyword-based search engines over the presented query builders. We expect that our findings can serve as initial blueprints to guide the next generation of KG query builders.

The rest of the paper is structured as follows: Sect. 2 reviews the functionality and limitations of current SPARQL query builders. Furthermore, we provide details of the three selected tools for the usability evaluation, and explanations as to why they were selected. Section 3 shows the design of our mixed-method approach. Then, in Sect. 4, we analyze the results of our user study and provide lessons learned summarizing the insights gathered and making suggestions for future query builder tools. Finally, Sect. 5 provides conclusion and future work.

2 SPARQL Query Builders

SPARQL query builders are tools that are specifically designed to facilitate the process of querying. A range of these tools are available, each with their own

[1] https://query.wikidata.org/.

varying purposes, querying approaches and target audiences [9]. In this section, we first categorize and analyze available tools. Then we select the most prominent tools for our usability evaluation, based on comparative criteria.

2.1 Categorization

Query builders can be categorized and differentiated based on many possible criteria. In this paper, we follow a pure user interface (UI) criteria influenced by Grafkin and Mironov [9], suggesting a categorization on the basis of the querying approach used in the query builders. Thus, we distinguish between *form-based*, *graph-based* and *natural language-based* querying approaches. It is important to highlight that some approaches combine different elements, following a "hybrid" approach [9]. Other existing techniques that can complement these approaches, such as AutoSPARQL [17], which uses (supervised) machine learning, are outside of the scope of this paper.

Form-Based Query Builders. Form-based querying is an approach that focuses on textual input fields and constructs a query one step at a time. The approach resembles SPARQL's triple pattern syntax and eases the process of query building. This is either enabled by suggesting relevant parts of the query to users or restricting them to selective inputs. A limitation of this approach is that it only allows for a limited set of queries. The classes and objects have to be suggested or enabled as a choice for the user to be able to use them in the query building process. Furthermore, these tools often do not allow for the specification of filters for the results, as they are limited by their input fields. Therefore, some tools are not able to formulate advanced queries [17].

Examples of form-based approaches are ExConQuer [1], the Linked Data Query Wizard [14], VizQuery[2] and the Wikidata Query Service. The ExConQuer Framework is a set of tools meant to explore, convert, and query linked data. In the ExConQuer query builder, users can navigate through classes, instances and properties in a way similar to facet-based browsing. It was deemed as useful both by experts and casual users for exploring and querying linked data [1]. However, it does not offer the full expressiveness of SPARQL.

The Linked Data Query Wizard [14] (LDQW) was designed as a web-based tool for exploring, filtering and analyzing data from SPARQL endpoints. Its approach is to turn the underlying graph structure into a tabular interface that enables interaction with the data set. This interface is meant to take advantage of the fact that many users are already familiar with search engines and spreadsheet applications. A user study conducted by the creators of the tool showed that it was very usable. However, users had difficulties with adding filters and the spreadsheet approach showing too many options [14].

The VizQuery tool is based on SPARQL triple patterns and used specifically for querying data from the Wikidata endpoint. It is a prototype that only offers

[2] https://tools.wmflabs.org/hay/vizquery/.

the simplest functionality for creating queries. VizQuery uses the Wikidata API to provide auto-completion and suggestions for Wikidata properties and items. Although it offers the functionality to use variables for more advanced users, the UI is very limited in its approach as it does not allow for the creation of more complex queries.

Finally, the Wikidata Query Service (WQS) is the official query service of Wikidata and offers a "Query Helper" that allows users to create queries through a form-based approach. As shown in Fig. 1, users can add items to the filter and get relevant suggestions and auto-completion for properties. The Wikidata API allows users to create queries even if the exact names for entities are unknown. Additionally, if users add an item to the filter, WQS will automatically assign a relevant property. However, the WQS does not offer the full expressiveness of SPARQL, and it is meant to be domain-specific as it can only reach Wikidata.

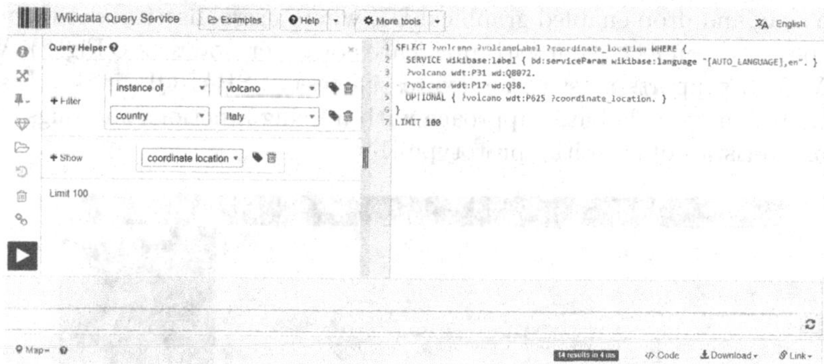

Fig. 1. Screenshot of WQS query builder

Graph-Based Query Builders. The graph-based approach consists of visual query builders and systems (VQS). This category describes tools that lower the difficulty of creating SPARQL queries by enabling a visual approach. The used visualizations are similar to the syntax of textual SPARQL queries. VQS supports users in creating syntactically valid queries by constraining and guiding their editing actions through the use of a graphical UI. A limitation of this approach is that users of these tools still need a rough understanding of the underlying schema to formulate a query. Without understanding how SPARQL queries are constructed users are not able to successfully visualize the queries in some tools [17].

Examples of VQS include iSPARQL[3], NITELIGHT [21], OptiqueVQS [22] and QueryVOWL [11]. iSPARQL and NITELIGHT allow for the whole expressiveness of SPARQL and are query builders for advanced users. Both tools extend the traditional SPARQL framework to enhance its functionalities and feature drag and drop interfaces to connect graph nodes and predicates. However, they

[3] http://dbpedia.org/isparql/.

use a complex series of buttons and options to incorporate all their features in the interface. Additionally, because of their complexity they require thorough knowledge of the underlying data [21].

OptiqueVQS [22] is primarily meant to be a product for end users with limited technical skills and knowledge. Therefore, it includes a simplified interface that is meant to enable users to address basic tasks. A criterion that differentiates OptiqueVQS from other query builders is that it was developed to meet industrial requirements and was evaluated with industrial users. It was, therefore, designed to provide a good balance between usability and expressiveness [22], although, it puts the focus on a very concrete profile of users.

Finally, QueryVOWL [11] differs from other graph-based tools because it uses the Visual Notation for OWL Ontologies (VOWL) [18] to visualize the queries. QueryVOWL enables casual users to build queries by combining the proven to be intuitive and understandable VOWL with matching SPARQL mappings. It offers a drag and drop enabled graphical UI, where users insert nodes through a search box and connect them with predicates or other nodes (see Fig. 2). While QueryVOWL supports most of the expressiveness of SPARQL, it is still somewhat limited in its node-based approach with missing functions and bugs, inherent characteristics of an initial prototype [11].

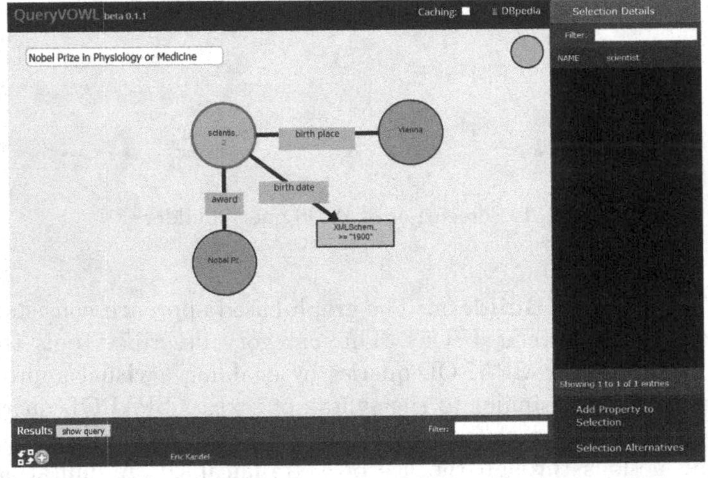

Fig. 2. Screenshot of QueryVOWL query builder

Natural Language-Based Query Builders. Natural language (NL) approaches offer users the convenient and valuable option of using natural language for querying. NL-based approaches enable the user to form precise queries by providing the high expressiveness of terms that users are familiar with. As NL-based approaches interpret natural language phrases, linguistic considerations have to be taken into account. Tools of this variety are often limited by linguistic ambiguities and variability. Furthermore, the development of accurate NL interfaces is complex and requires considerable implementation efforts.

Therefore, NL tools are often domain-specific or tailored to applications making them hardly adaptable to other ontologies [15].

Examples of NL-based tools are NLP-Reduce [16] and SPARKLIS [8]. The NLP-Reduce tool is meant to facilitate the querying of linked data for users with no prior knowledge by using a reduced set of natural language processing functionalities. The system allows for a non-restrictive query language that can consist of keywords, sentence fragments or full sentences. NLP-Reduce was deemed as easy to use without any training. However, as the simple approach avoids complex linguistic and semantic technology it does not allow for the expressiveness of SPARQL [15].

SPARKLIS [8] is a natural language-based web tool that offers the full expressiveness of SPARQL and is usable for casual users. As shown in Fig. 3, the query in SPARKLIS is represented as a NL sentence in a tree structure and the user can focus on different parts of the query to refine it. The selection of parts is guided by suggestions that are enabled by SPARKLIS to allow the user to see relevant options. If a query element is inserted at the focus, the NL sentence is verbalized into a readable form to adapt to that change. Because of its navigational approach and the way suggestions are generated, SPARKLIS has some problems regarding loading and response times [8].

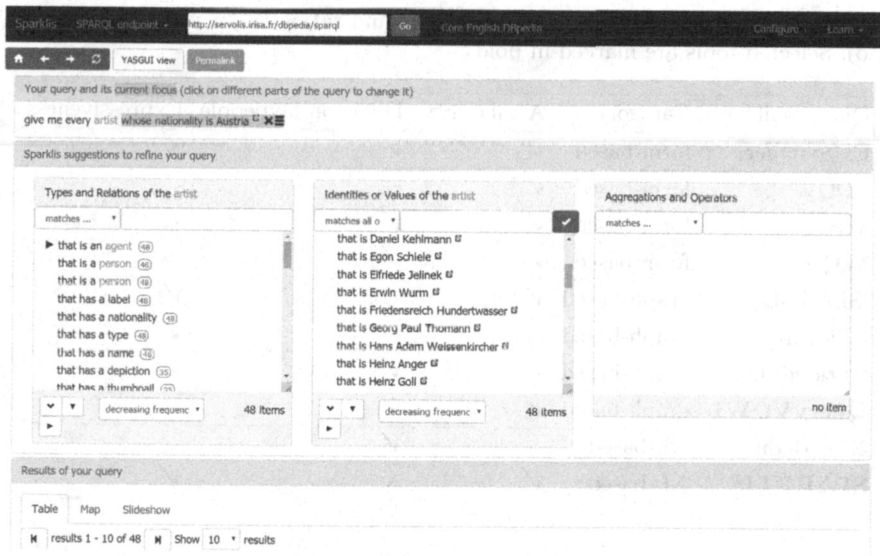

Fig. 3. Screenshot of SPARKLIS query builder

2.2 Selected Tools for Our User Study

We select representative tools for our study, based on criteria, summarized in Table 1. One of the most important factors of the selection was the *availability* of tools. As many tools were either not available or operational anymore, such as ExConQuer or NITELIGHT, they could not be evaluated. Web tools were preferred because casual users could theoretically find them on the web by themselves and use them to query data. The ease of use or *focus on laypeople* was important as a pre-selection criteria[4], to enable the evaluation with casual users. We considered a tool with a focus on laypeople, (i) if it was specified as designed for casual users in the companion research paper(s) describing the tool, or (ii) if initial examination tests with laypeople revealed a considerable facility when performing simple tasks.

Thus, our user study finally considers WQS, QueryVOWL and SPARKLIS as prominent (and available) query builder representatives of form-, graph- and NL-based query approaches, respectively. Out of all three tools the WQS offers the lowest amount of expressiveness and is furthermore the only tool meant to be domain-specific as it can only reach Wikidata. QueryVOWL has an intuitive graph-based web tool and allows for a certain extent of expressiveness of the SPARQL language. Finally, out of all three selected tools, SPARKLIS offers the most features of SPARQL and therefore the highest expressiveness, although the overload of information and options can negatively influence its usability. The following sections provide an extensive usability evaluation of the three selected query builders: WQS, QueryVOWL and SPARKLIS.

Table 1. Examined tools with selection criteria and rating (✓ = yes, ∼ = partially, - = no). Selected tools are marked in bold

Query builder	Category	Availability	Focus on laypeople	Expressiveness
ExConQuer	form-based	-	✓	∼
LDQW	form-based	✓	∼	-
VizQuery	form-based	✓	✓	-
WQS	form-based	✓	✓	∼
iSPARQL	graph-based	✓	-	✓
NITELIGHT	graph-based	-	-	✓
OptiqueVQS	graph-based	-	✓	-
QueryVOWL	graph-based	✓	✓	∼
NLP-Reduce	NL-based	-	✓	-
SPARKLIS	NL-based	✓	∼	✓

3 Evaluation Design

Our usability evaluation follows a mixed-method evaluation design, consisting of both a quantitative and qualitative part. It is meant to use the results of one method to clarify the results of the other method and therefore to increase

[4] Note that the final usability is evaluated in the next section, here we just select the representative tools of each category.

the meaningfulness of results by capitalizing on the inherent strengths of both methods. This ensures the comparability of quantitative data while it also allows for the informative value found in qualitative approaches [10]. We first show the quantitative and qualitative data considered in our study. Then, we present the participants, test plan and tasks in our study.

3.1 Quantitative Data

For the quantitative data, a suitable conceptual model has to offer measures that can be collected and analyzed in an easy way, while still being meaningful and usable for the evaluation of query builders. In our evaluation, the decision falls on the software engineering standard ISO 9241-11 [4]. In particular, we consider a combination of ISO 9241-11 factors with measurable attributes, as follows. First, we use the *effectiveness* factor, i.e., the success in achieving goals. For the context of the study this factor is further decomposed into the *accuracy* (i.e., amount of hints given to the user during task completion) and *completeness* (i.e., task completion rate) of the tasks performed by the users. Then, we consider the *efficiency*, which describes the amount of resources that users spend to achieve their goals [4] and is measured by the time spent to complete a task. Finally, we use the *satisfaction* factor, i.e., the user's positive attitude towards the tool [4]. In our evaluation, we make use of the System Usability Scale (SUS) questionnaire[5] [6], to provide a quantitative measurement about the users' perceived usability of the tool, facilitating a comparison.

3.2 Qualitative Data: Think-Aloud

Qualitative data that are collected in usability evaluations typically consist of observational findings about the usability of design features. We make use of the think-aloud method [7], i.e., users are asked to voice their thoughts while trying to solve a predefined task. Their thoughts are then gathered in the form of a think-aloud protocol. This method has proven to be a reliable source of information, yet its application offers some challenges. In a realistic scenario, some users will have problems with voicing their inner speech. To counter this, we include a brief explanation of think-aloud in the pretest introduction and *prompt* participants to voice their thoughts during task completion. The think-aloud protocol on its own would be too inaccurate as it is often missing thought processes that are not verbalized. Thus, *retrospective questioning* is used in the evaluation, directly after testing the query builders, to insure that participants are still able to remember their thoughts. Participants are asked to recall their thoughts and opinions on certain points in an unstructured interview.

Typically, experts would evaluate systems or tools on the basis of so-called usability heuristics [19] and through that be able to find problems in UIs. We follow this approach in our evaluation, and analyze the think-aloud protocols based on the ten usability heuristics by Nielsen [19] that provide general principles for

[5] Available at: https://bit.ly/2YuQyHJ.

the design of UIs. The heuristics observed in our evaluation are: *visibility of system status* (i.e., keeping users informed of the process), *match between system and real world* (i.e., speaking the user's language), *user control and freedom* (i.e., enabling users to control their workflow and undo and redo actions), *consistency and standards*, *error prevention*, *recognition rather than recall* (i.e., minimizing the user's memory load), *aesthetic and minimalist design*, and *help and documentation*.

3.3 Participants

While an evaluation of systems such as query builders is typically carried out by field experts, our test users have to have no prior knowledge regarding LOD or SPARQL, so that the usability for casual users can be analyzed. Thus, our selected target group is digital natives that are versed in dealing with web tools and interfaces.

We follow Nielsen's studies on UI evaluations, estimating that the optimal number of participants for a medium-large project should include 15 users [20]. Thus, 15 bachelor students, ranging from 18 to 25 years old and evenly split between genders are finally selected to participate in our usability evaluation. The participants had never heard of or worked with SPARQL.

3.4 Usability Evaluation

The evaluation took approximately an hour per person and consisted of three parts: (i) the introduction that explained the test procedure to the participant, including the topic and evaluation approach of the user study; (ii) the testing of the query builders and the corresponding tasks; (iii) a debriefing where participants were able to verify their think-aloud messages and to add something to their protocols based on the ability to compare all tools. The order of the three tools was randomized before the evaluation. The tasks were printed out on a sheet of paper, and read aloud by the participants so that any questions could be clarified before users started the evaluation.

The participants received the following tasks: (i) show all Austrian artists; (ii) show all volcanoes in Italy and their location (on a map); (iii) show all scientists born in Vienna after 1900 that have been awarded a Nobel Prize in Physiology and Medicine. The first task introduces the participants to the query builders and encourages them to interact with the interface and create a list of results. The second task is similar to the first one in that it combines a single object with one relation to a subject, however, it introduces the location. As QueryVOWL does not offer an option to show the location on a map, the task is changed to output the location attribute. The third task is the most complex one as it is meant to show the expressiveness of the tools. It includes three objects that have to be put into relation with one another and a filter based on the birth date. For WQS the task was changed to search for humans instead of scientists, to output the items, as the corresponding results are saved differently in Wikidata. Furthermore, because the tool is missing a function to filter the results, the WQS

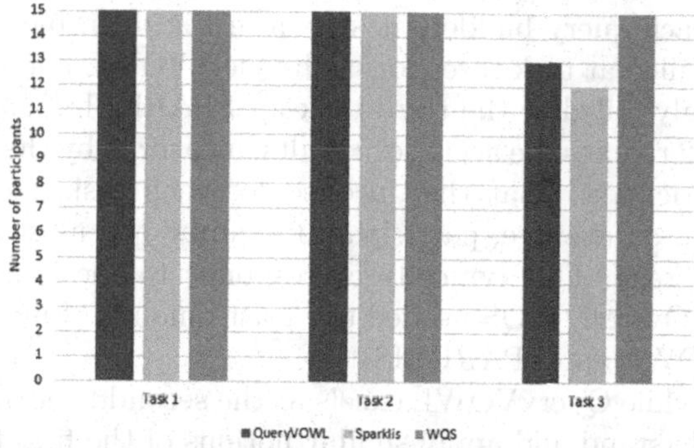

Fig. 4. Task completion (over a total of 15 participants)

Table 2. Average hints per query builder and task

Query builder	Task 1	Task 2	Task 3	Total hints
WQS	**1.07**	0.87	**0.67**	**2.60**
QueryVOWL	1.93	**0.60**	1.73	4.27
SPARKLIS	1.80	1.20	1.53	4.53

task was changed to additionally output the birth year instead. Hints that were given to users in the tasks were mostly based on the way the relations or filters were created. Users were never told where to click but were instead made aware that they had made an error and that their current approach would not work. If users were not sure about which relation they had to choose, a keyword was given to them, which was not counted as a hint. After finishing the tasks for one tool the participant fill out the SUS questionnaire and shortly answer the retrospective questions for the think-aloud protocol.

4 Usability Results

In the following, we present the results[6] of the user study divided into the usability metrics and heuristics that were gathered through the quantitative and qualitative parts of the user study respectively. We then provide a discussion assessing the selected tools.

4.1 Usability Metrics

The usability metrics are analyzed by comparing the quantitative data of the corresponding query builders.

Effectiveness. The effectiveness is comprised of the completeness and the accuracy. Regarding the completeness, most of the participants were able to complete

[6] All fine-grained results are available at: https://bit.ly/2YuQyHJ.

all the tasks for each query builder, as shown in Fig. 4. In particular, the same two participants failed at task three for both QueryVOWL and SPARKLIS, and one participant only failed at the third task for SPARKLIS.

In turn, Table 2 reports the accuracy results, measured by the average number of hints (per participant) that they needed for each task and query builder. Results show that, on average, participants required the most amount of hints to finish the first task. This typically corresponds to the familiarization with the environment. Overall, WQS needed the least amount of hints, about half as much as QueryVOWL and SPARKLIS.

Interestingly, while QueryVOWL excels at the second task (i.e., users seemed to accurately understand and apply similar notions of the first task) it provides the worst results for the most complex third task. Finally, it is worth mentioning that no participant was able to finish all the tasks of a query builder without at least one hint.

Both completeness and accuracy show that WQS offers the best effectiveness. It required the least amount of total hints and achieved the best task completion rate. The effectiveness of QueryVOWL and SPARKLIS showed only marginal differences.

Efficiency. The efficiency was measured by the amount of time that was spent to complete a task. The results in Table 3 show that, as expected, participants needed the most time to finish task three (i.e., the most complex one). In turn, users required the least amount of time to finish the second task, because of the aforementioned learning effect and its similarity to the first task. Overall, efficiency results are in line with the accuracy. Thus, users spend the least amount of time per task in WQS, while the results of QueryVOWL and SPARKLIS are similar to each other.

System Usability Scale. As mentioned in Sect. 3, we measure satisfaction through the System Usability Scale (SUS) [6], in the range 0–100. The results in

Table 3. Average time spent per query builder and task (in mm:ss)

Query builder	Task 1	Task 2	Task 3	Total time
WQS	**01:31**	**01:45**	**01:52**	**05:09**
QueryVOWL	02:42	01:53	03:08	07:44
SPARKLIS	02:26	01:48	03:06	07:21

Table 4. Average System Usability Scale (SUS) score per query builder

Query builder	SUS score	Rating
WQS	**61**	'OK'
QueryVOWL	50.5	'Poor'
SPARKLIS	48.5	'Poor'

Table 4 show relatively similar scores for each tool. WQS reports the highest SUS score of 61, which can be interpreted as an 'OK' result using the adjective rating of the scale [3]. In contrast, the similar scores of QueryVOWL and SPARKLIS can both be rated as 'Poor'.

4.2 Usability Heuristics

The think-aloud protocols were clustered via the so-called usability heuristics [19] (see Sect. 3). We exclude the heuristics that were missing in the protocols and were not directly observed. In the following, we briefly summarize the results that were most frequently mentioned.

Most QueryVOWL users complained about a lack of **visibility of system status**. The graph-based construction was lacking appropriate feedback in some cases and users were not able to see that input has been received. The NL-based SPARKLIS approach had less problems with the visibility, as feedback was provided instantly in NL form. However, users complained about the loading and response times of the tool.

As for the **match between system and real world**, some users of WQS had problems deciphering the meaning of the used terms. As WQS only offered an option to add items as well as properties through the use of the filter button, it resulted in some mistakes for the users. The terms that were used in QueryVOWL were taken directly from SPARQL and were confusing for some of the users. For example, users had problems deciding between using 'artist' as a class, individual or property, because they had no idea of the underlying data model. SPARKLIS managed to speak the user's language through the use of non-system-oriented terms and a natural language query.

Regarding the **user control and freedom**, most users complained about the missing undo and redo buttons for WQS and QueryVOWL. SPARKLIS offered the best user control (e.g., undo and redo) and freedom for participants.

As for **consistency and standards**, WQS and SPARKLIS offered standard buttons and users were able to use them easily. In contrast, none of the users was familiar with the visual style of QueryVOWL.

Regarding **error prevention**, all tools offered suggestions, enabling users to pick from available options. However, WQS was the only tool that offered spell checking and suggestions based on the input, a feature that users were missing in the other tools. For example, if 'geolocation' was entered, it still showed 'coordinate location'.

Concerning **recognition rather than recall**, users described some options of WQS as hidden away. Users complained about QueryVOWLs options, in the nodes and sidebar, which were not selectable and visible in some cases.

As for the **aesthetic and minimalist design**, most users complained about the clutter of information in parts of the interface of WQS, such as the suggestion box. QueryVOWL was described as minimalist to the point of missing necessary information. Users complained about the amount of options and features that were shown at once in SPARKLIS. This led to them feeling overwhelmed and not in control at first.

Table 5. Summary of usability results per tool (bold values show the best tool for each metric)

Query builder	Completion rate (%)	Average hints	Average time (mm:ss)	SUS score (0–100)	Usability problems
WQS	**100**	**2,60**	**05:09**	**61**	4
QueryVOWL	95,56	4,27	07:44	50,5	7
SPARKLIS	93,33	4,53	07:21	48,5	**3**

Finally, as for **help and documentation**, users liked the example queries of WQS and SPARKLIS; and QueryVOWLs video. However, they would have preferred integrated tutorials over the available documentation of the tools.

4.3 Discussion

The results of the evaluation are summarized and discussed for each tool. An overview of the results, including the number of extracted usability problems, is shown in Table 5.

WQS. WQS had the best results regarding the usability metrics. Users were able to achieve the best effectiveness and efficiency by a wide margin. The analysis of think-aloud protocols revealed four usability problems: the use of confusing terms, missing user control, non-selectable options and the complexity of parts of the UI. The problem that most participants encountered was the clutter of parts of the UI, such as the suggestion box. Furthermore, buttons and input fields were described as hidden away and led to confusion among users. Overall, WQS had the best results in this user study, most likely, based on the easy to use form-based approach with recommendations and suggestions enabled by the Wikidata API. However, it offered the lowest amount of expressiveness and was the only tool that was domain-dependent.

QueryVOWL. In short, regarding both the amount of hints given and the time per task, the first task of QueryVOWL had the highest average of all tasks and tools. It was apparent that users had difficulties understanding the visual approach and the interface of the tool. The think-aloud protocols showed that both the frustration and difficulties that users experienced could be explained by the uncovered usability problems. Seven usability problems could be extracted from the protocols: the lack of appropriate feedback, use of confusing terms, missing user control, non-familiar visuals, missing error prevention, non-selectable options and the UI missing necessary information. One of the most substantial problems was the missing visibility of system status and appropriate feedback. This, combined with the use of confusing terms and the lack of error prevention, led to making mistakes. The absence of undo and redo functions only amplified these problems. However, it is important to note that the tested version of QueryVOWL was a prototype meant to demonstrate the querying approach.

SPARKLIS. Both the completion rate and the average total amount of hints were marginally worse than those of QueryVOWL. Three usability problems could be extracted from the think-aloud protocols: the lack of appropriate feedback, missing error prevention and the overwhelming UI. Most users were overwhelmed by the amount of options and input fields that SPARKLIS offered and suggested a more minimalistic interface. SPARKLIS results were interesting in that the usability metrics results differed from the statements and think-aloud protocols of users. Most users were satisfied with the tool, and users that were not, said that they liked its approach after seeing all tools. This combined with the low amount of usability problems speaks for the usability of the tool. The think-aloud protocols showed that a better tutorial or a beginner friendlier interface would have led to a more usable tool.

4.4 Lessons Learned

Based on our results and the similarities regarding usability problems and user suggestions, we summarize key aspects for designing a query builder for knowledge graphs.

First, results show that the querying approach is not as important for the usability of the tool as it may seem. User satisfaction and preference was mostly influenced by the interface design and ease of use of the tools. For example, 4 users preferred the graph-based approach of QueryVOWL even if they did not grade the tool itself as usable.

Regarding the ease of use, the availability of suggestions had a great impact on users. Casual users are inexperienced and suggestions allow them to see possible queries and subsequently understand the way queries are built. Participants suggested that tools could offer their most frequently built queries as examples, as (initial) queries built by casual users most likely would not differ too much.

An important point for the interface design was not to overwhelm the user with options. The results of think-aloud protocols show that most participants disliked having too many options or fields for query input. In contrast, important functionalities should not be hidden away from users. The features that are likely to be used often, should be visible and selectable at all times.

Regarding the usability heuristics, some features had a great impact on users. The ability to undo and redo parts of the query was praised when it was available and criticized when it was missing by a majority of participants. Casual users are especially prone to a trial and error method, which is why the possibility to undo errors as well as error prevention methods are so valuable.

Concerning the documentation, participants of the study said that they were not likely to read tutorials or watch videos longer than a few minutes. A majority of users suggested to integrate tutorials in the query builder interface. The availability of tooltips could also improve usability.

Finally, it should be noted that for most casual users the alternative to building a SPARQL query to gather information is the use of traditional keyword-based web search engines. A majority of participants said that if they had the choice they would still use those search engines instead of any query builder to solve tasks such as those of the user study. Therefore, query builders still need to somehow compete with this traditional mindset, keeping high usability standards while offering advanced functionalities to exploit the expressivity of SPARQL and the rich fine-grained information of (potentially interconnected) knowledge graphs.

5 Conclusion and Future Work

This paper presents a usability evaluation of SPARQL query builders for laypeople, i.e., users that want to explore knowledge graphs but have no prior knowledge of SPARQL. We first categorize and analyze query builders based on their querying approach (i.e., form-, graph-, and natural language-based). We then select and evaluate three prominent representatives: the Wikidata Query Service (WQS), QueryVOWL and SPARKLIS.

Our user study is based on a mixed-method usability evaluation with three increasingly complex tasks (i.e. queries). On the one hand, we measure the effectiveness, efficiency and the System Usability Scale (SUS) score as quantitative data. On the other hand, we make use of the think-aloud method as qualitative data, clustering results based on usability heuristics.

The results show that the form-based WQS offered the best usability of the three selected tools. However, usability problems were found for all tools, mostly concerning the difficulty of understanding and efficiently performing the query building process. Irrespective of the querying approach, users were mostly influenced by the interface design and ease of use of the tools.

Finally, we extract key aspects for the interface design of future query builders. These include the availability of undo functions and error prevention methods as well as integrated tutorials, examples and suggestions to understand how queries are constructed for the underlying knowledge graphs.

Our future work considers to expand the user study with a broader spectrum of queries and users, and the application of the lesson learned to build the next generation of query builders for knowledge graphs.

Acknowledgements. This work is supported by the EU's Horizon 2020 research and innovation programme: grant 731601 (SPECIAL), the Austrian Research Promotion Agency's (FFG) program "ICT of the Future": grant 861213 (CitySPIN).

References

1. Attard, J., Orlandi, F., Auer, S.: Exconquer: lowering barriers to rdf and linked data re-use. Semant. Web **9**(2), 241–255 (2018)
2. Auer, S., Bizer, C., Kobilarov, G., Lehmann, J., Cyganiak, R., Ives, Z.: DBpedia: a nucleus for a web of open data. In: Aberer, K., et al. (eds.) ASWC/ISWC -2007. LNCS, vol. 4825, pp. 722–735. Springer, Heidelberg (2007). https://doi.org/10.1007/978-3-540-76298-0_52
3. Bangor, A., Kortum, P., Miller, J.: Determining what individual sus scores mean: adding an adjective rating scale. J. Usability Stud. **4**(3), 114–123 (2009)

4. Bevan, N., Carter, J., Harker, S.: ISO 9241-11 revised: what have we learnt about usability since 1998? In: Kurosu, M. (ed.) HCI 2015. LNCS, vol. 9169, pp. 143–151. Springer, Cham (2015). https://doi.org/10.1007/978-3-319-20901-2_13
5. Bonatti, P.A., Decker, S., Polleres, A., Presutti, V.: Knowledge graphs: new directions for knowledge representation on the semantic web (Dagstuhl seminar 18371). Dagstuhl Rep. **8**(9), 29–111 (2019)
6. Brooke, J.: SUS: a retrospective. J. Usability Stud. **8**(2), 29–40 (2013)
7. Charters, E.: The use of think-aloud methods in qualitative research anintroduction to think-aloud methods. Brock Educ. J. OLD **12**(2) (2003)
8. Ferré, S.: SPARKLIS: an expressive query builder for sparql endpoints with guidance in natural language. Semant. Web **8**(3), 405–418 (2017)
9. Grafkin, P., Mironov, M., Fellmann, M., Lantow, B., Sandkuhl, K., Smirnov, A.V.: SPARQL query builders: overview and comparison. In: BIR Workshops (2016)
10. Greene, J.C., Caracelli, V.J., Graham, W.F.: Toward a conceptual framework for mixed-method evaluation designs. Educ. Eval. Policy Anal. **11**(3), 255–274 (1989)
11. Haag, F., Lohmann, S., Siek, S., Ertl, T.: QueryVOWL: visual composition of SPARQL queries. In: Gandon, F., Guéret, C., Villata, S., Breslin, J., Faron-Zucker, C., Zimmermann, A. (eds.) ESWC 2015. LNCS, vol. 9341, pp. 62–66. Springer, Cham (2015). https://doi.org/10.1007/978-3-319-25639-9_12
12. Harris, S., Seaborne, A.: SPARQL 1.1 query language, March 2013
13. Heath, T., Bizer, C.: Linked data: evolving the web into a global data space. Synth. Lect. Semant. Web: Theory Technol. **1**(1), 1–136 (2011)
14. Hoefler, P., Granitzer, M., Veas, E.E., Seifert, C.: Linked data query wizard: a novel interface for accessing SPARQL endpoints. In: Proceedings of LDOW (2014)
15. Kaufmann, E., Bernstein, A.: How useful are natural language interfaces to the semantic web for casual end-users? In: Aberer, K., et al. (eds.) ASWC/ISWC - 2007. LNCS, vol. 4825, pp. 281–294. Springer, Heidelberg (2007). https://doi.org/10.1007/978-3-540-76298-0_21
16. Kaufmann, E., Bernstein, A., Fischer, L.: NLP-reduce: a naive but domain-independent natural language interface for querying ontologies. In: Proceedings of ESWC, pp. 1–2 (2007)
17. Lehmann, J., Bühmann, L.: AutoSPARQL: let users query your knowledge base. In: Antoniou, G., et al. (eds.) ESWC 2011. LNCS, vol. 6643, pp. 63–79. Springer, Heidelberg (2011). https://doi.org/10.1007/978-3-642-21034-1_5
18. Lohmann, S., Negru, S., Haag, F., Ertl, T.: Visualizing ontologies with VOWL. Semant. Web **7**(4), 399–419 (2016)
19. Nielsen, J.: Enhancing the explanatory power of usability heuristics. In: Proceedings of the SIGCHI conference on Human Factors in Computing Systems, pp. 152–158. ACM (1994)
20. Nielsen, J., Landauer, T.K.: A mathematical model of the finding of usability problems. In: Proceedings of INTERACT and CHI, pp. 206–213. ACM (1993)
21. Smart, P.R., Russell, A., Braines, D., Kalfoglou, Y., Bao, J., Shadbolt, N.R.: A visual approach to semantic query design using a web-based graphical query designer. In: Gangemi, A., Euzenat, J. (eds.) EKAW 2008. LNCS (LNAI), vol. 5268, pp. 275–291. Springer, Heidelberg (2008). https://doi.org/10.1007/978-3-540-87696-0_25
22. Soylu, A., et al.: OptiqueVQS: a visual query system over ontologies for industry. Semant. Web **9**(5), 627–660 (2018)
23. Vrandecic, D., Krötzsch, M.: Wikidata: a free collaborative knowledgebase. Commun. ACM **57**(10), 78–85 (2014)

QUANT - Question Answering Benchmark Curator

Ria Hari Gusmita[1(✉)], Rricha Jalota[1], Daniel Vollmers[1], Jan Reineke[1], Axel-Cyrille Ngonga Ngomo[1,2], and Ricardo Usbeck[1,2]

[1] University of Paderborn, 33098 Paderborn, Germany
{ria.hari.gusmita,rricha.jalota,daniel.vollmers,jan.reineke, axel.ngonga,ricardo.usbeck}@uni-paderborn.de
[2] University of Leipzig, 04109 Leipzig, Germany
{ngonga,usbeck}@informatik.uni-leipzig.de

Abstract. Question answering engines have become one of the most popular type of applications driven by Semantic Web technologies. Consequently, the provision of means to quantify the performance of current question answering approaches on current datasets has become ever more important. However, a large percentage of the queries found in popular question answering benchmarks cannot be executed on current versions of their reference dataset. There is a consequently a clear need to curate question answering benchmarks periodically. However, the manual alteration of question answering benchmarks is often error-prone. We alleviate this problem by presenting QUANT, a novel framework for the creation and curation of question answering benchmarks. QUANT supports the curation of benchmarks by generating smart edit suggestions for question-query pair and for the corresponding metadata. In addition, our framework supports the creation of new benchmark entries by providing predefined quality checks for queries. We evaluate QUANT on 653 questions obtained from QALD-1 to QALD-8 with 10 users. Our results show that our framework generates reliable suggestions and can reduce the curation effort for QA benchmarks by up to 91%.

Keywords: Benchmark · Question answering · Knowledge base

1 Introduction

Question answering (QA) engines are at the core of an increasing number of human computer interfaces, including personal assistants and chatbots [9]. The development of accurate QA frameworks for (RDF) knowledge graphs has hence become an endeavor of increasing importance and popularity [14,16]. Consequently, the provision of means to evaluate the performance of QA systems on *current datasets* is critical to (1) monitor the improvement of the state of art over past approaches and (2) provide realistic insights in relevant improvements for question answering systems on current challenges found in datasets. Benchmark series such as the Question Answering on Linked Data (QALD) series [15] address

M. Acosta et al. (Eds.): SEMANTiCS 2019, LNCS 11702, pp. 343–358, 2019.
https://doi.org/10.1007/978-3-030-33220-4_25

this need for objective evaluation. They support QA researchers and developers by providing new versions of their benchmarks periodically. However, maintaining high-quality and current benchmark datasets is a challenging endeavor. In particular, changes in the knowledge base underlying the benchmarks (as well as metadata annotation errors) lead to a large proportion of the queries in previous benchmarks not being executable on current versions of datasets. Table 1 gives an overview of the extend of the degradation of the QALD benchmarks over time. A significant proportion of the SPARQL queries that were not modified over time degraded (i.e., could not be executed) with newer versions of the knowledge base underlying QALD. For example, more than 30% of the QALD-4 benchmark cannot be executed on DBpedia 2014, which was release a mere year after the publication of QALD-4.

Table 1. Degradation of QALD benchmarks against various versions of DBpedia (in %). The numbers in brackets indicate total number of questions.

DBpedia version	QALD-1 (44)	QALD-2 (87)	QALD-3 (88)	QALD-4 (177)	QALD-5 (262)	QALD-6 (350)	QALD-7 (215)	QALD-8 (219)
3.6	18.18							
3.7	25.00	16.09						
3.8	31.82	20.69	17.05					
3.9	54.55	41.38	40.90	25.99				
2014	50.00	39.08	40.90	30.50	24.43			
2015–04	36.36	27.58	23.86	18.08	13.74			
2015–10	36.36	26.44	23.86	18.08	12.59	10.57		
2016–04	36.36	26.44	25.00	20.90	14.88	14.00	4.19	
2016–10	43.18	33.33	32.95	25.99	20.23	20.00	12.09	0

Addressing the challenge of updating a QA benchmark to the current schema of a dataset is a tedious, time-consuming and error-prone endeavor (see Sect. 4 for numbers). In this paper, we alleviate this problem by providing *QUANT, a framework for the intelligent creation and curation of QA benchmarks.* QUANT regards the ith version B_i of a QA benchmark as a pair (D_i, Q_i) composed of a dataset D_i and a set of questions Q_i. One of the core functions of QUANT is the generation of intelligent suggestions for benchmark curators (i.e., users annotating and improving a QA benchmark): Given a query $q_{ij} \in Q_i$ with zero results on D_k with $k > i$ (i.e., on a newer version of D_i), QUANT's suggestions aim to provide a small number of modifications to q_{ij}, such that the modified q_{ij} i.e. q'_{ij}, can be executed on D_k with non-zero results. We call this modification process for queries *porting* the queries from version i to version k. With these smart suggestions, QUANT aims (1) to ensure that queries from B_i can be reused for B_k (e.g., as training queries) and (2) to speed up the curation process as compared to the commonly used manual and text-editor-based creation and curation process [15]. To achieve this goal, QUANT (1) supports *the creation of SPARQL queries* answering a particular information need as well as the execution of said query against a predefined endpoint or knowledge base.

Moreover, QUANT checks (2) *the validity of benchmark metadata* as well as (3) the *spelling and grammatical correctness of questions* across multiple languages both in their natural-language query and keyword form.

To demonstrate the usability of QUANT and the efficiency of the smart suggestions, we performed two extensive evaluation campaigns. First, we analyzed the performance gain using QUANT over the tradition manual curation process with 3 experts. The results show that we decreased the required curation time by 91% while keeping the inter-rater agreement at 0.82. Second, we used QUANT to create a new joint benchmark from 8 QALD datasets. The smart suggestions were accepted by 83.75% of the users on average, indicating their usefulness. The novel, large and high-quality QA benchmark dataset, called QALD-9, is available at https://github.com/ag-sc/QALD/tree/master/9/data.

2 Related Work

The work on QUANT is related to three research areas, namely (1) workshops and evaluation campaigns, (2) datasets for QA over knowledge graphs and (3) curation tools for benchmarks.

2.1 Workshops and Evaluation Campaigns

A number of challenges and campaigns attracting researchers as well as industry practitioners to QA have seen the light of day over the last two decades. Since 1998, the TREC conference, especially the QA track [17], aims to provide domain-independent evaluations over large, unstructured corpora. The CLEF campaigns on information retrieval has a more than 10-year tradition in evaluating IR systems [1]. The well-known QALD (Question Answering over Linked Data) [15] campaign, currently running in its 9th instantiation, is a diverse evaluation series which include questions, of which the answer can be computed (1) based on a single RDF knowledge base, (2) by combining RDF and textual data, (3) using several knowledge bases. The benchmarks cover several domains, including encyclopedia knowledge and music. Given that this series of benchmarks is openly available and widely used ([5,7] points to 30 systems, which were evaluated using QALD), we will use the QALD datasets to evaluate QUANT.

2.2 QA over Knowledge Graphs

Other QA datasets emerged apart from the above-mentioned challenges. LCQuAD [13] is one of the largest QA over knowledge bases benchmarks with 5000 questions and their corresponding SPARQL queries over the 2016-04 version of DBpedia.[1] It also provides a framework for generating natural language questions and their corresponding SPARQL queries, minimizing the domain expert intervention. However, these questions are often grammatically incorrect and

[1] http://dbpedia.org.

require manual paraphrasing. Out of the 5000 LCQuAD SPARQL queries, 2570 queries could not be answered by the 2016-10 DBpedia version and interestingly, 456 queries were not answered by the 2016-04 version. We performed this evaluation before LCQuAD was updated.[2] Free917 [3] and WebQuestions[3] are widely used in the Semantic Web as well as Deep Learning community. Cai and Yates [3] manually created the Free917 dataset consisting of 917 questions and their logical forms, tailored to around 600 Freebase properties. Berant et al. [2] generated the WebQuestions dataset by using the Google Suggest API to collect 1M questions and got a subset of them (100K) labeled on Freebase by Amazon Mechanical Turk works. Yih et al. [18] built the WebQuestionsSP dataset[4] by re-annotating the WebQuestions dataset. WebQuestionsSP, unlike its parent dataset, contains the natural language questions, their semantic parses in the form of SPARQL queries and the derived answers. For annotating the dataset with SPARQL queries, they designed a dialog-like user interface to fasten the process which is unfortunately no longer available.

2.3 Curation Tools for Benchmarks

Since both manual curation and crowd-sourcing for benchmark creation are tedious and time-consuming tasks, there is a need for tools that speed up the process while reducing annotation errors. Jha et al. [8] built Eaglet, a semi-automatic benchmark curation tool for named entity recognition and entity linking (NER/EL). The framework checks for anomalies in a gold standard, based on the rules derived from the existing gold standards for annotating documents for NER/EL. Duan et al. [6] introduced an RDF storage benchmark generator to convert any dataset into a benchmark dataset (to reduce the gap between real and benchmark RDF data) for evaluating the performance of RDF stores, by formulating the benchmark generation problem as an integer programming problem. It is capable of generating data that resembles the characteristics (structuredness, size, and content) of real datasets with user-specified data properties. Lance [11] is a domain-independent, generic benchmark generator for Instance Matching systems; supports semantics-aware transformations with varying degrees of difficulty and creates a weighted gold standard for a better evaluation of the performance of instance matching tools. The interface accepts user-provided specifications to generate a benchmark. All the above-mentioned tools are similar to QUANT in the sense that they make benchmark generation easier for end users and employ strategies derived from an analysis on previous gold standards to improve the quality of the resulting dataset. However, to the best of our knowledge, there is no tool similar to QUANT in the domain of QA over knowledge bases.

[2] http://lc-quad.sda.tech/.

[3] https://goo.gl/93iqgC.

[4] http://aka.ms/WebQSP.

3 Approach

3.1 Architecture and Workflow

QUANT has a modular design comprising (1) a preprocessing module to eliminate duplicates in case several datasets get loaded, (2) a machine translation module to automatically translate text into 10 languages, (3) a keyword generation module to make the QA datasets suitable even for keyword-based information retrieval evaluations, and finally (4) a curation module to serve smart suggestions as can be seen in Fig. 1.

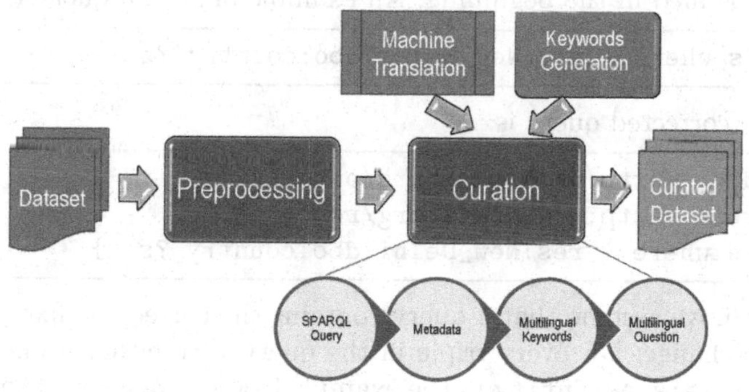

Fig. 1. QUANT's modular architecture

A curation process consists of (a) a user logging into QUANT, (b) determining an endpoint URI and version for the target knowledge base, (c) uploading a (QALD-JSON formatted) dataset. A user can then either d) create, (e) delete or (f) curate questions using smart suggestions. Finally, a user can export the curated dataset into the widely accepted QALD-JSON format [16]. Examples of a dataset formatted using QALD-JSON are available herein.[5]

3.2 Smart Suggestions

The most distinctive features of QUANT which enhance the overall curation productivity are smart suggestions for every attribute (SPARQL query or metadata) in case they contain a wrong value. That is, the system automatically detects the presence of potentially incorrect entries and offers hints pertaining to how to correct them. In the subsequent paragraphs, we explain how we provide smart suggestions for (a) question to SPARQL mappings as well as for (b) metadata attributes, and (c) question or keyword translations.

[5] https://github.com/ag-sc/QALD/tree/master/9/data.

SPARQL Suggestion. There can be various reasons for a SPARQL query (S) that worked on a previous version of the knowledge base to not work against another version or another endpoint. If QUANT is not able to fetch results from the current SPARQL endpoint, it activates the SPARQL Correction and Suggestion curation module. QUANT either suggests a new SPARQL query or renders the failure case if the correction module fails, to allow for a manual curation by the user. The cases that we applied for SPARQL Correction have been described below.

- Missing prefixes: QUANT first checks whether the query (S) fails due to missing prefixes. We call a prefix missing if it has been used in the query but not been defined in the beginning. An example of such a query is,

```
select ?s where { res:New_Delhi dbo:country ?s .}
```

  where the corrected query is:

```
PREFIX dbo: <http://dbpedia.org/ontology/>
PREFIX res: <http://dbpedia.org/resource/>
select ?s where { res:New_Delhi dbo:country ?s .}
```

  Henceforth, we assume that a query contains the correct prefixes.
- Predicate change: For every triple in the query with either a known subject or object (`pre:knownEntity` in the example below), we check if the predicate changed in the underlying knowledge base. The original predicate is preserved and a new SPARQL query (S') is formed to search for all the predicates that are associated with either the known subject or the known object. However, if in a SPARQL triple, both subject and object are unknown, then all previous triples (if present) (`prevSubject prevPredicate prevObject.`) are added to the new SPARQL query (S'). That is, if the triple being checked is of the form `?s pre:Predicate ?o` and there exists a triple preceding it, that provides the value for either the unknown subject (`?s`) or the unknown object (`?o`) , then in the new SPARQL query (S'), the previous triple is used to limit the search space for predicate testing. The new SPARQL query (S') can have one of the following forms.
  First form:

```
select ?p where { pre:knownEntity ?p ?o }
```

  Second Form:

```
select ?p where { ?s ?p pre:knownEntity }
```

  Third Form:

```
select ?p where { ?unknownSubj prevPredicate prevObject. ?
    ↪ unknownSubj ?p ?o.} or
select ?p where { prevSubject prevPredicate ?unknownObj. ?s ?p
    ↪ ?unknownObj.} or
```

```
select ?p where { ?unknownSubj prevPredicate prevObject. ?s ?p
    ↪ ?unknownSubj.} or
select ?p where { prevSubject prevPredicate ?unknownObj. ?
    ↪ unknownObj ?p ?o.}
```

All the resulting predicates that match or contain the original predicate's label are stored. By replacing the original predicate with each of these stored predicates in the original SPARQL query, we check if the query produces non-zero results. If it works, we suggest this newly formed query to the user. Note, if we need to apply the third case, it is a match against all predicates in the knowledge base that arise from the result of the previous triple(s).

- Predicate Missing: If none of the resulting predicates match or do not contain the original predicate's label, the user is informed about the missing predicate in the triple for manual curation.
- Entity Change: Each known entity (subject or object) in the triple is checked in the knowledge base. In DBpedia, if the entity is not found and belongs to a YAGO class, we append 'Wikicat' (which is a YAGO-specific update on DBpedia's later versions) at the beginning of the entity label and check again. If this new YAGO class is present in the knowledge base, we check if the SPARQL query works with it and suggest it to the user, if it does. If the missing entity is not a YAGO class, we check if there is a redirection on DBpedia for this entity by using the following SPARQL query:

```
select ?redirect where
{ <entityToBeChecked> dbo:wikiPageRedirects ?redirect. }
```

  If a redirect is found, the updated SPARQL query is tested against the endpoint and suggested to the user, if it returns an answer. Note, we were aware that this method is highly tailored towards DBpedia but can be adapted to any Linked Data knowledge graph using standard attributes such as `owl:sameAs` and `skos:related`.
- Entity Missing: The user is informed about the missing entity in the triple if the procedures to find an alternative entity fails.

If there are no suggestions generated after performing the checks above, QUANT permutes the order of the triple patterns within the conjunctive clauses to which they belong and reruns the SPARQL correction pipeline. While the order of the triple patterns in such clauses does not matter, it does affect the search space when we test for entities and predicates. Hence, by changing the order of triples, we can either narrow down or broaden the search space and increase the probability of correcting the SPARQL query and returning a suggestion.

The following examples depict SPARQL suggestions or messages returned by QUANT when it receives an outdated query.

- Entity change:
  Degraded SPARQL query:

```
SELECT ?uri WHERE
{ ?uri rdf:type yago:CapitalsInEurope }
```

QUANT suggestion:

```
SELECT ?uri WHERE
{ ?uri rdf:type yago:WikicatCapitalsInEurope }
```

- Predicate missing:
  Degraded SPARQL query:

```
SELECT ?uri WHERE
{ ?subject rdfs:label "Tom Hanks".
?subject foaf:homepage ?uri }
```

QUANT suggestion:

```
The predicate foaf:homepage is missing in ?subject foaf:
    ↪ homepage ?uri
```

- Predicate change, Query Permutation:
  Degraded SPARQL query:

```
SELECT ?date WHERE
{ ?website rdf:type onto:Software .
?website onto:releaseDate ?date .
?website rdfs:label "DBpedia" . }
```

QUANT suggestion:

```
SELECT ?date WHERE
{ ?website rdf:type onto:Software .
?website rdfs:label "DBpedia" .
?website dbp:latestReleaseDate ?date . }
```

Metadata Suggestion. QA benchmark metadata can be used to tailor benchmarks to the needs or research directions that a QA system follows, e.g., to ignore questions which need aggregation operations or to especially focus on them [5,7]. QUANT provides formal checks for the metadata entries found in QA benchmarks.

For example, the *answer type* tag corresponds to the data type of the answer returned by the SPARQL endpoint. There are five possible data types (i.e., Boolean, Date, Number, Resource, and String). If the existing value of answer type is not suitable for the returned answer, QUANT will suggest the correct one based on a regular expression. The *aggregation* tag defines whether the SPARQL query contains one or more aggregation functions such as COUNT, SUM, AVG, MIN, MAX, SAMPLE, GROUP_CONCAT, VECTOR_AGG, and

COUNT DISTINCT.[6] If the SPARQL query contains at least one of these functions, *aggregation* must be set to true, otherwise it is set to false. QUANT detects the presence of these functions in the query and suggests the correct value. The *hybrid* metadata entry describes whether it is required to search not only the Linked Data knowledge base but also textual data to produce an answer. The SPARQL query of a hybrid question will mostly contain the phrase `text:query` or `if:contains` in it. In this case, this attribute must be set to True. *onlydbo* is a binary flag which states whether the SPARQL query contains URIs which belong exclusively to the DBpedia namespace. QUANT examines all the URIs, both long forms and abbreviations,[7] in the SPARQL query to check if they belong to DBpedia and suggests the correct value for this field. *out-of-scope* tag denotes a SPARQL query that is not able to retrieve answers from a SPARQL endpoint or when the answers are not semantically correct. If this is the case, *out-of-scope* must be set to true.

Multilingual Questions and Keywords Suggestion. To enable multilingual QA evaluation campaigns and foster more active research in this area, QA benchmarks are often made available in several languages. However, translating queries across languages in a consistent way entails a significant amount of manual effort. In the case of missing or incomplete translations, QUANT first applies stopwords and question-word removal techniques to generate missing keywords. Here, we rely on technique similar to those implemented in FOX [12]. Secondly, our framework applies an automated machine translation tool called Translate Shell[8] to provide translation-suggestions in 10 other languages for both questions and keywords. As machine translation is not perfect, the completion of the final translation remains the curator's task.

Figure 2 shows a screenshot of the framework which displays curation process.

4 Evaluation

Our evaluation had three goals: (1) compare the curation time using QUANT with manual curation time, (2) investigate the effectiveness of smart suggestions, and (3) determine how capable QUANT is in providing a high-quality benchmark dataset.

4.1 Efficiency Evaluation

First, we analyzed the performance gain using QUANT versus a manual curation. Our annotators were three graduate CS students with a good working knowledge of Linked Data. To avoid any inherent bias, the three graduate students

[6] https://www.w3.org/TR/sparql11-query/#Aggregates.
[7] https://www.w3.org/TR/2013/REC-sparql11-query-20130321/#sparqlSyntax.
[8] https://www.soimort.org/translate-shell/.

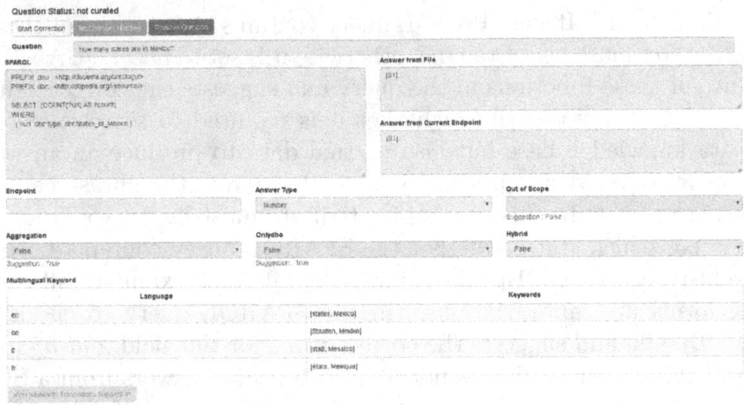

Fig. 2. Screenshot of QUANT's curation process

worked sequentially and without any prior knowledge of the data. They had to curate 50 questions manually and subsequently curate 50 different questions using QUANT. The results show that we decreased the needed time by 91% while keeping the inter-rater agreement from two of the users at 0.82, which stands for almost perfect agreement [4]. On average, users needed 23 min (between 22 and 25 min) using QUANT as opposed to 278 min (between 240 and 330 min) on average (more than 10×) using a manual curation approach.

4.2 Smart Suggestion Evaluation

Second, we used QUANT to create a new joint benchmark by joining the past 8 QALD datasets together and unifying them. We divided 10 expert users (Ph.D. students and senior researchers) into 5 pairs. The members of each pair had to curate exactly the same questions. The first four user pairs curated 130 questions, while the user pair worked on another 133 questions. This resulted in 653 questions, see also Sect. 5.

We monitored the number and types of suggestions accepted by the users throughout the curation process. Our evaluation results show that from 2380 suggestions provided by QUANT in total the acceptance rate from all the users was 81.04% on average (see Fig. 3). As seen in Fig. 4, most users accepted suggestions for the out-of-scope metadata, which, after correcting the SPARQL query, entailed a change to the questions' metadata.[9] Keyword and question translation suggestions yielded the second and third highest acceptance rates. We got higher acceptance rates (over 90%) mostly on questions from the later versions of QALD (QALD-7 and QALD-8), i.e., by users 1, 2, 9, and 10. Despite the fact that the questions are handed out to the curators in chronological order, we saw no effect of this ordering in the acceptance rate. Interestingly, the acceptance

[9] Note that if a user changed the SPARQL query manually using the hint from the suggestion, it is not added to the statistic.

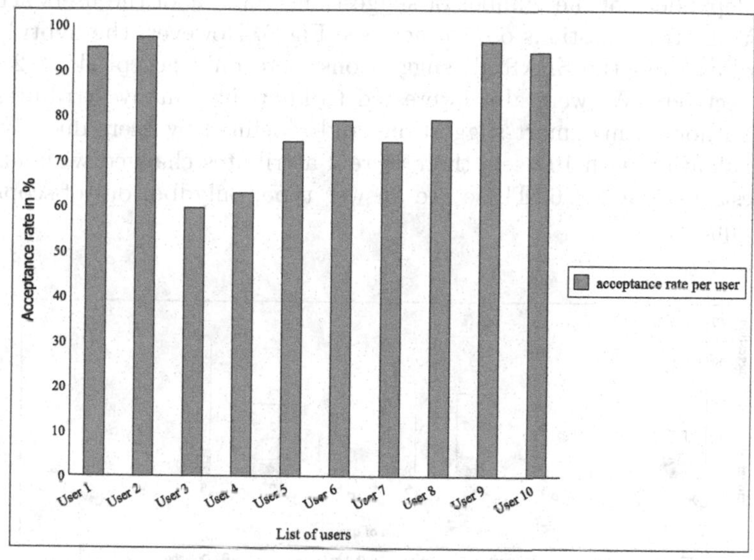

Fig. 3. Acceptance rate of all users

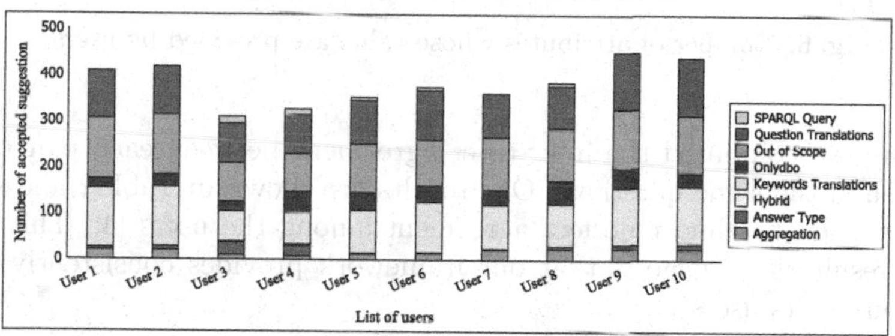

Fig. 4. Number of accepted suggestions for each attribute from all users

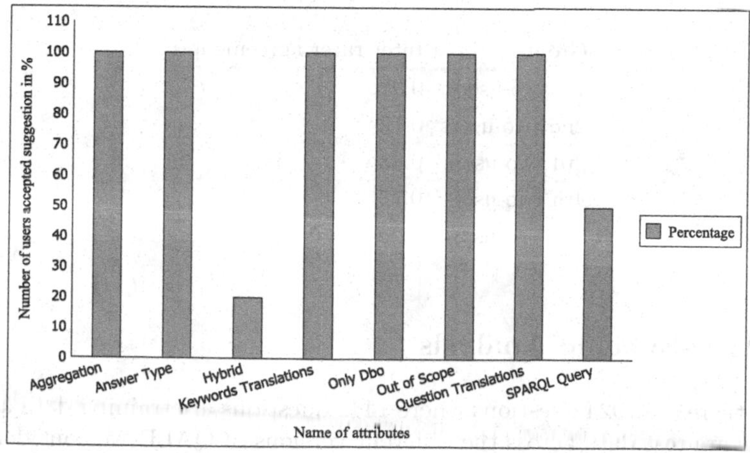

Fig. 5. Number of users accepted suggestions for each attribute

rate is independent of the number of suggestions. 83.75% of the users accepted QUANT's smart suggestions on average, see Fig. 5. However, the hybrid metadata attribute and the SPARQL suggestions were only accepted by 2 and 5 users respectively. We were also interested to know how many attributes were changed without using smart suggestions and redefined by users directly. During the evaluation with 10 users there were 4 attributes changed without using the suggestions, see Fig. 6. These are answer type, onlydbo, out-of-scope, and SPARQL query.

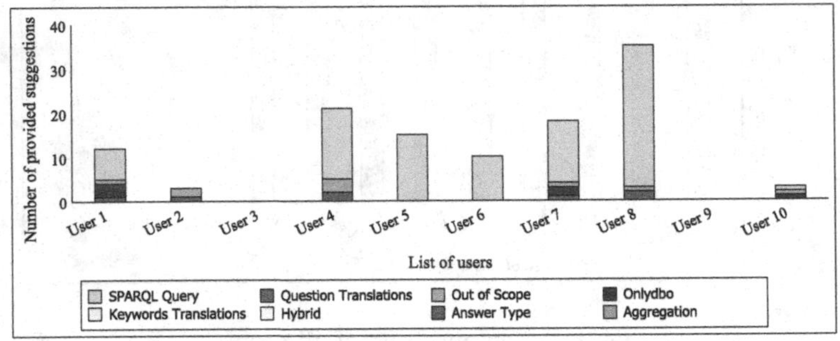

Fig. 6. Number of attributes whose value are provided by users

Finally, we computed the inter-rater agreement between each pair of users which shared the same questions. Our results are shown in Table 2 and suggest from very good to almost perfect agreement among the users [4]. This is very positive result as it suggests that our framework provides consistently helpful suggestions to its users.

Table 2. Inter-rater agreement over 5 annotator pairs curating at least 130 questions

Group	Inter-rater agreement
1st two-users	0.97
2nd two-users	0.72
3rd two-users	0.88
4th two-users	0.77
5th two-users	0.96

5 QALD-Specific Analysis

In total, there are 1924 questions where 1442 questions are training data and 482 questions are test data across the different versions of QALD we considered. So far, novel QALD train datasets were created by merging the test and training questions of the previous QALD version. The test dataset for a new QALD version is normally based on completely new questions extracted from search engine or chatbot log files [15]. It can be seen in Fig. 7 that the real distribution of QALD-train dataset in almost all versions unfortunately does not represent the ideal distribution. The change of the knowledge base contributes in the sense it causes several questions become unanswerable so that they have to be removed from dataset.

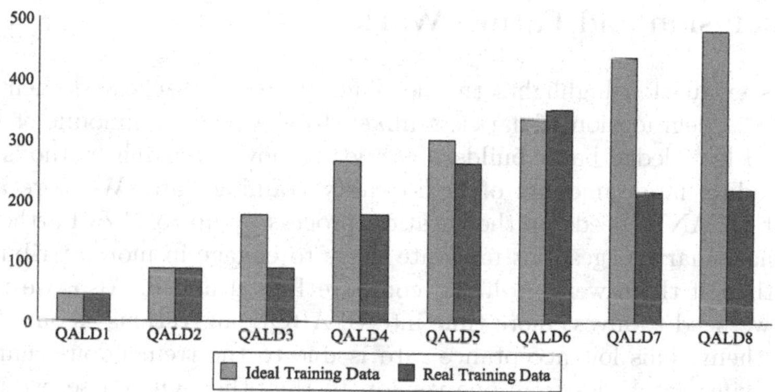

Fig. 7. Ideal and real distribution of QALD training data in all versions

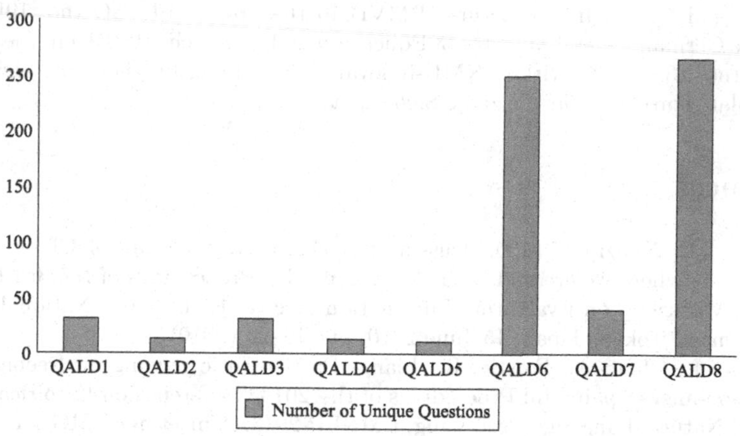

Fig. 8. Distribution of unique questions in all QALD versions

Our analysis discovered there are many exact duplicates, i.e., questions which were exactly the same in all attributes, in most QALD versions. We solved this problem by taking the one from latest version as it is more mature with respect to correctness and completeness of the question's attributes. Furthermore, there were only 655 unique questions as seen in Fig. 8. Sequentially, we removed 2 semantically similar questions so that finally we have 653 questions in total.

After applying the smart suggestions via 10 expert users, QUANT was able to produce a QALD-JSON formatted dataset of 558 total benchmark questions, increasing the size of QALD compared to QALD-8 by 110.6%. This dataset forms the QALD-9 dataset [10]. In particular, questions previously marked as out-of-scope in past challenges were curated such that they are now a valid question, and are thus treated as novel questions in this new QALD dataset.

6 Conclusion and Future Work

QUANT's evaluation highlights the need for better datasets and their maintenance. The degradation of datasets linked to the growing amount of Linked Data-based knowledge bases builds a barrier to novel research methods which are demanding large amounts of high-quality training data. We were able to show that QUANT speeds up the curation process by up to 91%. Furthermore, we saw that smart suggestions motivate users to engage in more attribute corrections than if there were no hints, compare Figs. 4 and 6. Also, we pointed out that we need to invest more time into SPARQL suggestions as only 5 users accepted them. This low acceptance rate is due to the tremendous changes in the underlying ontologies from one version to the other. Of course, we plan to support more file formats based on our internal library.[10]

Acknowledgments. This work was supported by the German Federal Ministry of Transport and Digital Infrastructure (BMVI) in the project LIMBO (no. 19F2029I) and by the German Federal Ministry of Education and Research (BMBF) in the project SOLIDE (no. 13N14456) within 'KMU-innovativ: Forschung für die zivile Sicherheit' in particular 'Forschung für die zivile Sicherheit'.

References

1. Agosti, M., Nunzio, G.M.D., Dussin, M., Ferro, N.: 10 years of CLEF data in DIRECT: where we are and where we can go. In: Proceedings of the 3rd International Workshop on Evaluating Information Access, EVIA 2010, National Center of Sciences, Tokyo, Japan, 15 June 2010, pp. 16–24 (2010)
2. Berant, J., Chou, A., Frostig, R., Liang, P.: Semantic parsing on freebase from question-answer pairs. In: Proceedings of the 2013 Conference on Empirical Methods in Natural Language Processing, EMNLP 2013, A meeting of SIGDAT, a Special Interest Group of the ACL, Grand Hyatt Seattle, Seattle, Washington, USA, 18–21 October 2013, pp. 1533–1544 (2013)
3. Cai, Q., Yates, A.: Large-scale semantic parsing via schema matching and lexicon extension. In: ACL 2013, Volume 1: Long Papers, Sofia, Bulgaria, 4–9 August 2013, pp. 423–433 (2013)
4. Chaturvedi, S.R.B.H.: Evaluation of inter-rater agreement and inter-rater reliability for observational data: an overview of concepts and methods. J. Indian Acad. Appl. Psychol. **41**(3), 20–27 (2015)

[10] https://github.com/dice-group/QUANT.

5. Diefenbach, D., López, V., Singh, K.D., Maret, P.: Core techniques of question answering systems over knowledge bases: a survey. Knowl. Inf. Syst. **55**(3), 529–569 (2018)
6. Duan, S., Kementsietsidis, A., Srinivas, K., Udrea, O.: Apples and oranges: a comparison of RDF benchmarks and real RDF datasets. In: Proceedings of the ACM SIGMOD International Conference on Management of Data, SIGMOD 2011, Athens, Greece, 12–16 June 2011, pp. 145–156 (2011)
7. Höffner, K., Walter, S., Marx, E., Usbeck, R., Lehmann, J., Ngomo, A.N.: Survey on challenges of question answering in the semantic web. Semant. Web **8**(6), 895–920 (2017)
8. Jha, K., Röder, M., Ngonga Ngomo, A.-C.: All that glitters is not gold – rule-based curation of reference datasets for named entity recognition and entity linking. In: Blomqvist, E., Maynard, D., Gangemi, A., Hoekstra, R., Hitzler, P., Hartig, O. (eds.) ESWC 2017. LNCS, vol. 10249, pp. 305–320. Springer, Cham (2017). https://doi.org/10.1007/978-3-319-58068-5_19
9. Malyshev, S., Krötzsch, M., González, L., Gonsior, J., Bielefeldt, A.: Getting the most out of wikidata: semantic technology usage in Wikipedia's knowledge graph. In: Vrandečić, D., et al. (eds.) ISWC 2018. LNCS, vol. 11137, pp. 376–394. Springer, Cham (2018). https://doi.org/10.1007/978-3-030-00668-6_23
10. Usbeck, R., Gusmita, R.H., Ngomo, A.C.N., Saleem, M.: 9th challenge on question answering over linked data (QALD-9). In: Semdeep/NLIWoD@ ISWC, pp. 58–64 (2018)
11. Saveta, T., Daskalaki, E. Flouris, G., Fundulaki, I., Ngomo, A.N.: LANCE: a generic benchmark generator for linked data. In: Proceedings of the ISWC 2015 Posters and Demonstrations Track co-located with the 14th International Semantic Web Conference (ISWC 2015), Bethlehem, PA, USA, 11 October 2015 (2015)
12. Speck, R., Ngomo, A.N.: Ensemble learning of named entity recognition algorithms using multilayer perceptron for the multilingual web of data. In: Corcho, Ó., Janowicz, K., Rizzo, G., Tiddi, I., Garijo, D. (eds.) K-CAP 2017, pp. 26:1–26:4. ACM (2017)
13. Trivedi, P., Maheshwari, G., Dubey, M., Lehmann, J.: LC-QuAD: a corpus for complex question answering over knowledge graphs. In: d'Amato, C., et al. (eds.) ISWC 2017. LNCS, vol. 10588, pp. 210–218. Springer, Cham (2017). https://doi.org/10.1007/978-3-319-68204-4_22
14. Unger, C., Ngomo, A.-C.N., Cabrio, E.: 6th open challenge on question answering over linked data (QALD-6). In: Sack, H., Dietze, S., Tordai, A., Lange, C. (eds.) SemWebEval 2016. CCIS, vol. 641, pp. 171–177. Springer, Cham (2016). https://doi.org/10.1007/978-3-319-46565-4_13
15. Usbeck, R., Ngomo, A.-C.N., Haarmann, B., Krithara, A., Röder, M., Napolitano, G.: 7th open challenge on question answering over linked data (QALD-7). In: Dragoni, M., Solanki, M., Blomqvist, E. (eds.) SemWebEval 2017. CCIS, vol. 769, pp. 59–69. Springer, Cham (2017). https://doi.org/10.1007/978-3-319-69146-6_6
16. Usbeck, R., et al.: Benchmarking question answering systems. Semant. Web J. **10**(2), 293–304 (2018)
17. Voorhees, E.M., et al.: The TREC-8 question answering track report. TREC **99**, 77–82 (1999)
18. Yih, W., Richardson, M., Meek, C., Chang, M., Suh, J.: The value of semantic parse labeling for knowledge base question answering. In Proceedings of the 54th Annual Meeting of the Association for Computational Linguistics, ACL 2016, Volume 2: Short Papers, Berlin, Germany, 7–12 August 2016 (2016)

Simple-ML: Towards a Framework for Semantic Data Analytics Workflows

Simon Gottschalk[1(✉)], Nicolas Tempelmeier[1], Günter Kniesel[2], Vasileios Iosifidis[1], Besnik Fetahu[1], and Elena Demidova[1]

[1] L3S Research Center, Leibniz Universität Hannover, Hanover, Germany
{gottschalk,tempelmeier,iosifidis,fetahu,demidova}@L3S.de
[2] Smart Data Analytics Group (SDA), Universität Bonn, Bonn, Germany
guenter.kniesel@uni-bonn.de

Abstract. In this paper we present the Simple-ML framework that we develop to support efficient configuration, robustness and reusability of data analytics workflows through the adoption of semantic technologies. We present semantic data models that lay the foundation for the framework development and discuss the data analytics workflows based on these models. Furthermore, we present an example instantiation of the Simple-ML data models for a real-world use case in the mobility domain.

1 Introduction

The creation of a *Data Analytics Workflow* (DAW) demands significant data science expertise. This expertise is required to integrate data from heterogeneous sources, to extract features for *machine learning* (ML) tasks, to configure the DAW and to optimize its parameters. The Simple-ML framework, which we currently develop to address these challenges, aims to enable a robust, efficient and reusable DAW configuration through seamless integration of semantic information in all typical DAW components, making it a *Semantic Data Analytics Workflow* (SDAW). The adoption of semantic information, such as a domain model and semantic dataset profiles, substantially differentiates Simple-ML from existing data science frameworks such as RapidMiner or Microsoft Azure.

In this paper we present Simple-ML and illustrate its adoption to data analytics for urban mobility. Popular problems in this domain include short-term road traffic forecasting [5], the prediction of congestion patterns [7] and impact prediction of planned special events [8]. The corresponding SDAWs require a variety of heterogeneous data sources, including but not limited to traffic and mobility data streams, map data (e.g. OpenStreetMap), knowledge graphs containing events and spatial entities (e.g. EventKG [3] and Wikidata), as well as traffic warnings, accidents, weather conditions and event calendars [5,8].

Our contributions are as follows: (i) We propose the Simple-ML framework for SDAWs: a semantic-driven approach that aims at increasing the efficiency of the workflow configuration, as well as robustness and reusability of DAWs using semantic technologies. (ii) We introduce a domain-specific semantic data model

M. Acosta et al. (Eds.): SEMANTiCS 2019, LNCS 11702, pp. 359–366, 2019.
https://doi.org/10.1007/978-3-030-33220-4_26

that provides semantic descriptions of the application domain and domain-specific relevant datasets (i.e. dataset profiles). (iii) We illustrate an application of the Simple-ML framework to a real-world use case in the mobility domain.

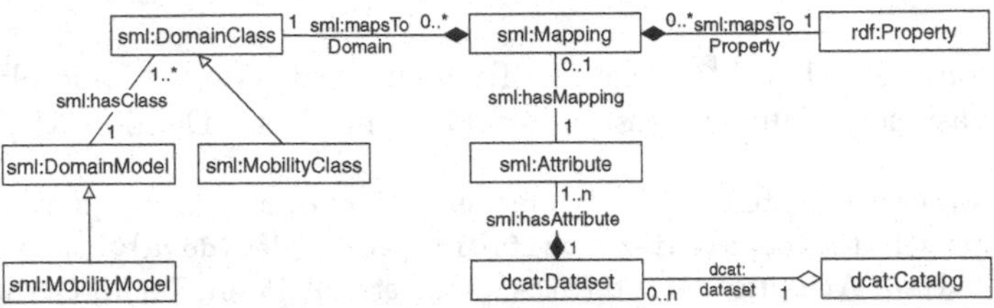

Fig. 1. An UML class diagram illustrating the Simple-ML domain model, the data catalog and a partial instantiation of the domain model in the mobility domain.

2 Semantic Models for SDAWs

The goals of Simple-ML are realized through a domain model (Fig. 1), semantic dataset profiles and the SDAW. We conduct the modeling in RDF[1] reusing existing vocabularies (e.g. `dcat`[2]), where possible. The terms specific to Simple-ML are defined in the Simple-ML vocabulary, denoted using the `sml` prefix[3].

Domain Model: In Simple-ML, the *domain model* describes relevant concepts, their properties and relations in the specific application domain. The class `sml:DomainModel` represents the model of an application domain. The domain-specific concepts are modeled as instances of the class `sml:DomainClass`.

Dataset Profiles: *A dataset profile* is a formal representation of dataset characteristics (features). *A dataset profile feature* is a dataset characteristic. Such features can belong to general, qualitative, provenance, statistical, licensing and dynamics categories [1]. In Simple-ML, the goal of the dataset profiles is to define dataset characteristics required to facilitate SDAWs, including information required for data materialization.

Dataset profile: A dataset profile is modeled as an instance of `dcat:Dataset`. General dataset profile features as well as provenance and licensing features are described using the DCMI Vocabulary (`dcterms`) Statistical dataset profile features (e.g. the number of instances) can be provided at the dataset and the attribute levels.

Dataset attributes: The attributes of the `dcat:Dataset` are modeled as instances of `sml:Attribute`. An attribute is described through its statistical characteristics at the instance level (e.g. the mean value `sml:meanValue`), along with the access

[1] Resource Description Framework (RDF): https://www.w3.org/RDF/.
[2] Data Catalog Vocabulary (DCAT): https://www.w3.org/TR/vocab-dcat/.
[3] The list of the adopted namespaces and the data catalog are available online: https://simple-ml.de/index.php/data-catalog/.

information to the underlying data source (e.g. the column name in a relational database) to facilitate data access and materialization.

Dataset access: Simple-ML supports access to datasets through dedicated attributes that represent physical storage location and data format (e.g. `sml:fileLocation` and `csvw:separator`). Currently, relational databases (`sml:Database`) and text files (`sml:TextFile`) are supported.

Mapping between the Dataset Profile and the Domain Model: Dataset attributes are mapped to the concepts in the domain model (`sml:DomainClass`) through the `sml:Mapping` class, as illustrated in Fig. 1. This mapping adds domain-specific semantic description to the dataset attributes and facilitates their use in the SDAWs. The class `sml:Mapping` provides two properties: `sml:mapsToProperty` to map a dataset attribute to a property in the domain model, and `sml:mapsToDomain` to specify the `rdfs:domain` of this property, which is an instance of `sml:DomainClass`.

Data Catalog: Dataset profiles are organized in a domain-specific data catalog. The extensible Simple-ML data catalog is modeled as an instance of `dcat:Catalog`. The data catalog schema including representations of dataset profiles and the mapping to the domain model is illustrated in Fig. 2.

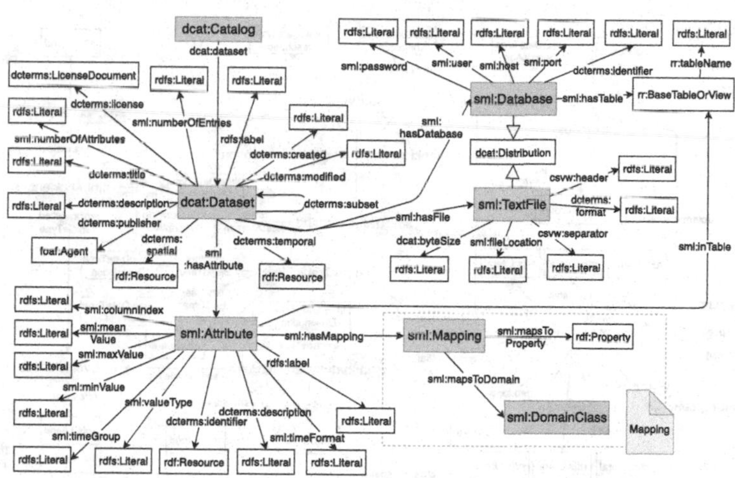

Fig. 2. The data catalog schema based on the `dcat` vocabulary. Arrows with an open head denote the `rdfs:subClassOf` properties. Regular arrows denote the `rdfs:domain` and `rdfs:range` restrictions. Blue boxes denote the key `dcat` and `sml` classes. (Color figure online)

3 Semantic Data Analytics Workflow (SDAW)

Figure 3 depicts an overview of a *Semantic Data Analytics Workflow* (SDAW). A SDAW consists of several steps discussed in the following.

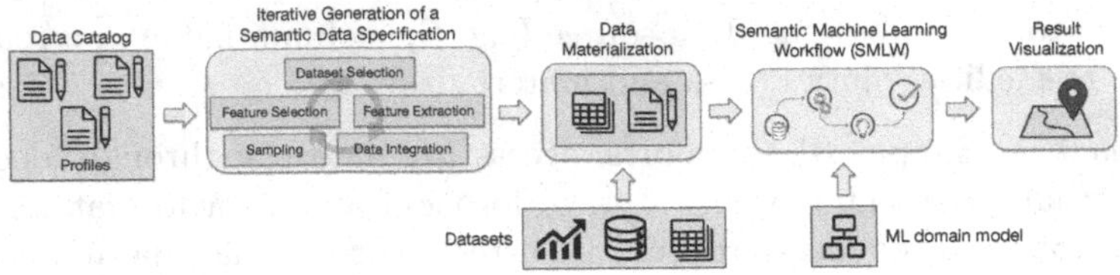

Fig. 3. An overview of the Simple-ML Semantic Data Analytics Workflow (SDAW).

Iterative Generation of a Semantic Data Specification: In this first step, the user defines the semantic specification of the data to be used in the workflow. The input in this step is the data catalog. The specification is defined through the selection of the operations to be applied to the dataset(s) in the data catalog and their attributes. Possible operations include dataset selection, sampling, feature selection, feature extraction and data integration. These operations can be applied iteratively in a user-defined order. The Semantic data specification is defined at the metadata level using dataset profiles and does not require any physical data access. The specification can be stored to facilitate reusability.

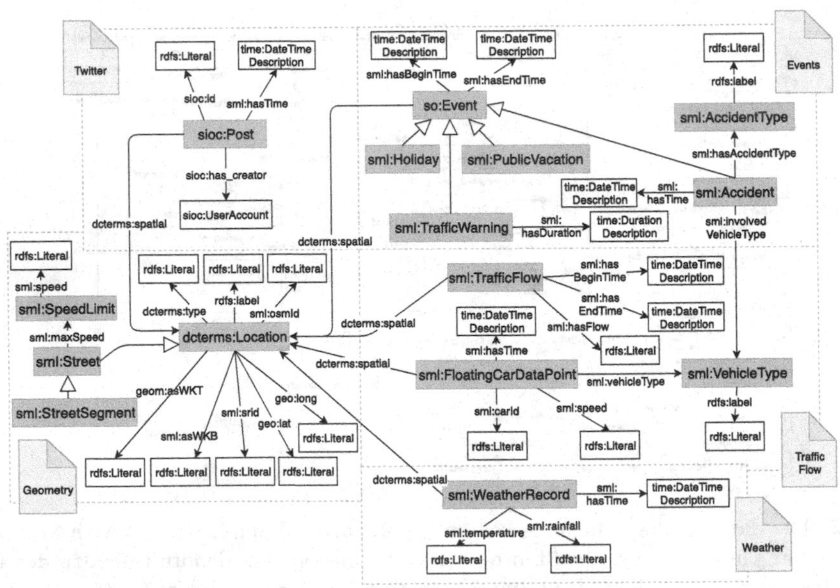

Fig. 4. An example domain model for the mobility domain. The arrows with an open head denote the `rdfs:subClassOf` properties. Regular arrows denote the `rdfs:domain` and `rdfs:range` restrictions. Classes in green boxes are sub classes of `sml:MobilityClass`.

Data Materialization: The data specification configured during the previous steps is applied to the physical datasets to materialize the integrated data.

Semantic Machine Learning Workflow (SMLW): The domain model is complemented with a ML domain model that captures the essential properties of ML concepts and their implementation in specific frameworks. A domain specific language (DSL) for SDAWs and SMLWs will include an advanced type system that will use metadata from the application domain to describe datasets and the intermediate results of data processing on one hand, and the metadata of the ML domain to describe the ML processing steps. This will enable statically checking the correctness of applying particular ML methods to particular data. To this extent, we will build upon previous approaches aiming to integrate ontologies into existing type systems (see e.g. [4]). We will go one step further, by designing a language dedicated to the data analytics and ML domain and including data models both for the data and also for the ML processes.

Result Visualization: The domain model can be used to automatically suggest suitable visualizations for specific data types.

4 Domain Model for Mobility

Figure 4 exemplifies an instantiation of the domain model in the mobility domain. This model includes the following classes:

- `sml:FloatingCarDataPoint`: A vehicle's type, position, time and speed.
- `sml:TrafficFlow`: Vehicle count statistics (e.g. from road sensors [7]).

```
sml:SimpleMLCatalog a dcat:Catalog ;
    dcat:dataset sml:FCDDataset .
sml:FCDDataset a dcat:Dataset ;
    dcterms:title "Floating Car Data" ; sml:hasFile sml:FCDDatasetFile ;
    dcterms:temporal [  so:startDate "2017-08-01"^^xsd:date ;
                        so:endDate "2017-12-31"^^xsd:date ] ;
    sml:hasAttribute sml:FCDDatasetAttribute1 .
sml:FCDDatasetFile a sml:TextFile ;
    dcterms:format "text/comma-separated-values" ; csvw:separator ";" .
sml:FCDDatasetAttribute1 a sml:Attribute ;
    rdfs:label "vehicle id"@en ; sml:columnNumber "0"^^xsd:integer ;
    sml:hasMapping [    sml:mapsToProperty sml:carId ;
                        sml:mapsToDomain sml:FloatingCarDataPoint ] .
```

Fig. 5. An excerpt of an example data catalog in the mobility domain.

```
SELECT ?columnNumber  ?attrName ?mapProperty ?mapDomain WHERE {
    sml:FCDDataset sml:hasAttribute ?attribute .
    ?attribute dcterms:identifier ?attrName .
    ?attribute sml:columnNumber ?columnNumber .
    OPTIONAL { ?attribute sml:hasMapping [
        sml:mapsToProperty ?mapProperty ; sml:mapsToDomain ?mapDomain ; ] . } }
```

Fig. 6. SPARQL query to select attributes of a given dataset (here: `sml:FCDDataset`).

- `so:Event`: Mobility-relevant events, their time and geographical location.
- `sioc:Post`: Social media posts modeled using the SIOC ontology[4].
- `sml:WeatherRecord`: Temperature and rainfall at location and time.
- `dcterms:Location`: Spatial information with geographical coordinates.
- `sml:SpeedLimit`, `sml:AccidentType`, `sml:VehicleType`: Classes that represent categorical values for speed limits, accident types and vehicle types.

These classes are sub classes of `sml:MobilityClass`, which is a sub class of `sml:DomainClass` and thus allows the use of `sml:Mapping` as shown in Fig. 2.

Figure 5 provides an excerpt of an example Simple-ML mobility data catalog.

5 Simple-ML Application to Traffic Speed Prediction

We illustrate the iterative generation of a semantic data specification for the problem of traffic speed prediction for a specific road segment at a given time.

Dataset Selection: The user selects a Floating Car Data (F) and OpenStreetMap (O) datasets. Figure 6 shows the SPARQL query to retrieve F's profile.

Data Specification: (i) *Feature Selection*: The user selects four features based on the domain model: `sml:maxSpeed`, `sml:hasTime` from (F) (class `sml:FloatingCarDataPoint`), and `rdf:type` and `sml:maxSpeed` from (O) (class `sml:StreetSegment`). (ii) *Feature Extraction*: The user selects the following temporal features that are suggested by the system: week day, hour of day from (F). (iii) *Data Integration*: A mapping between the vehicle positions in (F) and the street segment coordinates in (O) is suggested by the system and chosen by the user.

Data Materialization: Using the data specification, relevant features are materialized, with example instances shown in Table 1. The resulting data can then be used in the SMLW to train a supervised traffic speed prediction model.

Table 1. Example instances generated using the semantic data specification

FloatingCarDataPoint (F)				StreetSegment (O)	
Type	Speed	Time (day)	Time (hour)	Type	maxSpeed
1	74	Sunday	23	motorway_link	80
0	84	Sunday	16	motorway	*none*
1	17	February	8	secondary	70

[4] https://www.w3.org/Submission/sioc-spec/.

6 Related Work

Recent works [2,4,6] aim to combine semantics and ML to address a variety of real-world problems. Simple-ML goes one step further and makes use of semantics in the entire DAW. Simple-ML employs dataset profiles and domain-specific data models. The survey [1] provides a comprehensive overview of RDF dataset profiling methods, tools, vocabularies and features partially utilized by Simple-ML. We illustrate the use of Simple-ML in the mobility domain. Mobility has seen many challenges and use cases for data analytics [5,7,8]. In Simple-ML, the mobility domain is modeled in a light-weight, data-driven manner that facilitates compatibility and reusability of the SDAWs across use cases and datasets.

7 Conclusion

In this paper we presented our current development towards the Simple-ML framework. Simple-ML adopts semantic technologies to support the efficient creation, configuration and reusability of robust data analytics workflows. We illustrated an application of the framework to a real-world use case in the mobility domain.

Acknowledgements. This work was partially funded by the Federal Ministry of Education and Research (BMBF), Germany under Simple-ML (01IS18054) and Data4UrbanMobility (02K15A040).

References

1. Ellefi, M.B., et al.: RDF dataset profiling - a survey of features, methods, vocabularies and applications. Semantic Web **9**(5), 677–705 (2018)
2. Esteves, D., et al.: MEX vocabulary: a lightweight interchange format for machine learning experiments. In: Proceedings of the SEMANTiCS (2015)
3. Gottschalk, S., Demidova, E.: EventKG: a multilingual event-centric temporal knowledge graph. In: Proceedings of the ESWC (2018)
4. Hartenfels, C., Leinberger, M., Lämmel, R., Staab, S.: Type-safe programming with OWL in Semantics4J. In: Proceedings of the ISWC (2017)
5. Lv, Z., Xu, J., Zheng, K., Yin, H., Zhao, P., Zhou, X.: LC-RNN: a deep learning model for traffic speed prediction. In: Proceedings of the IJCAI 2018 (2018)
6. Merkle, N., Zander, S.: Using a semantic simulation framework for teaching machine learning agents. In: SEMANTiCS, pp. 78–89 (2018)
7. Nguyen, H., Liu, W., Chen, F.: Discovering congestion propagation patterns in spatio-temporal traffic data. IEEE Trans. Big Data **3**(2), 169–180 (2017)
8. Tempelmeier, N., Dietze, S., Demidova, E.: Crosstown traffic – supervised prediction of event impact on urban traffic. GeoInformatica (2019)

Semantics in Blockchain and Distributed Ledger Technologies

Incorporating Blockchain into RDF Store at the Lightweight Edge Devices

Anh Le-Tuan[1,3(✉)], Darshan Hingu[1], Manfred Hauswirth[1,2], and Danh Le-Phuoc[1]

[1] Open Distributed Systems, TU Berlin, Berlin, Germany
anh.letuan@tu-berlin.de
[2] Fraunhofer Institute for Open Communication Systems, Berlin, Germany
[3] Insight Centre for Data Analytics, NUI Galway, Galway, Ireland

Abstract. RDF stores provide a simple abstraction for publishing and querying data, that is becoming a norm in data sharing practice. They also empower the decentralised architecture of data publishing for the Web or IoT-driven systems. Such architecture shares a lot in common with blockchain infrastructure and technologies. Therefore, there are emerging interests in marrying RDF stores and blockchain to realise desirable but speculative benefits of blockchain-powered data sharing. This paper presents the first RDF store with blockchain that enables lightweight edge devices to control of the data sharing processes (personal, IoT data). Our novel approach on the deep integration of the storage design for RDF store enables the ability to enforce controlling measures on access methods and auditing policies over data elements via smart contracts before they fetched from the sources to the consumers. Our experiments show that the prototype system delivers an effective performance for a processing load of 1 billion triples on a small network of lightweight nodes which costs less than a commodity PC.

Keywords: Blockchain · Linked Data · RDF store

1 Introduction

User-generated and sensor data is being widely used by various applications to make them smarter and better. While such applications are using the data for nearly free, such consumer data from both public and private sources is incredibly valuable to corporations, marketers, investors, and individuals. For example, American companies alone are estimated to have spent over $19 billion in 2018 acquiring and analysing consumer data, according to the Interactive Advertising Bureau.[1] There are recent recurrent questions of how users can take control and make the benefit out of it. It is obvious that in order to take control

[1] https://www.iab.com/news/2018-state-of-data-report/.

A. Le-Tuan and D. Hingu—These authors Contributed equally to the work.

M. Acosta et al. (Eds.): SEMANTiCS 2019, LNCS 11702, pp. 369–375, 2019.
https://doi.org/10.1007/978-3-030-33220-4_27

of one's data, there must be an ability to accurately account for ownership, and similarly account or keep a record of all transactions, exchanges and permissions while in a secure and tamper-proof manner.

The arrival of blockchain technologies gives the promise to get your data out of a corporation's centralised database to store your own devices or your encrypted storage of your choice at the edges of networks. This will be critical in helping develop transparency and accountability in data sharing as we take ownership of our data. Blockchain provides a number of substantive benefits. It provides a layer of transparency and accountability for data ownership and transactions. It can also minimise the influence of data middlemen in any consumer data transaction while putting the data back in the hands of the consumer. This means users can regain control of who uses our data, when our data is used and our compensation for it.

In parallel, the recently emerging trend of edge computing paradigm for IoT-driven information systems makes it much more feasible to push computation and data management operations closer to the data sources. Being able to store and query data at the edges of networks offers opportunities to improve performance and to reduce network overhead, but also flexibility for the continuous integration of new IoT devices and data sources. This motivates us to build a novel distributed RDF store which leverages blockchain benefits for data publishers at the edges of networks. To the best of our knowledge, our system is the first of this kind. The system design will be presented in Sect. 2, the implementation report will be followed in Sect. 3. Our experimental results in Sect. 4 show that a small cluster of Raspberry Pis (cost less than a commodity workstation) can efficiently handle 1 billion RDF triples of IoT data.

2 System Overview

To store and to share RDF data on the edge with the guarantee of the data ownership and the compensation for shared data, we marry a distributed database system and blockchain. Confronting the decentralised edge networks, the distributed database system allows any members to share their data, resources

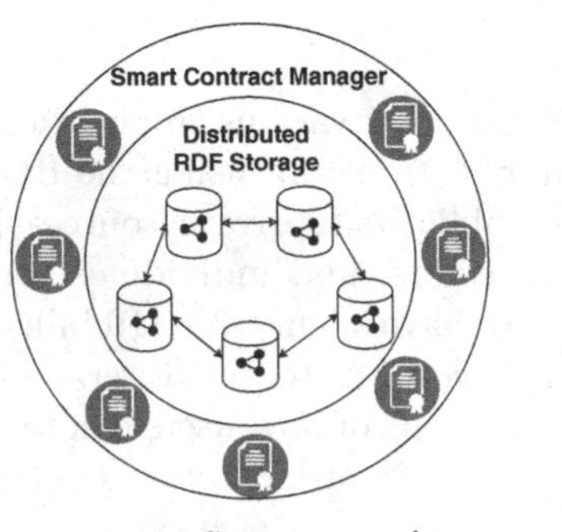

(a) System overview

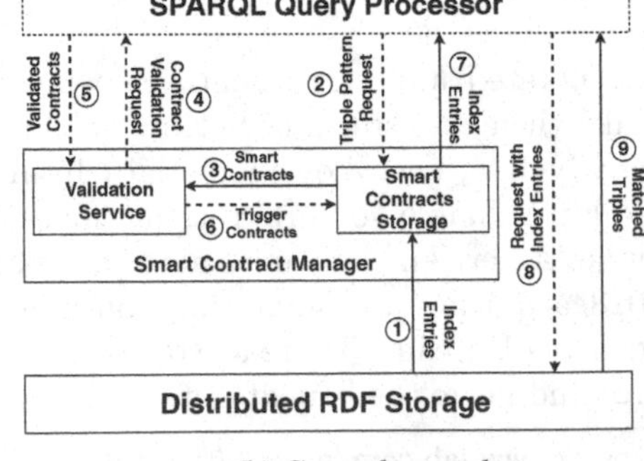

(b) General procedure

Fig. 1. System overview and general procedure

while maintaining their autonomy and independence from centralised servers. A feature of blockchain technology is the smart contract which allows the data owners to control the access to their data (e.g., who can have the access or how much to pay to gain the access).

Our system (Fig. 1a) consists of two subsystems: a *Distributed RDF Storage (DRS)* and a *Smart Contract Manager (SCM)*. The DRS takes responsibility to store RDF data among connected devices in the network physically. Meanwhile, to secure the ownership of the data, the access to the data in the distributed storage is encrypted into smart contracts which are published and managed by the SCM. The basic principle of the system is that when a provider wants to trade his/her data, she/he publishes the data partitions (e.g., a set of sensor readings) associated with smart contracts. A smart contract contains the meta information of a published data partition, for example index key, and a contract that can be used to specify terms like price scheme and access control policy on data to be fetched to clients.

Considering that to answer a SPARQL query, the SPARQL query processor performs graph pattern matching over RDF datasets. The graph matching operator executes join operations between RDF triples that match the triple query patterns. Therefore, to retrieve query pattern matched data, we organise RDF data in the similar way as RDF4Led [4] does. We store RDF triples in three storage layouts as sorted permutations of triples: SPO (Subject - Predicate - Object), POS and OSP. Each layout is a sorted list and is partitioned into chunks called data blocks. The first triple of each data block and the physical address of the data block are formed an index entry which is kept in the main memory. The triples of the index entries are the keys for searching the data blocks that potentially contain the matched triple of a query pattern. However, instead of storing the data blocks in the local file systems as in RDF4Led, we use distributed file systems to create the DRS subsystem. The distributed file systems provide scalable data distribution and sharding featured associated with distributed data structures like DHT [1]. In such data structure, each data block that is stored is mapped to a unique identifier. The identifier space is partitioned among the nodes. Each node is responsible for storing all the data blocks that are mapped to identifiers in its portion of the space. Hence, data is distributed and resource consumption is balanced among the edge nodes. Furthermore, instead of keeping the unique access identifiers of data blocks in index entries openly, we allow publishers to encrypt them into smart contracts and keep them in the *Smart Contracts Storage (SCS)* of the SCM (see Fig. 1b). In the Smart Contracts Storage, the smart contracts are kept sorted by the triple, therefore, the corresponding smart contracts that hold the query pattern matched triples can be searched as described in [4]. Finally, a data block can be fetched only when the access identifier is revealed, in consequence, only when the smart contract that holds identifier of the block is triggered.

The general workflow of the system is visualised in Fig. 1b. When a client starts sharing her/his RDF dataset, the system indexes the data, partitions the indexes into data chunks, stores the data chunks in the DRS and sends the index entries to the SCM (1). The SCM encodes the arriving index entries into smart contracts and stores these contracts in the Smart Contracts Storage. From the given triple requests (2), the SCM searches in the SCS for the contracts that hold the accesses to the requested data. Later, these contracts are sent to the *Validation Service* which developed with blockchain technology (3). The Validation Service verifies the if contracts are validated, and navigates validation requests to the SPARQL Query Processor (4). When the contracts are validated (5), the Validation Service triggers these contracts (6), returns the opened index entries with access identifiers the SPARQL Query Processor (7). With these index entries and access identifiers, the SPARQL Query Processor should be able to fetch the matched triples from the DRS to join operators (8) (9).

3 Implementation and Deployment

To implement the system, we extended the Java code base of RDF4Led [4] that allows RDF data processing tasks (e.g., parsing, indexing) to execute on the edge node. The DRS subsystem is implemented by re-engineering the Physical Layer to store the data blocks (which contain RDF molecules) in the p2p file system IPFS [1]. IPFS is a secure, high-throughput, distributed block storage model with content-addressed hyper links. It allocates a unique hash for each stored block of data. In IPFS, the data blocks are identified and retrieved by their IPFS hashes. In SCM, the SCS is stacked on top of the Buffer Layer. The smart contract and related features are implemented with Ethereum[2]. However, instead of using an in-memory caching of RDF4Led, the index entries which also keep the address of their corresponding smart contracts are stored in Redis[3]. Redis is a distributed in-memory key-value data that allows data is clustered in memory of multiple devices. When a devices join the network, it also contributes its computational

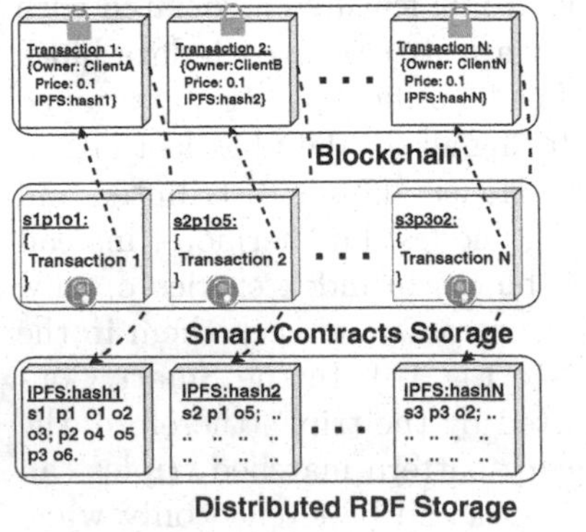

(a) Physical data organisation

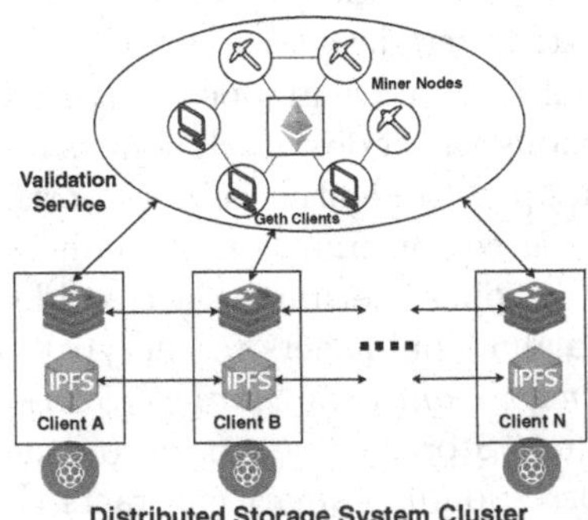

(b) System deployment schema

Fig. 2. Physical data organisation and System deployment schema

[2] https://www.ethereum.org/.
[3] https://redis.io/.

resources to the whole system. To communicate the Validation Service with the Ethereum's blockchain network, we use Web3j of Ethereum.

Figure 2a illustrates the physical data organisation of SPO index layout in our system. In the DRS layer, sorted list of triples are partitioned, compressed as molecules and stored in IPFS as byte arrays. The associated IPFS hash of RDF molecules are packed with addresses of the smart contracts. The smart contracts are stored in Ethereum blockchain and are programmed to return the stored IPFS hashes if the transactions are triggered. In the SCS, each entry contains the first triple of each molecule and its smart contract id. These entries are kept in sorted list of Redis which provides the key-range search that allows index lookup in the same fashion as in RDF4Led.

Figure 2b depicts our system's deployment strategy. The nodes are installed with IPFS and Redis which make our SCS and DRS layer respectively. A node's IPFS and Redis clubs with another node's IPFS and Redis to form a cluster respectively within the network to provide a decentralised distributed data storage. The *Validation Service* Cluster is implemented using Ethereum's Private Blockchain using Geth which in turn is configured to use Proof-of-Authority consensus mechanism. The remaining nodes are set up as full-nodes clients, which provide additional storage to the service.

4 Evaluations

This section presents our evaluation on the deployment as presented in Fig. 2b. We created a network of 15 Raspberry Pi 3 model B (ARMv7 Quad-Core 1.2 GHz CPUs, 1 GB RAM, 64 GB SD card, Raspbian OS), each node costs approximately €50. *Note that the total cost of the whole setup is less than a commodity PC.* The RDF dataset for the evaluation is generated by mapping sensor readings from NOAA[4] dataset to RDF using SSN/SOSA ontology [3]. The schema of our data set is provided a long with the implementation in our Github repository[5].

We evaluated our system with two experiments. Experiment 1 consists of two tests on two system settings. Firstly, we fixed the cluster size at 10 nodes and measured the average throughput per node when inserting more data. Secondly, we observed the increasing of the throughput when adding more node. A billion and 100 million triples dataset was used respectively in the first experiment. In Experiment 2, we measured the response time for searching the matched triples of single query patterns on 1 billion triples dataset.

Figure 3a represents the first setting's result with the accumulated throughput of a fixed number of nodes. As predicted, the throughput gradually decreases when data stored in the storage increases. After 500 million inserts, we can see a stagnant flow in the graph. The result of the accumulated throughput of a varying number of nodes in the cluster is presented in Fig. 3b. Here, we plot throughput (triples/seconds) in thousands against the number of nodes participating. It appears as the number of processing nodes in the cluster increases, the

[4] https://www.ncdc.noaa.gov/.
[5] https://github.com/anhlt18vn/Semantic2019.

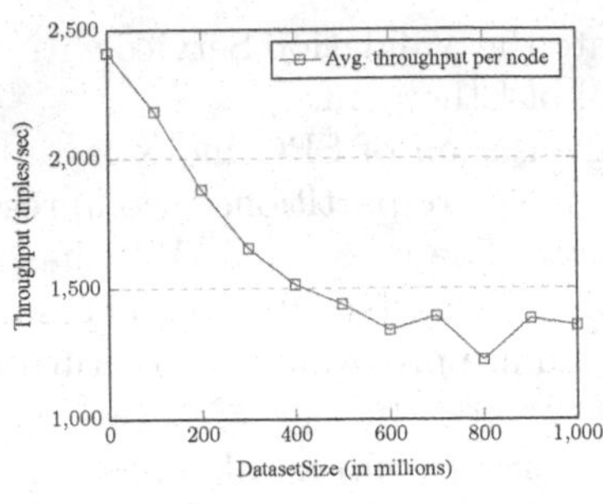

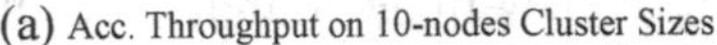

(a) Acc. Throughput on 10-nodes Cluster Sizes

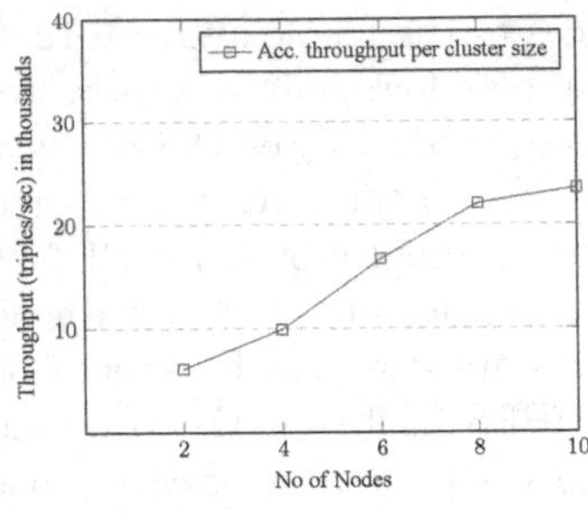

(b) Acc. Throughput on Varying Cluster Sizes

Fig. 3. Insert throughput results

throughput also increases. After reaching a peak point, the growth has minimised due to the decentralised nature of the system.

From both the tests, we can observe that the system is competent in handling a large dataset due to its decentralised ecosystem. We have also seen that the system's performance becomes stagnant after attaining peak. It is mainly because the decentralised system adheres to the network latency, which occurs due to its replication and distribution strategies. With the current architecture, the system has proven highly scalable, though it is acknowledged that there has been a trade-off in terms of performance to achieve this nature of the degree of scalability.

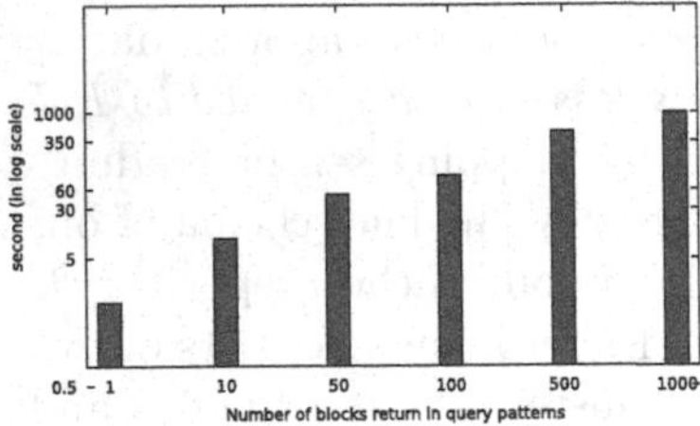

Fig. 4. Query response time

Figure 4 shows the result of experiment 2. We can see that the system deliver very good performance for the query that needs data from 1–10 blocks on the 1 billion dataset. However, the response time increases linearly to the number of fetched blocks. From our analysis, the delay is mainly contributed by the throughput/delay of processing multiple transactions on Ethereum.

5 Conclusion and Outlook

This paper presents the first implementation of a novel RDF distributed store with blockchain technology for the decentralised edge network. The experiments proved that the system can be deployed on a network of lightweight edge devices such as Raspberry Pis. With a network of fifteen nodes of Raspberry Pi, the system is able to host a dataset up to a billion RDF triples. The cost for deploying such system is quite competitive and flexible as a Pi node costs less than €50 and the number of nodes can be elastically increased or decreased at runtime. Next step, we will increase tenfold in the number of nodes to study the scalability and limitations. For the shortcomings shown in Fig. 4, the processing throughput causing long delays on the queries that use a large number of data blocks can be increased by new achievement of transaction throughput, e.g. 20 k transactions/second in [2].

Acknowledgements. This work was funded in part by the German Ministry for Education and Research as BBDC 2 - Berlin Big Data Center-Phase 2 (ref. 01IS18025A), Irish Research Council under Grant Number GOIPG/2014/917 and Marie Skodowska-Curie Programme H2020-MSCA-IF-2014 (SMARTER project) under Grant No. 661180.

References

1. Benet, J.: Ipfs - content addressed, versioned, p2p file system. arXiv:1407.3561 (2014)
2. Gorenflo, C., Lee, S., Golab, L., Keshav, S.: Fastfabric: scaling hyperledger fabric to 20,000 transactions per second. arXiv:1901.00910 (2019)
3. Haller, A., et al.: The modular SSN ontology: a joint W3C and OGC standard specifying the semantics of sensors, observations, sampling, and actuation. Semant. Web **10**(1), 9–32 (2019)
4. Le-Tuan, A., Hayes, C., Wylot, M., Le-Phuoc, D.: Rdf4led: an rdf engine for lightweight edge devices. In: IOT 2018 (2018)

Verifying the Integrity of Hyperlinked Information Using Linked Data and Smart Contracts

Christoph Braun and Tobias Käfer(✉)

Institute AIFB, Karlsruhe Institute of Technology (KIT), Karlsruhe, Germany
uvdsl@student.kit.edu, tobias.kaefer@kit.edu

Abstract. We present an approach to verify off-chained information using Linked Data, Smart Contracts, and RDF graph hashes stored on a Distributed Ledger. We use the notion of a Linked Pedigree, i.e. a decentralised dataset for storing hyperlinked information, as modelling foundation. We evaluate our approach by comparing different ways to build the Smart Contract. We develop a cost model and show, based on our implementation, that for managing multiple Linked Pedigree instances, a single larger Smart Contract is superior to multiple smaller Smart Contracts for supply chains shorter than 50 participants.

1 Introduction

Chained value-creation networks are commonplace in many industries. Consider e.g. supply chain networks in logistics or production systems, where goods and services are handed over decentrally between different independent parties to deliver goods and services to the customer. In such networks, transparency is gaining importance. Customers demand verifiable[1] information on where their food comes from (track & trace), or recall campaigns need to be organised fast and specifically. Recently, distributed ledger-based solutions have gained attention, e.g. TradeLens by IBM and Maersk for global trade networks[2]. But sharing information on a distributed ledger may not always be desirable: As in a distributed ledger, every participant stores a copy of the whole ledger, data sovereignty and privacy become an issue. Moreover, storing data on the distributed ledger is expensive, which calls for so-called "off-chaining" of data [1], i.e. storing data outside of the distributed ledger while keeping the distributed ledger in the loop by storing hashes on the ledger. For off-chaining, to not complicate matters, a uniform access mechanism would be desired. Linked Data is a

[1] To verify: "Make sure or demonstrate that (something) is true, accurate, or justified." (Oxford Living Dictionary) We assume truth of the information on the distributed ledger to be established. Then, we allow for verification that the information has not been changed.

[2] "IBM teams with Maersk on new blockchain shipping solution", https://tcrn.ch/2vRLFLT.

M. Acosta et al. (Eds.): SEMANTiCS 2019, LNCS 11702, pp. 376–390, 2019.
https://doi.org/10.1007/978-3-030-33220-4_28

light-weight standard-based way to publish data in a decentralised fashion, where access control can be easily implemented. Hence, we ask: Can we combine the verification capabilities of the distributed ledger with Linked Data management?

Transparently provided information is important, e.g. in the food sector, where society demands more transparency regarding details on products and their transportation[3]. More general, in retail, the transparency in production and transport of consumer goods and retail products is a important factor of customer decisions[4,5]. Regulation authorities discuss such product transparency and documentation to be required in the future[6]. But that information needs not just to be public. Customer trust needs to be ensured, where structural assurances [2] such as the mathematical foundations of distributed ledgers can serve as basis. Publicly shared information has high economic potential in the logistics domain, e.g. by addressing the bullwhip effect, but is hindered by the need for privacy of businesses [5,7]. Hence, a more cautious approach to share data, like disclosing data only to a selected number of persons, may unlock some of the benefits. But even if organisations are willing to share information, interoperability of the information systems is an issue [5,7,12]. Hence, the flexible data model of RDF and the standardised light-weight protocol HTTP can reduce friction. If RDF is not available yet in an organisation, lifting of existing data to semantic models has been proposed for the supply chain domain in [4].

Previous works in the intersection of Semantic Web and Distributed Ledger, e.g. at the Linked Data and Distributed Ledgers workshop series (LD-DL)[7] have not considered off-chaining of data. Previous works in off-chaining of data are often built using distributed hash tables [1], where the problem of data sovereignty arises just like with storing data on the chain.

Our approach consists in the following parts (this unique combination and 2, 4, 5, and 6 are the contributions of this paper):

1. We use Linked Data, i.e. RDF accessible using HTTP to store data off-chain in a decentralised fashion. Access control for data privacy can be layered on top, e.g. using HTTP authentication, or more recent approaches such as Web Access Control[8] or WebID+TLS[9].
2. We present a vocabulary that extends the Linked Pedigree ontology [10] to describe a product's handover history and the Ethereum Ontology[10] to describe an Ethereum distributed ledger.

[3] https://www.forbes.com/sites/gmoanswers/2015/11/30/transparency-no-longer-optional/.
[4] https://www.labelinsight.com/hubfs/Studies%20and%20Reports/2016-LI-Food-Revolution-Study.pdf.
[5] https://www.pwc.de/de/handel-und-konsumguter/assets/bevoelkerungsbefragung-rueckverfolgbarkeit-als-kaufargument.pdf.
[6] https://www.euractiv.com/section/agriculture-food/news/food-safety-midnight-deal-for-revised-general-food-law.
[7] Browse with http://events.linkeddata.org/ldow-lddl/ as entry point.
[8] https://www.w3.org/wiki/WebAccessControl.
[9] https://www.w3.org/2005/Incubator/webid/spec/tls/.
[10] http://ethon.consensys.net/.

3. We use the RDF graph hashing approach of [3] to connect the off-chained data with the distributed ledger.
4. We present a link-traversal based querying approach for verifying data on a Linked Pedigree off-chain.
5. We present a Smart Contract, i.e. code that can be executed on the Distributed Ledger, for verifying data using the Distributed Ledger.
6. We present a protocol to apply all of the above.

The paper is structured as follows:First, we survey related work (Sect. 2). Next, we present an example (Sect. 3), which also introduces the protocol. Subsequently, we present the foundational definitions, on which we base our approach (Sect. 4). Then, we describe the components of our approach (Sect. 5), that is the vocabulary, the smart contract, and the graph traversal. We next evaluate our approach (Sect. 6) by developing a cost model, which we instantiate using an implementation. We then discuss our findings (Sect. 7). Last, we conclude (Sect. 8).

2 Related Work

In the intersection of supply chain and distributed ledger, there are two major initiatives started in collaboration with IBM. Both initiatives are based on the distributed ledger Hyperledger: TradeLens for global freight companies, and FoodTrust for agricultural goods. Both approaches have similar characteristics: All information (e.g. document filings, supply chain events, authority approval status, ...) is stored on the distributed ledger. As all nodes that are part of the distributed ledger have a full copy of the ledger, this hints at scalability issues. Both solutions support access rights to this data on the ledger. TradeLens is citing data interoperability as a challenge. While they incrementally move to UN's CEFACT vocabulary[11], our approach allows for using semantic technologies to achieve data interoperability using mappings between schemas. Similarly, provenance.org, an online service for track and trace of goods using a distributed ledger, stores all data on the ledger.

In the intersection of semantic technologies and distributed ledgers, different ontologies have been proposed to describe a distributed ledger: There is, e.g. GraphChain [11], BLONDiE[12], and EthOn[13]. Our approach uses parts of EthOn. Besides defining an ontology, the GraphChain [11] approach also allows to distribute RDF data onto a distributed ledger. Our approach however requires data to be provided as Linked Data, irrespective of the back-end.

In the intersection of semantic technologies and supply chain, the Linked Pedigree approach has been developed [10]. Linked Pedigrees are RDF graphs to describe trails of ownership of goods provided via HTTP. Moreover, the paper contains a protocol for using the thus described data in a supply chain.

---

[11] https://blog.tradelens.comascomm/news/why-interoperability-matters/.
[12] https://github.com/hedugaro/Blondie.
[13] http://ethon.consensys.net/.

Our approach adds verification using distributed ledger technologies and hashing to Linked Pedigrees.

3 Example

We next describe an example to illustrate our approach. Imagine the following three steps in a simple supply chain:

Item Creation: A fisherman creates an item, i.e. some fish.
Item Handover: The fish is handed over between supply chain partners, e.g. from the fisherman to a trucker to a local supermarket to the consumer.
Item Verification: At the store, the consumer verifies information about the fish as a decision-making support for the purchase. Verification could also be performed during each handover.

For the illustration, we look at the information transferred during these three steps: Within the first two steps, i.e. item creation and item handover, the item's physical history is described and published as Linked Data. The third step of item verification solely corresponds to the verification of that published information, and does not involve checking on the physical item itself. For brevity of the example, we leave out verification during the handover steps. The overall protocol is depicted in Fig. 1. The top left group starting with "create item" in bold relates to the item creation. The next group starting with "transport item" relates to the handover. With "store item", the step for verifying the data starts, ending in the actual purchase.

3.1 Item Creation

The fisherman creates an supply chain item by catching the fish. They record information on the item and the catching process, e.g. fishing ground and time, builds an RDF graph from the information, and publishes the graph via HTTP. Thus, the initial part of the Linked Pedigree on the fish is formed. From this point, the creation procedure is the same as for any item handover in the supply chain.

3.2 Item Handover

When the fish is handed over, e.g. from the fisherman to the trucker that carries the fish to the market, an RDF graph with information on the hand over is created and stored in the Linked Data store of choice of the party that owns the fish before the hand-over. The information is linked to the RDF graph describing the previous Linked Pedigree part, which contains an event that concerns this fish. Thus, we form a hyperlinked graph of the fish's product trail. Additional information may be included *ad libitum* in each step, e.g. information on the item's creation. For later verification purposes, a hash of the information is put into the Distributed Ledger using a Smart Contract.

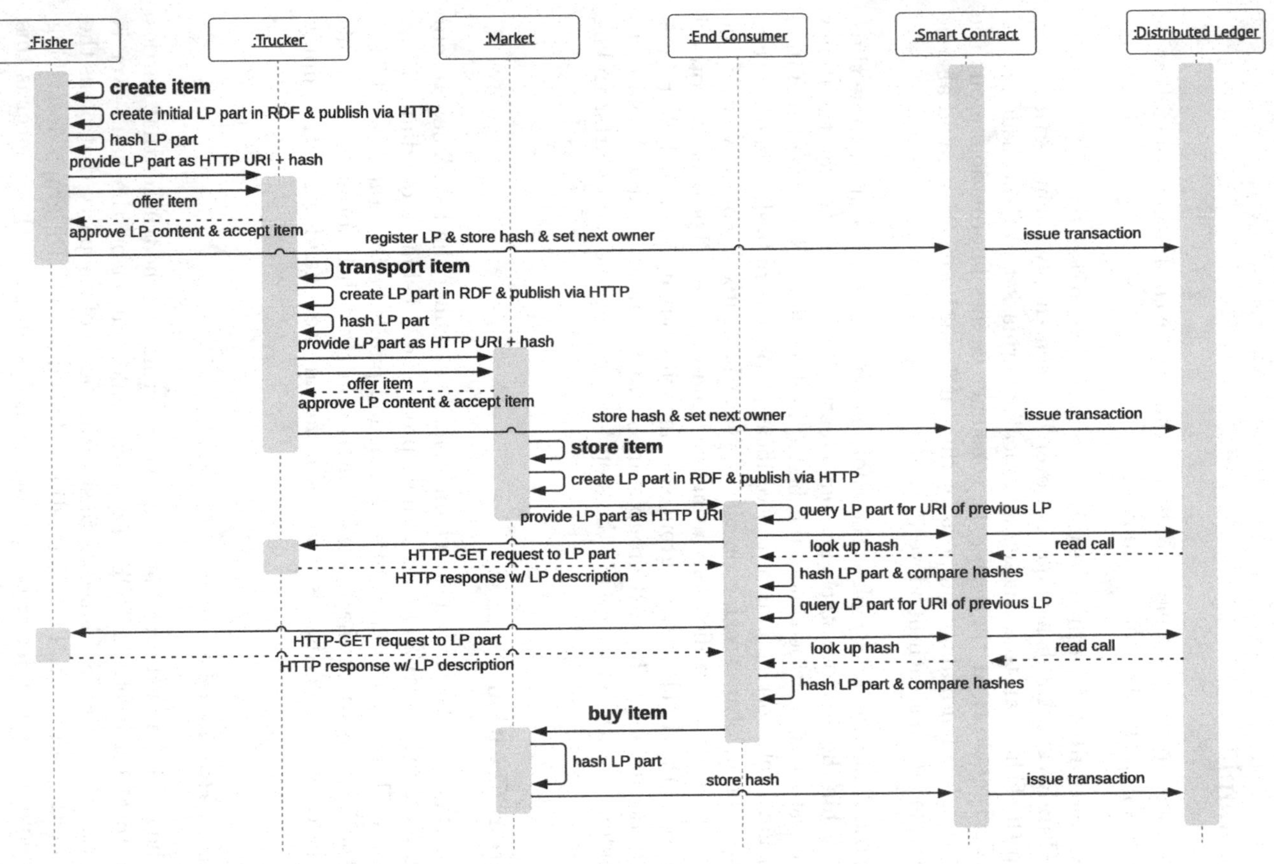

Fig. 1. Protocol for managing and verifying data along a supply chain.

3.3 Item Verification

Before actually buying the fish, the consumer may want to ascertain if the fish's information has not (maliciously) been tampered with, e.g. a retrospective adjustment to the cooling information was made. To this end, the consumer looks up the fish's information, which the supermarket provides in the form of a URI of a Linked Pedigree part. This Linked Pedigree part contains a reference to the previous part, which the end-consumer now dereferences. Consulting a Smart Contract, the customer can determine whether the retrieved information has not been changed since it was first published. By following the links in a Linked Pedigree to the respective previous Linked Pedigree and by dereferencing the corresponding identifiers, the customer can go back in the information trail on the fish right until the very beginning, i.e. the catchment. In each step, the customer can consult the Smart Contract to verify the integrity of the information provided.

This verification can be performed analogously at any point in the supply chain by any participant, starting at different points in the traversal.

4 Preliminaries

We base our approach on Linked Data, i.e. we make use of URIs, and provide hyperlinked RDF graph via HTTP. We build Linked Pedigrees in the form of RDF graphs. We store RDF graph hashes in a Distributed Ledger based on Ethereum using a Smart Contract.

4.1 Linked Data, URIs, RDF, and HTTP

We following the Linked Data principles[14]: We use Uniform Resource Identifiers[15] (URIs) as names for things. We use graphs expressed according to the Resource Description Framework[16] (RDF) to describe things. An RDF graph is defined as a set of triples. With $\mathcal{U}$ as the set of all URIs, $\mathcal{B}$ as the set of all blank nodes, and $\mathcal{L}$ as the set of all literals, a triple t can be defined as $t \in (\mathcal{U} \cup \mathcal{B}) \times \mathcal{U} \times (\mathcal{U} \cup \mathcal{B} \cup \mathcal{L})$. In our examples, we use CURIEs[17] that allow to abbreviate URIs using prefixes[18] . We use the Hypertext Transfer Protocol[19] (HTTP) to dereference URIs and assume dereferencable URIs.

---

[14] https://www.w3.org/DesignIssues/LinkedData.

[15] https://www.ietf.org/rfc/rfc3986.txt.

[16] https://www.w3.org/TR/rdf11-concepts/.

[17] https://www.w3.org/TR/curie/.

[18] We point to prefix.cc for resolving the prefixes. Moreover, we use `p:` as short for http://purl.org/pedigree, `e:` as short for http://ethon.consensys.net/, and `x:`, as short for http://people.aifb.kit.edu/co1683/2019/ld-chain/vocab for our extensions

[19] https://www.ietf.org/rfc/rfc7230.txt.

4.2 Linked Pedigree

A Linked Pedigree [10] is a trail of ownership of a product published as Linked Data described using terms from the OntoPedigree ontology. Each Linked Pedigree consists of different parts, i.e. instances of the class `p:Pedigree`, which reflect the different owners. The parts are assumed to be linked using the `p:hasReceivedPedigree` property. As each owner of a product may choose a storage provider of their liking, the Linked Pedigree can be regarded as a decentralised dataset. Each part of a Linked Pedigree bears a status, `p:Initial`, `p:Intermediate`, or `p:Final`. We show the terms of the OntoPedigree ontology that we use in this paper as part of Fig. 2.

4.3 Hashing RDF Graphs

To hash RDF graphs, we apply the approach of Hogan [3]. The approach allows for determining stable hashes of RDF graphs in the presence of isomorphism-preserving transformations of the graph, i.e. triple re-ordering and blank node renaming.

4.4 Distributed Ledger Technologies

Distributed Ledger Technologies is the umbrella term for distributed ledger concepts like blockchain or transaction-based directed acyclic graphs [6]. A distributed ledger is a distributed database in a decentralised network, where changes to the database, i.e. transactions, have to be approved by network nodes via a consensus algorithm [8]. This allows for secure processing of transactions between parties that do not trust each other. Furthermore, when new data is appended to the distributed ledger, timestamps and hash-based references to previous data are included. This meta data leads to a high degree of data integrity and imposes a high effort on retrospective modification of data [8]. In addition, as the database is replicated in full, every network participant can query their instance of the distributed ledger. Hence, all data and all associated changes are transparent to the entire network.

Ethereum Blockchain. For our work, we choose Ethereum, a well-established blockchain implementation, that allows for the deployment of decentralised applications via Smart Contracts[20]. Ethereum allows for building private proof-of-work blockchains. Proof-of-work is a consensus algorithm based on expensive compute operations, which need to be executed for the approval of blocks of transactions. Participating in the consensus creation, i.e. approving blocks of transactions following a specified algorithm, here proof-of-work, is also referred to as "mining".

[20] https://github.com/ethereum/wiki/wiki/White-Paper.

Closely connected to the mining process in an Ethereum network is Ethereum's internal cryptocurrency called "Ether". Ether is used to pay transaction fees. Whenever a transaction is issued, the miner who approves the transaction is to be compensated for lending his computing power to the network. This network utilisation is measured in "gas", ether's internal utility value. Therefore, costs are typically given in gas. However, in private blockchain networks the amount of computing power necessary for proof-of-work based consensus can be set to a reasonably low level, such that transaction fees as well as energy cost for computation of the proof-of-work algorithm are kept within limit.

Ethereum Smart Contracts. Ethereum also allows for the deployment of Smart Contracts. Smart Contracts allow for defining application logic that can be executed directly on the distributed ledger. Applications built as Smart Contracts are thus sometimes called "decentralised applications". A Smart Contract can be regarded as application logic that executes automatically during mining when the conditions of the contract are met [13]. From a programming perspective, a Smart Contract is a piece of code that is stored on a distributed ledger and executed in a decentralised manner, i.e. local execution, then synchronising and consenting on the resulting database change, if any, with the network.

5 Technical View on Key Components

In the following, we will present our approach from a technical perspective. We first elaborate the model of a Linked Pedigree and its Ontology to model an item's creation and handovers among supply chain partners. Then, we outline the implemented Smart Contract's functionality that enables for the item verification process. Finally, we present our Linked Graph Traversal algorithm, thereby explaining the procedure of item verification and Linked Pedigree retrieval in detail.

5.1 Vocabulary

In each Linked Pedigree part that is not an initial Linked Pedigree part, the property `p:hasReceivedPedigree` specifies the respective previous Linked Pedigree part by its URI. When additional information is desired to be verifiable as well, additional triples can be added *ad libitum*. For verifying the information on the Linked Pedigree using the Distributed Ledger, we have to add information on where to verify the information. To this end, we built an ontology by taking selected parts from the OntoPedigree ontology, added terms from the EthOn ontology, and invented new terms. A depiction of our overall data modelling can be found in Fig. 2.

5.2 Smart Contract

Our Smart Contract offers three functions: First, RDF graph hashes of Linked Pedigree parts can be stored together with their URI on the distributed ledger.

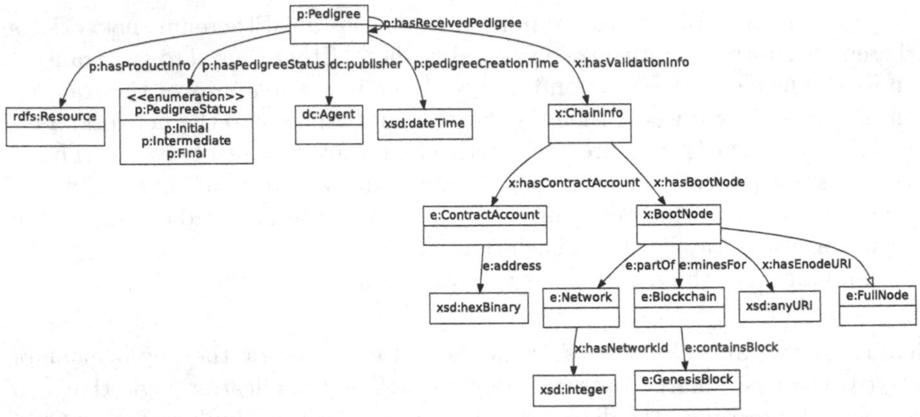

Fig. 2. The vocabulary we use for our approach. We use an UML class diagram to illustrate modelling in RDFS using the following correspondence: UML's class, association, and inheritance map to rdfs:Class, rdfs:domain and rdfs:range of an rdf:Property, and rdfs:subClassOf relationships respectively

Further, these hashes can be looked up from the distributed ledger using their associated URI. Finally, the URI of a single Linked Pedigree part can be looked up using its direct successors' URI.

Storing Hashes. An agent, requesting the Smart Contract to store a hash of a Linked Pedigree part, must provide the following arguments:

- The hash itself
- The URI of the Linked Pedigree part (required to enable for look ups of the hash by its Linked Pedigree part URI)
- The URI of the previous Linked Pedigree part (needed in order to append the current part's URI to the correct Linked Pedigree)
- The wallet of the next owner (required for rights management, specifically we thus can restrict writing information on this Linked Pedigree to the next owner)

In Fig. 1, the calls that "issue [a] transaction" are storing hashes. Once stored, the Smart Contract does not allow for hashes to be altered or removed.

A request for storage of a hash results in a transaction on the distributed ledger issued by the Smart Contract. Therefore, the requesting agent has to pay a transaction fee in order to compensate for the required network utilisation.

Retrieving Hashes. To enable for a verification process by hash comparison, a hash can be retrieved for the RDF graph of a Linked Pedigree part by calling the Smart Contract using the part's URI. Such look-ups are characterised using "read call" in Fig. 1. Since this look up can be carried out without a transaction to the network, no transaction fee applies here.

Retrieving URIs. An agent may not be able or authorised to dereference the URI of a Linked Pedigree part. The Smart Contract offers a fall-back function for looking up the corresponding previous part's URI. This way, unavailable Linked Pedigree parts can be skipped, thereby keeping the traversable chain of URI references intact. Again, since any agent ought to be able to look up URIs, retrieval of URIs via the Smart Contract is unrestricted. We omitted such calls to the Smart Contract from Fig. 1. As for retrieving a hash, the Smart Contract for URI retrieval does not need to invoke transaction, again, no transaction fee applies.

5.3 Link Traversal and Data Verification

To retrieve and verify a specific Linked Pedigree, an agent starts with the URI from the Linked Pedigree they know to be the last in the chain. They can then obtain the RDF graph that describes this Linked Pedigree part using an HTTP GET request. From this RDF graph, the agent calculates a hash value using the blabel approach from [3]. We use the implementation available online[21]. At the same time, the agent retrieves the stored hash for this URI from the Distributed Ledger using the Smart Contract. The agent can then verify the information by comparing the hash they generate to the hash retrieved from the Smart Contract.

To go further in the history of the item, the agent performs Link Traversal-based querying intertwined with verifying as just described: For a part p, the agent queries the RDF graph about the p for triples with p as subject and `p:hasReceivedPedigree` as predicate. Then, the agent finds the URI of the previous Linked Pedigree part in object position. With this URI, the agent performs dereferencing, verifying, and querying as described, until the initial Linked Pedigree part, i.e. the part with `p:Initial` status, is reached.

The traversal algorithm may terminate exceptionally, e.g. when Linked Pedigree parts are unavailable due to outages, or insufficient rights for the agent. However, for each Linked Pedigree part URI the previous Linked Pedigree part's URI can be looked up using the Smart Contract. This allows for skipping of unavailable parts.

By traversing backwards on this chain of URIs, the item's whole Linked Pedigree is retrieved, see the HTTP-GET requests from the End Consumer to Trucker and Fisher in Fig. 1. If all hash pairs match, the whole Linked Pedigree can be regarded as verified. Additionally provided links can be looked up for more information, e.g. on the item itself, its production or its transportation, if corresponding access rights are granted.

6 Evaluation

To evaluate our approach, we focus on finding the best way to implement our concept within the chosen environment of a private Ethereum proof-of-work

[21] https://blabel.github.io/.

network. We do not compare our approach in technical terms, e.g. transactions possible per second, to an existing DLT-based solution, since our approach only uses a standard Ethereum implementation as infrastructure. When choosing a different infrastructural environment, e.g. a permissioned blockchain or a proof-of-authority consensus, other evaluation criteria may apply.

We contrast two ways of achieving the presented functionality using Smart Contracts. Looking at our supply chain example, we ask if the deployment of a Smart Contract for the whole supply chain network, or a more fine-grained approach of multiple Smart Contracts is more beneficial. For clarity of the presentation, we name the approach with a Smart Contract that manages hashes and URIs for *multiple* items in the network, a "Multi-Item-Contract" (MIC). The alternative, a "Single-Item-Contract" (SIC), is a Smart Contract that is used for validating one item exclusively.

For the evaluation, we first build a cost model to compare two approaches regarding operating cost and storage overhead. We then instantiate the cost model experimentally.

6.1 Cost Model

Let $\mathcal{C}$ denote a set of Smart Contracts that is deployed on the blockchain. Let $\mathcal{I} \subset \mathcal{U}$ denote the set of URIs that identify single item instances, for each of which a Linked Pedigree exists. Let $\mathcal{P} \subset \mathcal{U}$ denote the set of URIs that identify single Linked Pedigree parts.

We define a function $g : \mathcal{P} \to \mathcal{P}$ that maps a Linked Pedigree part $p_k \in \mathcal{P}$ to another $p_j \in \mathcal{P}$, where $k \neq j$. Thus, function g appends the Linked Pedigree part p_k to a previous Linked Pedigree p_j. This results in chains of Linked Pedigree parts that we formally describe as n-tuples. A single chain, i.e. n-tuple, forms an item's Linked Pedigree. Be Λ the set of all Linked Pedigrees is $\Lambda \subset \mathcal{P}^n$. An item i's Linked Pedigree $\lambda_i \in \Lambda$ is then an n-tuple of the form:

$$\lambda_i = (p_0,\ p_1,\ \dots\ ,\ p_n) \in \mathcal{P}^n$$

Each Linked Pedigree has an initial element $p_0 \in \mathcal{P}$, where

$$(g(p_j) = p_0,\ \exists p_j \in \mathcal{P})\ \wedge\ (g(p_0) = p_x,\ \neg\exists p_x \in \mathcal{P})$$

and consists further of n-1 elements $p_k \in \mathcal{P}$, where

$$g(p_k) = p_{k-1},\ \forall m \in \{1,\ 2,\ \dots\ ,\ n\}$$

Further, we define h as the bijective mapping between an item's URI and its Linked Pedigree $h : \Lambda \to \mathcal{I}$. Last, we define the funtion $e : \mathcal{I} \to \mathcal{C}$, which maps an item $i \in \mathcal{I}$ to a Smart Contract $c_j \in \mathcal{C}$, since each item is validated by a Smart Contract.

We thus defined three dimensions of our approach, which we use in the evaluation: the set of deployed Smart Contracts $\mathcal{C}$, the set of items $\mathcal{I}$ (Linked Pedigree equivalent), and the n-tuples of Linked Pedigree parts (each forming a Linked Pedigree):

$$\{\mathcal{C}, \mathcal{I}, \mathcal{P}^n\}.$$

6.2 Applying the Cost Model

Applying the model $\{\mathcal{C}, \mathcal{I}, \mathcal{P}^n\}$ to the question at hand, whether a MIC or a SIC approach is preferable, we make the following assumptions:

The number of deployed Smart Contracts $|\mathcal{C}|$ is variable. Further, the number of supply chain items is growing over time due to ongoing business:

$$\lim_{t \to \infty} |\mathcal{I}| \to \infty.$$

The same holds for the total number of Linked Pedigree parts, since

$$|\mathcal{P}^n| = dim(\mathcal{P}^n) \times |\mathcal{I}|,$$

each item having a Linked Pedigree with n elements. For our evaluation we will assume a constant average size of a Linked Pedigree $dim(\mathcal{P}^n) = n$.

In the following, we compare two approaches regarding operating cost and storage overhead: The first one is a MIC approach with a constant $|\mathcal{C}| = 1$. The alternative is a SIC approach with an over time growing $|\mathcal{C}| = |\mathcal{I}|$.

Operating Cost. When deploying the Smart Contract or issuing a transaction, the computing power lend from the network's miners needs to compensated by a transaction fee. Therefore, the usage of Smart Contracts is associated with operating cost.

To compare the operating cost of a MIC approach and a SIC approach, let d_a denote the average deployment cost for approach a. Let r_a denote an item's average registration cost of for approach a, which is simply the cost of storing the initial Linked Pedigree part. Let s_a denote the average cost of storing a hash of an intermediate Linked Pedigree part for approach a. Then for an approach a, the cost function

$$p_a(\mathcal{C}, \mathcal{I}) = d_a \times |\mathcal{C}| + (r_a + s_a \times (n-1)) \times |\mathcal{I}|, \ a \in \{MIC, SIC\}$$

applies. For the MIC approach, we have $|\mathcal{C}| = 1$ resulting in the MIC cost function

$$p_{MIC}(\mathcal{I}) = d_{MIC} + (r_{MIC} + s_{MIC} \times (n-1)) \times |\mathcal{I}|.$$

For the SIC approach, we have $|\mathcal{C}| = |\mathcal{I}|$ since there is a deployment of a Smart Contract per item. This results in the SIC cost function

$$p_{SIC}(\mathcal{I}) = (d_{SIC} + r_{SIC} + s_{SIC} \times (n-1)) \times |\mathcal{I}|.$$

By comparing the two cost functions, we can see that a growing $|\mathcal{I}|$ leads to higher operating cost for a SIC approach due to deployment cost typically being far greater than function execution cost. So, an increasing number of supply chain items $|\mathcal{I}|$ favours a MIC approach.

Further, equating both cost functions $p_{MIC}(\mathcal{I}) = p_{SIC}(\mathcal{I})$ leads regarding the number of supply chain items to

$$|\mathcal{I}|^*(n) = \frac{d_{MIC}}{d_{SIC} + (r_{SIC} - r_{MIC}) + (n-1)(s_{SIC} - s_{MIC})}$$

with $|\mathcal{I}|^*(n)$ being the number of supply chain items, where both approaches are at equal operating cost, dependent on the number of parts in a Linked Pedigree. $|\mathcal{I}|^*(n)$ shows that the more parts form a Linked Pedigree instance, i.e. the greater n, the less desirable is a MIC deployment due to the slightly lower storing cost of a SIC.

For our implementation, the following estimated[22] gas cost apply:

$$d_{MIC} = 1,065,000\ ;\ \ r_{MIC} = 95,000\ ;\ \ s_{MIC} = 185,000$$

$$d_{SIC} = \ \ 750,000\ ;\ \ r_{SIC} = 80,000\ ;\ \ s_{MIC} = 170,000$$

These estimated gas costs lead to

$$|\mathcal{I}|^*(n) = \frac{1,065,000}{750,000 + 15,000 \times n}$$

Here, $n = 50$ is the vertical asymptote of $|\mathcal{I}|^*(n)$, meaning that for a Linked Pedigree length of less than 50 parts per single Linked Pedigree a MIC-based approach outperforms a SIC-based one.

Storage Overhead. When deploying a Smart Contract, the Smart Contract's code is stored on the distributed ledger. Every network participant with a full node[23] stores therefore a copy of that Smart Contract's code.

To formally compare the storage overhead of a MIC approach and a SIC approach, let s_a denote the storage space needed per Smart Contract for approach a. Let u denote the storage space needed per URI (item plus Linked Pedigree part), which is independent of the approach taken. Let further h denote the storage space needed per hash, which is also independent of the approach taken. Then for an approach a, the following storage overhead function applies for one network participant:

$$o_a(\mathcal{C}, \mathcal{I}, \mathcal{P}^n) = s_a \times |\mathcal{C}| + u \times (|\mathcal{I}| + |\mathcal{P}^n|) + h \times |\mathcal{P}^n|,\ a \in \{MIC, SIC\}.$$

When omitting approach independent variables, one network participant's storage space overhead function for deployed Smart Contracts remains

$$\hat{o}_a(\mathcal{C}) = s_a \times |\mathcal{C}|, a \in \{MIC, SIC\}.$$

For our (granted simple) implementation, the Smart Contracts lead to the following (in bytes):

$$s_{MIC} = 3,300\ ;\ \ s_{SIC} = 2,300$$

Obviously, for our implementation a MIC approach is superior to a SIC approach already for only two supply chain items.

[22] Estimates for URIs of 100 characters length.

[23] As opposed to a light node, which only stores a flat copy, i.e. hash values, of the distributed ledger.

7 Discussion

Applying the cost model on operating cost and storage overhead, we show that using network wide MIC is economically preferable as opposed to using a SIC if we consider networks with average supply chain length below 50. Above 50, the cost of an additional SIC, including deployment and Linked Pedigree storing, is smaller than the overall cost of storing an additional Linked Pedigree in a MIC. Note, that the length of 50 is the number of hops of an item between supply chain participants. In contrast, the network's size, i.e. the number of participants in general, does not affect our model.

There may be special use cases, where deploying multiple Smart Contract instances may be desirable in general, e.g. when the Smart Contracts are required to interact with each other or when functionality does not fit all participants' needs. With that, a SIC-based seems to be more flexible than a MIC-based. However, also in a MIC-based deployment, updates can be performed, yet they then need to appeal to the entire user base.

It is then in any case the obligation of the business partners to agree on which Smart Contract instance to use. Especially in large supply chains, this might cause significant overhead cost. Therefore, proposing a standard Smart Contract, that is already deployed and ready for usage, might facilitate business making in the network.

8 Summary and Conclusion

We presented an approach to verify the integrity of hyperlinked information using Linked Data and Smart Contracts, where Linked Data is used to store data off the chain. We showed a protocol for the verification in the presence of the transfer of physical goods, outlined the technical aspects of our approach and evaluated our approach using a cost model we developed. The implementation of our approach can be found online[24].

We see wide application possibilities of our approach in decentrally organised logistics networks with many participants of small size who desire on-premise data storage and acces control. As our presented approach allows for verifying information published as Linked Data, we contribute to the often neglected layer *trust* of the semantic web stack [9].

Acknowledgements. We acknowledge the support of Björn Leuthe and Christian Merker in an early draft of the work presented.

References

1. Eberhardt, J., Tai, S.: On or Off the blockchain? insights on off-chaining computation and data. In: Proceedings of the 6th European Conference on Service-Oriented and Cloud Computing (ESOCC) (2017)

[24] https://github.com/uvdsl/LinkedData-Logistics.

2. Gefen, D., Karahanna, E., Straub, D.W.: Trust and TAM in online shopping: an integrated model. MIS Q. **27**(1), 51–90 (2003)
3. Hogan, A: Skolemising blank nodes while preserving isomorphism. In: Proceedings of the 24th International Conference on World Wide Web (WWW) (2015)
4. Huang, C.C., Lin, S.H.: Sharing knowledge in a supply chain using the semantic web. Expert Syst. Appl. **37**(4), 3145–3161 (2010)
5. Jharkharia, S., Shankar, R.: IT-enablement of supply chains: understanding the barriers. J. Enterp. Inf. Manag. **18**(1), 11–27 (2005)
6. Kannengießer, N., Lins, S., Dehling, T., Sunyaev, A: What does not fit can be made to fit! trade-offs in distributed ledger technology designs. In: Proceedings of the 52nd Hawaiian International Conference on System Sciences (HICSS) (2019)
7. Lotfi, Z., Mukhtar, M., Sahran, S., Zadeh, A.T.: Information sharing in supply chain management. Procedia Technol. **11**, 298–304 (2013)
8. Nakamoto, S: Bitcoin: A Peer-to-Peer Electronic Cash System (2008). https://bitcoin. org/bitcoin.pdf
9. O'Hara, K., Alani, H., Kalfoglou, Y., Shadbolt, N.: Trust strategies for the SemanticWeb. In: Proceedings of the Workshop on Trust, Security, and Reputation on the Semantic Web at the 3rd International Semantic Web Conference (ISWC) (2004)
10. Solanki, M., Brewster, C.: Consuming linked data in supply chains: enabling data visibility via linked pedigrees. In: Proceedings of the 4th International Workshop on Consuming Linked (COLD) at the 12th International Semantic Web Conference (ISWC) (2013)
11. Sopek, M., Gradzki, P., Kosowski, W., Kuzinski, D., Trójczak, R., Trypuz, R.: GraphChain: a distributed database with explicit semantics and chained RDF graphs. In: Proceedings of the 3rd Workshop on Linked Data & Distributed Ledgers (LD-DL) at the Web Conference (29th WWW) (2018)
12. Steinfield, C.: Inter-organizational information systems. In: Topi, H., Tucker, A. (eds.) Computing Handbook Information Systems and Information Technology, vol. 2, 3rd edn. Chapman and Hall/CRC, New York (2014)
13. Szabo, N: Smart Contracts (1994). http://szabo.best.vwh.net/smart.contracts.html. Offline, but available in the Web Archive

Author Index

Printed in the United States
By Bookmasters